Introducing Women's Studies

Also by Diane Richardson

Women and the AIDS Crisis
Safer Sex: The Guide for Women Today
* *Women, Motherhood and Childrearing*
Theorising Heterosexuality: Telling it Straight

* *Published by Macmillan*

Introducing Women's Studies

Feminist theory and practice

Second edition

Edited by

Victoria Robinson

and

Diane Richardson

MACMILLAN

First edition 1993
Reprinted four times
Second edition 1997

Published by
MACMILLAN PRESS LTD
Houndmills, Basingstoke, Hampshire RG21 6XS
and London
Companies and representatives
throughout the world

ISBN 0–333–68469–9 hardcover
ISBN 0–333–68470–2 paperback

A catalogue record for this book is available
from the British Library.

10   9   8   7   6   5   4   3   2
06 05 04 03 02 01 00 99 98 97

Copy-edited and typeset by Povey–Edmondson
Tavistock and Rochdale, England

Printed and bound in Great Britain by
Creative Print and Design Wales, Ebbw Vale

03/02/99

For my mother and father and in memory of my grandmother, Fannie Hinchliffe

(Diane Richardson)

For my mother, Sandra Robinson, my nana, Nellie Robinson, and in memory of my grandmother, Winifred Thompson, for their strength and dignity.

(Victoria Robinson)

Contents

Acknowledgements

We would like to thank all those involved in the preparation of this book. Special thanks go to Joanne Crossland and Marg Walker in the Department of Sociological Studies at Sheffield University for their help in typing the manuscript and sorting out the Bibliography – a nightmare task! We would also like to thank our publishing editor Catherine Gray and the production staff at Macmillan, and Jo Campling as consultant editor. Thanks, too, to Wendy Bolton and Val Ashforth for their practical support. I must also thank, for sharing their ideas and enthusiasm, students at the University of Sheffield who have taken the Sexuality and Gender Relations course over the years, as well as PhD students. My colleague Chris Middleton has also been an important source of support and deserves to be thanked. I'm also (still) grateful to Vicki Robinson, who originally had the idea of writing this book, for asking me to co-edit it with her. The fact that our friendship has continued to grow and has survived a second edition is testimony to the fact that, despite a lot of hard work, we've had enormous fun in the process; sharing ideas about all manner of things from feminist theory and politics, to colour charts and chocolate. Last, but most certainly not least, my thanks to my family and friends for their continued friendship and emotional support, in particular Sarah Bishop, Jean Carabine, Hazel May, Carol Standish, Helen Thompson and Ann Watkinson.

Sheffield   DIANE RICHARDSON

I would like to thank Maggie Murdoch, Jenny Hockey and Heather Symonds for their continued friendship and intellectual support as well as the students on the BA Women's Studies at the Division of Adult Continuing Education, University of Sheffield, particularly Christine McGregor who brought me back material from the USA. All those who have helped with childcare for my son including Christine Proctor, Lesley Allen; Andrew, Kevin and Robert Marples and particularly my mother, Sandra Robinson, as well as Marjorie Marples for both deciphering my hieroglyphics and her love of theory and Rod Pollard for style advice. As usual, Diane Richardson for her professionalism, humour and energy and the fact that we have remained friends over approximately 300 000 words. Colin Gibberd, Joe Picalli and my son Eddie Joe Robinson (almost two), for amusing himself while I wrote and edited and lastly, my Nana, Nellie Robinson, who died whilst we were working on this book, and who, throughout my life, gave me only unconditional love.

Sheffield   VICTORIA ROBINSON

Notes on the Contributors

Kum-Kum Bhavnani is an Associate Professor in the Department of Sociology at the University of California at Santa Barbara, Santa Barbara. She returned to higher education as a student in 1983, and received her PhD from King's College, Cambridge University. She has written, amongst other things, on issues of racism in feminist theory and youth cultures, and is presently working on a three-nation project, with Angela Y. Davis, on incarcerated women and alternatives to incarceration. She is the author of *Talking Politics* (1991) and co-editor, with Ann Phoenix, of *Shifting Identities, Shifting Racisms* (1994).

Lynda Birke is a biologist in the Centre for the Study of Women and Gender at Warwick University, where she teaches courses exploring feminist issues in relation to science and technology. After doing biological research for fifteen years, she now focuses on social studies of science. She has published extensively in feminism and science, having become interested in it as a result of the tension between being a scientist and her activist work in the women's movement. Her published work includes *Women, Feminism and Biology* (1986), and *Feminism, Animals and Science* (1994).

Gill Frith is a lecturer in English Literature at the University of Warwick. She has worked extensively in adult education, specialising in women's writing and feminist theory, and has published several essays on the relationship between reading and gender. She is the author of *Dreams of Differences: Women and Fantasy (*1992) and is currently completing *Foreign Friends*, a book about female friendship and national identity in novels by women writers.

Jalna Hanmer is Professor of Women's Studies and Co-ordinator of the MA/Dip. Women's Studies (Applied) at the University of Bradford. She is co-author of *Man Made Women: How New Reproductive Technologies Affect Women*, editor of *Issues in Reproductive and Genetic Engineering, 1988–1992*, and has undertaken research for the European Commission on women's perspectives on the Human Genome Project. She also researches and publishes on violence and crime and is co-author of *Well-Founded Fear: A Community Study of Violence Against Women*, and of *Women, Violence and Crime Prevention* (with Sheila Saunders), and co-editor of *Women, Violence and Social Control* (with Mary Maynard). Her current research addresses police and inter-agency responses to the repeat victimisation of women by known men.

June Hannam teaches Women's Studies and labour history at the University of the West of England, Bristol, where she is head of history. She has published articles on feminist and socialist politics in the nineteenth and early twentieth centuries and has written a biography, *Isabella Ford, 1855–1924*. She is now working on a book (with Karen Hunt) entitled *Debating Socialist Women, 1880–1930*.

Marsha Henry is in the Centre for the Study of Women and Gender at Warwick University, where she is doing a doctorate in Women's Studies. After a first degree in her native Canada, she came to Warwick to do the MA in Gender and International Development. Her research focuses on the discourses of science and technology, and their impact on women in the Third World; she is particularly interested in sex preselection in India and the development of new reproductive technologies.

Jenny Hockey is a social anthropologist teaching health studies in the Department of Social Policy at the University of Hull. She has a particular interest in women and health. Her publications include *Experiences of Death. An Anthropological Account* (1990) and (with Allison James) *Growing Up and Growing Old. Ageing and Dependency in the Life Course* (1993).

Stevi Jackson is Senior Lecturer in Sociology and Women's Studies at the University of Strathclyde. She is the author of *Christine Delphy* in the 'Women of Ideas' series (1996). She has co-edited *Women's Studies: A Reader* (1993), *The Politics of Domestic Consumption: Critical Readings* (1995) and *Feminism and Sexuality* (1996). She has also published a number of articles on romance, sexuality and family relationships. Forthcoming books include *Concerning Heterosexuality* and *Childhood and Sexuality Revisited*.

Margaret Marshment lectures in Media and Cultural Studies at Liverpool John Moores University. She has also taught on the Women's Studies MA at the University of Kent, and the Popular Culture and Changing Experience of Women courses for the Open University. She is co-translator, with Grazyna Baran, of *Fat Like the Sun*, a volume of Anna Swir's poetry; and co-editor, with Lorraine Gamman, of *The Female Gaze* (1988). Her research interests are in the fields of feminism, representation and popular culture.

Mary Maynard is a Senior Lecturer in the Department of Social Policy at the University of York, having previously been Director of the Centre for Women's Studies there. She has published widely on many aspects of Women's Studies and is currently completing a book on feminist social research and developing a project on widowhood. Some recent publications include: *Researching Women's Lives from a Feminist Perspective* (1994) (with June Purvis); *The Dynamics of 'Race' and Gender* (1994) (with Haleh Afshar); *(Hetero)sexual Politics* (1995) (with June Purvis); and *New Frontiers in Women's Studies* (1996) (with June Purvis).

Paula Nicolson is Senior Lecturer in Health Psychology at the University of Sheffield. Her research interests are concerned with women's sexual and reproductive health and women's experience of working in organisations. She is author of *Gender, Power and Organisation: A Psychological Perspective* (1996), and *Postnatal Depression: Psychology, science and the transition to motherhood* (1996).

Diane Richardson is a Reader in Sociology in the Department of Sociological Studies at the University of Sheffield and has been a Visiting Scholar in Women's Studies at Murdoch University, Australia, and at Harvard University. Her other books include *Women and the AIDS Crisis* (1989), *Safer Sex: The Guide for Women Today* (1990), *Women, Motherhood and Childrearing* (1993) and, as editor, *Theorising Heterosexuality: Telling it Straight* (1996). She is currently working on a book on social theory, social change and sexuality.

Victoria Robinson lectures in Women's Studies at the University of Sheffield where she has established it as a field of study in the Division of Adult Continuing Education and in local communities. She has recently published articles in the areas of sexuality, particularly heterosexuality and non-monogamy and developments in Women's Studies, gender studies and men's studies. Her most recent published work is in the area of masculinity.

Christine Skelton is a lecturer in Education at the University of Newcastle upon Tyne, where she teaches on Primary and Secondary PGCE (Post Graduate Certificate in Education) courses. Her previous research includes an ethnography of an initial teacher education programme and a life history study of the careers of male teachers of young children. She is conducting PhD research on masculinities in the primary school.

Jackie Stacey lectures in Women's Studies and film studies in the Department of Sociology at Lancaster University. She is co-editor of *Off-Centre: Feminism and Cultural Studies* (with Sarah Franklin and Celia Lury, 1991), *Working Out: New Directions in Women's Studies* (with Hilary Hinds and Ann Phoenix, 1992), *Romance Revisited* (with Lynne Pearce) (1995) and author of *Star Gazing: Female Spectatorship and Hollywood Cinema* (1994) and *Teratologies – A Cultural Study of Cancer* (1997). She is also a co-editor of the film and television studies journal *Screen*.

Liz Stanley is Reader in Sociology and Director of Women's Studies at the University of Manchester. Working class by birth, a lesbian by luck and a northerner in England by choice, her interests focus around epistemology. Recent books include: *The Auto/Biographical I: Theory and Practice of Feminist Auto/Biography* (1991); *Breaking Out Again: Feminist Ontology and Epistemology* (1993, with Sue Wise); *Sex Surveyed 1949 to 1994* (1995); and *Knowing Feminisms: On Academic Borders, Territories and Tribes* (1996).

Fiona Williams is Professor of Social Policy in the School of Sociology and Social Policy at the University of Leeds. She has also been Visiting Professor in Women's Studies at the Queen's University of Belfast. She has written widely on social policy and social divisions, especially in relation to gender, 'race', class and learning disability. She is best known for *Social Policy: A Critical Introduction. Issues of Race, Gender and Class* (1989, revised edition forthcoming). Her current research interests are in comparative social policy and in social policy and the politics of intimacy.

Jan Winn is a lecturer in Sociology at Teeside University. Previously she has taught on the Women's Studies BA and MA courses at Sheffield Hallam University. Her teaching and research interests include feminist theory, male sexual violence, and sexuality. She is currently engaged in research on female violence, including notions of 'serial murder'.

Anne Witz is Senior Lecturer in Sociology at the University of Strathclyde and has recently been Marie-Jahoda International Visiting Professor in Feminist Studies at the Ruhr University, Bochum in Germany. She is the author of *Professions and Patriarchy* (1992), co-author (with Susan Halford and Mike Savage) of *Gender, Careers and Organisations* (1997), and co-editor (with Mike Savage) of *Gender and Bureaucracy* (1992). She has also written on gender and contemporary nursing, women's work in nineteenth-century coalmining (with Jane Mark-Lawson), women survivors of child sexual abuse (with Liz Ross), and gender and class analysis. She is currently working on a book, *Gendering the Social*, which explores the impact of feminism on sociology.

Introduction

Women's Studies has become established as an important field of study in many countries across the world. It continues to be a rapidly expanding area both in terms of the number of courses available and in the proliferation of feminist theories from a variety of perspectives. Also, other academic disciplines such as Sociology and Literature have been transformed, to varying extents, as a result of the debates and ideas that have emerged from within Women's Studies.

Despite these developments, when we wrote the first edition of this book, in 1993, there had been few attempts to provide a Women's Studies textbook that offered a comprehensive overview of past, present and future developments in feminist knowledge and theory. Since that time, a number of books which cover diverse aspects of Women's Studies have been published (for example, Kramarae and Spender, 1993; Evans, 1994; Evans, 1996; Stanley, 1996). This includes introductory texts to Women's Studies such as Cosslet, Easton and Summerfield (1996) and Madoc-Jones and Coates (1996); Readers in Women's Studies such as Jackson, (1993), as well as books dealing specifically with current debates about the teaching and learning process in Women's Studies (for example, Griffin, 1994; Griffin, Hester, Rai and Roseneil, 1994; Ang-Lygate, Corrin and Henry, 1996; Maynard and Purvis, 1996). This proliferation of materials is to be welcomed as part of the necessary and continued development of Women's Studies as a field of enquiry and, for many, a form of political practice. However, there is still a clear need for an up-to-date introductory text which covers the major debates in a comprehensive and accessible manner. This is one of the reasons why we felt it was important to provide a revised and enlarged second edition of *Introducing Women's Studies*. Further, when we first edited the book we acknowledged that there were some important gaps and omissions. In our aim to extend the scope and therefore the usefulness of this collection for students and tutors of Women's Studies, we have incorporated new chapters on social policy, feminist critiques of science and technology, and feminist methodologies. Nevertheless, it remains the case that no one book can do justice to the variety and richness of the diversity of feminist ideas available within the broad parameters of Women's Studies. What this book does offer is a comprehensive overview of the key themes and issues in major subject areas within Women's Studies, from an inter-disciplinary perspective. It introduces the main feminist ideas and perspectives on such issues as sexuality, the family, work, 'race', history, violence, reproduction, science and technology, feminist theory, motherhood, health, education, language and literature, representation, and debates within

Women's Studies itself to students of Women's Studies, and those studying feminism and gender relations on other courses. Each chapter benefits from the writer's specialist knowledge of their subject, and contains a summary of the research and a critique of the main arguments, highlighting differences between feminists. At the end of each chapter there are suggestions for further reading. These recommended texts are useful overviews or collections, allowing the reader to explore the issues raised in each chapter in more depth.

For those new to Women's Studies there are a number of dictionaries available which are useful in helping to explain and expand upon concepts and terminology used in this book (Kramarae and Treichler, 1985; Humm, 1995). In addition, there is the *Feminist Encyclopedia* in four volumes (Kramarae and Spender, 1997). The use of the term 'race' in quotes is to indicate that 'race' is a socially constructed category rather than a biologically determined one. Also, the word Black with a capital is used in some chapters to indicate that it is a political category rather than purely a descriptive term, referring to the experiences of racism directed at non-white people. The term Women of Colour rather than Black is preferred by some authors.

Finally, we would hope that this second edition of Introducing Women's Studies informs and inspires a new generation of feminist scholars who will be committed to theorising and challenging the position of women both locally and globally. Our aim is that this book will stimulate further discussion and analysis, taking Women's Studies into the next century.

DIANE RICHARDSON
VICTORIA ROBINSON

1

Introducing Women's Studies

Victoria Robinson

But if I wish to define myself, I must first of all say: 'I am a woman'; on this truth must be based all further discussion – de Beauvoir, 1949, p. 15.

In the late 1990s, Simone de Beauvoir's statement is open to question. This questioning has come from post-modernists who have deconstructed the category 'woman', from those who prefer to think in more neutral terms of women as genderless human beings and from still others, particularly some men, who fear the assertion that being a woman is not irrelevant but fundamental to our efforts to theorise women's position in diverse societies, their subjectivity and material circumstances, as well as the nature of knowledge itself.

Despite the unstable political climate worldwide, an international back-lash against feminism and continued media hostility to and caricaturisation of feminists, Women's Studies has continued to (critically) engage with the notion of 'woman', to connect knowledge to power and to transform the intellectual landscape radically.

Women's Studies has been difficult to define, partly because of the diversity of feminist thought and positions and also because it has no straightforward parallel to other subjects. (See Madoc-Jones and Coates, 1996, for an attempt to define Women's Studies.) Pioneering feminist voices from the early 1980s attempted to explain why Women's Studies had been necessary:

> Fundamental to feminism is the premise that women have been 'left out' of codified knowledge; where men have formulated explanations in relation to themselves, they have generally either rendered women in-visible or classified them as deviant . . . The description and analysis of the omission of women as autonomous human beings has been one of the most significant contributions made by feminism. (Spender, 1981, p. 2: see also Kramarae and Spender, 1993)

This recognition has entailed the setting up of Women's Studies pro-grammes and also attempts to characterise them:

To introduce feminist insights means to challenge radically the generation
and distribution of knowledge; it means changing the whole shape of the
course, or the problem – or the discipline . . . Autonomous Women's
Studies, as we define it, has the potential to alter fundamentally the nature
of all knowledge by shifting the focus from androcentricity to a frame of
reference in which women's different and differing ideas, experiences,
needs and interests are valid in their own right and form the basis for our
teaching and learning. (Bowles and Klein, 1983, p. 3)

If a fundamental feature of Women's Studies is the simple yet radical
belief in an approach to knowledge which places women at the centre of
analysis (challenging an androcentric/phallocentric notion of knowledge
which can be defined as men's experiences and priorities being seen as
central and representative of *all*), then this realisation of a theoretical
dishonesty has profound implications for how we organise, structure, teach
and research within the disciplines and the academy in general. This 'simple'
shift in theorising and teaching recognises the politics of theory in terms of
the so-called objectivity of knowledge, which has failed to recognise and
validate the diversity of experience of over half of humankind.

Post-modernist claims that to pursue a total theory is mistaken and
essentialist, given that to do so inevitably means to generalise and universalise, have informed this feminist theorising. (See Crowley and Himmelweit, 1992; also Cornwall and Lindisfarne, 1994.)

An aspect of post-modern theory which has affected feminist ideas about
the production of knowledge has been the premise that 'no one can make
claim to have privileged insight into any objective truth' (Crowley and
Himmelweit, 1992, p. 3). This 'objective' knowledge has served men's
interests and purposes. Feminists though have also had various concerns
about the critique of epistemology made by post-modernism. (See Nicholson, 1990, for instance, and also Lennon, 1995, and Charles, 1996, for
further debates on the issues this has raised.)

The emphasis on a feminist perspective meant a realisation of the power
relations inherent in current knowledge frameworks and practices, in terms
of who had access to that knowledge, how it was distilled and evaluated and
how meanings were 'encoded', so creating 'men's studies' (Spender, 1981).
Though feminists have made (critical) use of past male theorists despite their
gender blindness, it was recognised that it was necessary to develop feminist
theories and concepts which saw women as primary to theorising. (For
further discussions on feminist theory and knowledge production in the
context of the 1990s, see Harding, 1992; Rose, 1994; Lennon, 1995; Morley,
1995b; Charles, 1996.)

In this chapter I will briefly situate the development of Women's Studies
in a historical context before raising some epistemological issues (that is,
theoretical issues and problems in the production of knowledge) and

discussing some of the central characteristics of Women's Studies as a field of study. As suggested, the radical implications of feminist theory and practice inform the curriculum and teaching and learning, so it is necessary to examine the relationship of students and teachers to Women's Studies and the dynamics of the classroom. Central debates both between Women's Studies and the academy and within Women's Studies itself are discussed, followed by a consideration of emerging areas, such as gender studies and men's studies.

What is Women's Studies?

The women's movements of the 1960s and 1970s in the Western world had a fundamental impact on the establishment of Women's Studies courses in adult and higher education (Lees, 1991). This connection of the academic world to a social movement meant that the setting-up and teaching of such courses was a profoundly political act; theoretical analysis was seen as being intimately connected to social change, which was broadly defined as the recognition and analysis of women's oppression, and therefore as how to end their subordination in patriarchal and capitalist societies.

There has been debate over whether Women's Studies is an extension of the women's movement or if 'it is now structurally (and, some would maintain ideologically) distinct from that movement' (Sheridan, 1990, p. 36). So it could be argued that the links with the women's movement have changed or lessened, particularly in the 1990s, when some would argue that the women's movement is in disarray. A connected debate in the late 1990s is whether feminist political practice and academic feminism are connected. (See Radford, 1994; Morley and Walsh, 1995; Warwick and Auchmuty, 1995; Charles and Hughes-Freeland, 1996.) But it must be acknowledged that the feminist insistence on the importance of sisterhood, the personal being political, the false separation of public and private spheres, a recognition of the common oppression of women and their diversity in terms of 'race', ethnicity, sexuality, class, age and levels of dis/ability, as well as the acknowledgement of the importance of women's historical and immediate experience and the idea of the development of a feminist consciousness, were central concepts to the women's movement and began to inform the development of Women's Studies in the establishments. (Though some of these assumptions, such as a universal sisterhood, the use of the category 'woman', and a simplistic notion of difference and diversity have been greatly challenged and inform contemporary debates within Women's Studies.) (See Chapter 3; Lugones, 1993 and later in this chapter.)

Women's Studies as a formal area of study emerged in the USA in the late 1960s (see Cramer and Russo, 1993). In Britain, women involved with left politics and the women's movement in the 1960s and 1970s began to set up

Women's Studies courses within higher education and in an adult education context, and it was in the latter where, for instance, women's health, history and self-assertiveness courses developed. The constraints of formal assessment and required qualifications which characterised higher education did not apply to community-based education, allowing women more control over the educational process.

Though some courses in Britain had been established within polytechnics and universities, it was not until 1980 that the first MA was offered in Women's Studies, at the University of Kent. Gradually other postgraduate courses followed and then undergraduate programmes, so that it is now possible to study for a degree in Women's Studies in Britain. (For more detail on course development from the 1970s onwards, see Davies and Holloway, 1995, and Warwick and Auchmuty, 1995, as well as Smyth, 1995, on Women's Studies in Ireland; see Zmroczek and Duchen, 1991, for a discussion of Women's Studies progress in the UK in a European context, as well as Corrin, 1992; Bjørhoude, 1993 on Norway; Malečková, 1996, and Kupryashkina, 1996, on Women's Studies in post-communist Europe, see Sheridan, 1991, for Australian developments and Lee, 1995, on Korea.) Access courses and further/adult education programmes have also been important in terms of entry to higher education for groups such as Black and working-class women (Kennedy and Piette, 1991) and so have feminist higher education courses in local communities (Coulson and Bhavnani, 1990).

Despite continuing hostile political and economic conditions, Women's Studies exists as both autonomous programmes and as courses and modules within different disciplines in further, adult and higher education. It is established in varying degrees in North and South America, Europe, Australia and New Zealand, Asia and the Arab world, where feminist scholars are seeking to transform both academic disciplines and women's lives (Klein, 1991). Many of these courses, however, are often established despite underfunding, opposition and prejudice against Women's Studies and as a result of intense and prolonged struggle with the system (Hanmer, 1991).

Women's Studies encompasses the deconstruction of traditional disciplines in terms of their subject matter and their structure. Teaching, learning and research are all transformed by a questioning of conventional knowledge claims to objectivity and 'truth' and the separation of experience from theory. Women's Studies practitioners have also attempted to produce theories and concepts which reflect feminist concerns and principles. Most, though not all, research has been within the social sciences and arts/humanities areas, with increasing work being done in areas such as science and technology (see Chapter 10 and Birke, 1994b).

When discussing the discipline of sociology Pamela Abbott and Clare Wallace asserted:

Instead it is seen as necessary to reconceptualise sociological theories – revolution, not reform, is necessary. This is both because existing theories are sexist beyond reform by mere tinkering and because feminist research actually challenges assumptions and generalisations made from male-stream research. What is needed is a total and radical reformation of sociology so that it is able to incorporate women adequately. (Abbott and Wallace, 1990, p. 10)

(See also Abbott, 1991; Charles, 1993; Stanley, 1993; Abbott and Wallace, 1996, for debates on whether sociology has been reformulated.) Women writing of different disciplines have argued that the acceptance of feminist critiques in their specific knowledge frameworks has varied (Campbell, 1992, and Kramarae and Spender, 1993). How far the feminist intellectual revolution has indeed forced other disciplines to transform has also been discussed by Moore, 1994, on anthropology; Wilkinson, 1991, and Nicolson, 1992, on psychology; Thom, 1992, on history and Kabeer, 1992, on feminism and development.

The organisation of knowledge into separate and distinct disciplines meant that the new questions and methods of feminist enquiry that emerged from the 1970s onwards, from putting women at the centre of theoretical discourse, were not adequately answered or dealt with. The crossing of theoretical boundaries – multidisciplinary, interdisciplinary or transdisciplinary (going beyond the disciplines) – allows an issue or area to be examined from a variety of intellectual standpoints and has been seen as the most appropriate to Women's Studies. Some women have questioned the possibility of a truly interdisciplinary approach, or have pointed out the potential difficulties of such an approach with scholars trained in single disciplines (Bowles, 1983; Campbell, 1992; Hinds, Phoenix and Stacey, 1992; Morley, 1995a; Madoc-Jones and Coates, 1996). (For a comparison of disciplinary, interdisciplinary and transdisciplinary approaches and the debates involved, see Sheridan, 1991.)

It has also been argued that Women's Studies itself constitutes an academic discipline, both for intellectual reasons and for survival within the institutions. Other feminists would not wish to see feminist scholarship constrained by the limits of a discipline and prefer to see it as a field of study. Some non-feminists within the academic world would still argue that Women's Studies is not a distinct, legitimate subject area, given that it 'thieves' like a magpie from a diversity of sources, but the new generation of students who now hold undergraduate and postgraduate degrees (including PhDs) and the proliferation of Women's Studies centres, would suggest otherwise.

Women's Studies started by filling in the gaps and exposing the silences, adding women into disciplines which were not reformulated from a feminist perspective. This 'add-on' approach was not sufficient, though, and it was necessary to develop autonomous Women's Studies with its emphasis on the *feminist* basis of its evolving theories and methodologies; the recognition of men's power to define knowledge and practice. This is not merely adding another piece to the patriarchal jigsaw, but it is in effect starting a personal, educational and political revolution at both an individual and a structural level. This being the case, there is still an argument for using the term 'Feminist Studies' instead of Women's Studies, but it is often avoided for practical reasons (for example, the academy's resistance to the term) and because it is not self-evident which 'feminisms' are being referred to. Some Black women have also preferred the term 'womanist', arguing that feminist has referred to white women only. Whatever name is used, the male educational hierarchy should both fear and welcome these transformations in theoretical certainty, for to truly take on the full implications of this has started to mean the giving-up of power as well as gaining in intellectual integrity.

If Women's Studies was initially concerned with contesting masculine knowledge, gender-blind and gender-biased scholarship, linked to women's political agendas (Maynard and Purvis, 1996), then Joanna de Groot and Mary Maynard (1993) have argued that the Western Women's Studies endeavour has involved three connected processes: those of recuperation, reconstruction and reflexivity. Maynard and Purvis have interpreted this as first asking why and how women had 'disappeared' from academic concerns. Women's Studies also evolved its own concepts, themes and methodologies to attempt to counteract this situation, and these two aspects generated reflexivity, self-awareness and self-criticism which characterises Women's Studies in the 1990s.

Who engages with Women's Studies?

Studying Women's Studies can be simultaneously exhilarating and painful, as well as illuminating and disconcerting, making women's experience of oppression, which was once seen as opaque and individual, into something approaching a collective sense of oppression and struggle. So who decides to engage with it and why do they choose to?

Women's historical exclusion from education for both ideological reasons and practical ones, such as lack of childcare facilities, as well as their underachievement at different levels, has been well documented (Spender, 1993 and Chapter 14). Another central reason for the relative lack of working class and/or Black women in higher education, for instance, has been that intellectually the subject matter has not spoken directly to their experiences. The idea that traditional subjects and research have been *about* and not *for* women is counteracted by Women's Studies' insistence on the notion that women's experiences as workers, mothers and carers is not left outside the classroom, separate from the 'serious' job of theorising. Learning therefore connects with the 'mundane' world of women's daily lives as well as with their sexuality and emotional life. Women who left education at an early age or who have been on traditional courses speak of the vital nature of learning in the feminist classroom which contrasts with earlier experiences.

Students of Women's Studies vary in terms of 'race', ethnicity, age, class, sexuality, able-bodiedness and nationality. They may be connected with the women's movement and associate strongly with a diversity of feminist ideas, or they may not view or define themselves as feminist, even subscribing to media stereotypes of feminists as 'strident, man-hating harridans' (see Griffin, 1994; Warwick and Auchmuty, 1995). Sue Lees points out that the accounts of women students who came on to a foundation course in Women's Studies in the mid-1980s revealed reasons that are similar to those of women joining consciousness groups in the late 1960s. The accounts quoted reveal women's different reasons and relationship to feminism. She concludes:

> Do these accounts suggest we have reached the period of post feminism? Over and over again women maintain that they come on courses for themselves, for their own development, rather than to gain any particular qualifictions. Some are already graduates, some even have postgraduate qualifications, but do not feel their previous education has had relevance to their lives. (Lees, 1991, p. 94)

(See also Griffin, 1994b.)

Some students, however, have an image of feminism which stereotypes not only Women's Studies courses but also their students and tutors. What is important is that the feminist classroom affords the possibility of dialogue between women with different conceptions of and relationships to feminism, and that the idea of contradiction between women's lived experience and perceived feminist ideas is creatively explored.

As Women's Studies becomes more mainstream and students start to take Women's Studies as just another course, as they would (say) literature or economics, rather than as a conscious political or exploratory act, then the need for students and teachers to problematise this becomes imperative. This can lead to situations where women who define themselves as feminist are in the minority (Arpad, 1993). Theoretically, for example, students can produce technically proficient essays covering all the right issues but which in reality are only masquerading a supposed feminist empathy, as they have not reflected on the debates in a personal context. So the feminist insistence on the personal being political can be obscured when students take Women's Studies purely for the qualification (although more students are taking Women's Studies for vocational, amongst other, reasons). Also, first-year undergraduates' conceptions of Women's Studies may be vastly different from mature students' engagement with feminist issues: the latter group make up a large percentage of students on Women's Studies courses (Griffin, 1994; Madoc-Jones and Coates, 1996). If currently the majority of students and teachers of Women's Studies are women, then we need to be aware and discuss the implications of more men being involved at various levels (see Kramarae and Spender, 1993; Walter, 1994), as well as recognising the diversity of Women's Studies students in general. Students then, choose to do Women's Studies for a variety of reasons (not necessarily mutually exclusive) and expect different things from the experience. They may take it for profoundly political reasons; out of a curiosity to engage with feminism, or to help them combat sexism at work; for a qualification, or because it looks like an interesting course, when it becomes mainly an intellectual exercise. Some students use courses primarily for consciousness-raising, others as an opportunity for critical analysis of the situation of women, and others still for both these reasons.

Students also have a range of home backgrounds and personal relationships so some may have support from family and partners for their studies, while others may face hostility and misunderstanding of what Women's Studies is. Mature women students also have to negotiate study with responsibility for childcare and domestic work (Adams, 1996). The consciousness-raising aspect of Women's Studies in whatever context – a women's health course in the local community or an MA in Women's Studies – can and does change students, and this needs to be reflected on as part of the course itself (Griffin, 1994). Students initially hostile to feminist ideas may, at the end of a course, identify with feminist views. Students generally may find through Women's Studies a new confidence and become more articulate as a result. Students can also question and analyse the roles and relationships they are in as a consequence of taking on feminist ideas, and this can have a profound impact on students' self-perceptions and values as well as on their conceptions of educational practices such as student-teacher relationships. Like tutors, they may bring into the classroom anti-lesbian and racist attitudes and assumptions, so course content and teaching methods need to acknowledge the problems and potential of exploring them. Women's Studies classrooms will be charged with a whole range of emotions and feelings – hurt, anger, passion and revelation – and both students and teachers need to incorporate these into feminist theoretical and pedagogical practices (de Groot, 1994; Warwick and Auchmuty, 1995). As Jalna Hanmer says: 'On Women's Studies courses, women students can behave in new ways. They often feel able to demand, discharge and disclose in ways unthinkable on traditional discipline, or interdisciplinary, or professional courses. This can be critical for student academic development' (Hanmer, 1991, p. 113). It is important, as Hanmer says, that the course gives students space and time for 'student-initiated informal groups with opportunities to sit and discuss anything and everything'. If the constraints of the course do not allow this, then students may form their own groups out of class time, which serve both a social and intellectual function.

Many Women's Studies courses in the UK are part-time, increasingly modularised, and allow students to combine work, family and study as effectively as possible. It is important that the needs of women, often mature and/or part-time students, are considered when planning courses. The timing of courses and the reasons why students are not always able to adhere rigidly to assessment deadlines are important to consider, along with the incorporation of study skills into courses, as women may have had negative educational experiences which reinforce feelings of inadequacy and lack of confidence in academic matters. Childcare provision, which has not been a priority in higher education (though adult and community courses have recognised the necessity), is and continues to be unrecognised, but is crucial if women are not going to be denied access to education as in the past. Students studying part-time have often also to cope with lack of financial help.

If students endeavour to theorise women's position in circumstances which are far from ideal, then the staff involved in setting up and teaching courses often make decisions from similar contradictory positions, and quite possibly in the context of resistance to and lack of understanding of what Women's Studies actually is, as well as economic constraints.

Teachers of Women's Studies arrive at their intellectual destination from a variety of sources. Many have been working from within individual disciplines to transform the theory and methodology of their subject matter, as well as dealing with colleagues' resistance to feminist ideas. They have often faced the double burden of teaching within their own subject and developing Women's Studies in an intellectual and practical sense. Commitment by female staff, mirrored by students' perseverance, needs to be placed in the context of attitudes which have refused to see Women's Studies as academically respectable or rigorous, where an honest admitting of feminist bias has been seen as evidence of political indoctrination and abandonment of objectivity and reason. Women teachers who have done postgraduate work in an interdisciplinary programme of Women's Studies, together with the new generation of women on current undergraduate programmes, may well see themselves as scholars of Women's Studies as opposed to defining themselves as an economist or historian, for example, who has a specific interest in feminist theory. Such a woman would be able to teach courses on women and sexuality, psychology, feminist theory and women and the media, and would be a truly interdisciplinary scholar. The diversity of tutors' backgrounds can be creative, but can also lead to tensions and disagreements over the nature of what Women's Studies is. Tutors (like myself) may well be on part-time or temporary contracts without tenure, and access to the decision-making process as well as institutional and research resources is often limited. So staff who are marginalised within the institution in terms of power, because they are women, can be doubly so if involved with a subject which may still have neither status nor support.

Teachers themselves come from different classes and 'races' and may be lesbian or heterosexual, struggling with their own and others racism and anti-lesbianism, and so the ways in which their personal identities interact with institutional constraints and student expectations are all part of the dynamics of the feminist and non-feminist classroom, and the academy in general (Squirrell, 1989; Kitzinger, 1990; Mirza, 1995; Rassool, 1995).

If Women's Studies within the academic sphere has been seen as too radical, then some in the women's movement argue that teachers of Women's Studies (and Women's Studies itself) will and have (has) been deradicalised as they/it enter(s) the mainstream, in terms of political vision and connection to the wider movement. Women's Studies' practitioners can be seen to be corrupted by a male hierarchy that demands obedience to a patriarchal orthodoxy and have been seen as careerists, or not connected to the women's movement, by those women who see them as merely token feminists (see Taking Liberties Collective, 1989; Coulson and Bhavnani, 1990; Morley, 1995b).

It is necessary to recognise, however, that to associate with feminism and Women's Studies can also be detrimental to women involved in courses in terms of careers and academic 'respectability' (see Kramarae and Spender, 1993; Brown Packer, 1995). Also, such distinctions between Women's Studies and the women's movement deny the political principles of women involved in setting up and teaching such courses: the fact that this can be a feminist political act, and also ignores the political energy needed to survive in the institutions. On this issue, when discussing the work of Alex Warwick and Rosemary Auchmuty, Gabriele Griffin writes: 'It is clear from their chapter that to see Women's Studies as separate from or inferior to other forms of feminist activism is misleading and undermining.' (Griffin, 1995, p. 5; see also, Stanko, 1991; Griffin, Hester, Rai and Roseneil, 1994; Morley and Walsh, 1995).

Teaching and learning in the Women's Studies classroom

If a feminist perspective on education meant radically changing the curriculum, it also necessitated a reflection and transformation on how we teach and learn. From the beginning of the setting up of Women's Studies courses in the early 1970s, feminist pedagogy has, to some extent, been on the agenda, particularly in the USA (see Maher and Thompson Tetreault, 1994, for instance), but it is only relatively recently in Britain that we have started to discuss the diversity and complexity of feminist approaches (McNeil,

1992). For example 'On the other hand, women can take pleasure in the knowledge that working together to transform traditional ways of teaching and learning, evaluation and assessment, and knowledge production, creates an excitement which sustains hope, energy and affection even inside academia' (Walsh, 1995, p. 96).

Ideally, the Women's Studies classroom is about creating a situation where students can engage with such feminist principles, where they can learn to evolve as autonomous scholars, and listen to and respect others. What is the reality of such a classroom when the contradictions of struggling with our own prejudices, the difficulty of dismantling and reconstructing previously comforting educational practices and the diversity of student and teacher expectations are ever present within far from radical establishments? The central relationship to have received consideration is the one of student and teacher.

The idea of the tutor as all-knowing expert with students as empty vessels to be filled with pearls of wisdom was criticised by 1970s theorists such as Paulo Freire in *Pedagogy of the Oppressed* (1970), but the gender dimension did not inform these preconceptions. There has been acknowledgement that both students and teachers enrich the classroom and theoretical discourse with the immediacy and vitality of their experience, and a dialogue should ensue, not a hierarchy of opinion. The concepts of authority and power associated with the relationship have been analysed, and the negative aspects of these dynamics: their misuse and antithesis to feminist philosophy in terms of hierarchical learning and non-collectivity meant an initial rejection of, for example, the right of teachers to assess students' work. Clare Ungerson (1988) felt that we can expect that some women have the experience to grade and judge written work. This has paralleled a feminist redefinition of power and authority to entail an acceptance of the teacher's role as possessor of knowledge, empowerer and nurturer, so that patriarchal pedagogic patterns are not reproduced. Tutors themselves, as well as students, are participating in the learning experience (Lubelska, 1991; Walsh, 1995). We need therefore to redefine our notions of power, and talk instead of empowerment. Power can be seen as necessary for personal realisation and thus to achieve collective ends, but still needs further analysis (McNeil, 1992).

This recognition of power and attempts to challenge hierarchical notions of assessment and learning can be seen in the paradox of education's insistence on graded work to ensure standards of achievement. Students and teachers may attempt to challenge this by incorporating collective working methods with joint student essays and presentations, dissertations or research as opposed to exams, by team-teaching and by including non-traditional methods of discussion and assessment, such as collective marking, experiential accounts and women's autobiography and multimedia within courses. (See Humm, 1991, 1994; Lubelska, 1991; Kenrick, 1994;

Pearce, 1994a; Walsh, 1995; Warwick and Auchmuty, 1995, for a discussion of some of these issues.)

Students may choose not to know what grades they have been getting for their written work, but the paradox remains that teachers may well have to exercise institutional power and formally assess work, since not to do so would devalue Women's Studies courses in terms of the status they have within institutions and in terms of students' need and desire for a qualification. It is important that the process of evaluation and marking is discussed openly and the politics of the criteria used by teachers recognised. These issues of power are reflected in all aspects of Women's Studies, from entry to courses, curriculum development, the format of classes in terms of small group work (Hobby, 1989), in the participation at conferences (Griffin, 1994a), and in equal representation of all groups (in the production of journals, for example). It is necessary to problematise the contradictory position students and teachers occupy in relation to each other, the academic world, and the principles of the women's movement in course feedback and class discussion, so that our classrooms reflect movements to an equality of power.

Vital work in exploring the political implications of feminist pedagogic issues has been the recognition of the need for students and tutors to work creatively with differences between women, and to struggle to analyse and overcome racism, heterosexism, classism and ageism, both in the classroom and the academy. Students and tutors may be heterosexual or lesbian (out or not). They may be struggling to address their own prejudices (or questioning their backgrounds and allegiances), and feminist theory is still not sufficiently developed to fully account for the interactions of capitalism, 'race', age, heterosexism and gender. Working therefore with difference and women in a dynamic sense can lead to frustration and anger in the classroom. Racism in the academy, on Women's Studies courses, and the issue of a Black feminist pedagogy, has been raised and discussed (Haraway, 1990; Squire, 1990; Jarrett, 1996; see also Chapter 2 below). Anti-lesbianism, heterosexism and lesbian students and tutors have also been analysed (Crumpacker and Vander Haegen, 1987; Kitzinger, 1990; D. Epstein, 1995; Walsh, 1995). The needs of older (see Carpenter, 1996) and differently-abled students and tutors (see Begum, 1992a; Potts and Price, 1995), long neglected, crucially still need to be discussed in terms of feminist pedagogic issues.

As Women's Studies progresses into the mainstream and feminist students may become the minority, we need to make explicit the contradictions involved in feminist teaching and learning in the mixed (women and men) or mainstream classroom (Cameron, 1989; Philips and Westland, 1992). Not only do we need to make explicit our teaching strategies, but we should develop feminist pedagogies at all educational levels, including teaching feminist issues in schools (Weiler and Mitchell, 1992); we must also continue to address feminist pedagogical issues more fully, particularly the interaction of differences in the feminist classroom (V. Robinson, 1993).

Debates within Women's Studies

The master's tools will never dismantle the master's house. (Lorde, 1984b)

Women's Studies is an evolving, fluid and dynamic area of study connected to the women's movement (even if that connection is conceptualised differently, as I have mentioned), with its own plurality of political positions and aims. It is also a political act against phallocentric knowledge-making, ironically being constituted within the walls of the academy it is attempting to transform through feminist perspectives. It is of little wonder, then, that there are intense debates within Women's Studies itself, and there are parallels with the dialogues taking place in different countries despite cultural differences.

The question of whether, as women, we should engage with theory at all was initially posed as Women's Studies developed. Theory was seen by many as a male weapon of oppression, wielded by those who would ridicule and silence women. Women's energy then was seen as best directed at practical moves to help the community of women. But such views ignore the fact that women have always theorised, despite traditional pairings of men with logic and reason and women with intuition and emotion. Theory itself is not inherently male, even if it has been used to justify women's position of inequality (Spender, 1983b; Wilton, 1995a). What we need to do is to redefine theory and the act of theorising. What is necessary is accessibility to theory and the recognition that knowledge is power and must not be produced only for the influential, or knowledge producers themselves alone. (Though even now there are debates between feminists on the validity of certain male theorists. For example, some feminists would still argue that Freud is too patriarchal, even misogynist, to be of use to feminist theory, whilst others – such as Mary Evans – would argue there has been 'a reacceptance by feminism of Freud and psychoanalysis': Evans, 1994, p. 4.)

Different countries have different traditions regarding feminism and its relationship to theory in terms of the relative importance attached to descriptive, empirical or analytical work (Moi, 1987). Some women feel that theory which is inaccessible to most women and elitist in terms of the language used is anathema to the women's movement's principles of collective access and sharing of knowledge. For instance, theorists who have embraced a psychoanalytic theoretical language have been seen to replicate male patterns of theorising, 'the equivalent of strapping on a phallus' (Greer, 1988). Other women insist on the importance of theory, which will sometimes of necessity be complex, but which needs to be made available to as many women as possible, combining subjectivity and objectivity utilising non-traditional learning methods, and at the same time ensuring that theory is connected to social action. Accessibility of complex theory is still a key issue for students and tutors (particularly in relation to post-modernist writing: see Coulson and Bhavnani, 1990; Campbell, 1992; Walsh, 1995; Madoc-Jones and Coates, 1996). But some women still feel the need to engage with such academic terminology at the same time as making it accessible: 'We see it as a case of "beating them at their own game": if the debates of academic feminism are to be carried out in the medium of a language as complexly baroque as old German (and sometimes as silly as Franglais), then we intend to help as many as possible to become proficient speakers of it, but not believers in it' (Stanley and Wise, 1993, p. 231).

This reconceptualising of theory also extends to feminist research methodologies, which recently have received much feminist scrutiny (see Chapter 9 below).

An epistemological issue which has been central to both feminist theory and research methodology has been the traditional academic separation of theory and experience, and emotion and reason. A fundamental issue about the nature of feminist theorising has been the insistence by feminists on redefining an academic notion of objectivity. At one level, this has led to accusations that Women's Studies practioners are 'biased', indoctrinating students with political (and worse, feminist!) dogma, or that they are not sufficiently rigorous or academic, (see Lyndon, 1992; Cramer and Russo, 1993; Spender, 1993; Morley and Walsh, 1995).

In a classic early study, Dale Spender (1981) charted the way women initially defended the subjective (and by implication women), and moved to a critique of objectivity, which was, in effect, a critique of men themselves:

Women came to realise that the knowledge which men constructed about women (from their deviant physiology and psychology to the definition of women as non-workers) was frequently rated as 'objective' while the knowledge women began to construct about women (which has its origins in the role of a participant rather than a spectator) was frequently rated as 'subjective'. (Spender, 1981, p. 5)

So feminists challenged the 'objectivity of objectivity' and recognised that subjectivity was a valid part of theorising. (For a discussion of whether that means feminism has to abandon objectivity, see Sydie, 1987, and for further, more recent discussions of objectivity, see Harding, 1990; Kramarae and Spender, 1993; Stanley and Wise, 1993; Lennon, 1995.)

Personal experience, then, is a vital starting point to explore differences and similarities between women. Within the context of Women's Studies, women can locate that experience within a theoretical context, to combine reflection on the personal with analysis and critique. Such a combination is not without tension. Students sometimes feel that there is either too little or too much experience informing theoretical debate.

If in the 1970s it was seen by some women as necessary to stress the theoretical side of feminist theorising in an attempt perhaps to achieve academic credibility, then in the 1980s the experience/theory debate was still an issue. Veronica Beechey asserted that 'the concept of "experience" which remains the bedrock of a feminist analysis for some writers is criticised by others for being subjectivist' (Beechey, 1986, p. 1). Others saw that it was not enough to refer unproblematically to experience (Weedon, 1987). Certainly, individual experience which is not reflected on, or challenged, can be at best limiting, and could, for instance, be racist, if I as a white woman use my experiences alone for constructing a theoretical framework or world view (see also Chapter 2 below). In other words, the unreflexive use of women's experience can be seen to universalise the category 'woman' which ignores differences of class, 'race' and sexuality amongst others (Kitzinger, 1994). Other, later criticisms have emerged from feminist post-structuralists who have asserted that there are difficulties with the conceptualisation of experience as authentic truth (Lennon, 1995; Roseneil, 1996).

In a pedagogic context, women have reflected on ways to incorporate experience into the context of courses: for example, by working imaginatively with students' autobiographies and analysing the concept of experience itself, as well as examining experience in relation to feminist epistemologies (see Humm, 1989, 1991; Hollis, 1995; Pearce, 1994a; Adams, 1996) and by feminist academics reflecting on autobiography in knowledge production (Stanley, 1995a), and the continued idea that rationality is not the only way of knowing (see Roseneil, 1996).

If we accept the need to theorise, where is the best place to offer a sustained and rigorous critique of patriarchal knowledge and women's position in society? Some women have felt that the contradictions involved in situating Women's Studies within formal academic settings are too problematic in terms of accepting and working within imperfect conditions, and the concessions needed to remain there too great (Griffin, 1994a; Morley, 1995b). Women's Studies is seen as best constituted outside formal education, and within informal community-based situations where curriculum control and women-only spaces are easier to obtain. (Even Women's Studies itself is not seen as the most appropriate place for feminist scholars because women's energies, some have argued, could be directed instead at, for example, helping women in the community.)

Virginia Woolf, as early as 1938, saw the dangers of entering male-dominated and male-defined educational institutions. Much later, Hester

Eisenstein (1984) interpreted Mary Daly in *Gyn/Ecology* (1978) as asserting that Women's Studies programmes were merely 'gifts of the patriarchy, rather than concessions won in struggle' (p. 115).

In fact, some women initially left the academic sphere or have suggested that a separate women's academy or university would enable Women's Studies to realise its aims in a principled manner, ensuring control over curriculum, staff and resources: a return in a sense to women-only colleges. Others have acknowledged the contradictions of Women's Studies in higher education, but have stressed the necessity of engaging in mainstream institutions (Kramarae and Spender, 1993).

A central debate around Women's Studies within mainstream education evolved in the late 1970s and the 1980s over whether we should put our energies and resources into autonomous Women's Studies courses or into integrating feminist perspectives and methodologies within the other disciplines, and ultimately transforming them. Separatists argued that separate Women's Studies does not necessarily mean a distancing from power in terms of status and resources (as supporters of integrated Women's Studies have argued in the past). Separateness has been seen as a political stance chosen from a position of strength, not marginality or weakness, and integration is viewed as assimilation, with the woman-centred aspects of Women's Studies being lost. The 'mainstreaming' implications of integration are also discussed by Marian Lowe and Margaret Lowe Benston (1991) in terms of the contradictions involved regarding power and feminist principles. Autonomous Women's Studies means not having to rehearse old arguments and waste valuable time on anti-feminist views. Others have felt that the enclave of autonomous Women's Studies has allowed the mainstream to assert that women have 'been done', leaving male-defined theories, methodologies and teaching practices untouched by feminist insights and allowing students and staff, both female and male, to refuse and/ or ignore engagement with feminism. This view though still has its supporters: 'Even today it seems that the main areas where women are encouraged to be different are in the *ghettoes* [my emphasis] of "women's studies" and Feminist practices,' (Campbell, 1992, p. 17).

These two stances simplify the debate as many women argue the need for the simultaneous development of autonomous Women's Studies and feminist approaches within the disciplines (Hinds, Phoenix and Stacey, 1992). Others have seen Women's Studies as a strategy, not as an end in itself: thus Women's Studies is, in effect, signing its own death warrant when the other subjects are truly transformed. Gloria Bowles and Renate Duelli Klein (1983), in an important early collection, summarised the autonomy/integration debate, pointing out that supporters of both approaches have different views on how change takes place, that few women would want to argue for one strategy only, and how other factors (such as the nature and size of the college, and the resources available) are important influences when deciding which course of action to pursue. Susan Sheridan (1990), writing as an Australian, surveyed the literature on the 'mainstreaming' or independent, interdisciplinary 'discipline' debate, particularly as it has emerged in the USA, and utilising D. Rosenfelt, concluded:

> There are few voices to be heard now defending the view that women's studies will 'wither away once the curriculum is transformed, should that happy event ever come to pass', while there is a variety of proposals about the kind of autonomous existence it might lead in the future as a discipline or body of knowledge (Rosenfelt, 1984, p. 168). (Sheridan, 1990, p. 49)

Though the debate in the 1990s generally has subsided, in some countries it is still an issue. See for example Bjørhoude (1993) for comments on the Norwegian situation.

Moving in from the cold: problems and possibilities

Connected to this debate is the idea that Women's Studies is gradually moving in from the margins and becoming more mainstream. Though still very marginalised in some respects, for example in terms of the funding it attracts, hostility towards it and lack of understanding of what it is (Aaron and Walby, 1991; Davies and Holloway, 1995; Walsh, 1995; Warwick and Auchmuty, 1995), Women's Studies is gradually gaining academic respectability and status within the institutions, and the growth of new courses at different levels is rapid. If it is accepted that Women's Studies wants to move out of the margins to the centre, towards acceptance, academic credibility, and (arguably) more power, then its development should be celebrated. But crucial questions, such as where exactly we are shifting to, and whether such a move entails deradicalisation and co-option, still need to be asked.

In 1981, Adrienne Rich wrote:

> The question now facing Women's Studies, it seems to me, is the extent to which she has, in the past decade, matured into the dutiful daughter of the white patriarchal university – a daughter who threw tantrums and played the tomboy when she was younger but who has now learned to wear a dress and speak almost as nicely as Daddy wants her to. (Rich, 1981, pp. 4–5)

In the late 1990s, the possibilities of respectability replacing rebellion, and of token Women's Studies courses, are real ones. Dale Spender and Cheris Kramarae conclude:

So the success story is double edged. Some of the insights about the nature of knowledge, about multiple realities (of female experience), of difference, of dominance, and the politics of research have been 'appropriated' by the academy without necessarily advantaging women or leading to positive changes within the discipline. (Kramarae and Spender, 1993, p. 2).

(For a thorough discussion of the contradictions of Women's Studies affecting change in the academy, both positive and negative, see Morley, 1995b).

Another irony inherent in the success of Women's Studies is that more male teachers and students, as well as anti-feminists, may have to or want to engage in it, so women-only, pro-feminist spaces will be lost. Lyndie Brimstone argues for the strategic importance of being in a marginal position, as going into the mainstream does not challenge the marginal/ mainstream hierarchical conception, so that 'When we leave the margins it must be because they no longer exist' (Brimstone, 1991). It is important to recognise, though, that with the increasing acceptance of Women's Studies into the mainstream of scholarship, we need to develop strategies which enable us to use the power and position we gain from entering, and still authentically challenge the academy with a diversity of feminist approaches. This could be through independent Women's Studies programmes and transformation of individual disciplines. Anti-feminism in the academy though, must not be underestimated. (See Clarke *et al.*, 1996, for discussions on the backlash against feminists and Women's Studies in the academy in the USA.) Assimilation and backlash are both possibilities for Women's Studies worldwide.

A central question of the 1990s has been, and is, whether we are developing and transforming as a distinct area of study informed by the diversity of women's experience which feminism in the 1980s claimed to represent. Reflecting debates and divisions within the women's movement, the most fundamental dilemma of Women's Studies has concerned the marginalisation of Black, working-class and lesbian perspectives amongst others, and often in opposition, it has been argued, to the prioritising of the needs and experiences of white, middle-class Western women. The title of Adrienne Rich's early book, *On Lies, Secrets and Silence* (1980c), could be used to illustrate how Women's Studies, up until recently, has largely been silent on the question of the diversity of women's experiences and interests. In a theoretical sense, for example, Black perspectives have often been ignored or added in a superficial manner without informing concepts or debate in a systematic way (Carby, 1982; hooks, 1991; Watt and Cook, 1991; Lorde, 1992; Simmonds, 1992; Bhavnani and Phoenix, 1994; Bhopal, 1995; Jarrett-Macauley, 1996; Maynard, 1996; Young, 1996; and Chapter 2 below). In a pioneering work, Hull, Scott and Smith (1982) revealed the existence of a diverse Black women's tradition, and how Women's Studies had refused to be influenced or reconceptualised by this or to acknowledge Black women's contradictory position in the wider Black community. Even when subjects such as history recognised class and 'race' issues, the omission of Black women as opposed to Black men was still apparent (Higginbotham and Watts, 1988). If 'woman' is not seen as a unified category,[1] then it becomes possible to see the differences between Black and white women in terms of their history, economic position and culture, for example. It also means that 'Black' is not a unified category either, revealing differences between Black women also.

Patricia Hill Collins in *Black Feminist Thought*, though specifically referring to African-American women, deliberately placed Black women's experiences and ideas central to her analysis: 'In this volume, by placing African-American women's ideas in the center of analysis, I not only privilege those ideas but encourage white feminists, African-American men, and all others to investigate the similarities and differences among their own standpoints and those of African-American women' (Collins, 1990, p. xiii).

Lesbians have also revealed the heterosexist nature of much feminist theory in terms of course content and format which refuses to critique heterosexuality and which often conflates lesbianism automatically with radical separatist feminism. Lesbianism is often separated off from general feminist issues and discussed in the context of a narrow definition of sexuality. The insights gained from discussing heterosexuality, for example, in a sexuality module, often do not inform feminist theory generally. Lesbian issues and lesbians themselves have been seen to be marginalised in Women's Studies (Wilton, 1996). An absence of lesbian perspectives is to be found in the lack of (out) lesbian teaching staff, as well as in the content and style of what is taught on Women's Studies courses (Taking Liberties Collective, 1989).

In the same way that some feminists have argued that 'whiteness' needs to be deconstructed by white people as a social category (charles, 1992; Bhavnani and Phoenix, 1994), then it is also argued that heterosexuality should be discussed and theorised, so that even within feminist theory it is not taken for granted or assumed to be a 'natural' institution and experience. (See, for example, the special issue of *Feminism and Psychology* (1993) and Richardson, 1996e.)

Working-class women have illustrated how their needs and expectations of Women's Studies courses have been subsumed under the assumption that all women have the same access to courses in terms of finance, and that middle-class women have defined the feminist theoretical agenda in terms of curriculum and conference organisation, for instance (Taking Liberties Collective, 1989; Hapke, 1995; Stanley, 1995a; Strom, 1995). Other groups of women, such as revolutionary/radical feminists, older women, differently-

abled women and women involved with feminism outside the academic
arena, have voiced dissatisfaction with Women's Studies courses' failure to
include and validate their views and political situations. For instance, on the
exclusion of older women and ageing, see Arber and Ginn (1995), Ingrisch
(1995), McMullin (1995); and on differently-abled women, see Begum
(1992a); Potts and Price (1995); and on young women and feminism,
Morgan (1995).

A central issue for Women's Studies in the late 1990s is to discuss more
systematically how the categories of 'race', ethnicity, class, lesbianism and
heterosexuality are connected and not necessarily mutually exclusive (Brah,
1991; Brimstone, 1991; Simmonds, 1992; Bhavnani and Phoenix, 1994;
Moore, 1994; Ang-Lygate, 1996; and Chapter 2 below). This connects up
to the issue of difference, and how we have started to reformulate this in
more sophisticated and complex ways.

Women's Studies has begun to recognise the need to work creatively with
the concept of difference between women, which ensures that feminist
theory is a synthesis of those differences in a dynamic sense so that we
have meaningful dialogue around both differences and similarities; not
guilty avoidance and angry accusations by women, or a hierarchy of
oppressions, or an undynamic pluralism of positions which does not
recognise power differences. But if the 1980s was about an eventual
recognition and reflection on this, the 1990s and beyond still need to be
about the need for Women's Studies courses to make those reflections
become a reality in terms of feminist theorising: syllabus content (Cramer
and Russo, 1993), teaching methods and the involvement of all students and
teachers in feminist projects. For instance, Mary Maynard (1996) decon-
structs the concept of difference and how it has been used in Women's
Studies, and the associated dangers of its inflexive use. We still have not
fully analysed the framework of difference within feminist theory on issues
around 'race', racism, nationalism, migration and identity (Maynard and
Purvis, 1996); see also Griffin *et al.,* (1994) on difference and the chapters in
Maynard and Purvis (1996).

Some women (and men) have felt the necessity to establish separate Black,
lesbian and Jewish Women's Studies courses as well as gay studies, and we
need to talk openly about the reasons for such programmes (for example,
the failure of Women's Studies adequately to make visible these groups and
their diverse perspectives, and the racism and heterosexism of the institutions) and the implications of them, both in theoretical and resource terms.
(For discussion of some of these issues see Escoffier, 1990.) For example,
should Lesbian Studies and Black Studies courses be integrated into
Women's Studies programmes, or should they be autonomous, or both?
Rose Brewer (1993) concludes that Black feminists have forced real changes
in the field of Black Studies as they have generated a Black women's
standpoint there, which has resulted in Black Women's Studies where they

have placed 'gender, race, and class in intersection at the center of the discipline' (Brewer, 1993, p. 68). This has been partly because Women's Studies has not given voice to Black women.

Similarly, some lesbians have asserted that neither Women's Studies nor lesbian and gay studies have offered an intellectual or political framework for either lesbians or lesbianism (Wilton, 1995a). (See Wilton, 1995 for an attempt to set an agenda for Lesbian Studies, and a formulation of its relationship to Women's Studies.) As with Women's Studies, there is the fear that increased visibility can mean 'enhanced vulnerability and political incorporation' (Morley, 1995b, p. 175) for Black Studies and Lesbian and Gay Studies. Others have outlined strategies to ensure Lesbian Studies do not replicate some of the methodological and ideological failings of Women's Studies (Staddon, 1995: see also Abelove, Barale and Halperin, 1993).

The question of men, both male students and staff, and their relationship to Women's Studies, has gained in relevance as the subject has developed (Philips and Westland, 1992). Ironically, much feminist energy has been spent working out whether men can be feminists or not and devising strategies for coping with them, whether hostile or genuinely interested in Women's Studies. Men, like women, have a variety of reasons for taking up Women's Studies, which range from authentic interest to intellectual curiosity, and include negative reasons such as the wish to 'master' the theories involved, to put down the arguments of feminists more effectively, and the 'need to understand women better'!

An inherent danger is of men studying and teaching feminist perspectives, but not taking on their implications at a personal level, refusing to acknowledge their own power as men or how they use that power in their daily lives and relationships. Some male academics have, for instance, appropriated feminist criticism but do not engage with it; their interest is, for women, 'both gratifying and unsettling' (Showalter, 1987), given that most men still do not even engage with feminist theory at all (see also Walter, 1994). Elaine Showalter quoted Gayatri Spivak who is 'sharply skeptical of the motives of "straight white male intellectuals" who have turned to feminism' (p. 118). Certainly, now that feminist theory has gained some respectability, and is even seen as fashionable, some men see feminist critiques as acceptable, and think that engaging with them can perhaps be a good career move. Some have not acknowledged the theoretical debt they owe to Women's Studies in terms of the hard-won insights of feminist theory. Others in the 1980s reflected productively on their position as teachers of Women's Studies (Bezucha, 1985; Schilb, 1985; Snock, 1985), but the question remains whether men should be teaching and studying Women's Studies at all.

However, supportive men have at times ensured that Women's Studies courses have flourished when non-feminist female staff's lack of interest has been apparent, or when no feminist women tutors have been available. Specific situations have meant the principle of only women teaching the courses has been impossible if Women's Studies courses were to be established at all, though many courses have tried to ensure that, if men are teaching, then wherever possible students choose through options whether to take a male-run course. Men, however sympathetic, do change the nature of the classroom in terms of what can be discussed and what kind of atmosphere can be achieved. Some women in the 1980s, like Pat Mahony (1983), argued the case that Women's Studies needs to be taught in single-sex groups because some men monopolise discussion. She made the point that women in mixed groups will themselves often come to this conclusion. Writing later in the 1990s, Philips and Westland (1992) argue that a younger generation of women students do not always see mixed groups or male students as an issue, though some students continue to do so.

If it is accepted that men as socially constructed subjects need to examine the issues Women's Studies raises in both a personal and theoretical way, then the question arises of what is the best way for them to do this. In the 1990s, many of the questions about men in Women's Studies have been raised in relation to men's studies, writings on masculinity, and gender studies. Men can join Women's Studies classes, take options within their subject areas on feminist issues, or take gender studies courses and some have asserted the need for the setting-up of men's studies courses where they can explore the deconstruction and reconstruction of masculinity, which traditional disciplines have not done (Brod, 1987: Introduction). Some men have supported the view that 'Men's studies doesn't seek to supplant women's studies. It seeks to buttress, to augment women's studies, to complete the radically redrawn portrait of gender that women's studies has begun' (Kimmel, 1988, p. 20).

Though the USA has seen the initial growth of such courses, other countries – such as Britain – have started to emphasise men's studies and masculinity sections in bookshops and publisher's catalogues (see Robinson and Richardson, 1994). Some women, whilst supporting the need for men to take responsibility for self-inspection and effecting personal change, as well as theorising male power, view such courses with suspicion (see Hanmer, 1990; Cornwall and Lindisfarne, 1994; V. Robinson, 1996). The very name is unfortunate, given that it assumes Women's Studies and men's studies are complementary, and its existence, before the security of Women's Studies courses is established, will, ironically, put the focus back on men, who may ignore feminist work and possibly divert resources away from Women's Studies.

Feminists have asked where were the men who are involved in men's studies *before* it became academically advantageous to study masculinity, as well as pointing out that there are other ways men can show support for feminism and women's position, for instance, within traditional disciplines, without creating their own area of study (Canaan and Griffin, 1990). Feminists have called for self reflection by men: 'A central concern is whether this new and evolving interest by some men in the construction of masculinity challenges male power and privilege, as well as allowing men to redefine sexuality in new and diverse ways' (V. Robinson, 1996, p. 110).

Feminists have seen the establishment of men's studies and interest in masculinity as potentially progressive, but have also been concerned about its failure to deal with differences between men in terms of 'race', class and sexuality. (L. Robinson, 1993; V. Robinson, 1996.) It needs to be acknowledged, though, that some men have recognised the dangers of labelling such an area 'men's studies' and prefer 'The critical study of men' instead (Hearn and Morgan, 1990). Others acknowledge the debt to feminism and feminist theory which men's studies has (Morgan, 1992). Diverse groups of men interested in masculinity and with various relationships to feminism include academic men interested in contributing to the growing field of masculinity writing, Robert Bly's writings (1990), the men's therapy movement, anti-sexist men and men in the men's movement, amongst others.

Another new development in the 1980s and 1990s is gender studies. Gender studies has been growing within the disciplines in Britain and more recently as an area of study in its own right. New journals have appeared which include the word 'gender' in the title. Any development which sees gender divisions as socially constructed, and therefore liable to change, is to be welcomed. The increase in awareness of gender as being as important a variable as class in theory generally, is also to be seen as positive. But an emerging concern is for the tendency of gender studies to be seen as a more politically safe option than Women's Studies. Feminists have argued that the concentration on gender as opposed to placing women as the main category of analysis means that we see both women and men as equally oppressed, and the power imbalance is obscured, thus depoliticising the relationship between the sexes. Men's power and their personal and structural responsibility for women's oppression is no longer of primary importance, and individual men do not have to examine their own beliefs and behaviour, or confront male power at the level of society, if they feel they are equally subordinated. This can happen in both gender studies and men's studies. Gender studies can also allow men to argue that men should be involved in teaching in this area, and (for some) it can be an opportunity to devalue and stereotype feminist theories and Women's Studies (see, for example, Mike Roberts, 1994).

Some feminists and others have welcomed the increased use of gender as a category of analysis (Bem, 1993; Walter, 1994), arguing it is more inclusive: 'The move towards gender studies hence seems in general to be a progressive and fruitful one' (*Polity Reader in Gender Studies*, 1994, p. 3). Another argument is that it is more likely to be accepted in the establishments than Women's Studies as it is seen both as less threatening and as a less restricted field of study. Others (including Evans, 1991; Braidotti, 1992; Richardson and Robinson, 1994) have voiced concerns, amongst others, that the move to gender studies is worrying because the notion of gender is theoretically inadequate, despite others still seeing it as a more encompassing term.

Conclusion

If in the late 1990s we are still, as Bowles and Klein (1983) urged in the early 1980s, scrutinising the roads we take in our search for knowledge, still asking if they are suited to making our visions come to life, then we need to reflect explicitly on how the feminist knowledges we create inform and connect to women's lives, as well as to social and political movements. Women's Studies is still mainly established in higher and community education. We need to think about how feminist insights can enrich and empower younger women in schools and other contexts. This chapter has both stressed the importance of theory and that Women's Studies itself can be seen as a form of activism, but we need actively to formulate strategies so that feminist ideas and research inform the media, popular debate and policy. Feminist ideas have already done this, on the issue of domestic violence, for example, despite this not always being recognised. I have also argued that we may be out of the margins in some respects, but the intellectual landscape is far from transformed. Despite the high profile of Women's Studies in publisher's catalogues, for instance (see Robinson and Richardson, 1996), the move to gender and the importance given to men's studies in some countries ensures that critical self-awareness and continued honest and non-caricaturing debates between different feminists are never more important than now, when patriarchal knowledge is showing signs of theoretical fatigue. Indeed, showing the continued necessity of Women's Studies, for those who would believe we are now in a post-feminist age, is also a concern at this time.

If it can be said that in the 1990s we started to engage with some differences in a more meaningful way, then central challenges to any perceived idea of having 'done' differences comes from those feminists who argue against 'the hegemony of Western feminist discourses' (Jung, 1994, p. 208), and the need for Women's Studies 'to situate itself within a global political and economic framework' (Maynard, 1996, p. 22). As So-Hee Lee (1995) asserts 'Forging the missing link of commonality beyond difference now becomes the confronting issue of 1990's women's studies' (p. 73).

Note

1. Post-modernist theory has led to the concept of 'woman' being destabilised and questioned. This has, in many ways been positive, allowing us to work more

honestly and creatively with differences between women, although this has also engendered criticisms that the related post-modernist idea of the acknowledgement of fragmented identities, which is inherently critical of identity politics, characteristic of the Western women's movement since the 1960s, has meant that the focus has been on differences between women and not on action or alliances. (See Bhavnani and Phoenix, 1994, and also Charles, 1996, and Roseneil, 1996, for discussions on whether the debate needs to be polarised in these positions.) Post-modernism has influenced much, though not all, of recent feminist thinking, and some women still reject it as a body of thought. This is also true of the influence of psychoanalysis and post-structuralism. So though 'post-modernism has disrupted absolute certainties about definitions of feminism' (Evans, 1994, p. 8), there are still disagreements over its influence and relevance for feminist theory. In the late 1990s, Caroline Ramazanoglu (1995), for example, when discussing certain aspects of post-structuralism, warns against dismissing the notion that there are some common aspects of women's experiences of the body, as a recognition such as this can enrich feminist theories. It remains to be seen whether post-modernism will continue to provoke such interest and controversy in relation to Women's Studies and feminist theory in the twenty-first century. This point could also be made in relation to other theoretical developments such as Queer Theory. (See Chapter 7 below and Richardson, 1996e.)

Further Reading

Jane Aaron and Sylvia Walby (eds) *Out of the Margins: Women's Studies in the Nineties* (London, Falmer Press, 1991).

Hilary Hinds, Ann Phoenix and Jackie Stacey (eds) *Working Out: New Directions for Women's Studies* (London, Falmer Press, 1992).

Mary Kennedy, Cathy Lubelska and Val Walsh (eds) *Making Connections: Women's Studies, Women's Movements, Women's Lives* (London, Taylor & Francis, 1993).

Gabriele Griffin, Marianne Hester, Shirin Rai and Sasha Roseneil (eds) *Stirring It: Challenges For Feminism* (London, Taylor and Francis, 1994).

Magdalene Ang-Lygate, Chris Corrin and Millsom Henry (eds) *Desperately Seeking Sisterhood: Still Challenging and Building* (London, Taylor & Francis, 1996). These books, which are collections of papers given at recent Women's Studies Network (UK) conferences in Britain, reflect (as the titles imply) some of the key debates in feminist theory and practice in relation to Women's Studies.

Mary Maynard and June Purvis (eds) *New Frontiers in Women's Studies: Knowledge, Identity and Nationalism* (London, Taylor & Francis, 1996). An interdisciplinary collection which focuses on the parameters of Women's Studies knowledge in relation to a white Western Women's Studies and how it might be challenged, as well as focusing attention on women's experiences of nation, migration and nationalism.

Gabrielle Griffin (ed.) *Changing Our Lives: Doing Womens Studies* (London, Pluto Press, 1994). An edited collection which explores the experiences of Women's Studies students and practiners from different ages, backgrounds and sexualities.

Particularly useful for those considering studying Women's Studies, and those already doing Women's Studies who want to make sense of their diverse experiences.

Cheris Kramarae and Dale Spender (eds) *The Knowledge Explosion: Generations of Feminist Scholarship* (London, Harvester Wheatsheaf, 1993). An anthology which surveys the disciplines and shows how feminism has influenced and challenged traditional ways of thinking, which is particularly useful as it is in an international context.

Beryl Madoc-Jones and Jennifer Coates (eds) *An Introduction to Women's Studies* (Oxford, Basil Blackwell, 1996). An accessible 'taster' for students new to Women's Studies which is a useful learning resource, highlighting particular areas of women's experiences and incorporating exercises and questions to encourage students' active learning.

2

Women's Studies and its Interconnection with 'Race', Ethnicity and Sexuality

Kum-Kum Bhavnani

Feminism is the political theory and practice that struggles to free *all* women: women of colour, working class women, poor women, disabled women, lesbians, old women – as well as [Western] white economically privileged heterosexual women – Smith, 1982, p. 49

Introduction

In 1990 Meg Coulson and I published an article on Women's Studies which was called 'Making a Difference – Questioning Women's Studies' (Coulson and Bhavnani, 1990). In that article we suggested that while Women's Studies was beginning to deal with issues of difference – both in its rhetoric as well as in its courses – many (mainly white, but not exclusively so) teachers and students of Women's Studies had not yet incorporated the rhetoric or course material into their political practice outside academic work, or, at times, inside their academic work. In sum, we argued that too many 'women's-studies-people' had rarely attended to the 'race'/ethnicity aspects of equal opportunity or affirmative action policies, but instead had focused on the gender aspects of these policies. Since then, I have written a chapter, entitled 'Talking Racism and the Editing of Women's Studies' (Bhavnani, 1993a) in which I argued that processes of Erasure, Denial, Invisibility and Tokenism combined together to reproduce one form of racism within Women's Studies. In that chapter, I suggested that if academic writers and political activists (who may be one and the same at times) paid serious attention to international issues, epistemological concerns, and difference, then, perhaps, the practice of Women's Studies would be shifted away from editing women of colour[1] out of feminist thought and towards a Women's Studies agenda which was of value to all women.

27

Five years later, in writing *this* article, I now wish to emphasise that the task for Women's Studies is to examine the *interconnections* of 'race', ethnicity, class, and sexuality, for it is this examination that can allow categories of inequality to be engaged with. That is, the project of Women's Studies could be to see these categories as ones that overlap each other, sometimes contradict each other, and also, at other times, work together. In other words, in this chapter, I will argue that while the processes of Editing still do occur within Women's Studies, five years later, and almost two decades after the publication of *This Bridge Called My Back* and *Some of Us Are Brave*, the focus of Women's Studies in both the academy and outside should be to concentrate on how 'race', class, ethnicity and sexuality shape and influence each other, alongside gender.

It is clear that 'race' and ethnicity are issues that are central to contemporary discussions of inequality, which include gendered inequalities. For example, although the 1991 Anita Hill and Clarence Thomas Senate hearings were ostensibly about sexual harassment, the clear context for the events was one of 'race' in the USA (Morrison, 1993).[2] Given the acknowledged importance that 'race' and ethnicity have now acquired in many discussions of the social, one question which arises is 'how can these categories be understood as being in a *dynamic* relationship with gender?' My argument is that it is possible to see the dynamic and shifting nature of these relationships if Women's Studies in the industrialised countries, and hegemonic feminisms (Sandoval, 1991) explicitly focus on Third World feminisms.

Racism

Racism is a system of domination and subordination based on spurious biological notions that human beings can be fixed into racially discrete groups. Racism is identified as a 'natural' process, and is seen to be a logical consequence of the differentiation of human beings into 'races'. Given that there is no sound evidence from the natural and biological sciences to justify the assumption that the human species can be divided up into separate 'races', both 'race' and racism come to be economic, political, ideological and social expressions; in other words, 'race' is not a social category which is empirically defined; rather it is created, reproduced and challenged through economic, political and ideological institutions.

My analysis of women's exploitation and oppression, which is an adaptation of Juliet Mitchell's classic writing (Mitchell, 1971), is that such exploitation and oppression is created and reproduced and, therefore, also resisted, through five domains: production, reproduction (to include social reproduction, biological reproduction, as well as reproduction of the labour force), caregiving, socialisation/representation and sexuality. Thus, this analysis demonstrates that the racialised structurings of capitalism and patriarchies, along with analyses of imperialism and colonialism, are central to discussions of women's exploitation and oppression. Because women's relationship to each of the five domains is contingent – on economic, politics, history, ideology as well as culture – 'race'/ethnicity, along with sexuality and class, is one important feature of this contingency.[3] It therefore becomes clear that all women cannot be subsumed into a singular or unitary category of 'woman'. The unity of women has been a theme through which issues such as sexuality, violence against women and reproductive rights have been, and continue to be, explored. But it has also been the case that the 'unity of women' has not been the *only* means by which gendered inequalities have been discussed. Women's location within economic production, the role of the state and in the nuclear family has been discussed consistently within Women's Studies, which has meant that 'class' inequalities and issues of sexuality have been engaged with, albeit in rather a limited way. Rarely, however, have these class and sexualised inequalities been interrogated for how they inform and are informed by racialised and gendered inequalities simultaneously.

Background

Women's Studies courses in colleges and universities have created an area of intellectual enquiry known as Women's Studies or Feminist Studies or Gender Studies (see Chapter 1 for a discussion of the different implications of each of these). In so doing, Women's Studies has critiqued academic enquiry within the 'mainstream' by examining how women's contributions have been erased from much academic work, for example, within history. While journals such as *History Workshop*, in defining themselves as socialist and feminist, have attempted to put right this *erasure*, it is evident that erasure will continue until gender divisions are located centrally within historical (and other forms of) enquiry. An erasure of women's contributions then means that another process comes into play: that of *denial*. In this process, writers deny the particular ways in which women can both contribute to, and challenge, the existing social order. For example, work on revolutions often denies the differing ways in which women and men contribute to such social change (such as Skocpol's classic work of 1979) although some more recent writings have attempted to counter such a denial (such as Foran, Klouzal and Rivera, 1996). As a consequence of denial, women get made *invisible* within 'malestream' analyses. This invisibility is a familiar process: for example, women are absent in much social theory. Yet the invisibility may be noticed only when well established academic feminists such as Nancy Fraser (1989) write about gender in contemporary social theory. Sometimes, work which tries to make women visible does so by an additive process in order to avoid being categorised as 'malestream' (see Abbott and Wallace, 1996 for examples and critiques of such an additive – as distinct from transformative – approach). An additive approach can, however, create a type of *tokenism* because, whilst it includes women as a topic, it does not place gender divisions centrally when analysing economic, political and social relationships.

The four processes of *erasure, denial, invisibility,* and *tokenism* are basic to feminist critiques of much academic writing and analyses. Given that Women's Studies courses are informed by feminist writings, these four processes also frequently form the organising principles for developing curricula in Women's Studies.

For those who are students and teachers of Women's Studies, and many others, the identification of the above four processes is no longer new or controversial. In practice the processes represent part of the rationale for the existence and continuing appeal of Women's Studies, which is thus considered to be a challenge to much academic work. The problem with this view, however, is that to write about a single feminism – through which both capitalism and patriarchy can be challenged – implies that all feminists have common interests, and these assumed common interests are seen as more important than the differences of interests amongst us. In other words, to write about feminism in the singular feeds into the old, and now often-critiqued, discourse that 'sisterhood is global'. For if there is only one feminism, then, it follows that all women must be able to unite within it, thus subsuming their differences.[4]

These differences of interest were nicely captured in a song written by Sweet Honey in the Rock called 'Are My Hands Clean?' in the mid-1980s. Sweet Honey in the Rock is a group of African-American women living in the USA and the song mentioned above contains lines such as 'I wear garments touched by hands from all over the world' and 'Far from the Port au Prince palace/Third World Women toil doing piece work to Sears' specifications/For three dollars a day my sisters make my blouse' (words cited in Enloe, 1990, p. 158). These words demonstrate the complexity of women's exploitation, and how the interests of some women (to buy cheap clothes) can work against the interests of other women (to be paid a pittance for their labour). Thus, the words show how women living in the Third World[5] can have differing priorities from women – of colour and white – living in the industrialised nations, who, in turn, may have differing interests among themselves.

I use the example of this song to briefly demonstrate that the category 'woman' is not a trans-historical or trans-geographical one, for it shows that all women's interests are not always and automatically coincident (see Bryan, Dadzie, and Scafe, 1985; Lewis, 1993) and it thus becomes clear that the meanings of 'feminism' and 'woman' can only be usefully analysed within their particular geographic, racialised and historical settings (Mani,

1990). If woman is not a trans-historical category, and all women's interests do not coincide, then it follows that feminism, the political movement which aims to liberate all women, is also historically and geographically specific. Thus, there are many feminisms – that is, there are many ways of understanding and analysing women's exploitation and resistances – and therefore there are many ways of transforming this subordination.

Just as 'woman' and 'feminism' are not concepts which have unchanging meanings, so the term 'race' has specific origins and a specific trajectory depending on its geographical and historical meanings. 'Race' does not have a biological validity, for all human beings are members of the same race, *Homo sapiens*. However, it is clear that 'race' does have a social power, for it is on the basis of assumed racial differences that human beings are categorised as being of colour or white in Britain. The development of 'race' as a spurious *scientific* category is a consequence of imperialism and colonisation; it is this 'scientificism' which informed (and still informs), prevailing ideologies of biological superiority and inferiority among human beings on the basis of 'race'. But people are not merely categorised; racism – one consequence of the category 'race' – means that there are power inequalities embedded within these categories, which thus become historically specific systems of domination. In other words, human beings are located within relationships of subordination and domination and these relationships simultaneously shape, and are shaped by racialised, economic, and gendered inequalities. That is, as we argued a decade ago, capitalism is not only a form of class based inequality, but is also patriarchal, sexualised and racially structured (Bhavnani and Coulson, 1986).

In this chapter I will suggest that, despite the plethora of discussions of 'difference', processes of erasure, denial, invisibility and tokenism operate to exclude women of colour from much of the rhetoric and practices of hegemonic feminism – which, on the whole, is racially unselfconscious – and, therefore, these processes reproduce racism. I will then discuss 'difference' in relation to Women's Studies and, finally, I will show why it is necessary to shift the centre of hegemonic feminisms towards Third World feminisms. The overall goal of this chapter will be to argue that the goal for Women's Studies at the end of the twentieth century could be to focus on the *interconnections* amongst categories of inequality such as gender, 'race'/ ethnicity, class and sexuality.

Erasure within Women's Studies

The challenges to feminism have come from a wide variety of perspectives and most have originated (but not exclusively) from women of colour. The initial direction of these challenges can be summed up as follows: By and large within the Women's Movement today, white women focus upon their oppression as women, and ignore differences of race, sexual preference, class and age. There is a pretence to a homogeneity of experience covered by the word *sisterhood* that does not in fact exist' (Lorde, 1984a, p. 114). Audre Lorde, who died in November 1992 and has been described as 'a lesbian, feminist and activist poet' (Lewis, 1990, p. 101), emphasised the creativity which differences among women can fuel. And in doing this, she addressed some of her writings to white women:

> Some problems we share as women, some we do not. You fear your children will grow up to join the patriarchy and testify against you, we fear our children will be dragged from a car and shot down in the street, and you will turn your backs upon the reasons they are dying. (Lorde, 1984a, p. 119)

This brief extract from Lorde's prose writing, in addressing white women, captures the process of racial *erasure* ('some we do not') as well as her way of examining the differing and often contradictory experiences of Black and white women. Whilst she acknowledges that all women who are mothers have fears for their children, she is arguing that the fears of Black women simultaneously include a fear that white women will refuse to look at the *reasons* that may cause Black children to be shot.

Erasure was a key theme in *Ain't I A Woman?* (hooks, 1982). The title of that influential book used the now famous words of Sojourner Truth – the only black woman present at a Women's Rights Convention held in 1851 at Akron, Ohio – who, in her address to the Convention, used that phrase as a refrain.[6] In this way, Sojourner Truth made the point that racism as well as class bias were embedded within the nineteenth-century women's movement (Davis, 1982). Since then, Patricia Hill Collins (1990) has shown that in questioning the norms by which white women were defined, that in demonstrating that femininity was actually specific to white middle-class women (for example, being helped into carriages, helped over ditches, not having strong arms), Sojourner Truth was, in fact, deconstructing 'woman' as a category; that is, this well-known speech can be read as a commentary on the seemingly universal notions of 'woman' and 'femininity', and not merely as an assertion that Black women are different from white women. The implication of deconstructing 'woman' means that the 'solution' which follows is not a simplistic one of adding (in this case Black) women in. Rather, by raising the charge of racial *erasure*, women of colour are presenting a means for redefining 'womanhood' and 'femininity'.

This point may also be drawn from Rosina Visram's (1986) historical account of Indians in Britain from 1700 to 1947, in which she demonstrated that the history of Britain rests on the contributions of women and men from India, from at least over two centuries ago. She noted that women frequently came as ayahs – (live-in housekeepers and carers of children).

Visram's documenting of this pattern of migration for some Indian women shows how white women, who were the memsahibs, negotiated their roles as mother and homemaker by using the labour of non-white, poor women.

It is these examples which can begin to show how the interconnections amongst imperialism, class and 'race' inform the many definitions of womanhood. From these examples it can be seen that definitions of 'woman' are often contradictory and it is these contradictions which may be rightly accentuated as the histories of women of colour are reflected upon.

In the past decade, following critiques similar to the above, there have been a number of attempts to counter racialised/ethnicised erasure, as, for example, in the anthology produced in the USA by Women of the South Asian Diaspora (1993). This collection of over 100 pieces (which includes poetry, short stories and critical commentary) was produced by women students at the University of California at Berkeley who came together in 1991 because they felt estranged from other forums of women of colour in the USA. They were students from Ethnic Studies, Development Studies and Anthropology and the book came about because 'we have come to understand that South Asian women's solidarity throughout the diaspora is necessary to increase our visibility' (Women of the South Asian Diaspora, 1993, p. xvi). This sentiment is echoed in the Foreword by Jane Singh: 'This anthology comes at a critical point in South Asian American history. As one of the least-studied ethnic groups in the United States, people of South Asian origin have been overlooked by historians and social scientists as well as by scholars of Ethnic and Women's Studies' (p. vii).

An attempt to undermine such erasures also underlies the book by Valerie Mason-John and Ann Khambatta (1993), in which the authors interviewed 16 Black[7] lesbians about their lives in England. The book provides quotes from the women who were interviewed on matters such as whether Black lesbians should dissociate themselves from white lesbians; whether lesbian sexualities were expressed more freely in Africa, Asia, the Americas and the Caribbean before colonisation; on relationships with white women; racism; S/M politics; and the use of 'queer'. The authors have successfully shown in this work that the range of opinions within Black lesbian communities is wide ('neither of us fits neatly into prevalent, one-dimensional notions of black lesbian identity', p. 10) and draw skilfully upon the interviews to demonstrate this point very clearly. For example, in discussing relationships with white women they quote Marlene Bogle: 'I thought I would never have a relationship with a white woman but I did. Although it didn't work out, we did have some common ground' (Mason-John and Khambatta, 1993, p. 31). They also quote Hope Massiah: 'Relationships with white women are fraught with difficulties. I've been in relationships with white women, and although they were good, the issue of racism was always there. You cannot escape from racism' (Mason-John and Khambatta, 1993, p. 30); and Femi

Otitoju: 'White lesbians often say: let's all be comfortable together and let it all be nice and not too difficult. They conveniently ignore that we are different, and that we have a different experience' (Mason-John and Khambatta, 1993, p. 45). The book also takes the reader through a history of Black lesbianism in Britain over the past 20 years, including the OWAAD[8] conferences, the development of *Outwrite* in 1982 – a newspaper produced by women of colour – which folded in 1989, the development of the Black Lesbian Group in 1982, as well as events such as the 1984 Black Feminist Conference in London, the appearance of *Mukti* (an Asian feminist magazine) in 1984, the Zami I and II conferences (for women of colour lesbians) in 1985 and 1989, and the development of conferences and groups outside London from the late 1980s on.

More recently, there has been an anthology edited by Valerie Mason-John (1995) which is compilation of writings by lesbians of colour in Britain. This anthology examines a range of issues in addition to the interconnections amongst 'race'/ethnicity, gender and sexuality such as age, representation, and everyday life. The above books – one is an interview study and two are edited collections – demonstrate that women of colour are still busy producing literature to counter our/their erasure from the rhetoric and practices of Women's Studies.

Denial within Women's Studies

Racial *erasure* implicates white women. Thus, not only are white women racist, or, implicated in institutionalised racism, but there is also a simultaneous *denial* of whiteness as a racialised category. White skin frequently signifies power and privilege – 'the rightness of whiteness' – and this is often accompanied by a silence on the part of white women about their privilege as inscribed within political, economic and ideological inequality. This silence can mean denial and this denial can then lead to a lack of focus on examining whiteness, and its role in perpetuating power inequalities. What can also happen is that in not analysing whiteness, it can then be assumed that all hegemonic feminisms have to do in order to engage with 'race' is to focus simply on the experience of Black women. However, if whiteness is unpacked, it may then be possible to see more clearly how gender privilege and inequality are expressed through racialised contexts, as well as vice versa.

There has been some work in the 1990s which examines whiteness. For example, Ruth Frankenberg in her book *White Women: Race Matters* shows that white women in the USA can reflect on whiteness as part of their personal biographies and also shows how 'Growing Up White' (a title of a chapter in the book) is a crucial practice of whiteness which shapes women's experiences. This 1993 book was shortly preceded by *Beyond the*

Pale, a book written by Vron Ware and published in 1992, on white women and their historical complicity with British colonisation. Both of these books argue that the privilege which is accorded to white women has much of its roots in the historical circumstances of colonisation and immigration, and suggest that until whiteness is viewed as a racialised category, it will be difficult for much of feminism and for white feminists to overcome their racism.

Denial over the power and privilege which whiteness often provides is perhaps most likely to be encountered within particular strands of radical feminism. This is because radical feminism argues that the key antagonism in human social relations is that men, as a group, profit from women's oppression, and that this is a primary antagonism that is the source of all other inequalities (Humm, 1995b). A logical consequence of such a politics for both Black and white radical feminists is that sisterhood becomes the main goal for which all women must struggle and, in this way, women's difference can be easily sidestepped. This is not to say that liberal or socialist and Marxist feminisms always deal adequately with racism, although the work of Angela Davis (1981) is one example of an analysis which takes Marxism, socialism and feminism seriously within a context of racialised inequalities. My argument is that it is a radical feminist, and related, analysis that is most likely to lead to a denial of differing and contradictory interests between women of colour and white women.

One consequence of the denial of the privilege of whiteness is that there can then be an implicit assumption that all women ultimately have the same material interests: overcoming patriarchy. For example, when a white woman falsely accuses a Black man of raping her, the issues that frequently come to the fore are ones which pit women against men. In such cases, there can be a simultaneous silence about the fact that such accusations are shaped by patriarchal and racialised structuring simultaneously. One of the clearest expressions of this is the now classic statement by the Combahee River Collective:

A combined antiracist and antisexist position drew us together initially, and as we developed politically we addressed ourselves to heterosexism and economic oppression under capitalism . . . We believe that sexual politics under patriarchy is as pervasive in Black women's lives as are the politics of class and race. We also often find it difficult to separate race from class from sex oppression because in our lives they are most often experienced simultaneously . . . We struggle together with Black men against racism, while we also struggle with Black men about sexism. (Combahee River Collective, 1981, pp. 212–13)

Fifteen years later, as I write this chapter, I would also like to add one more sentence: 'We struggle together with white women against patriarchal oppression while we also struggle with white women about racism and imperial domination.'

A *denial* in relation to 'race'/ethnicity, and the privilege of whiteness, can lead to an opposition of white women against Black men. Such a pitting is not just confined to past events (see Angela Davis's 1981 analysis of the Scottsboro Nine events in the USA in the 1920s). The 1995–6 trial of O. J. Simpson in the USA is a case in point. In this trial Simpson, an African-American man and an ex-footballer, well known to many people for his prowess at football, his sports commentaries and his acting roles, was accused of murdering his white ex-wife, Nicole Brown Simpson. He was also known to have physically abused his wife a number of times (through telephone calls she made to the Los Angeles Police Department). Much of the commentary and writings on the trial stated that public opinion on the trial was overwhelmingly informed by two mutually exclusive oppositions: either that one section of public opinion sided with white feminists who wanted to eliminate domestic violence and therefore were certain that Simpson was guilty of murder, or that another section of public opinion sided with African-American people who wanted to eliminate racism, and so considered him to have been framed, and therefore not guilty of murder. There seemed to be no room for feminists (of colour, for example) who abhorred his brutal beatings of his ex-wife, but who also argued that he should be allowed to have a trial which did not reproduce the institutionalised racism that is overwhelming in the USA, particularly when African-American men are brought into the legal system.

The trial began on 7 November 1994 and was televised in its entirety, with the first major event being jury selection: a procedure that lasted almost two months. During this time, much was made in the media of the idea that a predominantly Black jury would automatically side with a Black defendant, despite statistics which show that 'race' of victim and 'race' of defendant are not factors that influence jury decisions in spousal murder cases. Almost nothing was said about the number of women on the jury, and how that might influence their decision. The 'not guilty' verdict was watched by 57 per cent of the adult population of the USA (Bill Carter, 'Executives are Cool to Idea of Pay-Per View TV Interview', *New York Times*, 5 October 1991).

As I said earlier, much of the commentary on this trial pitted Black men against white women. For example, in this trial, the prosecution, led by a white woman, drew upon prevailing cultural 'common senses' about Black men as emotionally uncontrolled people, particularly in relation to white women.[9]

A similar 'competition' between 'race' and feminist issues was also present in the Hill–Thomas Senate Hearings in the USA held in October 1991. The hearings were convened so that the United States Senate could examine evidence that had become available which suggested that a nominee for the

US Supreme Court – Clarence Thomas, a Black man – had sexually harassed a woman at his work place. The woman whom he was accused of harassing, Anita Hill, is also Black. These events have been discussed in many ways.[10]

During the hearings, a clear interconnection was established by Thomas between 'race' and gender through his use of the metaphor of lynching to describe his perception of the hearings. Clarence Thomas's reference to the hearings as a 'hi-tech lynching for an uppity black' (13 October 1991) has become fairly well known. However, less well commented upon is that he used the metaphor of lynching very early on, in the final sentences of his Opening Statement. He states there, 'I will not provide the rope for my own lynching or for further humiliation.' In drawing upon lynching, Thomas is not only presenting himself as a racialised victim but as a sexual victim too. This is because lynching connotes 'race' and sex simultaneously, for Black men in the USA were often castrated when they were lynched by white people. Also, lynchings were presented as an appropriate sanction when there were allegations that Black men had slept with white women. The fears and the horrors associated with miscegenation by white people were seen as adequate reason to conduct a lynching. So Thomas constructed an image of himself as a racial and sexual victim (Bhavnani, 1993b).

In drawing on racism, Thomas was able to rely upon a key tension within hegemonic feminisms, namely that gender and 'race' are mutually exclusive categories and therefore do not affect each other. He also implied that siding with him implied siding with anti-racists, and siding with her implied siding with white (racist) feminists. In implying that Anita Hill was a puppet of racists who might oppose his nomination, Thomas (unconsciously?) signalled the long and unfortunate history of US 'white feminisms' which suggest that gendered inequalities are more serious than racialised ones.

His invocation of the history of Black men being lynched overrode all of Hill's carefully presented arguments and persona about the allegations. What happened was that by introducing these discourses Thomas succeeded in devaluing the allegations of sexual harassment from a Black woman about the behaviour of a Black man. The apparent ease with which he was able to do this is due to the following processes. US feminist movements have rarely *engaged* with the charges of racism directed at them by Black and Third World women. Consequently, when Thomas organised his Opening Statement around the racism he had defied, these (hegemonic) feminist movements were unable to challenge his assertions. When, on occasion, some feminists writing in the press did discuss racism, they tended to view gender and 'race' as sources of inequality that are distinct from each other, rather than as intertwined axes of differing interests.

In other words, gendered inequalities are usually constructed both as discrete from, and in competition with racialised inequalities – either someone is Black *or* they are a woman – rather than as categories which are enmeshed and therefore interconnect with each other. If hegemonic feminist movements go along with such a separation, then women of colour come to be defined into or out of one of these categories, with the consequent erasure, denial and invisibility. And anyone who refuses the separation, who argues uncompromisingly that 'race' and gender are inextricably interlinked, ends up with arguments that are not attended to (see Bray, 1991). In this way, the *denials* elide into *invisibility*: the *invisibility* of Black women as racialised, sexualised and gendered subjects within capitalism.

Invisibility within Women's Studies

A racism within much of Women's Studies and feminist campaigns which is based on the *invisibility* of Black women is the target of many critiques. Some time ago Hazel Carby (1982) showed how 'feminist' analyses of the British welfare state which argued that women were dependent on men in Britain did not 'fit' for some women of colour. For example, many Afro-Caribbean women who were recruited to Britain after 1945 came as workers. Women of South Asian origin were more likely to enter Britain as dependents of men after 1945, but they were also subject to the controls of the British immigration legislation, a set of legislation which legitimated internal examinations of women at entry to Britain, and which led to severe restrictions on family life for Black people. Thus, 'classic' early feminist analyses ignored the relationships to the state which women of colour had, as workers as well as migrants, and also ignored the ways in which these corresponded with ideologies and political realities of women as dependents.

Fiona Williams (1989) attended to the points made by Carby in her book *Social Policy*, in which she reviewed the implications of the charge of racism and sexism in analyses of British welfare. Hers was one of the first books on social policy in Britain which explicitly attempted to integrate 'race'/ ethnicity, gender, class and sexuality with welfare provision. In other words, her arguments developed the points that Hazel Carby had made, thus showing the specific ways in which the erasure of women of colour led to a denial of the privilege of whiteness, which then made women of colour *invisible*.

Unfortunately, such invisibility is still an active component of hegemonic feminisms. This may be noted in the more recent publication by Maxine Baca-Zinn and Bonnie Thornton-Dill (1994), *Women of Colour in U.S. Society*, which aims to rectify invisibility.[11] The editors argue that their edited collection demonstrates that the urgent task for feminist scholarship is to study the diversity of women's experiences, which is the logical precursor to arguing that feminist scholarship could appropriately examine the interconnections of the categories of diversity and inequality with gender.

A key aspect of Women's Studies is that we develop academic enquiry and projects which overcome the invisibility of women, and thus stop us being hidden from history. Almost by definition, such work will not only 'add women in' to the information, but through such 'additions' it will be able to transform received ideas, and thus understand women's myriad resistances and forms of exploitation. For example, Angela Davis did this 25 years ago in her 1971 article, 'Reflections on the role of the black woman in the community of slaves', in which she analysed and so refuted the concept of the Black matriarch 'at its presumed historical inception' (Davis, 1971, p. 3). One section of her article dealt with resistances within the lives of the enslaved, and she argued that it was only within the 'home' (out of sight of the slave owners and overseers) that it was possible for the enslaved to assert a small amount of freedom. That is, it was through the performance of domestic labour that enslaved Black women came to be central in the creation of an arena through which some aspects of slavery could be resisted.

The work of Parita Trivedy (1984) attempted to do something similar through an examination of the documents which showed some ways women were involved in peasant uprisings in India in the 1940s. In her argument, she showed why it is important to study the Mahila Samitis who were women who organised around the specific forms of oppressions experienced by peasant women, and that organisation included being couriers as well as being involved in armed struggle. She also showed how such work can allow the present to be understood as dynamic rather than as being static.

However, it is not only the use of historical methods which can prevent *invisibility*.[12] If we can analyse, and then try to change how people are represented, in this case (women of colour), then that could be another means of undermining our invisibility. bell hooks (1992) has shown that there has been little change in the representations of Black people (women and men) and argues that it is important to struggle over representations which either deny the existence of Black people, or draw upon only negative representations. More recently, Reina Lewis (1996) and Lola Young (1996) have done just that. Lewis argues in her book that she is investigating a problem – the relationship between imperialism and culture and their relation to gender – by closely analysing the work of the artist Henriette Brown and the literary works of George Eliot. It is worth noting in her argument about Orientalism[13], which is nicely complex and nuanced, that she shows that while white women did not have an immediately obvious access to being Orientalist they were implicated in some of the constructions and repercussions of Orientalism.

Lola Young's work provides a critique of cinematic representation arguing that: 'The small number of critical accounts of British cinema which have addressed racial concerns have tended to privilege "race" without adequately exploring or indicating the place of gender, sexuality and class' (Young, 1996, p. 189). She also shows how an analysis of white women in terms of their ethnicity, alongside their gender, would provide new recognition of the ways in which 'race', class, sexuality, ethnicity and gender inform each other.[14]

The process of becoming invisible affects women of colour in many ways. It is not only our histories in relation to the histories of white women which work in conflictual and contradictory ways: it is also that our sexualities and our ways of expressing them – whether in an interracial setting, whether with white children, whether we live as single women or whether we choose to live as lesbians, or indeed, whether we live with a combination of these identities – get informed and influenced by invisibility. The invisibility can be undermined, as the examples above demonstrate, by making the invisible visible. This is needed not just to obtain a more complete or more accurate description (it is not just an 'adding-in' issue) but also because a consideration of issues of lesbian and gay sexuality can permit a more precise set of projections which can indicate the kinds of visions we have and want to create. That is, when we reflect on sexual institutions within societies, we can see that ideas of heterosexuality, monogamy, polyandry, for example, deeply implicate one set of structures for reproducing inequalities as distinct to others.

What much work which perpetuates or reproduces the invisibility of women of colour does is to demonstrate that it is important to name racism, whether that racism occurs through erasure, denial or invisibility, because when racism is named it then becomes possible to start to create the conditions to undermine that racism. Take as an example lesbians. Just as many white lesbians argue about the invisibility of lesbianism within feminist analyses and campaigns, so lesbians of colour have also commented on their invisibility for some time.

> G: But I also feel a joy and strength at seeing any Black and Third World women coming out because they all help to shatter the myth that lesbianism is a 'white thing'. (Carmen *et al.*, 1984, p. 56)

Clearly, such invisibility was not eliminated because of that one article. Yet since that piece, there have been a number of edited collections which address the interconnections between 'race', ethnicity and sexuality (see Ratti, 1993, which was explicitly put together to counter the invisibility of South Asian lesbians and gay men in the USA), and also articles and collections which focus on the relationship between ethnicity, 'race' and lesbianism (Trujillo, 1991; Kaahumanu and Hutchins, 1991.[15]). Films such as *Khush*, (made by Pratibha Parmar in 1991) opened up discussion about sexualities in both the Third and the First Worlds simultaneously, and there has also been the development of organisations such as Shamakami[16] which brings together South Asian feminist lesbians and bisexual women in the USA who may feel unable to live in some parts of the world because of their sexuality, only to then experience racism in other parts (Islam, 1993).

Tokenism within Women's Studies

Erasure, leading to *denial*, which are the precursors for *invisibility*, means that a solution which is often created is that of *tokenism*. Tokenistic practices may be viewed as a possibility of re-organising human lives along with economic, political and ideological institutions to include/integrate categories of inequality (such as sexuality, class, gender, and 'race'/ethnicity) that are often seen as distinct and discrete, while avoiding both victimology or pathology.

However, *tokenism* can also mean a lack. The problem, though, is that the acknowledgement of a lack can often prevent any further analysis and exploration of why that lack occurs. A case in point is Susan Faludi's 1991 book, *Backlash*, which was on the *New York Times* bestseller list for many weeks. In this work, she argues that the end of the twentieth century has led to a backlash against feminism, by which she means 'white' feminism. While I do not wholly agree with her analysis (Bhavnani, 1993b), my point here is that she mentions Black women of colour in a very tokenistic manner. For example, she has only five index entries for women of colour, in a book that is 552 pages long. The longest of these refers to the different experiences and locations of African-American women in the US labour force (pp. 365–6), with the others referring, extremely briefly, to the wages of African-American women (p. 364 and p. 374), to the fact that all women do not obtain positions in management or in men's departments in the retail industry (p. 388)[17], and a reference to the poverty levels amongst African-American women (p. 482) which is done only in the context of reproductive rights and anti-abortion movements. These entries suggest that she views racism, when she sees it, as being primarily about the relationship between African-American women and white women. Thus, she not only reproduces tokenism, but, in addition, she further inscribes the invisibility of other women of colour in the rhetoric of hegemonic feminism.[18]

Token acknowledgements, by their very nature, prevent deeper questions being asked (and analyses being produced) about whether there are differences – material, ideological and political – amongst women and, just as importantly, how such differences could be overcome. The reason for using Susan Faludi's book as an example is because it was very widely read and discussed, and if such books continue to define feminism, even implicitly, as only about (and for?) white women, then any references to women of colour necessarily become token references. That is, they become ways of only 'adding-in' women of colour, and not a means for suggesting how feminism could be transformed.[19]

Therefore, simply adding 'race' into gendered inequalities, rather than conceptualising them as enmeshed within each other, can produce a tokenism of the most unhelpful sort: we come to be 'perceived as token women in Black texts and as token Blacks in feminist texts' (Giddings, 1984, p. 5).

It is this 'adding-in' (which can suggest tokenism) that the philosopher Elizabeth Spelman (1988) has partly addressed in her thoughtfully written book, *Inessential Woman*. In one chapter she examined the arguments that lead to questions such as 'which is more fundamental – sexism or racism?' She shows that this is an unhelpful question, for it implies that each is a clearly bounded discrete category which is untouched by the other. In other words, the question is unanswerable for it is like asking, about the product of a multiplication, which of the two numbers is more fundamental to the answer. In the same vein, it is not possible to create a universal list that places oppressions in a hierarchical relationship to each other. Inequalities intertwine and intersect with each other such that it is impossible to establish general rules which dictate that one form of inequality is more severe than another. This can only be done in specific contexts and with specific situations. Categories of 'race'/ethnicity, sexuality and class inequalities reciprocally inform each other and inform gender and, because of this enmeshed nature of their relationships, it is not possible to say that one category is likely to lead to 'more' exploitation or oppression than another without specifying the historical, geographical, political and related dimensions as they pertain to the specific situation in which such claims are being made.[20]

Some of these complexities can be seen when thinking about identity. For example, I am not simply a woman, or Black or a woman of colour, or a university professor, or Indian, or a mother, or someone who teaches feminist studies and about Third World women's struggles, or an aunt, or heterosexual, or a socialist, for each of my apparently categorical identities is not what it appears. A woman of colour from Britain employed as a university professor in the USA, such as myself, is constantly negotiating some of the tensions and contradictions of symbolic and actual power, privilege, powerlessness and institutionalised discrimination when she is in her job. Some co-workers and students may want to categorise me as one or the other first, and I may elect, or have foisted upon me, a particular part of my identity in a particular situation. But if there are others which could have been selected, then the existence of those possibilities means that those other categories also inform my identity. So, categories of identity (and inequality) are not discrete and uninfluenced by each other. For example, when I teach, am I being seen (heard is probably more accurate, because of my English accent) as a non-American, a woman, a woman of colour?[21] My argument is that it is not possible to say which, if any, of these will be privileged above the others without analysing the specific contexts in which the identities are seen and named. In other words, it is not possible to think of 'woman' as a category without simultaneously reflecting on whether the woman is defined as white or not, an 'outsider' or not, how her sexuality is perceived, and what her class position and allegiances are assumed to be. There are, of course, many other identity markers, such as age and disability, which could also be used in the above example.[22]

Thus, the very processes by which Women's Studies claims that gender is ignored – *Erasure, Denial, Invisibility* and *Tokenism* – are ones that themselves act as *EDIT*ors of Women's Studies.

Is experience the way forward?

It is sometimes argued that experience – and specifically, differences of experience between white women and women of colour – is the way out of such *EDIT*ing. Spelman (1988) argues that 'a lively regard' (p. 131) for experience is crucial. Certainly, a key and major contribution of Women's Studies texts has been to record the importance of experience within academic analyses. This is a particular contribution by which feminists can tackle academic work in Women's Studies, for to examine experience may start a process of excavating suppressed and subjugated knowledges.

However, to privilege experience as a way into understanding women's exploitation and oppression can also hinder discussion and debate. For example, I can feel intimidated in white-only contexts, and white women could claim they feel intimidated when women of colour discuss racism for many hours, and make the white women feel guilty. Although the same word is used, it obviously does not express the same type of experience.

The argument about experience could also be used when reflecting on an assumed desire on the part of many people to feel at home, to have the experience of 'home'. Yet:

Where is home for starters? Can you call a country which has system-atically colonised your countries of origin, one which refuses through a thorough racism in its institutions, media and culture to even recognise your existence and your rights to that existence – can you call this country 'home' without having your tongue inside your cheek?

For Black women who are political or economic exiles from countries such as South Africa, Chile, Jamaica, India (the list could of course be endless) where is 'home'? . . . Home with such women becomes a place of mind, a place where she knows she cannot be. (Grewal *et al.*, (1988), p. 10)[23]

As Women's Studies, as an area of academic thought, has had such difficulty in persuading the academy that experience must be integral to social analyses, this insistence can mean that experience becomes privileged, and thus becomes *the* claim to an unchanging truth. As a result, it has often 'made sense' for experience to be constructed in opposition to objectivity, which itself has been, and continues to be, thoroughly interrogated in the past decade (Allen and Baber, 1992; Longino, 1993; Nicholson, 1994). In addition, feminist critiques have, in challenging 'objectivity', raised the question 'who can be a knower?' (see Code, 1991; Harding, 1991; Lather, 1991). Thus, feminist work has been important in raising questions about the possibility of a value-free knowledge. It has also been argued that the different ways in which different knowledges are framed is an *ideological* issue rather than one of objective analysis.[24] Yet there still seems to be an underlying theme that the 'experience'/'objectivity' binary should be inverted, and that this will ensure the subversion of mainstream knowledge.[25] The result of an argument like this is that 'experience' becomes *the* claim to truth; that is, it claims a place identical to the one that objectivity presently has/had, and 'experience' then becomes the only truth, silencing disagreements and argumentation.[26] It was a focus on commonalities of experience amongst women, to the exclusion of any discussions of difference, that underpinned the idea of a global sisterhood, with the result that power inequalities amongst women were sidestepped.

The outcome of the many challenges to an opposition between experience and objectivity is that it now becomes easier to see that individual experience is created in an active relationship to objectivity. Both create and inform, and are created and informed, by the other. For example my version of feminism leads me to *experience* anger about all human poverty, and this experience is informed by my *'objective' knowledge* that there is institutionalised injustice against poor people. In this way, my intellectual commitment to examine the causes and the perpetuation of poverty are informed by my experience of seeing people who have to beg for money being stripped of all human dignity and self-respect. I cannot say that my experience is more important than my 'objective' knowledge: each has informed the development and commitment of the other. It is an understanding of this relationship between experience and objectivity which could undermine the privileging of one form of knowledge over another, and so subvert the processes which create hierarchies of knowledge.

For example, Haraway's (1988) argument that objectivity is a 'particular and specific embodiment' rather than a 'false vision promising transcendence of all limits and responsibility' (Haraway, 1988, p. 582) is one example of such subversion. She argues that 'partial perspectives' are 'privileged ones', because 'feminist objectivity is about *limited* location and *situated* knowledge' (Haraway, 1988, p. 583; my emphasis). Limited location and situated knowledge are therefore the route into the creation of feminist objectivity. Such an elegant argument is not simply relevant for theoretical work, but also for feminist empirical work. I have engaged with Haraway's argument by suggesting criteria by which it may be used to develop feminist research strategies, the criteria being accountability, the micro-politics of research situations and engaging with issues of difference (Bhavnani, 1993b).

From the above, it can be seen that I argue that the reason for the *EDIT*ing of Women's Studies is not simply because the experiences of women of colour are different from those of white women, and that the former are omitted from hegemonic feminisms for, if that were the case, then 'adding-in women of colour' would be the solution. As we have seen, 'adding-in' is unsatisfactory since it leaves the category of 'feminist' itself as singular, universal, unquestioned and therefore intact.

A parallel point, but cast as the relationship between theory and practice, was made by Barbara Christian (1987). In that classic article she was arguing against an opposition between theory (which is treated as mediated analysis) and literature (which is treated as pure and authentic expression). Her argument focuses on the academic status given to theoretical analyses, and she argues that those who strive for the greatest academic respectability have to be defined as doing theoretical work. The ideas she presents have been discussed within the many women's movements all across the world – how theory and practice are intimately connected and that 'theory' is not of greater value than 'practice' – and yet contemporary discussions about the nature of feminist theory seem to ignore them.

Despite the cautionary note sounded above about experience being the only truth, it is clear that both theory/analysis and experience must remain central to any project that defines itself as feminist. One example of such integration is in the work of Dorinne Kondo (1991). The book is an ethnographic exploration of identity and its construction in a Japanese work place. The author, a Japanese American woman, provides the reader with a thoughtful account of her own feelings and ideas as to how her identity is perceived – she is seen as both an insider and an outsider to put it at its most simple – as she discusses the many social institutions that serve to shape the identities of the people she encounters. In this way she provides a wonderful set of insights on how conducting ethnographic work with a group with which one has a particular affinity leads to exciting complexities within the ethnography: complexities that make the work more true to the reality of the people's lives. Another example of ethnographic work which aroused considerable controversy in the USA because the writer claimed an affinity with the subject of her study is Ruth Behar's *Translated Woman* (1993). The controversy came about because Behar argued that the position of Esperanza – a poor woman who worked as a street peddler in a small town in Mexico, 500 miles south of the US border, whose story she tells – was similar to her own position as a Cuban woman in the USA employed as a university professor and seeking tenure in the US academy. Whatever the merits of the comparison, this book is another example of writing which draws upon feminist arguments to produce a book that integrates personal experience with theory.

Difference and Women's Studies

Both of the above writers tackle the issue of difference in their work, which is one of the most important issues for contemporary feminism.[27] Yet 'difference' itself is contested, and used in different ways by different analysts. For example, Henrietta Moore points out that 'such is the malleability of the term that almost anything can be subsumed under it' (Moore, 1994, p. 1). Her book is a collection of her writings on anthropology and gender which are united in an attempt to develop a 'specifically anthropological approach to feminist post-structuralist theory' (Moore, 1994, p. 7). It is often asserted that the discussions of 'difference' in the past decade have been the impetus for re-thinking Women's Studies as a unitary approach to knowledge. While it is true that the past decade has witnessed a significant growth in discussions of 'difference', it is also worth remembering that women of colour have been arguing about many of these issues, within second-wave feminisms, since the 1970s.[28] At one's most sceptical, one could argue that the reason 'difference' is now taken so seriously is because white analysts (both women and men) have engaged with it, whereas before they merely ignored it.

Since, the meaning of 'difference' is so malleable, it is necessary to examine the concept systematically. Avtar Brah has done just that by arguing that difference, in the context of discussions which examine the interconnections of 'race'/ethnicity with feminism, needs to be thought about in four ways: difference as experience, difference as social relations, difference as subjectivity and difference as identity (Brah, 1992). Mary Maynard (1994) has built on this and argued that while difference may be thought of as diversity of experience, it is the post-modern use of the term that now prevails in most academic discussions. She argues that because post-modern approaches emphasise fragmentation, and the idea of multiple selves, and thus a distrust of a metanarrative, there is a danger that such thinking examines what divides women to the exclusion of reflecting on what it is that also unites women. She is not arguing for a return to an 'all women are sisters' position, however. What she says is that the categories of 'race'/ethnicity and gender should be analysed not to make them disappear into a universal sisterhood but, rather, to illuminate the processes by which they interconnect, yet retain their distinct identities. Her solution is that feminisms should develop a politics of identification rather than a politics of difference (Maynard, 1994, p. 19). In arguing this, Maynard draws upon an earlier chapter by Avtar Brah (1991) which suggests that a politics of identification is one in which political coalitions are developed through the acknowledgement of struggles of groups other than one's own.

The complexities of examining difference, while still retaining ideas about how women *could* be united is a major theme in the writings by women of colour these days. For example, Ien Ang argues: 'For some time now, the problematic of race and ethnicity has thrown feminism into crisis' (Ang, 1995, p. 57). That opening sentence of her article takes the reader through a wide-ranging argument about the difficulties of dealing with difference for, she suggests, 'recognition', 'understanding' and 'dialogue' are not the answer. Her point is that if the goal is to achieve a resolution of difference, then feminism becomes similar to the idea of a multicultural nation (she is using Australia as her main example here) that has shifted its desire from assimilation of people of colour to one in which differences are to be celebrated and tolerated. That is, the desire to resolve difference means that feminism adopts a pluralist position towards 'race'/ethnicity. The problem with pluralism is that power inequalities are not always engaged with – pluralistic societies often imply that all that is needed is a tolerance of difference by permitting all differences to exist simultaneously – and many critics of pluralism argue that such a philosophy creates barriers to asking why it is that in plural contexts, values/cultures/politics are still, however, in a hierarchical relation to each other.[29] Ien Ang suggests that in this way of thinking, feminism becomes like a nation which 'invites' other women (for which read non-white women, on the whole) to join in, but only on the condition that they do not upset the fundamental basis of feminism. Her suggestion is to develop a 'politics of partiality' (Ang, 1995, p. 73) rather than a politics of inclusion.

Both Maynard and Ang seem to be arguing for different emphases in the starting point for feminisms: one for identification (as distinct from difference) and the other for partiality as distinct from inclusion. The way through these apparently oppositional arguments seems to be to argue for a feminism which begins with both the realisation that women have different material interests amongst themselves, but also, at the same time, acknowledges that such differences are not 'natural' but are socially/politically created. That is, my suggestion is to argue that feminisms can represent both current realities about women and our lives (that is, a politics of difference), and *simultaneously* represent the hope that such differences of interests may not always be the case (a politics of possibilities).

Donna Gabaccia (1994) has written a book which implicitly works from the starting point of a politics of partiality, but which also focuses on the ways in which 'race'/ethnicity, gender, class and sexuality are interconnected, and moves towards a politics of possibilities. Her study, which begins with the experience of migratory women, looks at the relationship between world development, migration and American immigrant life, and she specifically focuses on these interconnections to see how foreign immigrant women redefined the meaning of American womanhood. She expresses the hope that her work will 'encourage scholars in women's studies to continue submitting key concepts – from modernization and race to emancipation and patriarchy – to ever more intensive cross-cultural scrutiny' (Gabaccia, 1994, p. xiii). She argues that while gender was not 'the primary marker of the boundary between the U.S. and the other side' (Gabaccia, 1994, p. 128), it 'mattered in a variety of ways' (Gabaccia, 1994, p. 128). Her work also demonstrates that through an attention to gender it is possible to see the differences between African Americans and other minorities in the USA: how they are seen racially, but also in other ways. Her desire that gender be always examined along with 'race'/ethnicity, class, nationality and nativity is timely, and is yet another example of the excellent scholarship that can be produced when the *interconnections* amongst categories of inequality are scrutinised.[30]

Third World Women's Studies

One especially apt way to examine the interconnections of categories of inequality is to focus on women in the Third World – their situations, their movements, and their struggles of resistance – for their lives and writings encompass all the categories of inequality that I have discussed above.[31] The 1995 conference to mark the end of The Second UN Decade For Women – held amidst some controversy in Beijing – certainly tackled issues of sexuality, difference, ethnicity, identity, class, nationality and the state, and their interconnections with each other. That it was held in the Third World, with mainly Third World delegates present amongst the 30 000 women signifies the importance of Third World women's struggles for change, and also demonstrates that hegemonic feminisms, if they are to keep up with the issues raised by social movements, need to place such struggles at the centre of their work. In short, Western feminisms need to integrate non-Western perspectives into their theorising.

Cynthia Enloe's book (1990) began to do this by 'making feminist sense of international politics'.[32] In addition to changing the focus of theorising, it is clear that First World feminisms could learn much from writings produced by/about women in the Third World (such as the collection edited by Sangari and Vaid, 1989, and the work by Guzman Bouvard, 1996, on how women across the world are reshaping human rights). That there is such a shift in focus away from the First World may be seen in collections such as the recent one edited by Haleh Afshar (1996) which examines feminist politics in the Third World. This collection provides examples of new ways to understand not only feminism, but also ways to understand political strategies and struggles that are developed by women.[33] For example, the articles in this book range from an examination of the interconnections amongst women in the Third World with the state, the politics of aid, fertility, religion and authoritarianism. In this way, the work which is discussed demonstrates through analysing interconnections how feminist thought and critique transforms the very categories which it engages with, and suggests how women's resistances in the Third World can help First World women's struggles.

Saskia Wieringa (1995) tackles the experiences of resistance in her collection entitled *Subversive Women*, which is subtitled *Women's Movements in Africa, Asia, Latin America and the Caribbean*. This book, which was published in the USA, UK and in India simultaneously, discusses not only methods and epistemology in feminist research, but also the ways in which women resisted, and continue to resist, colonisation, imperialism, and economic and cultural inequalities through an examination of their roles as mothers, as producers of food, in theatre and through the writing of poetry.

The Wieringa book is unusual, along with the collection by Afshar, for much work which focuses on the Third World either operates with a conception of women as beings without agency, or does not analyse the roles played by women in both the public and private domains. In addition, most work also rarely comments upon how women's role in the private domain impacts upon the public domain.[34]

Conclusion

As Women's Studies scholarship continues to develop, it is clear that such development is not without its drawbacks. The most significant drawback is one that uses the very same processes – of editing, denial, invisibility and tokenism – which have kept feminist thinking out of the mainstream to keep women of colour out of hegemonic feminist thought. The way to move on beyond such drawbacks is for Women's Studies to both work with the idea of two types of politics – namely, a politics of difference alongside a politics of possibilities – as well as to take the lead in examining the *interconnections* between gender and other categories of inequality, so that the relationship amongst all categories of inequality can be seen to be contingent, shifting and enmeshed, rather than as mutually exclusive and in competition with each other. I have argued that issues raised by feminists and other women in the Third World, along with issues raised by feminists and women of colour in the First World, provide the means through which such interconnections may be analysed.

Notes

1. I will use the term 'women of colour' throughout this chapter to refer to women who are not white.
2. I will discuss these events later in this chapter.
3. It is clear that each category structures the others. As Zillah Eisenstein says: 'Racialized patriarchy that reflects the complex connections between racial and sexual privilege is differentiated by gender, while gender is differentiated in and through the racialized meanings of whiteness' (Eisenstein, 1994, p. 41).
4. 'That this way of conceptualising 'woman' is not merely an historical event, but continues today has also been argued by K. Robinson (1996) in her article about the lack of voice for Filippinas in discussions of their sexuality and gender relationships. She suggests that there is a 'presumption that women as a group have a transparent set of interests so that a (politically conscious) First World white woman can speak for all women' (K. Robinson, 1996, p. 57).
5. The use of Third World to describe nations which are poor, or 'underdeveloped', is controversial. However, I will use this term for it best presents the geographic and economic issues I wish to address when discussing the development of contemporary feminisms.
6. The extract from her speech which is most well known is as follows:

   'That man over there says that women need to be helped into carriages, and lifted over ditches, and to have the best places . . . and ain't I a woman? Look at me! Look at my arm! . . . I have ploughed and planted and gathered into barns, and no man could heed me – and ain't I a woman? I could work as much as any man (when I could get it) and bear the lash as well – and ain't I a woman? I have borne five children and seen them most sold off into slavery, and when I cried out with grief, none but Jesus heard – and ain't I a woman?'

7. The authors define 'black' as referring to people who are 'descended (through one or both parents) from Africa, Asia (i.e. the Middle East to China, including the Pacific nations) and Latin America and lesbians and gay men descended from the original inhabitants of Australasia, North America, and the islands of the Atlantic and Indian Ocean' (p. 9).
8. OWAAD refers to the Organisation of Women of Asian and African Descent. This organisation – which was set up in Britain in 1978 by women of colour, and whose first conference in London was attended by 250 women – folded in 1982, following an attempt at the conference to bring Black lesbianism into visibility in Britain.
9. I have analysed the Opening and Closing Statements in this trial and have suggested that this is true in the media reports as well as the legal arguments (Bhavnani, 1996). John Fiske (1996) also discusses some of the interconnections between 'race' and gender in this trial.
10. See Morrison (1993b) for a lively collection of articles on the many implications of these hearings.
11. In their Preface they write: The 'book grew out of a concern at the exclusion of women of color from feminist scholarship' (Baca-Zinn and Thornton Dill, 1994, p. xi).
12. A number of books have been produced in the past few years which aim to rectify this invisibility This is what Amina Mama (1995) does in her examination of subjectivities, which she does by interrogating Black femininity. Further, she draws upon social theory, as well as upon writings by psychologists, social theorists and psychoanalysts. Works such as hers, as well as many others (see

Jaggar and Rothenberg, 1993; Kauffman, 1993; Landry and MacLean, 1993; Evans, 1994) aim to transform feminism away from its previously narrow conception of gender to include a wider set of problems and issues.

13. The term 'orientalism' is derived from Edward Said's book (1978) which is a documentation and analysis, using themes from Foucault, that the Orient is an institution within contemporary thought and that Orientalism refers to the systematic knowledge by which the Orient is constructed as the Other.

14. There are other very important issues related to representation which are raised by, for example, Gayatri Chakravorty Spivak in her 1988 classic article 'Can the Subaltern Speak?' but which are beyond the focus of this chapter.

15. I was introduced to some of these anthologies, and others, by Peter Chua and Susana Peña.

16. Which is a Bengali way of saying 'love for your equal or same' (Islam, 1993).

17. This example uses a quote from a Black woman, who is described as such, but whose racialised identity is not discussed at all.

18. I am anxious to not appear to be setting a moral high ground for who can be more thoughtful on 'race' than whom. Catherine Stimpson (1988) wrote in the early 1970s: 'Race, to the dismay of many, to the relief of others has become a proper test for deciding who is best at certain intellectual as well as political activities'(p. 3). This sentiment captures a large amount of the tensions I feel when I write and argue about racism. It *is* proper that a racialised consciousness be central to all intellectual and political work. But I would not wish to caricature its importance to the point where my politics get understood as the politics of separatism rather than as what they are, the politics of autonomy. Further, it is clear that some (white) writers and political activists have taken racism seriously. For example, the journal *Feminist Review* gave over editorial control to a group of Black women in 1984; *Signs* produced an important special issue (1989) called 'Common Grounds and Crossroads: Race, Ethnicity and Class in Women's Lives'; and in 1994, *Feminism and Psychology* produced a Special Issue called 'Shifting Identities, Shifting Racisms'.

19. For example, Bhavnani and Coulson (1986) discussed how socialist feminism could be transformed.

20. Also see Thompson (1994) and Taylor, Gilligan, and Sullivan (1995) for social science work that tries to avoid tokenism.

21. I do also get considerable pleasure from some of these contradictions when they create the conditions for some change as well. My migration to the USA in 1991 has forced me to think more about the place of the migrant intellectual, and the complexities of my situation. For example, while I was, and still am, Black in the British context, in the USA, I am often treated as someone who comes from a privileged background because I am not a domestic minority, and hence am seen as not 'belonging'; in addition, because of my English accent (which often connotes a vast amount of cultural capital in the USA) I have also been treated, and told, that I am not 'truly' someone of colour. Such notions of my identity, and how it is related to in the USA is further complicated by the history of migration of South Asian populations to the USA which is a very different history from that of the South Asian population in Britain. The history of South Asian migration to the USA has produced stereotypes of South Asian populations there, and also we are frequently not included within the category 'Asian' here. See Bhavnani (1990, 1993b) and Phoenix (1994) for how some of these complexities about identity affect researchers and research projects.

22. Barbara Hillyer has written a book, *Feminism and Disability* (1993), in which she also briefly discusses the relation of 'race' and racism to this set of issues.

23. A recent collection, Thompson and Tyagi (1996), has developed this theme of 'home' and used it as a means of analysing personal identity and autobiography.
24. Alonso (1988) has referred to how history has acquired this truth value, for history is framed within hegemonic discourses as 'unmediated factuality' rather than as interpretive description (p. 37).
25. This argument has been dealt with – the opposition of experience and objectivity – by suggesting that to set them in opposition means that the knowledge/power hierarchy itself is unchallenged (Haraway, 1988), yet the consequences of Haraway's points are not always present in feminist writings.
26. I am grateful to Meg Coulson for helping me clarify my thoughts here.
27. 'Difference' has frequently been used to indicate differences between women and men, but, more recently, it is used to examine differences amongst women.
28. Maynard's argument seems to be the opposite of what Gayatri Chakravorty Spivak says: 'I would even say that these days, my interest as a teacher and in some ways as an activist is to build for difference' (in Shor and Weed, 1994, p. 155).
29. See Bhavnani and Bhavnani (1985) for a critical discussion of pluralism in relation to British multiculturalism; also Bhatt (1995).
30. Jenny Shape also does this in her work *Allegories of Empire* (1993).
31. Of course, this must be done without recreating Third World women as unitary and unified subjects (Mohanty 1988).
32. The subtitle of her book *Bananas, Beaches, and Bases.*
33. Also Kabeer (1995) for a new way to understand issues as they pertain to women and development using feminist analyses.
34. There is also some fascinating work done on sexuality in a colonial context by Jacqui Alexander (1991).

Further Reading

Shabnum Grewal *et al.*, *Charting the Journey: Writing by Black and Third World Women* (London, Sheba Press, 1988). This anthology provides a wide range of arguments and discussions raised by UK-based Black and Third World women. Similar anthologies in the USA would be *This Bridge Called my Back* edited by Cherrie Moraga and Gloria Anzaluda, (Watertown, Mass., Persephone Press, 1981), and *All the Women are White, All the Blacks are Men, But Some of Us are Brave: Black Women's Studies*, edited by Gloria T. Hull, Patricia B. Scott and Barbara Smith (New York, The Feminist Press, 1982). These last two volumes are also unusual for collections which originate in the USA, as they include writings by women of a range of ethnicities rather than focusing on just one ethnic/racial group.

Stanlie James and Abena Busia (eds) *Theorizing Black Feminisms* (New York, Routledge, 1993) provides a number of chapters in which African-American women discuss the state of feminism in the 1990s, and suggest what they consider to be the particularities of African-American feminism.

Reina Lewis *Gendering Orientalism* and Lola Young *Fear of the Dark* (both from London, Routledge, 1996) discuss how issues of 'race', ethnicity and representation are crucial for the development of contemporary feminist ideas.

Rakesh Ratti (ed.) *A Lotus of Another Color: An Unfolding of the South Asian Gay and Lesbian Experience* (Boston, MA, Alyson Publications, 1993); Carla Trujillo (ed.), *Chicana Lesbians: The Girls Our Mothers Warned Us About* (Berkeley, CA, Third World Women Press, 1991) and Valerie Mason-John (ed.), *Talking Black: Lesbians of African and Asian Descent Speak Out* (London, Cassell, 1995) are anthologies from the USA and Britain which examine the interconnections of sexualities with 'race', ethnicity and gender.

Saskia Wieringa (ed.) *Subversive Women: Women's Movements in Africa and the Caribbean* (London, Zed; New Delhi, Kali, 1995) is an excellent collection of articles which examines the experiences of resistance amongst Third World women.

3

Feminist Theory: Capital F, Capital T

Jackie Stacey

When I first encountered what might loosely be referred to as 'feminist theory' in the early 1980s it was presented to me as a series of competing explanations of women's oppression. The emphasis was very much upon how existing theories might be extended and reworked to provide answers to questions about how to challenge inequality. How and why had women been systematically excluded from power and from public life, and how and why had their contributions to culture been undervalued and trivialised; furthermore, how had their restriction to particular domains, such as the so-called more private spheres of domesticity, sexuality or informal labour, been organised against their interests? The aim was to explain the problems in order to transform the patriarchal relations of all spheres of social, cultural and economic life. In addition to adapting existing theories, feminists inside and outside the academy produced both new analyses of social exclusions and visions of a culture transformed. It seemed to me that 'feminist' was the central category and 'theory' was regarded through a more or less instrumentalist lens as a resource for our political purposes.

As I sit here now deciding on how to approach a chapter on 'feminist theory' in the late 1990s, I am struck by the level and breadth of theoretical knowledge demanded of a contemporary readership wanting to get to grips with this body of work. In order to introduce new readers to what continues to be a rapid proliferation of theoretical writing by feminists working within highly diverse frameworks and contexts, I am acutely aware of how much 'background' is necessary to make many recent contributions even the slightest bit intelligible to students new to Women's Studies. Furthermore, in an interdisciplinary context such as this, the task of such a theoretical mapping seems almost unimaginable for any one author. With the rapid growth in feminist scholarship both inside and outside Women's Studies, and an increased engagement with highly specialised theories in the academy, many would argue that there is now a sense in which the capital 'T' of Feminist Theory has come to take precedence over the capital 'F'. As the project of transforming academia has become a legitimate form of feminist labour, so the instrumentalist approach to Theory of earlier decades has given way to a new weighting (some would even say fetishising) of theoretical concerns for their own sake. What Feminist Theory so often signifies today is an engagement with Theory, capital 'T'. What is frequently assumed is that Theory means addressing what Rosi Braidotti ironically runs together as one word: 'Foucaultlacanderrida' (Braidotti, 1991). Braidotti quite rightly points to the increasing imperative for feminist theorists to be concerned with at least one, but preferably all three, of these infamously difficult canonised French writers who represent different aspects of post-structuralism and post-modernism.

Much recent feminist theory has drawn on these bodies of work in order to open up debates about the meaning of the category 'woman'. For post-structuralists, the notion of any fixed identity category is problematic and thus 'woman' should be regarded as a constantly shifting signifier of multiple meanings. Rejecting the assumption that identity categories have essential or constant meaning across time, place and historical context, post-structuralists see their task as interrogating how culture ascribes meaning to such categories. The term 'individual' is rejected as part of the liberal humanist belief system that we are autonomous beings, free to choose how we live and unconstrained by power structures; instead the term 'subject' is used widely to indicate that our sense of self is a construction and that we are positioned by sets of ideas and practices, or discourses: the subject here is seen as an 'effect of language', as 'positioned by discourse' (see Coward and Ellis, 1977; Henriques *et al.*, 1984; Weedon, 1987). In other words, rather than assuming that humans from particular groups are oppressed by an external culture that is imposed upon them, these models insist that our sense of selves as subjects is something that language systems produce; language thus speaks us, rather than the other way around. For some post-structuralists, subjectivity (the ways in which we understand ourselves as subjects) is not only fluid, fractured and fragmented because it is an effect of competing discourses, but also because of the disruptive impact of the unconscious. Lacanian psychoanalysis, for example, has been highly influential in suggesting a model of the split subject whose unity is a desirable but unachievable fiction (see Rose, 1986; Grosz, 1990). Post-structuralism, then, with its emphasis on the illusory character of a unified and coherent self and on the shifting and contradictory dimensions of identity, has posed a profound challenge to the authenticity, transparency and 'truth claims' of much experientially-based feminist theory.

Many of these theories of subjectivity and language overlap with post-modernism, which also questions the possibility of the authenticity of experience and the unified subject as the origin of meaning, emphasising instead the endless rehearsal and 'intertextuality' of cultural representations, styles and modes of expression. This loss of belief in the unique experience of the individual, and the capacity of language to represent it transparently to others, is part of a loss of faith more generally in the foundational beliefs of modernity. Importantly for feminism, the present 'post-modern condition' has been characterised by the collapse in the 'legitimating authority' of modernity's 'Grand Narratives': those ways of valuing modern science, rationality and development in the name of 'progress' (Lyotard, 1984). Whereas the narratives of 'the liberation of humanity' and of 'the pursuit of knowledge' combined to legitimate the scientific project in the past, in post-modern culture people have lost faith in such ideals. The significance of such a pronouncement for feminist theory is highly contradictory. On the one hand, many feminists would be the first to join in the celebration of the end of the myth of science as progress (given its oppressive constructions of gender, sexuality, 'race' and class); on the other hand, the narratives of liberation and of the pursuit of knowledge (and indeed the connection between the two) continue to inform feminism as a project. Post-modernist thinking, then, has produced some uncomfortable questions for many feminists: does self-knowledge lead to liberation; does feminism have its own progress narratives; and, is the notion of liberation separable from its liberal humanist and modernist foundations?

These post-structuralist and post-modernist theoretical frameworks have been widely utilised by some feminists in order to challenge what they see as the problematically humanist, essentialist and empiricist tendencies of previous (and, indeed, current) feminist work (see Weedon, 1987; Weed, 1989; Nicholson, 1990; Butler and Scott, 1992; McNay, 1992). My point here is not to underestimate the significance of this work, or to distance myself from it (for much of my own work engages with different elements of it), but rather to comment upon the impossibility of introducing much of it satisfactorily in a chapter such as this. There is a further issue here, though, which needs spelling out and which concerns the formation of academic canons. It is not just that much of this work addresses a long and complicated set of theoretical debates that are hard to sum up in an introductory chapter, but also that it has increasingly taken on a metonymic function: it has often come to stand in for the whole of Feminist Theory. Or to put it yet another way, feminist theory that does not engage with these theoretical traditions is often excluded from the capital 'T' category of Feminist Theory. This raises important questions about the hierarchy of disciplines in the production of what counts as legitimate Theory, and about the actual meaning of interdisciplinarity in Women's Studies. Are some subjects seen as more generative of Theory in the 1990s, and, if so, which ones? Is there more theoretical movement from Philosophy and Literature in the direction of Sociology and Psychology than vice versa? Or is our perception of this dependent upon our relative disciplinary locations?

In the first edition of this collection I began my chapter on feminist theory by explaining my decision not to write it as a rehearsal of the usual typology of feminisms (Stacey, 1993). I argued there, and elsewhere, that we need to move beyond the conventional 'Big Three' (Marxist, radical and liberal feminisms) as they had been constituted by many accounts in the 1970s and 1980s (Hinds, Phoenix and Stacey, 1992). Typically, the three classic feminist positions have been characterised as follows: radical feminism focuses on male violence against women and men's control of women's sexuality and reproduction, seeing men as a group as responsible for women's oppression; Marxist feminism, in contrast, sees women's oppression as tied to forms of capitalist exploitation of labour, and thus women's paid and unpaid work is analysed in relation to its function within the capitalist economy; and finally, liberal feminism is distinctive in its focus on individual rights and choices which are denied women, and ways in which the law and education could rectify these injustices. In some accounts, socialist feminism and Marxist feminism are distinct from one another; socialist feminism is less economically deterministic, and allows some kind of autonomy to women's oppression, yet retains a belief that women's liberation and socialism are joint goals. Black feminism (and sometimes lesbian feminism) are then usually attached as an addition, as if they were unified categories in need of no further differentiation. Whilst the contrast between these three perspectives proved a useful shorthand for the ways in which competing feminist explanations of women's oppression had their roots in different theoretical and political traditions, this particular typology not only became rather hackneyed in what it described, but also proved to be highly problematic in what it excluded: much feminist writing cut across these rigid divisions, rendering them meaningless.

Finding these accounts of feminist theory overly conventionalised, I decided instead to write the earlier chapter (in the first edition of this book), 'Untangling Feminist Theory', as an account of some of the problematic and unresolved theoretical debates within a range of feminist theories: debates about the usefulness of the term 'patriarchy', about universals and particulars, about the category 'woman' and about essentialisms and social constructionisms were taken as examples of theoretical problems across the disciplines. Given the opportunity to return to the difficult task of writing an introductory chapter on feminist theory, I am struck by an important change in how feminist theory is written about and, most especially, taught in Women's Studies. Whereas courses on feminist theory ten years ago were typically arranged around 'theoretical perspectives' or typologies (Marxist, liberal and radical, with a few extra tag-ons), now they tend to offer histories which track changes and developments, typically contrasting feminism in the 1970s with that of the 1990s. Twenty-five years of feminism seems to have marked the threshold that requires the writing of its theoretical history to begin: the previous typologies are starting to be replaced by a model of periods/phases in feminist thinking. In other words, the previously *synchronic* construction of respective feminist positions has been replaced by an increasingly prevalent *diachronic* construction of a history of feminist theory.

However, I find myself equally concerned about this mode of teaching and writing about Feminist Theory. Some of the same pitfalls exist in the accounts of feminist theory across the decades (the diachronic approach) as did in the perspectives in feminist theory (the synchronic approach). Whereas in 'Untangling Feminist Theory' I aimed to avoid reinforcing what I continue to perceive to be unhelpful stereotypes of particular types of feminisms and feminists in the 'perspectives' approach to feminist theory (socialist feminists are not concerned with sexuality, radical feminists are all essentialists and so on: see Richardson, 1996), I am now wanting to caution against some of the characterisations of past and present feminisms in the 'developments' in feminist theory approach. In this chapter I want to reflect upon the question of how accounts of Feminist Theory often constitute a very particular *historical narrative*. I am interested in how these theoretical histories are being written and in the kind of mythic constructions of past and present that are put in place in the process. This has important implications not just for the writing of a history of feminism, but also for the teaching of feminist theory courses within Women's Studies in higher education. Many of the characterisations that I use in what follows are drawn from my experience of teaching Women's Studies in Britain during the last decade; no doubt readers outside this context will recognise some of the general patterns, though I would expect them to take various forms in different national contexts.

Constructions of 'feminist theory today' tend to rely upon notions of feminist theory in the past. Indeed, such typifications are an inevitable shorthand: my own beginning to this chapter took as its starting point a rather crude contrast between what 'feminist theory' meant to me when I first encountered it in the early 1980s, and what it might refer to today. I read this shift in significance from the capital 'F' then to the capital 'T' now as indicative of institutional and political changes which continue to inform the meaning of the rather vague, but highly contested category which is the subject of this chapter: feminist theory. However, it is not the past/present dialogue *per se* that troubles me, but the commonsense stories, and in particular, their *narrative forms*, that are coming to characterise the construction of a history of feminism in the 1990s. Perhaps second-wave feminism has come of age, is entering middle age or is simply troubled by an ambivalent nostalgia; whatever the reason, accounts of feminist theory now tend to conform to a very specific narrative trajectory. The story that I have heard most frequently in discussions in Women's Studies classes maps a shift from 'naive and simplistic' feminist theory to 'wise and sophisticated' Feminist Theory. It follows a classically developmental model in which the subjects of feminism today present their theory in opposition to their version of feminist theory in the past, which is represented as rather unformed and crude. In its worst form, this history is a progress narrative of the most conventional kind; we are presented as the enlightened, knowing subjects at the end of a progressional history. It is this version of Feminist Theory that I wish to contest in this chapter.

These accounts of 'past feminisms' flatten out their complexities and contradictions and present a retrospective narrativisation that serves present purposes and legitimises the superiority of contemporary Feminist Theory: similarity, sisterhood and solidarity in the 1970s is contrasted with difference, diversity and dissent in the 1990s, for example. As I shall go on to illustrate, a mythic past is often constructed as the (often bad, but always unified) object against which the subjects of the present measure themselves. In particular, what has been called '70s feminism' has taken on a coherence, and often a *personification*, of mythic proportions. The '70s feminist', with all the media stereotypes that figure evokes, is so frequently referred to in Women's Studies classes today that I can only conclude her presence in a feminist imaginary to be highly significant. Now '70s feminism' has been constituted as a key player in the narrative genealogy of feminist theory. We are told that '70s feminism' was naively universalistic, it was anti-sex, it ignored differences among women (especially ethnic and national ones), it embraced experience unproblematically, it was humourless, it was anti-pleasure, it was homophobic and/or anti-lesbian, it was bourgeois, it was humanist, it was essentialist and it tried to speak for all women (for a discussion of younger feminist views of 'older' feminisms see Denfeld, 1995; Findlen, 1995.) But these criticisms (and I do not mean to suggest that none are valid or important, merely that some have become overrehearsed truisms) are often accompanied by a somewhat contrary set of nostalgic idealisations of past feminisms. Sometimes these inform rather different versions of the past and sometimes they can be seen lurking behind the more negative construction typified so far. Indeed, 70s feminism is sometimes also represented as the good object that has been irretrievably lost. It is also often taken to represent the good old days of political activism; it was a time of revolutionary vision and of optimism, a time when women felt they were 'making history'. In some ways 70s feminism is yearned for as a Golden Age; for all its faults it was the 'Real Thing' (Echols, 1989; Jeffreys, 1990).

What troubles me about these tendencies in my experience of discussions about feminist theory within Women's Studies in Britain is the extent to which we are in danger of reproducing some fairly conventional generational patterns of academic (and other cultural) practices. It would not be exaggerating to suggest that there is a certain Oedipal character to this kind of construction of past figures. This history of feminist theory as I have characterised it has been transformed into a personified teleology in which key players take their places. In the version critical of 70s feminists, they are represented as symbolic embodiments of the 'bad mother' against whom the new generation must rebel in order to prove the superiority of their knowledge. Just as 70s feminists, in embracing the aims of the women's movement, rebelled against what they perceived as the complicit or compromised values of their mothers, so many 90s feminists (as well as non-feminists) retrospectively construct their previous counterparts as hopelessly wanting. Today's accounts of developments in feminist theory no longer take 'masculine knowledge' as their opponents; rather, 70s feminism has come to replace that old enemy. This form of Oedipal rejection is not restricted to those who are new to feminism, or those who reject the label 'feminist' as off-putting or old-fashioned, but can also be found in the work of theorists who seek to establish a distance from their previous beliefs and former selves.

Whilst some readers will immediately recognise the scenarios I have represented, albeit somewhat exaggeratedly for polemical purposes, others, new to Women's Studies, may find themselves at this point wanting an example through which to trace my characterisation of the problem. I shall offer one brief illustration of my rather generalised claims, before moving on to the rest of the chapter. My example is the discussions that have formed around the emergence of so-called 'queer theory' (see also Chapter 7). In some ways this is a tricky case to use since there is no agreed body of work that could be pulled off the shelf and labelled 'queer theory'. In fact the subject of another chapter might be the speed with which this category has been constituted as a coherent object despite the extraordinary diversity of its remit and the tensions and incompatabilities within this so-called position. Its suitability in this context, however, lies precisely in the ways it has been represented as the 90s answer to the limits of previous theories of sexuality. It is hailed and scorned alike for representing the political and theoretical concerns of a new generation.

Queer positions

The use of the term 'queer' is itself taken to be emblematic of a new mood, a new sense of entitlement and a new defiance (see Butler, 1993; McIntosh, 1993; Braidotti with Butler, 1994). Reclaiming a despised category such as 'queer' has been seen as an expression of anger and frustration at the refusal of Western societies to respond to the needs of lesbian, gay and bisexual people. In particular, the term 'queer' was initially associated with HIV and AIDS activism in the USA which took the form of direct actions in which performances and staged politics accompanied the more conventional marches, petitions and demonstrations. To be queer in the 1990s is to be passionate about your sexuality and your politics and to adopt an 'in yer face' strategy or lifestyle which makes no concessions to mainstream tastes and sensibilities. Often set up in opposition to what is perceived as a lesbian and gay politics of the 1970s and 1980s that wanted integration and acceptance, queer celebrates the pleasures of the margins; it says to heterosexual culture 'You can be like us if you want, but we certainly don't want to be like you.' Queer thus sees itself as embracing diversity and perversity and establishing alliances between gays, lesbians, bisexuals, and indeed some 'like-minded' (oppositional, perverse, outrageous?) heterosexuals. Queer might be thought of not so much as an identity, but as a discursive position open to all.

The emergence of 'queer cinema' in the mid- to late 1980s illustrates this shift perfectly (Rich, 1994). Queer cinema offered a direct challenge to what was seen as the 'positive images' trap of lesbian and gay cinema of the 1970s and 1980s that appealed for acceptance through bids for normality, naturalness and common humanity ('we're all the same underneath'). Queer cinema defined itself very firmly instead as the cinema that dared to take risks, to explore deviance and to look at the 'underbelly' of sexual desire. Films such as *Swoon* (1991, dir. Tom Kalin) and *She Must Be Seeing Things* (1987, dir. Sheila McLaughlin) investigated questions of violence, jealousy, power imbalances, possessiveness and betrayal within gay and lesbian relationships. For some this shift from lesbian and gay to queer cinema has provided a welcome inclusiveness and a breaking-down of false boundaries around sexual identities; for others it has meant a return to male-dominated political arenas and the marginalisation of feminist and lesbian concerns (see Gever *et al.*, 1994; Rich, 1994; Wilton, 1995).

'Queer theory' echoes some of these characteristics but not in a straightforward or an obvious way. It refers to a theoretical move rather than a particular writer and there is much debate about who does and does not conform to such a label. Some might use the term 'queer theory' to refer to the widespread academic attention in the last decade to writings about homosexuality. The work of Jonathan Dollimore (1991) and Eve Kosofsky Sedgwick (1990) in particular has been seen as typifying this queer position in literary studies, which insists not just on taking gay writing seriously, but on the centrality of homosexuality to the literary canon more generally. These writers both 'queer' the canon in terms of acknowledging queers in the canon and by foregrounding the centrality of queerness to the canon. Other accounts of queer theory might take Eve Sedgwick's and Judith Butler's work in tandem and name them as queer theorists because of their shared concern with reframing sexuality within a post-structuralist epistemology (Butler, 1990, 1993; Sedgwick, 1990). Both writers emphasise fluidity and the repetitive reconstitution of the subjects of desire and caution against fixing the meanings of sexual identities. Others still might include the work of Teresa de Lauretis who edited a special issue of the journal *differences* on queer theory (de Lauretis, 1991). De Lauretis's own recent work (1994) might be taken to form a central part of queer theory insofar as she 'queers' psychoanalysis in search of a theory of the specificity of lesbian desire. All these writings vary enormously and there are very different versions of what queer means in each example. Queer theory refers to work on the centrality of homosexuality to heterosexual culture (the 'haunting of culture by queerness', as the subtitle of the 1996 Lesbian and Gay Studies Conference at the University of Warwick put it); it refers to the problematisation of all sexual categories from a post-structuralist position and to the queering of existing theories in search of alternative explanations of perverse desire.

Queer theory is, however, considerably more than the sum of its parts in terms of the work the category does in constructing theoretical histories. Queer theory has taken on a weighty, symbolic significance in debates about 'developments' in Feminist Theory. Queer writings have contributed to an already steadily growing field of studies in sexuality and yet are seen to mark a distinctive break with previous theoretical traditions. Feminist theories of sexuality, especially of lesbianism, tend to get positioned in particular ways in accounts of this distinctive break. Typically, in accounts of this history, lesbian feminist work (such as Rich, 1986) is contrasted with queer interventions (such as Butler, 1990) in relation to an attributed essentialism and a conservative identity politics in the former (see Richardson, 1996d). The essentialisms of these former 'naive' theoretical models of lesbian feminism are not seen as the more familiar ones based in biology or nature, but rather those based upon claims of unified and universal meanings to the category lesbian (see Stacey, 1993). Queer objections to feminist theories of lesbianism hinge upon a critique of lesbian feminist assumptions about the coherence, stability and permanence of sexual identity: the assumption, for example, that once lesbians have 'come out', they will never go back in again (either into the closet or into heterosexuality); or the assumption that lesbians everywhere share a common culture or heritage, and thus constitute a 'community'. Queer positions refuse to seek out trans-historical or cross-cultural instances of lesbian relationships or lifestyles. The well-known lesbian and gay pleasures of claiming and naming famous predecessors, for example, would be dismissed by queer critics for their essentialising tendencies (though they may be indulged in nevertheless for their campy gossip value). Accompanying this construction of feminist theories of sexuality as problematically desirous of unified and fixed identities is a queer challenge to the infamous power of the 'authority of experience' (see Fuss, 1989): that it is the exclusive prerogative of those who have experienced an oppression or a lifestyle to define its politics. Queer challenges have insisted instead on the multiplicity of identifications and meanings to sexual categories (emphasising activities rather than types of people) and have cautioned against any unifying impulses that characterise the search to establish identities in the face of their denial and repression by a homophobic and anti-lesbian culture.

This kind of characterisation of queer theory in relation to feminist theory constructs a linear progress narrative in which Theory (capital T) has rescued feminism from its early naivety. It representes developments in feminist theory as a journey from essentialism to fluidity, from ignorance to enlightenment. Such a representation of this past/present relationship reproduces just the type of narrative that post-modernists have identified as central to the project of modernity (Lyotard, 1984). Indeed, not only is such a construction troubling in terms of its Enlightenment structure, it also represents a problematic version of the contemporary feminist theorist as the wise and knowing subject placed at the end of this progression. As Foucault (1979) argues, our sense of ourselves as the enlightened subjects at the end of a repressive historical teleology is itself part of the discourse of liberation that characterises modernity. Thus it is particularly ironic that post-modernist 'queer' theory is so often positioned within such a classically modernist narrative framework.

A further issue is also raised by these theoretical histories: that is, the way in which the developments are characterised as a radical break between past and present. In these kinds of Enlightenment narratives the conservative past is replaced by the radical present. What concerns me is the lack of attention to the continuities in past and present feminist theorising. I do not seek to reveal an unbroken tradition in feminist thinking, but rather to caution against the 'radical break' characterisations because of the ways in which they ignore the continuing preoccupations of feminist theory that keep resurfacing, albeit in very different forms. I want to highlight the ways in which feminist theory returns to particular thorny questions but does so in the context of changing historical and political circumstances. In the following sections I shall take two case studies – 'writing the self' and 'embodied subjectivity' – in order to explore my claims further.

Writing the self

There has been a recent spate of publications in which feminists have sought to investigate representations of the self through combinations of personal and theoretical modes of writing. Although the crossing of the generic boundaries of writing has always been a preoccupation of feminist work (and indeed part of the politics of its project, as I shall discuss later) there has been a marked increase in the number of feminist texts that cannot be straightforwardly classified. It is hard to name these forms of writing precisely for this reason. Nancy Miller (1991) suggests the term 'personal criticism' to describe these kinds of feminist intervention. But, as she says, having listed a wide range of (largely American) examples, we need to ask:

Why personal criticism now? Is it another form of 'Anti-Theory'? Is it a new stage of theory? Is it gendered? Only for women and gay men? Is it bourgeois? postmodern? A product of Late Capitalism? Reaganomics? Post-feminism? It might be possible, and the reflexes of my structuralist training make me contemplate the project, to construct a typology, a poetics of the 'egodocuments' that constitute personal criticism: confessional, locational, academic, political, narrative, anecdotal, biographematic etc. But is it really a good idea? . . . [W]hat if what seems new and provocative just turned out to be another academic fashion? (Miller, 1991, p. 3)

What is significant about this 'autobiographical turn' in its more recent manifestations is indeed the influence of post-structuralism on its formation. And yet these new interventions undermine the 'theory versus experience' dichotomy endlessly rehearsed in such debates. For Miller, personal criticism is not turning one's back on theory but 'turning theory back on itself' (Miller, 1991, p. 5). As she goes on to argue, the introduction of more personal modes of writing into feminist theorising can disperse the public-private hierarchy that maintains masculine academic professionalism and indeed patriarchal cultural relations more generally. Rather than excluding the so-called personal from knowledge production, feminists have continued to find ways to introduce it into academic theory in such a way as to challenge the latter's status as scientific objectivity. Be it through the uses of accounts of 'experience', oral histories or autobiographical memory work, feminist innovations in writing theory have persistently undermined the masculine myths of neutrality that have characterised its truth claims (see, for example, Lorde, 1984a; Haug, 1987; Probyn, 1993; Kuhn, 1995).

For many feminists the introduction of personal criticism is a strategic disruption of the smooth surface of abstract universalising theories that have constituted woman as 'lack, invisibility, silence' (Miller, 1991, p. 7). The embarrassment that personal modes may introduce into academic settings touches on the sense that 'emotion', 'experience' and 'autobiography' have no place in the discourse of knowledge and should be kept outside the doors of the academy. The authority of theory relies upon the exclusion of the personal to maintain its status. For some, it is precisely these conventions, based in the traditions of objectivity and universal truth claims, that have been seen to protect the domain of Theory in academia as a masculine preserve (see Chapters 1 and 9). Barbara Johnson, for example, sees the reintroduction of the personal as a way of 'disseminating authority and decomposing the false universality of patriarchally institutionalised meanings'. For her, the equation of the personal with the feminine provides an imperative to challenge the patriarchal construction of both as 'other' to knowledge proper: 'Not only has personal experience tended to be excluded from the discourse of knowledge, but the realm of the personal itself has been coded as female and devalued for that reason' (Johnson, quoted in Miller, 1991, p. 15).

The challenge to the authority of academic Theory in terms of its exclusionary practices has motivated a number of Black feminists to cross the usual generic boundaries of writing. Writers such as Audre Lorde (1984a), Barbara Smith (1986) and Gayatri Spivak (1988) have used letters, dialogues and polemic to open academic theorising to personal and political questions of racism, anti-lesbianism and homophobia, and the reproduction of power in a (post-)colonial world. For some, abstract theorising in white academia has reproduced a hegemonic elite with little self-reflection upon its privileged position. Barbara Christian, for example, condemns the banishing of the personal and of the emotional in the traditions of academic writing that suggest 'the authors are dead, irrelevant, mere vessels through which their narratives ooze; that they do not work nor have the faintest idea what they are doing but rather produce texts as disembodied as the angels' (Christian, 1990, p. 573); for Christian, the use of this 'metaphysical language', typical of a particular kind of Theory, 'mystifies rather than clarifies our condition, making it possible for a few people who know that language to control the critical scene'; and ultimately, she argues that some critical theory 'is as hegemonic as the world that it attacks' (Christian, 1990, p. 572). Like other Black critics, Christian writes cynically of the ways in which such theoretical moves emerged 'just when the literature of peoples of color, of black women, of Latin Americans, of Africans began to move to 'the center'' (Christian, 1990, p. 572).

Women's Studies in particular has opened up institutional spaces that explore the intersection of 'private' and 'public' discourses of knowledge, personal and theoretical modes of writing and individual and collective experiences; indeed, such dichotomies have themselves been under critical deconstruction within such contexts. In some cases, innovative modes of pedagogy in Women's Studies have facilitated exploration of the interface between these different forms of writing, speaking and knowing. Whilst this has not been without its problems and controversies, and should not be read as indicating that Women's Studies invites an uncritical, untheoretical and unreflexive outpouring of confessional disclosure, where it has worked, students have produced work that not only has a particular significance to their lives, but that also pushes at the boundaries of academic thought more generally.

However, the danger of reappropriating that which has been banished as unsuitable (such as the personal in the name of feminism and anti-racism) is of course that this might be read as reinforcing precisely the associations which led to their original joint condemnation. For feminists who wish to follow Christian's lead, there is always the danger that such a challenge can be read as reinforcing inevitable or essential connections between emotions, femininity and Blackness (or indeed between theory, masculinity and whiteness). Should feminists then be wary of making claims that suggest a generalised sexual difference around the personal such as: 'what interests women is the personal' (Miller, 1991, pp. 12–13)? For Miller, this claim might be recast as the question: 'if what seems important (*"interesting"*) to women is personal, what seems important and interesting to men?' (Miller, 1991, p. 13). Despite the obvious risks of essentialism, Miller argues that something continues to draw her back to personal interventions such as those of Barbara Christian (1990) and Jane Tompkins (1989). What appeals to her is their attention to reading and writing practices and their insistence upon the 'positional' as well as the 'personal'; in other words, cultural location is made part of the textual exchange between readers and writers (Miller, 1991, p. 17; see also Skeggs, 1995).

These recent forms of 'writing the self' in feminist theory continue a long-standing concern with 'breaking out' of conventional forms of academic knowledge production (see Stanley and Wise, 1983; Stanley, 1990a). Rather than representing the history of these approaches to Theory as a shift from the early essentialisms of 'identity politics' and the 'authority of experience' to a newly-emergent sophisticated explorations of the fluidity of the self, exemplified in the progress narrative accounts, I want to argue that many of the recent examples of these personal modes of theorising have given previous feminist concerns a particular inflection through a reworking of post-structuralist frames. What is new and different about them, however, is the particular emphasis on the *textuality of self-representation* that has come to the fore in these forms of personal criticism. Miller's conceptualisation of personal criticism as 'an autobiographical act', for example, emphasises the notion of a rehearsed performance of the self to an anticipated audience. The self here is not just represented to the reader for affirmation or recognition: it is presented in many recent works as an invention, a self-fabrication, a strategic rhetoric or a narrativised memory.

In *Family Secrets: Acts of Memory and Imagination*, Annette Kuhn (1995) offers another example of a recent feminist investigation of the autobiographical self that is informed by post-structuralist theory, but also continues a concern with new modes of personal criticism. Kuhn highlights the patterns of memory formation and narrative retelling in her own autobiographical exploration of family photographs and the memories they prompt. Firmly situated within class, national and gender locations, Kuhn offers reflections upon her childhood through the simultaneous presentation and investigation of memory forms. For Kuhn:

> [T]elling stories about the past, our past, is a key moment in the making of our selves. To the extent that memory provides their raw material, such narratives of identity are shaped as much by what is left out of the account – whether forgotten or repressed – as by what is actually told. (Kuhn, 1995, p. 2).

For Kuhn, as for other writers using memories of the past to explore theoretical and personal questions, such as Carolyn Steedman (1986), memory cannot restore the past, but rather offers traces of self-formation that enable the subject to reflect upon past-present relationships. Kuhn offers both stories of her childhood based around a series of chosen photographs and a critical commentary on the configurations of memory that lead her to narrate these particular stories in particular ways. The reader is positioned at the interface of personal and theoretical discourses about self-representation. Thus, whilst the reader may well enjoy a sense of recognition or personal involvement in the narratives, these pleasures are accompanied by theoretical cautions that often undo the conventions of self-presentation even as they present the self.

'Experience' has not disappeared from feminist theorising in the 1990s, but its presentation to readers is accompanied by a warning: be wary of the truths we hold to be self-evident. Readers are required to hold together the personal and the positional, and these autobiographical disclosures, with a commentary upon their forms. This dual strategy produces a kind of reflexivity in reading as well as writing practices: personal experiences continue to inform the theory and yet are simultaneously interrogated in the retelling and in the reading process (see Pearce, 1997, forthcoming).

These parallel reading and writing strategies have come to characterise the writing of the self in much contemporary feminist work. Elspeth Probyn's work, for example, is centrally concerned with ways of writing the gendered self into feminist cultural analysis in such a way that recognises its discursive constitution but also includes accounts of experience. She writes, 'we cannot pretend that this is an easy thing to do, that there is an unmediated innocence to the self. The possibility of the self rests within a filigree of institutional, material, discursive lines that either erase or can be used to enable spaces in which "we" can be differently spoken' (Probyn, 1993, p. 4). In this way Probyn's project returns us to the crucial question of when the autobiographical subject of feminist work may lay claim to a more generalised 'we'.

The move from 'I' to 'we' is perhaps most contested in this kind of autobiographical writing. One of the changes that has taken place in feminist theorising is the decrease in confidence with which these claims of generality about gendered experience can be made. As I have previously detailed, the category 'woman' is as much the subject of critical interrogation in Women's Studies in the 1990s, as it is the starting point for assuming shared oppression (Stacey, 1993). Probyn offers a contemporary compromise: she does not return us to some of the more problematic 'we' claims produced by the desire for community, for solidarity and for unity that have been thoroughly criticised by those upon whose exclusion such fantasies were based, but neither does she leave us with the sense that the personal represents only the idiosyncratic individual account. Instead, she argues 'we have to construct ways of thinking that are marked by "me" but that do not efface actively or through omission the ways in which "she" may see differently. At the same time, neither she nor me can be disallowed to speak our experiences' (Probyn, 1993, p. 4). For Miller, too, the move from personal to collective pronoun continues to be a crucial issue. Whilst the caution against generalities (not to mention against universalisms) is well-placed, she suggests, it is nevertheless important to remember 'the historicity of that move from "I" to "we" – the sense of intellectual experiment and innovative practice of the late seventies in the United States, and the feeling of excitement the idea of community negotiates: the possibility that there might be enough feminist teachers out there to collaborate' (Miller, 1991, p. 16).

It is precisely the absence of a sense of historicity that concerns me in this chapter. Removed from any kind of location, 1970s and 1980s feminisms are frequently condemned as a unified block of misguided political and theoretical essentialisms. The use of personal experience and autobiographical testimony has often been taken to characterise feminist theories of these periods. The trajectory that I have seen rehearsed repeatedly in Women's Studies classes runs something like this: 70s feminists based their theories on their experiences, which they included in their writing as an authentic claim to a unified female identity, which they then generalised to include all women ignoring their own privileges as middle-class, heterosexual, white, Western women. Whilst I do recognise that there are problems with '70s feminism' and I do not want to be dismissive of challenges that have been made to its limitations, my point is that these versions of the past do not help us understand the complexities and contradictions of the relationship between the personal and the political, and the autobiographical and the theoretical. In fact, by lumping together all feminist work from the past in these kinds of dismissals, contemporary accounts of the history of feminist theory do both the past and the present a disservice. The 'writing of the self' that I have discussed briefly here poses a number of questions in this respect. First, we might ask whether 70s feminist theorists wrote predominantly in these personal modes. Miller argues that the 'authority of experience' was indeed a key current in feminist theory in the 1970s, but that 'despite that foundational construction, most academic women in the 1970s did not articulate that as a "new personalism" in their writing' (Miller, 1991, p. 14). Literary theorists of that time, she claims, may have been fuelled by a 'profound understanding of the consequences of taking the personal as a category of thought and gender as a category of analysis', but on the whole their writing was not littered with autobiographical anecdotes (Miller, 1991, p. 14).

Similarly, during the 1980s, when identity politics was supposed to characterise feminist theorising, there were (at least) two contradictory strands of 'development' in relation to the writing of the self. On the one hand, as Miller goes on to suggest, the 1980s saw the institutionalisation of 'feminist theory' as an (abstract and depersonalised) body of knowledge within the academy, and the emergence of Women's Studies as a field in its own right; on the other hand, there was a good deal of writing which disrupted the authorised and highly abstract discourses of knowledge at that time by including personal criticism in theoretical debates (see, for example, Marks and de Courtivron, 1981; Haug, 1987). Indeed, many of these interventions into the generic boundaries of expression came from women who did not conform to the conventional identity package of the 1980s white, middle-class, heterosexual academic feminist referenced above. The work of Carolyn Steedman (1986) and Valerie Walkerdine (1986, 1989) offered personal and theoretical challenges to theories of culture which failed, in various ways, adequately to address the intersections of class, gender and historical location. Audre Lorde's work powerfully inscribed the personal within theoretical considerations of power and desire (Lorde, 1984a). Her concern with conceptualising difference and with the interconnections between racism, sexism and homophobia is articulated through a mode that crosses conventional boundaries of writing, including the poetic as well as the polemical within feminist theorising. Lorde's biomythography, *Zami: A New Spelling of My Name* (1982), reworks the conventions of traditional autobiography to highlight its restrictive traditions of self-presentation. Elizabeth Wilson's autobiography, *Mirror Writing* (1982), also challenges autobiographical conventions of self-revelation and offers an account of her life that is informed by post-structuralist theories of writing and representation.

My point here is to emphasise some of the continuities of this aspect of feminist theorising: the writing of the self that seeks to combine the personal with the positional with the theoretical does have its roots in the 1970s (but this does not uniformly characterise feminist theory of this decade), it has continued to be rewritten during the 1980s (but not by a unified group of women who never questioned the problems of identity) and now in the 1990s there is a renewed interest in seeking to combine such modes of writing (but they have not entirely abandoned all the concerns of feminists from previous decades). Feminist theory that builds on the personal, then, might be seen to have been 'dismantled and renovated – to shape a variety of personal and less personal discourses at an oppositional angle to dominant critical positionings' (Miller, 1991, p. 14).

Embodied subjectivity

My second case study takes feminist theories of the body as its starting point. The 1990s have seen the publication of a plethora of feminist books about the body: Julia Epstein and Kristina Straub, *Body Guards* (1991);

Elisabeth Bronfen, *Over Her Dead Body* (1992); Yvonne Tasker, *Spectacular Bodies* (1993); Barbara Stafford, *Body Criticism* (1993); Judith Butler, *Bodies that Matter* (1993); Emily Martin, *Flexible Bodies* (1994); Elizabeth Grosz, *Volatile Bodies* (1994); Jennifer Terry and Jacqueline Urla, *Deviant Bodies* (1995); Elizabeth Grosz and Elspeth Probyn, *Sexy Bodies* (1995); Lisa Cartwright, *Screening the Body* (1995); Anne Balsamo, *Technologies of the Gendered Body* (1996). This list, which gives only an exemplary sample, is indicative of the ongoing concern with matters bodily in feminist scholarship, be they deviant, flexible, volatile or spectacular ones. Crossing conventional disciplinary boundaries, this work draws on film theory, sociology and anthropology, cultural studies, the history of science and literature. For example, Elisabeth Bronfen explores images of the dead feminine body in art and literature as a symptom of patriarchal culture's failed repression of death (Bronfen, 1992); Barbara Stafford examines the intersections of the arts and sciences in the historical development of particular notions of perspective in representations of the body (Stafford, 1993); and Lisa Cartwright examines the changing visual representations of the female body in the history of medical and cinematic technologies (Cartwright, 1995).

In so far as it ever disappeared, the body has returned to take centre stage in contemporary Feminist Theory. This renewed interest demonstrates a continuing preoccupation with the ways in which the body is inscribed within particular sets of power relations and can be read as a marker of difference (of gender, 'race', class and sexuality). Heavily influenced by post-structuralist and post-modernist theory, and yet also critically reworking it, much of this work explores the bodily materiality and physicality of subjects. It shows a continued feminist concern with the exploitation of the bodies of particular groups of people: for example, the exchange of black bodies and labour during slavery or the objectification of women's bodies through visual representation (see McClintock, 1995). It looks at how bodies are regulated and surveyed (for example, in science, in philosophy, in the cinema) and how the body is represented in culture (for example, in literature, in medicine, in art). But it also analyses how bodies exceed such control and can trouble representation. The body is thus seen to be both the site of pain and pleasure, suffering and desire.

So why has there been this renewed interest in the body in feminist theory during the last decade? One reason might be the perceived limits of the theories of subjectivity which preceded it. To generalise vastly, we might say that the emphasis on language as the central means of reproducing dominant culture that characterised much structuralist and post-structuralist thinking in the 1980s left the body out of the picture. The interest in how subjects are positioned by ideologies or discourses often marginalised questions of *embodiment*; indeed, some critics felt it constructed a notion of a disembodied and unlocated subjectivity. The ways in which we live our subjectivities in and through our bodies thus needed further elaboration.

A second reason for this return to matters bodily might be the continued presence of discourses of Nature in public debates about social inequalities (see Haraway, 1991; Strathern, 1992; Yanagisako and Delaney, 1995). No matter how often feminists have argued that the categories of gender, 'race', class and sexuality are socially and culturally constructed, and not biologically determined, the appeal to Nature continues to frame many public debates. In popular culture and media representations, for example, ideas about Nature are constantly invoked. Be it in the reinforcement of conventional notions of gender in discussions about 'artificial' reproduction (the so-called test-tube baby debate), or the naturalisation of 'race' and gender through the commodification of 'exotic other cultures' for consumption (such as in Benetton advertisements), or the reinvention of 'sexual natures' in studies of the Gay Gene (they really are born that way, after all!), ideas about 'the natural' are never far away, though they may be under continual reconfiguration (see Franklin, Lury and Stacey, forthcoming).

Accompanying the continued significance of Nature in popular cultural representations is the expansion of feminist studies of science and technology (see Franklin and McNeil, 1991, 1993; see also Chapter 10 below). This is a further reason for the increased interest in the body in Women's Studies. Although science and technology studies have been a crucial area of feminist concern for some time now, they have recently cross-fertilised other disciplines more obviously and developed very influential interdisciplinary approaches to the study of gender (see Haraway, 1989, 1991; Braidotti, 1994; Cartwright, 1995; J. Epstein, 1995; Franklin, Lury and Stacey, 1997; McNeil, 1997 forthcoming). Indeed, it would be true to say that research on the body is currently so visible on the feminist agenda because of the success of feminist science studies.

Having stressed the renewed interest in the body in current feminist theory, then, I want to state firmly that this is a *continued* interest for many. Indeed, the study of the control of the female body has remained one of the most fundamental concerns of second-wave feminism. In the early 1970s, feminist theory and politics saw the exploitation of the body as the key to the patriarchal control of women: what women's bodies could and couldn't do; what their bodies did and didn't feel; where their bodies could and couldn't go; whose body did and did not matter (Firestone, 1971; Greer, 1971; Boston Women's Health Collective, 1973; Dreifus, 1977). Although it was certainly not without its problems and limitations, this early work nevertheless placed the bodily dimensions of oppression firmly on the political and academic agenda. Like the more personal modes of criticism discussed in the previous section, these interventions challenged the foundations of patriarchal knowledge about women and, indeed, the conventional modes of abstraction of social and cultural theorising.

What was at stake in many of these early interventions was the status of knowledge, the legitimacy of expertise and the politics of entitlement to both (see McNeil, 1987). In fact, projects and then publications, such as *Our Bodies, Ourselves* (Boston Women's Health Collective, 1973), illustrate perfectly the power/knowledge relations elaborated in Foucault's work on medical and other discourses that has been such a strong reference point for much recent feminist work on the body (Foucault, 1973b, 1978). Beginning as 'the Doctors' Group' in the late 1960s, a number of women in Boston met to discuss the limits of doctors' knowledge about women's health (see Hockey, 1993, p. 264). Their work questioned conventional forms of medical expertise about women's bodies and began the ambitious project of collecting and collating alternative forms of knowledge through experiential and experimental methods. There could scarcely be a better example of 'contested discursive boundaries' (though nobody would have used that language then) than the story of the pot of natural yoghurt that has now become a feminist urban legend. A women's health centre in the USA was raided by police for using illegal and unrecognised medical methods; when an officer tried to seize a pot of natural yoghurt (now a well-known remedy for vaginal thrush) as evidence of the use of unlawful remedies, one of the women there refused to give it to him, protesting that it was simply her lunch. This story about an everyday object becoming state evidence in the struggle over the legitimacy of expertise perfectly condenses some of the ways in which early feminist interventions shifted the boundaries of the debates about medical knowledge. The clash between formal and informal, and between professional and personal, forms of knowledge about women's bodies and how to treat their medical problems has continued to be a fierce political and theoretical battle throughout the history of second-wave feminism (see Chapter 13 in this volume).

In addition to these often unexplored connections between early feminist work and recent theories of the body, there was also a continued interest in this area throughout the 1980s (see, for example, Haug, 1987). Much of this work still informs the theorising of bodily questions in the late 1990s. This is especially true of so-called 'French feminist theory' of this period (or rather, of those strands of it that concern themselves with culture, language and representation: see Marks and de Courtivron, 1981; Duchen, 1986; Moi, 1987). Although highly diverse in many ways, this theory might be described as being unified around the project of feminine writing, *l'écriture féminine*. A number of French feminist theorists in the 1980s contributed to a radical rewriting of the feminine subject (normally repressed within the Symbolic Order of patriarchal culture), posing a challenge to the conventional wisdoms of Freudian and, more particularly, Lacanian, psychoanalysis. As Gill Frith sums up, '[W]hereas "masculine" language is linear, finite, structured, rational and unified, "feminine" language is fluid, decentred, playful, fragmented and open-ended' (Frith, 1993, p. 170). Luce Irigaray (1985a; 1985b), for example, offers an ironic account of the significance of sexual difference based upon feminine sexuality and the specificity of the feminine body; and Hélène Cixous (1981) calls for the elaboration of a profoundly different feminine mode of expression based on writing the specificity of the feminine body. Julia Kristeva's work (see Moi, 1986) has also explored the relationship between perceptions of bodily difference and the construction of the sexed subject. Her interest in how the division between the 'semiotic' and the 'Symbolic' relates to the meanings of masculinity and femininity within patriarchal culture has placed beliefs about the mythical maternal body centre stage.

Despite being dismissed as 'essentialist' by many (see Stacey, 1993), the work of these writers continues to influence feminists concerned with theorising the body in the 1990s. Even those who challenge many of their ideas continue to engage with them in substantial detail (see, for example, Butler, 1990, 1993). Moreover, there are a number of recent publications that draw quite directly on this 1980s theory. I want to take one example, Kristeva's theory of 'abjection', to illustrate my claims briefly (Kristeva, 1982). Before moving on to the writers who have used this theory recently, I offer a summary of its most pertinent dimensions with respect to this context.

Kristeva's *Powers of Horror: An Essay on Abjection* (1982) offers a poetic/ theoretical account of how and why some bodies (or some bodily processes) have the power to horrify, to produce a physical shudder, a sense of both fascination and disgust. At the root of such responses, she argues, is the 'abject'. Neither subject nor object, the 'abject' reminds us of the impossibility of fixing permanent or immutable boundaries between each; it highlights the temporary character of our banishment of undesirable objects from our bodies and psyches. The abject haunts the subject, long after it has been banished. The abject:

> is the impossible object, still part of the subject: an object the subject strives to expel but which is ineliminable. In ingesting objects into itself, or expelling objects from itself, the 'subject' can never be distinct from these 'objects'. The ingested/expelled 'objects' are neither part of the body, nor separate from it. The abject (including tears, saliva, faeces, urine, vomit, mucus) marks bodily sites that will later become erotogenic zones (mouth, eyes, anus, nose, genitals). The subject must expel these abjects to establish the 'clean and proper body' of oedipalization. (Grosz, 1992, p. 198)

The abject is both separate from, and yet part of, the subject. It is that which we want to exclude, but which threatens to re-enter. As such, it is a constant reminder of the mutability of our borders and the vulnerability of the subject: 'It is thus not lack of cleanliness or health that causes abjection but what disturbs identity, system, order. What does not respect borders, positions, rules. The in-between, the ambiguous, the composite' (Kristeva,

1982, p. 4). Abjection is 'the horror of not knowing the boundaries distinguishing "me" from "not me"' (Chisholm, 1992, p. 439). It both summons and repels us and it both attracts and horrifies us: 'what is *abject* . . . the jettisoned object, is radically excluded and draws me into a place where meaning collapses' (Kristeva, 1982, p. 2). The abject can never be fully rejected: 'while releasing a hold, it does not radically cut off the subject from what threatens it – on the contrary, abjection acknowledges it to be in perpetual danger' (Kristeva, quoted in Creed, 1993, p. 8). It is the crossing of the border between I/other and between inside and outside that truly disgusts; not deaths then, but that which must be eradicated in order to live.

Kristeva suggests that the abject has been attributed to the feminine through its association with the maternal body. In reminding us of the borders between life and death it draws upon our ambivalence to our previous connection to, and dependence upon, the mother's body: '[The abject] signals the precarious grasp the subject has over its identity and bodily boundaries, the ever-present possibility of sliding back into the corporeal abyss from which it was formed' (Grosz, 1992, p. 198). To simplify, we might say that our desire to escape abjection has its roots in a fear of the mother's body.

Kristeva's theory of abjection has been challenged, but also reworked and elaborated in a number of recent feminist texts on the body (see Butler, 1990; Creed, 1993; Krauss, 1993; Mulvey, 1991; Grosz, 1994). Judith Butler and Elizabeth Grosz engage with it in the context of philosophical discussion about theories of the gendered body (though with very different conclusions); Mulvey and Krauss use it as a starting point for theoretical commentary on the 'Disgust Pictures' of American artist Cindy Sherman that explore themes of horror and fascination with bodily decay and of the blurred boundaries between the human and the non-human body; Barbara Creed (who aligns herself most closely with Kristeva's own position) traces the history of the connections between monstrousness and femininity in representation of the female body in popular horror films.

Building on Kristeva's notion of abjection in her own recent theory of the 'corporeality' of sexual subjectivity, Elizabeth Grosz asks:

> Can it be that in the West, in our time, the female body has been constructed not only as lack or absence but with more complexity, as a leaking, uncontrollable, seeping liquid; as a formless flow; as viscosity, entrapping, secreting; as lacking not so much the phallus but self-containment – not a cracked or porous vessel, like a leaking ship, but a formlessness that engulfs all form, a disorder that threatens all order? (Grosz, 1994, p. 203)

It is not that Grosz is suggesting that women *are* like this, but rather that their corporeality has been 'inscribed as a mode of seepage' within a patriarchal culture that reassures itself by fixing boundaries and borders as immutable (Grosz, 1994, p. 203). Grosz's book contributes to the many reworkings of a theory of abject and dangerous bodies as symptoms of the fears and desires of dominant culture, be they manifest in the visual images of the female body and its flows in the cinema (Creed, 1993), in the bodily dimensions of racist 'expulsions and repulsions' (Young quoted in Butler, 1990, p. 132), or the homophobic responses to HIV and AIDS as a sign of homosexual pollution (Watney, 1987; Butler, 1990). Grosz's model also provided a highly suggestive starting point for my own analysis of the cultural anxieties around disease, sexual desire and the gendered body in the construction of cancer and lesbianism as taboo categories (the C word and the L word: see Stacey, 1997 forthcoming).

I have taken Kristeva's theory of abjection as an example of how recent feminist work on embodied subjectivity continues to draw upon, and engage with, much earlier models of the gendered body. It would be easy to map a trajectory of the developments in feminist theories of the body that follows the progress narrative I have been criticising so far in this chapter: from early *essentialism* through *social constructionism* to the present *cultural constitution*. It is often the case that new work on the body defines itself in opposition to a more natural, taken-for-granted body of previous feminist theorists. Once again, removed from their political and historical location, early feminist theorists are frequently constructed as the bad objects, the essentialist predecessors, against which the more sophisticated theories of the body today are defined. But I have countered this character-isation not only because it has become so hackneyed, but also because, despite the current emphasis on discursive constitution, and all the fluidities that suggests, there are nevertheless long-standing, stubborn theoretical questions that continue to torment contemporary feminist work in the area. There are also, as I have indicated, frequently overlooked continuities in this area of theory that have persisted across the decades.

Heroines and stars

The problem with the tendency to construct a developmental model of Feminist Theory based upon a progress narrative is partly that it reproduces highly traditional notions of history. As I have argued, such representations of past-present relations position the latest contributions as the most enlightened in opposition to the early simplicities of past thinkers. This kind of history has been widely challenged for the ways in which its linearity, cause-and-effect logic and moves towards closure suggest mislead-ingly that the world is becoming a better and fairer place as we become more knowing and more rational subjects (Foucault, 1979; Lyotard, 1984). Indeed, these narratives of progress and development are ones in which the masculine values of rationality and of control are reinforced. To narrate the story of Feminist Theory along such lines is to strike an ironic chord when many feminist academics are themselves critical of the ways in which the narratives of modernity more generally follow a linear, progressivist pattern. For feminist theorists influenced by post-structuralism and post-modernism, for example, to be positioned as the Enlightened subjects at the end of a history of Feminist Theory is a contradiction in terms.

A further problem with this kind of account of Feminist Theory is that, like all progress narratives, it produces its own forms of heroism. Those who are perceived to be producing the capital 'T' of Feminist Theory are often seen to be the heroes at the apex of this narrative, fetishised through idealisation and idolisation. In the first edition of this book I explained why I wanted to avoid the 'key texts' approach to a chapter on feminist theory. I explained that such a project seemed to me to pose the problems not just of the idiosyncrasies of personal choice but, more importantly, of the necessary exclusions such a selection would entail. In short, I opposed the formation of a 'feminist canon'. To replace the Great Men of Theory with the Great Women of Theory may change the gender, and indeed the agenda, but would do little to challenge the fetishising of Great Minds and of Genius that has characterised the individualism of the history of ideas.

Accompanying the divisions and selections around what counts as Theory has been a very marked increase in the cult of personalities and the institutionalisation of a star system, not only within academia in general, but also within Women's Studies. The cult of the personality that produces a fascination with, an envy of (and even a hatred of) particular individuals has its own recognisable brand within the late twentieth-century academy. For readers new to feminist theory who have come to this chapter as a way to begin to explore unknown territory, I hope they will not go away with the idea that if they read *x*, *y* and *z*, they will have 'done' feminist theory. Rather, I hope this account might begin to engender a critical awareness of the ways in which feminist knowledges are constructed and contested within changing contexts, as well as of the politics of how certain kinds of writing are designated 'Theoretical', whilst others are not. In other words, Feminist Theory is not an object that can be neatly packaged and consumed, and neither is it the product of a few fetishised star contributors writing in a vacuum, but rather it is a process, and, I hope, one in which the capital F remains as crucial as the capital T.[1]

Note

1. Other chapters in this book have offered readers guidance through the selection of Further Reading in their subject areas; I have decided not to make such a selection, for the reasons discussed here.

4

Women, History and Protest

June Hannam

Second-wave feminism and women's history

Writing in 1972 when the women's liberation movement was gaining momentum, Anna Davin urged women to study their own history, 'for by showing that the role and nature of women changes with each society we are helping to defeat the argument "that's how it's always been"'. As Davin suggests, the writing of women's history cannot be separated from contemporary feminist politics. Women concerned to understand their specific inequalities and to challenge institutions which perpetuate their oppression have looked to understand the roots of that oppression in the past; to discover whether such challenges had been made before and what they could learn from them (Davin, 1972, p. 224). If women saw themselves as marginal in the past it would reinforce their view of themselves as subordinate and powerless in the present. Only if a woman's role could be shown to be socially constructed and rooted in a specific historical context, rather than natural and universal, could feminists hope to argue that it was open to change.

The first organised women's movement of the late nineteenth century had already inspired an earlier generation of historians to research into women's history. Finding that 'hitherto the historian has paid little attention to the circumstances of women's lives', writers such as Alice Clark, Barbara Hutchins and Barbara Drake carried out detailed studies of women's work, trade unionism and political activities (Hutchins, 1915; Drake, 1920; Clark, 1968). In the intervening years, however, their work became lost from view. This coincided with a fragmentation of the women's movement after the First World War. Many active feminists worked from within a variety of political groups, and feminist politics were often submerged as they grappled with issues of peace, fascism and war.

It was only with the revival of a feminist movement in the late 1960s that interest in women's history was awakened once more. This suggests that 'women's experience has to be remembered anew with each resurgence of feminist consciousness, for between times it leaves hardly a trace' (Alexander, 1984, p. 128). When feminists searched the history books they found that women were still largely 'hidden from history'. Nothing much seemed to have changed from when Virginia Woolf complained that although woman:

> pervades poetry from cover to cover, she is all but absent from history . . .
> Of our fathers we always know some fact or some distinction. They were soldiers or they were sailors. They filled that office or they made that law, but of our mothers, our grandmothers, our great grandmothers what remains is nothing but a tradition. One was beautiful, one was red-haired, one was kissed by a queen. We know nothing of them except their names and the dates of their marriages and the number of children they bore. (Woolf, 1929, p. 45)

As Woolf implies, women's invisibility stemmed partly from what has long been seen as historically significant: foreign policy questions, the development of formal political institutions and the growth of industry and commerce. Women did not have a high profile in any of these areas and this could be construed as an expression of the subordinate role that they played as architects of their world. It has been all too easy for historians, products themselves of a particular social context, to accept the Victorian model of women's essential passivity and domesticity, and to minimise their contribution to historical development. Consequently, women have appeared in mainstream histories either as objects of humanitarian concern or as problems affecting male workers or administrators.

Women have not been completely absent from the history books. We know about some women and some events, although this in itself can have a distorting effect. A few 'great women' have been singled out for attention – for example, Florence Nightingale, Elizabeth Fry, Josephine Butler and Elizabeth Garrett Anderson – but their lives and work have been seen as exceptional and their characters idealised to emphasise 'female' qualities of caring and saintliness. Women also tend to have been noticed when engaging in activities traditionally seen as important by historians, such as munitions work during the two world wars. It is no accident that the struggle for the vote, when women sought access to the formal political arena, has received the most consistent attention from historians and is the one campaign that is instantly recognisable to a wide audience.

Despite such exceptions, women's contribution to the development of social, economic and political change has been marginalised through their absence from mainstream historical studies (Lewis, 1981; Campbell, 1992). Feminist historians in the early 1970s set out to redress the balance, and over the last 25 years research and writing on aspects of women's history has steadily increased. This chapter will survey the developments that have taken place in the writing of women's history during this period. It points to changes in subject matter and approach, drawing attention to the way in which our understanding of women's lives has been altered by recent scholarship. The focus will be on British women's history from the late eighteenth century. Where appropriate, reference will also be made to research undertaken into American women's history. Here the approaches and concerns have often had a different focus, leading to a fruitful exchange of ideas between researchers in the two countries (Newton, Ryan and Walkowitz, 1983; Offen, Pierson and Rendall, 1991). Finally, recent trends in women's history will also be discussed.

Making women visible

Given the paucity of references to women in standard texts, one of the first tasks of feminist historians was to rediscover women's active role in the process of historical change. Sheila Rowbotham's pioneering study, aptly entitled *Hidden from History* (Rowbotham, 1990a), led the way and was followed by a series of monographs on aspects of women's lives, including employment, women's organisations, family life and sexuality. With the emphasis of the women's movement on consciousness-raising, feminists saw a knowledge of their past as a source of strength and therefore drew attention to women who had achieved in the public arena. If they looked hard enough, historians could find women at the work place, in trade unions and taking part in political and social reform movements where they canvassed for political parties, stood for election to public bodies and were militant at times of labour unrest (Lewenhak, 1977; Burman, 1979; Hollis, 1979). The American historian and feminist theorist, Gerda Lerner, described such an approach as contribution history; that is, one which sought to include women within an existing male-defined history, where activities in the public and political arena were seen as of greatest historical importance (Lerner, 1981).

Other feminist historians, in particular in the USA, were more interested in focusing on the development in the nineteenth century of a separate women's sphere. They explored the predominant ideals and values which underpinned women's social role and their sexuality, and produced studies of prostitution, images of women in art and literature, the double standard of morality, and contemporary debates about women's nature and femininity (Hartman and Banner, 1974; Vicinus, 1981). The dangers in such an approach were that women could too easily be seen as victims of male oppression and that historians would end up describing 'what men in the past have told women to do and what men in the past thought women should be' (Lerner, 1981, p. 149).

Both the research into women's activities outside the home and the interest in exploring the development of a separate sphere for women went beyond simply putting women back into an existing historical framework. It also meant a challenge to what should be seen as historically significant. The growth of social history in the 1960s and 1970s provided a context for such a redefinition. The expansion of higher education and the proliferation of social science courses encouraged historians to recognise the significance of subjects such as family structure and relationships, sexuality, popular culture, childhood and youth for an overall understanding of social, political and economic change (Perkin, 1976; Judt, 1979). Using insights from other disciplines, notably sociology and social anthropology, historians began to research new topics, such as the importance of etiquette and social rituals, or birth control and family size (Davidoff, 1973). They also began to examine the interrelationship between areas often seen as separate, such as work and family; or community, culture and class.

A new focus on 'history from below' placed an emphasis on those who had previously lacked a voice (Thompson, 1968; Samuel, 1981), in particular unorganised rank-and-file workers and the very poor. It was feminist historians, however, who ensured that women were included in this process of recovery, although they concentrated largely on the experiences of white middle-class and working-class women. It was not until later that the need to explore the history of Black women and lesbians was more fully recognised.

To trace the history of neglected, less powerful groups could seem to be a daunting task. Sources might at first sight appear not to exist, in particular to those historians used to relying on records of institutions, on government statistics, or on the extensive personal papers left to posterity by the wealthy and powerful. If lesbian, Black and working-class women's experience was not seen as important, either by themselves or by others, they were unlikely to have recorded it in their own right. Lesbians in particular may have destroyed written material in order to protect themselves and others, thereby helping to compound their invisibility. Parliamentary papers, social surveys, trade union and socialist journals were usually written by men, often drawn from the middle class, and therefore reflecting their preoccupations and biases.

Yet, by asking the right questions, historians have been able to find a surprising amount of material in already familiar sources on family life, living standards and the lives of women and children. Anna Davin found that 'accumulating information and details given incidentally in other contexts' was one of the best ways for historians to find out about ordinary life (Davin, 1972, p. 218). Police court cases in newspapers, the reports of charity and missionary societies, medical officers' reports, hospital records, journal articles and photographs, for example, can provide a mine of information on life histories, diet and childcare practices. Recent studies of Black women's history have shown that, far from being invisible, Black women's experiences can also be traced through a wide variety of sources, including the private papers of planters and missionaries, government enquiries, census data, newspapers and autobiographies (Higginbotham and Watts, 1988; Alexander, 1990).

Perhaps the single most well-known source and methodology to emerge from this interest in uncovering the experiences of 'ordinary' people has been oral history. Interviewing women and men about their past lives was not a new technique for historians, but it had been largely confined to those who had played a key role in events: for example, politicians, members of the armed forces and civil servants. In the 1970s, however, researchers sought out women and men who were not well known and interviewed them in large numbers about work, family life, childhood and sexuality.

The methodological questions raised by oral history have generated considerable debate (Gluck and Patai, 1991). Nevertheless, feminist historians have found oral evidence to be particularly valuable in providing an insight into the lives of those who have left few written records; in particular, lesbians, working-class and Black women, whose experiences might otherwise have been lost from view (Roberts, 1984; Hall Carpenter Archives/Lesbian History Group, 1989; Jewish Women in London Group, 1989). It has enabled historians to construct life histories, to discover networking and to 'explore the world of an individual's meanings and beliefs' (Gittins, 1979, p. 12). Personal testimony can raise unexpected issues, which lead the historian to ask new questions, and can add a more three-dimensional texture to the lives of 'ordinary' people than is usually found in the studies carried out by middle-class investigators (Booth, 1902–3). Penny Summerfield and Gail Braybon's study of the two world wars, for example, showed how oral evidence can be used to convey a sense of women's own experiences of home and work, unmediated by official policies and propaganda (Braybon and Summerfield, 1987).

From the discussion so far it would almost appear that women's history could simply have been subsumed in social history. The study of a hitherto neglected group, denied access to formal structures of power and thereby rendered invisible, and the challenge posed to notions of what is historically significant, could be seen as entirely compatible with the broader context and concerns of social history. But social historians have often failed to draw attention to women or to recognise the importance of sexual divisions.

Elizabeth Higginbotham and Sarah Watts, for example, have shown how the ground-breaking scholarship of the 1970s on the history of Afro-Americans failed to explore the specific experiences of Black women. It was only when feminist historians, building on the work of the activist and philosopher Angela Davis (1982), put Black women at the centre of their analysis that new insights were gained into women's community work, family life and paid employment. They were able to show 'the differential

effects of racial oppression on men and women' and to argue that Black
women as well as Black men played a crucial role in helping the community
to 'survive and resist the dehumanising impact of slavery' (Higginbotham
and Watts, 1988, p. 15).

As practised by feminist historians, women's history has developed a
distinctive character of its own. Far from seeking to find out about and
describe women's lives, and to incorporate their research into an existing
historical framework, feminist historians have argued that if women's
experiences, their values and the shape of their lives have often been
different from those of men, then women's history cannot be viewed as
just another version of men's history. Commenting on the studies undertaken in the 1970s, Gerda Lerner suggested that the key question to ask is
what history would be like if it were seen through the eyes of women and
ordered by values they define (Lerner, 1981). Such a woman-centred
approach would mean, for example, looking at the way in which culture
is transmitted to the young, at the building of social networks and at the
way in which these have provided continuity.

Women's lives were often bound up with family concerns, with emotional
support and personal relationships. Feminist historians have argued that
these personal, subjective experiences had just as much historical significance as the world of waged work and politics. They have questioned the
distinction usually made between public and private life and have sought
instead to explore the interconnections between them (Davidoff and Hall,
1987). In doing so they have found that 'inequalities in the domestic world
structure inequalities in the public sphere' rather than necessarily the other
way round (Lewis, 1986, p. 1). If women's experience of family and work
was different from that of men's, then the periodisation of their history
would also need to be different. It has been suggested that this difference
'may embrace not only the contents of historical experience, but also the
experience of time itself' (Bock, 1989, p. 8). Thus the rhythm of family lives,
including events such as marriage, childbirth and death, need to be
recognised (and interrelated with) the more familiar concepts of time as
affected by changes in economic and political structures (Hareven, 1982).

The distinctive approach of feminist historians has been to insist that
women as a social group have suffered a variety of controls and restrictions
on their lives which need to be explored historically. Women may be a
separate group because of their sex, or biological characteristics, but what
interests the historian is the 'cultural definition of behaviour defined as
appropriate to the sexes in a given society at a given time' (Lerner, 1986,
p. 238).

Feminist historians have argued that gender divisions and the power
relationships between women and men are crucial for an understanding of
the historical process, and that recognition of the importance of these
divisions must then lead to a reconstruction of history in the broadest

sense. Nonetheless, in seeking to rewrite history to take account of women's specific experiences, feminist historians differ in their emphases and approach. These differences relate both to debates within contemporary feminist theory and practice, and to the strengths of particular historical traditions in different countries.

Women's history and labour history

In the 1970s and early 1980s feminist research in the USA, for example, concentrated on a separate women's culture, the growth of all-female institutions, family history and sexuality. In Britain, where the study of labour history had long been a central concern, many feminist historians, working within a predominantly socialist tradition, focused on women's waged work, their trade union organisation and their role in labour politics. They sought to reconcile class and gender in their historical analysis, which was an uphill task in the context of a Marxist approach which emphasised the key role played by the struggles of organised male workers as agents of social change and which marginalised the role of women and their specific experiences (Davin, 1981; Sargent, 1981; Segal, 1989).

By recognising and highlighting the importance of the sexual division of labour feminist historians have made a distinctive contribution to the study of labour history. They have shown the extent to which working-class struggles and political movements were concerned with gender relations in both the work place and in the home (Rose, 1993). They have also drawn attention to the way in which the division of labour between men and women helped to structure work patterns and was an integral feature of broad changes in production. Writing in the 1970s about the history of working-class women, Sally Alexander noted that:

Feminist history releases women from their obscurity as the wives, mothers and daughters of working men. This does not just mean that family life, housework, the reproduction of the labour force, the transmission of ideology etc. can be added to an already constituted history, but the history of production itself will be re-written. For the history of production under capitalism, from a feminist perspective, is not simply the class struggle between the producer and the owner of the means of production. It is also the development of a particular form of the sexual division of labour in relation to that struggle. (Alexander, 1977, pp. 59–60)

Feminist historians have also raised the need to explain why the sexual division of work took the specific form that it did in different periods, and that it should not be seen as 'natural' (see Chapter 11). Detailed studies of women's occupations have suggested that the potential advantages to employers of mechanisation, prevailing definitions of skill, the power of male trade unions, and management practices all played a part in the definition of jobs as female or male (John, 1986; Glucksmann, 1990).

A crucial factor in this definition was women's identification with cheap labour, which in turn was closely related to their role within the working-class family. Women's work in the nineteenth century had a lower social and economic value than men's 'due to their primary association with reproduction rather than production and their responsibility for childcare and housework (with no economic value)' (John, 1986, p. 5). The low value placed on women's work then affected all aspects of their employment, including wages, conditions of work and the type of jobs assigned to them.

We now know, therefore, far more about the complex relationship between women's paid work, in particular outside the home, and their work within the family. In an edited collection of articles, Pat Hudson and Robert Lee suggest the need to explore aspects of women's work which tend to be less visible, for 'we know that much of women's work . . . has been concentrated outside of this formal economy in the vast range of tasks surrounding home and hearth and in irregular low status employments which do not readily enter historical record'. They also argue that women's work should be examined in relation to broader concerns, such as the creation of political identity, the maintenance of living standards and its impact on fertility (Hudson and Lee, 1990, p. 2).

Women's position as waged workers has been affected not just by their family context, but also by government policies. This can be illustrated by studies of women workers during the two world wars. While recognising that women's work was altered during the course of twentieth-century wars, the latest research questions the extent to which war had a long-lasting effect on the nature and extent of women's employment. Drawn into production because of the emergency of wartime, women's temporary status in the labour force was underlined both by government policies relating to the replacement of skilled male workers by less-skilled female workers, and by union agreements about the position of male workers once the war was over. War also led to an increased emphasis on the importance of motherhood, which served to reinforce women's marginal status in production and to promote domesticity. Although some women may have welcomed the chance to return home and give up their double burden, those who wished to remain at work found it much more difficult to retain their position in 'non-traditional' areas of female employment (Woollacott, 1994; Summerfield, 1995).

Feminist historians working within a socialist tradition have been concerned to examine the interaction between class, 'race' and gender, but their approaches have frequently differed. For some, the concept of patriarchy provided a way of coming to terms with the questions which arose when it was recognised that 'women have not only worked for capital, they have worked for men' (Newton, Ryan and Walkowitz, 1983, p. 3). Barbara Taylor and Sally Alexander, for example, used the concept of patriarchy as a way to develop a theory of sexual antagonism, since a Marxist theory of class conflict could not answer all their questions (Alexander and Taylor, 1981). Sheila Rowbotham, on the other hand, challenged the use of such a concept. She argued that it could not help to explain, and diverted attention from, those aspects of male-female relationships which are not simply oppressive, but include varying degrees of mutual aid. She pointed to periods in which 'class or race solidarity are much stronger than sex-gender conflict and times when relations within the family are a source of mutual resistance to class power' (Rowbotham, 1982, p. 367).

Other authors used 'dual systems' theory to link capitalism and patriarchy, suggesting that 'patriarchy was a thriving and vibrant aspect of capitalism and not a vestigial remnant from an earlier time' (Humphries, 1995, p. 87). Heidi Hartmann, for example, argued that trade unions played a key role in determining and reinforcing women's subordinate role in the work place. She claimed that women's status as secondary workers stemmed from the patriarchal relations between women and men which pre-dated capitalism. When capitalist labour relations threatened to destroy the family and male power over women's labour, organised male workers rejected women as co-workers in order to maintain their dominance in both the work place and in the home (Hartmann, 1981).

Sally Alexander and Sonya Rose, however, have suggested that exclusionary practices by male workers must be seen in more complex ways. Threatened with a reduction in wages and loss of control over the pace of their work, skilled men reacted by attempting to exclude less skilled men as well as women from their trades. They were reacting as workers as well as men and therefore gender was only one factor, albeit an important one, in their overall strategy of survival (Alexander, 1980; Rose, 1988).

Recent studies of the impact of industrialisation on women's lives and their economic and social status continue to address the question of the relationship between concepts of patriarchy, class, 'race' and the development of capitalism (Berg and Hudson, 1992; Rose, 1992; Berg, 1993; Humphries, 1995). The debate between Bridget Hill, a socialist historian, and Judith Bennett over continuities and change in women's history also addresses similar issues. Hill suggests if patriarchy is seen as central to women's history then the focus of attention will always be on the 'way in which patriarchal power has operated in the past to oppress women'. This misses the 'subtlety of the complex interaction of the many other factors that have shaped women's history. It will be to ignore the fact that it is not only men who have wielded power and that women have been oppressors and exploiters as well as oppressed and exploited' (Hill, 1993, p. 18). In her reply, Bennett asserts that her own view of patriarchy is a subtle one which rejects the notion that it is a static force. Instead she argues that 'patriarchy clearly has existed in many forms and varieties, and its history will, in fact, be a history of many different historical patriarchies' (Bennett, 1993, p. 178). Nonetheless, while recognising the interaction between economic systems and patriarchy she insists that while some women may wield more power than some men 'women as a group are disempowered compared to *men of their group*' (Bennett, 1993, p. 177).

In the early 1970s, when socialist feminists were grappling with the relationship between class, gender and the material conditions of women's oppression, radical feminists argued that women's experience of history was primarily determined by their sex. Although there were differences in the way in which patriarchy was analysed and defined (see Chapter 3), radical feminists used it as a conceptual tool for explaining women's oppression over time and saw male power over women as the key to understanding women's subordination (Rich, 1980c). They were more interested in sexuality and socialisation than with labour markets and the sexual division of labour, and emphasised the 'psychic, sexual and ideological structures that differentiate the sexes' (Kelly, 1983, p. 260).

Lesbian historians in particular have drawn attention to the way in which men's control over women's bodies underpins patriarchy and emphasise that male power has been maintained through the social construction of heterosexuality (Jeffreys, 1990, 1995; Jackson, 1994). Sheila Jeffreys has argued, for example, that sexuality should not be seen simply as an area of personal and private concern, but as a 'political relationship'. The sexual activity which takes place between a heterosexual couple 'represents an area in which men's power and control can be reinforced, and women's subordination reproduced' (Jeffreys, 1985, p. 178). In such a context, lesbianism can be seen as a form of strong resistance and women can form a 'female world of love and ritual' in which their strongest emotional and supportive relationships are with other women (Faderman, 1981; London Feminist History Group, 1986, p. 6).

Difference

It would be misleading, however, to suggest that there is a neat divide between radical and socialist feminists or between those concerned with sexuality and those who concentrate on class and labour relations. Not only is it difficult to fit historians neatly into categories of feminist thought, but the boundaries between liberal, socialist and radical feminism have become more fluid over time (Maynard, 1995). Sally Alexander's study of working-class movements in the early nineteenth century, for example, examined how the unconscious entered politics and how our understanding of self and sexual identity would change our understanding of class (Alexander, 1984).

In her writings on feminist biography, Liz Stanley explored the way in which her subjects were created through a process which is social, class-related and sexual-political (Stanley, 1987).

During the 1980s feminist history moved away from an approach which emphasised women's common experiences to one which increasingly explored the differences between them. It was recognised that the nature of men's power over women and the ways in which women offer resistance to that power were bound to be different depending on whether women are white, Black, middle class or working class, lesbian or heterosexual, which can then determine what kind of access they have to social and economic power (London Feminist History Group, 1986; Stanley, 1990a).

Lesbian historians in particular sought to rescue lesbian history from invisibility and produced detailed studies which reclaimed the lesbian past (Faderman, 1981; Jeffreys, 1985; Baum Duberman, Vicinus and Chauncey, 1991) More recent texts, however, have been concerned to integrate a lesbian perspective, which focuses on the social construction of heterosexuality as an integral part of the way in which male power is constituted and maintained, into a broader feminist history (Jackson, 1995; Richardson, 1996e).

An interest in questions of ethnicity, 'race' and Empire, which has produced studies of Irish, Jewish, Indian and Black women, has also emphasised the importance of difference (Burman, 1990; Luddy, 1992; MacCurtain and O'Dowd, 1992; Marks, 1994; McClintock, 1995; Midgley, 1995). Despite the growth of research into women's history over more than two decades the experience of Black women in Britain has been neglected. And yet Ziggi Alexander provides evidence to suggest that 'these islands had been home to thousands of Africans and their descendants since the time of Roman occupation' (Alexander, 1990, p. 22). Although information on Black women's lives can be pieced together from references scattered throughout different general studies, there is no one text which provides an overview. Alexander argues that white feminist historians themselves have been affected by the 'political preoccupations of the dominant culture'. Their interest in recovering women from historical invisibility, therefore, did not initially rescue Black women from obscurity.

Far more studies have been undertaken into the history of Afro-American women. These have revealed the active role that Black women played in the development and maintenance of Afro-American communities in both the public and the private sphere (Higginbotham and Watts, 1988). Evelyn Higginbotham also points out, however, that these studies make clear that 'factors of class and race make any generalisation regarding womanhood's common oppression impossible' (Higginbotham, 1990, p. 63). They highlight the need to explore Black women's lives through 'race', class and gender oppression, while also insisting that Black women themselves were not a 'monolithic' group, but had a diverse range of experiences and responses to the varied aspects of their oppression. This is reinforced by the oral history studies of Black and Indian women which have increased our understanding of their lives during the twentieth century (Wilson, 1978; Bryan, Dadzie and Scafe, 1985).

White women's involvement in Empire has also attracted considerable attention from feminist historians. Some women, such as Flora Shaw, became leading propagandists of Empire, whereas others criticised male imperial policy and 'developed a feminine vision of benevolent imperial social reform' which led them to support women's suffrage (Midgley, 1995, p. 262). Studies by Vron Ware and Antoinette Burton explore the complex ways in which British feminists related to the Empire. Burton, for example, suggests that white feminists saw themselves as having a civilising mission, whereas Ware suggests that they attempted to link their struggle against male supremacy at home with the struggle against racist domination in the colonies (Ware, 1992; Burton, 1995).

These studies have helped to undermine the view that Empire was an 'exclusively white masculine space' and have demonstrated the ways in which 'Victorian gender ideology and European women' had an impact on colonial societies and their populations (Burton, 1994, p. 487). In turn this has contributed to the development of a new approach to the study of domestic politics in which Empire is seen as as 'an active agent in the construction of cultural and especially social reform discourses' (Burton, 1994, p. 488; see also Poovey, 1988; Hall, 1992). Clare Midgley's study of women's involvement in anti-slavery movements, for example, shows the way in which anti-slavery politics helped to shape not only feminist but also more general political discourses in the nineteenth century (Midgley, 1992).

First-wave feminism

Over the last 25 years, therefore, our understanding of women's history has been enriched, both by the opening up of new areas of enquiry and also by the search for a conceptual framework to make sense of women's specific social position (Lerner, 1986; Riley, 1988). As a result, we now have a far more complex view of the factors which shaped women's lives, of their own aspirations and the extent to which they have experienced change. Some sense of this can best be given through examples drawn from recent work on the history of middle-class women and the organised women's movement in the nineteenth and twentieth centuries. This period is of particular importance since the Victorian ideology of separate spheres (in which men were to be breadwinners and active in the public sphere, while women were to be home-makers confined to the private sphere), and notions of what constituted masculinity and femininity, have had a long-lasting influence on the lives of women up to the present day, and on the interpretations of historians.

Our view of the Victorian woman has changed from that of passive victim to active agent in the process of historical change (Lewis, 1986; Rendall, 1987). Whilst not denying the importance of the Victorian ideology of separate spheres, historians have challenged the familiar stereotype of the middle-class leisured woman, confined to the private sphere. It has been argued that not only did a woman's role within the family contribute to broader economic and social developments, but also that women took an increasingly active part in public life and brought their own values to it.

Philanthropy, for example, has long been recognised as an area which middle-class women made their own. As a voluntary activity, and one which required caring qualities, it was seen as a suitable outlet for women's desire to do something useful with their lives for the good of a wider community (Prochaska, 1980). Research by feminist historians, however, has provided new insights into the motivations of female philanthropists and has re-assessed their contribution to the development of social policy. Mary Carpenter, Octavia Hill, Louisa Twyning and others were not just do-gooders, filling in time between social engagements. They took a serious approach to philanthropy, regarded their activities as purposeful work and helped to develop a professional standing for social work.

The consequences of their activities in redefining women's social role were more contradictory. Jane Lewis suggests that Octavia Hill, Helen Bosanquet and other social activists were all convinced that it was women's duty to serve the community and that they needed education and training for voluntary work. Their views were underpinned, however, by a belief in natural sexual difference and they were 'extremely sensitive as to where the boundary should be drawn in respect of their activities' (Lewis, 1991, p. 8). Octavia Hill, for example, thought that work amongst the poor should be 'quiet' and 'out of sight' and should not fall outside the bounds of propriety (Lewis, 1991, p. 9). Nonetheless, by speaking in public, directing the work of large organisations, taking part in committees and negotiating with politicians they provided a salient example for those who argued that women had a valuable contribution to make to the public sphere (Vicinus, 1985; Parker, 1988; Luddy, 1995).

In the nineteenth century, women increasingly organised together to challenge aspects of their unequal social position. The dramatic struggle for the vote has always been a well-researched area, but we now know that this was the culmination of a much broader struggle to achieve political, social and economic equality. Women fought to gain a measure of economic independence by seeking access to higher education and the professions; they dared to speak out in public about sexuality when they fought to repeal the Contagious Diseases Acts; and they sought to influence public afairs by standing for selection to School Boards, Boards of Guardians and local councils. From the beginning they also campaigned for the Parliamentary vote, partly on the grounds of natural justice and equality with men, and also because they saw it as a way to achieve other goals (Walkowitz, 1980; Banks, 1981; Levine, 1987).

In the last decade attention has focused on the importance of friendship ties between women involved in these campaigns and also on the framework of ideas which guided their actions (Spender, 1983a; Garner, 1984; Levine, 1990). The result is that we now have a much clearer and more complex view of the aims and dynamics of the nineteenth-century women's movement. In the context of separate spheres, women in the nineteenth century often found the greatest emotional support from other women, whether female relatives or friends, and created networks which linked their political and social lives. These support networks, and their importance for the development of feminism, have emerged most clearly as a result of the new interest in writing feminist biography.

Feminists have been concerned to use the biographies of individuals, or groups of women, to explore wider networks of friendship, the relationship between the public and the private, and the economic and social position of women more generally. In doing so they have questioned the approach of more traditional biography writing, with its emphasis on the great woman or unique individual, the description of her life from birth to death, and the possibility of knowing the innermost thoughts and definitive personality of the subject (Stanley, 1992b; Steedman, 1992). Feminist biographers have, instead, been concerned to locate their subjects within the broader social, political and intellectual context in which they lived, and to adopt a more thematic approach in their writings. Carolyn Steedman, for example, uses the life of Margaret McMillan to explore childhood in the late nineteenth and early twentieth centuries and the relationship between educational theories and reform (Steedman, 1990).

Feminists, therefore, have been at the forefront in developing new approaches to biography writing and in their critical appraisal of existing methodology. They have recognised the need to examine the relationship between the historian and the subject of the biography, and to think critically about the way in which diaries, letters and journals were produced and their use as a source (*Gender and History*, 1990). Both Liz Stanley and Kali Israel, for example, use the image of a kaleidoscope to convey some of the complexities of historical research into women's lives. Israel feels this is particularly important in the case of middle-class women, for their lives have been 're-fracted to us through the multiple mirrors of their contemporaries' texts and art works' (Israel, 1990, p. 39; see also Stanley, 1987). Feminist biographers are more willing than in the past to confront the unpalatable aspects of some women's lives, and to learn something from them, rather than to gloss these over in the search for perfect heroines (Birkett and Wheelwright, 1990).

Studies of leading women, including Olive Schreiner, Isabella Ford, Catherine Marshall and Elizabeth Robins, as well as more collective biographies of less well-known feminists, have provided important insights into the social background and motivations of those who were active in the late-nineteenth-century women's movement (Stanley, 1985; Hannam, 1989; Vellacott, 1993; John, 1995). Such biographies have shown important links between the struggle for women's rights and other social and political movements, such as anti-slavery, medical reform, animal welfare, temperance and socialism. Friendship ties sustained late Victorian feminists in their campaigns and cut across class and political boundaries, although the implications for the goals and character of the women's movement were complex. Philippa Levine has argued, for example, that social networks helped to create a distinct female identity and alternative set of values, which led women to emphasise the perceived differences between the sexes as well as demanding equality (Levine, 1987).

A shift of attention away from the manoeuvrings of various campaigns to a study of the ideas which underpinned these movements has again provided new insights into the motivations and aims of Victorian feminists. Throughout the period there was a tension in feminist ideas between a commitment to equal rights and an acceptance of gender differences. Concerned to be treated equally with men, feminists also accepted the importance of their role within the home as wives and mothers. They wanted the possibility of economic and social independence for women, in particular for single women, while at the same time demanding a recognition of the key importance of motherhood (Garner, 1984). Increasingly they used the notion of 'women's special qualities', of caring and purity, to justify their demand for entry to the public sphere and to reinforce their own sense of the importance of feminine values. In her study of women in local government in the late nineteenth century, Patricia Hollis has argued that separate spheres could be used in both conservative and radical ways; it 'reinforced stereotyping of women's nature' while encouraging women to claim a role in public life and to 'expand the contours of what elected authorities were there to do' (Hollis, 1987, p. 210).

The most recent studies of feminist ideas in the period caution against posing a simple dichotomy between equality and difference, and emphasise the importance of understanding feminism within the context of prevailing political and social thought (Caine, 1992; Rendall, 1994; Holton, 1996). Jane Rendall analyses the languages of suffragists in the 1860s and 1870s in the light of new interpretations of nineteenth-century liberalism which suggest that the pursuit of individual rights was inextricably linked to a language of duty and obligation. She concludes that mid-nineteenth-century feminists developed many different meanings of citizenship which not only challenged liberal assumptions about the separation of the public and the private but which were also limited by a 'nervousness . . . about democracy' and an ethnocentrism which were shared with male liberals (Rendall, 1994, p. 144). In her study of four leading members of the women's movement Barbara Caine also emphasises the complexity of their views; she suggests that there were similarities in their thinking which came from a shared intellectual and social context which stressed women's social and moral duties. She notes that they agreed that women were oppressed, but at the same time 'they disagreed about the basis and nature of this oppression and about how it should be reformed; about the nature of women and the extent to which the differences between men and women were innate or socially conditioned.' (Caine, 1992, p. 7).

Nineteenth-century feminists were not just interested in gaining access to the public sphere: they also sought to improve conditions for women within marriage, and saw the growing political interest in motherhood after 1900 as a movement which would reinforce their claims, as mothers, to play a part in the nation's affairs (Bock and Thane, 1991). They also sought to challenge the double standard of morality. Accepting the role assigned to them as moral guardians, they insisted that men should reform their own sexual practices rather than seeking a redefinition of women's own sexuality (Bland, 1995). This outlook, along with a reluctance to champion birth control and easier divorce, brought some criticism from 1970s feminists, whose goal was greater sexual and reproductive freedom for women (Rowbotham, 1990a).

More recently, when the potential gains for women from the 'sexual revolution' have been questioned, historians have begun to write more sympathetically about the first wave of feminists. Sheila Jeffreys, for example, argues that a reluctance to embrace birth control made sense in a period when women were socially and economically dependent, since they feared that this would give men greater control over women's bodies. Re-examining the work of leading sexologists of the period, such as Havelock Ellis, she argues that far from contributing to a climate of greater sexual freedom for women, they imposed a heterosexual norm which served to constrict women's lives, especially those of spinsters and lesbians (Jeffreys, 1985, 1995). Margaret Jackson argues that feminists theorised 'links between the sexual, political and economic aspects of women's subordination' and that through politicising sexuality they challenged the sexual basis of male power (Jackson, 1994, p. 182).

Lucy Bland also emphasises the importance of analysing late-nineteenth-century feminist writings and campaigns around sexuality, but she argues strongly that historians should recognise the differences between such women as well as their similarities, and make sure that they are aware of the context in which such ideas were developed. Unlike Jeffreys, she believes that feminist attempts to control male sexuality were defeated not simply by the rise of anti-feminist sex reform before the First World War, but also by the rise of eugenic and imperialist concern with the falling white, middle-class birth rate. She also argues that it is important to recognise the class nature of feminist writing, since it was often middle-class women writing about and attempting to regulate working-class sexuality (Bland, 1986, 1995).

What has become clear is that it can be very misleading rigidly to compartmentalise either individual women or the movements of which they were a part. Any attempt to divide women neatly into different categories, such as 'equal-rights feminists' or 'social maternalists' who sought to extend their domestic influence beyond the home, breaks down once their writings are examined in detail. The same woman could employ different sets of arguments according to the circumstances in which she was involved and not consider that they were contradictory. Moreover, even if they gave most of their energies to one cause rather than another, feminists tended to support a variety of women's rights campaigns and to see them as inter-linked.

Similarly, the links between the women's movement and other social and political movements have begun to be re-assessed. Clare Midgley, for example, examines the connection between women's involvement in anti-slavery campaigns and feminism in the 1860s, while a number of recent studies explore the connections between the women's movement and other political parties (Walker, 1987; Hirshfield, 1990; Midgley, 1992). From the mid-1880s, for instance, many feminists became involved in labour politics. They joined socialist societies, tried to draw the attention of the labour movement to the specific needs of working-class women and worked hard to bring the labour movement and the women's movement closer together (Hannam, 1992; Hunt, 1996).

Although it was more difficult for working-class women than their middle-class counterparts to take part in militant suffrage activities, since they could not afford to be imprisoned or separated for too long from their communities, Jill Liddington and Jill Norris have shown that Lancashire working women campaigned actively for the vote after 1900 (Liddington and Norris, 1978). The revived suffrage movement led to tensions in the labour movement between the claims of women as a sex, and class politics. It was argued that the demand for votes for women on the same terms as men threatened labour unity by emphasising women's common interests and would only enfranchise middle-class women. The refusal of the Labour Party to give support to a 'limited' franchise caused a dilemma for those women who were both socialists and feminists about where their priorities should lie. When the Labour Party finally adopted women's suffrage it was on the grounds of women's essential difference from men – the importance of their taking caring qualities from the domestic sphere into the wider community -and could be used to divert attention away from tackling women's inequality at the work place (Holton, 1986; Hannam, 1992; Hunt, 1996). By drawing attention to the rich interconnection between the women's movement and the labour movement, such studies have transformed our understanding of both movements and of the broader relationship between class, 'race' and gender.

Gender, history and post-structuralism

In 1979, Gerda Lerner argued that women and their activities in the past had been ignored because historians asked questions that were inappropriate to women. She suggested that to rectify this feminist historians should focus on a 'woman centred enquiry' and consider the possibility of the existence of a female culture within the general culture shared by men and women (Lerner, 1981, pp. 178–9). This was to be the first step in the move towards 'a new universal history, a holistic history which will be a synthesis of traditional history and women's history' (Lerner, 1981, p. 180).

After over two decades of research into women's history, what has been achieved? It is far easier now for those who are interested to study women's history. The development of journals, such as *History Workshop, Feminist Studies, Feminist Review, Gender and History* and *Women's History Review*, and the growth of a women's press has made research more readily available to a wide audience. Women's active contribution to historical change has been recognised; our view of what is historically significant has been altered; and some of the distinctions between public and private, production and reproduction have been broken down or blurred.

We are still a long way, however, from Gerda Lerner's vision of a new history which takes full account of women's experiences. Mainstream history texts and educational courses often ignore the latest research into women's history. There has been a tendency to view women's history as being separate from other developments and something which can be studied simply by enthusiasts, leaving other historians unaffected. This has led some feminist historians to move away from a focus on women's history, in order to construct a different type of history which encompasses women and men and takes account of the variety of experiences within both sexes.

Jane Rendall, for example, has argued that women's history 'need not be confined to separate shelves', but its themes should inform the history of men as well as women and should focus on the varied ways in which gender differences in different societies have been constructed and understood (Rendall, 1990). Leonore Davidoff and Catherine Hall's detailed study of family and work in Birmingham during early industrialisation is a good example of such a development, in which the intricate connections between family relationships, sex roles, work and the development of class identity are explored and seen to be gendered (Davidoff and Hall, 1987).

The first editorial of *Gender and History* claimed that the journal's intentions were to study male institutions as well as those defined as female and to address men and masculinity as well as women and femininity, in order to 'illuminate the ways in which societies have been shaped by the relations of power between men and women' (*Gender and History*, 1990). More recently Anna Clark, in her study of nineteenth-century working-class politics, has shown how the claim for the vote was gendered and that citizenship was equated by radical artisans with men and the construction of a male identity (Clark, 1995). This emphasis on a gender-centred history is not unproblematic. Feminist critics of such a development, both in history and in other academic disciplines, argue that the category of gender is a neutral term which implies that 'the interests of the sexes have now converged and that the differences in life changes . . . that exist between women and men are matters of choice' (Evans, 1991, p. 73). This undermines alliances between women and weakens their potential for challenging the dominant culture. It is suggested that a focus on women's history and women's experiences is the only way to ensure that sexual inequalities and the power relationships between women and men remain central to historical enquiry.

Post-structuralist theories have also influenced the debate around gender and the writing of feminist history. For post-structuralists, language and discourse are central, since 'no directly knowable reality exists, because the very language that we use to discuss and describe the social world at the same time inscribes and constructs it' (Maynard, 1995, p. 269). Joan Scott, for example, emphasises that women's representation of their own experience is mediated through their habituation of the discourses of their own day (Scott, 1988; Thom, 1992). Thus the implication is that the social meaning of gender can only be understood through an analysis of language and discourse. (Purvis, 1995).

According to Mary Maynard this implies a different approach to knowledge from that employed by second-wave feminists since an emphasis on deconstructing 'the discursive practices through which the social world is portrayed in key texts moves away from the notion that there is an objective reality which is knowable through scholarship' (Maynard, 1995, p. 269). This has profound implications for feminist history since it challenges old certainties about lived experience, the nature of women's subordination and the possibility of a unified feminist politics.

It has led to considerable debate between those who believe that a study of the discourses of gender relations can empower women by challenging masculine language and the male authorial voice, and those who are concerned that women's specific oppression and experience will be lost. The latter argue that lived experience is mediated not just through discourse and text, but also through material structures and relationships (Scott, 1988; Hoff, 1994; Maynard, 1995; Kent, 1996). Similarly, the use of the category 'woman' has also been challenged; Riley, for instance, suggests that '"woman" is historically, discursively constructed, and always relatively to other categories which themselves change' (Hall, 1991, p. 205). This more fluid, diffuse view of the female self has been welcomed by those who argue that woman as a unitary subject often meant the privileging of white, middle-class heterosexual women and the exclusion of others (Kent, 1996).

Such debates have contributed to new directions in the theory and practice of feminist history which are likely to continue to the end of the century. Recent studies focus on language, representation, symbolism, medical discourse and the female body, thus opening up new areas of enquiry as well as bringing a fresh approach to more familiar subjects of research. Judith Walkowitz's stimulating study of late nineteenth-century London focuses on narratives of sexual danger, such as the story of Jack the Ripper, in order to provide new insights into feminist sexual politics. She departs from a 'traditional narrative' in order to 'convey the dynamics of metropolitan life as a series of multiple and simultaneous cultural contests and exchanges across a wide social spectrum', while retaining a clear sense of women as active agents in making their own history (Walkowitz, 1992, p. 10). Attention to the gendered nature of language has also meant a new approach to the study of popular politics and social identity in which perspectives relating 'to gender and sexuality as well as nationalism, race, ethnicity and localism' are being used instead of class, which is narrowly defined. Hudson suggests that this enables the changing nature of social identity and political consciousness to be 're-examined in the light of female experience' (Hudson, 1995, p. 39).

As these discussions suggest, in the 1990s there continues to be a close relationship between debates within contemporary feminist theory and politics and the approaches and concerns of historians. It is this interaction between feminist politics and historical practice that has helped to ensure that the study of women's history can still excite its students, and remains open to change. The challenge for feminist historians is to use the new cultural history, with its emphasis on language and discourse, to gain a greater understanding of the multiple, often conflicting ways in which gender identities have been formed and have shaped women's lives, while not losing sight of the unequal power relationship between the sexes.

Further reading

Philippa Levine, *Feminist Lives in Victorian England* (Oxford, Basil Blackwell, 1990). This book studies the connections between women's public and private lives, and emphasises the importance of friendship for an understanding of the nineteenth-century women's movement. Provides a new interpretation through the use of collective biography.

June Purvis (ed.), *Women's History: Britain, 1850–1945* (London, UCL, 1995). A recent textbook which introduces the main themes and debates in women's history through chapters on different aspects of women's lives, such as health, politics, 'race' and empire, sexuality, education, work and literature.

A book which addresses lesbian history issues is Martin Baum Duberman, Martha Vicinus and George Chauncey, *Hidden From History: Reclaiming the Gay and Lesbian Past* (Harmondsworth, Penguin, 1991).

Margaret Jackson, *The Real Facts of Life: Feminism and the Politics of Sexuality, c.1850–1940* (London, Taylor & Francis, 1994). This study considers the social construction of sexuality over nearly a century, analysing the relationship between feminism, sexuality and male power.

Vron Ware, *Beyond the Pale: White Women, Racism and History* (London, Verso, 1992) examines issues around ethnicity, 'race', empire and women's history.

5

Women, Writing and Language: Making the Silences Speak

Gill Frith

This chapter looks at women and words: at women's writing and women's relationship to language, and at what contemporary feminist theory has had to say about these issues.

Why should we look at literature in terms of feminist politics? When I studied English Literature at university in the 1960s, the literary 'canon' (that selective list of texts considered worthy of academic study) consisted almost entirely of work by white men. My course included a tiny handful of books by women (Jane Austen, the Brontës, George Eliot), but we did not study these writers *as* women. Great Literature, we were told, was about 'universal truths'. Gender was irrelevant.

This picture was challenged by the emergence, in the late 1960s, of the contemporary women's movement. Feminist researchers began to uncover the vast body of neglected women's writing: forgotten reputations were retrieved, and long out-of-print texts republished by feminist publishing houses such as Virago and the Women's Press. But redressing the balance, proving that women's writing was 'as good as' men's, was not the only issue. The reconstruction of women's history has been a central concern for contemporary feminism, and the study of women's writing has played a vital part in that process. The rediscovery of pioneering feminist texts like Virginia Woolf's *A Room of One's Own* (1929/1977) led to the realisation that much of what contemporary feminists were saying had been said before. The area of fiction, in which women have been actively engaged in large numbers since the eighteenth century (Spencer, 1986; Spender, 1986), provided a particularly rich source of material about women's lives. Fiction, paradoxically, precisely because it is not 'true', provides a space for the writer to explore ambiguities, contradictions and dissatisfactions, which cannot be expressed openly. 'Classic' texts, as I shall be demonstrating, suddenly looked different when read from a feminist perspective.

However, even as the process of recovery and re-reading got under way, new questions emerged. Can literature tell 'the truth' about women's lives? Is it the case, as Virginia Woolf suggested, that the 'man's sentence' is 'unsuited for a woman's use' (Woolf, 1929, p. 73)? Is it possible to identify or devise an alternative, 'female language'? Don't generalised terms like 'the woman writer' and 'the female imagination' effectively marginalise Black and lesbian writers? Shouldn't we be challenging traditional modes of literary judgement, and looking at texts outside the canon: romantic novels, science fiction or thrillers, for example? And what of the 'woman reader'? What do books mean in women's lives? What about the reader's 'race', class, sexuality: aren't these also important elements in her response?

We may all look at the same words on the same page, but what we make of them depends upon what questions we ask. My aim in this chapter is to introduce the different questions which feminist critics have raised, and to show how changing the terms of the question affects the 'reading', or interpretation, of the text. Each section deals with a different strand within feminist criticism, but the approaches identified are not mutually exclusive. Most individual critics in fact 'belong' within at least two sections: there are Black lesbian critics, socialist feminist critics influenced by French feminism, and so on. Feminist criticism has become increasingly 'pluralist' in its nature, moving from an initial suspicion of 'theory' towards what is, in my view, a productive, but undoubtedly also sometimes bewildering, cross-fertilisation of ideas.

In the interests of clarification, I shall be focusing on a single text, Charlotte Brontë's *Jane Eyre*,[1] chosen partly because it is well known and easily available, but primarily because it has been discussed by so many feminist critics from diverse perspectives and can therefore highlight differences between feminists. Upon its first publication in 1847, *Jane Eyre* was perceived as a dangerously subversive text (Gilbert and Gubar, 1979, pp. 337–8), and the novel was still 'banned' in girls' schools in the late nineteenth century. Contemporary feminist critics have rediscovered those subversive qualities, but while most feminist readings of *Jane Eyre* identify a secret or 'repressed' text buried beneath the surface of the apparently simple tale of the governess who gets her man, the nature and significance of that hidden text is seen in very different ways.

I have concentrated upon feminist literary theory because this is often regarded as the most challenging and difficult area for the student new to Women's Studies, but I do not want to neglect the wealth of writing which is being produced by women today. At the end of the chapter, I shall move beyond *Jane Eyre* to indicate some recent trends and developments in contemporary feminist fiction.

Declaring it aloud: images and experience

'Wicked and cruel boy!' I said. 'You are like a murderer – you are like a slave-driver – you are like the Roman emperors!'

I had read Goldsmith's *History of Rome*, and had formed my opinion
of Nero, Caligula, &c. Also I had drawn parallels in silence, which I never
thought thus to have declared aloud. (*Jane Eyre*, p. 43)

Jane Eyre begins with an assault upon a girl by a male text, or, more
correctly, by a male *armed* with a text. Jane's pleasurable retreat into the
world of books is disrupted by the male heir of the household, who
dispossesses her of her book, flings it at her, and causes her to fall,
wounding her head. Pain displaces terror: in the outburst quoted above,
Jane breaks her silence and gives voice to her long-nurtured resentment and
rage. The two interlinked events – male assault and female response – may
be seen as representative of the two feminist approaches to literature which
were dominant in the early 1970s: the analysis of 'images' and the appeal
to 'experience'. Here, similar questions are asked in two rather different
ways.

'Images of Women' criticism asks: What have men's texts, and male
mastery over the text, done to women's heads? Kate Millett's *Sexual Politics*
(1970), with its witty exposure of the misogyny endemic in the novels of
D. H. Lawrence, Norman Mailer and Henry Miller, paved the way for many
later studies which looked at the books which have been 'flung' at women.
Feminist critics dissected the sexual stereotyping pervasive in male-authored
texts in the literary 'canon', in children's literature, magazines and popular
fiction. In contrast to the dominant, negative images – such as passive
woman and active man, self-sacrificing virgin and predatory whore –
feminists sought to identify and encourage alternative, positive images of
women (see, for example, Cornillon, 1972).

'Authority of Experience' criticism asks: 'What happens when a woman
speaks out, gives *her* interpretation of the text on the basis of a woman's
experience?' In her 1977 essay on *Jane Eyre*, Maurianne Adams emphasised
the cohesiveness of women's experience, and the reader's identification with
the novel's heroine. Adams made little distinction between author and
character, critic and reader: when 'we' read *Jane Eyre*, memories of our
girlhood reading, 'when we saw in Jane's dreadful childhood the image of
our own fantasies of feeling unloved and forever unloveable' interact with
'our more mature understanding' of the complexity of Jane's journey from
childhood to womanhood (Adams, 1977, p. 137). Jane is split: torn between
the need to love and be loved, and the desire for autonomy, 'to be
somebody in her own right'(p. 139). She is torn, also, between two
unsatisfactory images of women, as either spiritual and asexual, or furious,
passionate and mad. Jane is, according to Adams, an instinctive feminist
who suppresses her feminist awareness, only to have it surface in her
turbulent dreams.

As we shall see later, subsequent feminist theorists have questioned some of the assumptions behind these approaches, notably the idea that oppressive and 'false' images and readings can be replaced by an alternative, universal, woman-friendly 'truth'. But 'Images' and 'Experience' criticism reflected the two pressing needs of an emergent women's movement: to identify the sources of oppression, and to assert female collectivity. Together, they represented a radical challenge to the way in which English Literature, conventionally a 'woman's subject', was taught in schools, colleges and universities. By exposing the distortions and preconceptions which underpin the portrayal of women in literature, and by asserting a woman's right to speak about her reading as a woman, they questioned the assertion that the male-dominated literary canon offered a universal 'truth', transmitted by the (usually male) tutor to the compliant female student.

Opening the chamber: gynocriticism

The red-room was a spare chamber, very seldom slept in . . . (*Jane Eyre*, p. 45)

What happens to Jane in the red-room, that 'haunted' chamber to which the fiercely resistant Jane is conveyed by women, and where the sight of her own face in the mirror terrifies her into insensibility? According to Elaine Showalter in *A Literature of Their Own* (1978), Jane's ritualised imprisonment is both a punishment for 'the crime of growing up'(Showalter, 1978, p. 114) and an 'adolescent rite of passage' (p. 115), in which entry into womanhood is characterised by Victorian vigilance and control over female sexuality. The 'bondage' of the frenzied Jane in a chamber dominated by vibrantly contrasting reds and whites echoes Victorian fears of and fantasies about 'the lethal and fleshly aspects of adult female sexuality'(p. 115). Noting the recurrence of enclosed and secret rooms in the novels of women writers, Showalter suggests that the red-room, 'with its deadly and bloody connotations, its Freudian wealth of secret compartments, wardrobes, drawers and jewel chest' may be seen as 'a paradigm of female inner space' (pp. 114–15).

A Literature of Their Own is one of the 'classics' of feminist 'gynocriticism', a term coined by Showalter herself to define an approach concerned with the woman as writer, and including 'the psychodynamics of female creativity; linguistics and the problem of a female language; the trajectory of the individual or collective female literary career; literary history; and of course, studies of particular writers and works' (Showalter, 1979, p. 25). It is a broad definition which could encompass much of contemporary feminist criticism. In practice, however, 'gynocriticism' has come to be associated with the quest to identify a specifically female literary tradition. 'We think back through our mothers', said Virginia Woolf in *A Room of One's Own* (Woolf, 1929, pp. 72–3), a book which anticipated many of the questions asked by contemporary gynocritics. In the late 1970s, pioneering texts such as Showalter's book and Ellen Moers's *Literary Women* (1978) re-opened the 'spare chamber', and set out to provide a map of women's literary history, by rediscovering neglected texts and reinterpreting familiar ones, by analysing the lives of and connections between 'literary women', and by identifying shared themes, tropes (figures of speech) and plot-devices.

The value of gynocriticism should not be underestimated. By uncovering the rich legacy of a neglected female 'subculture' and emphasising its thematic coherence, it provided ammunition and substance for establishing the study of women's writing, not only in higher education, but in schools, extra-mural classes and informal reading groups. Gynocriticism has been much criticised for its 'essentialism' (Moi, 1985; Mills and Pearce, 1989), but it is notable that both Showalter and Moers question the idea of a 'female imagination', seeing the female tradition rather as a 'delicate network of . . . influences and conventions, including the operations of the market-place' (Showalter, 1978, p. 12). Showalter emphasises the conditions in which women's writing has been produced and received, placing *Jane Eyre* historically, within what she sees as a unified but 'disrupted', and specifically British, female literary tradition. *Jane Eyre* belongs to what Showalter calls the 'feminine' phase of British women's writing, in which the female 'subculture' is secret, ritualised, characterised by internalisation and self-censorship; women, united by the physical facts of the female life-cycle (menstruation, childbirth) but unable to express them openly, developed a covert symbolic language to explore the range of female experience.

Gynocriticism opens the secret chamber, but does not tell us how to arrange the furniture. Resistant to 'theory', preferring to rely on 'evidence', it provides no coherent framework for interpreting the rich and suggestive material it uncovers about women's lives and work. Showalter and Moers both draw upon Freud in interpreting the recurrent motifs in women's writing, but such psychoanalytic borrowings are random rather than systematic. While the idea of a female literary tradition can be a fruitful basis from which to research and study women's writing, it carries the risk both of perpetuating the traditional marginalisation of women's literary production, and of assuming that, at any point in time, a unified female subculture can be satisfactorily identified. The position of the writer or reader outside the white, heterosexual, middle-class 'mainstream' can too easily be ignored or subsumed under the enveloping banner of 'female experience'.

Secrets of nature discovered: radical feminist criticism

> They conversed of things I had never heard of; of nations and times past; of countries far away; of secrets of nature discovered or guessed at; they spoke of books; how many they had read! What stores of knowledge they possessed! (*Jane Eyre*, p. 105)

Radical feminism has been summarised as founded in the belief that 'the original and basic class division is between the sexes, and that the motive force of history is the striving of men for power and domination over women, the dialectic of sex' (Heidi Hartmann, quoted in Palmer, 1989, p. 43; see also Bell and Klein, 1996). Radical feminist literary criticism prioritises female experience and solidarity, by validating autobiographical and subjective responses and foregrounding the issues of 'woman- identification, feminist community, lesbian relations and relations between mothers and daughters' (Palmer, 1989, p. 160). 'Woman-identification' is central to Adrienne Rich's essay on *Jane Eyre*, published in 1973, before Rich identified herself as a radical feminist. Rich's analysis of Jane's relationships with women is framed within a 'humanist' reading of the novel: Jane journeys towards self-discovery, independence and equal marriage (Rich, 1980c). Nevertheless, Rich's reading stands in striking contrast to Elaine Showalter's, and illustrates how differently the novel may read when relationships between women are foregrounded.

Showalter interprets *Jane Eyre* as reflecting the impossibility of female solidarity when women are powerless; Brontë's women, she argues, 'police' one another as agents of patriarchal control. Rich sees Jane as encountering a succession of traditional female temptations, each of which is placed against an alternative: a positive female role model who offers Jane nurturing and support. At Lowood, Miss Temple (substitute mother) and Helen Burns (substitute sister) are protective figures who encourage Jane's moral development and intellectual growth. But for Rich, the key moment in the novel comes when Jane dreams of a visitation from the moon, who tells her 'My daughter, flee temptation'(*Jane Eyre*, p. 346). Now in touch with the matriarchal aspect of her psyche, Jane is able to resist the temptation to become Rochester's concubine, just as, later in the novel, she is saved from 'passive suicide' by Diana and Mary Rivers, maternal role-models whose names represent, between them, the pagan and the Christian aspects of the Great Goddess.

Although not presented as a lesbian reading, the essay anticipates Rich's later idea of the 'lesbian continuum' (Rich, 1984, p. 227), which does not limit lesbianism to the experience or desire for genital sexual experience, but encompasses a range of 'woman-identified' experience, including the sharing of a rich inner life, bonding against male tyranny and practical support. According to this (controversial) definition, Jane's relationships with women at Lowood and Moor House could be seen as representing a 'lesbian' impetus in the novel which is repressed in the conclusion.

Rich's essay also illustrates two concerns central to her later work and to radical feminist criticism in general: the reclamation and reworking of female myth, and mother–daughter relationships (such as Demeter and Persephone, mythical mother and daughter). In *Of Woman Born* (1977), Rich sees motherhood (once separated from its restrictive institutionalisation under patriarchy) as the primary source of female power and creativity. The celebration of motherhood is interlinked with the rediscovery of matriarchal myths, a project shared with Mary Daly (1978) and other radical feminist critics who see male violence as the chief instrument of patriarchy, to be countered by the establishment of a separate women's culture and the assertion of specifically female creative powers. 'Myth criticism' sets out to decode the myths selected and passed on by patriarchy, to expose their subtexts of mysogyny and male aggression, and to reclaim myths for women both by reversing male stories and recuperating and reformulating earlier, female-centred mythologies (Humm, 1994, 1995). Myth criticism is appealing for the same reasons as it is problematic: it offers a romantic, celebratory vision of a lost tradition of female goddesses and woman-bonding which conflates female 'nurture', female 'nature' and female creativity, and depends upon the assumption that women are naturally and uniformly *good*. Marina Warner, however, has developed myth criticism in a different way: in *Managing Monsters* (1994) and *From the Beast to the Blonde* (1995) she casts an erudite and ironic eye on the myths and fairy-tales that 'manage' our lives.

Perhaps the most significant contribution made by radical feminism has been on the question of language. In *Man-Made Language* (1980), Dale Spender argued that women constitute a 'muted group' in society because meaning has been controlled by men (but see Cameron, 1992). Language reflects male experience and perpetuates male power; 'feminine' words are negatively marked (think of the different connotations carried by dog/bitch, master/mistress, bachelor/spinster). Mary Daly and Adrienne Rich both experimented inventively with ways of wresting linguistic domination from patriarchal control. In *Gyn/Ecology* (1978), Mary Daly set out to create a language which will serve the interests of women by changing the syntax, reclaiming obsolete or pejorative words (Hag, Spinster, Harpy) and re-structuring familiar ones (as in 'Crone-ology'). Rich's methods are less drastic, but she too aims to repossess meaning for women by creating a language of the collective 'female body', by defining 'a female consciousness which is political, aesthetic and erotic' (Rich, 1980d, p. 18) and finding ways of 'converting our physicality into both knowledge and power' (Rich, 1977, p. 284). Such an unashamed affirmation of the links between female biology and female creativity contrasts interestingly with the work of Sandra Gilbert and Susan Gubar, for whom the female body is a haunted house.

Echoes in the chamber: *The madwoman in the attic*

> While I paced softly on, the last sound I expected to hear in so still a region, a laugh, struck my ears. It was a curious laugh – distinct, formal, mirthless. I stopped. The sound ceased, only for an instant. It began again, louder – for at first, though very distinct, it was very low. It passed off in a clamorous peal that seemed to echo in every lonely chamber. (*Jane Eyre*, p. 138)

The source of the laughter is Bertha, Rochester's mad wife, who is confined to an attic from which she occasionally, and dangerously, escapes. As the title of their book implies, Bertha is a central figure in Sandra Gilbert and Susan Gubar's *The Madwoman in the Attic* (1979). The book is 'gynocriticism', in the sense that it traces a female literary tradition, but I have considered it separatcly both because it gives a very distinctive interpretation of that tradition, and because it is still perhaps the most frequently cited text produced by contemporary feminist criticism.

It could be said that Gilbert and Gubar ask a single question: who is Bertha? The answer is that Bertha is Jane's 'truest and darkest double', her 'ferocious secret self' (Gilbert and Gubar, 1979, p. 360). Gilbert and Gubar point out that each one of Bertha's appearances in the novel is associated with an experience (or repression) of anger on Jane's part, and that the text draws a number of parallels between them. They suggest that Bertha is not only *like* Jane, but acts *for* Jane: when she attacks Rochester, tears the wedding veil, burns down Thornfield, she is acting as the agent of Jane's secret desires. The idea that Bertha is Jane's alter ego was not new: all of the readings discussed so far see Bertha as an expression of Jane's repressed passion and anger. The difference is that Gilbert and Gubar see Bertha as representative of the restrictions experienced by the woman *writer*. Their famous opening sentence – 'Is a pen a metaphorical penis?' (p. 3) – sets the terms of their argument. Creativity has traditionally been defined not only as male, but as generated by the male body. Women have been 'framed' by male texts which represent the creative woman as a monstrous transgression of biology, and thus suffer from a debilitating 'anxiety of authorship'. Like Showalter, Gilbert and Gubar see the house as a trope for the female body, but argue that it represents women's anxiety about enclosure within the patriarchal text: the 'house' of literature is a prison, and 'womb' is a metaphor for tomb. Trapped by biology and ideology, ill-at-ease in the patriarchal literary tradition but unable to speak directly as women, female authors resort to covert strategies. They come to terms with their feelings of fragmentation by conjuring up the figure of the mad or monstrous woman who, acting as 'the *author's* double, an image of her own anxiety and rage' (p. 78) seeks the power of self-articulation. *Jane Eyre* is an exemplary text, not only for the figure of Bertha, but also because of its recurrent motifs of enclosure and escape, first established when Jane is confined within the red-room. In this 'patriarchal death-chamber' (p. 340) – a place tended by women, but presided over by the spirit of a dead man – Jane sees in the mirror the trapped image of herself.

Gilbert and Gubar have been criticised, with some justification, for their representation of the woman writer as a spellbound victim. Paradoxically, though, the appeal of their argument is that, despite the emphasis on stifled creativity, the story they tell is an oddly comforting one. Women have been put down, but they have fought back. The writer-heroine, tied to the railway track, is crushed in body, constrained in mind, but free in spirit: she escapes the chugging wheels of patriarchal tyranny by declaring her resistance, if not exactly aloud, at least in ways that the reader can decode. Although the dazzling virtuosity of Gilbert and Gubar's reading is hard to imitate, they do offer a mode of reading which can be applied to almost any novel by a woman writer: any text is potentially a feminist text. The problem is there is only *one* text, and only one female author who, whatever her name, tells much the same secret story of repression and rebellion (Jacobus, 1981). There is, indeed, only one woman: in Gilbert and Gubar's reading of *Jane Eyre*, every woman becomes an aspect of Jane's rage; even Miss Temple and Helen Burns are seen as concealing, beneath their calm surface, 'sewers' of resentment and rebellion.

Madwoman deals with nineteenth-century British and American writers. Gilbert and Gubar's more recent, three-volume project on twentieth-century writing, *No Man's Land*, (vol. 1, 1988; vol. 2, 1989; vol. 3, 1994) shows some interesting shifts of emphasis. The pen is now a metaphorical pistol, signalling the battle between the sexes which the authors see as characteristic of the modernist period. *Jane Eyre* remains a key text, but it now reads differently: Bertha's echoing laughter expresses 'the alien urgency of female desire, with its threat to male potency'(1988, p. 137) and her attack on her husband is 'a kind of primal scene of sexual battle'(1988, p. 69). As Toril Moi has commented, Gilbert and Gubar's pervasive use of the term 'female' throughout *Madwoman* implicitly fuses the biological and the social (Moi, 1985, p. 65). So far in this chapter, I too have not distinguished between 'female' and 'feminine' (or 'male' and 'masculine'), because much early feminist criticism is hazy about the relationship between the two. In more recent feminist work, the distinction between the biologically 'female' and the socially constructed 'feminine' is crucial. In *No Man's Land*, Gilbert and Gubar define their project as an attempt to collate the individual narratives produced by 'a gendered human being whose text reflects key cultural conditions' into 'one possible metastory'(Gilbert and Gubar, 1988, p. xiv). In the sense that they now see the writer as a 'gendered being', whose writing reflects 'key cultural conditions' rather than the author's own experience, Gilbert and Gubar are speaking the language of post-structuralism.

Truth and the author: post-structuralism

I am merely telling the truth. (*Jane Eyre*, p. 140)

Jane's claim to be telling 'the truth' is linked to some caustic comments about the supposedly angelic nature of children, but its position in the novel is interesting. It comes just before the famous 'feminist manifesto' in Chapter 12, in which Jane declares that:

> women feel just as men feel . . . they suffer from too rigid a restraint, too absolute a stagnation, precisely as men would suffer; and it is narrow-minded in their more privileged fellow-creatures to say that they ought to confine themselves to making puddings and knitting stockings, to playing on the piano and embroidering bags. (p. 141)

Part of the attraction of *Jane Eyre* is its 'autobiographical' narrative, which leads the reader to feel that she is sharing Jane's experiences and that Jane is telling her 'the truth'. But Jane is a fictional character. Whose 'truth' does the novel represent? One answer is to see it as Charlotte Brontë's truth, rooted in her own experience, and to celebrate Brontë as a feminist heroine for telling it.

Such deference to the authority of the writer has been placed in question by what is called 'The Death of the Author'. In an influential 1968 essay of that title, Roland Barthes argued that 'To give a text an Author is to impose a limit on that text, to furnish it with a final signified, to close the writing' (Barthes, 1977, p. 147). The idea that the author's intention is an unreliable and inappropriate basis for interpreting the meaning of a text was not in itself new; it is central to that influential and long-established branch of literary criticism known as 'New' Criticism. But Barthes's essay went further, questioning the idea that *any* final meaning can be allocated to the text: a productive and revolutionary reading will, rather, refuse to assign 'a 'secret', an ultimate meaning, to the text' (p. 147) and will aim to disentangle its codes rather than decipher its message.

Such an argument has challenged the validity of two of the central preoccupations of the 'Anglo-American' approaches discussed so far in this chapter: to research the lives and works of individual authors, and to uncover the 'secrets' of female experience which lie beneath the surface of the text. The idea of 'the death of the author' has had an ambiguous impact upon feminist criticism, which, having laboured to find and restore the female author, has felt a less pressing need to kill her off. Taken to its logical conclusion, Barthes's essay renders the author's gender irrelevant. Feminist critics have continued, for the most part, to focus upon writing by women and to see the writer's gender as significant, but the influence of 'post-structuralism' has resulted in a new kind of analysis, which sees the text not as an authentic expression of experience, but as a site for 'the discursive construction of the meaning of gender' (Weedon, 1987, p. 138).

'Post-structuralism' is an umbrella term which encompasses recent developments within literary criticism, including work influenced by such diverse thinkers as Michel Foucault, Jacques Lacan, Jacques Derrida and Julia Kristeva. A central influence is 'semiotics': the study of discourse as a system of 'signs' which have no direct correspondence with the real world. The implication for the analysis of literary texts is that the meaning of terms is not derived from external reality, but is determined by the place of those terms within the structure of the text and by their relationship to other signs. (For example, 'female' takes on its meaning through the ways in which it is played against the term 'male' within a specific text.)

Post-structuralism develops these ideas to argue that: (a) meaning is neither fixed nor controlled by individual readers or writers: it is culturally defined, learned, and plural; and (b) human subjectivity is shifting and fragmented: the idea of the subject as a unified and free whole is the product of liberal-humanist ideology. For feminists, perhaps the most important point is that subjectivity is seen as changing and contradictory: gendered identity is not static and natural, but formed within language and open to change. Post-structuralist feminist analyses reject the idea of an authentic female voice or experience, but see the study of women's writing as a means of understanding patriarchy, mapping 'the possible subject positions open to women' (Weedon, 1987, p. 157). Meaning and culture, precisely because they are unstable and cannot be finally 'owned', are the site of political struggle and potential resistance.

As Elizabeth Wilson has warned, there is a danger that the post-structuralist flux of identity can become a modish, alternative 'higher truth' (Wilson, 1988, p. 42). How exactly feminism as a political practice is to survive the deconstruction of 'woman' as a unitary category in favour of 'a multiple, shifting, and often self-contradictory identity . . . made up of heterogeneous and heteronomous representations of gender, race, and class' (Teresa de Lauretis, quoted in Wall, 1990, p. 10) has been the subject of much debate, especially over whether it dilutes feminist politics (Jackson, 1992; Nash, 1994). But the challenge to the idea of a unitary 'woman's truth' has clearly been a necessary one, both fuelled by, and opening up a space for, the approaches I discuss in the next three sections.

Splitting the subject: socialist feminist criticism

Before I left my bed in the morning, little Adèle came running in to tell me that the great horse-chestnut at the bottom of the orchard had been struck by lightning in the night, and half of it split away. (*Jane Eyre*, p. 285)

For the Anglo-American critics of the 1970s, the 'truth' of *Jane Eyre* lies in its expression of feminist rage. Jane represents 'everywoman', homeless, oppressed and searching for autonomy, a quest finally rewarded by independence and equal marriage. Penny Boumelha (1990) questions such a 'heroinisation' of Jane, arguing that her movement from oppressed child to keeper of the patriarchal keys in fact confirms and reinstates the social institutions of class. Jane is always 'naturally' a lady, a displaced spiritual aristocrat whose apparent rise in social status only confirms what the reader knows to be already there.

While Anglo-American criticism emphasises the cohesiveness of female experience, socialist feminist criticism foregrounds contradiction, in the interests of identifying the complex ways in which gender intersects with class and 'race' within the literary text. Methods of maintaining the connection between the 'double trunk' of Marxism and feminism vary, but a characteristic mode of analysis may be seen in a ground-breaking essay by the Marxist Feminist Literature Collective (1978). The Collective followed the model of the Marxist theorist Pierre Macherey – focusing on the gaps, ambiguities, incoherences and evasions within the text – to locate the feminism of *Jane Eyre* in the novel's 'not-said'. What was most significant and controversial about the essay was the way in which it challenged Marxism's 'not-said', its silence about gender, by using Lacanian psychoanalytic theory. Psychoanalysis is not famous for its sensitivity to class or historical change, and may seem an odd instrument for socialist feminist analysis, but psychoanalytic theory has been attractive to socialist feminists (and others) because it provides a way of theorising gendered subjectivity as socially constructed, precarious, contradictory and capable of change.

The case for a synthesis between psychoanalysis, semiotics and a materialist feminist attention to class and 'race' has been persuasively argued by Cora Kaplan (1986b), one of the original members of the Collective. Such a synthesis, Kaplan argued, offered a way of analysing both the splits within the individual female psyche, and 'the splitting of women's subjectivity, especially her sexuality, into class and race categories' ('Pandora's Box', 1986b, p. 162). In her analysis of the 'feminist manifesto' in *Jane Eyre*, Kaplan pointed out that the language of the 'manifesto' defiantly links political and sexual rebellion even while distinguishing between them. But this temporary recognition of the congruence between women's subordination and the class struggle threatens to break up the class politics of the novel as a whole; Bertha's mocking laughter follows, warning us that to associate feminism with the class struggle leads to madness. This may sound like an 'Awful Warning', but Kaplan's point was that we need to remain alert to the social and ideological constraints which lie behind a particular text, while also recognising the instability of class and gender categories, and the fragmented character of the female psyche.

Socialist feminism's central contribution has been to emphasise that both fiction and its readers are the products of specific social structures. This emphasis on the material conditions in which culture is produced and received has led in two significant directions: first, towards the investigation of popular culture, questioning the division between 'high' and 'low' art, and analysing the relationship between gender and genre, a subject to which I return later; and second, towards challenging gynocriticism's picture of the marginalised and silenced woman writer. Nancy Armstrong's *Desire and Domestic Fiction* (1987) and Terry Lovell's *Consuming Fiction* (1987) both presented important correctives to the influential arguments of *The Madwoman in the Attic*, by emphasising the ways in which bourgeois domestic ideology facilitated the emergence of the middle-class woman writer. Armstrong saw the history of the novel as one in which competing class interests have continually been mapped on to the more containable, 'apolitical' arena of the struggle between the sexes. In *Jane Eyre*, she argued, the threat of social disruption is contained by being located on to the body of Bertha: political resistance is gendered, neutralised and reconceived as aberrant sexual desire through the spectre of the 'monstrous female'. Lovell emphasised the unevenness of literary history and the ways in which ideologies of domesticity have been simultaneously enabling and disabling. On the one hand, women have consistently played a central part in the production and reception of literary culture; on the other hand, women have been systematically reduced to the position of transmitters, rather than producers, of bourgeois culture. Women have been allowed to 'speak' but only on certain terms; a small number of female-authored texts have survived the process of literary 'canonisation' but, Lovell suggested, 'woman-to-woman' fiction has consistently been filtered out.

Listening alternately: lesbian feminist criticism

> I was fain to sit on a stool at Diana's feet, to rest my head on her knee, and listen alternately to her and Mary, while they sounded thoroughly the topic on which I had but touched. (*Jane Eyre*, p. 377)

Is *Jane Eyre* a lesbian text? As I have already noted, Jane's female friendships could be placed within Adrienne Rich's definition of the 'lesbian continuum'. Arguably, too, there is an erotic component in Jane's attraction to the dynamic Diana, and the pleasure she feels in yielding to her will. There has, however, been much debate within lesbian feminism about how exactly lesbianism is to be defined. Is it a question of political commitment or sexual desire? Does Rich's emphasis on 'woman-identification' eliminate lesbianism as a meaningful category? Does the lesbian challenge patriarchy precisely because she is *not* a woman according to heterosexist definitions of the term? (Zimmermann, 1986, 1992; Jay and Glasgow, 1990; Wittig, 1992; Palmer, 1993). Opinion over what constitutes a 'lesbian text' is similarly divided, but three main strands within lesbian feminist literary criticism may be identified here.

In *Images of lesbianism* criticism (Rule, 1975; Faderman, 1981), homophobic and voyeuristic stereotypes are identified and representations of lesbianism evaluated against the touchstone of contemporary lesbian feminist politics and experience. *Sapphocritics* represents the quest to identify a lesbian literary tradition. Whereas Faderman argued for a *political* rather than *sexual* definition of lesbianism which can embrace the passionate friendships of women in earlier eras, Sapphocritics focuses on recovering and re-evaluating writing by women identifiable as lesbian or bisexual. While Sapphocritics has uncovered much rich and illuminating material, it is inevitably a limited enterprise, since biographical evidence of the writer's sexuality is often hard to come by. *Lesbian stylistics* shifts attention from the lesbian *author* to the lesbian *text*, by decoding the codes and covert strategies characteristic of lesbian writing. The question of how far specific tropes or formal experiments can be clearly identified as 'lesbian' has been much debated, but such an approach has the advantage of extending the field to writers whose sexual identity cannot be known, and of opening up the possibility of a lesbian reading.[2]

Is *Jane Eyre*, then, open to such a reading? Marilyn Farwell (1990) suggests one direction which it might take. Farwell argues that the 'lesbian text' does not depend on the author's sexuality. Even a basically heterosexual novel may contain 'lesbian narrative space' if it includes an episode with erotic overtones in which the two women relate to one another in terms of 'sameness', defined by 'fluid instead of rigid boundaries', and in which the divisions between self and other, lover and beloved, subject and object, dissolve. Such episodes provide a critique of heterosexual norms by disrupting the conventional, male-centred dualities of 'difference': active/ passive, mind/body, male/female.

Brontë, it could be argued, offers just such a dissolution in Jane's relationship with the Rivers sisters. Diana teaches Jane German: 'I liked to learn of her; I saw the part of instructress pleased and suited her; that of scholar pleased and suited me no less. Our natures dovetailed: mutual affection – of the strongest kind – was the result' (p. 377). Jane teaches Mary to draw: 'Thus occupied, and mutually entertained, days passed like hours, and weeks like days' (p. 377). In this three-way relationship, Jane shifts between the position of teacher and pupil, subject and object; the fluid boundaries here not only imply a critique of the heterosexual relationships in the novel, but also prefigure the final form of Jane's relationship with Rochester. Jane's friendship with the Rivers sisters is founded upon free and animated talk: 'Thought fitted thought: opinion met opinion: we coincided, in short, perfectly' (p. 377). Jane's life with Rochester is described in this way: 'We talk, I believe, all day long: to talk to each other is but a more animated and an audible thinking . . . perfect concord is the result' (p. 476). The master–servant relationship of Thornfield is revised, at Ferndean, into a marriage founded upon the principles of female friendship.

It is arguable that such an analysis blurs the line between a 'lesbian' and a 'feminist' reading, but Farwell's essay reflects a significant shift within some lesbian feminist criticism away from the idea of a unitary lesbian identity and towards the concept of lesbianism as 'a position from which to speak', and away from the quest for 'authentic' representations of lesbianism towards the idea of the 'lesbian text' as one which challenges heterosexist structures and stereotypes. Lesbian feminist criticism has employed a wide range of approaches: experiential, biographical, psychoanalytic, deconstructionist, semiotic and French feminist (Jay and Glasgow, 1990; see also Lilly, 1990; Palmer, 1993). Currently the impact of 'queer theory' is making its mark on lesbian and gay studies, influenced by the pioneering work of Judith Butler (Butler, 1990, 1993) and Eve Kosofsky Sedgwick (Sedgwick, 1985, 1990, 1994).

Cultural and sexual identity, Butler argues, is something that we *perform*: there is no essential self, no 'real me'. Identity is, rather, constituted within the prevalent cultural codes, regulations and discourses. Its daily re-enactment involves exclusions and choices by which the subject defines the limits of her 'performativity'. But the performance of identity is not a free choice, to be adopted or relinquished at will. Any attempt to take up a new, resistant or subversive position is contingent: it can only reverse, mimic, parody or in some other way allude to the identities culturally available to the subject. Queer theory emphasises the range and diversity of sexual identies available. As Sedgwick puts it in *Tendencies*, 'queer' can refer to:

> the experimental linguistic, epistemological, representational, political adventures attaching to the very many of us who may at times be moved to describe ourselves as (among many other possibilities) pushy femmes, radical faeries, fantasists, drags, clones, leatherfolk, ladies in tuxedoes, feminist women, feminist men, masturbators, bulldaggers, divas, Snap! queens, butch bottoms, storytellers, transsexuals, aunties, wannabees, lesbian-identified men or lesbians who sleep with men, or . . . people able to relish, learn from, or identify with such. (Sedgwick, 1994, p. 8)

The heterogeneous politics of queer theory has been controversial. In one of the most important recent contributions to lesbian feminist cultural criticism, *The Apparitional Lesbian* (1993), Terry Castle questions whether Queer Theory erodes the specificity of lesbian experience and sexuality. As Castle demonstrates, there is a long cultural tradition in which the lesbian has been 'disembodied' or 'ghosted', presented as a spectral figure who appears only to disappear. Castle's project in *The Apparitional Lesbian* is to restore lesbian physicality: in a rich and engaging study of a wide range of literary and cultural texts, she makes the lesbian visible.

The field of lesbian feminist criticism has been much enriched by the proliferation and diversity of contemporary lesbian writing (Palmer, 1993). Jeanette Winterson's *Oranges Are Not the Only Fruit* (1985) has, arguably, currently overtaken Radclyffe Hall's *The Well of Loneliness* (1928) as the most-discussed novel in the lesbian literary canon. In her essay 'Written on Tablets of Stone' (Pearce, 1994b), Lynne Pearce suggests that Winterson's novel may be read as a re-writing of *Jane Eyre*, which offers a fundamentally different vision of romantic love. In both novels, Pearce argues, romantic love is posited against the institution of marriage, but whereas the relationship between Jane and Rochester moves from passion towards friendship, in *Oranges Are Not the Only Fruit* desire is posited as comradeship from the start, and love erupts within and alongside the institution of friendship. Winterson's novel, says Pearce, celebrates lesbian romantic love, but presents it as an 'absolute' whose realisation is necessarily deferred, since love between women – unlike the heterosexual romance in *Jane Eyre* – exists outside official institutions and discourses.

Freedom for bondage: post-colonial and Black feminist criticism

My hopes of being numbered in the band who have merged all ambitions in the glorious one of bettering their race – of carrying knowledge into the realms of ignorance – of substituting peace for war, freedom for bondage, religion for superstition, the hope of heaven for the fear of hell? Must I relinquish that? (*Jane Eyre*, p. 400)

Is *Jane Eyre* a racist text? In her analysis of the imperialist discourse which underpins *Jane Eyre*, Gayatri Spivak has scrupulously avoided posing this question, directing her rage, rather, at the 'imperialist narrativisation of history, that it should provide so abject a script' for Charlotte Brontë (Spivak, 1989, p. 176). Spivak uses the techniques of 'deconstruction'[3] to draw out the connections between imperialism's 'civilising' mission, as described by St. John in the quotation above, and the portrayal of Bertha – identified in the novel with the world of the West Indies – who is represented as subhuman and beyond the law. How, Spivak asks, does Jane move from her position as 'outsider' to acceptance and self-realisation? Her answer is that Jane's achievement of feminist-individualism depends upon the exclusion of the native female: she gets there over the body of Bertha, the 'woman from the colonies' who is sacrificed 'for her sister's consolidation' (p. 185).[4]

Post-colonial feminist critics have followed Spivak's lead in placing the novel in its historical context and identifying the imperialist subtext which lies at the heart of *Jane Eyre*. For Penny Boumelha, the 'dark' secret of the novel, represented by Bertha, madwoman and creole, is the 'maddening burden of imperialism concealed in the heart of every English gentleman's house of the time' (Boumelha, 1990, p. 61; see also Politi, 1982; Azim, 1993). In her book *Outside the Pale* (1993), Elsie B. Michie relates the representation of imperialism in the novel to the Victorian fantasy of the 'self-made man': while Patrick Brontë was able to *live* this fantasy, his daughters could only enter the masculine narrative of self-making in their fiction. Michie argues that the fantasies of class elevation in *Jane Eyre* and *Wuthering Heights* are underpinned by another Victorian fantasy: that social inequities which seemed intractable at home might be redressed in the wonderful world of the empire abroad. She concentrates on eliciting the colonialist stereotyping which lies behind the representation of Heathcliff and Rochester, and draws extensively on Victorian ethnography to argue that when Heathcliff and Rochester are 'down', they are associated with mid-nineteenth-century stereotypes of 'the Irish' as volatile, savage, dark and 'simianized' in appearance. When they are 'up', however, they are described as 'oriental despots': princes, sultans, emirs, paynims, Grand Turks.

Post-colonial criticism demonstrates the blind-spots in feminist 'heroinisation' of *Jane Eyre*, but it also provides an implicit commentary on more far-reaching omissions. In the 'classics' of gynocriticism, the writing of Black women, like the question of lesbianism, was conspicuous by its absence. In a pioneering essay published in 1977, Barbara Smith (1986) challenged that exclusion, arguing simultaneously for the establishment of a Black feminist criticism and a Black lesbian feminist criticism. Smith's reading of Toni Morrison's *Sula* (1973) has affinities with the essay by Marilyn Farwell discussed previously: *Sula*, she suggests, despite its apparent heterosexuality, works as a lesbian novel because of its critical stance towards heterosexual institutions. But Smith also emphasises the communality and specificity of Black women's writing, pointing to the recurrence of 'traditional Black female activities of rootworking, herbal medicine, conjure, and midwifery' and the use of 'specifically Black female language' (Smith, 1986, p. 174).

The history of the quest for a Black female literary tradition is comparable with that of Sapphocritics. On the one hand, the reclamation of 'literary foremothers' like Zora Neale Hurston, Nella Larsen and Gwendolyn Brooks has been paralleled and fuelled by the rich material provided by contemporary Black women writers such as Toni Morrison, Alice Walker, Maya Angelou and Audre Lorde. On the other hand, the viability of identifying a unitary Black female tradition has increasingly been questioned by those who emphasise the discontinuities, diversities and historical shifts within that 'tradition' (Carby, 1987; Wall, 1990). For some Black feminist critics, the influence of post-structuralism has resulted in a new emphasis on 'positionality' rather than 'experience', seeing theory as 'a way of reading inscriptions' of 'race', gender and class 'in modes of cultural expression . . . in order to raise questions about the way 'the other' is represented in oppositional discourse' (Smith, 1990, p. 39).

The idea of 'otherness' is central to Toni Morrison's *Playing in the Dark* (1993). Morrison's bold and revisionary account of the American literary canon deals with 'the ways in which a nonwhite, Africanlike (or Africanist) presence or persona was constructed in the United States, and the imaginative uses this fabricated presence served . . . It provides a way of contemplating chaos and civilization, desire and fear, and a mechanism for testing the problems and blessings of freedom' (Morrison, 1993, pp. 6–7). In *Black Women, Writing and Identity* (1994), Carole Boyce Davies also crosses conventional boundaries. She argues that it is 'the convergence of multiple places and cultures that re-negotiates the terms of Black women's experience that in turn negotiates and renegotiates their identities' (Davies, 1994, p. 3). Focusing especially on the importance of migration in Black women's lives, Davies identifies numerous forms of re-mapping, re-naming and cultural crossing in writing by Black women.

Since its inception, Black feminist criticism has questioned the distinction between 'high' and 'low' forms of art. Alice Walker (1984) echoes and extends Barbara Smith's emphasis on communal activity, to argue that the Black female creative tradition includes quilting, gardening and singing the blues. S. Diane Bogus (1990) takes the argument a stage further by identifying the 'Queen B' – the female blues singer who bonds with women – as a recurrent figure in Black women's writing, including Shug Avery in Walker's *The Color Purple* (1982). Charlotte Pierce-Baker (1990) takes up the quilting metaphor and applies it to the literary curriculum. Demonstrating the connections between *Jane Eyre* and Harriet Jacobs's slave narrative, *Incidents in the Life of a Slave Girl* (1861; reprinted 1988), she argues that studying the two rebellious, 'confessional' texts together creates a 'quilting of voices' which highlights the similarities and differences between two women from very different cultural backgrounds.

Another central concern in Black feminist criticism, the identification and validation of a Black female language, has been placed in question by post-structuralist critics, who see such a quest as essentialist and ahistorical. Mae Gwendolyn Henderson (1990) has inventively turned this argument on its head: what distinguishes Black women's discourse, she argues, is its heterogeneity and multiplicity. Black women's multiple and complex cultural positionality – simultaneously aligned with, and competing with, Black men, white women and other Black women – produces the ability to speak in diverse languages which Henderson calls 'speaking in tongues'.

Taking up French: women, language and French feminism

'Jane, what are you doing?'
'Learning German.'
'I want you to give up German and learn Hindustani.'
'You are not in earnest?'
'In such earnest that I must have it so: and I will tell you why.' (*Jane Eyre*, p. 423)

St. John's words may be seen as exemplifying both patriarchal domination over language and the displacement of a shared women's discourse: German is the new 'tongue' which Jane studies with Diana and Mary, and St. John's inflexible imposition of *his* chosen language upon Jane contrasts with the fluid and generous interchange which, as already noted, characterises her relationship with his sisters.

The relationship between language and gender has been much discussed by feminist theorists; I have already mentioned the ways in which radical feminists have set out to challenge patriarchal control over meaning. Here, I want to look at the influential school of thought associated with a particular strand of 'French feminism'. While there are some interesting overlaps between the two approaches, there is a central difference between the radical feminist vision of an oppositional, authentic language of female experience, and this strand of French feminist theory, which (drawing on the psychoanalytic model given by Jacques Lacan) sees 'woman' as unrepresentable within existing linguistic structures.

Within Lacanian theory the acquisition of gendered identity corresponds with, and is inseparable from, the acquisition of language. Entry into the 'symbolic order' of language and culture is an essential precondition of becoming 'human', able to communicate with other humans, but the symbolic order is a gendered order, which inscribes and confirms male dominance. Women remain marginal within culture, placed 'in a special relation to language which becomes theirs as a consequence of becoming human, and at the same time not theirs as a consequence of becoming female' (Kaplan, 1986a, p. 82). French feminism extends and revises this model to identify 'feminine' writing – *l'écriture féminine* – with what is repressed or rechannelled upon entry to the symbolic order, when the all-encompassing union between mother and child is broken. *L'écriture féminine* expresses both the free-floating pleasures of pre-linguistic, ungendered infancy, and the multiple, diffuse nature of female *jouissance* (orgasmic pleasure). Whereas 'masculine' language is linear, finite, structured, rational and unified, 'feminine' language is fluid, decentred, playful, fragmented and open-ended. *L'écriture féminine* is seen as revolutionary because it poses a potential challenge to the patriarchal order by subverting masculine logic and disrupting dominant linguistic structures. I say a 'potential' challenge because, after early childhood, the feminine is located in the unconscious; it cannot be fully expressed but only glimpsed, occasionally, in certain texts.

French feminist theory has been attractive to feminists because it offers a celebratory and inspirational vision of what might be, the subversive potential of women's words. There are, however, important differences between the three theorists who have had most influence upon English-speaking writers. Julia Kristeva (1986) sees 'semiotic' language (the rhythms, intonations and erotic energies characteristic of the pre-linguistic stage) as equally accessible to both men and women, since both have to repress the feminine upon entry to the 'symbolic'. For Hélène Cixous, 'writing the body' is an expression of what women have been forced to suppress, through a 'return to the body which has been more than confiscated from her, which has been turned into the uncanny stranger on display' (Cixous, 1981, p. 250). For Luce Irigaray (1985), *parler femme* expresses the 'doubleness' of female physiology: the two lips of the vulva speak a language more complex, subtle and diversified than that of male desire. British critics have tended to prefer Kristeva's separation of feminine language from female bodies, but it is arguable that women *do* after all have bodies, and that Cixous and Irigaray offer ways of representing (and challenging) the experience of the female body as socially and culturally mediated, rather than innate.

The impact of French feminism has been controversial (Moi, 1985; Jones, 1986). One problem is that to identify a particular kind of language with the 'feminine' is to risk perpetuating patriarchal notions of gender difference: order, logic, and control over language are 'masculine'; the irrational, the marginal, the contradictory are 'feminine'. As Deborah Cameron comments,

> feminists must have faith in the capacity of language to empower as well as oppress; linguistic resources may very often have been denied us and used against us, but there is nothing immutable about this or any other form of sexism. To place women 'outside language' in our theories is to deny ourselves something of crucial importance: the power to shape new meanings for a different and better world. (Cameron, 1992, p. 227)

French feminism privileges a particular style and form of writing, the *avant-garde*; it is the experimental, fragmented, open-ended text which approximates most closely to *l'écriture féminine*. While traces of *l'écriture féminine* can be found in *Jane Eyre*, such a reading works effectively by discarding the 'realist' elements of the text – the lucid, the orderly, the linear – in favour of its 'modernist' moments of fracture and rupture. The idea that the modernist text (in its refusal of linearity and closure) is intrinsically more subversive than the realist narrative has had much currency among feminist critics but, as Rita Felski has commented, multiplicity and indeterminacy are not necessarily feminist (1989, p. 7). To reject the realist text as colluding with the phallocentric order is to relegate much of what women have written – and, equally importantly, much of what women *read* – to the realms of the inauthentic.

The influence of Lacanian theory and French feminism is apparent in the analyses of *Jane Eyre* offered by Margaret Homans (*Bearing the Word*, 1986) and Elisabeth Bronfen (*Over Her Dead Body*, 1992), but neither Homans nor Bronfen sees the realist woman writer as 'inauthentic'. Both, rather, focus on the complex and competitive relationship between the 'literal' and the 'figurative' in Victorian discourse, and the problems which this conflict presented to the woman writer, who was faced with a 'dominant myth of language that excludes the possibility of women writing' (Homans, 1986, p. 68). Homans argues that, in nineteenth-century fiction, those experiences that were most specifically celebrated as feminine – such as childbirth or childcare – are consistently framed as antithetical to women's writing. Literal meaning and 'Nature' are identified with the figure of the mother, whose power must be relinquished or repressed upon entry into the symbolic order. Through an analysis of the dreams and the representation of motherhood in *Jane Eyre*, Homans argues that in order to find a voice as a writer, Jane must regress into childhood, betray the mother, and 'kill Mother Nature': 'the temptation to become part of a feminized nature, to become a feminized object like nature, amounts in Brontë's view to a temptation to die, for it would be to join the dead mother, to accept exclusion from what her culture defines as human' (p. 99). The cultural relationship between femininity and death is the central subject of Bronfen's book. She argues that the deaths of Helen Burns and Bertha Mason are an essential part of the process by which Jane emerges from her former position of social ambivalence. Helen and Bertha, marginalised figures in contrasting ways, are translated 'into figures of Otherness, of excessive purity or excessive pollution' (p. 223): their sacrifice is necessary before Jane can take up a fixed position within the masculine symbolic order.

Reader, I married him: gender and genre

Reader, I married him. (*Jane Eyre*, p. 474)

So far I have been focussing on *Jane Eyre* as a 'feminist text'. But Brontë's novel is also a romance, the 'mother-text' of all those novels – written, and read, primarily by women – in which innocent heroine meets brooding hero and lives happily ever after. Is it the case, as Germaine Greer once suggested, that romantic fiction is 'the opiate of the supermenial' (Greer, 1970, p. 188) and the romantic hero the invention of 'women cherishing the chains of their bondage' (p. 180)? More recent feminist studies have argued that romantic novels offer women readers a way of dealing with real anxieties and difficulties (male power and aggression, female dependence and confinement within the home) and a chance to fantasise alternatives: masculine tenderness, female power and desire (Modleski, 1982; Radway, 1987; Belsey, 1994, and see Chapter 6). (When reading *Jane Eyre*, for example, we know that no matter how cold and aloof Rochester may seem, he *needs* Jane.) Romance 'addicts', Radway emphasises, read selectively, not passively: their reading gives them 'space' for themselves and entry into a shared female subculture.

This re-assessment of romance is related to feminist interest in the relationship between gender and 'genre' (literary form), and in popular fiction by women (see, for example, Radstone, 1988; Carr, 1989; Cranny-Francis, 1990). Do certain genres offer particular possibilities for the woman writer? Violence, vulnerability, conflict and fear are central issues in the thriller, a field in which women have long been prominent (Coward and Semple, 1989); science fiction, while often regarded as a 'male' form, offers opportunities, which women writers have seized, for fantasising alternative worlds, whether terrifying or desirable (Lefanu, 1988; Armitt, 1991). Popular genres may be used for radical ends, which is not to say that they are necessarily progressive. As Light (1984) has shown, subversive explorations of female desire may be underpinned by conservative assumptions about class. But taking the 'bestseller' seriously challenges conventional assumptions about the inferiority of popular culture, and focuses attention upon the way in which culture is produced and received. Socialist feminists have been particularly active in this area; it is noticeable that several of the original members of the Marxist Feminist Literature Collective subsequently turned their attention to the analysis of the bestsellers written and read by women (Kaplan, 1986; Taylor, 1989), to the meaning which books actually have in women's lives and to the ways in which those meanings may differ, at different times or from within different cultural contexts (O'Rourke, 1989; Taylor, 1989). We need more work on the female reader, which still remains an underresearched area (but see Flint, 1993; Smith, 1993). But for now, I want to return to the woman writer, leaving *Jane Eyre* in order to look, necessarily briefly, at the impact of feminism upon contemporary women's fiction.

Writing as revision: contemporary women's fiction

In the early 1970s, the dominant feminist form was the 'consciousness-raising' novel: typically, a 'confessional' first-person narrative which traced the protagonist's movement from self-deluded dependence to autonomy and self-discovery. Novels like Marilyn French's *The Women's Room* (1977) – the 'novel which changes lives' – clearly met an important need, but the 'consciousness-raising' novel's claim to be 'telling the truth' for 'every-woman' and its focus on independent self-realisation have been criticised by some feminists (Coward, 1989; Gerrard, 1989; but see Felski, 1989). Gritty realism has increasingly given way to novels which draw attention to their own fictionality, a path pioneered by Angela Carter's 'magic realist' novels and the slippery, fragmented narratives of Doris Lessing and Fay Weldon.

Weldon's *Female Friends* (1977), like Michèle Roberts's *A Piece of the Night* (1978), exemplifies another characteristic feminist form: the 'patch-work' novel, which pieces together the lives of three or four women to uncover the hidden patterns of women's oppression across time and place. In these novels, 'fact' and 'fantasy' are often mixed. The continuity and cohesiveness of female experience is emphasised through the appropriation and reworking of myth and folklore, and through the stories passed on by mothers to daughters, as in two novels by Chinese-American writers, Maxine Hong Kingston's *The Woman Warrior* (1977) and Amy Tan's *The Joy Luck Club* (1989). The late 1980s, however, saw the questioning from within of some of feminism's most cherished 'truths'. Novels such as Leslie Dick's *Without Falling* (1987), Sarah Schulman's *After Delores* (1990) and Margaret Atwood's *Cat's Eye* (1989) set out to challenge earlier feminist sentimentalisation of 'woman-bonding', and to show that women are not always 'nice'. In *The Robber Bride* (1993), Margaret Atwood uses the patchwork form to question some of the assumptions of earlier patchwork fictions. Atwood's novel demonstrates the destructive effect of the demonic and spectral Zenia upon the lives of three other women: in this novel, the 'real world of women' is a harsh and vengeful place from which men, Atwood ironically suggests, must be 'insulated' (p. 110).

The re-telling of old tales has been a favourite enterprise: Angela Carter's *The Bloody Chamber* (1979) is a feminist revision of traditional fairy tales; Suniti Namjoshi's *The Conversations of Cow* (1985) is a lesbian reworking of Hindu myth, and the novels of Michèle Roberts have consistently and inventively transformed biblical legend and Roman Catholic iconography. Another dominant trend is the appropriation of popular genres. Feminist science fiction – such as Margaret Atwood's *The Handmaid's Tale* (1985) and Elizabeth Wilson's *The Lost Time Café* (1993) and *Poisoned Hearts* (1995) – comments on the present by envisaging alternatives, through utopian or dystopian visions of future possibilities for women. Wilson's novels combine fantasy, murder mystery and the exploration of gay and lesbian sexual identity, and indeed, the lesbian-feminist thriller has become a subgenre in its own right: Barbara Wilson, Mary Wings, Rebecca O'Rourke and Sarah Schulman have repeatedly used the murder mystery formula to explore and illuminate debates within contemporary feminist politics.

In the past decade, lesbian-feminist fiction has proliferated and diversi-fied. There has been a noticeable shift away from sombre realism and the 'politically correct' celebrations of sisterhood which were prevalent in the early 1980s towards more questioning, playful and erotic fictions in a variety of different genres (Hennegan, 1988; Palmer, 1993). Fiona Cooper's *Rotary Spokes* (1988), an exuberantly riproaring tale of lesbian self-discovery in a fantasised American Mid-West, Jeanette Winterson's unique blend of comedy, fantasy and confessional coming-out story, *Oranges Are Not the Only Fruit* (1985) and Jane DeLynn's short stories about sex and fantasy, *Don Juan in the Village* (1990) demonstrate a shift in feminist fiction as a whole towards a 'post-modernist' parodying and crossing of genres.

The post-modernist novel, as neatly summarised by Leslie Dick, 'uses strategies of plunder and purloinment, plagiarism, replication and simulation . . . to challenge the category of what an art work is' (Dick, 1989, p. 206). Angela Carter's *Wise Children* (1992) blends high and low culture, mixes identities and crosses time and space in a dazzling and teasing subversion of conventional assumptions about the line between fantasy and reality. In Michèle Roberts's *Flesh and Blood* (1994), the narrative moves from narrator to narrator, from present to past and back again, like 'a thread, unravelled, that I could wind as I wove my way into the labyrinth' (Michèle Roberts's, 1994, p. 7).

Perhaps the most dramatic development on the contemporary scene has been the achievement, and recognition, of Black women writers like Alice Walker, Toni Morrison, Paule Marshall and Toni Cade Bambara. While their work exemplifies the process of 'writing as revision'[5] – retrieving, reimagining, redefining – which is at the heart of contemporary feminist literature, it also demonstrates the importance of cultural specificity. History and culture are central preoccupations in Afro-American women's fiction (Willis, 1990), from Alice Walker's exuberant rewriting of the past in *The Color Purple* (1982) to Toni Morrison's haunting and powerful reclamation of the history of slavery in *Beloved* (1987). These novels foreground women's lives, tribulations and pleasures, but they do not claim to speak of all women, or even of all Black women.

The movement away from 'the woman's text' which seeks to encapsulate the specificity of female experience is also evident in recent British fiction. Feminist novelists have become more audacious and experimental in their representation of gender roles. In Jeanette Winterson's *Written on the Body* (1993) the gender of the narrator is never identified. In the past ten years, there has been a proliferation of novels by women with male narrators (Winterson, 1987; Tremain, 1990; Barker, 1991, 1993, 1995). Pat Barker's *Regeneration* trilogy, which includes the Booker prize-winner *The Ghost Road* (1995), focuses on male experience during the First World War; Kate Atkinson's *Behind the Scenes at the Museum* (1996) is set in the same period, but with a distinctively Yorkshire inflection. British feminist writers are turning their attention to the specificity of regional and national identity: there has been a sudden burgeoning of work by Scottish women (such as the novelists Janice Galloway and A.L. Kennedy, and the poets Kathleen

Jamie, Carol Ann Duffy and Jackie Kay) in which female experience is
explored but is located firmly (if sometimes ironically) in Scottish landscape
and culture. 'In my country', by the Black Scottish poet Jackie Kay, is a fine
example. The speaker is walking by the water when a woman passes round
her:

> in a slow watchful circle,
> as if I were a superstition;
>
> or the worst dregs of her imagination,
> so when she finally spoke
> her words spliced into bars
> of an old wheel. A segment of air.
> *Where do you come from?*
> 'Here,' I said, 'Here. These parts.'
> (Kay, 1993, p. 24)

The complex positions from which women may 'speak' are delicately and
humorously explored in the poetry[6] of Grace Nichols (born in Guyana and
living in Britain). I shall conclude with her short poem, 'Epilogue', which
speaks of a particular woman's experience, but also encapsulates the story I
have been recounting in this chapter:

> I have crossed an ocean
> I have lost my tongue
> from the root of the old one
> a new one has sprung.
> (Nichols, 1984, p. 64).

Notes

1. Numerous editions of *Jane Eyre* are available. Page references in the text of this
   chapter are to Charlotte Brontë, *Jane Eyre*, edited by Q. D. Leavis (Harmondsworth, Penguin, 1966).
2. For an interesting example of 'lesbian stylistics', see Paula Bennett's analysis of
   the clitoral imagery in the poetry of Emily Dickinson, 'The Pea That Duty
   Locks: Lesbian and Feminist-Heterosexual Readings of Emily Dickinson's
   Poetry', pp. 104–25 in *Lesbian Texts and Contexts*, edited by Karla Jay and
   Joanne Glasgow (New York and London, New York University Press, 1990).
   This collection also includes a useful bibliography of work on lesbian writing.
3. The central technique of deconstruction is to expose and undo the 'binary
   oppositions' (two apparently opposite terms of which one is in fact dominant) at
   work in the text. As Hélène Cixous has demonstrated, the binary system is not
   only hierarchical, but often privileges the term culturally associated with

masculinity. Among the examples she gives are: Activity/Passivity; Sun/Moon; Culture/Nature; Father/Mother; Head/Heart: see Cixous, 'Sorties', pp. 101–16 in Catherine Belsey and Jane Moore (eds), *The Feminist Reader: Essays in Gender and the Politics of Literary Criticism* (London, Macmillan, 1989).

4. Bertha's story is the central theme of Jean Rhys's novel *Wide Sargasso Sea* (1968), a fascinating 'rewriting' of *Jane Eyre* which Spivak also discusses in her essay.

5. I have borrowed this term from Adrienne Rich's 1971 essay, 'When We Dead Awaken: Writing as Re-Vision'. The essay also contains Rich's inspirational definition of the task of feminist criticism: to provide 'a clue to how we live, how we have been living, how we have been led to imagine ourselves, how our language has trapped as well as liberated us, how the very act of naming has been till now a male prerogative, and how we can begin to see and name – and therefore live – afresh' (Rich, 1980d, p. 35).

6. I am conscious that poetry and drama have been neglected in this chapter. For introductions to contemporary feminist work in these areas, see Jan Montefiore, *Feminism and Poetry* (London and New York, Pandora, 1987) and Helene Keyssar, *Feminist Theatre* (London, Macmillan, 1984).

Further reading

Belsey, Catherine and Jane Moore (eds), *The Feminist Reader: Essays in Gender and the Politics of Literary Criticism* (London, Macmillan, 1989). Excellent collection, primarily post-structuralist; includes important essays by Cixous, Kristeva and Spivak. Lucid introductory overview. For a fuller overview with useful chapters on French feminist theory, see Toril Moi, *Sexual/Textual Politics: Feminist Literary Theory* (London and New York, Methuen, 1985).

Cameron, Deborah, *Feminism and Linguistic Theory*, 2nd edn (London, Macmillan, 1992). First published in 1985; the 1992 edition is comprehensively revised and updated. Refreshingly down-to-earth guide to the complex field of contemporary linguistic theory.

Castle, Terry. *The Apparitional Lesbian: Female Homosexuality and Modern Culture* (New York, Columbia University Press, 1993). Readable and wide-ranging collection of essays, ranging from Greta Garbo and Brigitte Fassbaender to Anne Lister and Henry James. An important contribution to lesbian critical theory.

Mills, Sara and Lynne Pearce, *Feminist Readings/Feminists Reading*, 2nd edn (Hemel Hempstead, Harvester Wheatsheaf, 1996). Fully revised and updated edition of book first published in 1989. Distinctive for its practical application of theory to specific texts. Helpful glossary.

Sedgwick, Eve Kosofsky, *Tendencies* (Durham, Duke University Press, 1994). Stimulating collection of essays, ranging from eighteenth-century literature to contemporary politics, by a key writer of queer theory.

Showalter, Elaine (ed.), *The New Feminist Criticism: Essays on Women, Literature and Theory* (London, Virago, 1986). Primarily, but not exclusively, 'Anglo-American' in emphasis. Contains pioneering essays by Bonnie Zimmermann (lesbian feminist criticism) and Barbara Smith (Black feminist criticism). For more recent developments in these areas, see Karla Jay and Joanne Glasgow (eds), *Lesbian Texts and Contexts: Radical Revisions* (New York and London, New York University Press, 1990) and Cheryl A. Wall (ed.), *Changing Our Own Words: Essays on Criticism, Theory, and Writing by Black Women* (London, Routledge, 1990).

6

The Picture is Political: Representation of Women in Contemporary Popular Culture

Margaret Marshment

Represent, v.t. 1. call up in the mind by description or portrayal . . . 3. make out to be etc., allege that, describe or depict as . . . 5. symbolize, act as embodiment of, stand for, correspond to, be specimen of . . . 6. fill place of, be substitute or deputy for, be entitled to act or speak for, be sent as member to legislature or delegate to meeting etc. by . . . – *Concise Oxford Dictionary*, 1995

Representation is a political issue. Without the power to define our interests and to participate in the decisions that affect us, women – like any other group in society – will be subject to the definitions and decisions of others. These others (men, in this case) are likely to produce definitions and decisions that serve their interests rather than ours. This need not be a deliberate process of oppression: it may just seem to be 'common sense' that women should have babies and cook, that women cannot be company directors or bricklayers, that they should wish to totter around on high heels to make themselves attractive to men. This appears to be the natural order of things. So it just happens, 'naturally', that men are spared the drudgery of domestic chores, can have most of the best jobs and can expect women to want to please and service them.

The apparent naturalness of this social arrangement is evidence of the success of patriarchal ideology. If nineteenth-century feminism may be characterised by the struggle for the vote, for the right to be represented in a legislature that had power to determine so many aspects of women's lives, then the 'new-wave' feminism of the later twentieth century can be seen as enlarging the concept of politics to include the personal, the cultural and the ideological (see, for instance, Mitchell, 1974, pp. 99–182). This was not just a question of disillusion with the power of Parliament, but an awareness of the 'overdetermined' nature of women's oppression in society:

the way in which their subordinate position in a multiplicity of structures, institutions and value systems interacted with each other to lock women into an overall subordination. Among these structures are those concerned with producing representations of women: from school reading schemes to Hollywood films, from advertising to opera, from game shows to art galleries, women are depicted in ways that define what it means to be a woman in this society: what women are like (naturally), what they ought to be like, what they are capable of, and incapable of, what roles they play in society, and how they differ from men.

If these definitions do not fairly and accurately represent the real lives of women, and the reality of their potential as human beings; if women are being defined, for example, as wives and mothers to the exclusion of their work outside the home; if they are being judged by their sexual attractiveness to the exclusion of their moral and intellectual qualities; if they are being defined as inferior to men; then they are not receiving fair representation in society. So that while, for example, the law may no longer prevent women from entering certain professions, it might still be argued that if women are predominantly defined as naturally belonging to the domestic sphere, this could function just as effectively to prevent them from seriously pursuing careers. Ideology can be a powerful source of inequality as well as a rationalisation of it (see, for instance, Barrett, 1980, pp. 84–113).

This chapter will examine the concern shown by feminists over almost three decades with the issue of how women are represented in the media. It will suggest that, beginning with critiques of 'images' of women and of the female stereotypes promoted across a range of media, feminist work in this area has developed sophisticated analyses of how representation works, how meanings are created in and for a culture, and how people do or do not accept these meanings.

This is not to say that there is any *one* feminist approach to this question: on the contrary, there has been, and still is, considerable debate and disagreement not only over how to interpret particular images and texts, and how to evaluate, say, women's magazines, soap opera or romance fiction, but also over such issues as how, for example, feminism has affected the media in the past 25 years, whether women whether should work for inclusion in mainstream media or should set up autonomous organisations that challenge the mainstream, and what links (if any) exist between representation and social behaviour (between, for example, pornography and male abuse of women, or between the thinness of fashion models and anorexia).

Since there is a separate chapter in this volume on women and literature, this chapter will focus on material that can be described as 'popular', much of it visual as well as linguistic, such as film, television and women's magazines.

Resistance

The first widely publicised event of the women's liberation movement at the
end of the 1960s was the 'trashing' of accoutrements of femininity at the
Miss America pageant in Atlantic City in 1968 (Coote and Campbell, 1982,
p. 11). This was a protest against a particularly demeaning spectacle of
women judged (mostly) by men for their conformity to certain physical
criteria of femininity, which women in general were encouraged to aspire to
with the aid of the girdles, bras and mascara that were deposited in the
rubbish bin. This protest was itself the subject of media representation
(again mainly by men). The mythic 'bra-burning' became for years the
dominant cultural signifier of feminism: feminists were 'unfeminine', ugly
and frustrated, and therefore envious of the truly feminine bathing 'beau-
ties'. This event encapsulated many of the dilemmas confronted by women
in representing their own interests in the context of male domination of the
institutions and codes of representation. It was directed at male control of
definitions of women, but was interpreted as an attack on other women
defining themselves; it aimed to attack ideological stereotypes of female
beauty, and was interpreted as an attack on beauty itself; it was a protest
against the trivialisation of women, and was itself trivialised; it aimed to
challenge the power of men to define women and was itself defined by men.

In patriarchal culture, women are defined by those who subordinate
them. It is, for the most part, men who are, for instance, publishers, editors,
film directors or television producers, and who produce the images that
define women. And these definitions may be seen as ideological: as defining
women in opposition to, and as lesser than, men. It may be argued, for
instance, that it is in men's interests, as a group, for women to be confined to
the domestic sphere; not only does it reduce competition in the work place
and ensure a servicing for men at home that facilitates their work and leisure
activities, it renders women dependent on men, identifies women with the
'natural' world of the family and excludes them from those fields such as
science, politics, wealth-creation and the arts which are seen as characterising the achievements of humanity. Images of women cooing over babies and
floor cleaners are not therefore necessarily just limiting stereotypes; they
may be interpreted as encouraging a division of labour that favours men and
disadvantages women, while defining humanity as essentially male.

Women may themselves be seduced into accepting such images, both
because patriarchal ideology has achieved a general hegemony, and because,
however much they work against women's interests in the long term, in the
short term they may offer what benefits are available to women in a
patriarchal society. If, for example, single motherhood can mean poverty
and exhaustion, women may reasonably decide that marriage is the preferable option; so much so that they will desire marriage before contemplating

the alternatives.[1] And if definitions of femininity and heterosexuality demand that women wear make-up and high heels in order to be attractive to men, then not only might women wear them for this purpose, but they may well come to feel more confident, more beautiful, wearing them[2]. If, in this way, women come to be subordinated – even in their definitions of themselves and their desires – to the needs of patriarchy, it may be argued that this is because definitions of femininity appear to offer solutions to their material problems. 'Be pretty – get a man – escape poverty' is a crude reduction of what is a very complex process; but what is certain is that representation has an important part to play in it, and needs to be taken very seriously by anyone wishing to analyse, and change, women's subordination to men.

The internalisation of patriarchal values by women is also a reason why it is not necessarily a satisfactory answer for women simply to take control of the means of cultural production. It is obvious that if women are underrepresented in professions which produce and reproduce definitions of gender and gender relations, then they are not in a position to speak for themselves and in their own interests. It must therefore be a necessary, if not sufficient, project of feminist politics to work towards proportionate representation of women in the cultural professions of media production. And, as Anne Ross Muir has shown, much work remains to be done to achieve this (Ross Muir, 1988, p. 143). In recent years, women have become more visible as, for instance, newsreaders or presenters of arts and current affairs programmes, and a number of individual women have achieved eminence in various fields of media production. We could mention, as examples, Kathryn Bigelow (the film director), Lynda La Plante (the television script writer), Janet Street Porter and Jenny Abramsky as broadcasting executives, Glenda Bailey (the editor of *Marie Claire*) and Phillipa Giles (the television producer). It would, however, make little sense to produce a comparable list for men: there are just too many of them. Women are still massively outnumbered when it comes to positions of media power. And, of course, there is no female equivalent of Rupert Murdoch, or even Richard Branson: we may be thankful for this, of course, but it is an indication of where the power lies at this level.

However, not all women are feminists. Women who accept the ideas and values of what feminists define as patriarchal ideology will be more likely to reproduce it in their work than to challenge it. Women are overwhelmingly responsible for the writing of romantic fiction and for producing women's magazines, and, from Coco Chanel through Mary Quant to Katherine Hamnett and Vivienne Westwood, have constituted an influential minority in fashion design. There are also women editing tabloid newspapers and even pornographic magazines. These are all forms viewed with suspicion by many feminists, and with reason. The question is whether any woman can represent women's interests by virtue of being a woman, or whether a feminist analysis is essential, in which case we can also ask whether pro-feminist men can represent women equally well, and if not, why not?

Reflecting reality

Early feminist critiques of representations of women were often concerned with 'representativeness' in another sense: if most women were not like the stereotypes of femininity available in the media, then they were not being accurately depicted. Critiques by, for example, Mary Ellman on 'feminine stereotypes' (Ellman, 1968, ch. III) and Sue Sharpe on the media (Sharpe, 1976, ch. 3), compared media stereotypes of women as sex symbols, domestic drudges or virulent harridans with the real lives of real women and concluded that the misrepresentations amounted to an injustice that needed to be redressed by more 'realistic' representations. Elena Gianini Belotti, for example, sets a content analysis finding of gender roles in children's books against a sociological finding on women's work outside the home: 'In the 144 reading texts for elementary schools, mothers are seen in the kitchen; in reality 40 per cent of American mothers work in factories and offices.' (Belotti, 1976, p. 90). Sharpe also implied the desirability of reflecting social reality in her critique of children's readers:

> It is not only this portrayal which is wrong, but also the way that the conditions and standard of living are represented. Most children are nowhere near the upper middle-class world in which Peter and Jane live. Some primers have started to try to correct this fault, by recognising the modern world of tower blocks and supermarkets . . . However, the basic parts played by girls and women are little altered by their change in surroundings. Their place is still a domestic one. (Sharpe, 1976, p. 95)

This reflective model of representation has often been employed by social movements demanding more democratic regimes of representation. What is demanded is representations that show life 'as it really is', providing an accurate reflection of society and its people, including portrayals of members of dominated groups showing their position within the whole society, and their 'real' individual natures, as opposed to reproducing myths and stereotypes. This would mean, for example, not always depicting authority figures as white and male; not always showing *women* doing the housework, and not always showing them as happy and glamorous when they do. It would mean including in mainstream representation the whole range of roles and experiences of women, of whatever age, size, sexuality, class, 'race' or ethnic group; and portraying them as important in their own right, not just for their role in relation to the dominant group. The assumption behind this demand is that truth and justice are inseparable: only by accurately reflecting the shape of society and its members can the representation be seen as serving the needs of the whole society.

Women have always been faced with a peculiar problem in this respect. For, whereas it could be claimed that, say, working-class, Black, lesbian and gay communities were underrepresented in the works of upper-class white heterosexual artists, the same could hardly be said of women. Women have never been absent from the range of representations produced by men. The question was, rather, how well women were represented by them, and the answer was 'not at all well'.

Liberal liberation

What then was to be done? The obvious answer was that (a) women ought to be portrayed 'as they really were', and (b) such portrayals ought to promote the interests of women: that is, they should expose the oppression experienced by women under patriarchal capitalism, encourage social equality between the sexes, provide women and girls with positive role models and question ideological notions of sexual difference.

This may be described as the liberal approach to representation. The reflective model it employs has, as we shall see, been subject to considerable criticism in the light of more complex theoretical formulations of the relationships between representations and reality. However, we should perhaps not be too quick to dismiss its usefulness as a starting point for the analysis of these relationships. For, despite its complexity, there always *is* a relationship between representation and reality, and, even at the simplest reflective level, where this 'reflection' is felt to be accurate, the recognition involved can be a considerable source of pleasure: we all seem to enjoy the sense that an artist, in whatever medium, has 'got it right' in capturing the texture of real life experience, and are correspondingly irritated, or even angry, where a representation of something we know well is obviously wrong. It was an important moment, then, when the novel emerged in the eighteenth century as a form representing the newly dominant bourgeois class to itself. Another such moment occurred in the late 1950s, when British film and television picked up on developments in the novel and the theatre and screened works by working-class writers about working-class people and their lives. In works such as *Saturday Night and Sunday Morning* and *A Taste of Honey* in the cinema, and *Cathy Come Home, Z Cars* and *Coronation Street* on television, working-class viewers – almost for the first time – saw themselves represented as the subjects of serious drama, rather than as the objects of patronising comedy. For women to demand a comparable liberation from demeaning stereotypes was both legitimate and achievable.

If stereotypes of women still abound in the media, above all in the sexualisation of women in advertising and pornography, nevertheless the last 25 years has seen a significant shift in regimes of representation concerning gender. Many more mainstream fictional texts now feature women as the central protagonist, often dealing with women's issues such as rape and domestic violence, and/or often in roles which are invested with the authority of instutitions or of violence, which were previously seen as the monopoly of men. The same period has seen the emergence of a certain questioning of masculinity in portrayals of men as, for instance, caring parents (as *Three Men and a Baby*) or sexualised in advertisements for jeans or after-shave, as well as in the greater media visibility of gay men.

However, the liberal approach is flawed in its analysis and contradictory in its demands. First, how do we measure accuracy in representation? If particular images are accused of inaccuracy, by what standard are they being measured; by the writer's own experience, by other representations, such as sociological reports, history or journalism? And if so, what makes these sources more reliable as an account of reality than the particular material under review?

Second, what is meant by accuracy? Are photographs not accurate representations? Yes, but they can be set up, cropped, retouched. And does it not also matter who is photographed? Hillary Clinton, Princess Diana or Naomi Campbell cannot be said to represent the majority of women. Are we then asking that the experience of the majority of women should be represented? Yes . . . but, obviously not to the exclusion of minorities: women who are socially disadvantaged by, for example, class, 'race', disablement, sexuality or old age have a right to be represented. And so too do those atypical by virtue of their achievements in public life, the arts, sports and so on. In fact, we can legitimately ask for all women to receive due respresentation as regards whatever social groupings they may fall into.

However, numbers are not the only issue. Some women and groups of women are inherently more interesting to us: exceptional achievement, skill, courage, influence, or even notoriety, merit our attention, so that while we may be critical of particular criteria of, say, newsworthiness used by the media (the tabloids' excessive attention to royalty and entertainers, for example), we must also concede that a complete democracy of the image is extremely unlikely.

Third, it is not necessarily the isolated image or characterisation that is important. What is more significant is the regime of representation as it concerns gender in our society: the range and frequency of particular types of representation, the extent and nature of omissions, the meanings attached to particular types of representation (for instance, slim women are desirable, fat women are funny), the way these meanings are produced and re-produced in specific contexts, how context and assumed (and actual) audience contribute to the determination of meaning, and how representations of women compare and relate to representations of men.

In theory, the problem of establishing a 'truth' against which representations can be judged is an insuperable one. In practice, we accept that we must make judgements about how accurate and fair representations are. This does not mean accepting that 'reality' can ever be simply or fully 'reflected': all representation requires principles of selection; omission, emphasis, explanation and context are all processes that produce meaning, and it is not always of primary importance whether the end result accurately reflects reality or not (advertisements and pop videos, for instance, are not usually judged for their realism). What matters is to recognise that understanding the meanings that are produced, understanding what 'woman', 'femininity' and 'gender' (and indeed, 'man' and 'masculinity') mean in our culture, will require an analysis that acknowledges these as complex constructions rather than more or less accurate reflections of some given 'reality'.

The double bind

Liberalism's adherence to realist criteria produces a dilemma for itself. Asking for representations that are faithful to the reality of women's position in patriarchal society may risk demanding representations that show women predominantly in subordinate roles, as oppressed, as victims. Replacing stereotypic images of women with images of them as, for example, underpaid workers, bored housewives, battered wives, put-upon mothers, rape victims, may be more 'realistic' as evidence of the oppression of women under patriarchy, but they are not, in themselves, empowering images; less so, perhaps, even than patriarchy's stereotypes of women as desirable sex objects or all-nurturing mothers. The latter at least grant women a compensatory power.

A contrary demand from a similarly liberal perspective is quite the opposite: this has been for 'positive' images of women, showing what women can do, to act as role models to empower women in their sense of themselves and perhaps even in the conduct of their lives. But a constant stream of images of women as tycoons or gun-toting heroines can hardly be said to be realistically typical of women's experience: not only are such images unrepresentative of the majority of women's lives under patriarchy, but they may be accused of glossing over the grimmer reality of these lives by presenting a deceptively comforting image of how wonderfully women are doing. The spate of television advertisements beginning in the late 1980s showing glossy professional women driving company cars attracted feminist criticism on precisely these grounds, although it could equally be argued that these ads were doing what earlier feminists had complained they were not doing: showing women succeeding in the world of work, on men's terms. The question is, whether the token woman, even the token image of woman, functions as a trail-blazer, a thin edge of the wedge, or as a diversion from issues that affect the generality of women, a co-option of feminist values for commercial ends.

Whose values?

This brings us to another problem. A patriarchal society is one in which masculinist values have become general values. For women to be shown 'proving' themselves by these criteria is to confirm the validity of the very values which a feminist critique of patriarchy may be concerned to question; thus rather than challenging patriarchy, such representations may contribute to its validation. If a strong woman is one who is strong within patriarchal terms – say, rich, ruthless and invulnerable – this denies the strength of women (and those men) who are poor, compassionate and vulnerable.

A contrary feminist position would ask for a redefinition of the values of patriarchy: to redefine, for example, 'positive' and 'powerful' in feminist terms. This is a logical, and valid, answer to what I have called the liberal dilemma: representations that demonstrate the strength of women in enduring, subverting and challenging oppression may be seen as both 'realistic' and 'positive'. But they are still struggling against the signifying codes of power in our culture which have defined strength as those qualities possessed predominantly by men (such as physical prowess, institutional power, wealth) and then defined masculinity as connoting these qualities. This struggle for the redefinition of the meanings of words and the values of meanings (in so far as they can be distinguished) is a political one. To some extent we may claim, I think, that feminism has produced some significant shifts over nearly three decades in both meanings and values attached to gender.

It has done so both by laying claim to those qualities and values defined as masculine, and by questioning their worth. If the latter may appear the more radical strategy, the effectiveness of appropriating 'masculinity' for women should not be underestimated. Because women's subordination is overdetermined, a multiplicity of strategies is required to challenge its representational forms. We must remember that many of the more appropriative strategies, showing women succeeding in men's terms, occur in extremely popular forms, so that simply in terms of audience size their effect may be considerably more widespread than more radical and challenging forms which reach limited audiences. Of course, we cannot be sure that a figure like Alexis Carrington in *Dynasty* or Jane Tennison in *Prime Suspect* empowers women more than she validates the institutions of capitalism and/

or the police; but equally, we cannot be sure that she doesn't. It is arguably impossible to represent certain aspects of, say, power outside the context within which the culture has defined them. If definitions of 'woman' are to acquire a heterogeneity comparable to definitions of 'man', then representing women in conventionally masculine roles, with masculine qualities (positive *and* negative) can be welcomed as contributing to this process. The representations may not themselves qualify as 'feminist', but in extending definitions of femininity to include conventionally masculine qualitites they may serve to break down gender stereotyping.

Substitution

However, as Griselda Pollock argued (Pollock, 1977, p. 44), substituting male for female (or vice versa) within a text does not necessarily shift the meanings attached to one gender over to the other. As she demonstrates, a naked male in a woody glade does not have the same meaning as a naked female in the same scene, because the culture's regimes of representation inform the latter in ways they do not inform the former: the image of the naked woman is not an arbitrary element in the whole, it shares meanings of beauty, romance and naturalness with elements such as grass, flowers and sunshine that the image of the naked man does not possess. Simply replacing female with male will not imbue the image of naked man instantly with these meanings, although it might; but equally it might appear incongruous, even comic. The total image may acquire a quite different meaning as a result of substituting the one, crucial, element of gender.

Consider, for example, the different meanings of Alexis Carrington and J. R. as scheming tycoons; or of 'I am what I am' ('and what I am needs no excuses') sung by a Black woman (Gloria Gaynor) or by a gay drag artist (as in *La Cage aux Folles*). Lorraine Gamman argues that, while substititing female for male buddies in the television police series, *Cagney and Lacey*, does endow the women characters with the power associated with these authority roles, at the same time their femaleness alters the shape and concerns of the series, so that not only does it deal more with 'feminine' issues like domestic violence and child pornography, but also the interactions between the private and professional lives of the characters are dealt with in more depth, thus adding a dimension of soap opera to the genre. (Gamman and Marshment, 1988, p. 15). What happens, therefore, is that *both* the police series genre and definitions of femininity undergo some shifts as a result of the gender substitution of the leading protagonists. We may see comparable processes at work in other texts featuring female 'heroes', such as the films *Blue Steel*, *Alien* or *Thelma and Louise*, where the concerns of the narrative are shifted from those conventionally found in the genres of detective fiction, science fiction and buddy/road movies respectively. However powerful existing definitions of gender may be in determining the meanings of texts, as these examples demonstrate, they are not themselves unalterable.

White women's hegemony?

During the growth of feminism in the 1970s, feminism itself came under attack from women who felt themselves excluded from what they saw as a white, middle-class, heterosexual movement. It would probably be fair to say that most feminist cultural criticism assumes, by omission, a white heterosexual subject. This is in part a response to a media which has largely ignored the existence of Black and/or lesbian women, so that analyses of mainstream texts found it hard to do more than note the absences and carry on regardless. But a feminism that, even by implication – through practice rather than through intent – accepts an ideological definition of women as white and heterosexual, with black and lesbian women defined as 'other', is denying the fulness and complexity of the meaning of 'woman'. Developments in both media representation and feminist criticism with regard to Black and lesbian issues must be seen as involving a dialectic between feminism and the Black and gay movements respectively, each of which involved men as well as women. In each case, in fact, it was mostly men who featured first in shifting regimes of representation around ethnicity and sexual orientation and establishing a Black and a gay critical corpus.

Black women singers have long figured in popular music, although it could be said that until recently, with the exception of, for example, Ella Fitzgerald and Eartha Kitt, they were mostly confined to more 'minority' forms such as jazz and blues. The increasing general popularity of Black musical forms, from Motown to Rap, has made stars of, for example, Diana Ross and Salt 'n' Pepper respectively. In more recent years many Black women singers, such as Tina Turner and Whitney Houston, have become major stars in the field of popular music, a field which is still dominated by rock groups that remain generally both white and male.

In other popular cultural fields black women remain very much a minority presence. A very few Black women have attained international star status: we may mention Oprah Winfrey as a television talk show host, Naomi Campbell as a fashion model and Whoopi Goldberg in Hollywood film. In Britain, Cathy Tyson has made her mark in films such as *Mona Lisa* and television dramas such as *Band of Gold* (albeit in both cases playing a prostitute), while there has been a noticeable increase in the inclusion of Black women in minor roles in popular forms such as soap opera, talk shows or women's magazines. Despite the importance of Black male academics in the field, Black women are still relatively thin on the ground in academic media studies in Britain, compared with their activities as artists, film-makers, writers and performers. Collections of essays and in the fields of feminist and/or cultural studies do, however, increasingly include contributions by Black women writers, and Lola Young has recently published a study on the representation of Black women in film. (*Fear of the Dark*, 1996)

Given the importance of lesbianism as an issue in feminist politics during the 1970s, it is perhaps surprising that it has featured so little in issues of representation of women except, of course, in the tabloids' derogatory stereotypes of feminism, Otherwise, lesbians were mostly conscpicuous by their absence in mainstream media. Mainstream film had occasionally dealt sympathetically with lesbianism, as in *Children's Hour* or (more problematically) *The Killing of Sister George,* by treating it as a tragic flaw. In the 1980s, cinema saw little increase in the representation of lesbians, but at least films like *Lianna* and *Desert Hearts* presented it as a viable alternative sexuality. It was left to alternative cultural production, however, in films like *Thin Ice* and *Go Fish*, to celebrate lesbianism. Prime-time television, meanwhile, began to include sympathetic lesbian characters in genres such as soap-opera (*EastEnders* and *Brookside*), situation comedy (*Roseanne*) and police series (*Between the Lines*), as well as 'quality dramas' such as *Oranges are Not the Only Fruit*, while Channel 4, in line with its remit to appeal to 'minority' audiences, featured lesbian issues in its Out on Four magazine programmes. Lesbians attained a certain popular 'respectability' with the coming-out of prominent women such as Martina Navratilova and k. d. lang, while some mainstream forms, such as women's magazines, advertising and Hollywood film (for example, *Basic Instinct*) afforded them visibility in the guise of 'lipstick lesbians'. Feminist cultural criticism has taken cognisance of these developments, although it is lesbian collections like *The Good, the Bad and the Gorgeous* (edited by Budge and Hamer, 1994) that have given them prominence.

Feminine forms

Feminist criticism has demonstrated a particular interest in forms and genres specifically directed at a female audience. Genres such as soap opera, melodrama and romance fiction not only foreground the experience of women as their subject-matter, but also address women as readers/spectators. This is clearly of significance in a culture which assumes maleness as a norm; for in these works femaleness is the norm: heroines dominate the narratives, which deal with issues defined as feminine ones (romance and relationships, family and community). But romantic fiction, in particular, poses a problem for feminism. On the one hand, it is not only extremely popular among women readers, it is also largely produced by women. On the other hand, this fiction can certainly be accused of promoting stereotypical definitions of women as primarily concerned with emotional relationships, confined to romance and the family, and of doing so in terms which show women as subordinate to men socially and emotionally.

As long ago as 1971, Germaine Greer in her critique of the hero of romantic fiction, *The Female Eunuch,* held women responsible for their own oppression in this respect:

> This is the hero that women have chosen for themselves. The traits invented for him have been invented by women cherishing the chains of their bondage. It is a male commonplace that women love rotters but in fact women are hypnotized by the successful man who appears to master his fate; they long to give their responsibility for themselves into the keeping of one who can administer it in their best interests (Greer, 1971, p. 180).

That the message of romantic fiction appears to recommend marriage to a domineering man as the pinnacle of women's fulfilment, and that women, far from rejecting this message as so much sexist rubbish, consume such fiction in its hundreds of thousands, can lead to the conclusion that women are their own worst enemies. Critiques by, for example, Margolies (1982: romantic fiction is a plot to keep women unaware of their economic class oppression) or Snitow *et al.* (1984: romantic fiction is pornography for women), also suggest, if they don't actually say, that women readers, in their enthusiasm for such fiction, are colluding in their own oppression. 'Collusion' in domestic violence, 'contributory negligence' in rape: these are concepts feminism has reason to reject; must it not equally reject a cultural criticism that appears to write off millions of women as 'cultural dopes'?

Later feminist work on romantic fiction attempted to explain its appeal to women in terms of its, albeit utopian, engagement with real dilemmas faced by women in patriarchal society. Notable among these were the analyses of Tania Modleski and Janice Radway. Modleski suggests that the narrative of romantic fiction negotiates women's fears of men by interpreting the hero's indifference or hostility towards the heroine as motivated by overwhelming love for her, and that his ultimate submission to her may be read as a fantasy of revenge upon men for their treatment of women (Modleski, 1982, pp. 45–8). Radway's ethnographic study of women readers of romantic fiction focuses on the uses to which women put the practice of reading: these, she suggests, include having time for themselves away from the responsibilities of domestic routines that service men and children, and supplying a basis for a community of women exchanging and discussing the novels (Radway, 1987, pp. 86–7). Ann Gray's research on video-recorders in the home suggested that these functions were similarly served by women hiring 'women's' films to watch together, in a context where male choices dominated video viewing within the family and excluded genres considered to be 'feminine' (Gray, 1987). It has also been suggested that romance makes available to women the pleasures of the erotic in a socially acceptable form: a narrative of sentiment expressed in sensual language (Snitow *et al.*, 1984, p. 249). This is an erotic, however, which is exclusively heterosexual and most frequently informed with disturbingly masochistic implications. In recent years some genres of romance fiction have become more sexually explicit, and there has emerged the successful genre of blockbuster fictions, from Shirley Conran's *Lace* onwards, which makes a more direct address to women readers' desires for sexual fantasy (Lewallen, 1988, p. 101). Women's magazines, too, have become more explicit in their treatment of sex, to the point where not only do glossies like *Cosmopolitan* and *Elle* make stories and features about sex a major selling point on their covers, but the sexual content of magazines for younger readers became a matter of public debate, even in the British Parliament, in 1996.

Not so sentimental soap

It would seem that genres assumed to be addressed to women audiences – such as romantic fiction, melodrama or soap opera – have long served as measures of awfulness, with men (for the most part) deriding them, and women often admitting to liking them (when they do) rather apologetically. Interest in soap operas, however, has not been confined to female critics; the peculiar characteristics of this form (its endlessness, multiple plots, lack of a central protagonist) and its immense popularity (top of the television ratings almost every week) have attracted interest in cultural studies generally (see, for example, Dyer *et al.*, 1981). But, while 'soap' audiences in the 1980s became less gendered, with the inclusion of business plots in American prime time soaps like *Dallas* and *Dynasty* and the cult-like following among young people (male and female) for the daytime Australian ones like *Neighbours* (phenomena which may be linked to changing norms of masculinity) nevertheless, women have traditionally constituted the majority audience for soap opera, and perhaps continue to be considered as such.

Its appeal for women has been explained both in terms of its focus on family, friends and relationships, and its variety of strong female characters. Tania Modleski also saw parallels between the disjointed, repetitive form of 'soap' and women's domestic work (Modleski, 1982, p. 101), while Ien Ang conducted a study of European fans of *Dallas* in a sympathetic attempt to understand its phenomenal international appeal, especially to women (Ang, 1985, pp. 1–12). What these studies have raised are questions both about the criteria for analysing popular texts, and about the pleasures and purposes of those, especially women, who read/watch them. The criteria traditionally employed for evaluating the products of 'high' culture have proved inappropriate for analysing popular culture and its audiences. From assuming a coherently meaningful text which readers must strive to appreciate for their own moral and aesthetic enrichment, attention has shifted to analysing the ways in which, on the one hand, texts may rework ideological positions around, say, gender and gender relations, and, on the other, how readers/ audiences may negotiate their own understandings of these reworkings in deriving their own meanings and pleasures from them. Thus women might derive pleasure from texts reproducing sexist ideology by reading against the grain for humour or fantasy, say, or by identifying with the power of a villain such as the ice-pick murderess in *Basic Instinct*. How women do interpret and enjoy popular cultural texts has become the focus of the growing field of feminist audience studies, which challenges the assumptions of text-based studies that audiences are passive consumers of the media by emphasising the activity of women in reading or viewing in the context of their lives, needs and pleasures. Jackie Stacey's (1994) study of female fans of 1940s female stars is an example of work that has stressed the activity of women as consumers of popular cultural texts.

Women's magazines too are open to opposing interpretations. Here the work of Marjorie Ferguson and Janice Winship may serve as examples. Ferguson defines femininity as a cult, which is preached to women by its high-priestesses, the women's magazine editors. This is a cult which keeps women subordinate to men through its insistence on the sexual/domestic roles of women promulgated everywhere in the magazines from fashion and beauty to cooking and home decor to problem pages and features (Ferguson, 1983, pp. 11–12). Winship's study shows more awareness of the differences between the magazines (Winship, 1987, p. 148). Their historical development demonstrates that ideals of femininity change, though not necessarily entirely to women's benefit, unless it is assumed that pressures to be 'superwoman' in the 1990s are clearly less oppressive than the restriction of women's role to wife and mother in the 1950s. Differences between magazines in their address to women on the basis of age, class, wealth or (feminist) politics, may be seen either as demonstrating a media response to the heterogeneity of female experience, or, alternatively, as showing the extent of the media's co-option of that experience into a more flexible, but no less powerful, ideology of femininity; and one that, on the whole, omits the experience of women who are, for example, Black, lesbian and/or old.

Informing Winship's analysis of the contradictions of this popular feminine genre is the issue of pleasure:

I felt that to simply dismiss women's magazines was also to dismiss the lives of millions of women who read and enjoyed them each week. More than that, I still enjoyed them, found them useful and escaped with them . . . That didn't mean I wasn't critical of them. I was (and am) but it was just that double edge – my simultaneous attraction and rejection – which seemed to me to be a real nub of feminist concern. (Winship, 1987, p. xiii)

It is a 'double edge' that plagues feminist analysis of popular culture, as perhaps of popular culture analyses generally. Our own pleasures, and those of others, constitute a perennial thorn in the flesh of political critique. How are we to explain the pleasures derived from texts that are at best ambiguous, at worst downright reactionary, in respect of their representation of gender? Should we aim to destroy the pleasure because of the politics? Or rescue the politics because of the pleasure?

Comparable problems arise in relation to the politics of appearance. Men wear clothes, adhere to fashion and construct their appearance quite as much as women do;[3] but an *interest* in appearance has become defined as a specifically feminine one. Cultural definitions identifying femininity with an 'attractive' appearance compound this identification. An early, and continuing, feminist response to this has been a rejection of traditionally 'feminine' modes of dressing: the trashing of bras and girdles, for instance, in the first women's liberation media event, and the related development of feminists adopting a mode of visual self-presentation that resisted the feminisation of women: flat shoes, trousers, short hair, no make-up, for example. These could be justified on practical grounds (one cannot run in high heels) or on ideological ones (make-up pandered to the sexual desires of men), although in the end these rationales could probably not withstand logic much better than fashion itself.[4] Feminist challenges to dress codes were subject both to co-option by mainstream culture (as with dungarees, for instances) and to marginalisation through derogatory stereotyping (the tabloids' characterisation of feminists as 'dungareed dykes'). But there were problems from within feminism too: feminist dress can be criticised for aping masculine dress, and/or for establishing an alternative puritanical orthodoxy (see Young, 1988, pp. 178–9). Whether through feminist influence or not, shifts in fashion over the past 25 years have rendered this debate less acute. The greater heterogeneity of fashionable dress codes, with, for instance, flat shoes and loose trousers taking their place alongside mini skirts and lipstick as alternative fashions, means that women are less restricted in their self-definitions through appearance, while effacing any clear distinction between feminist and feminine dress.

The importance of dress as a feminist issue, however, is that it is the one area of representation in which all women participate. We are all obliged, constantly, to represent ourselves by the way we dress. We have to wear clothes, and clothes (whether we wish them to or not) always convey a meaning to others, which is socially constructed and understood, about such factors as age, class, fashionability and so on, and about our attitudes towards these factors. We cannot escape these meanings. At the same time, however, within constraints such as money, availability or work place rules, we can choose what to wear: we decide how to represent ourselves. We are all, therefore, practically and intimately involved in debates about the relations between ideology and pleasure, about defining sexuality, about the ethics of consumerism and, above all perhaps, about whether, and how, to reject or re-evaluate the 'feminine'.

Film form and content

Certain trends in feminist film theory, however, would seem to run counter to the dialectical potential of approaches to 'feminine' forms. While earlier feminist approaches to film, especially in the USA, adopted a liberal model that critiqued images of women in films, some British feminists drew upon French post-structuralist thought and psychoanalytic theory, as these applied to literature and film, and developed a theoretical approach which saw the relationship between form and content in film as so closely interlocked as to require a more radical strategy than merely calling for more 'positive' images of women.

The key article in this approach was Laura Mulvey's 'Visual Pleasure and Narrative Cinema' (Mulvey, 1975), in which she claimed that the cinematic forms of the dominant Hollywood cinema reproduce unequal gender relations through their construction of narratives based on an active male protagonist. The audience are invited to view the action through the point of view of this male protagonist, and – crucially – also to view the woman in the film, who is erotically coded for 'to-be-looked-at-ness', from this male perspective. The pleasures of this structure for the male spectator are divided between identification with the controlling gaze of the male character and the visual pleasure of looking at the body of the female character, a concept known, in Freudian psychoanalytic theory, as scopophilia. Through this organisation of looking in film, women's activity and subjectivity are denied: instead, they are subordinated to the look and the needs of the male. Film thus represents and reproduces the patriarchal power relations of society, in which men act and women are, men look and women are looked at, men's pleasures are served and women's are ignored (Mulvey, 1975, p. 20).

Mulvey therefore concluded that it was necessary not only to destroy the pleasures of mainstream forms through analysis, but also to construct alternative film languages which would deny audiences the familiar pleasures of narrative and scopophilia which depended on, and reproduced, patriarchal power relations (Mulvey, 1975, p. 26). Because these pleasures could not be separated from the artistic forms of patriarchal production processes, these forms could not be utilised for the creation of alternative meanings. In her own film-making practice – in works like *Amy* and *Riddles of the Sphinx* – Mulvey, and others, such as Sally Potter with *Thriller* and *The Gold Diggers* and Lizzie Borden with *Born in Flames,* produced challenging work that aimed to fulfil this brief.

One problem was, predictably, the audience. Distribution of films outside the mainstream commercial cinema circuits severely restricts the size of the potential audience. In addition, most people watch films for pleasure. An aesthetic that deliberately sets out to deny audiences pleasure is likely to confront difficulties. Feminist theory and practice in this respect was part of a general cultural debate in the mid-1970s that questioned the radical possibilities of realism – the most familiar and popular form for dramatised narratives – and recommended an *avant garde* practice in line with Bertolt Brecht's concept of 'alienation', whereby audiences were distanced from the spectacle and action and required not to identify *with* it, but to think *about* it. Using also Roland Barthes' distinction between *plaisir* (comfortable pleasure) and *jouissance* (ecstasy that disturbs) (Barthes, 1975, p. 14), radical critics called for texts to be 'open' rather than 'closed', to reject what Colin MacCabe called the 'hierarchy of discourses' whereby audiences are directed towards understanding a text to have one, unambiguous, meaning (MacCabe, 1976, p. 34). The 'closed' text is one which, by means of its consistent characterisation and/or realist *mise-en-scène,* and its coherent narrative, which is resolved at the end, directs the audience towards one particular meaning. This, it was alleged, was inherently conservative; a genuinely progressive text would discomfort the audience by requiring them to confront contradiction and irresolution, rather than fulfilling their expectations regarding narrative coherence and resolution. In so far as gender definitions are embodied in narrative forms and aesthetic regimes, it was therefore necessary for feminist work to reject these forms and regimes in order to destabilise cultural definitions of femininity and masculinity. A new, non-sexist society would require a new non-sexist conceptual order of meaning, value and aesthetics, which could not be created within forms that embodied patriarchal meanings, values and pleasures; a new language was needed.

The resulting deliberate denial of familiar sources of pleasure in these *avant garde* feminist works meant that even among the minority who saw them, there would be many who were frustrated and/or bewildered by a novelty of form which made them difficult to understand. In so far as the aim was to challenge and redefine the ways in which gender is represented, its radical impact could be seen as limited, not only by the size of the audience but also by its necessarily elite nature.

However, the development of alternative, feminist, venues for exhibiting these films – at women's events, in educational contexts, on British television's Channel 4 – has secured a significant and growing audience for these and other feminist films. It is, however, important to note that alternative feminist film practice has not been confined to the *avant garde.* The past 25 years in Britain, and more especially in North America, Europe and Australia, have seen a burgeoning of women's films in a variety of forms – documentaries, cartoons, educational films, and full-length feature films – which are neither *avant garde* nor mainstream entertainment. The development of video has been of great significance not only in facilitating the production of films relatively cheaply, but also in enabling them to be used in community and educational contexts. This has increased many women's awareness of what film can do, and of the narrowness of the codes and conventions within which mainstream cinema functions. It is also a powerful demonstration of how a range of approaches can interact to effect significant change: the political activism of women's groups, the establishment of Women's Studies, the exploration of theories of representation, the utilisation of new technology; all may be seen to be involved in this particular development.

Moving in on the mainstream

Meanwhile, mainstream cinema has itself extended the scope of its representations of women. Perhaps our perspective on film's portrayal of women has been skewed by the powerful stereotyping of the 1950s, for, as Molly Haskell (Haskell, 1973) and others have demonstrated, there were many strong, independent female stars and roles in movies up to and including the 1940s (Joan Crawford, Bette Davis, Katharine Hepburn, Marlene Dietrich, Barbara Stanwyck). However, even where the narrative did focus on the powerful woman, this was too rarely in a positive sense; most often she was morally flawed in ways that led to her death or defeat. Even rarer was the portrayal of female solidarity: except occasionally in melodrama (*Imitation of Life,* for instance) and comedy (for example, *Stage Door, Gentlemen Prefer Blondes*), women were shown as relating predominantly to men, or, if to each other, as rivals.

Perhaps in response to feminist pressure from within the industry, perhaps sensing a new demand from women audiences, commercial cinema, like television, now includes a significant minority of works which treat women and women's issues seriously. Notable among developments in the past two decades has been the portrayal of women as the central protagonist in a variety of narrative forms. Sigourney Weaver in *Working Girl,* the *Alien* trilogy and *Copy Cat*, Jodie Foster in *Silence of the Lambs* and *Nell*, Jamie Lee Curtis in *Blue Steel*, Whoopi Goldberg in *Sister Act*, Nicole Kidman in *To Die For* and Sharon Stone in *Basic Instinct* are just a small sample which may indicate the range of genres featuring strong female protagonists, while on British television the work of Lynda La Plante, in particular, has featured strong women on both sides of the law (*Widows* and *Prime Suspect*, for example). Women's issues have also received serious treatment in mainstream film and television drama. *The Accused* addressed the issue of rape; domestic violence was the subject of *Dirty Weekend, Sleeping with the*

Enemy and *Ladybird, Ladybird* and British soaps like *Brookside* have also had story lines dealing centrally with these issues. Perhaps equally important is the fact that mainstream forms tend increasingly not to use violence against women unproblematically as a source of entertainment, as was only too common in earlier film and television production, from the 'comic' effect of James Cagney thrusting a grapefruit into Jean Harlow's face to, for example, Clint Eastwood raping a woman who is 'asking for it' in *High Plains Drifter*.

From *Turning Point* and *Julia* in the 1970s to *Desperately Seeking Susan* and *Beaches* in the 1980s, and *Thelma and Louise* in the 1990s, we can now see portrayals of women as committed to and supportive of each other, including, as we have seen, some sympathetic portrayals of lesbian relationships. Most remarkable, perhaps, was Spielberg's adaptation of Alice Walker's *The Color Purple*. Here was a film centred predominantly and sympathetically on relationships between Black women, produced by a white man, which attained huge box office success (if also considerable critical controversy).

It may be argued that British soaps and sitcoms such as *The Liverbirds* and *Birds of a Feather* have established a tradition of women-centred communities. However, these are preceded and outweighed by such classics as *Hancock's Half Hour*, *The Likely Lads* and *Steptoe and Son* (all featuring forms of male bonding) and have continued to compete with heterosexual coupledom (for example, *Keeping Up Appearances* with its negative stereotype of a snobbish middle-aged woman) and male bonding in sitcoms such as *The Young Ones* and (more ambiguously) in *Men Behaving Badly*. American sitcoms too, such as *Kate and Allie*, *The Golden Girls* and *Roseanne*, increasingly featured women at the centre, and dealt with issues such as single-parenthood, old age and working-class family life.

Television, however, has also been a site for the development of female comedy (a notoriously male-dominated genre). From Victoria Wood, Dawn French and Jo Brand in Britain to Joan Rivers, Cybill Shepherd and Ruby Wax in the USA, female comics have now become household names, and if a disproportionate number of these were 'fat' women, we may also note the unforgettably scandalous image of middle-aged women created by Jennifer Saunders and Joanna Lumley in *Absolutely Fabulous*.

None of these mainstream developments, in fact, has been received by feminists without reservation. Many have been seen as sanitising or glamorising feminist issues; of having had to compromise too much with the commercialism of the project. Intervention in popular cultural production has continued to be a matter of debate within feminist criticism. Whether workers within the representational arts should strive for inclusion within the mainstream and risk compromising their principles, or should risk marginalisation by pursuing their artistic consciences, is a common dilemma for those excluded from mainstream cultural production. Rozsika Parker and Griselda Pollock's summing up of the problem for visual artists could apply to all women working in cultural production: 'Should women artists' energies be directed towards gaining access to the art establishment, demanding full and equal participation in its evident benefits, exhibitions, critical recognition, status – a living? Or, instead, should their efforts be channelled into their independent and alternative systems of galleries, exhibitions, educational programmes?' (Parker and Pollock, 1981, p. 135). Their conclusion is that these are 'differing strategies' rather than oppositions. Globally, this is clearly true: a multifaceted oppression requires a multifaceted response. But for individual women the choice and the judgement still remains to be made on an ongoing basis, in the context of their specific financial and other resources.

The problem is not fully solved in those cases where minority culture succeeds in entering the mainstream. Rather, new problems arise around issues of context and commercialism. Texts change their meaning according to context, so that when, for example, dungarees were taken up as high street fashion for all women, they ceased to be able to signify a feminist resistance to feminine dressing. Commercial success may similarly affect a work's political meaning. Cindy Sherman, for example, has expressed dismay at the popularity of her work:

'The more horrific works came out of a feeling that everyone accepted my stuff too easily. I was deliberately trying to be antagonistic towards collectors and critics. I thought, right, let's see if they want to shell out money for *this*' . . . As it turned out, all of New York wanted to shell out and cash in on Cindy Sherman. (Rumbold, 1991, p. 28)

The commercial success of some feminist fiction has raised similar problems. Angela Carter and Alice Walker are avowedly feminist writers whose work asks awkward questions within feminist debates. Carter tackles the dangerous ground of female desire in her fiction, so what happens when a male film director adapts a short story for a commercial film? Maggie Anwell has argued that the film of *Company of Wolves* distorts the delicacy of Carter's challenge to feminist debates around female sexuality (Anwell, 1988, p. 81). Walker's challenge, in showing Black women oppressed by Black men, has been to the male-dominated Black politics of the 1960s that subordinated Black women's struggle to Black (male) struggle; but in representing the Black woman's experience, she was also participating in the debate within feminism about the dominance of white women in defining issues concerning women. Whether or not the complexities of this debate were faithfully reproduced in Spielberg's film of *The Color Purple* (and this is much debated), it is significant that, with the exception of Whoopi Goldberg's subsequent films, Black women still feature in mainstream film culture rather less than do Black men.

Feminist critics, then, are far from agreed on particular texts or strategies. While there is some welcome evidence of feminist influence in the representations of women as powerful and independent in television series as different as *Cagney and Lacey*, *Prime Suspect* or *Absolutely Fabulous*, or in blockbuster fiction instead of Mills & Boon, in *Marie Claire* as opposed to *Woman's Own*, these works can alternatively be accused of having co-opted elements of feminism and harnessed them to a non-feminist message which, for example, reinforces patriarchial stereotypes or patriarchal values such as competitiveness. Not only might the sympathetic portrayal in fiction of a female cop or business tycoon be seen to validate the patriarchal hierarchies within which they operate, it can also be argued that the heterosexual glamour of the cop or tycoon reinforces women's need to be not only glamorous, but also competent and clever. Moreover, such images of superwomen do little to shift regimes of representation which exclude categories of women from being defined positively within the culture: old, poor or lesbian women, for example, receive no validation from images such as these.

However, it may sometimes seem that, in maintaining a necessary alertness to the possibilities of co-option by the dominant ideology, feminist criticism is bent on driving all cultural production into a no-win corner: damned if you do enter the mainstream, damned if you don't; damned if you show women succeeding, damned if you don't; damned if you show women as victims, damned if you don't.

Not that staying *out* of the mainstream solved the problem: Judith Williamson's criticism of Mulvey's film, *Riddle of the Sphinx* – a decidedly *avant garde* work (Williamson, 1986, pp. 131–44) – and the fairly widespread criticism of Judy Chicago's *The Dinner Table* (consisting of a huge triangular dinner table with place settings representing famous women throughout history) is evidence enough that, however consciously feminist in intention and uncompromisingly 'alternative' in form, no work can be guaranteed to deliver an acceptably feminist message to all feminists.

Post-modern Madonna?

One strategy for negotiating this impasse might be identified in the concept of post-modernism, which has proved to be of particular interest to feminist cultural criticism, although, again, not without reservations. Because post-modernism rejected the 'grand narratives' of human progress formulated by thinkers in the Enlightenment tradition, it led to the decentring of the Western male individual on which they were based. Previously marginalised as 'the other', women and Black people were, as a result, placed centre stage and seen to possess a perspective not only equal to, but privileged over, that of the now discredited 'norm' of white masculinity. This subaltern voice speaks both from within and outside the dominant culture, so that, unlike the singular vision of mainstream masculine rationality, it expresses a double consciousness. Post-modernist culture is thus characterised by irony, quotation and excess; it may be nostalgic, irreverent, playful, even super-ficial: all qualities which challenge rational assumptions that meaning can be produced or communicated in a straightforward way. To undermine the stability of meaning in this way is, it is claimed, to undermine the social order that it underpins. Post-modernism is therefore seen as facilitating a feminist critique of masculinist definitions of gender by destabilising the male-defined traditions of representation from within those traditions themselves. This is what Linda Hutcheon refers to as postmodernism's dual features of 'complicity and critique' (Hutcheon, 1989, p. 11: see also Chapter 3).

We may take as an example the star image of Madonna, which can be read as a post-modern text that plays with cultural definitions of femininity so as to undermine them. By combining in her attire such disparate signifiers as lace gloves, crucifix, leather jacket and mini skirt, Madonna calls into question the ability of these items to define women as particular types. By having performed in underwear that resembles armour, with suspenders as outerwear, she displayed a female sexuality that, in its aggressiveness, mocks men's assumptions that women's sexuality is a spectacle for their benefit. (The male reviewer of her Blonde Ambition tour who complained that he didn't find her outfit attractive would seem to illustrate the point rather nicely!) The frequency with which Madonna changed her image might itself be read as an ironic comment on a society that focuses so much on 'image', or as depicting the unstable and fragmented identity of contemporary life, or as mocking social constructions of femininity. If Madonna's images, like her performances, are multiple and ironic, then her display of sexuality can be enjoyed for its outrageousness: if this is woman displaying her sexuality for the delight of men, it is simultaneously mocking that display.

Or is it? Might it not equally be interpreted as an excuse for reproducing the same old sexist stereotypes which we can now enjoy again, precisely because we 'know' (don't we?) that they are not to be taken seriously? The 'complicity and critique' of post-modern cultural production enables it to offer the pleasures of popular forms while simultaneously mocking them, thus undermining the ideologies embedded in them. But the question is, of course, whether the mockery really does challenge the ideology, or whether, as with kitsch, we can have our cake and eat it. Did Madonna, for instance, offer a mockery of conventional femininity, or just another way to be fashionable and 'sexy'? Did she present a parody of stardom, or a model of it?

Perhaps post-modern cultural theory may be accused of underestimating the critical potential of popular cultural texts. If Madonna's pastiche of Monroe in her 'Material Girl' video is post-modern irony, what of Monroe's original performance in *Gentlemen Prefer Blondes*? Is this not also ironic about female sexuality in its display of a glamour addressed to men combined with cynical advice addressed to women, and in a film featuring female solidarity at its centre, with the Jane Russell character controlling the gaze?

Developments in cultural studies have demonstrated that few texts are entirely straightforward: there is always some degree of polysemy, some room for disagreement about meaning, some element of internal contradiction, some potential for an interpretation that goes against the grain of the apparently intended meaning. Ideology is inherently contradictory, and sexism is no exception. Where earlier feminist analysis concentrated on identifying the reproduction of gender ideologies in representations of women, later work has also been concerned to reveal the contradictions in these representations, and to demonstrate that, however sexist a text may appear to be, it cannot conceal all the contradictions of the ideology it embodies.

Janey Place, in her discussion of *film noir* heroines, concluded that, while the narratives often destroy the sexually aggressive woman, the films' visual style reinforces an image of the women characters as 'deadly but sexy, exciting and strong' (Place, 1980, p. 54). Similarly, it has been argued that it was the resistance of, say, a Doris Day role to the machinations of the predatory male, or, as in *Calamity Jane*, to the social demands of femininity, that characterised her star image rather than the 'happy ending' in which she submits to marriage and femininity (Clarke *et al.*, 1982, p. 36). Many star images have embodied contradictions that problematise, even if they do not mock, social constructions of gender: Garbo and Dietrich, for instance, with their suggestions of androgyny; the strength of a Bette Davis or Joan Crawford; the *femme fatale*'s control over men; even Monroe, sold as a sex symbol for male consumption, but appropriated both as a symbol of male exploitation of women and of capitalist exploitation of the individual. Or audiences may 'use' a text in unintended ways: the male gay appropriation of Judy Garland, for example, or the phenomenon of the 'cult film'; and did audiences take Johnny Weissmuller's Tarzan any more seriously as a model of masculinity than contemporary audiences do the excesses of a Stallone or a Schwarzenegger?

Inasmuch as narrative depends on some form of conflict, or at least the rectification of a disruption in order, knowledge or control, then the mere *fact* of this conflict or disruption puts in question the values that the ending will resolve; that the resolution is necessary at all is presumably because the values are, or are *felt* to be, in question. If the hero has to prove his masculinity through victory of some sort, then his masculinity cannot be taken for granted. If the romantic heroine has to work, through the narrative, to get her man, then it cannot be assumed that heroines automatically do get 'their' men. Underlying the simplest narratives then, such as an adventure story or a romance, is an unspoken insecurity: there would be no story if there were no doubt about the outcome. Perhaps in some genres there appears to be no doubt, even from the beginning (we know the detective or the romantic heroine will 'get his/her man'); and in less formulaic works there can be no doubt by the end of the narrative, once the hero or heroine has triumphed or failed. Narrative forms work precisely to conceal the doubt that men are necessarily masculine and heroic, or that women are necessarily feminine and desirable, and to affirm a *natural* connection between biological sex and cultural constructions of gender. If, in a global sense, they are often successful, still there lurks within them, at some level, their own negation.

This applies to other cultural forms. Consider, for example, Mulvey's point about the controlling male gaze: in analysing the structure of looking in mainstream cinema, she demonstrates how women may be seen as subjected to the male gaze (Mulvey, 1975, p. 19); but may we not also read this relation of looking as one where the woman simultaneously controls the desire of the man, so that what we are dealing with here is less simple than a one-way power relationship? Is one necessarily in control of a situation because one is in control of the gaze? Are gazes – even male ones – always, as she assumes, 'controlling'?

Conclusion

In a society characterised by gender inequality, we are likely to find this inequality reproduced in representations. We are also likely to find challenge and change, though with unevenness and contradiction. If this means that we can never find an instance of totally feminist representation – by which I mean one that is not only not sexist, but also counters all forms of oppression of women, omitting no woman's plight – then we would be in danger of feeling that feminism confronted an impossible task. But if we recognise that sexism itself, however ubiquitous, is also a leaky system, then we can admit that its contradictions give rise to some privileges for some women: queens, prime ministers, film stars, heiresses, leisured upper-class wives; and, at more mundane and ambiguous levels, women's greater rights to custody of children, their greater choice of dress styles, their lower incidence as prisoners, their greater facility for forming expressive relationships and freedom to express their emotions. Such 'privileges' do not come without a price, or, usually, without a struggle; but the possibility of struggle, the mere existence – let alone the achievements – of feminism, demonstrates the 'leakiness' of patriarchy.

At the representational level too women are not without their 'privileges': the tradition of using women as symbols of nations, virtues, trades; fictional heroines from Shakespeare's Rosalind to Tolstoy's Anna Karenina; the mythic status of stars like Garbo, Callas or Monroe. Feminist appropriation of the culture's language and images about women has not had to rely entirely on reversing negative meanings. There has always been sufficient ambiguity in the culture's regime of representations overall to enable feminism to find ammunition within them that can be turned against the patriarchal system of meanings; these reversals may constitute very small victories, or ones liable to further co-option, but they are victories nevertheless, interventions in what is not, in effect, a totally closed system.

This is not to deny that feminists still have far too much to be angry about: racism in its myriad manifestations continues to oppress Black women; heterosexuality functions as a norm that constantly marginalises lesbians; women in general are still the victims of poverty and sexual violence. In the field of representation, 'serious' news and current affairs is still predominantly presented by men; 'page 3' is still a feature of Britain's most popular daily newspaper and the pornography industry continues to prosper. It may be difficult to regard representational strategies such as role reversal or post-modern irony as adequate responses to such injustices. And feminism is about finding adequate political responses to the oppression of women, whereas popular cultural representations are not only about politics and ideology, but also – and embedded within these – about pleasure and aesthetics.

In seeking to use the media which patriarchial society has established as embodying pleasure and beauty, or in challenging them through the forging of alternatives, feminism is confronted with contradictions and risks. But then, would we be content to hope for a feminist culture which doesn't take risks? Much of the most challenging work which has engaged with gender issues, whether avowedly feminist or not, is that which has taken the greatest risks and has attracted criticism, including from feminists; contradictions produce controversy. And without contradictions, without debate and difference, feminism, like any other movement, would die. The Greenham women took risks; the women who disarmed a bomber destined for genocide in East Timor took risks. And writers like Angela Carter, exploring women's sexuality, take the risk of confirming myths about female masochism; Fay Weldon did not allow her 'She-Devil' a wholesome recovery from her husband's betrayal, but drove her instead to an agonising pursuit of physical beauty and a deplorable revenge; Alice Walker took the risk of feeding racist myths by writing about Black men's abuse of Black women. Artists like Judy Chicago use vaginal imagery and the traditionally feminine 'crafts' of embroidery and pottery and (it seems) other women's labour: is this celebratory of female identity, or a reduction of women's experience to the genital, or – in the hushed environment of a gallery – an ironic comment on the masculine norms of the art establishment? Photographers like Jo Spence and Cindy Sherman use themselves as models in images that can be accused of being narcissistic, embarrassing, ugly, to challenge our conceptions of what a photograph is or should be. Film-makers like Marleen Gorris (*A Question of Silence, 1982*) confronting women's violence or Rose Troche (*Go Fish*, 1994) depicts lesbian sexuality. Jennifer Saunders and Joanna Lumley created caricatures of middle-aged femininity. k.d. lang and Della Grace risk reinforcing stereotypes of the 'masculine' lesbian. All these are examples of feminist cultural producers who do not offer us easy answers. Rather, they challenge us to confront the difficult questions that feminism itself presents us with; they force us to think about what it means to be a woman in our society, whether we want to change that meaning, and if so how. And this, I think, is how we would wish to be represented, to ourselves and to others: as fully conscious human beings, struggling with the contradictions of our existence. This is, in fact, who we are, and it is in our interests that feminist culture should represent us as such.

Notes

1. This is not intended to imply that women are always somehow coerced into relationships with men; only that even our most intimate decisions may not be quite as 'free' from social forces as we might assume.
2. See, for instance, Sheila Rowbotham on her relationship to mascara, in Rowbotham (1973) pp. 44–5.
3. Consider, for example, the daily construction of men's faces through shaving.
4. It is not, for instance, self-evident that trousers are always more comfortable than skirts, and dungarees in particularly are decidedly inconvenient at times.

Further reading

Baeher, Helen & Ann Gray (eds), *Turning It On: A Reader in Women and Media*, (London, Arnold, 1996). A useful reader which discusses many key issues and theoretical approaches to the study of women and the media.

Cook, Pam & Philip Dodd (eds), *Women and Film: A Sight and Sound Reader*, (London, BFI, Scarlett Press, 1994). An anthology with a diverse selection of essays on women and film from cinema's earliest days to the present.

Gamman, Lorraine and Margaret Marshment (eds), *The Female Gaze: Women as Viewers of Popular Culture* (London, The Women's Press, 1988). A collection of essays produced in response to Mulvey's argument about the 'male gaze', examining popular film and television texts.

Zoonen, Liesbet van, *Feminist Media Studies* (London, Sage, 1994). This book gives a critical introduction to the relationship of gender, media and culture, outlining major themes and feminist theory and research in various areas.

7

Sexuality and Feminism

Diane Richardson

In recent years there has been a growth of interest in sexuality within and across many academic disciplines: for instance, in cultural studies and literary criticism (Butler, 1990, 1993; Sedgwick, 1990, 1993; Garber, 1993), geography (Bell and Valentine, 1995), architecture (Colmina, 1992), sociology (Giddens, 1992; Hawkes, 1996) and social policy (Cooper, 1994; Carabine, 1995, 1996b). A great deal of the impetus for this new interest has come from feminist research and theory on sexuality, as well as from lesbian and gay studies. It is not difficult to see why this should be so. Sexuality has long been a major issue within Women's Studies, feminist theory and politics. Feminists, in examining specific issues such as prostitution, birth control, sexual violence, pornography, AIDS, heterosexuality and lesbianism, have asked the question 'What is the relationship between sexuality and gender inequality?' Indeed, it is this question which perhaps more than any other has provoked discussion and controversy within feminism.

Most feminists would agree that men's power over women, economically and socially, affects sexual relationships; generally speaking women have less control in sexual encounters than their male partners and are subjected to a double standard of sexual conduct which favours men. Where feminists tend to differ is over the importance accorded sexuality in understanding women's oppression. For many radical feminists sexuality is at the heart of male domination; it is seen as a key mechanism of patriarchal control (Rowland and Klein, 1996). Indeed, some writers have argued that it is *the* primary means by which men exercise and maintain power and control over women. Catharine MacKinnon's work, for example, has been significant in the development of such an analysis (1982/1996). Others have been reluctant to attribute this significance to sexuality (for example, Segal, 1987, 1994; Rowbotham, 1990b).[1] They prefer to regard the social control of women through sexuality as the outcome of gendered power inequalities, rather than its purpose. What is less agreed upon, then, is the extent to which sexuality can be seen as a *site* of male power, as distinct from something patriarchal power acts upon and influences.

This tendency to see sexuality as constitutive of male power has its roots in radical feminism. Central to most radical feminist accounts is the view that sexuality, as it is currently constructed, is not simply a reflection of the power that men have over women in other spheres, but is also productive of those unequal power relationships. In other words, sexual relations both reflect and serve to maintain women's subordination. From this perspective the concern is not so much how women's sex lives are affected by gender inequalities but, more generally, how patriarchal constructions of sexuality constrain women in many aspects of their lives. It may influence the way we feel about our bodies and our appearance, the clothes we wear, the work we do, our health, the education we receive, our leisure activities, as well as the relationships we feel able to have with both women and men.

For instance, it is becoming clearer how sexuality affects women's position in the labour market in numerous ways; from being judged by their looks as right (or wrong) for the job, to sexual harassment in the work place as a common reason for leaving employment (see Chapter 11). Other writers have examined the ways in which girl's educational opportunities are restricted by the exercise of male sexuality. Sue Lees's work (1986, 1993), for example, shows how boys control girls' behaviour in the classroom through their use of the sexual double standard. Women's social lives and leisure opportunities are also affected by fears of sexual violence, especially around being out alone after dark (Green, Hebron and Woodward, 1990). Such fears police women's behaviour in other ways: for example, restricting their access to public space, where they choose to sit on a bus or train, how they sit and who they avoid eye contact with. Also, when we talk about reproductive rights we are not simply talking about better health service delivery or sex education, we are also talking about the role (hetero)sexuality plays in the oppression of women. As Jalna Hanmer points out in Chapter 16, the focus on the control of women's fertility through contraception, abortion and sterilisation masks the issue of men's assumed 'right' of sexual access to women. Related to this, women's health concerns reflect men's power in sexual encounters. As Holland *et al.'s* (1992, 1994) study of young women and sexual risk demonstrates, this is a major constraint on women's ability to protect themselves against AIDS through practising safer sex.[2]

These are some examples of how sexuality, as it is currently constructed, functions in the social control of women. However, the forms of control of women are likely to be different in different cultures and historical periods. For example, in the past, control over women's sexuality was linked to hereditary rights. If a woman had sex outside marriage there was no way that her husband could be sure that any children she had were his rightful heirs. For the wealthy at least, this is one reason why great emphasis was placed on the need for female chastity. Nowadays women may no longer be encased in chastity belts, but the notion of women's sexuality as the property of men still underpins many laws and social customs. The view that a husband cannot be guilty of raping his wife is a classic example of this (a view which the English courts upheld until 1991, when rape within marriage became unlawful).

Equally, sexuality as a mechanism of patriarchal control will not have the same significance for all women in any given historical period or culture. There may be important differences between women in relation to class, 'race', age, ethnicity, sexual identity and being differently bodied. For example, under slavery in the USA, Black women were generally considered to be the property of male white slave owners and, as will be discussed later, were often sexually exploited and abused by them (hooks, 1982). We therefore need to recognise and examine how racism, as well as class position, intersects with gender and sexuality. As Patricia Hill Collins (1990, 1996) has pointed out, for Black women racism informs their experience of male control of women's sexuality; they are subject to sexualised forms of racial oppression and racialised forms of sexual oppression. Thus, for example, sexual violence has specific meanings for Black and white women. When a Black woman is sexually harassed or abused by a white man, for instance, it is often racist sexual violence that she experiences (Hall, 1985). (For further discussion of related issues see McClintock, 1995; also Chapter 2 in this volume.)

Analyses of sexuality as a mechanism of social control are not new within feminism. Many nineteenth-century feminists were concerned with how women's lives were controlled by 'male lust' and sought to change sexual relations between women and men. They attacked the sexual double standard and drew attention to the ways in which sex was dangerous to women; in particular through the debilitating effect of repeated pregnancies and infection from venereal diseases such as syphilis. The proposed solution was male sexual control; hence the slogan 'Votes for Women and chastity for men'. Few feminists at that time demanded a wider knowledge of birth control and the availability of contraceptives, which would have reduced the risk of unwanted pregnancy. On the contrary, many feminists opposed contraception. They were concerned to protect women from the unwanted sexual demands of men and the possible consequences of an increase in men engaging in extra-marital sex, in particular the risk of getting sexually transmitted diseases and the loss of financial and emotional security if the marriage broke up (Jeffreys, 1985; Gordon and DuBois, 1992). In the early twentieth century there were signs of a shift in emphasis; support for access to contraception grew and there was a greater insistence by some feminists on the importance of sexual pleasure for women (although for the most part this was defined in terms of heterosexual relationships).

Since the nineteenth century then, debates and divisions have existed among feminists over the issue of sexuality. More recently, as I have indicated, feminists have debated the significance given to sexuality in understanding women's oppression, as well as specific issues such as pornography and heterosexuality. However, before examining some of these debates in more detail, we first need to ask which theories of sexuality predominate.

What is sexuality?

At first glance the answer to this question might seem obvious. Sexuality is often talked about as if it were simply a case of 'just doing what comes naturally'. This is often referred to as an *essentialist* view of sexuality. From this perspective, sexuality is conceptualised as an instinct or drive which demands fulfilment through sexual activity. A further assumption is that it is 'normal' and 'natural' for this instinctual urge to be directed at the opposite sex. It is, essentially, a heterosexual drive. Sexuality is, ultimately, a reproductive function, with vaginal intercourse *the* sex act. Society, in so far as it is seen as having an effect, modifies the expression of sexuality through repressing or controlling drives or urges that are pre-given and pre-social. Sexuality is a 'natural phenomenon'; universal and unchanging, something that is part of the biological make up of each individual (although it is assumed that men, in general, have a stronger sexual drive than women). There has also been a division of sexual attributes based on 'race' and class as well as gender. Historically, Black women, particularly African and Afro-Caribbean women, have been portrayed as highly sexed, lascivious and promiscuous (hooks, 1996). Such ideas about Black women's sexuality, and related images of the Black male 'stud', reflect deep-rooted racist notions that Black people are less civilised and closer to nature, having an untamed, animal sexuality (Collins, 1996). Similarly, it has often been assumed in the past that the 'working classes' are less sexually responsible as a result of being less able to control their sexual 'urges' (Weeks, 1990).

This essentialist model of sexuality has been critiqued by feminists and others who have argued that sexuality is socially constructed. To say that sexuality is socially constructed means that our sexual feelings and activities, the ways in which we think about sexuality, our sexual identities, are the product of social and historical forces. Just as with other aspects of social life, sexuality is shaped by the society and culture in which we live; religious teachings, laws, psychological theories, medical definitions, social policies, psychiatry and popular culture all inform us of what sexuality is. Moreover, we learn not just patterns of behaviour, but also the erotic meanings associated with those behaviours in any given social and cultural context.

This is not to say that biology has no influence on sexuality; clearly there are limits imposed by the body. The point is that the body, its anatomical structure and physiology, does not directly determine what we do or the meaning this may have. The capacities of the body gain their power to shape human sexual behaviour through the meanings given them in particular historical, cultural and interpersonal contexts.

Consider, for instance, the 'discovery' of the G-spot first described by Ernst Graffenburg in the 1950s and subsequently popularised as 'the G-spot' by Ladas, Whipple and Perry (1982). This term refers to a region of the front wall of the vagina which swells during sexual arousal and, it is claimed, is highly sensitive to stimulation. The fact that it is a sensitive part of a woman's body does not, by itself, motivate us to seek it out and touch it. Indeed, many women still do not know it exists. That some have spent time searching for their G-spot (and there are books and equipment to help them in their quest), and enjoy being touched there as part of their experience of sexual desire, is a good example of the social construction of sexuality. The G-spot is physiologically the same as it was before it was 'discovered', but it has a different social significance. By giving sexual meaning to a particular bodily region or function we produce sexuality; we construct desire.

Within the umbrella term 'social constructionist' there are a variety of different perspectives, including discourse analysis, psychoanalytic and symbolic interactionist accounts. They all adopt the view that patterns of sexual behaviour may vary over time and between cultures, and that 'physically identical sexual acts may have varying social significance and subjective meaning depending on how they are defined and understood in different cultures and historical periods' (Vance, 1989, p. 19). A kiss is not just a kiss, as time goes by!

Anthropological studies have demonstrated that there is enormous cultural variation in what is defined as 'sex'; why people have sex; how often they have sex; whom they have sex with; and where they have sex (Caplan, 1987). Historical studies of sexuality have also provided support for this perspective. For example, work on lesbian and gay history suggests that far from being 'natural' and universal categories, heterosexuality and homosexuality are social constructions. Although there is some disagreement between writers as to precisely when the idea of the homosexual person emerged, the general belief is that, in Europe at least, the use of the term 'homosexual' to designate a certain type of person is relatively recent, having its origins in the seventeenth to nineteenth centuries, with the category lesbian emerging somewhat later than that of the male homosexual. A seminal paper on this was by Mary McIntosh (1968), reprinted in Stein (1992). Further discussion of the emergence of such categories can be found in Foucault (1979), Faderman (1981), Jeffreys (1985), Weeks (1990), Baum Duberman, Vicinus and Chauncey (1991) and Plummer (1992). See also Bleys (1996) for an historical account of how racialised views of non-Europeans are linked with the modern construction of homosexual identity.

Such analyses allow us to see female sexuality as socially constructed rather than as repressed (a view which, as will be seen later in the chapter, was evident in early feminist work on sexuality). These arguments suggest that in many historical periods and cultures a woman who has sex with another woman may not think of herself, or be regarded as a lesbian. Whilst same sex behaviour may have always existed, it seems that an identity as lesbian or gay or, by implication, heterosexual, is historically and culturally specific. Ideas about, and the experience of, sexuality shift historically.

The view that sexuality is socially constructed is central to most feminist analyses of sexuality. Indeed, it reflects the conceptualisation of sexuality as a political issue: if sexuality is socially constructed then it can be reconstructed in new and different ways; sexuality need not be coercive or oppressive, it can be changed. However, even within feminist work, questions of essentialism have arisen. For example, critics have pointed to problems of essentialism within some feminist reworkings of psychoanalytic theory (Stacey, 1993). There has also been an unfortunate tendency to misrepresent radical feminist analyses of sexuality as essentialist or biologically determinist. (For a detailed discussion see Thompson, 1991, 1996; Richardson, 1996b). What this also highlights is that essentialism and social constructionism are not two distinct and opposing positions (Fuss, 1990). These are relative terms (though I would suggest it may make more sense to talk of theories being more or less essentialist than more or less constructionist) and it may be more helpful to think of a social constructionist/ essentialist continuum along which theorists may be placed. For instance, some 'social constructionists' may accept the notion of an innate sexual drive, albeit a drive that takes different cultural forms.

The most radical form of social construction theory suggests that there is no 'natural' sexual drive which it is said, to varying extents, we all possess as part of our biological make-up and is either expressed, or repressed. Sexual drive is itself a historical and cultural construction. John Gagnon and William Simon's (1973) early work on 'sexual scripts' adopted this position. Writing from a symbolic interactionist perspective, they argued that not only do we learn what 'sex' means, and who or what is sexually arousing to us, but we also learn to want sex. Whilst they acknowledged that biologically the body has a repertoire of gratifications, which includes the capacity to have an orgasm, Gagnon and Simon claimed that this does not mean that we will automatically want to engage in them. Certain gratifications will be selected as 'sexual' through the learning of 'sexual scripts'. A particular experience, say kissing, would not be repeatedly sought after in the absence of any meaningful script. It is the giving of social meaning to bodily functions and activities, pursing our lips and moving them about, which creates the motivation to repeat the experience. From this perspective, socialisation is not about learning to control an inborn sexual desire so that it is expressed in socially acceptable ways, but the learning of complex sexual scripts which specify the circumstances which will elicit sexual desire and make us want to do certain things with our bodies. What we call 'sexual drive' is a learnt social goal.

Unlike Sigmund Freud, who claimed the opposite was true, Gagnon and Simon's early work also suggested that sexuality is a vehicle for expressing non-sexual motives and desires; in particular, those linked to gender roles. Thus, they argued that men frequently express and gratify their 'need' to be masculine, a 'real man', through sexuality. Feminist theories of sexuality do not generally disagree with this: they do, however, explain it in the context of a wider understanding of structural inequality. Feminist theories of sexuality are not only concerned with describing the ways in which our sexual desires and relationships are shaped by society; they are also concerned to identify how sexuality, as it is currently constructed, relates to women's oppression. From this perspective, the way men behave sexually is not seen as simply the result of a certain form of upbringing, a certain kind of 'sexual script' learning to which notions of gender are central; it is also a product of gendered power differences (Holland *et al.*, 1996).[3]

The discursive challenge to essentialist theories of sexuality, characterised by the work of Michel Foucault and his followers, does engage with questions of power. Foucault (1979) argues against the notion of a biological sexual drive. He claims that by taking 'the sexual' as their object of study various discourses, in particular medicine and psychiatry, have produced an artificial unity from the body and its pleasures: a compilation of bodily sensations, pleasures, feelings, experiences, and actions which we call sexual desire. This fictional unity, which does not exist naturally, is then used to explain sexual behaviour and sexual identity.

Foucault also rejects the idea that this so-called essential aspect of personality has been repressed by various kinds of discourses on sexuality; for example, the law or the Church's teaching on sexuality, or medical and psychiatric accounts. It is not that sexuality has been repressed, he argues; rather it is through discourses on sexuality that sexuality is produced. In the case of women's sexuality, for example, Foucault argues that it has been controlled not by denying or ignoring its existence, through a 'regime of silence', but by constantly referring to it. It is discourses of sexuality which shape our sexual values and beliefs. 'Sex' is not some biological entity which is governed by natural laws which scientists may discover, but an *idea* specific to certain cultures and historical periods. Thus, what 'sexuality' is defined as, its importance for society and to us as individuals, may vary from one historical period to the next.

Foucault believes then, as do interactionists, that sexuality is regulated not only through prohibition, but produced through definition and categorisation, in particular through the creation of sexual categories such as 'heterosexual', 'homosexual', 'lesbian' and so on. He also draws attention to the fact that the history of sexuality is a history of changing forms of regulation and control over sexuality. For example, over the last hundred years there has been a shift away from moral regulation by the Church to increased regulation through medicine, education, psychiatry, psychology, social work, the law and social policy.

In theorising sexuality, many feminists have made use of Foucauldian perspectives (for example, Hollway, 1984; Smart, 1992; Carabine, 1996b). A major appeal of Foucault's work for feminists, 'lies in his radical anti-essentialism and his view of power as constitutive of sexuality, rather than merely repressive' (Jackson, 1996b, p. 25). At the same time, feminists have also found Foucault's work problematic (see Ramazanoglu, 1993b). A major criticism is that he is gender-blind in failing to examine the relationship between gender inequality and sexuality. Neither does his account of the different discourses on sexuality pay much attention to the fact that women and men often 'have different orientations to sexuality, even different discourses' (Walby, 1990, p. 117). In Foucault's work, sexuality is not understood as gendered; it is a unitary concept and that sexuality is male. Feminist critics have also pointed out how Foucault's account of the construction of the 'homosexual' category similarly ignores lesbians, implicitly encoding homosexuality as male (Fuss, 1990).

The psychoanalytic challenge to essentialism is associated with the reinterpretation of Freud by Jacques Lacan. For Lacan and his followers sexual desire is not a natural energy which is repressed; and it is language rather than biology which is central to the construction of 'desire'. Lacanian psychoanalysis has had a significant influence on the development of feminist theories of sexuality (see Grosz, 1990; Chodorow, 1992). The early work of Juliet Mitchell (1974, 1982), Jane Gallup (1982) and Rosalind Coward (1983), among others, as well as that of French feminist writers such as Julia Kristeva, Hélène Cixous and Luce Irigaray, have all been influenced by Lacan's work at some stage, even if they have subsequently moved on.

Although it is the Lacanian tradition which has usually been drawn on most in feminists' attempts to use psychoanalytic theory in understanding sexuality, some feminist writers have placed greater emphasis on pre-Oedipal traditions in psychoanalytic thinking (Benjamin, 1990). Others, writing from a post-modernist perspective, have also been critical of Lacan's work, especially his ideas on the signification of the phallus. Judith Butler's work (1990, 1993) has been particularly important in this respect. In a similar vein, some have criticised feminist psychoanalysis for privileging heterosexuality and failing to rescue lesbianism from being seen as a pathology (Hamer, 1990) although more recently, feminist writers such as Elizabeth Grosz (1991) have examined ways of 'stretching the limits of psychoanalytic theory' in order to explore its usefulness in developing lesbian theory. For a discussion of recent uses of psychoanalytic theory in feminist analyses of sexuality see Hollway (1996).

Sexuality and power

As I have already noted, feminists have critiqued essentialist understandings of sexuality and have played an important role in establishing a body of research and theory which supports the view that sexuality is socially constructed. However, it is not enough simply to say that sexuality is socially constructed, we have to decide what it is constructed from. It is argued by feminists that sexuality has been constructed in the interests of men and, consequently, is defined largely in terms of male experience.

This was an important aspect of feminist analysis of sexuality in the early 1970s; the main problem was that sexuality was 'male-defined', privileging male pleasure and defining 'women's sexuality as existing to serve male sexual "needs"' (Jackson and Rahman, 1997, p. 206). Women were encouraged to 'reclaim' their own sexuality for themselves; a sexuality that had been suppressed and denied them. As Sheila Jeffreys comments: 'These early feminist thinkers saw sex as something that women had been shut out of. Women had not been allowed the delights that men had taken for granted. Sex was an equal rights issue' (Jeffreys, 1990, p. 236).

Many feminists in the early 1970s also made a connection between what they understood to be the suppression of women's sexuality and social powerlessness. They believed that (re)discovering one's 'true sexual potential' would empower women, giving them greater confidence and strength in other areas of their life (Segal, 1987, 1994). With hindsight, many feminists have since questioned how beneficial the so-called 'sexual revolution' of the 1960s was for women (Campbell, 1980; Ehrenreich, Hess and Jacobs, 1987; Jackson and Scott, 1996b). More fundamentally, some have criticised the association of sexual liberation and women's liberation, asserting that sexual liberation has never been in women's interests (Jeffreys, 1990, 1994). Others would claim this is too pessimistic a view, which undervalues the significance for women of certain 'gains' of sexual liberalisation during that period, such as changes in abortion and divorce laws and attitudes towards lesbians (Walby, 1990; Segal, 1994).

The end of the 1970s saw a change of emphasis in feminist theory and practice regarding sexuality. The focus shifted from an attack on the sexual double standard and the assertion of women's right to sexual freedom and pleasure, towards new analyses of male sexuality and its material effects on women, involving a more detailed analysis of the relationship between sexuality and power (see, for example, MacKinnon, 1982). In particular, feminists debated the sexual objectification of women in pornography and its effects, the institution of heterosexuality, and sexual abuse and violence, drawing parallels between 'normal' ideas and practices of (hetero)sexuality and the latter. Feminists claimed that power and domination were central to the current construction of both male and female sexuality. They highlighted how, as part of their socialisation, boys learn that having sex with a woman, but more especially vaginal intercourse, is a central aspect of becoming and being masculine (see, for example, Jackson, 1982).[4] That this remains the case is clear from recent feminist research (for example, Lees, 1993; Holland *et al.*, 1996), which has highlighted how sexuality continues to be an important means of boys and men proving themselves as 'real men', with all the privileges, status and rewards that implies. By being (hetero)-sexual, a man affirms his status and power over others and his identity as masculine.

In drawing attention to the connections between sexuality and power, feminists also critiqued the idea that male dominance in sexual relations is 'natural': that men are naturally the 'dominant' or 'active' partner, whereas women are sexually 'submissive' or 'passive'. Within the works of sexologists and sex-advice writers, for example, there is a long history of assuming the relationship between sex and power to be natural, normal and inevitable; essential to sexual arousal and pleasure (Jackson, 1994). In criticising ideas and assumptions contained in essentialist discourses of sexuality, feminists have sought not only to develop alternative perspectives but, moreover, to show how such discourses are implicated in women's subordination, pointing out, in this case, how the idea that it is natural for men to sexually dominate women, and that women want and enjoy this, can easily be used to legitimate sexual violence.

Feminists have directly challenged other traditional, taken-for-granted assumptions about sexuality. As implied above, female sexuality has conventionally been defined as different from, yet complementary to, male sexuality. Sex is seen as both more important and uncontrollable for men than it is for women, this being the result of men's greater sexual 'urges'. The message is that men have powerful sexual urges which they find difficult to control. Women, who are not so troubled, should be aware of this and should not provoke men to a point where they can no longer be held responsible for their actions.[5] This is evidenced in the way that women often get blamed if men sexually harass them, and in the way men's sexual violence against women has often been seen as an understandable, if not acceptable, reaction to female 'provocation'. Common myths are that women provoke men by the way they dress, by leading men on, and by saying no when they really mean yes (see Chapter 8). An important consequence of such ideas, then, is that, by deflecting responsibility from men, women are placed in the role of 'gatekeepers', with responsibility for both their own and men's sexual behaviour. Arguably, this enables individual men to deny responsibility for sexual abuse and insist that they were misled or 'provoked'; victims of women or their own sexual 'natures'.

In much the same way, women have traditionally been expected to take responsibility for birth control, especially since the advent of the contraceptive pill. Similarly, underlying most 'safer sex' campaigns there appears to be tacit acceptance that men are 'naturally' less able to exercise self-control when it comes to sex than are women (Scott, 1987; Richardson, 1989, 1996a). Such ideas are important in understanding other forms of behaviour. For example, both pornography and prostitution are sometimes regarded as providing 'sexual release' for men who might otherwise be 'driven' to sexually harassing women or raping them.

Feminist research, as I have already pointed out, has highlighted how essentialist understandings of sexuality serve to 'naturalise' certain forms of male sexual behaviour that are oppressive to women and function as a form of social control. They have also drawn attention to the ways in which they influence how women 'define, resist, cope with and survive their experiences' (Kelly, 1988a, p. 34). For example, it is not uncommon for women who have experienced sexual abuse and/or violence to blame themselves initially. Similarly, the belief that men have strong sexual desires which women are responsible for controlling or 'provoking', coupled with the expectation that women have an obligation to meet men's sexual 'needs', helps to explain why women can find it difficult to refuse unwanted sex and/or insist on the kind of sex they would like. They may also find it difficult to refuse men because they fear the consequences: for instance, the threat of (or actual) violence or their partner rejecting them. It is for these sorts of reasons that many feminists cannot accept the liberal view that 'anything goes' between consenting adults in private. In the context of unequal power relations between adults in terms especially of gender, 'race' and class the notion of 'consent' remains problematic.

In recent years there has been a shift in focus in feminist perspectives on sexuality towards greater discussion of sexual pleasure (there are echoes here of the late 1960s and early 1970s when, as I have already outlined, many feminists saw the search for women's sexual satisfaction as an important feminist goal). This was signalled by the publication of the edited collection *Pleasure and Danger. Exploring Female Sexuality* (Vance, 1984/1992), which contained papers from a controversial conference on the politics of sexuality held at Barnard College, New York in 1982. In arguing for greater recognition of sexuality as pleasure, many writers claimed that too much emphasis had been placed on sexual danger during the late 1970s and early 1980s; in particular feminist debates about sexual violence and the meaning and effects of pornography. (The disagreements and divisions over the issue of sexual pleasure – often referred to now as the 'feminist sex wars' – crystallised in the 1980s over issues such as sadomasochism and 'feminist pornography', as well as defences of sexual roleplaying.) The contemporary emphasis on pleasure, however, would seem in many cases to represent a more explicit rejection or backlash against earlier (especially radical) feminist work, which is accused of being sex-negative or anti-sex. (This and other (mis) representations of radical feminist work is discussed in more detail in Richardson, 1996b: see also Chapter 3 in this volume.) Other feminists are concerned about the focus on sexual pleasure, because they regard 'pleasure' as a problematic concept for women under patriarchy and question the emphasis on the right to sexual pleasure as counterproductive to women's liberation (MacKinnon, 1982, 1996; Jeffreys, 1990, 1994).

On this and on other sexual issues it is clear that as well as many common themes running through feminist analyses of sexuality, there have been, and still are, major disagreements between feminists over what a feminist sexual politics should be. Nowhere have these been more apparent than in feminist debates over heterosexuality and pornography.

Heterosexuality

The view that heterosexuality is a key site of women's oppression (see, for example, Walby, 1990; Delphy and Leonard, 1992) is widely accepted within feminism; indeed, some have argued that it is *the* most important institution of patriarchy (Brunet and Turcotte, 1988). Within most feminist accounts, heterosexuality is seen not as an individual preference, something we are born like or gradually develop into, but as a socially constructed institution which structures and maintains male domination, in particular through the way it channels women into marriage and motherhood. Similarly, lesbianism has been defined not just as a particular sexual practice, but as a form of political struggle; a challenge to the institution of heterosexuality and a form of resistance to patriarchy.

Having said this, the critique of heterosexuality, and its role in the control and exploitation of women, has been one of the major areas of disagreement/debate between feminists. This was particularly evident during the 1970s with the emergence of critiques which highlighted heterosexuality as an oppressive institution. This represented a far more fundamental critique of heterosexuality than the previous focus on sexual practice. Indeed, some feminists argued that, if heterosexuality is key to male dominance, feminists should reject sexual relationships with men. In the USA, the classic 'Woman-Identified Woman' paper by Radicalesbians, written in 1970, asserted that 'woman-identified lesbianism' was the political strategy necessary for women's liberation and the end to male supremacy. The implication for heterosexual feminists was that they should give up relationships with men and put their commitment, love and emotional support into relationships with women (Radicalesbians, 1973). In Britain, similar ideas were put forward in a paper, first published in 1979, by the Leeds Revolutionary Feminist Group (Onlywomen Press, 1981). The paper, entitled 'Political lesbianism: the case against heterosexuality', proposed 'political lesbianism' as a strategy to resist patriarchy.[6] It stated that all feminists can and should be political lesbians because 'the heterosexual couple is the basic unit of the political structure of male supremacy . . . Any woman who takes part in a heterosexual couple helps to shore up male supremacy by making its foundations stronger' (Onlywomen Press, 1981, p. 6). A political lesbian was defined as 'a woman-identified woman who does not fuck men'; it did not necessarily mean having sexual relationships with other women. In some ways this compares with the strategy of those nineteenth century feminists who advocated voluntary celibacy and spinsterhood as a form of resistance to the sexual subjection of women.

Within hegemonic heterosexual relationships women are expected to service men emotionally and sexually. Men also gain from material servicing; it is women who are primarily responsible for housework and for the work of caring for family members, including male partners (VanEvery, 1995, 1996). This has implications for women's economic independence, in terms of the relationship between women's unpaid domestic labour and their position in the labour market (see Chapter 11). Clearly for women to withdraw *en masse* from such relationships *would* be revolutionary, even if some men could afford to pay for such services. However, as many feminists pointed out at the time, 'political lesbianism' is not a choice that is equally open to all women. This is another way of saying that heterosexuality and, by implication, lesbianism is structured by 'race', class, ethnicity, and age. For instance, is it an accident that nineteenth-century spinsters were, in the main, from middle-class backgrounds; or that 'celebrated' lesbians such as Radclyffe Hall and Lady Una Troubridge in the 1920s and 30s, were white women of independent means who could afford such a lifestyle?

In addition to the charge of ignoring differences and divisions between women, many heterosexual feminists were extremely angry and critical of such analyses of heterosexuality, arguing that they contravened the women's liberation movement's demand for the right to a self-defined sexuality (an argument that has been used in more contemporary feminist debates around pornography, butch/femme and sadomasochism). What right had one woman to tell another what to do sexually? Some also argued that heterosexuality could be a political practice or choice, a view which has emerged more recently in attempts by some heterosexual feminists to theorise heterosexuality (see, for example, Robinson, 1993).

Some lesbian feminists also reacted angrily to the arguments for political lesbianism (see Onlywomen Press, 1981). Part of their concern was that lesbianism was becoming associated with a critique of heterosexuality, a rejection of men, and feelings of sisterhood with other women, rather than a 'specific sexual practice between women, with it's own history and culture' (Campbell, 1980, p. 1). Nevertheless, the suggestion that 'Any woman can be a lesbian' did represent an important challenge to traditional assumptions about lesbianism as an immature or pathological condition of a minority group of women. By providing a political analysis of sexual relationships between women, feminism not only helped to destigmatise lesbianism, it also broadened its meaning. In other words, the women's movement not only helped lesbians to feel more positive about themselves and to 'come out', it also 'opened up the possibility for lesbian relationships for many women who had previously considered their heterosexuality a permanent feature' (Stacey, 1991).

In focusing on the 'political lesbianism' debates, we should not ignore the fact that, as I indicated earlier, in the early 1970s many heterosexual feminists as well as lesbians voiced criticisms of heterosexuality; however, this was largely as a form of sexual practice. In particular, they challenged the centrality of sexual intercourse in heterosexual relations, pointing out that very often this is not the major or only source of sexual arousal for women. Anne Koedt, for example, in a now-famous article, criticised 'the myth of the vaginal orgasm' and stressed the importance of the clitoris for female pleasure (Koedt, 1974/1996). However, despite Koedt's acknowledgement of the implications for lesbianism, such discussions were often focused on how to get men to be better lovers through improving their sexual technique, rather than on any fundamental criticism of heterosexuality. The important concern was establishing women's right to sexual pleasure, primarily within a heterosexual context.

In a radical and highly influential article first published in 1980, Adrienne Rich examined the institutionalisation of heterosexuality, suggesting that heterosexuality may not be a 'preference' at all but something that 'has had to be imposed, managed, organised, propagandised, and maintained by force' (Rich, 1981, p. 20). She went on to describe some of the factors which 'force' women into sexual relationships with men rather than women. For example, a sexual ideology which presents heterosexuality as 'normal' and lesbianism as 'deviant'; the unequal position of women in the labour market; the idealisation of heterosexual romance and marriage; the threat of male violence which encourages women to seek the 'protection' of a man; and men's legitimising of motherhood.

It is often felt that heterosexual women are being criticised by feminists who argue that heterosexuality is oppressive to women; but this is to miss the point. It is the *institution* of heterosexuality, which creates the prescriptions and conditions in which women 'choose' heterosexuality, which is being challenged. Related to this, it is also important to understand that critiques of heterosexuality, particularly those by lesbian feminists, are not aimed simply at getting a better deal for lesbians through challenging heterosexual privilege. The argument is that heterosexuality as it is currently constructed restricts *all* women's lives, albeit to varying extents.

Having said this, there has been a distinct lack of heterosexual feminist work on this subject and, until very recently, almost all feminist analysis of heterosexuality was written by lesbians (Douglas, 1990). In the last few years however the picture has begun to change with a growth in feminist writing on this subject (see, for example, articles in Wilkinson and Kitzinger, 1993 and Richardson, 1996e; Segal, 1994; Jackson, 1996b, 1996c; Smart, 1996a, 1996b). In addition to re-examining 'old' questions such as whether being a feminist and heterosexual is tenable, this recent output of work has tended to focus on sexual experience and practice, particularly on desire and pleasure, both in terms of a critique (Kitzinger and Wilkinson, 1993; Jeffreys, 1996) and a defence (Segal, 1994; Hollway, 1993, 1996). Some writers, however, have been more concerned with theorising the ways in which heterosexuality is institutionalised in society; how this is implicated in women's subordination and how heterosexuality as social practice constitutes gender (Carabine, 1996b; Richardson, 1996c; VanEvery, 1996). A good summary of recent analyses of heterosexuality within feminist theory is Jackson (1996b).

In addition to critiques of heterosexuality as an institution and a form of sexual practice, some feminists have also challenged the heterosexual bias of social theory, including a great deal of feminist work (see Sedgwick, 1990; Richardson, 1996c). For example, writers like Susan Cavin (1985) and Monique Wittig (1992) have criticised many theories about the origins of women's oppression because they assume heterosexuality to be universal. Other feminist work can be similarly criticised for assuming the universality and normality of heterosexuality. For example, much of the feminist work on the impact on women's lives of providing family and informal care can be criticised for its focus on the heterosexual family (Carabine, 1992).

There have also been similar attempts by proponents of queer theory to problematise heterosexuality. Queer is associated with the emergence of a new politics of identity in the 1990s which emphasises the fragmentation and fluidity of identity. New political movements concerned with sexuality, especially the impact of AIDS, have arisen; for example, ACT UP, Outrage, Lesbian Avengers and, in the USA, Queer Nation. In part, this shift is associated with the influence of post-modern critiques of earlier feminist and lesbian/gay thinking about gender and sexuality, especially the focus on disrupting binary categories such as woman/man, feminine/masculine; heterosexual/homosexual, straight/gay (for a discussion see McIntosh, 1993a; Wilton, 1996; see also Chapter 3). In trying to achieve this, some writers have emphasised subversive gender performance as disruptive of conventional sexual and gender binary divisions (see Butler, 1990; Doan, 1994); especially through parody (as distinct from imitation) and 'playing with gender', in particular through butch, femme and drag. This has prompted questions about the usefulness of subversive performance as a political strategy and, related to this, whether transgression is necessarily transformative. For further discussion and critiques of such developments see, for example, Wilson (1993a); Lamos (1994); Jeffreys (1996).

In terms of queer theory, as distinct from queer politics, there are both differences and overlaps with feminist critiques of heterosexuality. Feminists tend to privilege gender – the woman/man binary – and regard sexuality and gender as analytically interconnected. The focus is on how the construction of heterosexuality both privileges and disempowers women. Queer theorists, on the other hand, tend to privilege sexuality – the heterosexual/homosexual binary – and, whilst acknowledging the importance of gender, suggest that sexuality and gender can be separated analytically. The focus here is on how the construction of heterosexuality privileges some women *and* men and disempowers others. (Gayle Rubin's controversial early work (1984) raised similar questions within feminist debates on sexuality.) Michael Warner (1993) provides a useful account of attempts within queer theory to theorise heterosexuality.

The attempts by both feminists and proponents of queer theory to problematise heterosexuality have helped to deconstruct heterosexuality as a monolithic category. Although, within feminism, the focus has been on the interaction of heterosexuality and gender, more recent work has emphasised the need to examine how the experience of institutionalised heterosexuality informs, and is informed by other social divisions, especially 'race' and class position (see Richardson, 1996c and Chapter 2 in this volume).

Heterosexuality as a form of oppression has also been shaped by the history of racism, and consequently it does not take the same form for Black and white women. Racist stereotypes of Black people as primordially sexual have provided white men with a way of deflecting responsibility for racial sexual abuse and exploitation on to Black women; white man's desire for Black women has been blamed on her sexuality, her lasciviousness (Collins, 1990, 1996). They have also fuelled white racism directed at Black men, as well as patriarchal control of women's sexuality. For instance, under slavery Black women were often forced to have sex with white slave owners; those who resisted risked being tortured and punished. Sexual exploitation was part of their enslavement (hooks, 1992, 1996). While white men assumed the 'right' to have sex with their Black women slaves, it was considered unthinkable that white women should do the same thing with Black men. Indeed, Black men were likely to be severely punished if it were suspected they had made a sexual advance towards a white woman. For example, in the USA earlier this century many Black men were lynched and publicly castrated as a way of 'protecting white womanhood' (Simson, 1984). White fascination with and fears about Black male sexuality, although likely to be different for white women and for white men, continues to influence social attitudes and practices (for instance, the belief that Black men are more likely to perpetrate sexual assaults or rape).

The fact that sexual ideologies are racialised – and vice versa – has different implications for Black women and for Black men. (Having said that, the dominant view of Black sexuality as hyper-*hetero*sexuality helps to render both Black lesbians and Black gay men invisible.) The association of 'masculinity' with 'virility', and male sexuality with power and dominance, means that being stereotyped as a 'stud' is likely to have a certain appeal to many men, especially if opportunities to achieve social and economic status are restricted. The sexual double standard means that the attraction for

Black women of being defined in sexual terms is limited; often eliciting contempt and sexual harassment/abuse. Black feminists in particular have addressed these issues, criticising some Black men for their deployment of dominant images of Black masculinity (Bryan, Dadzie and Scafe, 1985).

Pornography

The anti-pornography movement, which emerged in the USA in the late 1970s, was a dominant issue for feminists in the West during the 1980s. Unlike opponents of pornography on the 'moral right', who object to its sexually explicit nature and its lack of religious values, feminist opponents object to the sexist and misogynist (woman-hating) nature of most pornography, which frequently depicts women as 'commodities' for male consumption who enjoy being dominated and humiliated. Some feminists have also drawn attention to the racist imagery in pornography (Forna, 1992). Patricia Hill Collins (1990) argues that an analysis of racism is essential to an analysis of pornography; it is not simply that racism has been 'grafted onto pornography', it is fundamentally implicated in its symbolic depictions, most obviously in the frequent use of master-slave imagery.

Most feminists would agree that pornography is sexist and racist; where disagreements often arise is over how important an issue pornography is for feminism. Opinion differs as to whether pornography actually causes women's oppression, or is merely a reflection of men's greater power in society generally. Andrea Dworkin (1981), in an early influential work, argued that pornography is the principal cause of women's oppression, because it legitimates women as the property of men and as subordinate to them. She claimed that it is a violation of women as human beings and an encouragement to men to treat women as inferior and in abusive ways. More recently, feminists such as Catherine MacKinnon (1989), Catherine Itzin (1992), Diana Russell (1993) and Kathleen Barry (1995, 1996), as well as Dworkin herself (1996), have continued to argue for feminist action against pornography on the grounds that it is a core dimension of the oppression of women. Other feminists, however, regard the significance attached to pornography by feminists such as these as misguided; they argue that although pornography may mirror the sexism of society, it does not create it (see, for example, Rodgerson and Wilson, 1991; Segal and McIntosh, 1992).

Another long-standing debate within feminism is whether there is a direct link between pornography and men's violence against women. Anti-pornography feminist writers have argued that pornography causes violence towards women (both involved in or abused as a result of pornography; see Brownmiller, 1976; Dworkin, 1981; and see also Everywoman, 1988; Itzin, 1993). Others claim that the evidence for this is unclear and unconvincing (Segal 1990a). (See also King, 1992, for a critical review of studies which attempt to demonstrate a relationship between pornography and sexual violence.) Some feminists would also claim that, whether or not it can be proven that there is a connection between consuming pornography and subsequent acts of violence, pornography should be opposed on the grounds that it is violence against women (Dworkin, 1981, 1996; Barry, 1996).

Even if it is not easy to prove conclusively a direct connection between the reading or viewing of pornography and specific acts of violence, it can still be argued that pornography is harmful in perpetuating a system of ideas and beliefs which are constitutive of male power. Deborah Cameron and Elizabeth Frazer (1992), for example, argue for moving beyond simplistic 'cause and effect' notions towards a more sophisticated analysis of the links between representation and behaviour, suggesting that pornographic representations provide scripts which violent men can utilise. In other words, some anti-pornography feminists would also claim that, at a less direct yet wider level, pornography harms women as a social group, by shaping male attitudes towards women and sexuality which are implicated in their subordination.

Also hotly debated is the question of what strategies should be used to oppose pornography. Some feminists want to make the production and sale of pornography illegal. In the USA, anti-pornography ordinances (laws which apply only to specific cities) were drawn up in 1983 by Andrea Dworkin and Catherine MacKinnon. The laws were aimed at preventing the distribution of pornography on the grounds that it is a violation of women's civil rights and the right not to be sexually discriminated against (Smart, 1989a). Although their attempt subsequently failed, it provoked fierce argument between feminists who support the introduction of laws against pornography and those who describe themselves as anti-censorship. Feminists against censorship believe that the introduction of such laws would be both ineffective (a ban on pornography would simply push it underground) and dangerous to women's interests, in so far as such laws could be co-opted by conservative, right-wing movements to censor feminist opinion, as well as lesbian and gay materials. Women's health books, for instance, containing information about issues such as birth control, abortion or lesbianism might be deemed pornographic and banned. Some have cited the *Butler decision* in Canada as evidence of this possibility[7]. Related to this, some feminists have also argued that there is a danger of an apparent alignment with religious and right-wing movements (Segal, 1990b; Rodgerson and Wilson, 1991), some going so far as to say that feminists campaigning against pornography are in collusion with them (Smith, 1993). Anti-pornography feminists have insisted that pornography is a political, not a moral, issue, thus distancing themselves from comparison with the right. In the UK, feminists who are anti-pornography campaigners have also been at pains to deny charges of collusion with the right (Jeffreys, 1990; Kelly, 1992b), some arguing in turn that feminists against censorship can be seen as aligning with libertarians and pornographers.

Instead of seeking anti-pornography legislation, feminists against censorship advocate restricting public access to pornography and increased public discussion to stimulate awareness of why feminists object to it. In reply, anti-pornography feminists would ask why feminists against censorship have not taken a similar stand against laws aimed at preventing racial hatred? As Andrea Dworkin comments 'why they think race hate laws aren't censorship laws, why it's all right to propagate agitations of hatred against women but not on the basis of race' (Dworkin, 1991).

There has not been a campaign in Britain on a par with that in the USA; nonetheless a similar division of opinion exists, though perhaps not to the same extent as in the USA, between feminists involved in the Campaign against Pornography (CAP), and Feminists Against Censorship (FAC).[8] Whilst the latter are critical of attempts to use the legal system, others argue that it is possible and necessary to press for changes in the law. A recent focus of concern has been the 'globalisation' of pornography, through the widening availability of pornography through new mediums such as video, but more especially computer imagery and the Internet (Butterworth, 1993).[9] For further discussion of the historical differences between feminists over the issue of pornography and suggested strategies to oppose it, see Chester and Dickey (1988).

Other feminists have criticised the focus on pornography as a 'single issue', and have argued for the need to incorporate feminist action against pornography within a wider critique of representations of women, such as in advertising, films and television programmes. More contentious is the suggestion that feminists should produce 'feminist pornography' (McIntosh, 1996). Providing critiques of the views of women and sexuality contained within pornography, and their possible effects, is not enough. It is argued that we need to create alternative forms of erotic representation, in order to produce a feminist pornography/erotica which expresses women's sexuality in words and images of our own choosing, and transforms the meanings and power relations typically manifested in pornography and other representations of sex in the process (see also Myers, 1989; Smyth, 1990). (The issue of what is pornography and what is erotica, and whether it is possible to make a distinction between the two, is another area of debate between feminists.) Such arguments are associated with a more general shift towards deconstructive, post-modern accounts in feminist theory and a currently fashionable 'politics of signification', which suggests that we can effect social change through transgressive or subversive representations (performances) of gender. This stance is often associated with Judith Butler's work (1990, 1993), though she has since disputed this reading of it (see also Jeffreys, 1996c; Richardson, 1996, for further discussion). It is in this context that we have witnessed the emergence of pornography and erotic fiction by and for women, but more especially lesbian pornography/erotica (Reynolds, 1991; Bright and Posener, 1996; Nestle, 1996). As with the subject of pornography generally, the question of whether there can be a feminist erotica or pornography has been hotly contested. Similarly, where lesbian pornography and erotica are concerned the arguments have, at times, been deeply divisive (Dunn, 1990; Richardson, 1992).

Conclusion

In this chapter I have tried to show how over almost three decades 'second-wave' feminists have been concerned, in various ways, with analysing and politicising sexuality. Feminists have emphasised how sexuality, which is commonly regarded as something that is private and personal, is a public and a political issue. They have challenged traditional assumptions about sexuality (for instance, the notion of sex as equalling intercourse and women as sexually passive), and proposed new ways of understanding sexual relations. In particular, feminist theory has problematised heterosexuality and redefined lesbianism. As well as giving new meaning to these sexualities, feminists have engaged in a whole variety of debates and campaigns around sexuality. As part of the desire for greater knowledge and control over our own bodies, feminists have campaigned for access to free contraception and abortion, as well as better sex education for women. Sexual violence has been placed on the public agenda largely as a result of the efforts of various feminist groups who have campaigned for changes in the law (over marital rape, for example), as well as for changes in policy and practice. Feminist services have been developed: refuges for women who have been sexually abused, rape crisis lines, and self-help groups for women who are survivors of sexual violence. Feminists have also campaigned against pornography, for the rights of lesbians, and for an end to sexual violence, as well as the right to sexual pleasure. They have drawn attention to issues such as sexual harassment at work and in education, and to the fact that many of women's health concerns are closely connected to sexuality.

Despite these achievements, it is clear that we need to continue to develop feminist critiques of sexuality. Many issues have not been adequately explored or theorised, such as the way in which heterosexuality interacts with other social divisions such as 'race', class and age, and the effects of 'globalisation' on sexuality: in particular, the impact of travel and sex tourism by especially Western males, sex in Cyberspace and its effects on sexual identities and communities, the impact of changing notions of citizenship and national status, as well as challenges to the sexual/social binary. Part of achieving this is to advance the current debate on sexuality. As Jackson and Scott (1996a) note, this is fundamental to feminism and Women's Studies.

If we are to appreciate the complexity and diversity of women's lives and the relationship of sexuality to other aspects of women's subordination, a great deal more work needs to be done. (Jackson and Scott, 1996a, p. 26).

Notes

1. This strand of radical feminism has also been criticised for underestimating the significance of other factors, such as women's unequal position in the labour market and their domestic roles within the family (for example Segal, 1987, 1990b; Rowbotham, 1990b), although such criticisms are rendered less significant if we acknowledge the interrelationship of those factors with sexuality (see, for example, Chapter 11). Some feminists have also suggested that other forms of oppression may be experienced as more significant for Black women (see Chapter 2). Women who stress sexuality as a form of social control have also been criticised for neglecting the pleasures of sexuality (Vance, 1992; Hollibaugh, 1996).

2. A wider discussion of the issues raised by AIDS for feminist theory and practice can be found in the edited collection *AIDS: Setting a Feminist Agenda* (Doyal, Naidoo, and Wilton, 1994).

3. In this respect many feminists would criticise Gagnon and Simon and others for relying on socialisation as the explanation of male sexuality and lacking a concept of power. Another criticism made of symbolic interactionist accounts like Gagnon and Simon's is that they fail to explain where these 'sexual scripts' come from. In particular, in describing different sexual scripts for women and men they do not provide an analysis of why they differ and why they take the form they do, as well as the functions this may serve. Some of these criticisms are addressed in an elaborated version of 'scripted theory' in Simon (1996).

4. This is evidenced in the way men often brag about sexuality and talk of sex as if it were about totting up 'scores'. The language used to describe sexual encounters also reflects this; boys and men often talk of 'having' or 'taking' a woman. It also manifests itself in many forms of harassment of women, from wolf whistles to sexual gestures or comments.

5. Such assumptions influence how we define women's sexuality in the broadest sense. For example, the view of sex as something that is done to a woman by a man implies that lesbian relationships are not an authentic form of female sexuality. Indeed, hegemonic ideas about heterosexuality structure and organise understandings of lesbian relations (Butler, 1993; Richardson, 1996c), as, for example, copycat relationships built upon masculine and feminine types.

6. A similar debate occurred in France at this time, focused around the publication of Monique Wittig's *The Straight Mind*. For a brief discussion see Jackson and Scott (1996a), and Wittig and Dhavernas in that volume.

7. In 1992, the Canadian Supreme Court's *Butler Decision* unanimously adopted an equality approach to pornography's harms to women. For a discussion of this ruling and how it differs from the anti-pornography ordinances they drafted, see MacKinnon and Dworkin (1996).

8. Another campaigning group is the Campaign Against Pornography and Censorship, which broadly shares CAP's analysis but also is against censorship. Having said this, feminists in CAP do not necessarily support censorship. For an outline of anti-pornography initiatives in the UK see the Appendices in Itzin (1993).

9. There is also concern that different regulations within the European Union, in the context of a 'free market economy', will lead to a shift towards liberalising restrictions on access to pornography in many countries, as has been witnessed in recent years in many Eastern European countries following social and political reorganisation.

Further reading

Sheila Jeffreys, *The Lesbian Heresy. A Feminist Perspective on the Lesbian Sexual Revolution* (London, The Women's Press, 1994). This book examines debates concerning sexuality within lesbian feminism, including the controversies surrounding the impact of sexology on the construction of lesbian identity, the politics of lesbian erotica, S/M, butch and femme roleplaying, drag and transsexualism. It also looks in a critical way at the impact of post-modernist ideas, in particular at the politics of transgression. As in her earlier work, *Anticlimax: A Feminist Perspective on the Sexual Revolution* (London, The Women's Press, 1990), Jeffreys posits the view that the 'sexual revolution', far from bringing liberation and fulfilment, has actually upheld male power and reinforced women's subordination. Also useful is Margaret Jackson, *The Real Facts of Life: Feminism and the Politics of Sexuality* (London, Taylor & Francis, 1994).

A very different stance is taken by Lynne Segal in *Straight Sex: Rethinking the Politics of Pleasure* (London, Virago, 1994). This book explores the shifts and divisions in feminist thinking and practice around sexuality and desire since the 1960s. In seeking to rethink sexual liberation as 'progressive' in terms of contemporary feminist politics, Segal explores a range of issues, including debates about heterosexuality, pornography, the influence of sexology, pychoanalysis and discourse theory on theorising sexuality, the contribution of lesbian and gay studies, as well as post-modern influences such as queer theory.

Carol Anne Douglas, *Love and Politics: Radical Feminist and Lesbian Theories* (San Francisco, ism Press, 1990). This book provides an overview of radical and lesbian feminist theoretical positions over 25 years, and looks at ideas on love and sexuality as well as divisions between feminists on these issues.

Stevi Jackson and Sue Scott (eds), *Feminism and Sexuality. A Reader* (Edinburgh University Press, 1996). This Reader brings together feminist writings on sexuality representing key issues and debates over the last 25 years. The readings are arranged around four main themes: Essentialism versus Social Construction; Affirming and Questioning Sexual Categories; Power and Pleasure; and Commercial Sex; they cover issues such as pornography, prostitution, sexual violence, heterosexuality and lesbianism, AIDS, Cybersex, queer theory, and the international sex industry. There is a useful introductory essay by the editors which summaries feminist debates on sexuality since the 1970s.

Diane Richardson (ed.), *Theorising Heterosexuality* (Buckingham, Open University Press, 1996). This book provides a critical examination of recent debates about heterosexuality, in particular within postmodern, feminist and queer theory. As well as examining the relationship between heterosexuality and feminism, heterosexuality is theorised in terms of its institutionalisation within society and culture, as sexual desire and practice, and as identity.

Gail Hawkes, *A Sociology of Sex and Sexuality* (Buckingham, Open University Press, 1996). This book offers a historical sociological analysis of the development of ideas about sex and sexuality, from Classical Antiquity and early Christianity to the present. Although not written from an explicitly feminist perspective, it explores many relevant issues including the politics of reproduction, debates about hetero-sexuality and post-modern influences on thinking about sexuality, including queer theory.

8

Women, Violence and Male Power

Mary Maynard and Jan Winn

This chapter will examine the higher profile of the issue of male violence against women and children in the domestic setting which has arisen out of the political practice of activists in the women's liberation movement and feminist research deriving from this. It will also address the growing popular interest in female violence. In some of the literature these are treated as separate topics. Here they are treated as part of a spectrum or spectrums of violence which have an impact and consequence on women's lives. Its persistence as an area of experience in women's lives is one of the reasons why violence is such an important topic for Women's Studies today.

Feminism and violence: tracing historical connections

The analysis of male violence has been a central feature of women's political activism and feminist theorising for many years. For instance, Elizabeth Pleck (1987) chartered its significance in America going back over three hundred years, and Anna Clark (1988) has described a similar situation in England for the period 1770–1845. Victorian feminists fought for women's rights to both divorce and legal separation on the grounds of a husband's violence and the successful culmination of this in Britain with the 1878 Matrimonial Causes Act provided an important means of escape for women involved with abusive partners (Walby, 1990). Similarly, in America, many nineteenth-century women, supported the temperance demand for restrictions on alcohol because excessive drinking was seen as contributing to wife-beating (Rendall, 1985). In Britain, in 1878, Frances Power Cobbe (1987) referred to wife-beating as 'wife torture'. She derided the fact that it was considered a source of humour and denounced the devalued way with which men regarded their wives. Along with others, she saw violence against women not as the pathological behaviour of a few 'sick' men; rather it was the extension of a system of practices and laws which sanctioned men's rights to regard women as their property and therefore to keep them under their control (Maynard, 1989). In many ways, 'first-wave' feminists' analyses of incest and wife-beating are very reminiscent of feminist writing on male violence today. For instance, they argued that incest was part of a generalised pattern of male violence manifest also in acts such as rape and domestic violence (Hooper, 1987).

As feminism developed in the late 1960s and early 1970s, the significance of violence in women's lives started to emerge. Feminists began to examine their own experiences of abuse, and provide support for other women who had been victims of violence. As a result, the first rape crisis line was established in the USA in 1971 and the first refuge for battered women opened in England in 1972 (Kelly, 1988a). Subsequently, the issue of violence against women has become an important focus for feminist theory and action. Support groups for women who have been abused now exist in many countries. New issues, particularly those of incest, child sexual abuse and sexual harassment, have been raised. Women from different countries have tackled forms of violence specific to their culture as well as violence which is familiar to Western women. For example, in India there have been campaigns against 'dowry deaths': women being killed by their husbands and in-laws for not having provided sufficient money or goods on marriage (Kishwar and Vanita, 1984). In Egypt and Africa women have challenged the custom of female circumcision (el Saadawi, 1980; Koso-Thomas, 1987). In Tanzania in 1991, a women's crisis centre was founded to take up cases of women subjected to sexual harassment, violence and discrimination (Gawanas, 1993). As Liz Kelly has remarked, the amount of effort, frequently unpaid, put in by women around the world to counter violence against them has been 'incalculable' (Kelly, 1988a, p. 2).

Concern over the sexual abuse of children is also not just a contemporary phenomenon. Research on incest dates back to the late nineteenth century, and public anxiety over child sexual abuse has erupted intermittently ever since (Hooper, 1987; Violence Against Children Study Group, 1990). It was, however, only in the 1980s that child sexual abuse gained a higher profile, due in large part to 'speakouts' by women survivors of sexual abuse and, subsequently, feminist analyses (Bell, 1993). There are other aspects of male violence which have been central to feminist theory and practice including rape, sexual harassment, pornography and murder, and feminists have often enhanced our understanding of such forms of violence by considering them together and acknowledging the interrelationship between different kinds of violence.

Although there is no single feminist perspective on male violence, it is in the work of radical feminists that the most detailed analyses are to be found. At the core of their approach is the view that violence is both a reflection of unequal power relationships in society and serves to maintain those unequal power relationships. It reflects and maintains the power that men have over women in society generally and also, therefore, within their personal relationships. The term 'patriarchy' is usually invoked as a way of conceptualising the oppression of women which results. The exact meaning of the term remains the subject of much debate. However, a useful definition, which acknowledges that both the nature and degree of patriarchal control varies within and across societies, is provided by Adrienne Rich:

> Patriarchy is . . . a familial-social, ideological, political system in which men – by force, direct pressure or through ritual, law and language, customs, etiquette, education, and the division of labour, determine what part women shall or shall not play, and in which the female is everywhere subsumed under the male. It does not necessarily imply that no woman has power, or that all women in a given culture may not have certain powers. (Rich, 1977, p. 57)

Broadly speaking, then, radical feminists see male violence as a mechanism through which men as a group, as well as individual men, are able to control women and maintain their supremacy. It is not simply a result of women's subordination in society but also contributes to the construction of that subordination and is thus instrumental. Anne Campbell (1993) argues that men in fact hold an instrumental view of violence, whereby violence does indeed have its own social and/or material rewards which include social control, normative approval and management of (masculine) identity. Radical feminists argue that, in order to be able to capture the extent of the impact of violence upon women, it is important not to predetermine the meaning of the term. To do this it is necessary to know about women's experiences of violence and the boundaries which they draw around them. Liz Kelly has extended this argument to child sexual abuse, arguing that: 'if we are to reflect in our definition . . . the range and complexity of what women and girls experience as abusive we must listen to what they have to say' (Kelly, 1988b, p. 71). Kelly (1988a) used accounts of women's own experiences, based on in-depth interviews, to define violence from the women's point of view. She shows how the kinds of abuse which the women described, and which they had experienced both as adults and as children, are reflected neither in legal codes nor in the analytical formulations often used by professionals. Along with other researchers, Kelly points to the wide range of male behaviours which women perceive to be threatening, violent or sexually harassing: many more than are conventionally regarded as abusive (Hanmer and Saunders, 1984; Stanko, 1985). She suggested that our common-sense definitions of what constitutes violence reflect men's ideas and limit the range of male behaviour that is deemed unacceptable to the most extreme, gross and public forms. Thus women often find themselves caught between their own experiences of behaviour as abusive and the dominant beliefs which define such behaviour as normal or inevitable. This leads Kelly to introduce new categories, such as 'pressure to have sex' and 'coercive sex'. Such terms are used to challenge the assumption that all sexual intercourse which is not defined as rape is, therefore, consensual.

Feminist researchers have also documented how the law's definition of violence routinely takes precedence over women's definitions (Edwards, 1981; Brophy and Smart, 1985; Stanko, 1985; Smart, 1989a). They have examined the mechanisms through which the law is able to define the 'truth' of things in rape, child sexual abuse and other cases, in the face of evidence which quite clearly contradicts this understanding. Although the law is supposed to be gender-neutral, its ability to be able to decide what does or does not comprise a violent act gives it tremendous power. The consensus of feminist opinion is that this power works against the interests of women and in the interests of men instead. This is because, by discounting the views and definitions of women, the law is giving legitimacy to those of their female and male assailants. In failing to challenge the latter, the right of all men to abuse women is upheld.

One aspect of the feminist definition of violence which should be emphasised is the inclusion of the threat or fear of force as well as its actual use. In her early pioneering article on the subject, Jalna Hanmer argued that the fear of violence both compels and constrains women to behave or not to behave in certain ways (Hanmer, 1978). It affects what they can do, where they can go, and with whom they can go. In other words, both the reality and the threat of violence act as a form of social control. It is therefore necessary to include both in any understanding of what violence is about. Thus it can be seen that the issue of violence is wide-ranging and cuts across a number of others dealt with elsewhere in this book (for example to do with sexuality, the family, education and employment).

With this in mind, radical feminists have attempted to develop a much broader definition of violence which links together a number of different forms through which it occurs and is experienced. The term 'sexual violence' is used to distinguish these on the grounds that they are acts directed at women because their bodies are socially regarded as sexual. Kelly defines sexual violence to include: 'any physical, visual or sexual act that is experienced by the woman or girl, at the time or later, as a threat, invasion or assault, that has the effect of hurting her or degrading her and/or takes away her ability to control intimate contact' (Kelly, 1988a, p. 41). This definition encompasses a wide spectrum of behaviour including rape, sexual assault, wife-beating, sexual harassment (including flashing and obscene phone calls), incest, child sexual abuse and pornography. (For a discussion of the relationship between pornography and violence see Chapter 7.) They are linked by virtue of the fact that they are overwhelmingly, though not exclusively, male acts of aggression against women and girls; they often use sex as a means of exercising power and domination; and their effect is to intrude upon and curtail women's activities. Radical feminists argue that they are thus mechanisms through which women are socially controlled.

One of the most obvious feminist responses to male violence against women has been the establishment of refuges, centres and groups as places where the abused can seek shelter, counselling and support (Dobash and Dobash, 1987). Hostels for battered women, rape crisis centres and telephone lines, incest survivors and self-help groups have been important in providing help in those areas where state agencies have been particularly inadequate. Although frequently underfunded, these developments have constituted an important intervention in dealing with violence practically, suggesting the benefits to be gained from feminist collective work.

Such activities have also led to a change in some aspects of feminist thinking about violence. In the early years, feminist analysis tended to portray women as the passive victims of male abuse. However, the testimony of the women themselves has led to a change in emphasis from woman as 'victim' to woman as 'survivor' (Macleod and Saraga, 1988). The point of this change is not semantic, and neither is it meant to detract from the traumas through which abused women go. Instead, it is a signal that those who have been beaten, raped and sexually assaulted can develop strategies to enable them to cope with their ordeals and that they may be able to devise techniques of resistance. The notion of 'survivor' is much more positive than that of 'victim', asserting as it does women's ability to continue with their lives despite the experience of sexual violence.

Feminists have also been at the forefront of various kinds of campaigning relating to sexual violence, arguing for changes in police practice and attitudes, more government funding for anti-violence projects, and a recodification of the relevant laws. Although some feminists are sceptical about the gains to be had by working from within the existing system, others argue that it is both possible and necessary to work with and refine the practices of legal and welfare agencies and press for reform in procedures adopted by the police and the judiciary (Kelly, 1985; Hanmer, Radford and Stanko, 1989). These issues have been central to feminist work in the area of violence in the domestic setting.

Violence in the domestic setting

Defining violence in the domestic setting

In Britain, it is common for domestic violence to be regarded as violence between adults who are in an intimate or familial relationship, most often a sexual relationship between a woman and a man (Hague and Malos, 1993). Out of 530 000 incidents of domestic violence in England and Wales recorded by the British Crime Survey in 1992, 80 percent involved female victims (Mayhew, Maung and Mirrlees-Black, 1993). Other research projects estimate that between 90 and 97 per cent of domestic violence is perpetrated by men on women (Hague and Malos, 1993; Grace, 1995). As the definition of domestic violence includes adults in intimate relationships, the remaining instances may well be accounted for by the victimisation of adult male children or male relations by other men in the household. However, some violent incidents will be perpetrated by women who may be the instigators of such violence or may be responding to violence. Nevertheless, because the majority of reported violence in the home involves a male perpetrator and female victim, feminists are critical of the use of the term domestic violence and argue that the gender of the perpetrator is hidden by the term (Morley and Mullender, 1994). Even the terms 'battered wives' and 'woman abuse' are seen as problematic as they do not fully capture the significance and dynamics of gender in violence occurring in the domestic setting (Smith, 1989). The problem lies in the fact that these terms focus on the position of women and thus hide the fact that we are actually discussing male (gendered) power and male violence. Despite these problems, the term 'domestic violence' is common to discursive frameworks utilised by the state, the criminal justice system and society generally.

Seriousness of and response to violence in the domestic setting

On some occasions violence in the domestic setting can lead to the death of a woman. In Britain, in 1994, over 100 women were killed by their partners or ex-partners compared to 28 men killed by their partners in the same year (HMSO, 1994). In Canada, about 30 women a year are killed by their partners (Came and Bergman, 1990). Between 1980 and 1984, 52 per cent of all women killed in one-to-one homicides in the USA were killed by male partners of some description (Holmes and Holmes, 1994). However, it is more common for domestic violence to include one or more of the following elements: verbal abuse, emotional abuse, economic abuse, physical abuse and sexual abuse. Much of this violence is hidden as many women may not define their experiences as violent and may not acknowledge abuses of power. It is quite common for women not to report attacks to the police, especially if the attacker is known to them, since they do not expect to be treated seriously or sensitively. They may also face further violence from their abuser as a repercussion of such a report, especially in societies where the police are reluctant to intervene in what they see as 'domestics' and consequently do not remove the attacker. Evidence from Australia, Britain, Canada and the USA has indicated the police's unwillingness to get involved if violence takes place in the setting of a woman's home because of a tendency to see it as simply 'trouble' in a personal relationship (Hanmer, Radford and Stanko, 1989).

Attempts to uncover the 'dark figure' or hidden aspect of crime have had little success in improving our knowledge of the incidence of violence towards women. The British Crime Surveys, for example, are designed to find out how much crime goes unreported and why people choose not to go to the police, by asking individuals directly about their experience of criminal behaviour. So far this has shown a very low rate for rape and other sexual offences, and Home Office researchers involved have readily admitted the difficulties in obtaining information. They explain this in terms of women's shame or embarrassment in talking to any interviewer about such matters and the possibility that the assailant may be in the same room at the time of the interview (Hanmer and Saunders, 1984). It is even more difficult to assess the number of lesbians in violent relationships given the marginalisation of lesbians and the invisibility or erasure of many violent behaviours committed by women.

By contrast, feminist researchers have begun to uncover the extent to which violence against women is hidden, by using female interviewers and more sensitive interviewing techniques. These studies, along with similar research, indicate that violence towards women is far more extensive than official figures might lead us to believe. They demonstrate that, whereas sexual violence is often trivialised and regarded as insignificant it is, in fact, an important, complex and ever-present threat in the lives of many women. However, it is difficult to judge whether abuse is actually increasing or whether heightened awareness of its existence is making cases (which would previously have been hidden) more visible.

Amina Mama (1993) addresses several concerns about the position of Black and Third World women experiencing violence which encompass and expand those addressed by white feminists. She notes that in Britain Black women are extremely reluctant to call the police even when serious or life-threatening crimes are perpetrated against them. When the police do attend they are reluctant to enforce the law and there is evidence to suggest that the police themselves perpetrate crimes against Black people. Ultimately Black women suffer a lack of protection within the community, are particularly isolated in white areas where stereotypical views of Black behaviour as 'normally' violent abound and may not be protected by the law because of evidence of police racism (Southall Black Sisters, 1993; Mama, 1993). This indicates that there are problems in defining what might constitute violence for the individual woman concerned and wider society, and this in turn affects responses to such violence. Mama states that Western, white feminism has failed systematically to address the issue of violence across anything but patriarchal and sexual violence axes. In doing this many white feminists are said to have largely ignored the differential problems faced by Black and Third World women and have therefore ignored the connections between class, racial and cultural differences. Beth Richie (1996) argues that gender, 'race'/ethnicity and violence in intimate relationships intersect and provide an effective system of organising Black women's behaviour in a way which leaves them incredibly vulnerable to private and public subordination. The complexities of the relationship between gender, class, 'race' and/or cultural oppressions are profound and far-reaching. The Hill/Thomas and O. J. Simpson cases in the USA illustrate the problems of relying on one axis in relation to male violence and the extraordinary divisions and alliances which can be formed as a consequence of such cases (see, for example, Morrison, 1993b and Chapter 2 in this volume).

Over the past ten years, violence in lesbian relationships has been explored by feminists (Lobel, 1986; Kelly and Scott, 1989; Renzetti, 1992; Taylor and Chandler, 1995). Just as the response to Black women's experience of violence is largely based on racial stereotypes, people's opinions of violence in lesbian relationships is often based on stereotypical views of the role and nature of lesbians and the view that lesbians merely mimic heterosexuality. The range of violences and abuses of power reported within lesbian relationships are similar to those reported by women in heterosexual relationships and include physical assaults, sexual assaults, destruction of property, psychological or emotional abuse, and economic control (Hart, 1986). An additional abuse is named by Hart as 'homophobic control'. For instance, the abuser may threaten to disclose the victim's sexuality to family, friends, work colleagues and so on. The abuser may also tell the victim that she deserves all she gets because she is a lesbian, that no one will believe her or that she has no option because the homophobic (anti-lesbian) world will not help her (Hart, 1986).

Joelle Taylor and Tracey Chandler (1995) argue that the issue of violence in lesbian relationships has been used to undermine arguments fundamental to feminist theory and to our understanding of the complex structures which underlie male power. This is a theme common to any discussion about female violence and can be used by anti-feminists to argue that women are as bad as, if not worse than, men and therefore the whole basis of feminist analyses of violence should be dismissed.

For instance, David Thomas (1993) criticises what he perceives as feminists' reluctance to discuss female violence towards their male partners, using this example of female violence to undermine feminist theories of male violence. However, it could be argued that Thomas fails to recognise that such violence remains hidden because of society's reluctance to perceive men as victims, except when other men are the perpetrators. He relies on the assumption that feminists do not recognise that women can be violent and abusive and implies that the focus should shift from male violence and incorporate female violence in such instances. This is clearly problematic as all dominant models, including feminism, focus on male power and violence and it is extremely difficult to synthesise oppositional symbolic meanings into one all-encompassing model at this point in history. The meanings attached to women or children who kill differs from those attached to men who kill. For instance, when two young boys killed two-year-old Jamie Bulger in the UK,[1] the very 'nature and essence' of childhood was examined in social, cultural and political arenas as society tried to negotiate the potential shift in cultural meaning of childhood this case raised. In contrast, the 'Dunblane Massacre'[2] seemed to raise questions about the ownership of firearms or the perpetrator's mental stability rather than the 'nature and essence' of manhood/masculinity. In many ways, the latter indicates society's tacit acceptance of male violence and the response to this incident relied heavily on traditional explanations of male violence which are typically a process of dissociation, whereby known violent men are separated from other 'normal' men. For example, the conventional liberal/psychological view of male violence sees it either as the behaviour of a few 'sick' or psychologically deranged men or as 'invited' by flirtatious or masochistic women. This approach thus focuses on the pathological or deviant characteristics of individuals and tends to ignore social, cultural or contextual facts. For example, men who batter have been presented as mentally ill, neurotic or disturbed (Dobash and Dobash, 1992). Rapists have been described as experiencing sexual frustration in their relationships with women due to problematic childhoods and disrupted family backgrounds (Stanko, 1985). Men guilty of child sexual abuse have been characterised as having suffered a chaotic family life, with resulting emotional deprivation (Driver, 1989). Frequently, it is suggested that men who are abusers have themselves been abused. However, some research suggests that only 10 per cent of male abusers may have been abused in childhood (Waterhouse, Carnie and Dobash, 1993). The problem with such explanations is that they do not hold when more general evidence is taken into account. For instance, as has already been noted, the incidence of violence against women is far greater than most advocates of the liberal/psychological view acknowledge, so that it ends up offering 'an exceptionalist explanation of a universal problem' (Smith, 1989, p. 24).

Although such explanations may be useful in understanding a few specific cases, liberal/psychological approaches cannot provide a theory to explain the general phenomenon. Further, such an approach is rendered gender-blind and does not explain why it is primarily men who are violent to women. There also tends to be serious methodological problems with the research upon which such arguments are based. Most of it comprises small, unrepresentative samples and there is little work using control or comparison groups (Walby, 1990). Additionally, there are in any case other empirical studies which challenge the legitimacy of individual explanations. Work by Murray Straus (1980) and by Richard Gelles and Clark Cornell (1985), for instance, showed that men who have hit their wives do not exhibit a particularly high degree of psychological disturbance, and neither, as Cathy Waldby *et al.* (1989) indicate, can sexual abusers of children claim to be mentally ill. For all these reasons we need to be wary of accepting explanations which focus on the attributes of individuals alone.

We should also be critical of arguments suggesting that women provoke violent behaviour towards them. It has variously been put forward that women incite domestic violence by behaving in such a way (for example, nagging, being too talkative or too extravagant) as to actually cause it or that women are engaged in a form of masochistic self-punishment (Dobash and Dobash, 1992); that women invite rape by deviating from the norm of femininity and acting provocatively (Stanko, 1985); and that child sexual abuse is the result of children being abnormally seductive (Driver, 1989). Feminist work disputes such accounts, pointing out that 'blaming the victim' in this way serves as a strategy for failing to take the totality of violence towards women seriously and decreases men's responsibility for it. In this perspective men are regarded as helplessly driven by their innately aggressive and sexual natures; or as sick, thus requiring treatment; or they themselves become the 'victims' of women and children who invite abuse. If we try to use such an approach to explain violence in lesbian relationships we are also denying the female abuser's responsibility. The only way we can use such a model is by using symbolic masculine meanings attached to lesbians. But, as Taylor and Chandler (1995) argue, when a lesbian beats or sexually abuses her lover she is still a lesbian, and she is still a woman.

It is important that distinct theories of female violence are constructed in order to highlight the different places women and men occupy in society, whether violence can be observed or not. Moreover, if feminism is a social and political movement for women it needs to provide theoretical frameworks which enable women to understand their own access to and use of power, aggression and violence. As we will see later, this has already started to occur for some forms of violence and feminists, and others are addressing the issue of women who kill their violent male partners.

Feminist responses/campaigns

The state has been slow to react given the wealth of evidence which has supported feminist claims. Feminists' arguments that the violence which was beginning to surface was but the tip of an iceberg were dismissed, amidst claims of exaggeration, provocation and lying on the part of women. Yet, subsequently, the feminist contentions have been upheld, with the seriousness of rape and domestic violence having been increasingly recognised (Dobash and Dobash, 1992). Yet, although violence to women has received an increasingly high public profile, the practical response of state agencies has been very patchy. It also appears that even those laws passed with the precise aim of assisting women in their fight against male violence have been relatively ineffective. Reporting on the situation with regard to domestic violence legislation in Australia and Britain respectively, Suzanne Hatty (1989) and Kathy McCann (1985) have described how reactionary judicial interpretations of such laws have limited what can be achieved under them.

This is because of the unsympathetic attitudes towards women held by the police and the courts who are the gatekeepers to the legislation.

Grace (1995) points out that the need to improve police response to domestic assault in Britain was recognised by the police themselves and by the British Home Office. She concluded that on the whole, British police are not yet dealing with domestic violence in a sensitive and serious manner. Thus, although the welfare, criminal and judicial agencies of the state have begun to respond to violence against women, the consensus of feminist opinion is that major problems still remain. Feminists played a significant role in raising the profile of sexual violence. They must continue to participate in the dialogue about it and be vigilant in monitoring how it is treated, if their influence is not to be undermined.

The Zero Tolerance campaign, co-ordinated by the National Association of Local Government Women's Committee, and supported by feminist activist groups, has been mounting an offensive against violence against women throughout Britain (*Rights of Women Bulletin*, 1994). The Zero Tolerance campaign in Edinburgh was inspired by and took its name from, a $136 million 'Family Violence Initiative', founded by the Canadian Federal Government. Roz Foley (1993) describes how the Edinburgh District Council Women's Committee launched the campaign in November 1992 after consultation with a range of women's groups. The campaign primarily took the form of numerous posters which depicted familiar daily domestic scenes and provided empirical data relating to various violent crimes committed against women and children by men. For instance, one poster showed an older woman and a young child with the information that '*From three to ninety three, women are raped*'. The majority of posters contained the assertion that '*Male abuse of power is a crime*'. The aim of the Zero Tolerance campaign then was to ensure that domestic violence became part of the public agenda. The relative success of such campaigns (see Kitzinger and Hunt, 1994) indicates that feminist theory and activism relating to the nature of gender and violence may have had some influence in terms of challenging and informing people's attitudes towards gender roles, gender expectations and violence.

Women's responses to male violence

Another area where feminists have increasingly become involved is the challenging of the criminal justice system's treatment of battered women who kill their violent male partners. Central to feminists' understandings and explanations of battered women who kill are ideas about the instrumental and systematic nature of male violence in the domestic setting. For feminists, female violence in this context would not occur but for the problem of male violence, a factor which is largely ignored, erased or distorted within the criminal justice system.

The roles of woman, mother and wife have important implications for the lives of women and contribute substantially to their subordination at home and in the labour market. If we consider these elements of subordination in combination with male violence in the home we can see that women who are being abused face enormous problems in trying to support themselves and their children independently. This makes it very difficult for women to leave violent men and they face very practical problems. At least four categories of basic needs have to be dealt with in order for women to lead independent lives and thus escape violence; adequate housing, financial support, medical advice and treatment and emotional/physical safety (Kirkwood, 1993). These problems are compounded by the response of the police if and when they attend incidents of 'domestic violence'. As stated earlier, the police are often reluctant to take any action and thereby contribute to any escalation of violence by failing to confront violent men's actions. Research in the USA shows that in many cases where a woman kills a violent male partner the police have attended their homes on several occasions (Buzawa and Buzawa, 1990). Other studies in the USA show that the police may have attended between 80 to 95 per cent of homes where an homicide later occurs (see, for example, Holmes and Holmes, 1994). The reluctance of the British police to take any action when they do attend is well illustrated by the highly publicised case of Sara Thornton, who killed her husband Malcolm.[3] The police attended the Thornton household on many occasions and rarely took any action. On one occasion her husband punched her in the face in front of two work colleagues, who intervened until the police arrived. As Malcolm Thornton had calmed down when the police arrived they left without taking any action (Nadel, 1993).

The problems do not exist solely in relation to the police's response to domestic violence, but in the criminal justice system as a whole. In Britain, the Southall Black Sisters were instrumental in highlighting the bias in the law in relation to women who kill violent male partners through their campaigning in the case of Kiranjit Ahluwalia.[4] The work of Southall Black Sisters and Justice for Women has led to the identification of several discriminatory aspects of British law relating to homicide, arguing that legal defences to murder have historically been created and developed to deal with male defendants.[5]

The problems lie in the fact that the law relies on gendered ideas about how the threat of force, diminished responsibility and provocation are experienced. Sara Macguire (1993) points out that women use the diminished responsibility defence more than any other. This may be because it is easier for all those involved in the case to believe that violent women are suffering from an abnormality of mind rather than defending themselves or suffering provocation. However, there are problems with this defence particularly in light of the current debates about 'battered wives syndrome' (Dobash and Dobash, 1992; Naylor, 1995). This diagnosis is given to indicate that a woman has eventually been driven to kill her abusive male partner because the abuse has somehow rendered her crazy or helpless (Dobash and Dobash, 1992). Some feminists appear to have ambiguous feelings towards the notion of 'battered wives syndrome'. Susan Edwards (1993), for example, believes that 'battered wives syndrome' does, at least, give women a voice and thus a defence to murder, even if it is problematic as a concept. Other feminists are very critical of a concept which relies on stereotypical views of women as 'crazy' or 'helpless'. For example, Sibusiso Mavolwane and Jill Radford (1993) argue that 'battered wives syndrome' is defined by the medical profession and ultimately empowers them to determine which women are suffering from a medical condition. Moreover, it allows such 'experts' to appropriate the power to define women's responses to domestic violence.

The defence of provocation is also problematic. The courts have consistently held that provocation is a 'sudden and temporary loss of control'. Ultimately feminists argue that the physical differences between women and men and the differing ways in which they are socialised to deal with anger and violence lead to different gendered outcomes. Thus, a woman may experience provocation differently and may not have the physical means to respond immediately and fulfil the criteria of a sudden loss of control. Instead, many feminists are campaigning for a change in the law whereby 'self-preservation' becomes a partial defence. Simply put, self-preservation is recommended to be adopted in cases where a person kills a partner or intimate who has been repeatedly racially, sexually or physically abusive and/or the person subjected to that abuse sees no alternative (Radford, 1993).

Similar debates about the law and the problems of medicalised models have been ongoing in the USA. Patricia Gagné (1996) identifies the strategies and tactics utilised by feminists in Ohio in securing clemency for 26 women convicted of killing violent male partners. Feminists there engaged with and worked within political and social institutions, adopting a 'self-limiting radicalism' which, it is claimed, created 'contexts of opportunity'. That is, they were in structural positions which enabled them to encourage the Governor to implement a review process of cases where a woman killed a violent male partner. Feminist activism in this instance was 'on the job', and the goals of the women's movement and career advancement of those activists were firmly bound together. In adopting an 'insider' stance feminists were able to influence and co-ordinate police and judicial responses to battering and support legislative change. This is particularly important as the social climate in 1990, when clemency was granted, is typically seen as either 'post-feminist' or as a period of 'backlash' towards feminism (Faludi, 1991). It is worth noting that activists utilised: the notion of (gendered) difference, seen as central to cultural and eco-feminism; the assumption that women rarely kill unless under duress; and ideas about 'peaceful families'. This had a cultural resonance with dominant ideas about family and gender difference. However, suppositions about female empowerment and the eradication of violence against women were still central and ultimately 26 women were granted clemency and released.

Fundamentally, feminist campaigns and theorising of battered women who kill is a continuation of similar work undertaken in an ongoing project aimed at ending male violence against women. As such the primary concern is the systematic nature of male violence, power and control. Female violence in this context does not undermine feminist theories of male violence or gendered relationships, rather it is considered that women would not kill their male partners if they were not subjected to violence.

Child sexual abuse

Defining child sexual abuse

Feminist theory and practice has also been crucial to developing our understanding of child sexual abuse. In many studies of child sexual abuse during the past 30 years men are believed to commit between 97 and 99 per cent of all cases reported, leaving women responsible for between 1 and 3 per cent of reported sexual abuse (de Francis, 1969; Groth, 1979; Mrazek, Lynch and Bentovim, 1981). More recently, research in both the USA and Britain has repeatedly indicated that males are the perpetrators in about 90 per cent of reported cases of child sexual abuse (Finkelhor *et al.*, 1990; Kelly *et al.*, 1991). Coons *et al.* (1989) conclude that girls are primarily the victims of child sexual abuse. However, other research suggests that this is not the case, Eugene Porter (1986) reports that perhaps 40 to 50 per cent of victims could be boys. It does seem that males are predominantly the abusers whether the victims are boys or girls.

There are, however, difficulties if we try to compile material which focuses around a category called 'child sexual abuse'. In Britain, for example, there is no offence called 'child sexual abuse'; rather it comprises a number of different sexual offences (Viinikka, 1989). Some of these, such as unlawful sexual intercourse, are age-specific and linked to the legal age of consent for heterosexual sex with girls, which is currently sixteen years. Others, such as rape, apply to both adults and children. The crime of incest is also defined in heterosexist terms, since it is regarded only as taking place between members of the opposite sex, must involve vaginal penetration and is restricted to certain kinds of familial relationships (Macleod and Saraga, 1988). It is thus confined to what is conventionally seen as 'normal' heterosexual activity. Use of the term 'incest' has been criticised by some feminists for focusing attention on who is involved rather than upon what is happening. They prefer terms such as 'father-daughter rape' instead, since it emphasises that the child is experiencing an act of aggression in which she is denied her self-determination (Ward, 1984). Other feminists employ 'incest' in a wider sense to include all abuse committed within the family or by any relative however distant (Nelson, 1987). The legal definitions relating to certain kinds of child sex abuse and rape are even more problematic in relation to female abusers as the overreliance on heterosexual definitions of sex fails to account for penetration by anything other than the penis, which is absent in female-female sexual violence. Even Elizabeth Ward's (1984) redefinition of incest as father-daughter rape fails to account for such abuse and denies these kinds of sexual agency when expressed by women, as well as the self-determination of the victim.

The sexual abuse of children is fundamentally related to the power disparity of the adult-child relationship. Macleod and Saraga (1988) have argued that definitions of sexual abuse should contain three key elements: the betrayal of trust and responsibility; the abuse of power; and the inability of children to consent. However, as they point out, this definition can be criticised for not including the idea that force or the threat of force may be used. The notion of 'informed consent' is also problematic for feminists since it assumes that the ability to say 'yes' or 'no' in abusive situations is a relatively straightforward affair, when in fact it is frequently complicated by relationships of power and emotional blackmail; frequently male abusers take great care to 'groom' their victims (Pringle, 1995). Additional difficulties with the definition are produced by the terms 'developmentally immature' and 'sexual actions'. The former implies that only younger children can be sexually abused, with the implication of consent and complicity for older ones.

Some feminists claim that, for girls, child sexual abuse has a particular function in terms of enforcing the institution of heterosexuality (Jones, 1985). As with male violence towards adult women, child sexual abuse is seen as perpetuating a status quo of male domination and female submission and is thus instrumental. Consequently masculinity in certain idealised forms is seen as intensely problematic by feminists and by male theorists who draw on feminist theory. For example, Keith Pringle (1992) argues that masculinity is the most important causative factor in the majority of cases of sexual abuse. David Jackson (1995) argues that Jon Venables and Robert Thompson, the two boys convicted of murdering Jamie Bulger[6], acted out fantasies of masculinity and power which are embedded in British and Western culture. Pringle (1992) does not present masculinity as being biologically determined, but as a socially constructed concept and role which can be reformulated.

Once again we also need to be aware of the complex issues which are raised in relation to sexually abused children from various racial and ethnic backgrounds. Audrey Droisen (1989) has argued that for Black and Jewish children the prejudices of racism and anti-semitism can compound the abuse and leave the child uncertain as to whether feelings of unworthiness are related to the abuse or the racism/anti-semitism. Again, stereotypical views of Black people may come into play when abuse is detected and state intervention can have dire consequences on a child who may be removed from her community, thus losing a crucial source of support.

Whilst most, if not all, feminists are critical of child sexual abuse, some feminists (such as sexual libertarianists) offer a future vision of a society where cross-generational sex may be just one formulation of erotic desire. For example, Kate Millett (1992) talks of such possibilities, stating that 'intergenerational sex could perhaps in the future be a wonderful opportunity for understanding between human beings' (p. 222). However, she goes on to state that adult/child relationships at present precludes any sexual relationships between adults and children which are not in some sense exploitative. In the same volume, Gayle Rubin is seemingly supportive of cross-generational sex, which is seen as occupying a similar social space to homosexuality, promiscuity, transsexuality, sadomasochism and other sexual practices described as 'bad' or 'abnormal' in Western societies. Again the notion of consent is particularly important, and it is difficult to see how children and young people can fully consent when a generational power disparity exists.

In recent years, the issue of female child sexual abuse, like violence in lesbian relationships, has been used to undermine feminist theories of male violence towards children. For instance, Michelle Elliott (1993) believes that child sexual abuse is not 'political' and thus dismisses feminist analyses which present male violence and abuse of power in multiple contexts as politically significant. Her focus on female child sexual abuse is presented as supporting this assertion, but this works if we believe that power only functions in a gendered context. However, as we saw earlier in relation to Black women's experiences, the abuse and use of power can lead to oppressive practices and violence in a variety of social contexts and relationships.

The issue of female child sexual abuse is starting to gain theoretical momentum in mainstream theory, and debate should provide opportunity to re-assess what being a woman means. How can abusive females be theorised and what effect will this have regarding theories of sexuality, femininity and violence? Can/should feminist theories incorporate women who engage in child sexual abuse, and what effect would this have on feminist theories of gender and sexuality? On the other hand is this relatively new area of concern about child sexual abuse another shift in the discourse of child sexual abuse, which has shifted from 'collective denial' to more recent notions about 'false accusations' and 'false memory syndrome' (K. Beckett, 1996)? The idea that adults who disclose abuse in childhood are making false accusations or that they have false memories (maybe even that they are 'fantasising') is very reminiscent of Freudian notions of 'hysteria' common at the turn of the century.

That aside, women do sexually abuse children and account for between 1 and 3 per cent of reported cases. Droisen and Driver (1989) concluded that when women do sexually abuse they are vilified for transgressing their gender role, indicating tacit assumptions are held by wider society that men are more powerful and more sexual than women. Val Young (1993), for example, challenges accepted theories of child sexual abuse, especially those connecting child sexual abuse and power relations. Despite this, she does recognise that child sexual abuse can be about 'the misuse of power'. She states that child sexual abuse can also be about . . . 'anger, self-gratification, objectifying children, comfort, possessiveness, a distorted type of love, transference of the abuser's suppressed sexuality, immaturity, sadism, making money out of pornography, aggression, a form of sexual addiction, and frequently, the misinterpretation of a child's natural sensuality and sexuality' (Young, 1993, p. 112).

Some feminists might argue that most of the above examples are related to power and the social construction of gendered relationships and sexuality. For example, anger can be the basis of attempts to misuse power or a reaction to the resistance to perceived power and control. Anger can be used to maintain or reinforce a power relationship, as indeed can the objectification of children or women.

On a very basic level it seems that some acts perpetrated by women are common to male abuse. For example, Olive Wolfers (1993) reports that in research carried out in 1990, on ten women abusers, seven went to great lengths to set the scene for 'bizarre' acts including bestiality and bondage. She took this to indicate that female child sexual abusers can be seen to be as physically and sexually violent as their male counterparts. That said, she goes on to discuss the possibility that women's involvement in child sexual abuse may be the attempt to achieve control in powerless situations. She seemingly draws on feminist theories about the experiences of women in relation to their own abuses and societal expectations of them (presumed powerlessness). This creates a conflict for women which they potentially resolve by engaging in violence. The resonance with explanations of male abuse which rely on the idea that abuse leads to abuse are clear, and it echoes some social/structural models of male abuse. In these models, male violence is explained in terms of social class, and is regarded as a response to such factors as frustration, stress and blocked goals caused by poor economic conditions, bad housing, relative poverty, lack of job opportunities and unfavourable work conditions (Smith, 1989). On this basis, it has been claimed that men who are violent towards women are disproportionately drawn from the lower classes, since they are more likely to suffer deprivation. Such a view has been advanced by a number of researchers on domestic violence in the USA. They have argued that men resort to violence when aspirations, which they are encouraged to hold regarding work and living standards, fail to be reached (Gelles, 1983).

Research on rape has also focused on its supposed prevalence amongst working-class men. For instance, in an early book on the subject, Menachem Amir (1971) discusses how men at the bottom of the social order reject dominant cultural values if they find these difficult to achieve, adopting instead alternative standards which are easier to attain. Amir argues that a deviant subculture of violence then emerges in which attributes such as machismo and physical superiority are particularly valued and where rape is one way of expressing this. Amir's claims that rapists are disproportionately drawn from working-class and Black groups have been challenged as classist and racist by feminists (Walby, 1990). However, some socialist feminists who have written about violence – for example, Elizabeth Wilson (1983) and Lynne Segal (1990b) – have, in the past, put forward the view that the deprivations of class and 'race' positions are responsible for male violence, with its ultimate cause being the inherent inequalities of a capitalist society.

A particular variant of the liberal/psychological perspective on violence is also to be found in a widely accepted explanation for child sexual abuse and other violence in the domestic or 'family' setting, which has had an important influence in professional groups such as social workers (see, for example, Kingston and Penhale, 1995; Cahn and Lloyd, 1996). Known as the family dysfunction approach, it is in some ways different from that so far discussed in its professed concern for the family rather than for the individuals who may have abused or been abused (Macleod and Saraga, 1988; Waldby *et al.*, 1989). The argument is that abuse occurs in families which are not operating 'properly' and where the 'normal' family hierarchies based on age and sex have broken down. Women are blamed for being dysfunctional as wives by failing to meet their husbands' sexual demands, or having too many interests outside the home, and are blamed for being inadequate mothers who have failed to be protective of their children (Waldby *et al.*, 1989). Sometimes it is suggested that mothers collude in child sexual abuse. This type of approach has been criticised for failing to account for power disparities within families and the fact that much abuse occurs outside the 'nuclear' family (Pringle, 1990; Kelly *et al.*, 1991).

The difficulty with such arguments is that once we look at other evidence, and not just at research based upon violence reported to the authorities (upon which most social class explanations are based), a different picture emerges. Studies of battered women who have sought shelter in refuges indicates that domestic violence occurs in all social classes and groups (Pahl, 1985). Similarly, community-based studies of rape and child sexual abuse do not indicate any obvious correlation with class position. For instance, Beatrix Campbell, a socialist feminist, who wrote about child sexual abuse in the county of Cleveland, England, says that there was no evidence that it was simply an expression of the area's economic deprivation.[7] She concluded that the abusers were: 'the men we all know, not so much the outcasts as the men in our lives: respectable dads, neighbours, stockbrokers and shop stewards, judges and jurors' (Campbell, 1988, p. 5). They are men of all ages, 'races', religions and classes. There is no evidence from research undertaken in the area of child sexual abuse to suggest a link between social class, stress or geographical location (Glaser and Frosh, 1993). The discrepancy between the two sets of conclusions, one of which supports social/structural explanations and one which critiques such conclusions, is likely to be due to the unrepresentativeness of the samples used in that research which advocates a social class position (Smith, 1989). This is due to the underreporting of the violence which women and children experience, as previously discussed, and to the fact that lower-class and Black men are more likely to be arrested, to appear in criminal statistics and, when convicted, to be made available for academics and professionals to study. Moreover, families who rely on the welfare state to survive economically are more likely candidates for scrutiny by welfare agencies, and thus more visible than their middle-class counterparts.

An additional problem with the social class approach, as Walby notes, is that little attempt is made to explain why men who are frustrated at their class or 'race' position avenge themselves on women (Walby, 1990). She asks why such men do not attack their more obvious class or 'race' enemies instead, pointing out that it does not even appear to be the case that men attack women of the superordinate class or 'race'. Walby suggests we must find the argument that social deprivation breeds male violence wanting. She concludes that 'its fundamental flaw is that it is unable to deal with the gendered nature of this violence' (Walby, 1990, p. 134). Similarly, the forcing of women into a similar framework or model ignores the possibility that in the adult-child relationship the adult woman may be more powerful. Why is this so difficult to accept when it is seemingly accepted in the case of male abusers?

There appears to be evidence that women do sexually abuse both female and male children, and that some of the physical manifestations of that abuse are similar to men's abuse (Elliott, 1993; Wolfers, 1992, 1993). However, it is not yet clear how many of the reported cases were committed by females in collaboration with males, and neither have the potential difficulties in unpacking who did what to whom and why been sorted out. The question of whether female abusers would have abused without the presence, perhaps insistence, of a male is not adequately addressed, or the idea that many female abusers actually report themselves to the authorities. So whilst Wolfers (1992) reports details about her sample of ten women abusers, it should be seen in a particular context: seven abused with, or at the insistence of, a man.

The problems in providing an all-encompassing theoretical definition of child sexual abuse are great. This undoubtedly contributes to the problems in determining what acts by females constitute sexual abuse. If we cannot determine what is meant by sexual and/or abusive behaviour in a universal way regarding male child sexual abuse, the inclusion of female abuse is problematic. However, if we argue, like Macleod and Saraga (1988), that definitions of sexual abuse should contain three key elements – the betrayal of trust and responsibility, the abuse of power, and the inability of children to consent – we can see that this could include women. What we can theorise or discuss is the idea of power in a particular context. In this case it would be power in a generational and/or gendered context and it would also include abuse by men and women who are not familially connected to the child (see Pringle, 1995). This incorporates the criticisms of Mama (1993) mentioned above and allows us to theorise about several contexts at the same time. This may mean that contradictions and tensions between the general and the particular can be gainfully employed when try to understand the problem of human violence, particularly the predominance of male violence.

Conclusion

It appears that, although much progress has been made in highlighting the extent and severity of the issue of male violence, a great deal still remains to be done in terms of how it is treated and dealt with. Most material is overwhelmingly about male violence towards white, apparently heterosexual women, and where there has been research which includes women from other backgrounds, this tends to ignore issues of racism and heterosexism in analysing its findings. In addition, the violence experienced by lesbians, both as women and as a result of anti-lesbianism, is largely ignored. It is thus vital that the parameters of research are broadened in order to be able to include those factors that may affect women's differing experiences of violence.

As previously stated, much of the theory relating to male violence has grown out of radical feminism. However, radical feminists are not a homogenous group and may approach the issue of male violence from differing perspectives. A major problem of the 1990s within feminism is the dismissal of many radical feminist perspectives which have important implications for certain issues like violence (Richardson, 1996d). There are also critiques of feminist analyses of male violence which argue that men are the victims of feminism (Bly, 1991; Thomas, 1993; Farrell, 1994). There is little doubt that the perception or representation of some strands of radical feminist theory and practice, centred on male violence, also causes some feminists a great deal of discomfort. For example, Camille Guy (1996) offers some poignant 'troubled thoughts' on developments within feminism in New Zealand over the last two decades, and documents her beliefs that a radical feminist 'orthodoxy' closed off debate in several areas, including sexual abuse. This may be connected to the misrepresentation of radical feminism as essentialist, specifically where male violence is concerned, and the characterisation of radical feminism as reactionary and/or moralistic (Richardson, 1996d). It is, arguably, an embittered impasse which will be difficult to bridge because of emotive and highly charged separations which exist within feminism. However, many feminists from various feminist 'camps' continue to argue that violence towards women is a gender issue and a product of the social construction of masculinities across class and 'racial' differences.

An interest in, and a concern for, understanding masculinity has only recently become part of the intellectual and political agenda as a distinct topic (Hearn and Morgan, 1990; Jackson, 1995; Pringle, 1995; V. Robinson, 1996). As Arthur Brittan has pointed out, a boy's genitals are the first sign of his potential membership of the category 'male' (Brittan, 1989). However, such categorisation does not just mean the simple acquisition of a label. Rather, it affects the whole way in which a male defines his difference from the category 'female'. In Western societies this notion of difference is heavily charged with symbolic meaning. Thus, men are taken to be more aggressive, competitive and sexual than women and, in order to demonstrate the strength of their masculinity, these are the characteristics to which they are encouraged to aspire (Miedzian, 1992). This means that masculinity and power, as presently constructed, are inherently interlinked (Cornwall and Lindisfarne, 1994). In fact, masculinity is a form of power and, to the extent that it is formulated in opposition to femininity, masculinity enables men to act out this power in the subordination and control of women. In one sense, then, to become masculine is to become an oppressor. Yet man as oppressor is not 'born' with his gender characteristics biologically and innately given, a perspective which does nothing to explain why some women are aggressive and violent and some men are not. Rather, these are socially and culturally 'constructed', since the so-called 'facts' of biology are always interpreted in the context of previously established meanings and beliefs. They are not immutable, and the role of men's capacity to choose to behave in oppressive and violent ways needs to be considered (Pringle, 1995).

Thus in our anxiety for the 'victims' and 'survivors' of violence we must not allow the question of men and masculinity to disappear off the agenda. We need to think through the strategies for how to get men to change and what the roles and responsibilities of men themselves are in this. A significant part of this process is the necessity for men to take seriously the issues discussed in this book. Politically, feminism has always been concerned with transforming knowledge and with generating alternative practices. Nowhere is this needed so much as in the area of violence to women and violence perpetrated by women.

Notes

1. Robert Thompson and Jon Venables, both under twelve years of age, were convicted of murdering two-year-old Jamie Bulger, in 1993, David Jackson (1995) argues that they were trying to achieve an idealised masculinity through their actions.
2. In 1996, Thomas Hamilton entered Dunblane Primary School with various firearms. He shot and killed 17 people, primarily young children aged between five and six years.
3. In 1990, Sara Thornton was convicted of murder and received a mandatory life sentence. She appealed on several occasions and was, after a re-trial, convicted of manslaughter. She was sentenced to five years' imprisonment which effectively meant that she was released in 1996 having already served her sentence.
4. As in the case of Sara Thornton, Kiranjit Ahluwalia was originally convicted of murder and sentenced to a mandatory life sentence. She was granted leave to appeal in 1992 and was convicted of manslaughter due to diminished responsibility. She was immediately released, having already served her sentence.
5. Homicide is basically the unlawful killing of another person and is defined as murder if they caused the death of another person and meant to either kill the victim or cause grievous bodily harm. In Britain, a conviction for murder carries a mandatory life sentence. However, there are full and partial defences to murder. A full defence relies on one or both of two elements. Either the person is killed by accident (no intention whatsoever), or was killed when the defendant defended themselves using force proportional to the force threatened. The partial defences include diminished responsibility, where the defence has to prove diminished responsibility on a balance of probability rather than beyond reasonable doubt, and provocation. For the latter it is the responsibility of the prosecution to show that the defendant was not provoked once enough evidence is put forward to show that provocation may have existed.
6. See note 1 above.
7. In the first six months of 1987, two paediatricians at Middlesborough General Hospital diagnosed sexual abuse in a total of 165 girls and boys. The series of events which unfolded thereafter (the 'Cleveland Crisis') led to a judicial inquiry. The resultant Butler-Sloss report (1988) acknowledged that the sexual abuse of children was a serious social problem, and, despite criticisms of the diagnostic technique (anal dilatation) propounded by various medical and public figures, Lord Justice Butler-Sloss exonerated the technique. The primary concerns voiced by Butler-Sloss related to the management of the crisis rather than the problem and causes of sexual abuse. Campbell (1988) states that 'A sexual crisis became a management crisis and politics became procedures' (p. 210).

Further reading

Liz Kelly, *Surviving Sexual Violence* (Cambridge, Polity, 1988). Based on in-depth interviews with 60 women, this book focuses on women's experiences of a whole range of forms of sexual violence over their lifetimes. The book emphasises the importance of allowing women's own views and definitions as to what constitutes violence to have a voice. In it, Kelly develops the concept of a continuum of violence to show that women's understanding of what is violent, and the significance of violence in their lives, can differ quite drastically from legal and other professional perspectives. The book concludes with a discussion of the implications of the study for feminist services and political organisations.

Marianne Hester, Liz Kelly and Jill Radford (eds), *Women, Violence and Male Power: Feminist Research, Activism and Practice* (Buckingham, Open University Press, 1995). This book highlights the issues and questions that have become central to recent understandings of sexual violence and abuse, and the new directions in which research in this area has developed.

Gill Hague and Ellen Malos, *Domestic Violence: Action for Change* (Cheltenham, New Clarion Press, 1993). The book explores the issue of domestic violence examining definitions and exploring the response of the police (including the notion of a public/private divide). The authors examine legal remedies, the problem of housing for the victims of domestic violence, and the response of statutory agencies and interagency co-operation. Finally they critically assess the founding and aims of 'battering' men's programmes.

Amina Mama, *The Hidden Struggle* (London, London Race and Housing Research Unit, 1993, 2nd edn.). This book examines statutory voluntary sector responses to violence against Black women in the domestic setting. It examines the initiatives of various states to such violence and provides theoretical and practical perspectives which offer a crucial critique of the marginalisation of Black women within previous research, and the response of various agencies to the violence they face.

Jill Radford and Diana E. H. Russell (eds), *Femicide: The Politics of Woman Killing* (Buckingham, Open University Press, 1992). Draws together a wide range of literature which examines the systematic torture and murder of women within different cultures throughout history. Defines femicide as the sexist torture of women. Different authors examine the dangers of the domestic setting. The links between femicide and racism are drawn out as is the role of the mass media, pornography and representations of physical violence/'snuff movies'. Examines problems within the criminal justice system in relation to male violence and documents how some feminists have protested and campaigned for change.

9

Methodology Matters!

Liz Stanley

Introduction

What is a chapter on methodology, specifically on how questions of methodology relate to the production of knowledge, doing in an introduction to Women's Studies? After all, isn't methodology boring and much less important than feminist theory or the ideas of women's history or economics, feminist literary criticism and so on? And anyway, isn't it just a matter of learning about techniques, such as how to carry out interviews or design surveys?

Women's Studies encourages us to ask interesting and centrally important questions. These include: what makes an idea 'feminist' or not? How can Women's Studies be taken more seriously within the academy? Why is 'gender', a concept which is easy enough to understand when reading about it, so difficult when it comes to understanding and changing our relationships and feelings? And why are some people's ideas and some kinds of feminism taken more seriously than others?

Methodology is important, methodology *matters*, because it enables us to ask, and also to begin to answer, these interesting and important questions. This is because 'a methodology' is, at its simplest, a set of linked procedures which are adopted because they specify how to go about reaching a particular kind of analytic conclusion or goal. Therefore, while questions of methodology are often presented in a purely 'technical' way, at root they are concerned with the 'getting of knowledge' and, within Women's Studies, with how knowledge is debated between different kinds of feminism, and also between feminism and the mainstream of the academy. Methodology matters, then, within feminism, because it is the key to understanding and unpacking the overlap between knowledge/power.

This chapter is concerned with exploring this complex and fascinating relationship between methodology and questions concerning the nature of feminist knowledge and, relatedly, with the claims that can be made for this as precisely *knowledge* (rather than, for example, opinion or feeling).[1] It does so by making four closely related arguments about feminism and methodology and exploring their ramifications for how we proceed in creating Women's Studies within the academy:

(a) debates about 'method': in the broadest sense of 'the getting of knowledge', are absolutely central to 'what feminism is about', for 'how we know what we claim to know' is the ethical and political heart of feminist thinking;

(b) the 'methodology debate' within feminism has been frequently mis-represented as a narrow proposal that there is a distinct and unique 'feminist method', whereas work carried out here is in fact constructing an approach which positions methodology as the central component of knowledge and so of feminist epistemology (an 'epistemology' is a theory of what knowledge is, and will be discussed in more detail later);

(c) binary ways of thinking about methodology are unhelpful, while approaches which emphasise methodology as largely a matter of epistemology play down the analytic importance of investigatory procedures which are concerned with observing, describing and ex-plaining the social world;

(d) Women's Studies should be concerned with the production of accoun-table feminist knowledge, and with encouraging real debate rather than operating the same kinds of closures as the academic mainstream.

These four arguments will be explored in the successive sections of the chapter, which begins with some observations about methodology broadly conceived.

Re thinking as a feminist methodology

In 1994 I gave a seminar at the University of Sussex in the UK, hosted by the Mass-Observation Archive, which was concerned with issues in reading documents, using as my example a set of day-diaries written in the later 1930s. More specifically, the seminar dealt with how feminist researchers read 'gender' around such documentary analysis, pointing out that the argument had relevance for the analysis and interpretation of contemporary materials as much as historical ones. Pieced together inductively from these particular documents, by adding together the differences between the content of the diaries of the women and the diaries of the men, I suggested that gender could be summarised as 'women have servants and men never eat' (Stanley, 1995b). Whatever else, this is clearly a very different notion of gender definitions and differences from that which exists within Women's Studies or feminist history, or indeed more widely. My conclusion was to the effect that what comprises 'gender' is a matter of 'reading' (or hearing, or seeing): that is, it is the product of particular interpretive frameworks. Gender is not an *a priori* characteristic of social life or of people or of the content of documents; it is not 'in' these as a 'by definition' component of them, but is instead a construction, one capable of being construed differently in different times and places, by different commentators, using different (or indeed the same) evidences.

The first comment made about what I had argued in the seminar was 'But this isn't revolutionary.' What interests me about this is what a 'revolutionary' argument might look like: is this how an argument or statement is formulated or defined? Can something be rejected as 'not revolutionary' when it had not claimed to be such? Is what is new or challenges convention revolutionary, or does the 'revolutionary' lie in some other kind of quality, and, if so, what might this be? Can we now recognise what is revolutionary, or would the genuinely revolutionary be perceived by contemporaries as odd or disturbing or trivially unimportant?

An instance of the practical utility of asking such apparently abstract questions concerns the history of my PhD oral examination, in 1976. My thesis was concerned with how gender was and might be conceptualised, performed and understood, and during the oral I was asked what Harold Garfinkel's (1967) discussion of the ways the apparently intersexed Agnes presented 'herself' might add to a feminist conceptualisation of gender. My response at that time, I now blush to remember, was to the effect that Garfinkel was admirable for 'admitting' he had been fooled by Agnes into thinking she was a 'real woman'. Thinking about this again a few years later, I 'heard' the question in a very different way, more as I think the examiner had intended it, as being about the performative aspects of gender as revealed by the 'deviant' rather than the conforming in gender terms. Later still, I 'heard' it in yet another way, around Garfinkel being unable to recognise that 'real women' too consciously give (different) gender performances of their 'true' gender, and that this is not reserved for those people who are deviant from the gender order (or rather, as Goffman, 1976, recognised, we are all deviant from the gender order, which is a convention rather than a prescription).

In addition to these thoughts, also running through my mind but not articulated during the Sussex seminar, was my rejection of the 'ideas as unique productions of great minds' approach, instead insisting that ideas are socially produced in particular times and places, and are shared endeavours or productions. I wanted to say that with regard to ideas there is no revolutionary and individual, only the evolutionary and collective. I also wanted to say, but didn't, that the evolution of a feminist mainstream within the academy, with its own canonical ideas, texts, and theoreticians, meant that what I'd said was likely to be new for many of those present, and correspondingly difficult to comprehend because it went against the grain of this emergent feminist canon. In the circumstances I felt unable to say either.

A few weeks before the seminar, I had gone with friends to see a production in Manchester of James Baldwin's play, *Blues for Mr Charlie*. By the end of the performance I felt torn between an admiring response to the extremely powerful stage presence and acting ability of the key women members of the cast, and the diametrically opposed depiction of women and the responses of the male characters to them which aroused my anger towards 'the play', but also towards its author, as I perceived some consonance here with other writings of his. Baldwin's play seemed to me to position black women as complete objects to (all) men, white women as by definition contemptible, white men as synonymous with power and this with the penis (termed as men's 'pecker' in the play), which (all) black men wanted parity with or superiority to. There was more than sexism here, I thought: there was misogyny and an accompanying denial of the salience of gender by subordinating it to issues of (men's) 'race' and racism; however, my attempts to discuss this with my companions led them quickly on to the plays of other male playwrights and their difficulties in creating 'other sex' characters.

The problematics I came away from this occasion with revolved around, on the one hand, how to understand gender, specifically its relationship with 'race'/racism, and on the other with what can be said in the face of intellectual orthodoxies. The 'correct' response articulated by my companions seemed to be that my reaction could be taken note of only as a reaction to the text, and that nothing could be said about the author and his attitudes even by comparing this particular 'text' with others he had written. There are questions here that interest me a good deal: how and in what ways can those of us involved in Women's Studies, gender studies or critical studies of men and masculinities interpret and respond to texts as repositories or representations of sexism or misogyny or racism? What does it mean to propose that a text which inscribes a very strong preferred reading of gender/racism can be, indeed should be, responded to and analysed separately from the role of an author in producing it? How can the relationship between gender and 'race'/racism be understood if the responses of audience members are ignored or denied when these reject the preferred reading and/or propose an alternative?

These vignettes of the seminar and the play point up the broad ideas I am concerned with. The first emphasises that the feminist preoccupation with 'gender' masks difficulties in how gender is apparently 'discovered' in social life, and that these 'operational' aspects of how we think about the political and intellectual issues involved constitute 'methodology' in the most fundamental sense of the term: 'how we think about X, Y or Z as important aspects involved in exploring what A is all about'. The second proposes that how 'texts' are thought of and analysed, whether in ways divorced from the role of their author in their origination (for example, the 'death of the author' argument) or as having connections (to put it no stronger) with authorial intention and accomplishment, is both a methodological matter of how we proceed in thinking about such complex matters, and also politically resonant regarding the nature of feminist analysis. Both vignettes explore similar issues:

(a)   that how to think about gender, and its interconnections with other social structural indicators of systematic inter- as well as intra-generational difference, such as 'race' or class, should not be treated as self-evident;

(b)   how these issues are thought about, and the related adoption of a particular position about the interconnections, provides a framework which signal how a 'package' of information about someone will be understood as indicating where they are to be positioned, socially, politically, intellectually and so on;

(c)   how these issues are presented and explored (that is, the procedural or methodological approach adopted in thinking about feminist issues) is something which *matters* because it affects what is understood as knowledge and who is seen to possess knowledge.

Fundamental here, I have so far implied rather than stated explicitly, is *thinking*. 'Thinking' in the sense I am using it includes how we conceptualise something, how we go about investigating it, how we determine satisfactorily what is sufficient evidence, where the boundaries of the topic of investigation are seen to lie, and how we rethink the 'same' topic from different vantage-points and over time. In discussing these matters, I have been exploring 'methodology' within a feminist frame, as it were 'from the bottom up': that is, by working from what might be termed its 'procedural fundamentals', the most basis and fundamental procedures we adopt in 'finding out', and I have argued that thinking is the most fundamental aspect of a feminist, indeed of any and every, methodology. I now turn to a discussion of the form in which 'feminism' and 'methodology' have been related in a more formal sense, by looking at the debate concerned with feminist methodology which has taken place within Women's Studies since the later 1970s.

Two versions of the 'feminist methodology' debate

There are now a large number of journal articles, textbooks and edited collections concerned with different aspects of 'feminist methodology' and its connections with questions of method on the one hand and issues concerning epistemology on the other. There are a number of ways in which the key ideas, which have been the subject of debate, could be introduced here. Rather than attempting to review all of this literature, this section instead looks at the nature of the debate that has occurred, focusing on what *kind* of debate has taken place; and here two different accounts of this debate are 'compared and contrasted' in order to introduce some of the key issues which have been involved. Following this, Sandra Harding's (1987) influential account of the relationship between method, methodology and epistemology is introduced; and some problems with her emphasis on epistemology, rather than methodology, are outlined.

The first version of the 'feminist methodology' debate to be discussed consists of a set of writings which position this debate in a way which concentrates upon method, and I refer to it as 'the critics' version' of this debate. The critics' version, advanced by a number of influential feminist social scientists,[2] proposes that in the later 1970s the debate started with 'male methods' being specified by some feminist social scientists as almost synonymous with so-called 'hard' or quantified approaches (particularly the survey), and characterises the alternative these feminists preferred as being those methods identified as 'soft' or qualitative approaches (particularly the unstructured in-depth interview). The critics' version suggests that the debate developed as a proposal that there was a distinct feminist method, and this is disapproved of because this is seen as politically as well as intellectually suspect, for two main reasons. The first is that any notion of a 'distinct feminist method' is assumed to be both separatist and essentialist: it could only be adopted and used by women and, relatedly, because only women could be feminists. The second is that it is also treated as relativist because its concern is with the social construction of meaning, with this being seen as a denial of material reality.

There is a 'politics of location' (Rich, 1986) surrounding this critics' version of the 'feminist methodology' debate which is usefully explored here, for it pinpoints some interesting methodological issues as well as providing a means of understanding the 'shape' or form that the debate has taken. Within academic life, it has become a fact of life that students read short accounts of complex bodies of work produced and criticised by third parties, rather than read the original pieces of writing. However, this is no replacement for reading what the original writers have said (those who are the proponents of an argument or position) rather than the critics of it. This is because secondary texts inevitably simplify, not least by shortening and summarising. They often simplify in another sense as well. The intellectual location from which debates and arguments are assembled and presented to an audience constitutes 'a point of view' – and the point of view of a critic is inevitably different from that of the proponent or originator. Recognising this is important, because 'a point of view' is both unavoidable and also indicates the existence of *perspective*: a particular way of seeing which highlights and brings into focus some thing as salient. However, as Ann Oakley (1974) has noted, 'a way of seeing is also a way of not seeing', for bringing some things into focus of course means that others stay in the background and are perceived as less (or not) salient. An example will help to convey this point.

I have expressed my argument here by using an analytic term introduced by Adrienne Rich, 'the politics of location', and for some readers this may be taken to mean I am thereby 'a radical feminist' of a particular kind and will hold the views and beliefs associated with such a position. However, if I had turned the frame a little and instead introduced the same kinds of ideas by reference to Donna Haraway's (1988) term of 'situated knowledges', then, for those readers familiar with this term and Haraway's work more widely, I would have been perceived as a feminist of a different hue, holding different ideas and convictions. Whether rightly or wrongly, the use of particular kinds of reference group is taken to indicate very different points of view, and from these other things are seen to follow: including what political or ethical problems are accorded greatest significance, and how these are perceived, analysed and understood, as well as what strategies are proposed.

While 'the politics of location' and 'situated knowledges' are terms which highlight somewhat different aspects of the same set of feminist issues, nonetheless both convey the fact that different knowledges about the 'same' thing are possible, and also that knowledge is specific because grounded in the 'point of view' of those producing it. Both are concerned to point out that knowledge is a *material* product of particular kinds of social systems, as well as of particular 'epistemic communities' (that is, a set of people sharing an epistemology and so ideas about what 'real knowledge' is). This way of thinking about and theorising knowledge – as something which is specific to time and place and person, and so which is contextual, grounded and material, as well as being rooted in the 'point of view' of particular knowledge-producers who share these ideas with a group of other people who think similarly – is a fundamental contribution which feminist thinking has made. It constitutes the basic aspects of a specifically feminist epistemology, and it also emphasises the importance of how the methodological aspects of knowledge-production are conceived and understood, for it disputes the 'foundationalist' or 'positivist' assumption that sees scientific knowledge as grounded in objective investigation independent of the perceptions of observers, knowing a reality seen as single, 'out there' and entirely independent of the 'point of view' of the investigating scientist.

I have noted in passing above that these ideas are basic to a 'feminist epistemology', to the way that feminism itself theorises what 'knowledge' consists of, how it is produced and by whom, how it can be distinguished from mere opinion, and how adjudicating knowledge claims are to be investigated and by whom. But, working out from these basic ideas, different kinds or styles of feminism interpret what they mean and how they should inform methods of social investigation very differently. This can be seen by pointing out that the 'feminist methodology' debate can look very different indeed when viewed from a different point of view, so that the first, critics', version I introduced above is seen not as 'what actually happened', but as simply a *version* about this, one version among a number of possible ones, as neither the only nor necessarily the best way of understanding these matters. I now turn to explore some aspects of an alternative version of the 'same' debate, comparing the 'critics' version' with the 'feminist methodologists' version'.

The methodologists' version of the feminist methodology debate also starts with the 1970s adoption by some feminist academics of an effectively binary approach to considering methods of research, and it too perceives that there was an association of 'hard' quantified methods with men and masculinity, and 'soft' qualitative methods with women and feminism. The feminist methodologists' version, however, came into existence at the same point in time, and as a *countervailing* set of ideas which insisted upon the complexity of reality and the corresponding need for complex and flexible methodological apparatus for understanding and analysing it in feminist terms. Again, the main people involved in promoting this were feminist social scientists, but social scientists who did not work within structuralist paradigms such as Marxism but instead within broad interactionist terms.[3] This work centred on the notion of 'consciousness', looked at interactionally or phenomenologically: that is, in a grounded and material way which focuses on the analytic procedures used by both 'the subject' and 'the researcher'. It also recognised that both researcher *and* subject were concerned with investigation, analysing and theorising the social world and people and behaviour within it. Perhaps the most contentious aspect of this approach was its insistence that 'subjects' enquire, investigate, analyse, theorise and conclude, and not just researchers, for the critics' version saw feminist researchers as a kind of intellectual vanguard, and 'women' as simply experiencing their lives rather than theorising them as well.

This strand of phenomenologically- or interactionally-focused feminist writing is now not particularly well known, even though the ideas associated with it have become part of the common currency of intellectual and academic life. An example will show why this is so: Dale Spender's (1978) working paper on 'feminist perspectives', which provided an early analysis and rejection of binary ways of thinking, was never published because of the hostility this discussion roused among many feminists who heard it orally or who read the written version. At the time it was seen to be saying something so ridiculous that no one could take it seriously. Of course, subsequently post-modernist and deconstructionist ways of thinking have become topical, and so an approach which rejects binary ways of thinking is not only no longer considered as odd or disturbing or trivially unimportant, but has become part of 'required ways of thinking'.

However, in the 1970s things were different, and there was a widespread feminist rejection of such ideas. But this did not bring about the demise of this way of thinking about methodological matters within academic feminism more widely, and from the early 1980s on there was an increasing interest in analytically exploring what the main ramifications of these ideas were for a feminist epistemology, and this occurred at more or less the same time that similar ideas associated with post-modernism and deconstructionism were gaining currency within social theory. The most important ideas of this kind which were associated with work within the feminist methodologists' version being produced at that time were:

(a)   knowledge is constructed from where the researcher/theoretician is situated and so feminist knowledge should proceed from the position of the feminist academic within the academy, working outwards;
(b)   academic feminism is implicated in the creation of gender binaries through the kinds of models or theories it promotes, which tend to over-dichotomise the social world;
(c)   the social world, including in its gendered aspects, is complex, and equally complex means of investigating and knowing it are required which reject dichotomised or binary ways of thinking;
(d)   producing accountable feminist knowledge requires analytic means of looking at the detailed processes of knowledge production;
(e)   what is analytically, ethically and politically important are the broad methodological procedures which underpin social investigation.

The work represented in this version, the feminist methodologists' version, did not argue in favour of a distinct or unique 'feminist method'[4] as the critics' version had suggested. Indeed, method in the sense of technique was never a matter of concern for its proponents, for this approach is instead concerned with presuppositions (ways of seeing and understanding), methodological procedures (broad ideas about suitable approaches to investigation), and epistemological claims-making (claims about the knowledge seen as resulting from such procedures).

Standing back from the 'bones' of these two versions of the feminist methodology debate, it is striking how different they are. Although both see feminist statements about 'hard' and 'soft' methods in the 1970s as the starting point for such debates, thereafter they diverge considerably. What is less obvious is how this difference relates to epistemological claims-making: who is claiming what kind of knowledge and how those who disagree with them are positioned.

Version one, the critics' version of the feminist methodology debate, comments upon the debate and criticises work associated with it, rather than being situated within it and being a part of it. It presents the culmination of the debate as the specification of a distinct and unique 'feminist method', something which is depicted as objectionable and/or ridiculous in its aspiration and failed in its accomplishment. The claims-making of the critics' version is centred upon its right to 'name' the terms of the debate and to make evaluations of what is 'failure'. This is seen in the critics' version in other ways as well: it presents itself as outside and detached; and it highlights aspects of the content of the debate, and in particular the supposed 'feminist method', which had no importance or relevance to those who were actually involved.

Version two, the feminist methodologists' version of the debate, is firmly situated within the debate, and is a central part of it. The concern here is not to criticise from the outside, but instead to explore how in feminist terms it might be possible to link 'methodological procedures' with 'epistemological presuppositions', and to do so in ways that can inform feminist research practice. The claims-making of the feminist methodologists' version focuses on the nature of knowledge as seen by feminists, and with how claims to generate and possess knowledge are 'grounded': that is, what kind of evidence, generated in what kinds of ways, and under what kinds of research circumstance, is seen as 'necessary' and 'sufficient'. It has also pointed out that feminist knowledge claims cannot be treated as 'by definition' superior to other kinds of knowledge claims; there are no grounds for assuming that 'feminist knowledge' is by definition, and *a priori*, preferable, and it should be subject to the same kinds of critical enquiries, including by feminists, as other kinds of knowledge claims-making are.

Does the difference between these two contrasting versions of the feminist methodology debate matter? After all, I have already argued that knowledge differs according to point of view, so perhaps this difference should be seen as simply an example of this and nothing more. However, the difference *does* matter, because it has consequences for what 'the debate' is seen to consist of and to be about, and also the kinds of evaluations that are made of work produced within it:

(a) because version one is formulated as a critique, as a critics' version which emphasises problems and weaknesses, this puts the ideas and arguments of version two, the feminist methodologists' version, in a subordinate position: being commented on and found wanting;

(b) however, the critics' version contains few ideas and arguments of its own, and it is largely dependent for its 'ideas content' on criticising the positive contributions of others;

(c) nonetheless, the critics' version claims the right to evaluate ideas and to treat contrary views as wrong.

This way of arguing, associated with the critics' version of the feminist methodology debate, is itself methodological in basis; and it consists of a set of procedures in which (a) single elements are abstracted from a broader context of work seen as 'other' in some way, then (b) these elements are treated as though they are not only closely related but also stand for the totality, and then (c) these are presented in ways which depict them as self-evidently wrong or false. Marx and Engels in *The German Ideology* (1970) referred to this process as the production of ideology, while Dorothy Smith (1974b) has termed it the 'ideological three-step', which first, abstracts a few aspects of an argument, second, treats these as though they are related and also the whole of the argument, and third, then criticises the argument for being simplistic. The critics' version, version one, operates a closure device: it inhibits proper debate by associating 'opponents', the proponents of version two, with extremism, separatism and essentialism; and this in turn helps to create and maintain a hierarchy of knowledge and knowers and thus of power relations within academic feminism. As this example shows, methodology can be politically and ethically resonant because there are consequences for how different viewpoints are evaluated when these are placed in a 'hierarchy of credibility'; and the closer a set of methodological procedures is to the 'ideological three-step' outlined above, the more politically resonant these procedures are in this sense.

So far in this section of the chapter I have provided an account of the 'feminist methodology' debate by looking at two of the different positions within this, and I have also argued that the debate itself has methodological aspects and consequences. Methodology matters are not optional extras which can be taken into account or left on one side: they are central to discussions of epistemology, ethics and politics, for they provide the grounding for what we think, but also how we think it, how we proceed to go about the business of finding out and thus of knowing, and they also specify the relationships that exist between different and competing positions. 'Epistemic privilege' is involved when one viewpoint claims a super-ordinate position over another or others, and, while there can be many bases for claiming such privilege, the positioning of another viewpoint as by definition wrong because different is both commonly made use of and is methodological as well as ideological in nature.

However, there are of course other accounts of 'the feminist methodology' debate than the two outlined here, and at this stage it is worth outlining Sandra Harding's (1987) discussion, which distinguishes between:

(a)   'method' in the sense of a specific technique such as a survey, interview or ethnography;
(b)   'methodology' in the sense of a theory or conceptualisation; and
(c)   'epistemology' in the sense of a theory of knowledge.

Harding's discussion starts by rejecting what she perceives as the emphasis on 'feminist method'. This demonstrates the impact of the critics' version of the debate over and against that of the feminist methodologists, who, as I have discussed, have actually been concerned with questions of methodology and epistemology, and not those of method. Harding's work too is concerned mainly with epistemology, and she outlines what she sees as the three main epistemological positions within academic feminism, positions which came into existence in the following order of development:

(a) 'successor science' – a foundationalist form of feminism which is concerned with investigating and presenting 'real science' rather than the faulty science seen as resulting from masculinist assumptions and ways of working;

(b) 'standpoint' – an approach concerned to investigate and theorise the social world 'from the standpoint of women'; and

(c) 'post-modern' – an epistemology which rejects the idea that there is a 'real reality' independent of interpretation and which highlights the existence of interpretational disputes.

Harding's discussion provides another starting point for thinking about such matters although, as with any simple 'heuristic model', or set of 'boxes' which simplify and divide up arguments and positions, there is the temptation to think that this is how feminists actually understand and theorise knowledge 'on the ground'.[5] However, the methodology debates within feminism cannot be fitted into Harding's model, for a number of reasons: first, all three of these kinds of argument about the nature of knowledge from a feminist viewpoint have co-existed since the late 1970, even though they may not have been given these labels. Second, the ideas and approach described as 'post-modern' and a late arrival on the scene were actually central to version two, the methodologists' version of the feminist methodology debate, and which indeed were a large part of why it was so dismissively criticised by the critics. And third, both version one, the critics' version, and version two, the methodologists' version, contain elements of all three of the epistemological ideas which Harding divides up and allocates to mutually-exclusive 'boxes' within her model.

However, this does not mean that Harding's work should be rejected, but rather that it should be treated cautiously as a *model*, in the way I suspect she intended, instead of as a *description*, in the way that many of her readers have done. My particular interest in it here is concerned with her discussion of method and methodology as derivative of epistemology and therefore to be 'bracketed' (safely placed on one side) while the 'real question' for feminism of epistemology is considered. This is certainly a plausible argument, and one I and Sue Wise have adapted and used from Harding's work (Stanley and Wise, 1990), but more recently I have begun to re-think its utility in the light of the issues introduced through the two vignettes I began this chapter with. This re-thinking is connected with the different ways Sandra Harding and I use the term 'methodology'.

For Harding, methodology is a term which corresponds with the social science notion of 'perspective': a theory which contains within it a specification of how the theory is to be applied in particular grounded research areas. However, I see it as instead a set of linked 'procedural' or 'operational' elements which provide the grounding for 'investigating', in the broad sense I used this term at the start of the chapter. My emphasis has been upon these operational procedures 'for investigating', and with looking at how these link together epistemological presuppositions with what are deemed satisfactory procedures for establishing knowledge. Harding's emphasis is, in contrast, upon the conceptual aspects of methodology, rather than these operational and procedural aspects. For Harding, 'theory and method' are seen as consonant, with theory specifying appropriate method, whereas my view is that methodology is potentially and sometimes actually independent of formal theory, for the suppositions grounding methodological procedures adopted in grounded research situations can be (and often are) at odds with those of a theoretical position which is derived from 'the literature'.

This might seem at first sight like splitting hairs, but in fact this difference in emphasis is consequential. Harding's approach rejects method as a sphere of analytic attention; and it shifts feminist analytic attention away from methodological procedures for investigating, and towards epistemological concerns. However, my approach foregrounds methodological procedures as analytically crucial for feminism in their own right, because they can provide the grounds for producing accountable feminist knowledge. Focusing on 'actual methodology', through a detailed analytic exploration of the phenomenology of emergent feminist consciousness within particular grounded research contexts, can make much clearer – and so make available for scrutiny by others – the grounds of the knowledge claims that feminist researchers make. I go on to discuss the importance of this in the next section of the chapter.

Some methodological 'isms'

As well as providing an account of ideas and debates concerning 'feminist methodology', I have also introduced and explained a number of technical terms, including 'methodology' itself, but also 'epistemology' and 'method'; 'foundationalism', 'positivism', 'knowledge claims', 'epistemic community' and 'epistemic privilege'; the 'politics of location', 'situated knowledges'; and 'methodological procedures' and 'epistemological presuppositions'. In doing so, my concern has been to scrutinise, explain and discuss what 'methodology' is within feminism, because it is surprisingly rarely that methodology is looked at in analytic detail: all too often, it is seen as simply not important enough to be discussed.

However, when 'methodology' is introduced to people, then the term is usually attached to a variety of qualifiers – methodological deductivism, holism, idealism – with most attention being paid to the qualifier, rather than the basic term itself. Moreover, these qualifiers are presented in terms of 'either/or' binary distinctions (methodological deductivism versus inductivism, holism versus individualism, realism versus idealism). These qualifying terms offer apparently convenient ways of pigeon-holing persons, ideas and positions; however, their convenience lies in their simplification of matters which are in my view too complex, as well as too important, to be reduced to binary choices. A brief discussion of the three main sets of qualifiers for methodology – methodological deductivism and inductivism, methodological holism and individualism, and methodological realism and idealism – will both introduce the terms and also show some of the problems here in feminist terms.

'Methodological deductivism' is usually contrasted against 'methodological inductivism'. Deductivism is positioned as an approach which involves devising a theoretical account formed around hypotheses which are then 'tested' against research experience so that the theoretical model can be confirmed or revised. Inductivism is described as an approach in which theory is devised from the details of research, being seen as the result of such research rather than its origin. The deductivist model carries considerable 'clout' because this is the 'scientific method' seen to produce objective, reliable, generalisable, scientific knowledge. Within much feminist thinking the claims of 'objective science' have been rejected because they are clearly biased by masculinist assumptions and ways of working,[6] and inductivism has been presented as a suitable feminist alternative because it grounds knowledge in 'experience': theory is derived from practice, rather than proceeding it.

However, both deductivism and inductivism are models: they are not realistic descriptions of what actually happens when research is carried out, and neither is actually *possible*, let alone plausible, as a prescription for actual research practice. Although deductive models, theories and hypotheses can indeed be formulated and 'tested', doing this requires simplification of the social world and the knowledge that the researcher has of it; consequently in good research conducted within a deductive framework this 'extra knowledge' is in practice made considerable use of, both in underpinning the model and also in informing the analysis and interpretation of results. The notion of inductivism is similarly problematic. It proceeds from the assumption that researchers can have 'empty heads' as they start their research, so that what is 'induced' will not be preconceived through the lens of prior knowledge. This is an assumption which, once thought about, is clearly untenable; we can never 'empty our heads' of what we already know and this forms the backcloth of any new knowledge we gain, which is fitted into the existing framework. Moreover, feminist

variants of inductivism, like the 'standpoint' epistemology discussed by
Harding, tend to conflate the *subjects'* concepts and ideas with those of
researchers. Thus, for example, 'feminist standpoint' research often oscil-
lates between the views of its women subjects and the feminist views of the
researcher.

'Methodological holism' is contrasted against 'methodological individualism'. Holism is a position described as seeing social wholes as having their
own functions separate from the activities and purposes of individuals, and
which discounts the influence of individuals on social phenomena, while
methodological individualism is described as seeing social wholes as outcomes rather than essences and as insisting that individual understandings
and actions need to be taken into account. Holism is often presented as
though synonymous with Marxism, but it also includes functionalism and
other positions, including some within feminism, which ascribe determining
power in social life to abstract forces such as, for example, history,
capitalism, the unconscious, and indeed patriarchy. Methodological individualism is frequently presented by critics as though it is 'individualist' in
sense of being 'reductionist' and 'solipsist': that is, that it reduces society to
individuals, and that individuals are seen as each trapped in their own
subjectivities and entirely separate from each other.

However, there is in fact no need for the recognition that 'people make
history and society' to exclude the related recognition that this is not 'in
conditions of their own choosing', to paraphrase Marx's famous dictum
here. And neither does recognition of 'existential solipsism' (that we are all
alone inside our heads and feelings) require the adoption of 'methodological
solipsism' (for in practice it is possible to traverse this 'aloneness' because
common understandings can be and are reached between people). In fact,
most feminist ideas and arguments work from a position of methodological
holism; however, cries of 'individualism' are often used to criticise or even
dismiss contrary viewpoints. This has been an important element in the
feminist methodology debate, at least in the sense that the critics' version
has used charges of 'individualism' as a means of denying credibility to the
feminist methodologists' version, while the methodologists' version has
actually been concerned to argue that feminist ideas and viewpoints should
'work' at the level of actual people, not just at the level of large-scale
generalisations, and that feminist knowledge should not be 'alienated
knowledge' which dismisses people's own understandings and ideas if they
differ from the generalised tenets of 'theory'.

'Methodological realism' is contrasted against 'methodological idealism'.
Realism is referred to as the insistence that a material objective world exists
independently of any social construction, and, relatedly, that foundational
knowledge about this can be gained through suitable investigatory means
carried out objectively by dispassionate scientists. Methodological idealism,
in contrast, is presented as the view that it is impossible to know the material

world because all that exists is a welter of endless subjectivities which give rise to an 'infinite regress': a radical relativism of infinite relative pronouncements about the world, rather than any certain statement about the nature of reality or means of deciding which pronouncement captures this reality. This is certainly one of the criticisms that version one of the feminist methodology debate, the critics' version, has made of the feminist methodologists' position.

However, idealism is actually misrepresented here by being presented as denying the existence of a material reality and as a form of radical relativism: recognising the importance of interpretation in social life and of social construction of meaning and knowledge does *not* mean denying the existence of an external material reality and neither does it mean adopting a radical relativist position. Again, this is more a critics' version of what this set of arguments 'adds up to', rather than one belonging to people who hold a so-called 'idealist' viewpoint. This is demonstrated by looking at what the feminist methodologists have actually written, which suggests that social life is complex, and different interpretations of meaning exist which should be respected and explored even if not accepted. To reduce this to a denial that 'reality' exists is at best mistaken, while to propose that it is arguing in favour of radical relativism is a simplification of relativism.

These ways of thinking about and categorising methodological arguments and viewpoints – deductivism versus inductivism, holism versus individualism, realism versus idealism – are frequently used, including within feminist discussions, to characterise positions and indeed to describe and explain different bodies of ideas about methodology matters. However, they present what are actually highly complex issues, containing many shades of opinion with them, in terms of sets of *binary oppositions*. They result in a oversimplistic way of thinking about such matters, for it is usually less a matter of 'either/or', and more one of 'and/also', in thinking about such ideas. In addition, it should be noted that the 'subjugated' end of each binary pair here is used less as a description and more as a means of denying credibility to someone else's position, rather like the term 'essentialist' is used to discredit particular persons, pieces of work or bodies of ideas (Fuss, 1989). That is, the 'subjugated' end of each binary is not a proponents' view of what this is, but instead a view formulated from a contrary and dismissive position. No academic feminists claim themselves to be essentialists, while many are 'described' as being such by critics who reject their work. And similarly, few (if any) feminists claim to be, for example, idealists or individualists, but these terms are used to criticise many people's work by commentators who object to it and who use such terms to indicate its assumed inadequacies.

An example of their use in this way is Maureen Cain's (1990) presentation of her work as feminist realism which is also holist and deductivist, and in contrast characterising, indeed caricaturing, my work with Sue Wise (such as Stanley and Wise, 1983) as idealist in the sense of purportedly denying that a material reality exists, individualist in the sense of supposedly holding reductionist views, and inductivist because apparently eschewing theory. This ignores our explicit disavowal of idealism, individualism and inductivism. It also considerably exaggerates differences between her position and ours, and ignores the considerable similarities, by assigning them to opposing binary positions. The twin lessons here are that such binary devices are far too simplistic for thinking about methodological matters, and should certainly be avoided as weapons for attempting to discredit ideas with which one disagrees. Disagreement is an honourable matter for exploration and discussion, while misrepresentation through binary categorisation is not helpful because it inhibits the serious evaluation of ideas.

Accountable feminist knowledge

If these binary qualifiers are unsuitable means for thinking about methodology matters in feminist terms, what then might constitute better means of doing so? In discussing this, I return to the idea of 'accountable feminist knowledge'. In the wider sense in which I have been using the term, methodology consists of an investigation of the aims, concepts and principles of reasoning of some epistemological position; that is, epistemology is dependent on methodological precepts, or rather neither of these is separable from the other. There are three main areas of enquiry within methodology in this sense:

(a) observation;
(b) description;
(c) explanation.

Within social sciences and philosophy, the weight of scrutiny is generally placed on the first and last of these, but it is the second, description, which raises the most complex and interesting issues as well as those most germane to the notion of accountable feminist knowledge.

The idea of 'situated knowledge' within feminism, introduced earlier, indicates that there is *a person* who produces this knowledge, who investigates, observes, describes, theorises, concludes and explains. The notion of accountable feminist knowledge builds on this and related insights drawn from the methodologists' version of the feminist methodology debate. Central here is the insistence that the stance of the observer should be recognised, together with the insistence that interpretation is complex and different points of view are possible from the one reached. Relatedly, it is not possible adequately to account for 'the researcher' and the situated knowledge they produce without pinpointing more precisely the different activities involved in 'research': just what does it mean, to 'observe', to 'describe' and to 'explain'?

In conventional ideas about research, the act of *observation* is interpreted in terms of research methods or techniques, as being self-evidently what these methods 'capture'. However, it is more complex than this. *Description* is the act of observation represented in a form which can be commented upon by other parties (and which can be provided through numbers and pictures as well as words). Typically, description is 'bracketed', ignored as having analytic significance because of its taken-for-granted insignificance as a methodological and an analytic act in its own right. However, as Harvey Sacks (1963) pointed out many years ago, the literal description of social events is not possible, any more than description can exist in a one-to-one referential relationship to that which it purports to describe. Rather, description is a 'gloss', a typification of the presumed meaning of such events: 'I went to the meeting; there was a row between Mr X and Ms Y' is not actually 'a description', for it contains two glosses – 'a meeting' and 'a row' – which are provided instead of describing what actually happened. And also an explanation, even of a basic kind, about 'what happened' is also contained within these 'glosses'.

In thinking about the third component of methodology referred to above – *explanation* – and its relationship to description, 'an explanation' consists of three closely related formal elements:

(a)   the 'explans', or premises of the explanation;
(b)   the 'explanadum', or the thing to be explained; and
(c)   the conclusion itself.

'A description', as a theorised account of aspects of social life, contains within it the premises upon which the description is based, and because of this it thereby contains a crucial part of what 'an explanation' consists of , because such premises also define the problem to be explained and suitable conclusions which can be reached. 'A row' is an explanation of a piece of social behaviour, not just an observation or description. Explanations, of course, are not confined to the simple and causal: there are probabilistic, deductive, genetic and many other kinds of what 'a satisfactory explanation' can be like. However, the point I am making here is that the seeds or beginnings of an explanation are already to be found in the description of social phenomenon for which explanation is sought. Whichever way we approach it, description assumes central place as *the* site for enquiry of methodology matters.

If we want to produce accountable feminist knowledge, then, we need to take account of the issues involved in 'description'. How do we describe the social world and what preconceptions are built into this? And are contrary descriptions available and might these be in some way preferable? What status do feminist descriptions of the social world currently have, including for those whose lives we research? What are the limitations, if any, to accountability when 'our' descriptions clash with 'theirs'? These questions do not have easy answers, as a simple example will indicate. In a project where a feminist meeting was recorded and then transcribed (Poland, 1990), some of the participants insisted that the 'literal words' didn't actually describe what had taken place: yes, they had said those things, but, no, in the context of the meeting the people present hadn't interpreted the meaning literally. What does 'accountable feminist knowledge' look like here? Should 'the real words' override 'the meaning'? And if 'the meaning' prevails, then what would it mean to discount 'the real words' that were spoken? In fact the researcher here chose to discuss the issues involved and to emphasise how complex these matters are, a complexity which is often hidden because researchers deal in generalities rather than discuss in detail concrete issues of interpretation.

Tying together some of these issues and complexities, there seem to be a number of key elements to 'accountability' within feminist research, all of them 'methodological'. They involve:

(a)   the provision of retrievable data;
(b)   the detailed specification of the analytic procedures involved; and
(c)   the in-depth discussion of the interpretive acts that produce 'findings' and 'conclusions'.

'Retrievable data' is data which is presented 'on the page' for readers to interpret and to comment upon, so as to be able to compare their interpretations with those of the researcher. In a sense, then, this requires that feminist texts not only 'stick to the data', but also present the data that they stick to, and this is as much true for 'theoretical writing' as it is for 'research accounts'. The analytic procedures involved should be made 'transparent', in the sense of being presented and argued in the order in which they were pieced together (which is, of course, not necessarily the temporal order of their occurrence) and the findings and conclusions, and so explanation, reached so that readers can follow this and evaluate it themselves. Of course the act of writing transforms from the act of thinking, so that such 'transparency' in the provision of analytic procedures is a device of writing (that is, there is no guarantee that it will have actually have occurred in the way the writer 'describes'), but still, the provision of a written account of such procedures provides texts which are considerably more 'open' than academic texts, even feminist ones, are usually; and their 'openness' exists in the fact they are capable of detailed analytic interrogation by readers.

When the researcher's acts of interpretation are provided in detail, step by step, then readers can unravel the specific interpretive procedures involved, deciding which they agree with and which they do not, which they can follow and which they cannot, which are satisfactorily accounted for and which are not. An 'open text' in this sense permits feminist knowledge to become considerably more accountable by enabling readers to interrogate and evaluate the analysis made of the evidence provided.

Of course this is a very brief and schematic account of what 'accountable feminist knowledge' might look like. However, it does emphasise the importance, indeed the centrality, of methodology within this. Consequently, it also emphasises that for those feminist researchers who are concerned with issues of accountability, this cannot be reduced to any simple formula of 'taking the research back'; as I have noted, even 'the words themselves' do not necessarily settle the kinds of interpretational complexities involved.

Are conclusions to methodology matters possible?

Of course, what is 'accountable feminst knowledge' should be a matter for debate. However, a *real* debate about feminist methodology has not yet happened for the reasons outlined earlier, and in particular because of the use of binaries to produce acts of closure by mis/representing contrary positions, and through positioning critics hegemonically, as 'the knowers' of methodology matters within feminism. What is needed now is an actual, real, debate, one involving an exchange of ideas and the thoughtful interrogation of alternative approaches, so that the heuristic devices or models which divide up people, as well as approaches, and place them within fixed 'boxes' can be eschewed in favour of the contextualisation of knowledge and of methodology.

A 'conclusion' is the point at which the settlement of an issue or discussion is reached. There can be no conclusion in this sense to this chapter, because it is not yet clear even what the basic terms and issues of the 'feminist methodology' debate should be, or what kinds of evidence and procedures would be deemed necessary to reach such a settlement. This is in part of course a product of the nature of feminism, or indeed any other complex body of ideas: these matters remain open to debate; or, rather, they *should* remain open to debate, although too often closures have been operated by one variant of feminism over and against others here. In point of fact everything methodological remains at issue, which makes this a singularly interesting as well as crucially important area of feminist intellectual activity.

I have argued here that methodology is 'where the action is', analytically speaking, and consequently that there is a need to take considerably more seriously 'how we do what we do' within Women's Studies. My chapter has proposed that methodology matters within feminism, and indeed that there is no 'beyond methodology' possible (Fonow and Cook, 1991). Without methodology we cannot *think*, indeed we cannot *be*; beyond methodology there is death, silence, the end.

Notes

1. The chapter is concerned with methodology in the broad sense of 'procedures for investigation', and not with the uses by feminists of the range of 'methods' or specific research techniques which are available; this latter aspect is usefully discussed in Reinharz (1992).
2. These writings have emanated from sometimes different kinds of feminism, but the kinds of arguments advanced overlap sufficiently to warrant being referred to as 'a set' arguing a position in a similar way. Early contributions include Barrett (1986, 1987); Clegg (1985); Currie (1988); Currie and Kazi (1987); and later contributions include Abu-Lugod (1990); Game (1991); Gelsthorpe (1990); Hollway (1989); Weedon (1987). For reasons of space, these contributions are not discussed in any detail here, although they are reviewed in Stanley and Wise (1993), pp. 1–15 and 186–233.
3. Contributions here include: Bartky (1977); Cook (1983); Cook and Fonow (1986); Daniels (1975); Eichler (1980, 1985); D. Smith (1974a, 1974b, 1978, 1987); Spender (1978, 1981); Stanley and Wise (1979, 1983); Wilkinson (1986). Again, space considerations mean this work is not discussed here in any detail, although it is reviewed in Stanley (1990a) and Stanley and Wise (1990, 1993).
4. Shulamit Reinharz (1979) has been the main proponent of the notion of a distinct feminist method although, curiously, she has almost never been referenced in these debates.
5. As I and Sue Wise (1990) have argued, these are not accurate even as a depiction of those feminists whose work is seen as providing a paradigm instance of such positions (for example, regarding Dorothy Smith and the 'feminist standpoint').
6. The feminist critique of science, including by feminists who are also well-known scientists, has been a highly influential strand within the development of the feminist critique of academia and knowledge production more generally. Many of these ideas are reviewed in Rose (1994).

Further Reading

Martyn Hammersley (1992) 'On feminist methodology', *Sociology*, 26, pp. 187–206.

Caroline Ramazonoglu (1992) 'On feminist methodology: male reason versus female empowerment', *Sociology*, 26, pp. 207–12.

Lorraine Gelsthorpe (1992) 'Response to Martyn Hammersley's paper "On feminist methodology"', *Sociology*, 26, pp. 213–18.

Anne Williams (1993) 'Diversity and agreement in feminist ethnography', *Sociology*, 27, pp. 575–89.

A set of articles which debate the nature of feminist methodology, with Hammersley seeing this as both a search for a 'feminist method' and the source of an anti-reason bias, while Ramazonoglu emphasises the ways in which this argument is in fundamental opposition to feminist tenets about the masculinism of how 'reason' and 'science' are understood. Gelsthorpe argues that experience and reason are not polarised in the ways suggested, and Williams points out that, contrary to Hammersley's insistence on uniformity, feminist responses to questions of methodology are considerably more diverse and contain a range of positions concerning reflexivity, power and knowledge.

Sandra Harding (ed.) *Feminism and Methodology* (Buckingham, Open University Press, 1987).

A highly influential reader, the introduction of which is concerned with 'method, methodology and epistemology' and especially epistemology. The contributing chapters offer examples of the different feminist epistemological positions reviewed earlier by Harding: successor science, standpoint and post-modern.

Mary Maynard and June Purvis (eds) *Researching Women's Lives from a Feminist Perspective* (London, Taylor & Francis, 1994). A collection derived from a Women's Studies Network (UK) conference. Contains useful short and accessible contributions offering a wide variety of examples from people at all stages in their academic lives. However, not all feminist research is concerned with 'women's lives' necessarily, and so the utility of many of the ideas advanced needs to be considered in relation to research on men, gender relations and children.

Shulamit Reinharz *Feminist Methods in Social Research* (Oxford University Press, 1992). A useful overview of the feminist use of the range of social science methods available, although its roughly equal length chapters gives a rather skewed impression, for certainly in published work feminist use of the survey, followed by interviews, far outweighs the utilisation of other methods.

Liz Stanley (ed.) *Feminist Praxis: Research, Theory and Epistemology in Feminist Sociology* (London, Routledge, 1990a).

The introductory chapters look at 'the academic mode of production' from a feminist perspective and review in detail a wide range of contributions to the debate about feminist methodology. The other chapters discuss issues which arose in a very wide range of different kinds of feminist research projects, with an emphasis on looking at epistemology in an accessible and grounded way.

10

The Black Hole: Women's Studies, Science and Technology

Lynda Birke and Marsha Henry

To ignore, to fail to engage in the social process of making science, and to attend only to the use and abuse of the results of scientific work is irresponsible. I believe it is even less responsible in present historical conditions to pursue anti-scientific tales about nature that idealize women, nurturing, or some other entity argued to be free of male war-tainted pollution. Scientific stories have too much power as public myth to effect meaning in our lives – Haraway, 1991, p. 107

A great strength of Women's Studies is its interdisciplinarity; we can use the insights of different disciplines to cut across their boundaries and create new understandings. Yet it is also its weakness, in the sense that Women's Studies is not nearly as interdisciplinary as it ought to be. More precisely, there are substantial areas of academic enquiry that have not played as large a part in the development of feminist theory as they should. Science and technology are among these: only quite recently has much serious consideration of science and technology begun to enter feminist theorising.

Yet – as the quotation above from Donna Haraway emphasises – science is enormously powerful in our lives. To fail to engage with it, or to cast it as inherently tainted and apart from our lives, is deeply irresponsible. Precisely because of the power of science and technology, to engage with it, to try to change it, is a profoundly political act.

In this chapter, we want to begin by sketching out some of the early development of feminist critiques of science and technology. From there, we focus on some specific areas to illustrate the kind of work that is now emerging in feminist scholarship, particularly in relation to feminist work on the new genetics, on theorising the body and on developing global perspectives. Finally, we end by some speculation: what kind of new directions might feminist scholars pursue? What directions are needed?

The women's movement and science

Earlier phases of feminism certainly engaged with science. Nineteenth-century feminists, for instance, tried to deal with the social consequences of evolutionary ideas; among these, Antoinette Brown Blackwell wrote critiques in 1875 of social Darwinism (Blackwell, in Rossi, 1974). There was, too, feminist activism around scientific issues, such as the (ab)use of animals in experiments: links were clearly made by some nineteenth-century campaigners against vivisection between the abuse of animals and that of women (Elston, 1987; Birke, 1991).

At the beginning of 'second-wave' feminism, however, there was relatively little engagement with science. Women had, as Hilary Rose has pointed out, rather more pressing issues, such as the defence of abortion legislation, to contend with (Rose, 1994, p. 2). There was, too, some hostility towards science within the women's movement, which sometimes collapsed into hostility towards women scientists (as one of us well remembers). Yet simultaneously feminist practice was drawing upon science, at least in the form of the women's health movement. Women's self-help groups, given particular impetus by the transatlantic publication of the Boston Women's Health Collective book, *Our Bodies, Ourselves*, sought to develop our own knowledge of how our bodies work (also see Chapter 13 below). At the very least, women learned some physiology in the process.

While many women in the women's liberation movement of the 1970s were hostile to science (and with good reason), there were small numbers of feminists working in science. As they came together, groups were formed, such as the London Women and Science Collective and the Brighton Women and Science Group: neither of these was concerned solely with issues to do with the scarcity of women in science, but they dealt also with issues to do with how science conceptualised women. It was that wider focus which was quite radical. What made these analyses radical was precisely their questioning of the content and practice of science. It was not – and is not – women who are the problem when the dearth of women in science is under discussion: rather, a good part of the problem lies with science itself.

At the beginning of the 1970s, that recognition stemmed from the growing awareness of the part played by science in destruction. Unlike the pre-war optimism towards science in the 1930s, those who grew up after 1945 were only too well aware of the potential of science to destroy. The dreadful destruction and genocide of the Vietnam War further reminded us of the double-edged sword of scientific progress. Not surprisingly, then, feminist critiques of the 1970s focused intensively on the destructive power of science, whether that be power over women, over non-white people, over non-heterosexuals, over the environment, or over other creatures (see, for example, Brighton Women and Science Group, 1980).

After 1980, however, there was a perceptible (if slow) growth in feminist scholarship in science and technology. The work also became more nuanced and detailed; and other discussion/activist groups formed, at least for short periods. Feminist scholarship in these areas has developed, too, now including work on physics and much more on technology, as well as developing extensive analyses of epistemology.

Overview: feminist critiques of science and technology

The scientific revolution . . . provide[d] crucial support for the polarization of gender required by industrial capitalism. In sympathy with . . . the growing division between male and female, public and private, work and home, modern science opted for an ever greater polarization of mind and nature, reason and feeling, objective and subjective; in parallel with the gradual desexualization of women, it offered a de-animated, de-sanctified, and increasingly mechanized conception of nature. In so doing, science itself became an active agent of change. (Keller, 1985, pp. 63–4)

A great deal of feminist scholarship has, indeed, focused on the various ways in which science has both become gendered and in turn reinforced social conceptualisations of gender. To say that science is gendered is not – as Evelyn Fox Keller has repeatedly had to emphasise – to say that women are less able to do it, or that we necessarily do it differently. Rather, it is to argue that science, as a way of looking at the world, is conceptually gendered; the distancing stance of objectivity, for example, is stereotypically associated with masculinity in Western culture (Keller, 1985). That, of course, is likely to have an impact on who gets to do it in the first place. Not surprisingly, then, men have long outnumbered women in the research activities of science and technology.

Women continue to be underrepresented in the ranks of scientists. Whatever the reasons for that relative absence from science and technology, governments and industry have begun to wake up to the fact that over half the potential work force is women. One consequence of this growing concern is a flurry of activities and organisations whose aim is to promote women's interests or to encourage more women into science. In the UK there is, for example, the long-established Women's Engineering Society, and the more recent Association of Women in Science and Engineering; and women's issues have increasingly been appearing on the agendas of major science organisations, such as the British Association and the Royal Society.

One important strand of these various initiatives involves attempts to encourage women into science by various means, including changing the curriculum and its delivery. This has entailed, for example, developing 'girl friendly science' (in which examples might be drawn from activities girls are likely to have experienced, rather than from typically 'male' activities), and working with teachers to change classroom practice. It is important, for instance, for teachers to ensure that girls really do get a chance at 'hands-on' activities; otherwise, boys will hog the apparatus, expecting the girls to take the notes. One such project was the Manchester-based Girls into Science and Technology initiative (GIST; see Whyte, 1986b). Sue Rosser has written extensively on the kinds of initiatives that are needed to bring more women into science. As she insists, we can go only so far if we merely open the doors to women; we must also change curricula and make teachers of science more aware of how gender-insensitive their practice can be. And, she points out, we need also to encourage teachers to recognise how gendered is much of the content of the science they teach (Rosser and Kelly, 1994).

Challenging the content is, of course, rather more difficult. It is also rather threatening to many scientists, including many women scientists, and particularly so when feminists assert that science is masculine and needs to be changed. In the context of speaking about feminism and science to a meeting of the British Association in 1985, one of us encountered hostility from a woman scientist in the audience: 'But if you succeed in changing it', she agonised, 'it would no longer be science'. Indeed: it would no longer be the kind of science that so many of us have criticised.

Another strand of feminist work on women's place in science has been to reclaim history: women have been as hidden from the history of science as they have been elsewhere. Think for a moment about women in science – how many can you name? Most people, including most feminists, rarely get further than citing Marie Curie.

Feminist scholars have now begun to uncover the history of women's role in science to document where women have worked and the processes by which they were excluded (see, for example, Merchant, 1982; Rossiter, 1982; Alic, 1986; Schiebinger, 1989, 1994; Rose, 1994). This work shows that there were, indeed, many women working in the history of science: it also shows how they were excluded in the history of organisations like the Royal Society, set up in the 1660s (Schiebinger, 1989; Rose, 1994).

Yet the exclusion of women is not the only aspect that we need to note. This important scholarship also illustrates how, early in the scientific revolution, science itself was conceptualised as a masculine activity, 'thrusting' into (female) nature's secrets. This hierarchical notion of gender gradually came to supersede a more equitable one, in what Londa Schiebinger (1989) has called a 'battle for scholarly style', in which images of masculinity ousted more feminine ones almost entirely. Thus, although traces of Scientia, the goddess of wisdom, remain in scientific iconography (for example, on the reverse of the Nobel medal), the images of an aggressively sexual male science have won.

Science, the story goes, epitomises the pursuit of objective truth, the exercise of supreme rationality; it seeks to tell the true story about the world out there. Feminist research has played a part in challenging this tale, insisting that what scientists produce has been only one interpretation, a partial truth (see Chapter 9). Feminist analyses of the content of science have mostly focused on biology, for it is biological ideas that so directly have framed theories about the 'inevitability' of existing gender roles. The queen of rationality and objectivity was, we found, rather inclined towards partiality, all too often representing the interests of those having more power: men, white Westerners, heterosexuals.

Most of the earlier feminist critiques of science tended to focus on issues of biomedicine (Hubbard, Henifin and Fried, 1979, 1982; Brighton Women and Science Group, 1980), asking questions about, for example, evolutionary theory, brain structure, and hormonal theories of lesbianism. These essays focused on various ways in which human behaviour was allegedly determined by underlying biology, and on the extreme reductionism of such arguments. Again and again, what we found was unwarranted assumptions, sloppy data, and flawed conclusions: so much for objectivity. Slightly later, more detailed feminist reviews appeared, offering in-depth analyses of biological theories about gender (for example, Bleier, 1984; Fausto-Sterling, 1985; Birke, 1986; Hubbard, 1990). What these works shared was a concern to uncover what Anne Fausto-Sterling called 'the myths of gender' in scientific accounts.

One important focus of much of this work was on hormones, and how the whole idea of 'gendered' hormones is problematic (and wrong). The ways in which scientific ideas about sex hormones developed historically and how they were discovered is analysed in detail, for example, by Marianne van den Wijngaard (1991) and Nelly Oudshoorn (1994). Other critics were more concerned with studies of animal behaviour, and the extrapolation to humans from what scientists claimed about certain species of non-human animals. Perhaps inevitably, the intersection of particular interests (including gender and 'race') and supposedly scientific studies is clearest in relation to primates, our closest relatives (see Haraway, 1989).

More recently, however, feminist analysis of the content of science has begun to turn towards the physical sciences and engineering – areas of enquiry that are much harder to analyse. For how easy is it to infer gender from studies of, say, black holes or atomic structure? Yet there are now feminist approaches to algebra (Campbell and Campbell-Wright, 1995) and to quantum physics (Barad, 1995). As Karen Barad points out:

Physics is not immune to feminist analysis simply because electrons are not obviously gendered . . . With a sense of human agency incorporated into scientific theories, perhaps physicists will no longer find it necessary to speak of elementary particles having attributes such as charm, beauty and strangeness, or to give seminars with topless, naked bottoms and exotic hermaphrodite states in the titles. (ibid., p. 71)

It is those twin elements – of criticism of sexist assumptions and of the denial of human agency – that form the core of feminist criticisms of science.

That denial of human agency, and insistence on what Donna Haraway (1991) has called the 'god's eye view' of the world – objectivity – contribute both to the benefits of science and to its destructive power. On the one hand, scientific method and experimentation have contributed to our ways of life, they have enabled powerful predictions that have contributed to the progress of technology and medicine, for example. On the other hand, of course, few or none of those have come to us unproblematically, and feminists are not alone in pointing to the destructive power of science. Indeed, there is a substantial feminist literature documenting how modern science, with its insistence on distancing the observer from the world observed, has contributed to environmental destruction (Merchant, 1982; Gaard, 1993; Plumwood, 1993), to the abuse of animals (Donovan, 1991; Adams, 1994; Birke, 1994) and to women themselves.

To take an example, Karen Messing and Donna Mergler (1995) examine the ways in which occupational health research is conducted in ways that ignore or play down the interests of workers; the research is deeply imbued with values of gender, 'race' and class, they point out. What matters is the pursuit of objectivity; so, carefully controlled trials matter more than the ethics of exposing a so-called 'control' group of people to danger. They conclude their chapter with a letter from a woman worker who had been made seriously ill by exposure to work place hazards; she knew that laboratory studies of rats exposed to the same chemicals showed how toxic they were. But, she concluded, 'the rat couldn't speak, but we can'. By so doing, the inhumanity of the research can be spoken. What perpetuates that inhumanity is precisely the 'god's eye' stance, in which objectivity matters more than considerations of ethics.

More abstractly, 'objectivity' and its pursuit poses other questions for feminists: how, in science, do we come to know what we know, for example? Sandra Harding, in her influential book *The Science Question in Feminism* (1986), outlined three broad epistemological strategies adopted by feminists. The first is feminist empiricism, founded on critiques of the content and methodology of science. Strategically, we have often had to do this: to critique, for example, the methodological flaws in studies of 'lesbian biology' as a means of challenging the underlying ideas. But, as Harding points out, doing so implies that the 'bad science' so uncovered can be improved, that there is a 'good' science to match. This would be to deny the social embeddedness of all knowledge; even 'good' science is still a science deeply enmeshed in particular social values.

Harding's second category draws upon standpoint theory, the idea that women might, through their oppositional stance(s) in a gendered society, share a standpoint (or standpoints). Her third category draws on post-modernist insights which might challenge the universalism implicit in standpoint ideas, and insist on difference. These two stances are clearly in tension: but that tension began to resolve by the end of the 1980s, Hilary Rose suggests (Rose, 1994; also see Longino, 1990), and towards a position of what she calls 'both/and': colloquially, having one's cake and eating it too.

The problem, she points out, is a central one for feminism: that is, we can deconstruct sexist claims to truth and point to their inherent biases (as post-modern approaches do). Yet that stance is problematic, for if we accept that knowledge is socially constructed, then so too must be our own version of truth; moreover, if we emphasise the social construction of knowledge, then what happens to the 'world out there'? Does it become merely another narrative? Another stance is to assume some degree of realism (that is, that there is a 'world out there': Ruth Hubbard's work (1990) is an example). We can thus insist on critiquing science while simultaneously insisting that feminist knowledges may be 'more true' in the sense of being more representative. We can both have our cake and eat it, it would seem.

What matters here to feminist theorising is the recognition that we might acknowledge the 'world out there', and the importance of context (both the social context of the observer of nature and the environmental context of the nature observed) in the processes of doing science. Indeed, recognising that context might shift science towards a stronger – because more socially inclusive – objectivity than the weak form that currently exists (Harding, 1992). Both context and the social location of the knower or observer matter.

One important reason why feminists have insisted on the need for context has to do with the political effects of simple reductionism which can lead to 'magic bullet' answers. So, rather than try to understand the complexity of a problem, scientists sometimes turn to surgery, drugs, or genetic solutions. As Ruth Hubbard and Elijah Wald (1993) have noted, concerning claims for genes for 'learning disability' or 'criminality', genetics can come in handy in letting institutions off the hook.

The global context

Until recently, most of the challenges to science and technology came from feminists working in the industrialised West about the West. Despite these efforts by many feminists, some women still remain invisible in the narratives of science. But that is changing; feminist writers such as Vandana Shiva (1989) and Val Plumwood (1993) have criticised the 'masculine' partiality in science and examined in some detail the impact of science and technology on the Third World. While reproductive technologies to contemporary developments on the Internet have become popular, news-worthy issues, the potential effects on women are all too often missing from the discussion. As many feminists have criticised feminism for not respecting the way in which women are different, it follows that women's experiences of the benefits or hazards of science surely differ. Inserting women and gender as categories into a world-wide picture is a necessary step in understanding the global implications of Western technologies. And – importantly – by examining the impact of Western science in the Third World, feminists can rightly challenge the dominant paradigms of Western 'development'.

Many scholars, mostly feminist, have criticised the view of science as the pursuit of systematic and ordered knowledge which is masculine, Western, dominant and universal (Nandy, 1988; Shiva 1989; Alvares, 1991). In particular Claude Alvares (1991) argues that from the earliest colonial expeditions in the Americas (approximately 1492), science has been part and parcel of imperialism. Along with the economic profits of imperialism, cultural hierarchies served to legitimate Western economic and social control and oppression in the colonies. As Western powers needed cultural evidence to legitimate their presence in 'other' worlds, the practice of science was often used as the measure of social and human worth.

Not only did the colonising science insist on naming the nature it found (often thus honouring the names of Victorian gentlemen in the process: Ritvo, 1987), but it constructed both the nature and culture it found as 'other'. In many instances, indigenous sciences were placed in opposition to the Western scientific paradigm (with its separation *from* nature) and their knowledges denied. But more often there was a Western perception that indigenous peoples of the Orient (or the New World) in fact lacked the moral and intellectual fibre to practise such a complicated discipline as science (see Shiva, 1988; Alvares, 1991). Non-Western theorists have thus criticised Western science for denying the relevance and importance of other forms of knowledge. From these critiques, many (mainly Indian) scholars have attempted to reinsert indigenous forms of knowledge into the contemporary literature on science, development and technology; a science that is relevant to the needs of developing countries must draw on the best of each form of knowledge. But, while Alvares (1991), for example, has examined the relationship between science and colonialism, gender has generally been missing from these accounts. In what ways do Western technologies affect women, especially Third World women? Among other things, Vandana Shiva (1988) points out, Western science damages the global environment, and harms the poorer people of the world in particular ways. One of these is the indiscriminate use of inappropriate technologies, which can serve only to exacerbate poverty: and, by encouraging changes in patterns of agricultural production Western technologies may impoverish women still further (also see Chakravarthy, 1992; Appleton *et al.*, 1995).

As Western science continues to grow in both scope and impact, it maintains a hegemonic place within the world. Constructed often as the only answer to development problems, science has been presented as ahistorical and apolitical. However, as science and its applications (mainly medicine, medical technology and other technologies) have been introduced to the Third World, it is obvious that science is far from being neutral.

Technology: ethnocentricity and measurement

While techniques are a way of making or doing something, technology encompasses the knowledge that goes into creating techniques (Faulkner and Arnold, 1985). Technology thus includes the social relations involved in creating or using knowledge of techniques. It is generally thought of as something modern, industrial, and Western (although many feminists would contest that that is so recent, arguing that women have for centuries been inventors and discoverers: Alic, 1982; Stanley, 1982). As technology plays a significant role in science, it follows that technological language has its roots in a similar ethno- and androcentric science (Wajcman, 1991; Benston, 1992; also see Woodward, 1994, for an analysis of ageism and technology). Thus, while some technologies might be suitable for Western science and development, they are often inappropriate to the specific histories and contexts of other parts of the world. Western developers and scientists have often applied technologies without considering the historical and cultural differences between the 'developed' world and those who are still 'developing'; indeed, that may in part be a consequence of the 'god's eye view' so intrinsic to science.

As an example of inappropriate technology transfer, reproductive interventions that have been successful in the West, such as the contraceptive pill, have largely failed in the developing world. In many cases the Pill failed because medical and development workers did not take into account the way in which women's experiences differ in the non-West. Furthermore, workers did not realise that many parents wanted to have large families to compensate for high infant mortality rates. Introducing a family planning method without first considering the way in which Third World women's experiences differ from one another as well as from Western women's, or even the reasons behind reproductive practices, has led to wasteful implementations of technology and often to the introduction of more coercive and dangerous contraceptive practices (such as sterilisation: Clarke, 1994; also see Diamond, 1994).

While some have suggested that Western science has violent foundations, Michael Adas (1989) has argued that machines, similarly, were often the measure of 'man' during Western colonial expansion; along with other measures of a society's worth, technological advancement did much to determine whether a society was deemed culturally progressive. But if 'man' is measured by technology, where does that leave women? How much do, or can, women use modern technologies?

Technology has come under increasing feminist scrutiny in recent years (see Kramarae, 1988; Kirkup and Keller, 1992). This work makes plain that women do use all kinds of technology, from domestic appliances, to computers in the office, to industrial machinery. As Cynthia Cockburn and Susan Ormrod suggest (1993), certain technologies have been 'gendered' into machines that are made with women in mind, and those made with men in mind. They note, for example, that domestic appliances are often painted in white, or light colours, and stereos and electrical tools in brown or black. The colour scheme, they suggest, and the design of the models is aimed at women's and men's 'traditional' characteristics and roles. That is, it is assumed that women like soft colours, clean and simple designs, while men like sleek, black, hard and complex machinery. Furthermore, those goods, either 'white' or 'brown', are labelled low and high technology respectively. This classification into low and high technology legitimates scientific ideas about women's 'inability' to use technology, and thus by implication to do science.

In the Third World context, women face difficulties when they must design new methods and implement technologies if resources are scarce. Bina Agarwal (1992) points out that women in many developing countries rely on wood as fuel for food preparation. When natural resources such as wood continually grow scarce because of environmental destruction, women are forced to develop or accept technologies that make more efficient use of supplies. Consulting women when designing fuel-efficient technologies is necessary, she argues, because it is mainly women that are gathering and using fuel. Thus, science and technology need to go hand in hand with gender-sensitive development. If women, who play a significant role in society, are not taken into account when applying these technologies, women continue to remain marginal to discussions that greatly impact on their lives.

Reproductive technologies are, of course, aimed ostensibly at women. But, as scientists develop reproductive technologies in the context of population policies aimed at further 'managing' reproduction, women do not necessarily stand to benefit. Indeed, it is mostly women who suffer the consequences of technological failures, including pregnancies and side-effects. Where governments face internal pressures, dangerous research experiments on reproductive technologies may be overlooked: but when women, who generally are the first to try new reproductive technologies, are reluctant because of the history of 'reject' contraceptives, they are constructed as ignorant and unwilling to accept Western aid (see Chapter 16 below).

Even in Western countries, new developments in reproductive technology may become commonplace while their disadvantages are played down; the introduction of in vitro fertilisation as a medical answer to infertility is one example (Basen *et al.*, 1993). Similarly, the injectable contraceptive drug

Depo-Provera was banned in North America and Britain in the 1970s, but was subsequently introduced into India and is now available in Britain (Ghandi and Shah, 1992).

Yet not all technologies designed for reproductive management have necessarily been harmful for women. Many contraceptive technologies have proved to be beneficial to women in controlling their sexual and reproductive lives. In particular, women in the developing world have embraced contraceptive methods which prevent them from having more children than they can afford to feed. Germaine Greer, in her book *Sex and Destiny* (1984), argued that many Western feminists have assumed that women in the Third World are 'victims' of technology while many of these women expressed general satisfaction with contraceptive technologies that were deemed dangerous inventions in the West. There is a real danger in so doing that Western feminists can be guilty of 'othering' other women as well as constructing science and technology as something fundamentally un-challengeable.

Expanding horizons: new feminist interventions in science and technology

One of the most important areas of expansion in feminist science studies is that being developed by women in developing countries. Here, we begin our look at new areas of intervention within this global context, before moving on to two other areas that are expanding rapidly: feminist analyses of information technologies, and in relation to how we conceptualise the body.

A particularly important aspect of non-Western feminist challenges to science and technology is that they bring to light many of the ways in which grassroots women's movements can act. Much of this work, like that of Vandana Shiva, centres on environmental issues, and has emphasised the important role played by women in protecting the environment and in managing sustainable agriculture. Thus, there are many examples of Indian women who have successfully challenged threats to their environments (Shiva, 1995).

Developments in biotechnology particularly pose challenges to women throughout the world. As Vandana Shiva (1995) points out, genetic engineering can create new organisms unsuitable for the environments into which they are introduced (as the green revolution did); in so doing, it can ignore women's traditional methods of crop management and pest control and encourage men's domination of Third World agriculture (Muntemba and Chimedza, 1995). Biotechnology also raises the issue of intellectual property rights. Who 'owns' the knowledge of the healing properties of particular trees in the rain forests? We can be sure that if battles for ownership ensue, it will not be the indigenous peoples who win (see Third World Network, 1995).

Genetic engineering is, moreover, beginning to challenge many of our culturally accepted ideas. One significant development is the multibillion dollar Human Genome Project, which seeks to 'map all known human genes'. The arrogant – and far-fetched claims – of many scientists defending that massive expenditure insist that it represents the 'search for the Holy Grail'. Only by mapping all human genes will we finally determine the 'secrets of man'. That this focus on genes excludes and ignores social tensions, locating human ills (or the 'secrets of man') firmly in the genes, has been commented upon by Ruth Hubbard and Elijah Wald (1993) and by Hilary Rose (1994). If social problems or diseases are fixed into the genes then tinkering with the genes might lead to a cure, and we can dispense with any ideas of social changes, such as better schools in the inner city. Apart from the social implications, these authors also stress how misleading is the view that 'genes are us', ignoring how genes work only in particular contexts.

The shift towards seeing 'the' gene as the explanation of everything is, critics insist, a dangerous one; to return to Hubbard's point made earlier, it lets institutional failures off the hook. It can also move us towards the slippery slope of eugenics, as feminist critics have often noted, in that there is already discussion about the search for the 'perfect child', available through pre-natal diagnosis of genetic disease (however that is defined). Where will this search for perfection end, critics ask? Aborting a foetus with a fatal, genetic disease might be one thing, but what about the foetus with (say) a cleft palate, or the 'wrong' colour eyes (Hubbard, 1990)?

These are important questions: new forms of biotechnology present new challenges to women and to feminist analysis. These must be carefully assessed, not only for their potential impact on our lives in the West, but perhaps more importantly for their global effects. What we women in the West might find a boon or even a mixed blessing might seriously damage women's lives elsewhere in the world.

The rapid development of computing and microelectronics is, arguably, one such case. In the age of the Internet, rapid communication around the globe is easy. Indeed, some feminists have argued that it helps to break down barriers, and to challenge stereotypes of gender (we will return to this point below). Yet simultaneously it relies on manufacturing processes increasingly located in the East, and carried out by women in harsh conditions of employment (Mitter, 1995).

Some Western feminists such as Margaret Lowe Benston (1992) and Gill Kirkup (1992) have suggested that computer technology is gendered and that women often have to adopt a masculine persona in order to interact successfully with computers. Does this analysis fit for the Internet? With information passing quicker than ever before, women outside the computer-based work force face isolation. With more and more information being passed through e-mail and bulletin boards, those who do not have time for and access to computers and computer language will miss out on a wealth of emerging knowledge (and, implicitly, power).

Furthermore, women living in the developing world face more immediate technological concerns, such as the need to obtain fresh water. This, of course, does not mean that the Internet is of no relevance to Third World women, or that it does not have an impact. But as information technologies take off in the West, does this mean that the need for what might be termed more basic technologies (of, say, food production) will be lost in the wake of Internet mania?

Surely the Internet and the emergence of new ways of transporting information have major consequences for women's movements globally. Will Third World feminists receive information and thus knowledge from the West, or will the development of computer technologies further alienate them from the scientific processes that most often affect Third World peoples? Also, if women in the Third World have recently managed to permeate dominant Western literature with texts of their own, will new techniques of writing and reading mean that their knowledges remain peripheral to Western knowledge-making? Or, alternatively, that their cultures and languages become part of a wider global network?

For the world's women, the Internet and other new forms of communication technology largely remain a mystery. But feminists interested in the Internet should also consider the advantages as well as the disadvantages for women in the global context as well as for those women that have access to computers. The Internet, for example, allows women to communicate and spread information across the globe: among other things, this mode of communication is relatively cheap and can dramatically expedite political actions by putting women quickly into contact.

As Sherry Turkle argues in her book, *Life on the Screen* (1995), some of the gender tensions between women and men can be erased in communications on the Internet. For example, as women and men take on 'personas' on the Internet, they can be to some degree gender-free, or gender-neutral. While it is difficult to 'play' with gender roles in 'real' life, being on-line gives women and men some invisibility of gender.

It is just these possibilities of new identities and alliances that are celebrated in 'cyberfeminist' writing. Sadie Plant (1996) has suggested that the Internet allows all kinds of possibilities, and opens up spaces for 'feminisation'. Plant's analysis of cyberspace has led her to believe that technology, contrary to being deadly for women as many feminists have averred, is deadly 'only for the white man', just because it opens up spaces of possibility for all those who have been defined as 'others'.

Yet the anarchy of the Internet also allows possibilities of pornography and sexual harrassment, but also of challenges to these forms of oppression. A recent case of Internet harassment in the USA was successfully challenged by women. Offensive material put on to the net by four male students led to an avalanche of protests, by phone and by e-mail. Commenting on the case, Ostrowski (1996) asks, 'Can we deny that the Internet has shown its potential for action on women's issues?'

In relation to feminist theory, women's invasion of cyberspace invokes the image of the cyborg (a human/machine combination). It is the stuff of myth, and figures large in science fiction. The cyborg as a metaphor with potential for women's politics is used, playfully, in Donna Haraway's vision (1991). Here, she speaks of 'polymorphous information' systems, which emphasise rates of flow across boundaries rather than bodily integrity. The metaphor of a cyborg thus stands for the cultural shift towards understanding bodies (and ourselves) in terms of information flow: 'Communications technologies and biotechnologies are the crucial tools recrafting our bodies. These tools embody and enforce new social relations for women worldwide', she notes (Haraway, 1991, p. 164).

Haraway intends to create a new story, our story, from the cyborg metaphor. To be sure, she acknowledges that the information age has also spawned such horrors as Cruise missiles; but it also offers new opportunities for breaching boundaries and making new alliances. As hybrids, already on the margins, cyborgs offer challenges to thinking in grand theories, she claims, precisely because they are *not* (as humans have tended to think of themselves) 'unitary'. As such, Haraway suggests, they threaten the troubling dualisms at the heart of modern Western culture, such as nature/culture, self/other and male/female.

On the other hand, the cyborg as an emerging hybrid of body and machine (in various guises, from pacemakers to other forms of electronic implant) cannot always escape the gendered culture in which it emerges. Anne Balsamo (1996), for example, combines analyses of body images in popular culture, including science fiction, with analysis of medical technologies of the body. The technobody (or cyborg), she concludes, is always marked by gender and 'race'; it does not escape just by being hybrid (also see Mason, 1995).

Like Haraway's influential work, other recent feminist studies have dealt largely with biology, and the kind of discourses that predominate. Much of the recent work focuses on specific areas of biology, using detailed analyses of the construction of ideas and language. What they have in common is a recognition that the language itself constructs concepts of gender. Nelly Oudshoorn's work on hormones is one example; another is Bonnie Spanier's in-depth study of molecular biology (Oudshoorn, 1994; Spanier, 1995; see also Keller, 1992). They point out how biological texts produce images of 'male' or 'female' molecules, such as hormones, or of bacteria that are 'feminine' because they receive genetic information from another bacterium.

What these various studies uncover is a genetic ideology built on concepts of mastery: DNA is, after all, called in most textbooks the 'master molecule'. This kind of linear, reductive thinking is deeply entrenched in scientific thinking. Commenting on this, Evelyn Fox Keller (1993) points out that:

> theories that structure our understanding in terms of linear causal chains – that posit ontological cores as master molecules, blueprints, or 'central offices' – serve to focus our attention on equally linear chains of consequences. With life relocated in genes, and redefined in terms of their informational content, the project of 'refashioning' 'life', of redirecting the future course of evolution, is recast as a manageable and doable project. (ibid., p. 108)

That the language of mastery and control is taken for granted in biology textbooks is a theme of Bonnie Spanier's (1995) analysis of molecular biology. It is not, she points out, only that DNA is cast as the master molecule; the language is much more pervasive than that. What genes do is the story, and everything else is relegated to bit parts. To take one of her examples, the idea that the 'language' built into DNA determines the manufacture of a particular protein is itself hierarchical; why, she asks, do we not think of proteins as produced from a whole complex of interactions among various parts of the cell? Why the focus on DNA? As Spanier notes, an important task for feminist science studies is to challenge this hierarchical model of mastery, and to insist on other readings of how nature works. This is, indeed, the task espoused by many biologists who oppose the mainstream, deterministic, accounts (Ho, 1988; Masters, 1995).

There is a similar co-existence, in recent feminist work on the body, between images of centralised control and images of fractured boundaries. Emily Martin's work has illustrated this tension well. Her book, *The Woman in the Body* (1987), documents the pervasiveness of the metaphor of control in how we think about how the body works. Control, overlain with sexist imaginings, helps to perpetuate the tale of 'heroic' sperm battling their way towards the helpless egg (see also Biology and Gender Group, 1989) so often found in textbooks. Control is built into the way in which bodily 'systems' (nervous, circulatory and so on) are conceptualised; controlling bodily constancy, rather than dynamism and change, is the *modus operandi* of physiology texts (see Birke, 1997).

Turning to the functioning of the immune system, Martin's subsequent work, *Flexible Bodies* (1994), examines the cultural transition between older thinking that spoke of immunity in terms of defending the body against germs, to a modern, post-AIDS, kind of thinking in which the immune system can be 'tuned up' and transformed in response to external challenges. It becomes, in the words of the credit card advertisement, a flexible friend. This discourse, Martin notes, has changed in both scientific narratives and in popular accounts. And it mirrors the changing language of corporate business: managerial flexibility is what matters in the 1990s. People, like immune systems, can be trained so they function better.

Donna Haraway, similarly, discusses concepts of immunity (Haraway, 1991). The post-modern immune system, suggests Haraway, is part of a 'network-body'; it is 'everywhere and nowhere' all at once (1991; p. 218) as a result of being tuned up through its responses to environments. She draws on material from the realm of biological writing, which suggests that 'the individual is a constrained accident, not the highest fruit of earth's history's labors' (p. 220). The body – as bounded, as the quintessential individual – is threatened even by the discourses of science itself. Its boundaries become permeable in this changing language of immune systems, opening it up to networks of influence both inside and out. Flexibility and fluidity, not bodies as fortresses, are the new watchwords.

Another approach to the prevailing notions of mastery is to insist on alternative accounts. Here, what matters is not so much the detailed analyses of mainstream scientific narratives, but advocacy of other narratives. There are several such approaches: for example, Judith Masters (1995) notes the assumptions made in many accounts of evolution, that organisms adapt to 'fit' the environment. Her alternative narrative draws on evidence suggesting a much more complex process of co-adaptation, in which 'the environment' (consisting also of myriad other organisms) adapts with the organism under consideration; thus, it is not individual species that adapt but communities.

In its insistence on complexity, this is a more feminist story. Similarly, Birke (1994) seeks to tell different stories about non-human animals as another way of challenging biological determinism (also see Haraway, 1989). Claims that (say) women's behaviour is biologically determined rest on particular cultural assumptions about what other kinds of animals are or do, she notes. So, if the cultural assumption is that other creatures are stupid, then we are bound to react to the linkage by denial. But there are other stories that might be told, tales of animal abilities; in doing so, we offer another challenge to simple claims that what we are is rooted in 'biology'.

These alternative narratives do not presume, in some relativist sense, that 'any narrative will do equally'. Rather, what they seek to challenge is what they see as the epistemological flaws in mainstream scientific accounts. As we have seen, the dominant narratives tend to perpetuate particular notions of hierarchy, of gender, 'race', species and so on. But – even within the evidence supplied by biological science itself – there are alternative ways of looking at things. What Judith Masters does is to provide a different story which, she argues, better accounts for evolutionary change precisely because it insists on complexity and agency: no organisms are passive victims in her vision of evolutionary change.

Future visions?

At present, then, feminist interventions in science and technology are taking place on many fronts. These include analyses of genetics and biotechnology, and of the body, of scientific narratives, of the potentials for change offered by new information technologies. Many of these are quite theoretical, staying firmly in the academy. Others, like cyberfeminism, might offer wider potentials for change through the anarchy, combined with communication potential, of the Internet. Still others, such as the challenges mounted by women's movements in less developed parts of the world, are challenges offered by women at the grass roots, by organising and activism. But what of the future? Where might we go now? We turn, somewhat speculatively, to these questions in our concluding section. These suggestions are, of course, our own: but what we seek to do is to provoke further development of these (and other) areas of feminist enquiry in science and technology.

Arguably, one of the most important developments in recent years has been the growth of debate from outside the West. Issues of patenting and intellectual property rights, brought to the fore by biotechnology, are central to this debate, as Vandana Shiva has insisted (1993, 1995). Not only do global women's movements need these debates, to shift the focus of enquiry from Western hegemony, but we also need more challenges from all of those peoples who have been classed as 'other' by the classifications of science. Even in the West, there is relatively little written to date, for example, by non-white feminists (although see Longino and Hammonds, 1990). What these debates continue to do – and must do, in our opinion – is to bring to discussion all the different contexts in which women might experience the impacts of science and technology.

A second area that needs to be developed further is the detailed examination of the discourses of science offered, for instance, by feminists such as Bonnie Spanier (1995). There are many other areas of science that could be fruitfully analysed. In particular, these narratives need further analysis in relation to feminist epistemological questions: how, for example, do the narratives themselves perpetuate or challenge persistent Western dualisms (such as gender, or nature/culture)? There has, however, been a focus in much of this work on the written word; we also need feminist deconstructions of, say, the visual images that are a critical part of science. To some extent, visual images have been scrutinised in other areas of science studies: they have yet to enter much feminist work (but see Keller, 1995).

Finally, we continue to be concerned about these academic enquiries and their relationship to feminist politics in two ways. The first of these is the ongoing exclusion of science and technology from many Women's Studies curricula: Women's Studies has long tended to be rooted in the humanities and social sciences, leaving detailed analyses of the natural sciences and technology out of syllabuses. The exception to this is much the same as it was 25 years ago, at the beginning of the women's liberation movement: Women's Studies does still include material on health and reproduction. Outside that, however, science and technology studies largely remain the Cinderella of the disciplines in the supposedly interdisciplinary world of Women's Studies.

Science and technology must be better integrated into the domain of Women's Studies. They are, to return to Donna Haraway's insistent voice, much too important; they have too much power as public myth. Like other narratives, they can be deconstructed as part of feminist opposition to 'grand narratives' which exclude women.

Yet there is another, perhaps more important, way in which the kinds of questions we have considered here must relate to feminist politics. Women's Studies, in the West, has to a large extent become separated from its roots in the liberation movements of earlier decades. Instead of taking to the streets, we now seem to take to the Internet. That in itself is a persistent challenge to feminists in the academy. As we have seen, however, it is not primarily Western feminists who are now mounting the activist challenges to scientific orthodoxies: rather, it is the poorer women of the Third World. In the West, we need to follow their example: science and technology are hugely powerful in the world at the end of the twentieth century. They affect the lives of all of us. Perhaps the feminist activism of the new century should take on more strongly the powerful, vested interests involved in new developments in technology, while Women's Studies in the academy takes on more fully the challenges of science and technology studies.

Further reading

Gill Kirkup and Laurie Smith Keller (eds), *Inventing Women: Science, Technology and Gender* (Cambridge, Polity, 1992). A collection of essays exploring feminist issues in science and technology, for the Open University course 'Issues in Women's Studies'. Covers a wide range of themes including the nature of science, our bodies, and producing and consuming science/technology. A good general introduction to the range of topics.

Gender Working Group, *Missing Links: Gender Equity in Science and Technology for Development*, United Nations Commission on Science and Technology for Development (London, Intermediate Technology Publications, 1995). Essays provide a wide coverage of the complex issues related to science, technology and gender in relation to global development.

Hilary Rose, *Love, Power and Knowledge: Towards a Feminist Transformation of the Sciences* (Cambridge, Polity, 1994). A clearly written book looking at the kind of questions raised within feminist theory about science and technology. Includes chapters discussing the nature of scientific knowledge, and on genetic technology.

Brighton Women and Science Group, *Alice Through the Microscope: The Power of Science Over Women's Lives* (London, Virago, 1980). This was one of the first books on feminist perspectives on science, and is of interest for that reason. It introduces several themes of interest to Women's Studies, including women and health, and lesbian issues. It was published quite soon after the first book in the USA: Ruth Hubbard, M. S. Henifin and B. Fried, *Women Look at Biology Looking at Women* (Cambridge, Mass., Schenkman, 1979), which includes essays on similar themes.

11

Women and Work

Anne Witz

The study of women's employment has been and continues to be of crucial importance in the feminist agenda for change. The analysis and explanation of processes which generate gender divisions and inequality in work has always been linked to feminist campaigns to end sex discrimination and inequality in the work place and, more generally, has occupied a central place in feminist theorisations of patriarchy or 'gender regimes' in modern societies (cf. Walby, 1990, 1997). Indeed, the steadily increasing participation of women in paid employment during the latter half of the twentieth century is arguably one of the most significant aspects of the transformation of gender relations (Walby, 1997). This chapter focuses on the distinctive ways feminists analyse women's paid work, as well as indicating some recent trends in women's employment.[1]

Feminist analyses of women and work developed mainly in sociology in the 1970s and were located within what might be termed the 'production paradigm' of the social sciences, which focused on the daily production of social life through labour or work activities and relations. It seemed to feminists that conventional approaches explained men's but not women's work. Hence the focus was on critiquing these conventional approaches. This focus also provided an important seed bed for the development of analyses of the intersection of gender divisions with those of class and 'race', both theoretically and empirically. The fortunes and fates of working-class women differ in important ways from those of middle-class women, just as those of Black working-class women differ from white working-class women. Feminist studies of the labour market have revealed how this is a site of complex and cross-cutting inequalities of class, 'race' and gender, and hence have proved vital in furthering feminist theorisations of differences between women, as well as of commonalities in women's position in and experiences of paid work (cf. Walby, 1990, 1997; Anthias and Yuval-Davies, 1992; Bradley, 1996).

Since the 1980s, feminist analyses of paid work have developed in new ways which explore issues of culture and identity, and move beyond the rather narrow economistic focus that characterised the 'production paradigm' of earlier feminist work. Feminists are now developing analyses of the

239

gendering of work place cultures and hierarchies, and the relationship between sexuality, power and embodiment at work. Feminists have also redefined the concept of 'work' to include unpaid domestic and caring tasks, as well as paid work, developing concepts such as 'caring', 'emotional' and 'sexual' work to grasp and analyse the gender-specific qualities that are loaded into tasks performed by women in the household and the labour market. Women balance their time and energies between household work and paid work in complex ways (Folbre, 1994), and there is an urgent need to renegotiate the gendered politics of time to care, time to work, and time to oneself (*Bulletin on Women and Employment in the EU*, No. 7, October 1995).

Gender segregation at work

The process of industrialisation created a new gendered division of labour that had two aspects. One was that men were occupied in paid work and women (ideally at any rate) in unpaid household work; the other was that the vast majority of occupations were exclusively male and those women who were employed did different jobs from men: that is, the labour market was rigidly gender segregated (Reskin and Padavic, 1994). By the beginning of the twentieth century, in Britain and the USA, women made up a lower proportion of the industrial work force than in the mid-nineteenth century. In the USA 6 per cent and in Britain 10 per cent of married women, and 40 per cent of single women in both countries, were in paid work (Hakim, 1979; Reskin and Padavic, 1994). In the USA, Black women were far more likely to be working, and only in the 1990s did white women catch up in their rate of labour force participation (Reskin and Padavic, 1994). It is important to bear in mind that the likelihood of women engaging in paid work is affected by 'race', class, age, marital status as well as whether or not they have dependent children. Nonetheless, the single most important change in the work forces of all industrial nations during the twentieth century has been the increasing participation of women in paid employment.

In the member states of the European Union (EU), women's employment is crucial to current and future patterns of employment. After decades of steadily increasing female employment rates, the EU female employment rate stood at 48 per cent in 1992, ranging from over 70 per cent in Denmark to only 31 per cent in Spain.[2] Women filled three-quarters of all new jobs in the decade from 1983 to 1992, when the female employment rate rose by 6 per cent and men's fell by 1.4 per cent. Part-time work has been a major factor in the growth of women's employment, as well as in the growth of total employment. In 1992 women accounted for 84 per cent of all part-timers in the EU. But full-time jobs also increased for women in all EU countries, whilst male full-time jobs declined in some countries. However, in nearly all EU countries female unemployment (10.6 per cent) is higher than male unemployment (7.9 per cent); only Ireland and the UK are exceptions. But conventional measures of unemployment distort the true extent of female unemployment, and it is increasingly necessary to distinguish carefully between 'employed', 'unemployed' and 'non-employed' or 'inactive'[3] men and women. Women are more likely than men to move out of employment into non-employment, and women's additional role in taking on the burden of non-market domestic and caring responsibilities means that they have higher non-employment or 'inactivity' rates than men (*Bulletin on Women and Employment in the EU*, No. 8, April 1996). Women move between employment, unemployment and non-employment more than men do, and it has been suggested that there are new, distinctly gendered mobility regimes emerging (Esping-Andersen, 1993).

Thus, the first aspect of the gendered division of labour – the male breadwinner/dependent housewife model – has been destabilised and no longer has as much empirical purchase, although it still retains considerable ideological purchase. The second aspect – the rigid segregation of men and women into different jobs – has proved far more resilient.

Gender segregation at work describes the concentration of women and men into different occupations, jobs and places of work (Reskin and Padavic, 1994). Despite the fact that over the past half century Western European and North American societies have enacted legislation to meet working women's long-standing demands for equal pay and an end to sexual discrimination in the work place, gender segregation has persisted. The analysis of gender segregation is an important focal point of feminist analyses of paid work. There are two dimensions of occupational segregation: horizontal segregation, which describes the fact that women and men are most commonly working in different kinds of occupations; and vertical segregation, which describes how occupational hierarchies are also constructed as gender hierarchies. As far as horizontal segregation is concerned, in Britain about a quarter of occupations are 'typically female', meaning that they have a higher proportion of female workers than in the labour force as a whole, whilst three-quarters of occupations are 'typically male' (Hakim, 1993). Women tend to be concentrated in a narrower range of occupations than men, namely catering, cleaning, hairdressing and other personal services; clerical and related occupations; and professional and related occupations in education, welfare and health. When we look at vertical segregation, then men tend to predominate in higher-level occupations, such as the middle and upper echelons of managerial and professional form of work, whilst women tend to be concentrated in lower professional and clerical jobs, as well as semi-skilled and unskilled manual jobs.[4]

Recently, a major comparative study of occupational segregation in eleven EU countries concluded that, overall, levels of occupational segregation are high and persistent, ranging from 0:48 to 0:59 (meaning that between 48 per cent and 59 per cent of women would have to move occupations before women and men were proportionately represented throughout the occupational structure: Rubery and Fagan, 1995). There are also important similarities in the pattern of gender segregation across member states. There is a low share of women in production and manual jobs, which means that there is limited evidence of women breaking into typically male-dominated jobs, and there is also a high share of women in clerical occupations, service occupations, sales occupations and professional occupations (particularly in education, health and welfare). Overall, there is a high degree of similarity in the structures and trends of gendered occupational segregation across all member states, although this should not be allowed to obscure important differences between countries (such as different labour market systems), as well as variations in female shares of particular occupations (such as the fact that women's share of clerical jobs ranges from 50 per cent in Greece and Portugal to between 69 per cent and 72 per cent in France, Denmark and the UK).

Other recent studies in Britain and the USA have nonetheless identified trends towards gender desegregation. In most Western countries, the level of gendered occupational segregation changed very little between 1900 and 1970, despite the fact that women were entering the labour force in increasing numbers, employers were re-organising work and introducing new technologies, and some occupations died out and others emerged. However, in the 1970s occupational segregation began to decline in the USA and this trend towards desegregation has continued, largely as a result of women moving into traditionally male spheres of employment, where they earn more than in traditionally female jobs (Reskin and Padavic, 1994). The evidence shows that occupations are becoming more 'feminised' and less 'masculinised'. Feminisation can have a number of outcomes, resulting in either genuine occupational integration, or the ghettoisation of women in particular specialities or jobs within an occupation, or re-segregation as men exit an occupation and leave it to women. Let us take two examples. In the USA, typesetting and compositing became re-segregated in the 1970s, flipping from being a male- to a female-dominated occupation after new computer technology changed the character of the work. In Britain, hospital pharmacy has become more integrated but also vertically segregated by gender as women tend to be ghettoised in lower-level, professional practitioner niches, whilst male pharmacists predominate in senior posts where they combine professional with managerial skills (Crompton and Sanderson, 1989).

The process of gender desegregation in Britain began later than in the USA; in the 1980s rather than the 1970s (Hakim, 1992, 1993). On the surface, however, there appears to have been little change in gendering of the occupational structure, as three-quarters of occupations continue to be male dominated and one-quarter female dominated. Nonetheless, the 1980s was a decade of gendered desegregation, with a greater (although by no means complete) integration of women at all levels of the occupational structure than in the 1970s. It must be stressed, however, that integrated occupations (defined as those with between 30 per cent and 50 per cent women) have only risen by 3 per cent between 1979 and 1990. As in the USA, desegregation is being achieved not by men moving into women's occupations, but by women moving into what were formerly almost exclusively male occupations.[5] This suggests a greater resistance by men to taking 'female jobs' and a greater willingness by women to enter 'male jobs'. For men, there is probably more at stake than simply the challenge to their masculine identity by doing 'women's work'; there is also the prospect of lower pay and the relative lack of autonomy that comes with 'women's work'. It is precisely because, as feminists have indeed argued, gendered occupational segregation has historically served to secure benefits for men at the expense of women that women have much to gain by entering formerly male preserves, like better pay and prospects, but men have little to gain by entering lower-paid female preserves.

Sylvia Walby (1997) also argues that there has been a significant change in the distribution of women through the occupational structure in the 1980s in Britain, resulting in a marked reduction in the extent of segregation and representing a significant restructuring of gender relations in employment. Most notably, women have increased their share of higher level occupations (see also Hakim, 1992, 1993), particularly professional and managerial occupations, where the number of women has increased by 155 per cent, compared with only a 33 per cent increase among men, shifting the gender composition of these occupations from only 21 per cent to 30 per cent female (Walby, 1997). The most important reason for these changes has been the increase in educational qualifications gained by women. Thus, women are gaining access to formerly male preserves by exercising the 'qualifications lever' (Crompton and Sanderson, 1989); or, rather, some women are. It is vital that feminists recognise the complex interrelationship between gender, class, 'race', ethnicity and age in structuring the fates and fortunes of women in employment. Women's position in the labour market is becoming increasingly polarised because of the ways in which these differences intersect. Around 85 per cent of women of the professional and managerial middle classes are economically active, with 65 per cent working full-time, compared to 68 per cent of women in the unskilled, manual working-class, of whom only 7 per cent work full-time (General Household Survey 1994, Table 7.11, p. 20, cited in Walby, 1997). It is also the case, that the racialised divisions are etched on to an already gender segregated labour market (Phizacklea, 1994), and employment levels vary considerably by ethnicity for women. In Britain, the women with the highest economic activity rate are white, closely followed by Black and Indian women, with a much lower rate for the Pakistani/Bangladeshi community

(Walby, 1997). Ethnic minority women are likely to be working longer hours, for lower pay, and are twice as likely than white women to be unemployed. Importantly, the gains being made by white women in higher grade jobs are not being shared by ethnic minority women. Instead, they are overrepresented in areas of occupational decline and underrepresented in growth sectors and occupations. Even when Black and ethnic minority women are skilled and experienced, they are twice as likely to be unemployed as white women (Phizacklea and Wolkowitz, 1995). Finally, there are major differences between women by age. Younger women are more likely to be in employment, to have educational qualifications, to be working full-time and to be in better jobs than older women, who are disproportionately taking up newly restructured, lower skilled, part-time and poorly paid jobs in services (Walby, 1997).

The feminisation and racialisation of work

The increasing polarisation of the female work force into full-time and part-time jobs, as well as differences between the experiences of white women and Black women in terms of the likelihood of working part-time or full-time, highlight the ways in which gender and 'race' intersect to generate distinctly feminised and racialised forms of work. Part-time work and homeworking illustrate this intersection exceptionally well.

The division between part-time and full-time forms of employment is a central feature of the gender structure of employment. Almost all the increase in women's employment over the past 25 years has been in part-time work. Between 1971 and 1995 in Britain the increase in women working full-time was only 3%, compared to an increase of 75% in women working part-time. The vast majority of Britain's part-time workers are women; almost half of all women in employment work part-time, compared to less than 10 per cent of men (Naylor, 1994; Walby, 1997). This concentration of British women in insecure, part-time employment is linked to the way part-time jobs are distributed across employment sectors. Only 7 per cent of employees in manufacturing – a male-dominated sector – work part-time compared with over a third of employees in services (a female-dominated sector), whilst in some services, such as hotel and catering, the majority of workers are part-time. The creation of part-time jobs in the 1950s and 1960s was a gender-specific strategy by employers to deal with labour shortages by tempting married women back into the work force, whilst not undermining the patriarchal division of labour within the family. Of course, the creation of part-time jobs has been an important factor in facilitating women's access to independent earnings, enabling them to combine paid with unpaid work associated with the demands of domesticity and childcare, as well as 'elder', care.[6] Feminist analyses have always seen women's access to earnings as an importance source of their greater autonomy and self-determination, because it lessens their economic dependency on male earners within family-households. New employer strategies of flexibilisation and casualisation of labour have mapped on to an already gendered structure of employment in Britain, where 39 per cent of workers in female occupations were already working part-time in 1971, rising to 43 per cent by the early 1990s (Hakim, 1993). Hence, the restructuring of Western economies and employment away from manufacturing and towards services, as well as the restructuring of employment into more flexible, predominantly part-time and casualised forms of employment is being achieved in gender-specific ways.[7] The restructuring of work is thus a key site of current transformations in gender relations because employment restructuring is overlayering new employment opportunities on top of already gendered structures of employment (cf. Walby, 1997).

Part-time work means different things in different European countries. In Britain it means an average of 18 hours per week in low-paying, insecure and unprotected employment.[8] In Scandinavan countries, where there are also high proportions of women working part-time, this more often means slightly reduced hours in full-time forms of employment. Ghettoised and feminised part-time jobs, inferior in every way to full-time jobs, have been constructed in Britain to meet employers' needs, and are not driven by an explicit gender equality agenda as in Scandinavian countries.

However, for feminists to focus on part-time employment as a distinctly feminised form of employment is to miss the impact of racialised factors on women's employment. Indeed, it has been argued that the emphasis white feminists have placed on part-time work as a determinant of gender inequalities in work can be seen as ethnocentric (Bruegel, 1989; Phizacklea, 1994). In Britain, ethnic minority women are far less likely to be working part-time than white women; 70 per cent of ethnic minority women work full-time compared to 50 per cent of white women (Phizacklea, 1994). This is particularly so for West Indian women, who are more likely to be the main or sole providers in a family, especially given high Black male unemployment. Whilst full-time work is associated with better pay and conditions for white women, the same is not true for Black women. Irene Bruegel (1989) has convincingly argued that white feminists need to seriously rethink their 'domestic responsibilities' model of women's disadvantaged position in the labour market, as the standard picture they present of the way women have negotiated their 'double burden' by taking part-time work does not necessarily apply to Black women.

Social inequalities of class, 'race' and gender are also replicated and reproduced in the homeworking labour force (Phizacklea and Wolkowitz, 1995). Homeworkers always have been and still are the most vulnerable, exploited and low-paid group of women workers, although there is a new form of homeworking known as 'teleworking', which describes the use of new information and communication technology (ICT) to work from/at home. Generally, though, homeworking, along with part-time and temporary employment, respresents another casualised and gender-specific form of 'flexible' work. The invisibility of homeworkers is strongly linked to the gender character of models of employment, which are biased towards the man working 'outside' the home for pay, rendering invisible both unpaid and paid work at home (Allen and Wolkowitz, 1987). In a recent British study, Annie Phizacklea and Carol Wolkowitz (1995) identify five groups of homeworkers: casualised employees, such as mainly Asian manual workers in the clothing industry and more typically white women clerical workers with relatively better qualifications and higher hourly earnings; *micro-entrepreneurs*, who are self-employed women engaged in 'craft' manufacture, such as expensive knitwear, or farm shop produce for specialist niche markets; *self-employed professionals*, often working from home in publishing, or as journalists, accountants and music teachers; and *technical* and *executive level employees*, usually 'teleworking' at home for the same employer for whom they had formerly worked full-time. It is important, then, to see traditional and new forms of homeworking as linked to women's 'constrained options', which are the combined result of external constraints (such as high unemployment, lack of qualifications or affordable childcare) and internalised expectations (such as women's paid work being subordinate to children's needs). Importantly, racialised divisions are etched on to forms of homeworking too, as Asian women homeworkers are segregated into a narrower range of jobs (particularly the traditional, casualised and low-paid forms of manufacturing work done at home) and work much longer hours than white women (Phizacklea and Wolkowitz, 1995).

Feminist explanations of gendered work

Early feminist analysis of women's paid employment was located within the 'production paradigm' of much social science. This paradigm has come under considerable attack since the 1980s as new theoretical paradigms have emerged, most notably those associated with post-structuralist and post-modernist feminisms. These have shifted the focus of much feminist analysis away from labour and production and towards culture, identity and consumption. There is a new concern with 'meaning' as well as 'materiality' (Bradley, 1996), with 'words' as well as 'things' (Barrett, 1992). In the 1970s and 1980s – dubbed as the era of 'classic' feminist accounts of gendered work (Adkins and Lury, 1996; Bradley, 1996) – the main debates amongst feminists centred around: (a) the relative importance of family and labour market structures in explaining women's clearly unequal and disadvantaged position in the labour market; (b) the relative significance of 'capitalism' or 'patriarchy' as the structural determinants of women's oppression in both the family and the labour market; and (c) whether gender divisions in work were rooted in 'ideological' (Barrett, 1980) or 'material' (Cockburn, 1983) processes. Since the late 1980s, shifts in feminist accounts of gendered work are most evident in new concerns with the 'cultural' rather than the 'economic', analyses of 'discourses of sexuality' rather than 'ideologies of gender', and the relationship between gender, sexuality, and embodiment in the experience of work within 'organisations' rather than the 'labour market'.

Early or 'classic' feminist debates about gendered work focused on the structural determinants of the sexual division of labour in employment. The term 'sexual division of labour' was preferred by those who traced the specific nature of women's position at work to the logic of capitalism; the term 'gender relations' came to be preferred by those who focused more on patriarchy as an explanation of gender divisions in employment. Classic feminist debates of the 1970s and 1980s disputed whether or not the dynamics of capitalism generated women's lower wages and gender-segregated labour markets, or whether the patriarchal practices of male workers had also played a part in securing male privilege in the labour market at the expense of women. Did we need a concept of patriarchy as well as capitalism in order to explain gender divisions and inequalities in the work place? From the very outset, this debate marginalised the specific nature of Black women's oppression and focused on the interrelationship between structures of oppression centred around gender and class, at the expense of 'race' and racism.

Importantly, these early attempts to explain gender-segregated and unequal work meant that feminists were simultaneously drawing upon and moving beyond existing attempts in the social sciences, particularly in sociology and economics, to explain the operation of labour markets and understand the world of work. Until the 1970s studies of employment operated with a heavily masculinist conception of work (Beechey, 1987), using a 'job model' to analyse men's experiences and attitudes to work in terms of the conditions of work itself, but adopting a 'gender model' to explain women's experiences of and attitudes to work, referring simply to their role in the family and extrapolating from this (Feldberg and Glen, 1979; Walby, 1997). As Jackie West (1978) neatly expressed it at the time, pre-feminist explanations of female employment were 'theoretically subordinated to the claims of domesticity'. In sociology, a voluntaristic framework predominated, which explained women's position in the labour market solely with reference to their position in the family and their allegedly greater 'commitment' to the family than to work. Equally, economists were largely content to explain women's lower wages in terms of their lower 'human capital' (such as levels of education and experience) because, as a result of rational decision-making within the family, women interrupt their working lives to bear and rear children, forgoing their (lower) wages for male partners' (higher) wages. From the point of view of feminists, this looked very much like a case of happy patriarchal families being cited as the sole explanation for a whole range of gender inequalities in the work place.

Consequently, early feminist work emphasised the need to look at the structure of the labour market in order to explain gender divisions and inequalities at work, and pioneered a shift from purely voluntaristic explanations linked to a simple 'domestic responsibilities model' (Bruegel, 1989) towards a more thoroughgoing analysis of processes located within the labour market itself. Feminists insisted that we could not simply 'read off' gender divisions in the public sphere of employment from those in the private sphere of the family household, arguing that the gender structure of work and employment was far more complex than this. Dual labour market theory offered feminists one way of understanding this complexity. Labour markets were seen as structured into two distinct sectors, where jobs in the primary sector were characterised by higher wages, more fringe benefits, recognised skills, opportunities for education and training, greater employment security and higher levels of unionisation than jobs in the secondary sector. It was employer 'preferences' or discrimination that led them to recruit women into secondary sector jobs, and this explained why women occupied inferior and unequal positions compared to men in the labour market. A similar explanation referred to segmented labour markets (Reich, Gordon and Edwards, 1980) which emerged as a result of employer strategies of control of the work force and attempts to fragment it. Segmentation by sex was identified as one aspect of this, but, defying explanation in terms of the dynamics of capitalist control itself, was said to have a 'separate dynamic' (which was never specified). It fell to feminists to think this one through, and Heidi Hartmann (1979) argued that this separate dynamic was a patriarchal, rather than a capitalist one. The introduction of the concept of patriarchy into feminist debates about how women's position in employment can be explained has been important for pushing feminist analyses beyond the limitations of gender-blind explanations of how labour markets work.

In particular, the concept of patriarchy was used in order to develop materialist explanations of gender divisions in work that pushed beyond the dominant, gender-blind, 'production paradigm' of Marxism. Generally, Marxist–feminist 'production paradigm' explanations of women's employment relied on the idea that women (particularly married women) made up a labour reserve (that is, a surplus population not yet drawn into wage labour) and that women were being drawn into new, de-skilled occupations (Braverman, 1974; Beechey, 1987). This kind of explanation did have the merit of pulling into view the relationship between the family and production, as it was argued that married women made up this labour reserve because their role within the family make them a cheap, flexible and disposable source of labour.[9] However, in the recessionary 1970s, women's higher job loss in manufacturing was linked more to strong male trade unionist protectionist strategies than to any logic of capitalism, and indeed women's employment opportunities as a whole did not actually deteriorate relative to men's, due largely to the continued expansion of service sector employment (Bruegel, 1979). It has become clear that economic restructuring away from manu-facturing and towards services has meant that men are more at risk of job loss whilst women are benefiting more from new forms of employment, as the search for flexibility by employers has meant the continued growth of female part-time employment and the decline of male full-time jobs. There is no doubt that women do form a 'labour reserve', but this argument has been developed more convincingly into a more general substitution thesis (rather than a disposability thesis) of the long term 'feminisation' of the labour force (Humphries, 1983; Humphries and Rubery, 1988).

None of the above explanations offers any clues as to why women were excluded from paid work in the first place, although the historical construc-tion of the 'male breadwinner' family model is clearly central to these analyses and it was argued that the struggle for a male 'family wage' was a crucial factor in securing both higher male wages and women's economic dependency in the working-class family (cf. Barrett and MacIntosh, 1980; Mark-Lawson and Witz, 1990) and that gender ideology had been pressed into the service of capitalism (Barrett, 1980).

An alternative way in which feminists developed explanations of women's employment, and particularly of gender segregation, out of the 'production paradigm' was by providing materialist analyses which pioneered the use of the concept of 'patriarchy' as well as 'capitalism'. This is often described as dual systems theory and owes much to the pioneering analysis of 'patri-archal capitalism' by Heidi Hartmann (1979, 1981), who argued that patriarchal relations of male dominance and female subordination, far from being destroyed, have been sustained within capitalist societies. The basis of male power is men's control over women's labour within both the family and the labour market. Heidi Hartmann argued that job segregation by sex has provided the main means through which male dominance in the labour market (and indeed generally throughout society) has been secured, and that the 'family wage' (a male wage high enough to support a wife and children) has provided the pivotal means enabling men not only to ensure that they receive higher wages than working women, but also to secure women's unpaid domestic labour and sexual services within the family. Hartmann emphasised the role of trade union organisation amongst working men as a means of gender struggles as well as of class struggle, as men secured gains for themselves at the expense of working women. The key move effected by dual systems theory was that of subjecting the interests and actions of men, and not just those of employers, to feminist scrutiny. Patriarchal practices have played a key role in creating the gender structure of paid work.

The concept of patriarchy has been particularly important in unpicking the complex, historical underpinnings of the current arrangement of gender-segregated jobs. Feminists drew upon the concept of patriarchal practices to specify how exclusionary strategies were used against women by male workers organised into trade unions or professional associations in the nineteenth and early twentieth centuries, and how demarcationary or segregationary strategies were used either alongside these or when exclusion failed (Cockburn, 1981, 1983; Walby, 1986, 1990; Witz, 1992). Feminists working with the concept of patriarchy (its acknowledged limitations notwithstanding) also pioneered structural analyses which challenged conventional explanations of women's position in the labour market as determined by their position in the family/household. Both Heidi Hartmann and Sylvia Walby have argued that it is gender segregation and patriarchal practices in the labour market that have proved vital in forging patterns of male dominance generally in modern societies. Sylvia Walby (1990, 1997) has developed an analysis of patriarchy which emphasises both its changing forms – the shift from 'private' to 'public' patriarchy – and its indeterminacy. Feminist analysis must be continually alert to changes in both the form of patriarchy and the corresponding nature and degree of inequalities between men and women, as well as differences between women based on age, generation, 'race', ethnicity and class. The role played by gendered forms of access to paid work stands at the centre of Sylvia Walby's account of the shift in patriarchy from its 'private' to its 'public' form (1990). This shift from a private, domestic gender regime to a public gender regime captures the modern trajectory of change in the overall system of patriarchy, signalling a transformation of gender relations, where:

> The domestic gender regime is based upon household production as the main structure and site of women's work activity and the exploitation of her labour and sexuality and upon the exclusion of women from the public. The public gender regime is based, not on excluding women from the public, but on the segregation and subordination of women within the structures of paid employment and the state, as well as within culture, sexuality and violence. (Walby, 1997, p. 7)

New directions in feminist studies of women's work

So far, the focus has been on the macro-level level patterning of gender-segregated work and on structuralist explanations of these patterns. The 'production paradigm' of classic feminist accounts of gender at work has been challenged by some recent developments. These are the development of a post-structuralist or 'culturalist' analysis of sexuality and power at work (Pringle, 1989); a shift in focus from gender and the labour market to an exploration of sexuality, gender, power and organisational cultures (Hearn *et. al.*, 1989; Cockburn, 1991; Mills and Tancred, 1992; Savage and Witz, 1992; Gerhardhi, 1995); the detailed, empirical analysis of micro-processes of the accomplishment of gendered work and identities in particular work place settings (Hall, 1993); and a focus on the embodied and sexualised aspects of gendered work (Acker, 1990, 1992; Adkins, 1995; Halford, Savage and Witz, 1997).

It should be noted, however, that feminists' concern with teasing out the ways in which class relations were fractured by gender and 'race' led to an early focus on the factory floor through empirical work place studies which excavated the everyday, lived realities and experiences of job segregation, the gender hierarchies of skill, and the intersection between class, gender and 'race' in the work place (Pollert, 1981; Cavendish, 1982; Westwood, 1984). Feminists were also engaged in something approaching the 'deconstruction' of the notion of skill before 'feminist deconstruction' was in vogue, arguing that the construction of a skill level of a job depended as much, if not more, on the gender of the person doing the job than on the content of the job itself (Phillips and Taylor, 1980). Recent feminist concerns with 'the body' or 'embodiment' were pre-figured by Cynthia Cockburn's (1981, 1983) analysis of the links between physical embodiment and skill, and particularly her emphasis on the 'physical' aspect of male power in the work place whereby, in staking claim to skills, men appropriate muscle, capability, tools and machinery, constructing themselves as strong and manually able, whilst constructing women as physically and technically incompetent. It is important, then, to recognise 'new directions' in the theorisation of women's and men's work as signalling a degree of continuity as well as change.

Rosemary Pringle's *Secretaries' Talk: Sexuality, Power and Work* (1989) marked a departure from the 'production paradigm' of classic feminist accounts of gendered work by relocating work in the context of debates concerning culture and sexuality. Working within a post-structuralist rather than a structuralist framework, Pringle locates her analysis of the boss–secretary relation within 'discourses of power' rather than 'the labour market', exploring the discursive construction of secretaries as a category, and the connections between domination, sexuality and pleasure. Pringle emphasises the role played by sexual and familial discourses in constructing the gendered subject positions of 'boss' and 'secretary' and in creating a structure of domination based on desire and sexuality. It is easier, she argues, to specify what a secretary is than what a secretary does, so urging us to see the processes of job definition, gendering and sexualisation as intertwined processes. Discourses of the 'office wife', the 'sexy secretary' and the 'career woman' have operated to define what a secretary is. Pringle shifts the focus in feminist analyses of work from a 'productionist' to a 'culturalist' paradigm, by looking at the ways in which power relations between women and men in the work place are discursively produced, the cultural meanings embodied in occupations, and the formation of work place subjectivities (Adkins and Lury, 1996). Cynthia Cockburn (1991) has also incorporated the analysis of sexualised discourses within her more materialist analysis of male power at work by exploring how sexualised discourses of difference are deployed by men to 'put women in their place' through highlighting their sexual and embodied difference, and deploying a 'politics of the body' to undermine the goals of equality politics in workplace organisations.

Again, we should note elements of continuity as well as change in studies of sexuality, gender and power in work place organisations, remembering that there was a small body of radical feminist work in the 1970s and 1980s which pioneered the analysis of how sexuality was deployed as a means of male control over women in the work place (cf. MacKinnon, 1978; Stanko, 1988), and was responsible for 'naming' sexual harassment as the unwanted and intrusive sexualisation and intimidation of women in the work place. Work place organisations are now seen as 'scenes of power, both gendered and sexual' (Hearn et al., 1989). The 'booming silence' on the topic of sexuality and organisations (Hearn and Parkin, 1986) has been superseded by a growing body of work which emphasises how, far from being banished from public arenas such as work place organisations, sexuality suffuses these organisations, although often in hidden ways. This new focus on sexuality and organisations has led to the more explicit analysis of masculinity at work (cf. Collinson and Collinson, 1989; Hearn et al., 1989; Roper, 1992) and has also rendered heterosexist forms of oppression and discrimination more visible. Lesbians and gay men experience discrimination at work, through employers' attitudes to recruiting and promoting lesbian and gay staff, as well as from co-workers, and can experience profound alienation within heterosexualised work place cultures. Lesbians in organisations experience 'double jeopardy' in terms of their gender as women and in terms of their sexuality, as the background buzz of heterosexist assumptions continually presents difficulties as to whether or not to disclose their lesbianism (Hall, 1989).

Another new direction in feminist analyses of work has been opened up by empirical, sociological analyses which explore the micro-politics of 'doing gender' as we 'do work'. Rather than treating gender as a ready made identity or set of behaviours that we 'import' into work place settings, gender is conceptualised as something we 'do' as we do work; it is an emergent feature of social settings, including work places (Hall, 1993; West and Zimmerman, 1987). Hall (1993) argues that we 'do gender' by performing jobs in certain ways because these jobs are structured to demand gender displays. In the female-dominated, yet gender-segregated, job of table servers, she shows how two distinct service styles demand gendered work performances: 'formal' service style in high-prestige restaurants is constructed as dignified and reserved and as demanding masculine gender performance; 'home-style' service style promotes a casual, familial form of interpretation and feminine gender performance. An extremely important aspect of this focus on 'doing gender' as we 'do work' is the insights it offers into the ways in which jobs become gendered *and* re-gendered. Gendered meanings are *loaded into* work behaviours (Hageman-White, 1987, cited in Hall, 1993), but different gendered meanings can be loaded into the same work tasks. Male nurses, for example, may attempt to load masculine meanings into the job of nursing, already loaded with feminine meanings (Williams, 1989), or male and female workers engaged in the same kinds of work behaviours (such as dealing with customers) can load these same tasks with differently gendered meanings (Leidner, 1991).

Finally, feminists have also begun to explore ways in which the work women do is embodied and involves 'emotion' or 'sexual' work, and how the very notion of a labour contract is a patriarchal or gendered construct. Joan Acker (1990) argues that, when we think of jobs and hierarchies in the abstract, we also assume that these can be filled with disembodied, gender-neutral workers. Yet, in reality, both the concept of 'a job' and 'a worker' are deeply gendered and embodied. This is because 'The closest the disembodied worker doing the abstract job comes to a real worker is the male worker whose life centres on his full-time, lifelong job, whilst his wife or another women takes care of his personal needs and his children' (p. 149). Acker (1990, 1992) introduces an analysis of embodiment alongside those of gender and sexuality as a key component in any analysis of gender, work and organisations. We might, therefore, see men's bodies as 'at home' and rendered invisible and unproblematic in organisations, whilst women's bodies, associated with reproduction, are ruled out of place and excluded, or are commodified as infused with sexuality as a way of including women within organisations (Halford, Savage and Witz, 1997). Discourses of embodiment may refer to reproduction or sexuality in order to mark women off as different from men in organisational contexts, where the male body is 'at home', hidden and normalised.

The concept of 'emotion work' has been developed through an analysis of the work done by airline stewardesses, who are trained in the management and control of emotions, feelings, attentiveness and appearance (Hochschild, 1983). The concept of 'sexual work' has also been developed by Lisa Adkins (1995), who explores the routine sexualisation of women workers in the leisure industry, arguing that women are not just required to be economically productive workers (as men are), but also sexually productive workers. Women exchange their attractiveness in return for employment; they are required to be constantly vigilant concerning their appearance and to routinely respond to the sexualised demands of male customers. In other words, women workers constitute a sexually commodified work force.

Conclusion

This chapter has drawn attention to how, as a result of deep-seated and ongoing structural changes in the nature and organisation of work – those associated with the deregulation of labour markets, the drive towards 'flexibility' by firms, the restructuring of economies away from manufacturing and towards services, the introduction of new information technology, and the 'casualisation' of work – there have been transformations in the gender structure of paid work (cf. Reskin and Padavic, 1994; Walby, 1997). The exclusive association of men with paid, 'productive' work in the 'economy', together with the exclusive association of women with unpaid, domestic work in the family/household, has been destabilised in late capitalist societies. And, as we have seen, although gendered occupational segregation remains high and persistent, there is also evidence of some desegregation. There are good reasons, nonetheless, for feminists not to jump to optimistic conclusions that these changes are indicative of the destabilisation of the gender order or regime of patriarchy. First, as many feminists have stressed, women still perform the bulk of servicing work, and their hidden labour is crucial in sustaining the fabric of everday lives in families, households, communities and voluntary networks of care (cf. Delphy and Leonard, 1992). Second, some women are benefiting more than others, and it is therefore vital for feminists to remain alert to the different structures of opportunity and constraint experienced by white women compared to Black women, by younger, qualified women compared to older, less qualified women and so on. (Walby, 1997). Third, the male breadwinner model of family organisation still dominates policy thinking and, as long as it does so, labour market policies are unlikely to bring about a new gender order which involves the more equitable distribution of waged work, domestic work and access to income (Lewis, 1993; *Bulletin on Women and Employment in the EU*, No.7, October 1995).

Feminists must contextualise their analyses and explanations of gendered work within a broader analysis of the transformation of the 'social', the 'economic' and the 'cultural' (Adkins, 1997). There are profound changes taking place in the ways in which we engage in, and constitute our identities through, paid work; these changes are linked to broader social processes. Many contemporary social theorists are capturing these shifts in the society and economy in terms of 'reflexive individualisation' and 'de-traditionalisation'. They are arguing that individuals are becoming increasingly agentic in the modes of their engagement in work and other aspects of their lives, such as building personal relationships and networks (cf. Beck, 1992; Beck and Beck-Gersheim, 1995), and that work is becoming 'de-materialised', shifting from the regimented, materially-based production of 'things' to an increasingly intangible knowledge-intensive form of innovation and culturally-based production (Lash and Urry, 1994; Heelas, Lash and Morris, 1996). In some of these accounts, 'traditional' structures, such as class, gender and 'race', are seen to have less of a hold on how individuals live their lives or forge their identities. Beck claims, for example, that 'people are being removed from the constraints of gender . . . men and women are released from traditional forms and ascribed roles' (Beck, 1992, p. 105).

We have looked at some of the ways in which processes of capitalist restructuring are impacting in gender-specific ways on employment in the Western industrial societies of Europe and North America. But what of the impact of the globalisation of capital on developing countries? Is there a gendered international division of labour? It is certainly the case that women all over the world are being pulled into capitalist production as workers, and that certain world-wide features of women's work are in evidence, particularly how women take the largest share of service sector jobs worldwide (although only a quarter in the developing world, compared to half in the rich world). As multinational corporations have moved into developing countries in free-trade zones, there is evidence of an overwhelming preference for young women workers. Just as in Western countries women's unpaid and paid work in the home is rendered invisible, so too in developing countries, as their role in agriculture in the informal economy has been unacknowledged and overlooked, particularly in aid programmes that have consequently benefited men at the expense of women (Joekes, 1987). Indeed, it has been argued that, on a global scale, the creation of a work force constructed in terms of the 'domestically defined female sex', rather than the creation of the 'free male proletarian', is becoming the prime strategy for multinational capitalist employers (Mies, 1986).

Are we to conclude, then, that the steadily increasing levels of women's engagement in paid work, as well as the trends towards desegregation in occupations, are symptomatic of the loosening of structures of patriarchy and the greater ability of women to engage as 'individuals' in the labour market? Are women, at last, getting just rewards for their labour? Feminists who are beginning to address these kinds of questions are advising caution in respect of such optimistic assessments. Yes, we can talk about 'gender transformations' (cf. Walby, 1997); but we must also be alert to the possibility that de-traditionalisation and individualisation are gendered processes. There may indeed be a process of re-traditionalisation in relation to gender, where new modes of 'individualisation' and the loosening of the self from structural constraints are mapping more easily on to typically male modes of negotiating their life courses, but becoming central to the current re-organisation of women's oppression (cf. Adkins, 1997).

Attempts to analyse these kinds of macro, societal level issues through an analysis of the gendered structure and organisation of work and non-work lives were once central to feminist analyses. However, we have also seen how feminists are forging new ways of analysing gendered work, ones which focus on the 'cultural' constitution of sexuality and gender *through* work, rather than the 'economic' positioning of men and women *in* work, as well as ones which explore the micro-processes of gender performativity in specific jobs, work places and organisations. These new directions enrich feminist analyses of women's paid work. Nonetheless, it is also vital that feminists continue to locate their analyses of paid employment within an interrogation of the re-gendering of the 'economic' and the 'social', as well as the 'cultural' (Walby, 1992; Adkins and Lury, 1996).

Notes

1. For a detailed analysis of recent empirical trends in women's work in Britain, see Walby (1997) and for a summary of the main features of gender segregated labour markets in Western European countries (specifically member states of the EU), see Rubery and Fagan (1995).
2. This compares to 72.5% for men and, although this seems much higher, the rates for men and women have been converging over the past 50 years, as men's rates are falling and women's are rising.
3. I prefer to use the term 'non-employed', as the term 'inactivity' – intended to describe those members of the population who are not available for or actively looking for work, such as pensioners or students – includes full-time housewives, who are, of course, anything but 'inactive'! The deconstruction and reworking of conventional androcentric language used in policy discussions and statistics is something feminists need to engage in. In addition, the changing structure of paid work means that conventional, androcentric terminology and statistical practices are no longer adequate in 'naming' and 'measuring' the gendered use of time over the life-cycle.
4. Most studies of occupational segregation provide broad-brush, macro-level pictures of which occupations are predominantly male or female (Hakim, 1979, 1992, 1993; Rubery and Fagan, 1995) and some recent analyses have begun to focus on processes of desegregation or integration (Reskin and Roos, 1990; Hakim, 1992, 1993). Studies of how and why particular occupations become gender segregated are relatively rare and usually qualitative. These have often taken the form of: historical studies of occupations such as engineering (Walby, 1986), printing (Cockburn, 1983), clerical work (Walby, 1986), and various health care occupations (Witz, 1992); or case studies of women's and men's relative positions within particular occupations, such as banking, accountancy, pharmacy, nursing, etc. (Crompton and Sanderson, 1989; Halford, Savage and Witz, 1997), and of the changing gendered composition of particular occupations (Reskin and Roos, 1990).
5. Whereas in 1979 nearly two-thirds of the male work force worked in occupations where 9 out of 10 workers were men, by 1990 less than half did; in 1979 nearly three-quarters of the male work force worked in occupations where 8 out of 10 workers were men, compared to less than two-thirds in 1990; and in 1979 three-quarters of the male work force worked in occupations where 7 out of 10 workers were male, but this had declined to 69% by 1990 (Hakim, 1992, 1993).
6. In the UK context of severely eroded public funded care for the elderly and infirm, as well as inadequate publicly funded childcare, part-time work does give women with caring responsibilities some employment options.

7. Although male part-time employment has been growing, by 1994 only 11% of men worked part-time, compared to nearly half of women in Britain (Naylor, 1994). Nonetheless, one aspect of the transformation of gendered work is the fact that over half of new men's jobs are also part-time (*Bulletin on Women and Employment in the EU*, No. 8, April 1996).

8. Until February 1995 in Britain, those who worked less than 8 hours and those who worked between 8 and 16 hours but had worked for less than 5 years with their current employer were not eligible for a variety of employment protection rights available to full-time workers, including the right to claim unfair dismissal, maternity leave, notice on dismissal, and statutory redundancy pay. In 1995, a European Court ruling led to a judgement in the House of Lords giving part-time workers the same employment protection rights as full-time workers. (*Employment Gazette*, February 1995, p. 43).

9. They were cheap because it was assumed that wives, unlike husbands, did not have to earn a 'family wage' high enough to support other family members, and they were disposable because they 'have a world of their very own, the family, into which they can disappear when discarded from production' (Beechey, 1977, p. 57).

Further reading

Rosemary Pringle, *Secretaries' Talk: Sexuality, Power and Work* (London: Verso, 1989). This is an important study of women's work which moved beyond the preoccupation with structures of women's employment and male power, and pioneered the application of post-structuralist ideas to an analysis of women's work. Rosemary Pringle looks in particular at the ways in which discourses of sexuality construct the jobs of bosses and secretaries.

Barbara Reskin and Irene Padavic, *Women and Men at Work* (London: Pine Forge Press, 1994). This is a very clearly written overview of the main aspects of women's work in modern societies, providing an introduction to the key concepts developed to explore women's employment as well as insights into the actual position of women in work in Western Europe and the USA.

Lisa Adkins, *Gendered Work: Sexuality, Family and the Labour Market* (Buckingham: Open University Press, 1995). Lisa Adkins critically reviews feminist and sociological analyses of employment, and develops a new way of understanding the gendered structure of the labour market. Drawing on an empirical study of gendered work in the leisure and tourist industries, Lisa Adkins extends the concept of 'labour' to include 'sexual labour', arguing that women are constituted as 'workers' through the commodification of their sexuality.

Sylvia Walby, *Gender Transformations* (London: Routledge, 1997). Developing her analysis of the shift from 'private' to 'public patriarchy' (*Theorising Patriarchy*, 1990), Sylvia Walby provides an excellent summary and analysis of the major changes in gendered employment in Britain today, exploring new divisions amongst women in terms of age, class, 'race' and ethnicity, and analysing changes in women's employment, as well gender relations more generally, in the context of the flexibilisation of work, the state, gender politics and citizenship.

12

Feminism and Social Policy

Fiona Williams

Introduction

This chapter is about the development of feminist ideas in social policy. As a discipline, social policy involves the study of the history, organisation and outcomes of the health and welfare policies and services, summed up by the term 'welfare state'.[1] Since the 1970s feminist work has had a growing influence upon the mainstream study of social policy in Britain, the USA and Europe. One reason for this hangs on the significance of social policies for feminism in particular and for women in general. What I mean by this can be illustrated by scanning the demands that emerged from the women's liberation movement in Britain at the beginning of the 1970s. These focused upon equal pay, equal work, equal educational opportunities, free abortion and contraception and free childcare facilities. (Later the right to a self-defined sexuality was added.) In other words, many of these original demands were claims upon the welfare state. In addition, the politics of feminism through the 1970s and early 1980s was the subject-matter of social policy, whether these were the Campaign for Legal and Financial Independence (which demanded an overhaul of the social security and taxation systems), the Working Women's Charter, campaigns for abortion rights and, later, reproductive rights, for women's refuges, for well-women centres, for rape crisis centres and for Black children's rights within schools. All of these campaigns were directed at the welfare policies of the state or local state, and what emerged from them was the beginning of a feminist critique of the welfare state.

At the centre of this critique is the acknowledgement that welfare issues are of central importance to women's lives and that women are of central importance to welfare: whether as *consumers or users* of welfare services; as *welfare workers*, both in a paid capacity (as nurses, cleaners, teachers and so on) or in an unpaid capacity as carers in the home; or as constituents who *campaign* over welfare issues. However, the nub of this relationship is its contradictory and uneven nature. On the one hand, the welfare state has the potential to offer women greater freedoms (by providing childcare, for example, so that women may take up paid work and achieve a degree of financial independence). On the other hand, it has the capacity to constrain, control and restrict women's lives (by, for example, restricting abortion to certain groups of women, or by forcing the sterilisation of other groups of women).

Within Women's Studies feminist social policy has for a long time represented the 'hard end' of evidence about women's material disadvantages, concerned as it is with issues such as poverty and homelessness. In so far as there has been something of a 'paradigm shift' within feminism, and reflecting that, within Women's Studies – arguably a shift from a focus upon 'things ' to 'words' (that is, from a focus upon structural inequalities to the texts and images of cultural representations: Barrett, 1992) – then feminist social policy no longer holds as central a place as it once did. At the same time, feminist social policy has itself undergone certain shifts, as I detail in this chapter. In addition, I would argue that a focus on the politics of poverty is not unconnected to the politics of pleasure; indeed they are two sides of the same coin in many women's lives these days. The restructuring of the welfare state, which in Britain has been driven by a New Right government since 1979, has directly undermined the living conditions of many groups of women, particularly lone mothers, older and disabled women, women on lower grades in the public sector, unskilled women workers and minority ethnic women. The politics of introducing markets, managers and a mixed economy into the welfare state has reduced many women's rights and access to services and benefits whilst increasing their responsibilities for the care of their children and their older and disabled relatives (see Mayo and Weir, 1993; May and Brunsden, 1996). At the same time, rather less successfully, the New Right has also attempted to create a moral panic around women's claims for their personal and financial autonomy. This has focused particularly upon young lone mothers who have been charged with generating a culture of dependency upon the state and with fostering a climate of moral irresponsibility. For this group of women, their struggles to develop individual and collective strategies of survival are intimately bound up with their identities, their lifestyles and their determination to develop relationships of their own choosing (see Campbell, 1993). The personal and the political, the structure and the image, the material and the textual are all interwoven.

Two key themes – the importance of welfare to women, and the contradictions it embodies – have been central to the development of feminist critiques in this area. The remainder of this chapter explores the development of feminist social policy in three parts. In the first part I look at the development of social policy and the ways in which different issues and perspectives have emerged. In the second part I illustrate the way in which feminist work in social policy generated new conceptual dimensions as well as critical refinements of mainstream concepts. In the final part I look at the impact of feminism upon new developments within social policy, with specific reference to comparative social policy. To begin with I present a brief overview of the sorts of questions feminists have asked about social policy.

Questions feminists ask

Whilst acknowledging the heterogeneity of feminist approaches within social policy and the important challenges posed by politics around 'race', disability and sexuality, it is possible to identify a number of new dimensions and perspectives that feminism in general has brought to the study of social policy. The initial contribution of the feminist critiques of welfare was to focus more intensely and critically upon areas of social reproduction (Pascall, 1986). This means not only the processes of bearing children but the physical, emotional, ideological and material processes involved in caring for and sustaining others. The conditions in which this takes place, and the consequences flowing from it, are crucial for women's lives and central to welfare policies. The questions feminist analyses have asked are: why do women play such a major role in social reproduction? What does this experience, and the way the state intervenes, mean for women? Does it mean different things for different women (single, working class, Black, older, disabled, lesbian)? Should it be changed, and if so, how? In other words, rather than simply taking for granted, as mainstream analysis had done, that women provide unpaid nurturing and caring because it is assumed to be natural or biologically-determined, or because it suits the accumulation needs of capital, feminist analysis has asked: *why women*? And in posing this question it has developed, most crucially, our understanding of the relationship between the private sphere of domestic life and the public sphere of paid work, politics and policy-making. In other words, it examines the specifics of the relationship between the family, the state[2] and the market and the impact of this relationship for women.

Following on from this feminists have raised important questions about *caring* (who cares for the family and why), about *dependency* (what roles do state policies play in constructing women's financial dependency), and about *power and inequality*. (How far do welfare policies sustain or reproduce unequal gender relations? How far are these experiences modified by other axes of power, around 'race', ethnicity, class, sexuality, age or disability? And how far are there variations in the way different welfare states in different countries have constructed these issues?) In their turn these issues have given rise to theoretical explorations into the construction of women's lives through state social policies and into explanations for the relationship between women and the state. Earlier explanations tended to explain this relationship in causal terms focusing upon patriarchy or capitalist patriarchy or patriarchal capitalism or a racially-structured patriarchal capitalism (Wilson, 1977; Barrett, 1980; Rose, 1981; Pascall, 1986; Williams, 1989). More recently feminist analyses have been less concerned with *causes* and have focused more upon the processes through which this relationship between women and the state is mediated by a multiplicity of social relations of power – of gender, 'race', class, disability, sexuality, age – in which women may be positioned differently at different times and within different welfare discourses (Langan and Day, 1992; Williams, 1992b).

Women's organisation around welfare issues has also raised important strategic issues. For instance, through campaigns in housing (women's refuges) and health care (well-women centres), women have attempted to organise in ways which are non-hierarchical and non-bureaucratic, which are neither racist nor sexist, and in ways which attempt to create a more equal relationship between users and providers. In this way they have, along with women trade unionists in the public sector, been influential in the development of equal opportunities policies and anti-oppressive strategies within public services as well as in developing empowerment strategies for users of welfare services.

Feminist analysis has also insisted upon the importance of tying economic policies to the needs of everyday life rather than the other way round (Ann Phillips, 1993). A further theme in feminist social policy writing has been the acknowledgement of the tensions between policies which meet women's needs in the here-and-now (an improved benefit for carers, for example) and transformative policies which give women greater power in the long term (policies which challenge the sexual division of labour in the home, for example). These reflect tensions in other areas: for instance, in policies rooted in women's claims to equality (as paid workers) and policies rooted in women's claims to difference (as mothers, partners or wives).

The development of feminist critiques in social policy

To some extent the development of feminist critiques in social policy mirrors the development of feminist ideas generally, so that from the late 1970s major areas of feminist research in Britain examined the ways in which the welfare state acted as a system of oppression, controlling women and holding them in a state of dependence within the family. Some of this early work was an attempt to refine Marxist theories of welfare. So, for example, Elizabeth Wilson (1977) and Mary McIntosh (1978) identified the state as maintaining (often in a contradictory way) a particular family form primarily for the benefit of capital but in a way that was oppressive to women. Central to these early analyses was an analysis of the family as the site of oppression, with the ideology of familialism permeating all areas of state provision and restricting women's role to that of wife and mother. Early campaigns focused upon policies that could bring women greater equality especially through employment: childcare, education and training opportunities, reproductive rights and so on. However, by the early 1980s, campaigns and analyses shifted more towards the local state and towards translating the inequalities of personal gender relations into political issues, especially around domestic violence, but also rape, and (later) child abuse. Although these campaigns involved women from different feminist perspectives, they were often initiated by radical feminists operating within a framework in which it was patriarchy and patriarchal social institutions as much as, if not more than, capitalism which were at the heart of women's oppression.

In terms of these different political perspectives influencing feminist analysis it is possible to identify at least five which influenced feminist debates in the 1970s and 1980s: a *right-wing libertarian feminism* which identifies women's success in the market place as the key to women's equality; *liberal feminism* with its focus upon equal rights and equal opportunities; *welfare feminism* which sees the welfare state as improving women's conditions, not as workers but as wives and mothers; *radical feminism*, which emphasises the need to challenge patriarchal social relations of welfare; and *Marxist/socialist feminism*, which sees welfare policies as combining capitalist and patriarchal interests but often in contradictory ways. In theory, these political differences stemmed from the analysis of the causes of women's oppression and the relationship between the family and the state. In practice, women of different political persuasions worked together on many welfare campaigns, such as those involving women's health and housing needs.

By the mid-1980s a number of shifts took place in both theory and practice. Two of these centred round the concept of difference. The first was a shift away from the striving of equality *with* men to an affirmation of women's difference *from* men. In welfare terms this was reflected in the development of alternative women's services run for and by women, and initially at least, operating outside the local state – women's refuges, rape crisis centres, well-women clinics, lesbian lines – which attempted to put into practice 'women-centred values'. Many of these services operated on lines which were non-hierarchical: they shared 'expert 'knowledge with the users, they offered users a say in the running of the services, and they stood in contrast and defiance to the paternalism of conventional state welfare services.

The second way in which the concept of difference began to refine analyses was through the development of the politics of difference, or 'identity politics', especially around 'race', disability, sexuality and age. Black feminist writers in the early 1980s began to highlight the processes by which Black women's experiences of the welfare state are rendered different from white women's (Bryan, Dadzie and Scafe , 1985). To begin with, Black women's experiences of paid work, family life, reproductive rights and sexuality are structured by 'race' and ethnicity as well as by gender and class. The simultaneous experience of racism and sexism, and the ways in which it may be mediated by social policies, reconstitutes Black women's experiences in specific ways, and these may be further compounded (or mitigated) by class positioning. For example, the struggle to establish Black women's refuges has involved confronting not only sexist practices in relation to domestic violence but also racist assumptions about Black family life and the needs of Black women within them; the stereotypes are of Asian families being self-sufficient, and African-Caribbean women being over-assertive (Mama, 1989). At the same time the issue of domestic violence challenges the inadequacy of low-cost housing for women on low or no income.

In relation to disability, disabled feminists have drawn upon and en-gendered theories of the social construction of disability, and also critiqued feminist theories of welfare (Keith, 1990; Morris, 1991). They have demon-strated how access to family life, motherhood, education and employment is structured differently for disabled women. The history of institutionalisa-tion and segregation of disabled people has generated oppressive notions of disabled people as passive, vulnerable, dependent, the objects of pity, charity or disgust. For women these discourses are compounded by ideol-ogies of gender (and also age, as many disabled people are older women). Discourses of sexuality often represent physically disabled women as asex-ual, whereas women with learning difficulties are often assumed to be, unknowingly, sexually promiscuous, and in need of protection and control (Begum, 1992b). Furthermore, far from liberating disabled people, the theories and practices of medical and social work professionals have had particular power in maintaining disabled people in a situation of depen-dency. In addition, as I explain later, feminist social policy writers have often assumed the interests of able-bodied women (in their campaigns and studies of women as *carers*) and obscured the interests of those who are *cared for*.

Critiques which focus upon the logic of sexuality within welfare have also drawn attention to the ways in which social policies generate a particular 'truth' – or dominant discourse – about sexual identity, lifestyle and practice which is, for the most part, based on the assumed 'naturalness' and universality of heterosexual coupledom and parenting (Carabine, 1992, 1996a, 1996b; VanEvery, 1991/2). This 'truth' changes over time, for example, in the greater acceptability of children born outside marriage; and it is also resisted and challenged more directly: for instance in the campaigns against Clause 28 of the 1988 Local Government Act which prohibited a local authority (through, say, schools) from promoting 'pre-tended' family relationships of lesbian or gay male partners or parents. At the same time, it can also serve to deny, marginalise or pathologise other forms of sexual identity or lifestyle: for example, in not extending the legal rights associated with heterosexual partnership and marriage (in relation to tenancies, insurance and pension policies) to same-sex relationships. A focus on sexuality both extends the analysis of social policy into the realm of intimacy whilst also demonstrating a further way in which the welfare experiences of women are not uniform but are constituted through differences in their sexual identities, practices and/ or experiences.

Finally, too, ageing is a gendered process: 'later life is primarily an experience of women' (Arber and Ginn, 1991, p. vii). Many of the first demands of the second wave of feminism expressed the interests of younger women for nurseries, abortion or contraception. However, in old age, many of the inequalities faced by younger women become intensified, particularly lack of economic resources (where earlier marginalisation from paid work is reflected in a lack of adequate pension provision). Older women also depend in different ways on welfare and health services for both care responsibilities (for partners) or care support and support for themselves and for their specific health needs.

The identification of differences has led to a more complex approach to the multifaceted ways in which women's lives, their needs and their experiences of welfare are constituted. In addition the multiple identities and divisions which structure women's lives have made the search for a single *cause* for women's oppression too obscure; instead feminist social policy has shifted towards an analysis which identifies the complex ways in which women's lives are both enabled and constrained by social policy discourses.

New conceptual dimensions

Feminist social policy has, inevitably, involved a critique of the mainstream discipline. In developing this it has added new conceptual dimensions to the study of social policy and reformulation of old concepts. In this section I look at three examples of new conceptual developments: the relationship of the private sphere of domestic life to the public sphere of the state and the market; the principle of care; and the principle of dependency.

The relationship between the private and the public

Mainstream analyses of social policy tend towards an understanding of the welfare state in terms of the relationship between the state and the market where the state intervenes to facilitate policies to, in traditional Fabian or social reformist terms, protect the working class from the worst excesses of the market (unemployment, poor housing). Thus, the political debates between different perspectives of welfare have focused upon how far the state should intervene to minimise the vagaries of the market (by providing unemployment benefit, pensions, public housing and so on). Traditionally, the Right has wished to minimise the role of the state, believing that welfare benefits lead people into a culture of dependency, whilst social reformists have believed such intervention necessary both for economic well-being but also in promoting a more just and harmonious society. Marxist analyses have seen the welfare state as the result of a truce between three key actors: capital in its pursuit of accumulation; the working class in pursuit of the amelioration of its conditions; and the state in pursuit of its own legitimacy. What all these analyses and debates take for granted is the role of the heterosexual family, and specifically the role of women in the family, assuming their primary role to be as wives and carers and their financial dependency on their husbands. They also take for granted the relationships within the family, assuming the interests of women, men and children to be unified and complimentary. In fact, the way in which the state intervenes to provide or facilitate, for example, maternity benefits, nursery care or day care for older people influences how far women carers are free to enter paid work in the market and whether they take part-time or full-time work. The extent to which they can earn an independent wage also affects the extent to which they are obliged to depend upon other sources of income (a partner or an income from the state).

In addition, the history of social policies has been as much about 'the state organisation of domestic life' (Wilson, 1977, p. 9) as it has been about men's working conditions. In most industrialised welfare states the establishment of national social insurance systems for unemployment and old age were followed swiftly by policies for mothers. Whilst in many cases these aimed to improve the conditions of motherhood, they also carried significant assumptions about the centrality of marriage and motherhood in women's lives. Indeed the issues of motherhood provide an interesting illustration of the ways in which women's lives, historically and today, are constituted differently by social policies and also how issues of 'race', disability, gender and sexuality intermesh. The development of maternity and child welfare services after 1918 met women's very real needs but, at the same time, served to consolidate women's place in the home. In addition, such policies elevated motherhood to a new dignity. It was not only women's duty and destiny to be 'mothers of the "race"' but also their reward (Davin, 1978, p. 13). Women's role in the family became tied to the development of the (British) 'race' and the British 'nation'. However, not all women were seen as potential bearers of the 'race'. The Mental Deficiency Act passed in 1913 led to the categorisation, grading and segregation of people with learning difficulties. Central to this act was the eugenic concern to protect society from the social, moral and racial threat that people with learning difficulties, and especially 'feebleminded' women, were seen to represent. These women were stereotyped as promiscuous, carriers of sexual diseases, bearers of deficient children and overfertile. Such stereotypes overlapped with medical ideas about poor working-class and migrant women. Indeed, many of those who were institutionalised and segregated (often for their whole lives) were working-class women who became pregnant outside marriage (Potts and Fido, 1990; Williams, 1992a).

Some of these eugenic ideas were carried into post-war medical practices whereby poor working-class and minority ethnic women were much more likely to receive the long-lasting drug Depo-Provera, or to experience sterilisation in lieu of contraception. A different and contemporary example of restricted eligibility to motherhood centres upon the conditions for acceptance for *in vitro* fertilisation (IVF) as laid down by the 1990 Human Embryo and Fertilisation Act which recommends that the woman should be part of a long-term heterosexual relationship (see also Chapter 16). Paragraph 16 of the guidelines to the 1989 Children Act also discourages lesbian and gay couples from fostering and adoption, although local workings of the Act may vary widely for there have been cases where lesbians have sought and been granted the right to be the resident parent.

A different working of the way in which the relationship between the welfare state and the family is mediated by 'race' can be seen in the experience of African Caribbean women recruited as migrant labour in the 1950s (Carby, 1982; Bryan, Dadzie and Scafe, 1985; Williams, 1989). Many were self-supporting and found themselves in low-paid jobs with long and unsocial hours (often in the newly developing post-war welfare services). In some cases this meant leaving children behind with relatives until there were resources and accommodation to bring them over, or it meant bringing children into a situation where there was no formal provision for working mothers and in which the separation of children from their mothers and the concept of working mothers was antithetical to the familial ideology of the time. Whilst these women were working under conditions imposed upon them as migrant workers they were seen to be failing in terms of the post-war ideals of motherhood. In this way, perceptions of the inadequacies of Black family life entered the discourses of welfare professionals albeit in contradictory and ethnically specific ways: African Caribbean women were seen as domineering, Asian mothers as passive and withdrawn. By the 1980s, evidence of this pathologisation began to emerge with the recognition of the disproportionate numbers of Black children who had been taken into care (ABSWAP, 1983).

These examples of the relationship between the family, the welfare state and the market reflect the fact that the welfare states in most industrialised countries emerged at the beginning of the twentieth century, when the gendered boundaries between the public sphere of paid work and politics and the private sphere of domestic life were most marked. It was also when medical and policy discourses began to define more clearly the contours of acceptable and unacceptable forms of sexual practice. Since that time welfare states have played a major role in drawing and redrawing these changing boundaries, in influencing the entry of women into the public sphere and the role of women and men in the private sphere, both in terms of the conditions and organisation of reproduction and intimacy as well as in the relationships of power between women and men in both spheres. In order to acknowledge these processes feminist social policy has given analytical space to the relationships between the *family*, the *state* and the *market*. However, this triangular relationship alone does not account for the differential experiences, such as those described above of minority ethnic women, and neither does it account fully for the discourses of exclusion around motherhood mentioned earlier. To capture these complexities we need to provide some analytical room for the role of the nation state in influencing the development of social policies. The development of the modern nation state was significant in constructing ideas about what constituted the nation, national unity and national identity. These ideas were extremely influential in policies affecting women, especially around motherhood, as discussed above, but they were also crucial in delineating the boundaries of inclusion in and exclusion from the 'nation' and the citizenship and social rights attached to nationality. It is possible, then, to understand the development of welfare in terms of three interrelated processes associated not only with the market and the family but also with the *nation state* (see Williams, 1989, 1995). Whilst the market signifies the development of industrial capitalism and associated patterns of mobilisation around class-capital relations, and the family signifies the material and ideological setting of the boundaries between the public and private spheres (as outlined above), the nation state expresses the significance of ideas of national unity and national identity which were constructed through an imagined cultural/racial/ethnic/linguistic homogeneity.

These three processes framed the backcloth to the development of the welfare state and wove their way into the organisation of and mobilisation for the new welfare benefits (forms of national insurance) and services (housing, maternal and infant health, education). So, for example, nationality and length of residence in Britain, or for non-British women, marriage to a husband with citizenship, increasingly became conditions of eligibility for welfare benefits. In practice these exclusions around nationality and residence were heavily racialised. By extending the framework for an understanding of social policy beyond the state and the market to inclusions and exclusions around the family and the nation, feminist social policy writers have widened the analysis to include gender and other social relations of power which reconstitute gender (see Williams, 1989, 1995; Lister, 1993, 1994, 1997). Two key new concepts to emerge from this wider and more complex analysis have been the principles of *care* and *dependency*, to which we now turn.

The principle of care

One important way in which welfare states construct the boundary between public responsibility and private duty is over the recognition, remuneration or socialisation of the care work (of children, disabled people, old and sick people) which is generally undertaken by women in the home. In so far as the principle of care is acknowledged this may be through state provision of caring services (nurseries, day centres, home helps) or through remunerating, subsidising or compensating for care work (such as family allowances or care allowances). On the other hand, some welfare states may regard such work as the responsibility of the family: that is, women. In this situation women who have financial resources may well turn to the market to buy in childminding or housekeeping services. In practice welfare states shift between all these options. Sweden and Denmark provide the highest degree of socialised care whereas in the USA or UK, while women are free to enter the labour market, this is highly conditioned by the fact that it is also seen as *their* responsibility to arrange for the care of their dependants. However, the UK offers token remuneration through Child Benefit and the Invalid Care Allowance. German social policies, on the other hand, encourage women to stay at home. The complexity of factors influencing these variations is discussed later in the chapter (see also Lewis, 1993; Sainsbury, 1994). Either way, where care is socialised, privatised, compensated or paid or unpaid, it is generally women who provide it. In addition, the degree of socialisation of care does not seem to have a major impact on the sexual division of labour for servicing household jobs, such as shopping, ironing or cooking (Bryson, Bittman and Donath, 1994).

Earlier feminist work on care in Britain began as a critique of the policy for community care and thus focused upon care of disabled and older people rather than children (although there is a steady stream of literature on the latter: see New and David, 1985). In 1980, Janet Finch and Dulcie Groves argued that community care was predicated upon a double equation: community care = care by the family = care by women. They suggested that the social construction of such work as duty or 'a labour of love' exploits women, keeps them in a situation of economic dependency and fails to recognise, reward or value a major contribution to the welfare state (Finch and Groves, 1983). Feminist writers also argued that policies for community care assume the continuing availability of women to provide care in spite of the rising numbers of women in paid employment and an increase in divorced and single women. In fact, whilst these numbers have increased, their caring duties have not dwindled. Surveys show that women do the bulk of caring work: 24 per cent of carers between the ages of 24 and 59 are women (compared with 16 per cent who are men, generally caring for a partner). Never-married or divorced women are more likely to care (HMSO, 1985).[3]

A further aspect of this feminist work has identified the costs of caring – emotional, physical and financial – to women. Caring often involves heavy physical work such as lifting; it may last up to 24 hours a day, and sometimes without any control over the conditions of that work. Carers often have to leave or reduce their labour market participation, which can involve not only loss of income but also loss of pension rights (Glendinning, 1992). In Britain, compensation for care – such as the Invalid Care Allowance introduced in 1975 – gave recognition to caring, but it is both low and restricted (only one-tenth of carers are eligible). Furthermore, until challenged in the European courts in 1986, it was not available to married or cohabiting women (on the basis that care would be part of their normal duties). Much of this early work focused on the exploitation of women as carers and, in a controversial article in 1984, Janet Finch pointed to the difficulties with strategies for care. The problem with paying carers is that, unless they are paid a market rate, then they are often trapped into poverty or dependency, and anyway such payments simply reinforce that idea that it is a woman's duty to care. She suggested that the solution was the 'residential route' where care is socialised and thereby transfers women's unpaid care in the private sphere to paid work in the public sphere. Here at least, it is argued, women have greater collective say and rights over their conditions of work (Finch, 1984).This argument subsequently faced substantial criticism especially by disabled feminists who argued that it completely disregarded the interests of those (often women) who are cared for (Morris, 1991).

By the mid-1980s the focus of feminist debates on care shifted away from the oppressive, exploitative aspects towards the *meanings* to women of caring. So, for example, Hilary Graham started to suggest that caring was not simply unwanted labour foisted upon women but that it 'is the medium through which women are accepted into and feel they belong in the social world' (Graham, 1983, p. 30). This was a theme that was taken up by Clare Ungerson in her study of the relationship between caring and identity for women and men (Ungerson, 1987). Ungerson tested the ideas raised by Carol Gilligan's *In a Different Voice* (Gilligan, 1982) where she suggests that there are gender differences in the moral frameworks within which men and women operate. Whereas men's moral frameworks guiding their actions are underpinned by a notion of *rights* which are subject to public and rational assessment, women's are underpinned by a notion of *responsibility* which are assessed in relation to individual circumstances. This means, to put the argument rather simplistically, that women define themselves within a context of relationships but also judge themselves in terms of their ability to care. However, Ungerson did not find significant support for these gendered distinctions in her research. Some of her female carers were happy and fulfilled, while others were resentful but dutiful. Some of the men, on the other hand, insisted that their caring sprang not from obligation, duty or rights, but from *love*.

The shift that this work on caring represents draws much more attention to the complexity of women's identities, to their agency and to the variations in meaning they may attribute to care. Nevertheless, much of this work at this time was exclusively gender-focused: that is to say, where differences existed and inequalities were recognised, these were generally those of a gendered nature; second, the site of care in much of this caring literature was taken-for-granted as the 'normal' heterosexual family (although Gillian Dalley did argue for more collectivised approaches to care: see Dalley, 1988). This is rather ironical since much feminist research aimed to uncover and challenge the unequal processes of family life, yet in so doing seemed to run the risk of overgeneralising the (white) heterosexual family as the *only* site of support and care. Third, by focusing exclusively upon the *carer* and care as *work*, what was ignored was an understanding of care as a relationship involving not only a carer but also a cared-for person, and constituting not only different *meanings* but also different *relations of power*. By the early 1990s these issues began to be explored and challenged. From the disability movement new *strategies* emerged which involved neither institutionalisation nor payments for carers, but a direct payment to the cared-for person to enable them to be able to pay a carer of their choice who would be in their employ, thus shifting the balance of power.

A number of studies also began to explore the different *contexts* in which the care of older and disabled people takes place, and the way these may be mediated by factors such as class, 'race' and ethnicity. For example, Yasmin Gunaratnam's study of Asian carers shows how lack of resources, inaccessible and inappropriate services, and the squeezing-out of minority ethnic voluntary organisations through greater competition amongst contracted-out services means that, for Asian carers, 'the move to community care is at some levels quite meaningless' (Gunaratnam, 1990, p. 122). In addition, Hilary Graham argued for a greater range of *sites* of care to be taken into account: both familial and non-familial, lesbian and gay as well as heterosexual, and including domestic service as well as informal caring (Graham, 1990).

These shifts in feminist understandings of care reflect the changes in feminist thinking generally, especially around an understanding of the different meanings attached to the act and process of care by differently-placed women. It is also possible to see in this some influence of post-structuralist thinking upon the area. In general, the influence of post-structuralism upon feminist social policy has been by way of selective osmosis, for there are some points where, by virtue of its very subject matter, feminist social policy analysts would find it difficult to wholly detach their analyses from a notion of broader structures and patterns of inequality and power. At the same time, a more complex enquiry into the different and diffused sites of power within the practice of welfare (as in Foucault's work) fits comfortably with some feminist approaches to social policy (Bell, 1993; Smart, 1995; Carabine, 1996a; for a general discussion see Williams, 1992b, 1996; Penna and O'Brien, 1996b). Writers on disability have, for example, interrogated the welfare discourse of 'care' in terms of the way it constructs disabled people as passive, their carers as invisible angels and welfare professionals as experts and agents of change (Morris, 1993). This approach marks a move away from seeing users of welfare as members of discrete, administrative categories (old, poor, disabled), but as agents of their own lives whose subjectivities and identities, as well as their social positioning influence their perceptions of their own needs and how they meet them.

The principle of dependency

The second principle which has underpinned British social policy is the principle whereby a woman is assumed to be, along with her children, dependent on her husband, the breadwinner. One consequence of this is that a woman's eligibility to benefits has often been in terms of her status as a wife and mother rather than as a woman or simply in her own right, as a citizen. The principle of male breadwinner and female dependant have their origins in the family wage system which assumes that the husband and father in the family earns sufficient to cover the needs of his wife and family. This formed the basis for male trade unionists' collective bargaining processes from the nineteenth century. Whilst on the one hand the family wage system gave more bargaining power to male workers, it also ensured that the balance of power and authority in the house was retained by the man.

These principles of male breadwinning and female dependency were at the heart of much of the subsequent policy on social security, as well as the practice of social work, education and training and housing. It was most clearly expressed in the Beveridge Report of 1942 in which the national insurance scheme gave married women the choice of not paying full contributions, forgoing their own entitlement to sick or unemployment benefits and so on, and relying on their husbands instead. This reflected Beveridge's view of the importance of women as wives and mothers in ensuring the continuance of the 'British "race"' (Beveridge, 1942, p. 49). While Beveridge insisted on marriage as a partnership of husband and wife as equals but different, married women were treated as dependent upon their husbands. The married women's option in unemployment insurance continued until challenged by equal opportunity legislation in the 1970s.

The family wage system was never, in practice, achievable by those in unskilled or semi-skilled work and therefore many married women have, by necessity, done paid work. Women have also been seen as an important source of low-paid labour by employers. Furthermore, not all women married or stayed married. In these ways there has always been an uneasy fit between the realities of the family and market and rhetoric of the state. Although the 1986 Social Security Act equalised the principle of liability (that is, gave the right to claim breadwinner status to a male or female partner) this still reinforces the model of a main breadwinner plus dependant for a heterosexual cohabiting couple. This has a particular negative impact on the wives/cohabitees of unemployed men since they are only allowed to keep £5 of any earned income whilst their partner receives benefit. Since this is unlikely to be used in travel and food expenses, the policy acts as a deterrent to take up employment.

Where women have an interrupted part-time working pattern they have fewer entitlements to occupational and earnings-related pension schemes. This makes women vulnerable to poverty in old age, particularly if they divorce. Current proposals plan to give divorced women rights to claim on their husband's pension funds. This will be an important reform but it will not solve the basic problem of pension systems which are based upon a male model of continuous employment rather than women's different employment patterns and caring responsibilities.

The phenomenon of the 'husbandless', lone mother is precisely one which exposes the inadequacies of a welfare system which assumes women's dependency, their responsibility for care, and a partial involvement in the labour market. In some welfare states lone mothers are treated as prospective breadwinners (for example, in Sweden and Denmark). In Britain, they are treated first and foremost as mothers since they are not required to register for work until the youngest child is 16 years. This means, however, that unless they can earn a sufficient wage which pays for childcare and other expenses they remain dependent on low state benefits. As such, lone mothers constitute one of the largest groups of those in poverty. Indeed, as Caroline Glendinning and Jane Millar have pointed out, it is the fact of being female which renders women at risk to poverty. They argue that a sexual division of labour which assigns to women a primary role in the domestic sphere and a secondary role in the labour market reinforces women's unequal access to income replacement benefits (for example, in pensions or unemployment benefits) in the private, occupational and public systems of welfare provision. 'And, of course, the inequalities of both the labour market and welfare systems are underpinned and legitimated by the ideology of dependency' (Glendinning and Millar, 1992b, p. 32).

Since the 1834 Poor Law the state has sought methods of transferring the dependency of lone mothers from the state to a liable relative. In addition, the rates of benefit have often been set at different rates for different kinds of lone mother: widows receive higher benefits than unmarried mothers. With the rise in the numbers of lone mothers, the most recent attempt has been the introduction of the Child Support Act in 1992 which gives the Child Support Agency powers to trace the biological father and make him liable for the maintenance of his children regardless of the mother's wishes.

Whilst this can be seen as a way of ensuring that men do not evade the financial responsibilities of fatherhood, it is also a clear move to shift the financial dependency of lone parents away from the state and on to the biological father of their children. Not only does this reinforce the concept of female dependency, but for some women this exposes them to a more risky and even dangerous dependency where there has been experience of domestic violence. As I mentioned in the introduction, this policy constitutes, and is partly a consequence of, a discourse of an emerging 'underclass' of state-dependent lone mothers and absent fathers. This 'underclass' discourse has been heavily influenced by American social scientists, especially the work of Charles Murray who argues that welfare programmes for single mothers in the USA have been responsible for the breakdown of the family and for enabling women to live without a husband or a job, and enabling men to leave their wives and children and lead lawless lives (Murray, 1990). In the USA, poverty, historically and today, is profoundly gendered and racialised and the majority of single mothers who depend upon welfare programmes are Black. This notion of an 'underclass' thus represents a heavily encoded attack upon African-American mothers as the threat to the stability and respectability of the American nation (see Gordon, 1990). In Britain, the discourse has so far been less racialised, but has still demonised single mothers' lifestyles and created a rationale for less rather than more social provisions to support lone parents (see Millar, 1992, for the issue of poverty and lone mothers).

The relationship between the state, the family and the market in Britain is a complex one as far as women's economic autonomy is concerned. On the one hand, many social policies have reinforced women's caring responsibilities and their dependence on their male partner. At the same time, increasing numbers of women have entered the work force and the government has not discouraged this. The economic activity rates of women over 16 years increased from 49.2 per cent in 1984 to 53 per cent in 1994, with a projection of 56.7 per cent in 2006, although this reflects an increase in part-time employment (HMSO, *Social Trends*, 1996). However, the government has not provided the sorts of facilities (childcare, especially) that could enable women with caring responsibilities to maintain or increase their earning power.

The uncovering of these two principles of care and dependency underpinning welfare state development has led to a questioning of an understanding of the post-war Keynesian welfare state[4] in Britain. Many commentators identified the welfare state with notions of universalism (the provision of benefits services to all) and a shift to egalitarianism. These notions have been questioned by feminist writers: in so far as the welfare state in Britain was built upon the notion of the white, male, heterosexual, able-bodied breadwinner-led family with dependent wife and children, then it constitutes a false universalism with limited egalitarianism. It was exclusive as much as inclusive. This critical perspective has led to a reformulation of some of the central issues and concepts in social policy. Here I look at citizenship.

Reformulating old concepts: citizenship

The concept of citizenship has been central to the development of post war theory on the welfare state (from Marshall in 1950 through to Esping-Andersen, 1990). T. H. Marshall's theory posited an evolutionary development from civil rights emerging in the eighteenth century and establishing individual freedom especially in the economic sphere, to political rights emerging in the nineteenth century (collective bargaining and universal suffrage), and on to social rights which emerged in the twentieth century through the development of a welfare state and which involved the right to be protected from want, destitution, ignorance and ill-health (Marshall, 1950). The concept of citizenship has enjoyed a revival recently; one of these is in the critical review of the concept by feminist writers and their attempt to pose a radical reformulation (Lister, 1993; Walby, 1994; Yuval-Davis, 1996).

Central to these critiques is the way Marshall (and many subsequent followers of Marshall's ideas) ignores (and thereby reinforces) the separation of public and private spheres, women's economic dependency and how these affect women's access to economic rights, to social rights and their participation in political rights. To begin with, the evolutionary pattern described by Marshall cannot be applied to women. Suffrage did not lead to women's involvement in the political sphere in the same way that it did for men. Furthermore, many aspects of social rights conferred on women, as we have already seen, the status of economic dependant rather than the economic freedom to earn a wage. Third, many women, especially mothers and carers, depend on the existence of social rights (such as care facilities) to be able to exercise their economic rights (to work) and to some extent their full political rights (to be, for example, an active trade unionist). Furthermore, some social rights (such as pensions) depend on a person's attachment to the labour market and, where women's attachment is weak, then their access will be minimal. Marshall's universal theory of citizenship demonstrates the false universalism of welfare state theory and practice.

The next step in these critiques has been to attempt to engender the concept of citizenship. However, engendering alone is not enough for, as Lister (1993, 1997) has pointed out, the process of exclusion of women from full citizenship rights applies in different ways to other social groups (minority ethnic and racialised migrant groups, disabled people, old people, lesbians and gay men, and poor people); these categories also include women. So the first conceptual and analytical question raised by an attempt at reconceptualisation is how to break with the false universalism embedded in the concept of citizenship. And is it possible to use the concept to bring together concepts of 'universality' and 'equality' on the one hand with concepts of 'diversity' and 'difference' on the other (Williams, 1992b; Lister, 1993)? The second question is: what does an active or participatory citizenship mean when we know that many groups are constituted in difference rather than commonality (I. Young, 1990; Ann Phillips, 1993; Williams, 1996). Rather than answer these questions in full, I shall indicate the sort of research that has contributed to their exploration. First of all, charting the different dimensions of inclusion in and exclusion from citizenship has been important: so, for example, the communities to which people belong may be defined in national (or supranational) terms which exclude certain racialised groups. Social rights may depend upon a test of residency or nationality. By the same token, admittance and confirmed residence to a country may depend on forgoing one's social rights: in Britain immigrants may be deported if they have 'recourse to public funds' (Immigration Act, 1988). Many immigrant workers in the EU now have 'denizen' status: that is, entitlement to most civil and social rights but no access to voting rights (Yuval-Davis, 1996). Sexual minorities (lesbians, gay men, transsexuals) may risk their employment if they bring their sexuality from the private to the public sphere. In addition, their failure to conform to dominant (or hegemonic presumed dominant) family forms may deny their access to certain services (joint tenancies, widows' and widowers' rights, parental rights and so on).

Once we begin to open up in this way the limitations of the very construction of civil and social rights then it is evident that the issue of citizenship is not just a question of conferring existing rights, obligations and entitlements to excluded and marginalised groups, but of finding ways in which groups can actively pursue their specific and common claims to entitlements. For example, to confer the right to be integrated into the community to disabled people does nothing to tackle the inequalities and discriminations that disabled people find in the 'community'. Without the capacity to actively pursue a 'participatory citizenship', the extension of existing rights to marginalised groups could actually reinforce existing relationships of inequality.

How far is this possible? One of the lessons from the implementation of equal opportunities' policies is the extent to which the specific claims from specific groups (Black, disabled, women and so on) ossified the differences between the groups, inhibited the acknowledgement of either cross-cutting or common interests, and fell too easily into competing claims, especially within the contexts of welfare restructuring. Yet, at the same time, we know that there are dangers based on following politics based on universal citizenship where a consensus may merely merely hide the specific needs of the most marginalised groups. One way out of this dilemma suggested by Yuval-Davis (1996), following on from the work of African-American feminist Patricia Hill Collins and Italian feminists Raphaela Lambertini and Elizabeth Dominini, is the politics of *transversalism* and coalition building:

> Transversal dialogue should be based on the principles of rooting and shifting – ie., being centred in one's own experiences while being empathetic to the differential positionings of the partners in that dialogue, thus enabling the participants to arrive to a different perspective from that of hegemonic tunnel vision. The boundaries of the dialogue would be determined by the message rather than its messengers. The result of the dialogue might still be differential projects for people and groupings positioned differently, but their solidarity would be based on a common knowledge sustained by a compatible value system. The dialogue, therefore is never boundariless. (Yuval-Davis, 1996, p. 18)

New issues in feminist social policy

The concept of citizenship has also been central to a new body of feminist work in social policy: the comparative study of gender welfare regimes. The impulse behind this work has been, on the one hand, the internationalisation of social policy (the establishment of supranational policy-making bodies such as the EU) along with an international restructuring of welfare and, on the other, a critique of mainstream comparative social policy whose analysis is based on limited conceptions of the state in relation to the market, and male-centred notions of citizenship (see Esping-Andersen, 1990, and the critiques by Langan and Ostner, 1991; Lewis, 1992; Orloff, 1993; Sainsbury, 1994). These critiques have since developed into sophisticated comparative analyses of the gendered welfare regimes of different countries. The importance of this work is that it provides us with an appreciation of the range of different policies to meet women's needs, and also of the range of dynamics which propel policy development in different countries. It thus enables us to identify commonalities as well as specificities in each country's development: for example, how far specific political, social and economic histories influence the acceptance of women in paid work. In this way it tempers the temptation to generalise or universalise the relationship between state policy, the family and the market from one's own national experience. In contrast, such comparison also helps us highlight generalisable aims, or indicators, for the common priorities in women's lives. So, for example, Ann Orloff suggests that one important indicator of social policies is how far they provide women with the capacity to form and maintain an autonomous household and offer women 'freedom from compulsion to enter potentially aggressive relationships in a number of spheres' (Orloff, 1993, p. 320).

One important example of a comparison of gendered welfare regimes is Jane Lewis's work (1992). She analyses the relationship between paid work, unpaid work and welfare in four countries (Britain, Ireland, France and Sweden). She argues that the model of the male breadwinner with dependent wife and children has been the basis of all modern welfare states, but one which has been modified in different ways in different countries. Her study examines the way these four countries have treated women as wives and mothers in terms of social security benefits, provisions for working mothers (such as childcare) and their position in the labour market. On this basis Britain and Ireland emerge as strong male breadwinner states, France as a modified male breadwinner state and Sweden as a weakened male breadwinner state. She also makes the point that it is often not the impulse for gender equality which weakens or modifies male breadwinner systems but rather the need for women's labour and pronatalism.

A slightly different approach is provided by Diane Sainsbury, who investigates the dimensions which contribute to the different ways in which welfare states are gendered (Sainsbury, 1994). Thus, for example, she includes (amongst other things), the nature of familial ideology; the basis of entitlement to benefits (for example, as breadwinner or as individual); who is prioritised in employment policies (men or men and women); whether care work is done in the home or socialised, and how it is paid. She sets up two contrasting ideal-type models of social policy, the breadwinner model and individual model, and uses this to compare policies up to 1970 in the UK, USA, the Netherlands and Sweden. Her conclusions suggest, perhaps surprisingly, that the Netherlands historically was closer to the breadwinner model than the USA or UK. However, it is about Sweden that her analysis departs from Lewis's. Sweden's social policies, she says, were historically grounded in a strong emphasis upon citizenship (male *and* female) as the basis to entitlement to benefits. So, rather than it representing, as Lewis suggests, a male breadwinner welfare state weakened by women's entry into the labour force, Sweden from the beginning weakened the influence of the breadwinner male. One crucial way it did this was by providing, from the 1930s, a comprehensive range of benefits for mothers, including child allowances, maternity grants and collective care and health provisions for children. The point is, Sainsbury argues, that it is necessary not only to look at the operation of the principle of *dependency* but also the principle of *care* in welfare regimes. We need to analyse how women receive benefits, not just on the basis of their being wives and workers (the principle of dependency) but also as mothers (the principle of care) and as citizens (the principle of need). Studies such as these which explore the gender logics of social policy are important. However, they pose problems: first, how to pursue the gender logic without falling into the trap of giving this primacy over other logics that affect women's lives, such as 'race', age, sexuality, disability? Sainsbury's ideal type 'individual model' stands at the positive end of 'women-friendly' models of welfare. Amongst its characteristics are a familial ideology which supports shared roles for husband and wife in financial support and care of the children. Expressed in these terms, it implicitly and unintentionally may well reinforce the hegemony of a household led by a heterosexual dual-earner couple. What guarantee is there that such a model serves those outside its frame equally, such as migrant mothers with a husband or children living in different countries; mothers in same-sex relationships; mothers with no relationships?

The incorporation of a differential notion of gender into comparative social policy is a complex task, but at least it enables us to raise important questions about the histories of male breadwinner models. Williams, for example, asks how far the capacity of countries to draw on labour from the colonies and poorer parts of the world after the Second World War enabled them to avoid using indigenous female labour which would undermine their male breadwinner welfare ideology? And how far is the dual-earner family now possible through the employment of migrant women in domestic service (Williams, 1995)?

Another approach to this question of difference is to focus upon those outside the dominant family model. Barbara Hobson's comparative study of policies for solo (that is, lone) mothers starts with the premise that the treatment of solo mothers represents an important barometer or litmus test of gendered social rights (Hobson, 1994). She finds that 'solo mothers are least disadvantaged when they are fitted into a policy frame that recognises them as the heads of legitimate households, within a policy logic of care as service or care as a facet of citizenship' (ibid., 1994, p. 185). Solo mothers are the *least* economically marginalised in Sweden and the Netherlands, though the policies in these countries are different. In Sweden, solo mothers receive benefits and services as working mothers (such as subsidised day care), as solo mothers (such as priorities and reduced fees in day care, payments where fathers are unable to maintain), as parents and citizens (such as child allowances) and as workers (such as parental leave, job protection). This is the parent-worker-citizen model. In the Netherlands, solo mothers receive a general unemployment benefit plus some solo mother benefits whose levels are high enough to keep them out of poverty. In addition, they are not required to seek work, or to forfeit benefit if they live with an income-earning partner. It is, in effect, a care wage which recognises them as head of the household, based on a mother-carer-citizen model. In fact, with the general austerity welfare budgeting occurring in Europe in the second half of the 1990s, policies in both countries may be cut back.

Conclusion

This final example of social policies in relation to lone mothers highlights a number of general tensions around the construction of policies to meet women's needs. Both sets of policies have in common their recognition of the individual rights of single mothers, yet they are based on different principles: one aiming for equality in the work place, the other recognising difference in the home. This raises the question of how far policies aiming for equality for women in the long term can be integrated with those acknowledging women's difference as women in the short term, particularly their responsibilities for caring? And how far can specific policies for women as women acknowledge the different ways in which women's welfare needs and rights are constituted? More generally, how far can welfare states develop universal services which encompass the diversity of needs generated by societies structured in difference?

As we go into the twenty-first century these questions have acquired a new context for women in Europe. This is the restructuring of welfare which involves, first, an enhanced role for the private, occupational and voluntary sectors; second, new forms of managerialised services; and third, an incorporation of the principles of the private market into the provision of welfare services. All these measures are designed to decrease public expenditure and, in many countries, have been accompanied by welfare cutbacks. They have also been accompanied by the development of the EU which has become a new supranational policy-maker in the field (Hantrais, 1995). In so far as welfare, as I have argued, is central to women's lives, then these changes directly affect the quality of women's lives and their employment opportunities. In those 'women-friendly' Scandinavian welfare states the defence of public sector services has become crucially a women's issue. In Denmark and Sweden many women voted against membership of the EU on the basis that this would mean submitting to lower standards of welfare provision.

In those less 'woman-friendly' welfare states such as Britain, welfare restructuring has served overall to consolidate increasing inequalities between different groups of women. Middle-class, professional women in dual-earner households are less affected by the withdrawal of care services, increased charges on services, cuts in the value of benefits, or the restructuring of full-time jobs to part-time, although this does not mean they are not affected at all (Mayo and Weir, 1993). Black women in particular have been adversely affected by economic and welfare restructuring: they work in occupations which are in decline or, as in the public sector, are subject to worsening pay and conditions (EOC, 1994). The development of stricter policies on immigration in the EU is also likely to affect minority women in Europe, and it raises the issue of how women now organise themselves to defend and challenge policies. For example, EU policy around poverty and social exclusion has little to say about 'race', ethnicity and migration within the EU. In 1992 women's groups across Europe campaigned to get the European Women's Lobby to take the position of Black and migrant women's issues seriously. This resulted in a report, *Confronting the Fortress: Black and Migrant Women in the European Community* (European Women's

Lobby, 1993) which highlighted areas of exploitation, such as homeworking, domestic work and the sex industry.

The development of a feminist social policy has opened up new areas of analysis in social policy, such as issues of care and dependency and the relationship between the public and private spheres; it has made us aware of the different ways social policies construct different women's lives and that the state is neither even nor even-handed in its responses to women's claims. It has also highlighted the way in which struggles for the redistribution of material advantages are bound up with struggles for the recognition of our different identities. The context in which these struggles and claims are constituted is now changing rapidly, creating new problems and possibilities. What is still clear is that welfare is as central to women's lives as women are to welfare.

Notes

1. Although 'welfare state' is usually used to designate these services, this can be misleading for two reasons. First, welfare services are provided not only by the state but also by the commercial, independent and voluntary sectors, and these sectors have grown in significance in most welfare states since the early 1990s. Second, the term 'welfare' carries different connotations in different contexts. In the USA, the term refers specifically to the means-tested and stigmatised benefits that go to the very poor who have no access to the benefits from private or national insurance systems, whereas in Britain it carries a much more general meaning.
2. The term 'the state' is resisted by many feminist writers as it implies a unitary and monolithic institution, whereas the state is often contradictory and uneven in its policy-making. A more suitable formulation would be 'state policies', acknowledging that these have different effects upon different women. I use the term 'the state' as shorthand.
3. Although these figures are over a decade old, they represent the first and most comprehensive national survey of caring activities carried out by the Office of Population Census and Surveys.
4. The Keynesian welfare state refers to the development of welfare provisions tied to a commitment to full male, white employment introduced in Britain after the Second World War.

Further reading

The classic text on women and welfare covering the history of the welfare state in Britain is Elizabeth Wilson's *Women and the Welfare State* (London, Tavistock, first published in 1977).

Gillian Pascall, *Social Policy: Feminist Analysis* (London, Tavistock, first published in 1986) offers a more detailed analysis of different areas of welfare in Britain from a feminist perspective. A second edition *Social Policy: A New Feminist Analysis* was published in 1996.

Fiona Williams, *Social Policy: A Critical Introduction. Issues of Race, Gender and Class* (Cambridge, Polity, first published in 1989) evaluates and critiques major theoretical perspectives on welfare, including different feminist and anti-racist theories. It argues for an integrated analysis of social policy which puts issues of 'race', gender and class at the centre. A new and revised edition, which takes into account shifts in feminist theory and politics, is due out in 1997.

Providing an analysis of women's experiences of the major areas of the welfare state in Britain in the 1990s, is Christine Hallet, *Women and Social Policy: An Introduction* (London, Prentice-Hall and Harvester Wheatsheaf, 1996).

One of the first collections of feminist critiques of comparative social policy, is Diane Sainsbury's edited volume covering research from Europe, the USA and Australia, *Gendering Welfare States* (Sage, London, 1994).

13

Women and Health

Jenny Hockey

During the last 25 years feminist authors have examined the effects of the conditions of women's lives upon their health; these include material conditions such as poverty, and ideological conditions such as stereotypical femininity. Indeed, the dominant conceptions of health which underlie the theory and practice of medicine can themselves be seen as one of the constraining conditions of women's lives.

To understand women's health we need to ask how social institutions, such as medicine, frame women's experience of both health and illness, and what part they play in maintaining women's subordination. Women's Studies participates in women's struggles to redefine 'health' and take control of their health care needs. This chapter examines both the conditions of women's health and women's roles, as academics, activists and practitioners, in challenging the gendered nature of health and illness.

The conditions of women's health

When women's health is compared to men's, they appear to experience more illness; that is, they have a higher level of morbidity. They also live longer. In 1993, British women's life expectancy at birth was 79 years, compared with 73 years for men (Central Statistical Office, 1996). Since the 1970s authors have sought explanations for this apparently contradictory state of affairs (Gove and Tudor, 1973; Nathanson, 1975; Graham, 1987b; Doyal, 1995). The lack of a fixed definition of illness, a failure to recognise differences between women based, for example, on class or ethnicity, and the lack of distinctions between illness behaviour, such as visits to the doctor and the experience of illness itself, have slowed their progress.

In an influential review article, Constance Nathanson examined the relationship between illness and the 'feminine role' (1975). Using survey data from Britain and North America, she showed that both women's morbidity and their utilisation of health services between the 1950s and the 1970s exceeded that of men's. This disparity persists, as evidenced in Mildred Blaxter's more recent study which showed that women's own assessments of their health were consistently worse than men's (1990). Acknowledging the difficulty of distinguishing illness from illness behaviour, Nathanson offered three explanations of women's higher levels of morbidity, despite living longer. First, it is culturally more acceptable for women to report illness; second, women's flexible domestic timetables allow them opportunities to visit the GP and to be ill; and third, it is women's demanding social roles that make them ill.

Not only did Nathanson raise these important questions; she also acknowledged the diversity of women's experiences. For example, she included Walter Gove and Jeannette Tudor's comparative work on married women and men (1973). This showed that married women experience more mental health problems, suggesting that marriage has a protective influence on men but not women. Women's lack of alternative gratification if engaged solely in unpaid domestic work; housework's low status; its lack of structure and visibility; the poor pay and conditions of women in employment and the conflicting role expectations faced by women; these are all cited as causes of mental health problems among married women. Nathanson argued that single women are even more at risk of ill health generally, highlighting their lower social status compared with married women in a patriarchal society. However, this ignores the risks incurred by married women; of domestic violence and lost employment opportunities as family carers.

Nathanson approached illnesses and their medical treatment as *social* events and processes, in that medicine frames mental and physical health in ways which are culturally and socially specific. Feminists have also highlighted the gendered social role of medicine and its oppressive effects on women. Thus, visits to the doctor may not reflect disease itself, but rather the medicalisation of stresses experienced by women as a result of poor housing or unemployment. Shared social problems which require a political solution are thus recast as the disorders of individual women, and therefore amenable to a medical cure. Similarly, women's lack of use of health care may not mean good health, but rather that social interactions with white, male doctors leaves many, especially working-class and Black women, feeling unworthy or inadequate.

Hilary Graham contrasts the health status of women from different classes and ethnic identities (1987). For example, the perinatal death rate (number of babies stillborn or dying in the first week of life per 1000 births) was twice as high among lower-working-class women in 1984 as among women belonging to upper social classes. Similarly, in 1990, the rate was 40 per cent higher among women born in the Caribbean or Asia than women born in Britain (Nettleton, 1995). Sexuality also influences health: for example, in the case of lesbians who may receive inappropriate gynaecological advice from doctors who assume they are heterosexual. Coming out to doctors about their sexual identity can be problematic as some lesbians fear their health problems will be seen as 'a pathological extension of their lesbian lifestyle' (Kenney and Tash, 1993, p. 121). Social class is also linked with long-standing illnesses among women, 47 per cent of lower-working class women having a chronic health problem, compared with less than half this percentage among women from upper social classes (Graham, 1987).

In addition, disability is more common among women, with two-thirds of the 4 million people who are disabled in Britain estimated to be female. This is partly due to women's longevity, later life being a period when disability is more common (Graham, 1987). Similarly women are more likely than men to either diagnose themselves, or be diagnosed, as having a mental health problem. Hospital admission and the prescription of mood-altering drugs is also more common among women than men (Ussher, 1991). These measures of the prevalence of disability and mental health problems among women do, however, ignore the diversity of women. Before we look more closely at this, we can compare Graham's and Nathanson's explanations for women's higher rates of morbidity.

Graham highlights women's physiological vulnerability to illness as childbearers and through their longevity. However, even during later life, biological vulnerability to illness is inseparable from the gendered *social* inequalities which older women face. Sara Arber and Jay Ginn note that older women are poorer than older men and have more difficulty in maintaining their accommodation, risking cold, damp conditions in order to save on heating. This inequality reflects their low pay or exclusion from the work force throughout their lives and therefore access to pension schemes (Arber and Ginn, 1991). Furthermore, Nathanson's work drew on studies which excluded the health care associated with reproduction, and still discovered higher rates of morbidity and greater consumption of health care among women. Nathanson's argument – that the sick role is more compatible with a feminine than a masculine social role – is challenged by Graham (1987), who shows that working-class women normalise and accommodate ill-health, prioritising the health needs of their families (Pill and Stott, 1982; Cornwell, 1984).

Nathanson also puts forward the argument that women's social roles are more demanding, a parallel with Graham's focus on the material circum-stances of women's lives as the cause of ill health. Thus, women's poverty affects them in ways which are not shared by men on low incomes. In addition to lower pay, they are also primary carers for dependent relatives throughout their lives. For example, children under five receive 87 per cent of the care from their mother (Kiernan and Wicks, cited in Oakley, 1995). Economic disadvantage invariably follows. Women in full-time work in 1990 earned 77 per cent of the hourly earnings of men, and the hourly rate of women in part-time work fell even more below the rate which men received (Equal Opportunities Commission, 1991). In 1993/4 women still earned, on average, only 80 per cent of men's incomes (Oakley, 1995). The cost and scarcity of childcare provision deters female lone parents from entering employment at all, and they constitute 90 per cent of lone parents (Coote, Harman and Hewitt, cited in Oakley, 1995). Christine Delphy and Diana Leonard's study (1992) revealed a lack of financial control among women with a male partner: whatever income they had went into a communal budget which was under their partner's control. Only the husband had personal spending money. Though poor women and men are both likely to face housing problems which adversely affect health, women's domestic and care work means longer hours in the home, combining material deprivation with social isolation. Finally, the health risks faced by women with poor housing, diet, environment and social support can be exacerbated by domestic violence from male partners (Hanmer and Maynard, 1987; Yllo and Bograd, 1988; Hanmer, Radford and Stanko, 1989; Dobash and Dobash, 1992).

While the diversity of women's positions in society and the associated implications for their health have therefore been recognised, Jenny Douglas (1992) still argues that research on Black women's health has overemphasised their experiences of maternity services and indeed made Asian rather than Afro-Caribbean women a primary focus. Family organisation and cultural practices associated with childbirth are often highlighted in a literature which either implicitly or explicitly portrays the Black family as deviant. Calling for research grounded in feminist methodology, Douglas argues that the issue of 'race' needs to be examined in research conducted by white women among Black respondents (Douglas, 1992).

Health is therefore constituted both through material conditions such as these – poor housing, diet, environment and social support – and through the ways in which women come to think about their bodies and minds. Case studies of mental health, disability, reproductive health and later life health issues among women show how the material and the ideological aspects of women's lives combine to produce particular experiences of health and illness. As we shall see, it is on both levels that women are disadvantaged within a patriarchal, capitalist society.

Women and mental health

In a classic study, Phyllis Chesler (1972) highlighted the ideological role of psychiatry in shaping conceptions of femininity and masculinity in Western societies. While madness appears ungendered, its attributes – passivity, emotionality, irrationality, dependency, need for support, lack of initiative – match stereotypical models of femininity. Dale Spender argues that one of Chesler's key points is that madness has a profile which threatens and controls *all* women, not just a troubled minority. There is little difference between 'mad' and 'normal' women in that it is male norms of behaviour which are equated with being mentally healthy (Spender, 1994, p. 282).

Being socialised into behaviours which, in men, might risk a diagnosis of mental illness, women stand in a double-bind relationship to psychiatry. Not only is madness characterised as an extreme manifestation of 'normal' feminine behaviour; it is also a label for women's behaviour which flouts such norms (for example, independence or aggression). Thus, women appearing before a criminal court are twice as likely to receive psychiatric treatment (Allen, .cited in Walklate, 1995). Jane Ussher notes that in being more likely to be sent to a hospital or regional secure unit, women who come before the criminal justice system risk a longer-lasting detention than men, for whom parole is automatic, with good behaviour, after two-thirds of a prison sentence (1991). Doubly deviant, having transgressed both the legal system and the limits of femininity, women's 'badness' cannot be accommodated within patriarchal frameworks of thought and is therefore categorised as 'madness'.

Chesler argues that the 'moral enterprise' of psychiatry is the subordination of women through pathologising and medicalising femininity's 'natural' attributes; and through labelling women who fail to conform to those attributes as deviant. Her work has had a profound effect, particularly in its influence upon the work of feminist psychologists such as Jane Ussher (1994) and Helen Bolderston (1994). However, an emphasis on madness as the product of an oppressive set of labels generated by a male-dominated psychiatric profession, which we see exemplified in Chesler's work, has met with criticism by other feminists. As Ussher (1991) argues, the intellectual unmasking of a system of labels does not relieve the very real mental or emotional suffering which many women experience; indeed, it may threaten the future of services which they stand to benefit from. Thus madness can be seen to exist, but as a predictable and indeed rational response to oppression, one which is controlled through the categories of psychiatric thought. Since women's madness disrupts and exposes a system of power, it becomes a focus for control through psychosurgery, electro-convulsive therapy and drug therapy. Thus, later feminists argue that women indeed experience mental health problems, often associated with their subordination to men. Busfield (1989) seeks a reconciliation between the apparently conflicting views that mental illness is either the construction of the psychiatrist, or the product of the conditions of women's lives. She argues that women do indeed experience mental suffering as an outcome of their circumstances. However, psychiatry's responses to disorders of this kind, in terms of both their constructs and their judgements, help to reproduce women's subordination.

These debates ignore differences between women, stressing that 'as women, madness affects us all; not just women who cry out in pain, or women who are caught in the psychiatric gaze, but all women' (Ussher, 1991, p. 288). By aligning femininity and madness within patriarchal discourse, a system of control is brought to bear upon every woman. However, there remain important differences between women's experiences of mental health and illness. Indeed the circumstances of specific women – married, lesbian, Black, Asian, older or disabled women – shed a clearer light on the systems of power which impact upon women's daily lives. For example, in 1988 a study by Littlewood and Lipsedge showed British-born Afro-Caribbean women to be thirteen times more likely to be admitted to mental hospitals with a diagnosis of schizophrenia than white women, while Afro-Caribbean men were seven times more likely than white men to receive this diagnosis. Sashidharan and Francis (1993) identify a similar pattern of admission to mental hospitals among Caribbean-born immigrants to the UK with symptoms diagnosed as schizophrenia. Thus, over the past two decades 40–52 per cent of admissions for Caribbean-born women and men have consistently carried a schizophrenia diagnosis, compared with 12–14 per cent of admissions among all individuals born in England (Sashidharan and Francis, 1993, p. 99). In an earlier work, Philip Rack (1982) argued that a Western psychiatric model of schizophrenia pathologises the normal responses of Asian and Afro-Caribbean people to stress. Angela Davis reports that Black American women have the highest rates of admission to psychiatric services, and health activists describe most adult Black women as living in a state of psychological stress (Davis, 1990, p. 21). Black women avoid resources such as feminist psychotherapy for fear of stereotyping: for example, the pathologising of the 'matriarchal' family structure (Boyd, 1990, p. 230). In these examples we find, again, a rational response to external demands being constructed as pathological, often according to the theories and practices of a predominantly white male body of knowledge, psychiatry.

Women and disability

Disabled women and men all face oppression in the form of unmet material needs and negative social attitudes, though social responses to disabled women cause them special problems (Lonsdale, 1990). For example, disabled women are assumed to suffer most through their failure to conform to stereotyped notions of sexual attractiveness, risking social and emotional isolation without a male partner. However, many women with disabilities enjoy satisfying sexual relationships, finding the barriers to such relationships are poverty and social isolation resulting from exclusion from mainstream education, public transport, work and leisure. This shows disability to be a socially constructed rather than biological problem. It is the social framing of bodily difference which handicaps disabled women, not the actual nature of their bodies (Morris, 1991). Disabled women with a male partner may, however, feel second best to an able-bodied woman and be particularly vulnerable to abuse. While many women face social and economic disadvantage by leaving an abusing partner, disabled women also risk institutionalisation if their partner was their primary carer. Bullard and Knight (1981) cite lesbianism as important for disabled women in that women are more likely to offer a supportive relationship.

Social invisibility is also felt strongly by women with disabilities (Lonsdale, 1990). As noted above, femininity is associated with passivity, and consequently women's frustration following the enforced passivity of disability may be overlooked. Unemployment is also viewed as less traumatic for women in general, making unemployed disabled women's poverty and isolation more invisible. These stereotypical assumptions cause research, policy-making and public opinion to focus mainly on men with disabilities. For example, the belief that men require penetrative sex has engendered a literature about the sexual needs of men with disabilities. Believed to be sexually passive, disabled women find a dearth of similar literature. Disabled women are further de-sexualised through loss of privacy in institutional settings and medical examinations. For example, Lonsdale reports that less care is taken to keep disabled women's bodies covered during medical examinations, a practice which customarily represents an acknowledgement of women's sexuality.

In summary, disabilities are not only more common among women; they also bring women special problems. This is particularly so among Black populations where 151 adults per 1000 Afro-Caribbeans are disabled as opposed to 137 per 1000 white adults. Reasons for this are complex. Social, economic and occupational factors all play a part in this disparity, as do health problems specific to Afro-Caribbeans, such as thalassaemia and sickle cell anaemia. As Lonsdale (1990) notes, the prevalence of disability within populations is difficult to ascertain since definitions of what constitutes disability vary. However, measures of disability at all levels except the lowest show that there are considerably more disabled women than men – 365 600 as opposed to 254 400. Women's greater longevity does not necessarily account for this difference since the prevalence rates among those over 74 are consistently higher among women. Explanations for this disparity, as in the case of Black people, are more likely to be poverty and poor housing, rather than age.

Women's reproductive health

Feminists have shown women's reproductive health to be one of the areas where medicine's ideological frameworks contribute most to the subordination of women (as Jalna Hanmer also notes in Chapter 16). This aspect of their lives brings many women into contact with doctors, since few women escape all the events or states associated with reproduction: menstruation, fertility, pregnancy, childbirth, breastfeeding and the menopause. Indeed the absence of conditions such as fertility often leads women to seek medical help. Even when women experience little illness, the normal changes which go on in their bodies still become *medicalised*; that is to say, a male-dominated profession extends its scope to an area previously seen to fall outside its remit. Ageing and sexual practice are other areas which have been medicalised. They are also more likely to involve women given their longevity and the tendency for women's sexual practice to fall under male control. Debates about medicalisation are divided between the view that extending the scope of medicine is to extend its scope for social regulation; and the alternative view, that long-term healing requires the treatment of the whole person and not just the disease (Nettleton, 1995). This bears on feminists strategies for reclaiming women's health which are divided as to whether it can ever be safeguarded within the existing system.

Childbirth, for example, has shifted away from female- to male-controlled delivery in line with the changing status of midwifery. Prior to the nineteenth century it was usually managed by women who had learned their skills through oral traditions. Indeed the term midwife means 'with women'. Nonetheless, as argued below, the medicalisation of childbirth allowed the developing male medical profession to consolidate its knowledge and status. Indeed, from the seventeenth century onwards male midwives restricted female midwives' work by differentiating between 'normal' and 'abnormal' deliveries, reserving for themselves those cases where instruments such as forceps were deemed necessary. This distinction persisted and was embodied in the 1902 Midwives Act which obstetricians supported as a way of regulating and de-skilling midwives through compulsory regulation, combined with their restriction to deliveries which required no medical intervention. It did mean that women delivering 'normally' gave birth without a doctor in attendance. However, medical criteria were used to distinguish normal from abnormal births and female midwives do not practise according to feminist principles *just* because they are women. Indeed, from a medical perspective all pregnant women are 'at risk', a 'normal' delivery being identified only in retrospect (Doyal, 1995). The *Changing Childbirth* report, discussed below, is at least in part the outcome of women's efforts in both professional and lay capacities to give women more choice about how and where their babies are delivered. In theory this should mean that, for some women, their desire for a home delivery is given professional support. Accounts of childbirth in more traditional societies also show the influence of patriarchal interests at the time of birth despite the presence of female birth attendants (Callaway, 1993). In Callaway's view, the future of any social group depends upon biological reproduction, so pregnancy and childbirth are appropriated by male interests, lest women lay claim to their own reproductive power.

Hospital birth rates have risen in this century, 98 per cent of women now delivering in a setting where they are susceptible to infection and the questionable interventions of medical technology, such as induced labours and routine caesarean deliveries and episiotomies (cutting the perineum lest it should tear at delivery: see Oakley, and Tew, cited in Nettleton, 1995). Lesley Doyal highlights the lack of evidence that hospital deliveries are safer (1995), while Ann Oakley (1980), in an earlier study, showed how doctors undermine pregnant women's knowledge of their bodies and trivialise problems such as insomnia.

Studies such as these have helped change health policy, as evidenced by the 1992 House of Commons Health Committee report *Maternity Services*. In response, an Expert Maternity Group produced a woman-centred report, *Changing Childbirth*, which questioned the centrality of medically-defined 'safety', highlighting the health implications of broader aspects of women's experiences of childbirth. Its policies aim to increase women's choice, coupled with community-based ante-natal care from a single midwife who is also present at the delivery. Like the 1902 Midwives Act, however, it leaves obstetricians to determine which women are 'at risk' and need the medical monitoring which community midwives cannot provide. *Changing Childbirth* policies therefore have to overcome obstetricians' vested interest in maintaining their status and economic wealth via a sufficient supply of patients (Foster, 1995). In addition, foetal medicine allows doctors to uphold the rights of the foetus despite opposition from the woman. In the U.S., poor Black women risk being forced to undergo medical procedures in the name of foetal rights. Affluent white women resist such pressures by purchasing care in a private clinic or from an independent midwife.

The medical management of childbirth is paralleled by the technologies which assist conception, such as IVF and gamete intra fallopian tube transfer (GIFT). Both services benefit women who, without such interventions, would not deliver the healthy baby they desire. However, feminists list many concerns about new reproductive technologies (NRT). For example, the cult of motherhood which incites women to unthinkingly undergo painful and emotionally debilitating courses of infertility treatment with limited success rates which, once started, are difficult to abandon; the vested career interests of medical researchers with business links with drug companies; the limited availability of National Health Service (NHS) fertility treatment, coupled with familialist policies which disadvantage women who are sex workers, single, older, lesbian, Black or disabled; and the exploitation of poor women as paid egg donors and surrogate mothers (Foster, 1995). Foster even cites the reported enthusiasm of an Australian specialist for using the corpses of brain-dead women as a source of eggs or a surrogate womb (1995). Finally, the possibilities for embryo selection puts female or disabled offspring at risk if they are viewed as a burden.

The value of medical interventions in women's reproductive lives cannot therefore be assumed. They can enable women to achieve self-selected goals; yet they threaten women's safety and autonomy whilst serving covert patriarchal interests. In later life women again face what some see as an apparently beneficial medical intervention: the development of hormone replacement therapy (HRT). Tellingly, the bodily changes which women may experience at menopause are medicalised as 'symptoms' to be 'relieved' by hormone implants, patches, pills or gels. Indeed, male gynaecologists have described menopause as a 'deficiency disease' (Foster, 1995, p. 73). While HRT promises protection against heart disease, stroke and osteoporosis (decrease in bone density), and the alleviation of hot flushes, insomnia, lethargy and depression, feminists have been sceptical. First, HRT medicalises or pathologises a life change traditionally seen as natural or even welcome. Second, it is not only aimed at alleviating women's health problems; it also promises to restore a youthful appearance and maintain sexual desire. Feminists point out that HRT therefore serves men's interests by enhancing their status through the presence of a youthful partner. It also advances careers in medical science and provides an expanding market for drug companies. Furthermore, HRT not only devalues women's maturity, but also brings possible health risks. Germaine Greer describes the conflicting research findings as 'the menopausal muddle' (cited in Foster, 1995, p. 67), there being few established links between HRT and women's specific health needs. In addition to its possible side effects (fluid retention, weight gain and nausea), women taking oestrogen alone increase their risk of endometrial (uterine) cancer. While oestrogen and progesterone combined protect against this form of cancer, they increase the risk of breast cancer. Though short-term use of HRT during the menopause is unlikely to cause these forms of cancer, protection against osteoporosis is gained only after extended use.

Many of the feminist concerns listed here turn on the decision-making processes which underpin the availability of services for women's reproductive health. For example, Foster (1995) cites the case of family planning clinics where women are more likely to be given advice from a *female* doctor about barrier methods of contraception which give them more protection against sexually transmitted diseases and cervical cancer. Cutbacks in the NHS are threatening the future of such clinics and indeed some areas have seen their closure, despite continued funding for high technology medicine within prestigious trust hospitals.

Older women's health

As noted, the changes which occur within women's reproductive systems are often cited as the cause of innumerable health problems, both physical and mental. However, many feminists have argued that the medicalisation of the ageing process merely deflects attention from the social problems which older women encounter by transforming them into individual pathologies.

Thus, in addition to the sexism to which they have been exposed throughout their lives, in one form or another, ageism is another *social* phenomenon which further undermines women's power and status. Barbara MacDonald (1984) provides a persuasive account of the social invisibility which she encounters as an older woman. Not only is her bodily appearance stigmatised and disregarded; her bodily functioning is also rendered taboo in that its changes foreshadow death. Social behaviour and attitudes therefore continue to be a source of threat to women's health throughout their lives. They also intermesh with material factors, as evidenced in findings from a British study commissioned by the Metropolitan Authorities Recruitment Agency to examine the position of older local government workers (Bernard, *et al.*, 1995). They show that by the age of 30 women begin to be categorised by managers as 'older workers', and their cut-off point for career progression comes ten years before that of men. Though the implications of sexist occupational cultures may be felt by women at all ages, in later life their effects result in poorer pay and diminished pension rights.

Material disadvantage also undermines their well-being, women over the age of 65 being one of the poorest groups within Western society. Among women over 60, the average weekly income is £58 compared with £108 for men of the same age and £80.59 for women aged 17–59 (General Household Survey 1991/2, cited in Vincent, 1995). Sara Arber and Jay Ginn argue that independence is crucially determined by personal income or control over household income. They cite studies to show that among women over the age of 75, twice as many are housebound when compared with men, and only 25 per cent of them have been medically assessed as fit, compared with 36 per cent of men (Hall and Channing, cited in Arber and Ginn, 1991). Nonetheless, women's health problems in later life are often understood in terms of changes in their reproductive systems, a tendency which reflects the foregrounding of women as primarily sexual/reproductive beings throughout their lives and, additionally, individualises the structural oppression of older women through a combination of sexism and ageism.

Defining health: providing healthcare

While Western medicine is linked with a male appropriation of women's healing role (O'Connor, 1987), this change in the gendered nature of healthcare is a complex process. During the seventeenth and eighteenth centuries the professionalisation of medicine involved a shift away from traditional domestic and community-based healing which occupied women in their roles as mothers, wives, midwives and cunning women (Stacey, 1988). In its place, there developed a market for medical remedies which had previously been used only as palliative treatments for dying people (Illich,

1975). Thus, by the eighteenth century, medical knowledge and skills acquired a new social and economic status, its practitioners extending their scope to the inner body after the lifting of religious prohibitions on dissection. This more scientific approach to medicine furthered the exclusion of women. Denied a university education since their establishment in the thirteenth century, women had no access to this key source of biomedical knowledge. Medical guilds, the precursor of the Royal Colleges, defined the boundaries of a set of elitist medical skills, reserving them as the practices of qualified men. Alongside these institutions, the Church outlawed women healers, in that medically unqualified female practitioners risked murder following a witchcraft accusation (Ussher, 1991, pp. 44–5).

The growth of 'lying-in' (maternity) hospitals during the eighteenth century also contributed to the development of a male-dominated medical profession (Versluysen, 1981). As sites within which male doctors could extend their expertise, such hospitals allowed the medical profession to restrict the work available for women midwives; to exercise control over women patients; to extend their knowledge and experience of childbirth; and to frame childbirth as a dangerous venture which required medical attendance. These factors meant that the male doctor who was once the subordinate of his wealthy, upper-class patients now occupied a clearly-defined position of power in relation to a lower social class population. This status persists today in that the higher ranks of medicine are dominated by men: 80 per cent of NHS consultants are men (Department of Health, 1994). As the major consumers of healthcare, women are therefore particularly likely to be exposed to a male-dominated health care profession. One result of this is that doctor-patient interactions can reinforce women's general sense of social powerlessness. The more serious her illness, the more likely she is to be treated by a male doctor, since men predominate in the higher status roles of consultant and registrar. Women are therefore at their most vulnerable when dealing with the powerful members of a male-dominated profession. Though women were important as healers before the seventeenth century, feminists have shown that it is as *patients* that they have contributed to the professionalisation of medicine.

Within the profession itself, women initially occupied only the subordinate role of nurse. Florence Nightingale embodies many of the inherent paradoxes of nursing during the second half of the nineteenth century. Doyal and Elston (1986, pp. 196–7) describe Nightingale as a shrewd politician who reconstituted nursing as a female-controlled profession. However, in keeping with her public persona as ministering angel she promoted the continued subordination of the nurse to the doctor (the naturally forbearing female servant of a male intellectual superior).

Though 53 per cent of all women are now economically active, 38 per cent of them having full-time employment (Central Statistical Office, 1996), nineteenth-century concepts of masculinity and femininity continue to inform the gendered division of labour within professional health care. Indeed, Nightingale's vision of a female-controlled profession of nursing has been threatened in two ways. First, the 1966 Salmon Report introduced a line management system for nurses which saw the creation of chief nurse and director of nurse education posts. Although men make up less than 10 per cent of the nursing population, 50 per cent of senior nurse manager posts are held by men (Blakemore and Symonds, 1993). Second, the Griffiths Report (DHSS, 1983) created another nursing-related post, that of district general manager. Discussing the introduction of general management, Nettleton argues that 'the general management structure has limited the influence of senior nurses in management decisions . . . nurses are increasingly managed by non-nurses' (1995, pp. 219–20). Only 3 per cent of general management posts have gone to women (Cousins, cited in Nettleton, 1995).

Other changes in nursing have a more radical aim. The 'new nursing' seeks to rework the nurse's traditional preoccupation with care, making it 'a skilled and indeterminate, theoretically informed activity at the core of the new nursing role' (Witz, 1994, p. 24). This principle is expressed in the *Project 2000* reform of nurse education and in the creation of a clinical career structure for nurses. Anne Witz argues that overall this represents an attempt by the members of a predominantly female profession to establish practitioner autonomy and resist remaining in a role subordinate to doctors. However, she argues that the professionalising of care is difficult precisely because the profession is female-dominated in a society where care is a highly gendered and *undervalued* activity. Furthermore, this strategy risks dividing those women who nurse into a steeply hierarchical career structure, where a small core of autonomous practitioners are supported by a peripheral work force of health care assistants.

Witz notes that the cost-cutting potential of such a division of labour may make it popular with employers (Witz, 1994). Clearly this has social and economic implications for lower-status female health care assistants, particularly since less qualified nurses tend to be Black. In 1992 the ratio of men to women employed as State Registered Nurses in England was 1:4 as opposed to 1:6 among less-qualified State Enrolled Nurses (Department of Health, 1994). Also, among the total of 217 553 women employed as nurses and midwives, over two-thirds (157 097) were women with part-time contracts. By contrast, among the 45 232 men employed in these posts, only 4 705 had part-time contracts (Department of Health, 1994). This suggests that, for many women, nursing is a career constrained by domestic demands. Gendered inequalities are compounded by the exploitation of Black and Asian women, an outcome of the recruitment strategies of the 1950s and 1960s when the British government sent senior British nurses to enlist cheap labour from Commonwealth countries. Peaking in 1970, such strategies resulted in the employment of 15 493 overseas nurses, 40 per cent of whom were from the West Indies, 29 per cent from Asia, 27 per cent from Africa and Mauritius and 3 per cent from Fiji, Tonga, the Seychelles and the Virgin Islands (Akinsanya, cited in Nettleton, 1995). Doyal (1985) argues that these nurses tended to accept poor conditions, low pay and rigid discipline at a time when British-born women had become more resistant. Among the women who currently fill lower-grade nursing or ancillary posts, many are Black women. Indeed, the NHS employs more people from Black and ethnic minority communities than any other British organisation (Ward, cited in Nettleton, 1995). Within one London hospital, Doyal *et al.* (cited in Nettleton, 1995) found that 84 per cent of domestics and 82 per cent of catering workers were born overseas. However, there are few studies of racism among health workers, a dearth compounded by the fact that the ethnicity of health workers is not routinely monitored (Nettleton, 1995). Nettleton also notes that 'there have been persistent denials of the existence of racism in the Health Service and a reluctance to implement monitoring of equal opportunities' (1995, p. 206).

Within medicine, gender and 'race' continue to structure the division of labour. Tandon (1987) describes the sexist and racist attitudes which marked her medical training, access to which required higher grades than her white male contemporaries. As a qualified doctor, she also found herself confined to short-term contracts. Though women and men enter medical school in almost equal numbers, women who qualify face both horizontal and vertical occupational segregation. In 1992 they made up only 20 per cent of consultants (Department of Health, 1994), even though they represented 60 per cent of doctors in the lower status specialism of public health medicine and 47 per cent of general practitioners under the age of 30 (Riska and Wegar, 1993). Women are grossly underrepresented on the Royal Colleges' councils and as British Medical Association negotiators, positions from which they could influence medical training. Domestic commitments, the 'old boy' system of patronage and the lack of part-time appointments have been cited repeatedly as barriers to women's career advancement in the NHS (Allen, 1988).

Excluded from positions of responsibility within the NHS, women none-theless feel pressured into taking responsibility when it comes to informal health care. With the shift away from institutional care during the 1960s and 1970s, many individuals have become primary carers for members of their own families. Care which takes place within the domestic sphere is difficult to document, though during the 1980s feminists such as Janet Finch and Dulcie Groves (1983) and Gillian Dalley (1988) were confident that 'the community' was a euphemism for a female relative. Graham (1987c) reported an estimated 1.3 million people acting as principal unpaid carer to a disabled adult or child, of whom 1.2 million lived with the dependent person. In 75 per cent of cases where an adult or elderly person was dependent, their carer was a female relative. In 100 per cent of cases where a child was disabled or chronically ill, the carer was their mother, while for adults with learning difficulties their mother was the carer in 80 per cent of cases. The 1985 General Household Survey (Green, and Arber *et al.*, cited in Maclean and Groves, 1991) appeared to cast doubt upon this strong gender bias, showing that where the spouse is the main carer it may also be a man. However, men's care work often has a different quality, tending to involve fewer heavy or intimate tasks such as bathing, toileting, feeding and laundry. Entertaining a dependent person, taking them to hospital, doing the garden or paying for treats are more characteristic of men's contribution to the care of a relative (Maclean and Groves, 1991; Twigg and Atkin, 1994).

The feminist literature of the 1980s has contributed significantly to the theorising of care from the perspective of women who are carers. For example, Finch and Groves (1983) highlighted the ambiguity of the notion of care, showing its dual reference to an emotion and to a form of work, a blurring of boundaries which often makes the financial cost of being a carer difficult to address. Gillian Dalley (1988) pointed out the gendered dimension of the way in which caring is viewed. Thus, men are seen to care for a relative when they finance the labour of others. Women must care directly, in a practical and emotional sense, if they are not to be castigated as uncaring.

The focus of research during the 1980s was therefore the experience of women who were informal carers. While they had previously been a largely hidden category, in terms of social research, social policy, and indeed their immediate social environments, feminists writing during the 1990s challenged this focus on women as carers, foregrounding the invisibility of women who were receiving rather than giving care. Their critique is exemplified in the work of Jenny Morris, a feminist and trade unionist, who became a wheelchair user after a fall damaged her spine. She argues that many of the studies of the 'caring relationship' which were published during the 1980s were entirely one-sided, so reinforcing relations of inequality and compounding the stigma and invisibility to which disabled women are subject in contemporary Western society (Morris, 1993). By privileging the interests of women who found themselves disadvantaged in the role of carer, the effect of this literature was that 'the category, woman, was constructed as non-disabled and non-elderly. There was no recognition that women make up the majority of disabled and older people, nor indeed that many disabled and older people are also informal carers' (Morris, 1993, p. 45).

In addition to providing primary care for a dependent relative, women also meet many of their families ongoing health care needs. Graham (1985) divides this role into providing for health, teaching for health and mediating professional health care, forms of work which have remained largely invisible both in practice and in the academic literature. It is nonetheless an important form of health care for which women have taken unbroken responsibility from medieval times onwards. Evidence from the nineteenth century and from more recent feminists, such as Mildred Blaxter and Elizabeth Paterson (1982) show women sacrificing their own health for the sake of their families. Not only must they maintain healthy habits, such as not smoking and providing a wholesome diet; they also risk censure from doctors when relatives are ill if they are seen to have failed to maintain a family member's health.

Women have also become a focus within the development of health promotion. Rather than addressing the political or environmental sources of illness, such as bad housing or airborne pollution, health promotion charges women with the tasks of attending ante-natal and child welfare clinics, breastfeeding throughout babyhood and giving up the use of drugs, alcohol and nicotine which may represent their only sources of support or pleasure (Daykin and Naidoo, 1995). Doyal and Elston (1986) report that the high infant mortality rate in nineteenth- and early twentieth-century Britain was also attributed to the 'ignorance' and 'fecklessness' of women, thereby downplaying a social and economic context of poverty and insanitary housing.

Reclaiming women's health

In charting the appropriation of women's healing role by a male-dominated medical profession, feminists with a particular interest in ethics have highlighted the paternalism which underpins doctors' decision-making on behalf of female patients (Sherwin, 1996). Aware of women's lack of knowledge, the women's movement of the 1970s and 1980s addressed this gap by generating handbooks such as *The New Woman's Survival Catalog* (Grimstad and Rennie, 1973), *Our Bodies, Ourselves* (Phillips and Rakusen, 1978/ 1989) and *The New Women's Health Handbook* (MacKeith, 1978). This literature is based on women's own accounts of their bodies, grounding strategies for action in women's personal experience (Williams, 1987). For example, the Boston Women's Health Collective's *Our Bodies, Ourselves* was born out of small group discussions at a Boston Women's Conference in 1969. White, middle-class Western women were the main audience for these handbooks during the 1970s; little material was addressed to the health care needs of Black, lesbian and working-class women who were more at risk of illness, both from their material and social environment and within existing systems of health care. Only in the late 1980s were books such as *Alive and Well: A Lesbian Health Guide* (Hepburn and Gutierrez, 1988) and *The Black Woman's Health Book* (White, 1990) published. *Women's Health*, a newsletter published by the Women's Health Collective in London, has been addressing feminist health matters since the late 1980s, giving women access to current medical research in issues devoted to Black women's health; adddictions; ageing; international women; women in prison; and women in Ireland. As noted, women's role as guardians of family health causes them to seek information on health, though often what they need is empowering support rather than directive medical advice (A. Williams, 1987).

Central to feminist debates around health has been the requirement that women take control of their own bodies and minds. This view has not however been without its critics. Susan Sontag (1983) has argued that concepts of illness which require the sufferer to take back responsibility for their own illness and its healing are not only punitively victim-blaming, but also misleading in that they deflect attention from the state's failure to provide health services for all society's members. At present there is a danger that doctor and patient are locked into a narrow sphere of discourse where, for example, doctors attribute cervical cancer or HIV/AIDS to sexual risk-taking among women, and women blame doctors for not allowing them access to available treatments. Feminist demands that women take responsibility for their own health therefore need to be wary of echoing health promotion messages that health should be seen as the outcome of a responsible *individual* lifestyle. Instead, women's involvement in strategies ranging from Green politics and the peace movement to feminist therapy represent a more collective approach to the social causes of illness.

As noted, feminists are divided as to whether health care provision for women can come from within existing services. If Women's Studies has unmasked the hidden political agenda of conventional medicine, as Chesler's argument suggests, should conventional health care be abandoned in favour of feminist-conceived and controlled women-centred healing? Well-women clinics and breast, ovarian and cervical screening are key forms of preventive health care for women, yet they are available only in limited ways within the NHS. Feminist health care needs to prioritise such services, alongside feminist therapy and counselling, particularly in relation to HIV/AIDS, sexual abuse and abortion. The implementation of such policies must also address the differing values and needs of lesbians, disabled women and Black women, currently unmet within an NHS which assumes the lifestyles of heterosexual, white, able-bodied individuals can provide a model for all forms of health care.

Doyal (1995) documents women's history of challenging the existing system from within. As a source of both health care and employment, the NHS is important in many women's lives. NHS cutbacks affect women particularly badly. Women have therefore joined trade unions and worked in women's health groups run by feminist health workers such as the radical nurses' group, the radical midwives' group, the radical health visitors' group and WIM (Women in Medicine), the national group for women in medicine. As informal carers, women have overcome their social isolation through organisations such as the Association of Carers. Despite evidence that women suffer as a result of the ways in which the NHS operates, both at macro and micro levels, feminists still argue that the state must take responsibility for health care provision, rather than leaving it to particular interest groups. As it stands, however, there is strong evidence that while some women do benefit from the NHS, others are severely disadvantaged. Doyal (1985) shows that working-class women consult their GPs more frequently, but that their needs so far exceed those of middle- and upper-class women that merely counting visits is no measure of the proportion of overall resources working-class women receive in relation to their requirements. The resources available to GPs also vary by region, more affluent areas receiving more resources. Finally, studies have shown that middle-class people in general are given more time in consultation with their doctors (Cartwright and Anderson, 1981). Cervical screening, birth control and abortion are all services which meet the needs of working-class women less effectively. Sterilisation operations and hysterectomies are, however, offered more readily to working-class and Black women; Doyal has argued that this is on the basis of a medical perception of them as 'ignorant' or 'feckless'. Women without alternatives sometimes find themselves offered abortions only if they agree to simultaneous sterilisations. Language difficulties compound the failure to meet some Black women's needs adequately, coupled with instances of institutional racism, evidenced in cases such as the use of injectable contraceptive drugs such as Depo-Provera, at times without the knowledge or consent of the woman herself (Doyal, 1995). Institutional racism is also evident in the use of NHS staff during immigration procedures where vaginal examinations and X-rays are used to verify the age and marital status of women. Indeed, the withholding of health care from individuals not proven to be 'ordinarily resident' in the UK is likely to undermine the health of Black people.

Feminist research which highlighted the creation and maintenance of gender, 'race' and class-based forms of social inequality, has now broadened to explore influences on women's health which lie outside the NHS. Alongside the links made between women's roles as carers, their poverty and their health, are studies of women's patterns of leisure which reveal the material and ideological constraints on their access to facilities (Green, Hebron and Woodward, 1990); the reproduction of women's subordination within the world of sport (Boutilier and San Giovanni, 1985; Hargreaves, 1985); and the health risks incurred by women using computers (Downing, 1983; Lewin and Olesen, 1985). The belief that the home is a safe haven for women ignores the rape, violence and accidental injury suffered by women confined within domestic space (O'Connor, 1987). Laura Goldsack (1994) highlights the paradox that while police personal safety campaigns target the street as the place where women risk attack, the home is often more dangerous, especially where it is barricaded with 'security' devices which hamper a woman's escape from a violent partner into the safer space of the street. Ann Oakley (1989) offers a critique of health professionals' response to women's smoking. She points out that prominence is given to female smokers' production of low-birth-weight babies rather than to women's health itself. Furthermore, in that the remedy put forward is individual lifestyle change, women who continue to smoke are perceived to be morally at fault. As Oakley stresses, clear links have been identified between women's smoking, their social class position and the demands placed upon them as carers, yet medical responses to smoking continue to ignore those aspects of women's lives.

Women's risks in the face of HIV/AIDS is a final area of neglect within existing services. Estimates vary from between 40 to 50 per cent as to the proportion of AIDS deaths which are likely to be women (Sack, 1992, and Richardson, 1989, cited in Foster, 1995). The World Health Organisation estimates that three million women are currently HIV infected and expected to die by the year 2000 (Bury, cited in Foster, 1995). UK figures might seem to indicate that HIV/AIDS remains less a woman's than a man's problem. Doyal, Naidoo and Wilton, (1994), for example, cite figures of 2 370 HIV virus infections among women compared with 16 640 among men; and 466 women with AIDS compared with 6 463 men in January 1993. However, as they stress, the incidence of AIDS is increasing more rapidly among women than men. The Communicable Disease Report (1993) cites an 18 per cent increase among women between January 1991 and December 1992, compared with only an 8 per cent increase among men. In addition to the numbers of women at risk, HIV/AIDS carries gendered implications in that women's reproductive rights, their sexuality and their role as informal carers are all likely to be affected. Campbell (1990) reports that mothers are often expected to care for gay sons dying of AIDS, given the negative reactions of male relatives. Indeed, stigma impacts strongly on women who are infected or who care for someone living with AIDS. As stressed in other areas of women's health-related experience, the incidence of AIDS reflects the diverse forms of women's oppression. Therefore, whether as someone who has AIDS or as the carers of people with AIDS, women's experience not only differs from that of men and reflects the diversity of women's social position; it also reflects their vulnerability within patriarchal and capitalist systems of power (Richardson, 1989).

More recently, health promotion workers have adopted a view of HIV/AIDS which resists targeting 'high risk' groups such as gay and bisexual men and intravenous drug users, recognising the danger that other groups will see themselves as immune. However, Foster (1995) argues that the economic disadvantage and relative poverty of many women does put them at higher risk of contracting the virus. Thus it is a disproportionate number of poor Black and Latino women and men who are dying of AIDS in

America in the 1990s (Panos Institute, cited in Foster, 1995). The Women and AIDS Project (1991) report that for every white woman dying of AIDS in America, there are 13.2 Black women and 8.1 Hispanic women. In the Caribbean, young women and children are particularly at risk. Campaigns which put responsibility for safer sex through condom use in the hands of women ignore the 'race' and gender-based inequalities which underlie such relationships. Women who carry condoms are at risk of being labelled 'easy' and women carrying condoms can be stopped by the police as suspected sex workers (Foster, 1995). Yet, as Doyal, Naidoo and Wilton (1994) point out, heterosexual intercourse, globally, is the most common route for the transmission of the HIV virus.

Though the social construction of gender, and indeed 'race' and sexuality, together put women at particular risk of contracting the HIV virus, the lessons learned from the women's health movement have been integral to activist interventions in the spread of the virus. Not only have Positive Women groups been set up throughout First World countries (and, indeed, among minority women), but feminist issues – such as Western scientific medicine's ideological agenda, the hierarchy of the medical profession and the relative powerlessness of marginalised social groups (intravenous drug users, sex workers and gay men) – have again become a focus for resistance (Wilton, 1994).

The documentation and theorisation of women's health and illness experiences within Women's Studies has been important in terms of responses not only to HIV/AIDS but also to a whole range of threats to women's well-being. It is via an understanding of the interrelationship between material and ideological oppression that thinking and practice has been challenged. Access to health care involves engagement with a male-dominated system of health care, one which previously resided within women's own hands. Carol MacCormack (1989) highlights women's continued role as healers, midwives and paramedics outside the West, something which development workers often ignore, failing to provide them with access to and control over medical technology.

In this, as in other areas, recommendations for the future include the monitoring of women's health-related employment through agencies such as the NHS Women's Unit, which advances the careers of women seeking influential management roles; women's working conditions generally; and informed choice for women in the use of medical technology. Only through possession of such information can women's experiences of health and illness be evaluated and transformed. Gains made in the broad area of women's health can be linked directly to the sustained work of the women's health movement in documenting, theorising and making interventions in issues ranging from reproductive health, through to HIV/AIDS and heart disease.

Further reading

Sue Wilkinson and Celia Kitzinger, *Women and Health: Feminist Perspectives* (London, Taylor & Francis, 1994). This collection has a clear feminist orientation towards women's health, coupled with contributions from a range of disciplines: psychology, sociology, social policy, social anthropology and economics. Framed by chapters which address the operation of male power in medicine, the chapters follow women's health experiences at different periods within the life course.

Lesley Doyal, *What Makes Women Sick: Gender and the Political Economy of Health* (London, Macmillan, 1995). This volume focuses on the economic, social and cultural aspects of women's lives which make them sick. Explicitly feminist, the book aims to identify and change such conditions. Though women's health is foregrounded throughout, particular attention is given to the diversity of women's lives globally. Women's domestic labour and paid employment, their sexual and reproductive lives and their exposure to the dangers of tranquillisers, eating disorders, alcohol and smoking are all addressed, followed by an extended discussion of the multiplicity of ways in which women are taking action on their own behalf.

Denise Russell, *Women, Madness and Medicine* (Cambridge, Polity, 1995). This volume challenges the knowledge base and practice of 'biological psychiatry', arguing that women are harmed by psychiatric treatment which claims biological causes for mental illness and disorder. Russell examines trends in psychiatric diagnosis and discusses the relationship between women, psychiatry and criminality, setting this material alongside the alternative perspectives of feminists such as Phyllis Chesler and Luce Irigaray.

Phyllis Noerager Stern (ed.), *Lesbian Health: What are the Issues?* (Washington and London, Taylor & Francis, 1993). Though the contributors to this volume are almost entirely American, important issues for lesbians in the UK, Europe and America are addressed. These include childbearing and child custody, alcohol abuse and health care, homophobia among health care professionals and lesbian social invisibility. The volume offers review articles of existing health research and campaigns; it also contains a series of chapters grounded in specific research studies among American lesbians.

14

Women and Education

Christine Skelton

In recent times the yearly publication of GCSE exam results in England and Wales has shown a steadily widening gap between the achievements of girls and boys. Girls outperform, or are on a par with, boys in the majority of subject areas. Even in those subjects in which girls have traditionally 'underachieved', such as physics and chemistry, an analysis of the results shows that the discrepancy comes not in girls' achievements, but in the fact that they do not opt for these areas in the first place. For example, 8 per cent of boys and 5 per cent of girls took GCSE physics with the result that 7 per cent of boys and 4 per cent of girls were awarded a pass (grades A–C: DFEE 1995). Does this mean that schooling has fulfilled the aspirations of both first- and second-wave liberal feminists who called in the late nineteenth century for a 'common standard' (Davies, 1868) and in the 1970s for an 'equal' education (Byrne, 1978) for girls? The answer to this is 'no'. Whilst many, but not all, girls appear successful in terms of academic achievement at the age of sixteen, as far as higher education and the labour market are concerned any apparent advantages rapidly disappear, with the result that fewer females than males occupy places in traditional universities and career opportunities are limited (see above Chapter 11). As higher education and careers are areas which occur after compulsory schooling has ended it might seem unreasonable to look to the school for explanations of why girls' outward success is not carried through into their post-16 education and work lives. However, the schooling of girls does have a significant part to play as discriminatory structures and practices are deeply embedded in the British educational system, and ultimately affect girls' future education and career opportunities.

To illustrate how schooling inhibits women's and girls' confidence, skills and abilities this chapter will focus on four themes. The first section will consider the history of girls' education in order to show how an 'education for girls' was for a long time regarded as needing to be different from an 'education for boys'. The second section examines the research into schooling which identifies the different and unequal experiences of girls and boys. Issues related to sex education, sexuality and sexual harassment have been brought to the fore through the work of radical feminists and their findings

303

will be discussed in the third section. The final section will look at where we are now by considering the impact of the Education Reform Act 1988 on gender and schooling. Inevitably many areas are not covered: for example, the experiences of women teachers, the teaching trade unions, and women in adult, and higher education. These areas are thoroughly documented in two series of books: the *Gender and Education* series (published by Open University Press) and the *Gender and Society: Feminist Perspectives on the Past and Present* series (published by Falmer Press). Both series consider the implications of education for *all* women in Britain; that is, the focus is not solely on white, middle-class females but encompasses issues of 'race' and social class.

History of girls' education, 1870–1975

The first Education Act (Forster Act, 1870) introduced a national system of state schooling for children between the ages of 5 and 10 through establishing school boards in districts where there were no suitable schools. These schools were intended primarily for working-class children, but there is evidence that they were used by some lower middle-class children. Attendance was made compulsory in 1880 but school boards could continue to charge any child who attended school a weekly fee (until 1890, when free schooling was introduced). The Forster Act was a major achievement for all those who had been campaigning for 'education for all', but particularly so for feminists. Educating upper- and middle-class boys had long been an accepted (and expected) feature of boys' preparation for adulthood, but providing an education for girls was a controversial topic.

Opposition to the idea of educating girls came mainly from the clerical, medical and scientific professions who based their arguments predominantly on concepts of 'natural' differences between males and females. Concerns for the effect that education might have on the 'female physique' were not confined to these three professions. Elizabeth Sewell, a teacher and novelist, wrote in 1865:

> The idea of making a boy's attainments the standard by which to measure the girl's is indeed obviously unfair . . . Not one girl in a hundred would be able to work up the subjects required for an Indian Civil Service examination in the way which boys do. Her health would break down under the effort . . . if she is allowed to run the risks which to the boy are a matter of indifference, she will probably develop some disease which if not fatal, will at any rate be an injury to her for life. (quoted in Spender, 1987, pp. 144–5)

One forceful argument put forward by such feminist historians as Carol Dyhouse (1981) and June Purvis (1995) to explain girls' inclusion in compulsory schooling has focused on women's domestic roles. They suggest that mass schooling was intended to impose upon working-class children a middle-class family form of male breadwinner, economically dependent wife and mother. Schools could teach working-class girls certain skills which they could, in later life, employ in the home and with their families. Consequently, in the early 1870s girls would spend as much as one-fifth of their time in school doing needlework (Sharpe, 1994). A concern that a falling birth rate and a high mortality rate had grave implications for the future source of recruits needed to maintain the British Empire prompted a rapid expansion in domestic subjects (Purvis, 1991, 1995). The Education Department influenced the elementary curriculum through the provision of grants, so in 1878 domestic economy was made a compulsory subject, and in 1882 and 1890 grants were given for the teaching of cookery and laundry respectively.

For middle-class girls the situation was different. Few attended any form of elementary school. If education did take place it was more than likely to take place in the home by the family, or be added to the teaching responsibilities of her brother's governess. Middle-class girls had more opportunities than working-class girls to attend secondary schools, but the curriculum offered by private schools was as restrictive as that offered to working-class girls in elementary schools. Often the emphasis was on acquiring useless accomplishments which would supposedly make them more attractive to potential husbands. The curriculum of one private girls' school consisted of deportment, drawing, callisthenics, foreign languages and English, but the latter was given low priority. Girls would study history and geography on alternate weeks, and they received nine lectures on science delivered by a gentleman in a public room (Purvis, 1995). It is clear that, from the outset, mass education for all children was never intended to cater for all the social classes, or to provide girls and boys with the same skills and abilities. Boys had to be equipped for their future in the labour market, while girls had to acquire the skills to support and make life comfortable for their menfolk and to care adequately for their children.

Education in the early part of the twentieth century lacked the benefit of feminist analysis, and so continued to provide an 'appropriate curriculum' for girls. The idea that an 'appropriate curriculum' for girls was firmly located in the domestic sphere was clearly evident in the Education Act of 1944 (the Butler Act). This Education Act was particularly significant because of its focus on equal opportunities. The aims of the Act in terms of equal educational opportunities were two-fold: first, to encourage social class mobility all children were provided with the right to free secondary education; and second, 'the meritocratic structure of the education system would guarantee that personal achievement and talent would be rewarded within a competitive setting, irrespective of the age, sex, and ethnic or class origin of individual students' (Troyna, 1987, p. 1).

The way these principles were construed militated against equal educational opportunities for all being put into practice. The decision as to the type of secondary school children went to rested upon their performance in the 11–plus examination. It was found that girls achieved higher scores than boys in this examination, which meant that more girls than boys would have been entitled to the more prestigious grammar school placements. To rectify this 'problem', girls' performances in the 11–plus examination were weighted differently from those of boys, so that girls achieved fewer places than their results demanded, and boys were awarded more places than their results merited (Deem, 1981; Evans, 1995). A further consideration is the interpretation of the phrase in the Act which called for schools to: 'afford for all pupils opportunities for education offering such variety of instruction and training as may be desirable in view of their *different* ages, *abilities* and *aptitudes*' (para. 8(b), my emphasis). As we have seen, girls' 'natural' future, irrespective of social class or 'race', was seen to be located in domesticity. Therefore, an interpretation of children's 'different abilities and aptitudes' could (and did) point to a different curriculum for girls and boys, with the former undertaking subjects suitable for homemaking and the latter receiving instruction in those subjects which would possibly lead on to higher education and/or certainly a 'good job'.

Subsequent educational reports, Crowther (1959) and Newsom (1963), continued to underline a girl's place as being in the home and a boy's in the work place. There were some slight changes in views; for instance, the Crowther Report showed awareness that some women might occupy dual roles (in the home and work force) but this was a possibility seen as only being available to middle-class women. (For an informative and detailed examination of these reports see Rosemary Deem, 1981). The 1960s and 1970s witnessed the emergence of many groups concerned with civil liberties, not least the development of a new feminist movement in Britain. Through a series of campaigns, various acts were passed dealing with inequality: that is, the Equal Pay Act, 1970, the Sex Discrimination Act, 1975, and the Race Relations Act, 1976.

The Sex Discrimination Act and government policy

At one point it seemed that the education service was not going to be covered by the Sex Discrimination Act. This was mainly a result of fervent opposition from the Department of Education and Science (DES: see Byrne, 1978; Rendal, 1985; Arnot, 1987). The DES (as well as the Department of Health and Social Security, Home Office and Civil Service) argued that legislation on the grounds of sex discrimination was unnecessary and inappropriate, as it did not exist in the education service. Despite this resistance education was included in the Act but, as Madeleine Arnot (1987) has said, a price had to be paid. First, single-sex schools and sport were exempted from the Act. Second, positive action could take the form of special access routes or courses only in the tertiary sector and not in general education. Third, the powers of the Equal Opportunities Commission (EOC), the quango set up under the auspices of the Sex Discrimination Act, were curtailed when it came to tackling discrimination in the education system. Finally, contract-compliance (for example, providing money for schools to increase laboratory facilities or for science materials) was omitted from the Sex Discrimination Act. The fact that no money was to be given to schools to facilitate the provision of equal educational opportunities was reinforced by the DES in the guidance it sent to Local Education Authorities (LEAs: Circular 2/76). The DES told LEAs to inform their schools that they should ensure that girls and boys had access to the same curriculum subjects. This was nothing more than a time-tabling exercise for most schools and would not tackle the discrimination taking place in the content of the curriculum.

The stance adopted by the DES in passing responsibility for implementing the Sex Discrimination Act on to LEAs explains the variety of approaches to equal opportunity issues which followed. Many LEAs developed Equal Opportunity policies which they implemented and monitored; others simply drew up policy statements which remained at the back of the filing cabinet; and a few did nothing at all (Skelton, 1989). It is worth mentioning here that the majority of policies were 'equal opportunities' rather than anti-sexist policies. The distinction between these approaches will be discussed later, but parallels can be drawn with these and LEAs' preferred perspective when it came to developing policies on issues of 'race'. In terms of both 'race' and gender policies there was (and is) a tendency to favour multicultural and 'equal opportunities' approaches rather than the more radical anti-racist and anti-sexist approaches, dealing as they do with issues of power (see Arnot, 1985; Troyna, 1993; and Siraj-Blatchford, 1995).

The Sex Discrimination Act is a milestone in the history of women's education. The Education Act 1944 may have put 'equal opportunities' on the agenda, but the Sex Discrimination Act took the theory and transformed it into a mode of practice. Putting to one side for a moment the opposition of the DES to a whole-hearted commitment towards eradicating gender inequalities from schooling, the endeavours of researchers, LEAs, and individual schools and teachers have illustrated where and how gender issues arise in the education system. A consequence of these endeavours has been the development of strategies which attempt to reduce the restrictive effects of discriminatory practices. The next section will identify *what* is meant by gender inequalities in schooling, *how* feminist theory has informed the questions that have been asked, and the resulting strategies.

Gender discrimination and schools

Until the passing of the Education Reform Act 1988 and the implementation of a National Curriculum, primary and secondary schools were characterised by many different features. The main impetus in secondary schooling was the development of a curriculum that encompassed both vocational training and 'subject knowledge', the aim being to equip all secondary students with relevant skills for their future in the labour market (for some, via higher education). The ethos of primary schooling (particularly since the Plowden Report, 1967) was child-centred, whereby children experienced an education appropriate to their individual needs, taken at their own pace and where 'discovery learning' was a key feature. Despite these differences, research into discriminatory practices showed overlaps between the two sectors. The intention in this section is to discuss those areas of gender discrimination which were found to be common to both.

Following the passage of the Sex Discrimination Act, 1975, the focus of research into gender inequalities was the secondary school. Large-scale studies of achievements in primary schooling clearly pointed to the fact that girls consistently outperformed boys (with the possible exception of mathematics), but when girls reached secondary school they started to fail (Measor and Sikes, 1992). This does not mean girls 'underachieved' in all subjects; rather, they were more successful at humanities and less successful in maths/science-based subjects. The question of whether girls did start to fail in certain subjects only upon the transition to secondary school, or whether the seeds had been sown during their primary years, prompted disagreement amongst researchers (Joffe and Foxman, 1984; Whyte, 1986; Abraham, 1995). What we do know is that the structures and practices of both primary and secondary schools have ensured that girls and boys experience different and unequal educational opportunities. The way in which schools contribute to this situation can be considered under four headings: organisation and management; resources and assessment; staffing structures; and teacher attitudes

Organisation and management

Segregation by sex as an administrative device dates back to Victorian times when the words 'Girls' and 'Boys' were engraved onto the stonework above separate school entrances. Research in the 1970s and 1980s showed schools dividing pupils into single-sex groups for official record cards, having separate registers (with boys' names first), cloakrooms and sometimes even playgrounds (Byrne, 1978; Deem, 1980; Skelton, 1988; Delamont, 1990). Dress codes were often found to be different for boys and girls. In order to socialise their pupils into the official culture many schools place great emphasis on the management of their appearance. Clothing, jewellery, hairstyles and, in the case of secondary schools, make up are closely controlled (Woods, 1990). Often these rules are different for girls and boys. It was found that in some schools female teachers and girls were not allowed to wear trousers (Whyld, 1983; Kessler *et al.*, 1987). Lesley Holly (1985) records how a male headteacher who espoused equal opportunities tried to ban girls from wearing shorts in the summer.

Evidence was also found of management strategies which relied upon sex/ gender differences. There were instances where teachers would encourage competition between girls and boys in terms of general knowledge quizzes, races as to who could finish their work first, and behaviour: for example, 'Which is the quietest line, the boys' or the girls'?' (Whyte, 1986; Windass, 1989; Thorne, 1993). Inevitably, it is the girls' line which is the quietest, and the subsequent praise from the teacher promotes the notion that girls are valued for their abilities to be passive and non-vocal. Occasionally, the opposite sex would be used as a threat to control pupils. Michael Marland (1983) writes that in one dance lesson the teacher told the girls that if they did not behave they would be made to dance with the boys! Similarly, researchers have found evidence where teachers 'punish' boys who misbehave by making them sit with the girls. There can be no greater insult to a boy's sense of masculinity than by referring to him as a 'girl' (Whyld, 1983; Miedzian, 1992; Salisbury and Jackson, 1996). It is important for teachers to be aware of and rectify these practices which differentiate between girls and boys because they frequently remind pupils that they are either female or male and help in the process of 'fixing' gender identity.

Teaching resources and assessment

There exists a wealth of evidence which shows that the vast majority of school materials have been gender biased. Analyses of textbooks in particular have attracted considerable attention. Women have been rendered insignificant or invisible in secondary-school English, social studies, history, geography and science books (Scott, 1980; Commeyras and Alvermann, 1996). The lack of females in school textbooks has been as prevalent in texts for 'female' curriculum subjects, such as English and history, as in 'male' curriculum subjects like maths and science (Turnbull, Pollock and Bruley, 1983; Abraham, 1995). Not only have women been notable by their absence but, when they are depicted, they are frequently given a submissive persona. For example, physics books have represented females as: 'women pushing prams, a woman floating on the Dead Sea, girls blowing bubbles, women cooking, women as radiographers, nurses or patients, women used as sex symbols in the same way they are used to sell cars, women looking amazed or frightened or simply women doing "silly" things' (Walford, 1980, pp. 224–5).

When research began into primary schooling it was found that the situation regarding gender-biased textbooks was the same. For all its emphasis on child-centred education, primary schooling was found to use 'boy-centred' resources. Glenys Lobban's (1975) research into reading schemes identified 33 different occupations for adult males but only eight for adult females. These were teacher, shopkeeper, housewife, mum, granny, princess, queen and witch, which meant that girls were presented with only two possible future role models in the paid labour market. In relation to maths textbooks, Jean Northam (1982) found the number of images of females steadily decreased, then disappeared, as the maths scheme progressed. Even more recent studies continued to find a disparity in images of females and males in maths schemes and history textbooks (Bailey, 1988; Cairns and Inglis, 1989; Osler, 1994). In their study of primary history textbooks, Joyce Cairns and Bill Inglis discovered an overemphasis on military and political history whilst cultural and religious history were neglected. Out of all the material in all the textbooks only 14.8 per cent dealt with women.

It has to be said that publishers have tried to address gender and 'race' imbalances in recent school textbooks, particularly reading schemes. However, the 'content-analysis' approach used to examine reading schemes for stereotyped images of gender, 'race' and social class has itself come in for criticism (Davies, 1989; Walkerdine, 1989). The argument is that whilst content-analysis critiques have been useful in identifying content bias, they have failed to engage with the text as a vehicle by which meaning is produced. Consequently, feminist analyses of stories need to consider not only the content, but the metaphors, forms of relationship and patterns of power and desire that are created in the text (Gilbert and Taylor, 1991; Christian Smith, 1993). When a content-analysis approach is applied to new and revised reading schemes such as *Flying Boot* (1994) and *Reading 360* (1994), it seems that the publishers have addressed feminist criticisms by including positive images of women in the work force and people from ethnic minorities. However, when the schemes are analysed using a post-structuralist approach (looking at forms of relationships, metaphors, and so on) then, far from making progress, a reverse situation sometimes occurs. For example, in the Janet and John (1949) reading scheme, Janet is portrayed as deferring to her brother, praising him and being of less interest to her parents than John, but she is given a name and does speak. In the first level of the revised Reading 360 (consisting of five books) readers are introduced to mum, dad, Ben and his dog Digger, whilst the girl, Ben's elder sister, is not named or allowed to speak until the next level (Skelton, 1995, 1997).

A further question tackled by researchers was whether this gender bias fed through into assessment procedures. In March 1985 the London GCE Board published a paper on bias and gender in examination papers and stated their disquiet about the potential bias against girls. This prompted the Fawcett Society to investigate all GCE papers for 1987, which involved reading 1000 papers in all. A number of problems were discovered. First, no account was taken of girls' interests and concerns. Boys' interests predominated where, for example, maths questions were placed in contexts like football games or car engines. Second, girls in maths papers appeared in stereotyped and frivolous contexts. Third, women were largely invisible. Of all scientists named in the science papers there was only one reference to a female scientist (Marie Curie). In English papers where the focus was on a female novelist's book (Brontë *The Tenant of Wildfell Hall*), the questions were on the male characters in the book. History papers asked questions on military and diplomatic history, ignoring social history and women's role in history. Fourth, the reversal of women's invisibility was to be found in the home economics papers. This issue had been recognised a few years earlier. A 1982 London 'O' level paper set the question:

> The average weekly expenditure on food is a major item in the family budget. How can *the mother* ensure that in a time of inflation *she* can provide nutritious and interesting meals for her family of husband and two teenage children? (Wynn, 1985, p. 204)

The neglect of girls' interests in these questions are as important as the differences in learning styles between boys and girls. Alienation from the content knowledge needed to answer a question, familiarity with assessed materials and preferred writing styles can all introduce a gender bias into the assessment procedures and subsequent results (Gipps and Murphy, 1994).

At the time much of this research was done (the late 1970s and into the 1980s), girls were outperforming boys at primary school and fell behind in many of the 'masculine' subjects at secondary schools. Pupils now undertake tests at the end of each stage of their schooling. Recent statistics show that in the 1995 tests for Key Stage One (that is, children aged between 5 and 7 years), girls noticeably outperformed boys; at Key Stage Three (children aged between 12 and 14 years) girls outperformed boys marginally in maths but outstripped them in English (School Curriculum and Assessment Authority, 1996). As was stated in the introduction to this chapter, a similar picture emerges when considering girls' achievements at GCSE and 'A' level. On the basis of this performance it could be, and indeed recently it has been suggested in television documentaries and most notably by the chief inspector of schools, Chris Woodhead, that it is boys we should be concerned about as they are the ones falling behind. However, there are other factors within the schooling experiences of girls which means that, despite their academic success at school, they are less likely to enter higher education on a full time basis. There has been no increase in the numbers of working-class and ethnic minority girls going to university and, in general, females from these groups have favoured the old polytechnics and colleges rather than the more prestigious traditional universities (R. Edwards, 1993; Pascall and Cox, 1993). When they do enter the labour market it tends to be in conventional female areas (EOC, 1996). So what messages are being transmitted to girls about how they should behave, what attitudes are appropriate and which careers they should choose?

Staffing structures

Before looking at gender-related issues arising from teacher-pupil interaction it is worth considering how gender impacts upon the position of women teachers in the educational hierarchy and what subjects they teach. Staffing structures of nursery, primary and secondary schools have presented (and still do present) a picture of 'male superiority', with males holding positions of authority. The Department for Education (DFE) statistics show that 52 per cent of secondary teachers are women but whilst 4 per cent of male teachers in this sector are headteachers the comparable statistic for female teachers is only 1 per cent (*Statistical Bulletin* 24/93). This imbalance is even more obvious at primary level. The number of women teachers in primary schools far exceeds the number of men teachers, yet 32.1 per cent of men teachers in the primary sector are headteachers compared to 7.3 per cent of women teachers (*Statistics of Education*, 1992). The subject areas taught and the posts of responsibility held also tend to be different for women and men teachers. Sixty per cent of all women teachers in secondary schools teach modern languages, art, drama, English and business studies (traditionally 'female' subjects), yet only a few teach design technology (DFE 24/93). Women teachers are also more likely to hold posts of responsibility which involve liaison, negotiating, training and out-of-school activities, such as heads of upper and lower school, in-service training (INSET), and heads of special education (de Lyon and Migniuolo, 1989; Ozga, 1993). These posts have a lower status than those of head of faculty, head of sixth form, deputy head and head of outdoor pursuits, which tend to be occupied by men teachers (Weightman, 1989; Hills, 1995). This image of males in higher status positions in education extends to ancillary staff, where the school caretaker is frequently male and in charge of an all-female cleaning staff. Similarly the part-time, and usually low-paid, positions of dinner attendants, teaching auxiliaries and school secretaries are occupied by women.

This evidence, of gender inequalities in school staffing structures, and that given in the previous section, illustrates how schools have reinforced notions of masculinity and femininity. However, this is only part of the story. Children are not passive recipients of school socialisation processes but active agents in their own learning (Delamont, 1990; Thorne, 1993). This means that the attitudes and beliefs of teachers and school pupils, and the interaction between and within these groups, are of crucial importance.

What do children learn about themselves through the attitudes of their teachers? Do teachers make judgements about children in their classrooms on the basis of gender?

Teacher-pupil interaction

This is a significant area in terms of explaining why girls later fail to maintain the potential they demonstrate at school. The message that is constantly being given is that whilst in school teachers expect girls to be more academically successful, yet wider society expects different (and unequal) attitudes and behaviour from its female population. To discuss the evidence of all the research findings in this area would occupy more space than is available here. A focus which highlights the effect on girls is that of teacher-*male* pupil interaction.

It has to be said that not all teachers hold or perpetuate stereotypical beliefs. There are many feminist teachers and teacher educators who constantly challenge biased attitudes (Weiner, 1985; Coffey and Acker, 1991; Frith and Mahony, 1994). Also, those teachers who do convey gender-stereotypical attitudes and expectations are not necessarily doing so on a conscious level. Rather, they may be conflating their *professional* values about, for example, how pupils ought to behave with their *personal* values about how each sex ought to behave (Levitin and Chananie, 1972). This point was clearly illustrated in my research on an initial teacher-training programme where student teachers, who were very conscious of sex discrimination at a personal level, were oblivious to the discriminatory attitudes and expectations that were actively 'taught' to them as part of their professional training. Consequently, their behaviour in the classroom towards pupils incorporated many instances of gender bias (Skelton, 1987, 1989). This behaviour included differences in the time given to boys and girls, which affected classroom management styles and, ultimately, contributed towards the holding of different expectations of girls and boys (Hodgeon, 1988; Cullingford, 1993).

Boys make greater use of verbal and non-verbal language which results in them taking up more of the teacher's time. Thus, boys get more attention in terms of teaching and instruction but also receive more reprimands and more praise than girls (Serbin, 1983; Browne, 1991; Attar, 1995). There is a notable domination by boys in any classroom discussion, although Jane and Peter French (1984, 1986) point out that it is not boys *per se* who secure the maximum amount of teacher attention, but one or two boys only. This 'skill' in attracting the teacher's time is achieved in several ways. First, boys are more mobile in the classroom and use more and larger body movements. One teacher observing her class reported: 'Even with an equal number of boys and girls, the boys dominated the discussion – not by strength of argument, nor even by their ability to articulate . . . But the boys added

power to their contributions by constant movement, jostling for attention
while, for the most part, the girls sat still' (Lee, 1990, p. 28). By making
greater use of non-verbal language than girls the boys literally gained space
and attention for their arguments.

There is a wealth of research evidence showing how many teachers assume
that boys will be more badly behaved than girls and adjust their management styles accordingly. Teachers have been known to select 'topics' which
are geared towards boys' interests in order to maintain their interest and,
thereby, facilitate classroom control (Clarricoates, 1978, 1980). At the same
time, boys are more likely to take 'risks', for example, putting themselves
forward to respond to a teacher's question even when they do not know the
answer (Spender, 1982; Whyte, 1986; Morgan and Dunn, 1990). Perhaps
because of their more boisterous behaviour in the classroom some teachers
seem to interpret 'more confidence' as 'more able', despite the fact that girls
consistently outperform boys (Clarricoates, 1987; Angela Phillips, 1993).
Such attitudes are continued into the assessment of children's work.
Margaret Goddard-Spear's (1989) research in this area found that the
majority of teachers she interviewed claimed they could distinguish between
the written work of girls and boys. She asked a group of secondary school
science teachers to grade samples of children's work on a number of
characteristics. These samples were taken from actual handwritten work
of a scientific experiment carried out by eleven-year-old children. The sex of
the pupils was altered so that each work sample was given to half of the
teachers as boys' work and to the remaining teachers as girls' work. When
teachers believed they were marking boys' work, higher ratings were given
for scientific accuracy, richness and organisation of ideas than to identical
work attributed to girls. Goddard-Spear's research also suggests that the sex
of the teacher was an influential factor, as the work of 'boys' assessed by a
female teacher produced a generous mark, whilst the most severe marking
was of 'girls'' work by a male teacher. School pupils are not oblivious to the
attitudes teachers have towards them, and these expectations strongly
influence their self-perceptions.

Many studies have highlighted how teachers' attitudes act in such a way
as to undermine girls' self-confidence. Michelle Stanworth (1981) coined the
phrase the 'faceless bunch' to describe the inability of many teachers to see
through girls' more passive approach and recognise them as individuals,
rather than as a conformist 'whole' group. Ultimately, this has led to a
situation whereby boys are more likely to be confident in their abilities than
are girls. Girls are far more likely to underestimate their performance in a
given task than boys, and they interpret failure in different ways. Boys will
accord their failings to lack of effort, whilst girls tend to attribute failure to
lack of ability (Jones and Jones, 1989; Stables and Stables, 1995). Significantly, whilst white and Asian girls are often perceived by teachers as
passive, and consequently 'faceless', the reverse is the case with Afro-

Caribbean girls. Several studies have shown how teachers' interactions with Afro-Caribbean girls are similar to those associated with boys: that is, they receive a disproportionately large amount of teacher attention which is generally negative (Fuller, 1980; Stone, 1985; Wright, 1987; Mac an Ghaill, 1988). As Cecile Wright (1987) notes, 'gender variables may operate quite differently in the multi-racial classroom from an all-white classroom' (p. 184). However, whether teachers' behaviours make girls feel 'invisible' or put them in a position of constantly challenging negative expectations, the result is the same in that negative teacher attitudes serve to curtail girls' educational opportunities (Mirza, 1995b).

These studies focused specifically on what happens within schooling, and so interventionist strategies used to tackle gender inequalities in education (such as Girls Into Science and Technology, or GIST, and the pre-National Curriculum Technical and Vocational Education Initiative, TVEI) have, consequently, been narrowly defined. These initiatives, located within an equal opportunities framework, had little effect on changing subject choice options of girls. For example, the GIST project was set up to address the 'problem' of girls' underachievement in science by raising teachers' awareness and making a traditionally male area 'girl-friendly'. The project ran from 1979 to 1983, during which time a team of researchers worked with ten coeducational comprehensive schools alongside teachers with responsibility for science and technology in the lower school. The aim was to encourage more girls to choose science at thirteen when children selected their examination options. The GIST Final Report (Kelly, Smails and Whyte, 1984) presented a range of disappointing outcomes. The project made very little impact on pupils' subject choices; there was only a slight change in girls' attitudes to science and technology, and the teachers, although generally supportive of GIST, felt that their own practices had not altered much as a result of it.

For some feminists, the reasons why gender inequalities continued to pervade girls' schooling experiences was obvious. The concept of gender-power dynamics (including issues of sexuality and sexual harassment) and its implications for classroom interaction was not a central feature of the majority of funded studies and interventionist strategies. The next section will consider the two main approaches, particularly evident in the early to mid-1980s, which were developed to tackle gender discrimination in schooling: that is, 'equal opportunities' and anti-sexism.

Feminist perspectives and education

Attempting to identify which of the feminist perspectives have had *the* most impact on education is an endeavour likely to generate fierce debate (Weiner, 1994). However, it is possible to identify the perspectives which are most frequently referred to in discussions on gender and education: that is, Black feminism, liberal feminism, radical feminism, socialist feminism and, more recently, post-structuralist feminism (Arnot and Weiner, 1987; Measor and Sikes, 1992; Acker, 1994). Rather than rehearse these perspectives which are fully discussed in the texts cited above and briefly in Chapter 3, my intention is to provide an overview of the two approaches developed to tackle gender discrimination at a *practical* level. Reference will be made to feminist perspectives where appropriate to show how the issues raised by the various feminisms have informed the 'girl-friendly' (equal opportunities) and 'girl-centred' (anti-sexist) approaches.

There has been considerable and understandable criticism in recent years from Black feminists of the fact that the majority of studies on gender and education have failed to address 'race' issues (Carby, 1982; Bryan, Dadzie and Scafe, 1985). More recent research and discussions have attempted to redress this imbalance (for example, Reay, 1991; Blair, 1995; Khanum, 1995). However, the two approaches developed to tackle gender inequalities in the classroom largely side-step the issue of 'race' and concentrate on gender.

Both 'equal opportunities' and 'anti-sexist' approaches share a common view – that education and schooling is geared towards white, middle-class males – but they differ as to how best to tackle the situation. Within an 'equal opportunities' perspective, girls' education is regarded as a 'problem' as they 'underachieve' (or did) in certain areas of the school system. The language of 'equal opportunities' is the language of liberal feminism. For liberal feminists the solution to gender discrimination is where a situation exists in which girls and women are provided with the types of skill and educational qualification that will enable them to enter areas of employment traditionally dominated by men; put crudely, a desire for equal numbers of female and male plumbers, pilots and politicians. The GIST project referred to briefly earlier was an example of a liberal (equal opportunities) approach with its emphasis on ensuring girls had equal *access* to science and technology subjects (Kelly, Smails and Whyte, 1984). A liberal feminist approach has been heavily criticised by Black, socialist and radical feminists for its neglect of structural inequalities (such as economic and social power) and its apparent wish to see women competing with, and acting like, men. On the positive side, liberal feminist ideas and values have been the basis for all central political and legal reforms achieved in the last hundred years, so its achievements should not be trivialised.

A 'girl-friendly' (equal opportunities) stance focuses on ensuring girls have *access* to school resources and educational benefits, whereas a 'girl-centred' (anti-sexist) approach is concerned with girls' *treatment in* and *outcome of* their schooling. The intention here is to place girls at the centre of the classroom in order to challenge the dominance of male experience (Weiner, 1986). Within an 'equal opportunities' framework girls are defined as 'the problem', whilst an anti-sexist position regards male power and privilege as 'the problem'. In their chapter in *Gender and the Politics of Schooling* (1987), Gaby Weiner and Madeleine Arnot have produced a table demonstrating the practical application of these ideas in schools. For example, an 'equal opportunities'/'girl-friendly' strategy would be persuading girls into science and technology, whilst the corresponding anti-sexist/ 'girl-centred' approach would entail recognising the importance of girl-centred study, focusing on girl- and woman-centred science and technology. Anti-sexist strategies have primarily emerged in response to the issues identified by radical feminist research into schooling.

Radical feminist research into girls' (and women teachers') educational experiences has highlighted two major concerns; the male monopolisation of culture and knowledge, and the sexual politics of everyday life. It has been shown how boys dominate teachers' time and attention, how they dominate the classroom in terms of space and securing resources and how their interests dominate the curriculum (Morgan and Dunn, 1990; Measor and Sikes, 1992). Importantly, the work of radical feminists has brought to the fore links between male power and sexual violence. The implications of the interrelationship of male power and sexual violence on the daily experiences of girls and women teachers in school has been widely explored (Mahony, 1985; Jones and Mahony, 1989; Lees, 1993; Larkin, 1994). Sexuality and sexual harassment are not issues which liberal feminism has traditionally engaged with, and yet they have been found to fundamentally effect girls' experiences of schooling.

Sexual harassment, sexuality and sex education

The fact that sexual harassment is a part of daily life for girls and women teachers in schools is well documented, yet it is a concept which is very difficult to define. Caroline Ramazanoglu (1987) suggests that one of the problems with defining the term is that an effective definition of sexual harassment incorporates behaviours which are widely regarded as an acceptable part of everyday life such as 'cleavage-gazing, personal remarks, blue jokes and friendly squeezing, rubbing, patting and propositioning' (Ramazanoglu, 1987, p. 65).

The majority of studies carried out in the 1980s on sexual harassment understandably focused on the abuse by boys and men teachers of girls and women (Mahony, 1985; Al-Khalifa, 1988; Herbert, 1989). It has been pointed out more recently that this has tended to suggest that sexual harassment is a heterosexual issue (S. Harris, 1990; Epstein, 1994). This is obviously not the case as there is ample evidence to demonstrate how gay and lesbian school students and teachers experience sexual harassment from pupils and colleagues (Trenchard and Warren, 1984; Gill, 1989; Rogers, 1994; Mac an Ghaill, 1995; Salisbury and Jackson, 1996).

Although there have been debates about sex education and how it should be taught, little has been said of sexuality. It is fair to say that the growth of interest in sexuality, particularly lesbian and gay studies (with a few notable exceptions), has not been mirrored in education (Wolpe, 1988; Holly, 1989; Jones and Mahony, 1989; Epstein, 1994; Mac an Ghaill, 1994). Debbie Epstein (1994) suggests that a reason for this neglect may be the division of what is public and what is private: education and schooling are public arenas, but sexuality is something which is private. However, as we have seen already, schools, and particularly co-educational schools, are sexual institutions in terms of heterosexuality: 'Some of us are now convinced that mixed sex schools are dangerous places for girls and women and that they exist to benefit boys as they establish their sexual domination over girls.' (Jones, 1985, p. 35). Right-wing political agendas over the past years have striven to keep sexuality out of schooling (Kelly, 1992a; Thomson, 1995). The advent of HIV/AIDS and the higher profile of child sex abuse has meant that some form of sex education in schools had to be undertaken. The Education Act of 1986 made explicit that where sex education was taught it had to be done within a heterosexual framework: 'Where sex education is given . . . it is given in such a manner as to encourage those pupils to have due regard to moral considerations and the value of family life' (Section 531, No. 7). What was particularly significant about the Education Act 1986 was that it removed sex education from the rest of the curriculum by placing responsibility for the decision as to whether and how a school taught this subject on to school governors.

Following on from this came the now notorious controversy over Clause 28 (later Section 28 of the Local Government Act 1988). Part 1b of Section 28 is headed 'Prohibition on promoting homosexuality by teaching or publishing material' and states that a local authority shall not 'promote the teaching in any maintained school of the acceptability of homosexuality as a pretended family relationship'. There was a tremendous outcry against this government edict for several reasons. First, it confused the sexual act with a person's sexuality. This was made evident in many of the comments made at the time Clause 28 appeared, which seemed to suggest that the mere mention of homosexuality would make young people want to practise it (de Lyon and Migniuolo, 1989; Sanders and Spraggs, 1989; Kelly, 1992a). The confusion of sex and sexuality missed the point that homosexuality, like heterosexuality, is a social and cultural phenomenon. Second, following the stance taken in the 1986 Education Act, the implication that teachers should not discuss sexuality with their pupils outside sex education lessons was unrealistic. It would be impossible for English teachers, for example, to discuss the work of many writers and dramatists without reference to sexuality (Epstein, 1994). As a result of the heated discussions about the implications of Clause 28 for education a subsequent Department of the Environment Circular (12/88) stated that, as Section 28 applied to local authorities, it did not impose any direct responsibilities on individual schools. Regardless of this, the message had been received by teachers that they needed to exercise extreme caution and self-censorship when it came to issues of sexuality and sex (Stears and Clift, 1990; Sex Education Forum, 1992).

The Education Reform Act, 1988, which introduced the National Curriculum, had little to say about the role of sex and sexuality in education. Although ostensibly school governors retained control of whether and how sex education should be taught, their decision-making powers were curtailed by the inclusion of reproduction (and, in 1991, HIV/AIDS) into National Curriculum Science.

Radical feminism (together with lesbian feminism) has helped to put the issues of sexuality and sex education on the agenda of schooling. Recently, feminist post-structuralist theory has brought new insights to girls' educational experiences (see Jackie Stacey, Chapter 3 for an explanation of feminist post-structuralism). Examples of feminist post-structuralist theory being applied to education can be found in work on children's understanding of feminist fairy tales (Davies, 1989), primary children's understanding of femaleness and maleness (Davies and Banks, 1995), the curriculum (Weiner, 1994) and reading schemes (Skelton, 1995, 1997). Whilst offering new ways of looking at gender and education by moving away from the notion of 'female-as-victim' or female as 'disadvantaged' in the educational system (Jones, 1993), a post-structuralist approach is by no means free from problems. It has been argued that a major difficulty with a feminist post-structuralist approach is that it precludes the development of political programmes (Weiner, 1994; Deem, 1995).

Where are we now?

At the beginning of this chapter I raised the question of whether girls' increased success at GCSE was a reason for feminist educators to sit back and celebrate. Whilst any improvement in girls' educational opportunities is a reason for celebration we certainly cannot 'sit back' and assume that girls' education has now been 'sorted'. To put this recent success into perspective requires a need to look at the statistics more closely, and also recent educational policy.

First, the statistics for GCSE cannot show the complete picture. Girls may be more successful than boys at GCSE but the statistics for 'A' level and degree qualifications note a reverse process occurring. Although girls continue to achieve at the same rates as, if not slightly better than, boys at 'A' level, they are more likely to opt for 'traditional' subject areas. For example, at GCSE girls achieve the same as boys at maths; in physics half as many girls as boys attempt the examination. At 'A' level, half as many girls as boys sit for, and achieve, maths, and in physics there is one girl for every four boys (DFE, 1994). By the time girls reach higher education the differences are even more marked. For example, in mathematics, for every one female with a maths degree there are five males. So a reading of the GCSE results which suggests that girls have broken out of the 'gender trap' is a false premise. Related to this is the question of whether *all* girls are more successful than boys at GCSE, irrespective of social class or 'race'. A consideration of the differences in achievement between middle-class and working-class girls necessitates a consideration of single-sex schooling.

The effectiveness and appropriateness of single-sex schooling for girls has been hotly debated since the beginning of this century (Brehony, 1984). Arguments in favour of single-sex schooling are that girls are more likely to pursue further and higher education generally; to take advanced science subjects; to have a more positive attitude to 'male' curriculum areas; and to experience women in positions of power (Colley, Comber and Hargreaves, 1994; Fisher, 1994). However, the studies which identify the value of single-sex schooling for girls have generally failed to include social class as an instrumental factor, although the *choice* of single-sex or mixed schooling has been an option largely confined to those sections of society that can afford it (Young, 1994; Kelly, 1996). Whilst girls generally do well in GCSE and 'A' levels, girls at single-sex schools do even better. Smithers and Robinson (1995) argue that the fact that single-sex schools do well in GCSE and 'A' levels is because single-sex schools attract academic girls with ambitious parents (by implication, middle-class), and not that co-educational schools are inferior. However, it should be noted that the research by Smithers and Robinson (1995) was funded by the co-educational group of the Head-masters Conference. The point here is that the debates surrounding single-sex schooling continue to rumble on because, in terms of *academic achievement*, girls and boys in single-sex schools perform little differently from children in co-educational schools.

Whatever stance is taken, single-sex schooling for girls is considered a legitimate demand by governments yet this does not hold true when it comes to separate schools for the Black population (J. Williams, 1987). As Jenny Williams goes on to suggest, whilst girls' schools have received some governmental support as a desirable alternative to co-education, the question of 'Black schools' is perceived as a threat to harmony and integration. The tensions which exist between anti-racism and anti-sexism have been a subject of much discussion (see Brah and Deem, 1986; Walkling and Brannigan, 1986). More recently it has been argued that these tensions might be overcome through interventionist programmes which are aimed at both policy and practice, and which consider structural, cultural and political dimensions (Siraj-Blatchford, 1993, 1995; Blair, 1995). In the current educational climate, brought into effect by the Educational Reform Act 1988, such interventionist programmes are unlikely to be developed.

This brings us to the second point made earlier; that we cannot assume girls' recent successes at GCSE will continue, and to understand why requires a look at current educational policy.

It was evident from the consistent use of 'he' to refer to pupils, teachers, school governors and so on, that the Education Reform Act (ERA) 1988 was not overly concerned with equal opportunities. In many ways ERA has helped to undermine equal opportunities policy initiatives developed by LEAs. First, ERA handed over responsibility for developing, implementing and monitoring equal opportunities programmes from LEAs to school governing boards. It cannot be assumed that school governors will consider equal opportunities to be an important aspect of schooling, particularly where school governing bodies are not representative of their local community (Miles and Middleton, 1995). Second, school governors have much more power and status under ERA and therefore individuals are required who possess particular administrative and financial skills. This could have the effect of discouraging many women, especially if they are working class or from ethnic backgrounds as they may feel they lack the necessary expertise. Third, any governing body without an awareness or understanding of equal opportunities could have an impact on the careers of women teachers, as well as on the girls in the school.

The National Curriculum itself is unlikely to open up new possibilities for equal opportunities. The introduction of a National Curriculum in 1988 meant that for the first time in the history of education in England and Wales, primary and secondary pupils would study the same subjects: maths, English, science, history, geography, art, design technology, physical education, music (and modern languages at Key Stages 3 and 4). However, although the introduction of the National Curriculum has opened up the overt curriculum to both sexes, it cannot tackle deeper inequalities. The National Curriculum concentrates on the formal provision of equal access but does not consider the kind of issues that have been raised by feminists and discussed in this chapter. Possibly the most significant aspect of ERA, which will disable attempts to develop interventionist programmes of the kind mentioned above, is the introduction of market forces into education.

ERA introduced market forces to education by implementing the notion of 'parental choice'. The idea is that schools will 'compete' for pupils, which means schools have to be more responsive to pupils and parents. As money will follow the pupils, more resources would be given to popular schools and unpopular schools would either close or change. As Geoff Whitty (1991) has argued: 'This will have particular consequences for the predominantly working class and black populations who inhabit the inner cities. While they never gained an equitable share of educational resources under social democratic policies, the abandonment of planning in favour of the market seems unlikely to provide a solution' (Whitty, 1991, pp. 19–20). Whitty is not alone in believing that the effect of market forces in education will provoke increasing inequalities across gender, social class and 'race' lines (see also Carlen, Gleeson and Wardhaugh, 1992; David, 1992; Ball, 1994). Inevitably, an uneven distribution of resources across schools must mean some pupils will lose out. As Stephen Ball (1994) has said, we cannot ignore the extent to which public monoply education has constructed sexist and racist practices but 'the market form and its attendant values and rhetoric . . . now legitimates and supports such bases of inequity' (p. 125). No doubt feminists will continue to make inroads through anti-sexist and anti-racist work as they did in the 1980s, when it became obvious that government reforms in Britain were being underpinned with a commitment to sustaining the social order through family, 'nation' and a new morality (Arnot, 1992; Arnot and Barton, 1992). However, there can be no doubt that, with government reforms in place which undermine egalitarianism, even the short-term gains (such as more girls entering and being more successful than boys at GCSE) will be more difficult to achieve for girls who are not white or middle-class.

Further reading

Liz Dawtrey, Janet Holland and Merril Hammer with Sue Sheldon (eds), *Equality and Inequality in Education Policy* (Clevedon, Multilingual Matters with The Open University, 1995). A collection of articles which discuss the history and gendered nature of education policies and the impact of those policies on practice in education in Britain and elsewhere. The book presents a range of views and approaches, demonstrating the complexity of the educational experience and the influence of gender, class, 'race' and culture on education.

Janet Holland and Maud Blair with Sue Sheldon (eds), *Debates and Issues in Feminist Research and Pedagogy* (Clevedon, Multilingual Matters with The Open University, 1995). This collection of articles presents the results of classroom research on issues of class, gender, 'race' and sexuality, and shows how these aspects continue to position students differently throughout their school lives.

Lynda Measor and Patricia Sikes, *Gender and Schools* (London, Cassell, 1992) provide an overview of research studies into gender and education. The book reviews the different approaches to the study of gender in schools and examines the interaction of 'race' and class with gender. Issues covered are gender socialisation, the implications of gender on achievement in schools, and inequality and education.

Iram Siraj-Blatchford (ed.), *'Race', Gender and the Education of Teachers* (Buckingham, Open University Press, 1993). The articles in this edited collection analyse the effects and implications of continued racist and sexist practices in teacher education. They consider how practitioners and policy-makers can provide equal opportunities for students and staff through courses, admission procedures, recruitment, school practice, administration and management.

15

Women, Marriage and Family Relationships

Stevi Jackson

Given the importance of family relationships in most women's lives it is not surprising that 'the family' has occupied a central place in feminist theory and research. Various aspects of family life have been identified as crucial to an understanding of women's subordination. Some feminists have emphasised male violence and men's control over women's sexuality and reproduction; others have looked at the economics of domestic labour and have discussed the contribution it makes to capitalism or the extent to which men benefit from it; still others have concentrated on the familial relationships which shape the construction of masculinity and femininity; and many more have examined the state regulation of family life. These issues have proved highly contentious. Indeed, the major debates between feminists on the interrelationship between patriarchy and capitalism have often been fought on the terrain of 'the family'. Recent discussions of differences among women in terms of class, 'race', ethnicity and sexuality have raised new questions for feminist analyses of family life.

Until the 1980s many theorists sought to locate the cause of women's subordination in the family, but it is now widely recognised that women's position within families is itself something which needs to be explained in terms of wider social processes and structures. This has resulted in a change of emphasis in feminist thinking. For example, where women's disadvantage in the labour market was (and sometimes still is) attributed to the burden of their domestic responsibilities, now women's domesticity is often seen as a result of gender segregation in waged work (Walby, 1986, 1990).

It has also become clear that the term 'the family' is itself problematic since it glosses over the historical and cultural variability of family forms and many different forms of family life that women today experience. The 'cereal packet' image of the supposedly 'normal' family – white and middle class with a breadwinning husband, domesticated dependent wife and two children – does not represent the normal or the typical. In 1993 married couples with dependent children accounted for only 25 per cent of British households and 41 per cent of the total population (CSO, 1995). Well over

323

half of these nuclear families have two breadwinners: two out of three married women are employed, as are three-fifths of mothers of dependent children (CSO, 1994). Cohabitation and divorce are both on the increase, and in 1992 around 38 per cent of marriages were remarriages for one or both partners. Growing numbers of women are living alone or rearing children independently; in 1991, 19 per cent of families with children were headed by single parents, most of whom were women. Almost one-third of British children are now being born to unmarried women, although the majority of these result from stable heterosexual relationships, and 24 per cent of children can expect to experience parental divorce before they reach the age of sixteen. In 1991, 23 per cent of children were not living with both of their natural parents and 8 per cent of children lived in households with a step-parent or step-sisters or step-brothers. (CSO, 1995).[1]

These figures should not be taken to mean that family life is no longer a salient feature of our experience. The majority of the British population, about 84 per cent in 1991, live in households based on marriage or parent-child ties (CSO, 1995). While less than half of us live in nuclear families at any one time, most of us have experience of this type of family at some stage in our lives. The point here is that families take varied forms and change over time with the birth or death of members, with children leaving home or marriages breaking down. Moreover, the term 'family' may be used in everyday life to cover households and relationships which do not fall within government definitions: for example, a lesbian couple with children may call themselves a family but will be hidden in official statistics under the heading of 'other households'.

Underlying the statistics on families and households are the varied and complex realities of women's domestic lives, the choices we make about the relationships we enter into and the many economic, social and cultural constraints on those choices. Understanding the differences among us, and especially the impact of class, ethnicity, racism and sexuality on family life, is essential to a feminist analysis. We need to draw attention to the persistent inequalities within families, but if we theorise women's subordination in terms of 'the family' as if it had only one form, we are in danger of perpetuating a version of the white heterosexual middle-class myth of the 'typical' nuclear family.

This is one of the grounds on which Black feminists have been critical of white feminists' preoccupation with the family as a basis of women's oppression (Carby, 1982; hooks, 1982; Bhavnani and Coulson, 1986). Black and white women's experience of family life are not the same, and there are differences between the various Black communities in Britain. South Asian households are more likely to contain more than one family with children than either Afro-Caribbean or white households. However, the proportion of nuclear family households among South Asians is also high (more than double that found among the white population). In 1989–91, over 60 per cent of households whose members are of Pakistani and Bangladeshi origin were based on nuclear families with dependant children, closely followed by over 50 per cent of households made up of people of Indian descent (CSO, 1993). Afro-Caribbean women, on the other hand, are more likely to head single-parent households than white or Asian women (CSO, 1995). In 1989–91, nearly half of Afro–Caribbean mothers were lone mothers, compared with around 15 per cent of white mothers and less than 10 per cent of those of Asian descent. (CSO, 1994). This is not just a matter of ethnic diversity, but also of the impact of institutionalised racism. Slavery, colonisation and, more recently, immigration and citizenship laws have had profound effects on Black families. Moreover, familial ideology has been central to racism, with Black families branded as pathological if they do not match white definitions of normality. Here racism and sexism converge in particularly damaging definitions of Black womanhood:

> the Afro-Caribbean family is seen as being too fragmented and weak and the Asian family seems to be unhealthily strong, cohesive and controlling of its members . . . Afro-Caribbean women are stereotyped matriarchs, or seen as single mothers who expose their children to a stream of different men while Asian women are constructed as faithful and passive victims . . . identified as failures because of their lack of English and their refusal to integrate. (Parmar, 1988, p. 199)

Black feminists have also challenged white feminist perspectives on the grounds that many Black women see their families as a base for protection from, and resistance to, racism rather than as the cause of their oppression. This highlights a more general point: in identifying the family as a site of women's subordination, the ambivalence of women's feelings and the contradictory nature of our experience of families should not be ignored. Patriarchal family structures may be oppressive for both white *and* Black women, but families may also supply women with their closest and most supportive relationships, not least in relationships between female kin.

Feminist criticism of the family, then, should not be read as a blanket condemnation of all aspects of family life, and neither is it an attack on those who live in families. Some feminists have experimented with alternative forms of domestic life, such as communal living, and with patterns of childrearing which challenge conventional sexist assumptions about girls and boys. Others have set up home with other women and have established support networks of friends which may be thought of in the language of kinship ties, as has been documented in some North American lesbian communities (Weston, 1991). Those who have actively chosen to live outside conventional families may be a minority, but their experiences can tell us a great deal about the limitations of individualistic efforts to change social and cultural structures and also about the potential for choice and resistance (Dunne, 1996; VanEvery, 1995).

Even if many of us do not live in 'normal' families, certain conceptions of normality predominate within our culture and underpin the framing of much state policy. Moreover, awareness of the diversity of family forms existing today, and sensitivity to women's ambivalent feelings about their families, do not invalidate feminist analyses of the inequality and exploitation structured into family relationships. What is clear, however, is that we cannot treat 'the family' as an isolated 'cause' of women's oppression, but need to relate family relationships to other aspects of society.

It is also important to challenge the commonly-held assumption that families are natural units, an assumption that is often used to justify women's subordination and which has informed functionalist sociological analyses of the family as serving universal human and social needs (Gittins, 1993). An appeal to 'naturalness' is often made as part of the Right's political defence of patriarchal family structures. For example, early in 1990 the then British Prime Minister, Margaret Thatcher, spoke of 'the right of the child to be brought up in a real family' (Family Policy Studies Centre, 1990, p. 5). A 'real family' is one based on a heterosexual couple. This is made explicit in Section 28 of the 1988 Local Government Act which stipulates that local authorities should not 'promote the teaching in any maintained school of the acceptability of homosexuality as a pretended family relationship'. Lesbians (and gay men), it seems, can form only 'pretend', not 'real', families. Such narrow definitions of the 'normal' family treat as natural, universal and trans-historical something which is, in fact, culturally and historically specific.

Cross-cultural and historical perspectives

If family forms vary in contemporary Western society, then we can expect much greater diversity to have existed historically on a world scale. There is no simple, single entity that can be defined as 'the family' and compared across cultures. What we are dealing with is not a fixed structure but a complex set of relationships and practices, each element of which can vary cross-culturally (Edholm, 1982).

Ties of kinship, which we usually think of as biological, are, in fact, social: 'relatives are not born but made' (ibid., p. 167). The way Europeans classify kin relationships is only one of many possible ways of deciding who is related to whom (C. Harris, 1990). The precise configuration of kin and non-kin who live together and co-operate economically varies greatly, as does the extent to which households are recognisable as distinct units within a society (C. Harris, 1990). Husbands and wives do not always live together, and children are not necessarily reared by either of their biological parents (Mair, 1972; Edholm, 1982; Moore, 1988). Marriage can be monogamous or polygamous; it may be an enduring relationship entered into after much negotiation or it may be a relatively informal arrangement (Mair, 1972).

Marriage usually confers some sort of legitimacy on a woman's children, but her husband need not necessarily be the father of those children and social fatherhood is not always conferred on a child's biological father (C. Harris, 1990). Motherhood is often regarded as a more natural role, but there are great differences in the meaning of motherhood from one society to another: in ideas about conception, birth and childrearing, and in the relationships between mothers and their children (particularly the extent to which mothers are solely responsible for the care of their own offspring: Edholm, 1982). Women as wives and mothers are not generally wholly dependent on men. One of the most pervasive myths about gender relations in Western society is that men are natural breadwinners and have provided for women since the dawn of human history. In most non-industrial societies, however, women make a substantial contribution to subsistence, and in many they are the main food providers (Moore, 1988).

Colonialism and world capitalism have had a major, and sometimes devastating, impact on the domestic structures of non-European societies. Such changes, however, should not be understood as a result of capitalism alone, or simply as social structures responding to the 'needs' of capital: 'These processes of transformation have been equally determined . . . by the existing forms of kinship and gender relations' (Moore, 1988, p. 116).

This is also true of the transition to capitalism in Europe. In understanding how modern family forms emerged it is necessary to keep in mind that they developed in a society which was already patriarchal. Women's family lives today have been shaped by the interrelationship between patriarchy and capitalism. The history of that interrelationship reveals both continuities and discontinuities in European patterns of family life.

Until the industrial phase of capitalism, most production, whether agricultural, craft or domestic industry, was centred on households. Everyone – men, women and children – contributed to the household economy. There was, however, a distinct sexual division of labour, and generally men controlled productive resources, including the labour of their wives (Middleton, 1983, 1988; Seccombe, 1992). With industrialisation the removal of commodity production from households reduced most of the population to wage labour, and separated family life from paid work. Among the bourgeoisie in the early nineteenth century these changes were associated with a new 'domestic ideology' which defined the home as women's 'natural' sphere (Davidoff and Hall, 1987; Hall, 1992). This ideology was subsequently adopted by sections of the working class. Male-dominated labour organisations sought to exclude women from many forms of paid work and to establish the principle of the male breadwinner earning a 'family wage'

(Seccombe, 1986, 1992; Walby, 1986; Mark-Lawson and Witz, 1990; Jackson, 1992b).

By the twentieth century, normal family life had come to be defined in terms of a breadwinning husband and domesticated wife, although this was not a pattern that many poorer members of the working class could afford to adopt. Even today, when the majority of married women spend a far smaller proportion of their lives rearing children than they did a century ago, the idea persists that a woman's purpose in life is to care for home, husband and children.

There have been intense debates among feminists as to whether this ideal of family life serves the interests of capitalism, patriarchy or both. I hope to demonstrate that, while male-dominated families may be functional for capital through producing labour power and providing a basis for social stability, men themselves are direct beneficiaries. I will concentrate my analysis on marriage, since other aspects of family life are covered elsewhere in this book. Moreover, it is marriage (and cohabitation) which binds many women into unequal relationships with men. This inequality is not intrinsic to relations between women and men in themselves, but is linked to wider social and economic structures and is sanctioned by the power of the state.

The economics of domestic life

The distribution of resources and the organisation of labour within families are interconnected, and related to unequal access to paid work. These economic processes are crucial determinants of women's subordination within families. Family ties are ties of economic co-operation, of support and dependency, but also of inequality and exploitation. In exploring these economic relations I will begin by looking at the income coming into families and how it is allocated.

The increasing number of female-headed households and the rising proportion of women in paid work has led feminists to question the myth of the male breadwinner. In 1993, around 70.8 per cent of women between 16 and 59 were employed or seeking employment, with slightly more married women having paid jobs than women without husbands. Women are also more likely to be employed if their husband is also in work. There are also ethnic differences here: 71.9 per cent of white women were defined as economically active in 1993, compared with 66 per cent of women of African and African Caribbean descent, 61.4 per cent of those of Indian descent and 24.8 per cent of those of Pakistani or Bangladeshi descent (CSO, 1995). For all these groups, except women in Pakistani or Bangladeshi communities, total dependence on a male worker is now a minority experience. Women's earnings make a vital contribution to the economic survival of most households and families (Land, 1983; Glendinning and

Millar, 1987, 1992b; Morris, 1990). It should not be forgotten, however, that women's work is generally lower paid and less secure than men's work, and that many women – especially those with young children – work part-time (see Chapter 11). Giving up work or taking part-time work in order to care for children has long-term effects on women's earning capacity, compounding the economic inequality between husbands and wives (Joshi, 1992). Hence women are likely to be at least partly financially dependent for most of their married lives. A number of studies have found, that even where women make a substantial contribution to household income, the importance of their earnings may be played down so that the man is still defined as the breadwinner. Women's wages, however essential, are often seen as covering 'extras' (Brannen and Moss, 1987, 1991; Mansfield and Collard, 1988; Pahl, 1989). There are potent ideological forces at work here whereby the financial role of women is downgraded and their domesticity is reaffirmed.

Feminist researchers and theorists have challenged the assumption that families are units in which all resources are distributed equally (Brannen and Wilson, 1987; Delphy and Leonard, 1992; Jackson and Moores, 1995). There is growing evidence that 'while sharing a common address, family members do not necessarily share a common standard of living' (Graham, 1987c, p. 221). Since husbands generally earn considerably more than their wives, they have potentially greater power in determining how family income should be allocated. Among married couples the degree to which men exercise direct control over domestic expenditure varies depending on the strategy adopted for apportioning that money. Whether women control the bulk of domestic finances, have a housekeeping allowance, draw from a common pool, or cover certain costs from their own wages, they generally spend little on themselves. Men, on the other hand, almost always have greater access to personal spending money (Graham, 1987a, 1987c; Wilson, 1987; Pahl, 1989, 1990; Brannen and Moss, 1991). Men and children have pocket money; women have housekeeping money.

This pattern is attributable both to men's greater economic power and to ideas about men's rights and needs. A couple may talk of the husband's wage as 'ours' rather than 'his', but in practice wives often do not see themselves as having an equal right to spend it, especially on themselves. One of the major attractions to paid work for married women is that it provides them with money over which they have direct control (Wilson, 1987; Pahl, 1989). The 'extras' they spend their earnings on, however, are usually for their children or the family as a whole rather than for themselves. Hence women generally contribute a higher proportion of their wages to housekeeping than do men (Westwood, 1984; Brannen and Moss, 1987, 1991; Pahl, 1990).

During the 1980s researchers uncovered considerable evidence of hidden poverty in families dependent on men. One telling indicator of this is that some studies found that a substantial proportion, sometimes as many as half, of previously married single mothers felt that they were as well off or better off financially than they were when with their partners (Evanson, 1980; Graham, 1987a, 1987c). This is surprising given that, during this period, two out of three lone mothers lived on state benefits and that households headed by lone mothers were three times more likely to be poor than two-parent households (Glendinning and Millar, 1987). It was not only men's spending on personal consumption that accounted for this, but also the greater degree of control lone mothers had over the total family budget (Graham, 1987a, 1987c). They could plan their expenditure, decide their priorities and make economies in the interests of their children and themselves without having to take a man's desires and demands into account. In part this represented a freedom to go without, since women were often prepared to make personal sacrifices which men were not, but lone mothers sometimes found that exercising their own preferences led to a more economical lifestyle (Graham, 1987a, 1987c).

The domestic distribution of money is unlikely to have changed substantially in the 1990s and serves to demonstrate a more general point: that consumption within families rarely takes place on the basis of fair shares for all. The same can also be said of patterns of work and leisure. Modern families are often seen as sites of consumption and leisure (Berger and Berger, 1983), but for women home is also a place of work. Men's participation in routine housework has increased slightly since the early 1980s, but women still carry most of the burden of domestic labour, whether or not they are in waged work (CSO, 1995).

It is still taken for granted, as an implicit element of the marriage contract, that women take primary responsibility for domestic work (Delphy, 1984; Delphy and Leonard, 1992; Gittins, 1993). This is evident from the beginning of married life. Among newly-wed couples interviewed by Penny Mansfield and Jean Collard (1988), women did most of the chores, even if they were employed full-time. They saw themselves as overburdened 'because of their working role and not because of their husbands lack of domestic involvement' (pp. 135–6). Being viewed as secondary breadwinners means that it is women who must make the adjustments necessary to ensure that both partners can go out to work (Westwood, 1984; Yeandle, 1984; Brannen and Moss, 1991). Men may be more inclined to 'help' around the house when their wives are employed, but their contribution is generally limited.

The work women do constrains their own leisure while making that of others possible. Men are usually able to go out more because of their greater financial independence as well as greater freedom from domestic responsibilities: they do not have to consider who is taking care of the children or whether there are clean clothes ready for the next day. Someone else is doing the work and taking the responsibility. Women's work thus creates men's leisure. Women not only have less leisure time than men, but they are more likely to spend it at home so that they are constantly 'on call' even when not actually working (Chambers, 1986). Women's time is a household resource drawn upon by other family members (Seymour, 1992). The consequent lack of segregation between work and leisure is one of the key features that differentiates housework from waged work.

Domestic labour

Feminists have sought to establish that housework is work. In the 1970s, for example, there was considerable discussion around the issue of wages for housework (see Malos, 1980). There are, however, a number of ways in which domestic labour differs from waged work. No other occupation is not only allocated to one gender, but includes almost all adults of that gender among its practitioners. No other job is so intimately bound up with personal ties or so grounded in an ethic of personal service. There is no fixed job description for domestic labourers, there are no agreed hours and conditions of work and no trade unions. Housework is work without boundaries or limits, with no clear beginning and end points, with no guaranteed space or time for leisure.

Research on housework has shown that women's feelings about it are profoundly ambivalent. Women commonly express dissatisfaction with the content, quantity and conditions of domestic labour. They frequently find it monotonous, repetitive, unstimulating, isolating, tiring and never-ending. They may resent the low status of housework within society at large, or feel that their work passes unnoticed and is taken for granted by other household members. They are often well aware that they carry an unfair burden, especially when they also engage in wage labour. These sources of discontent were documented in a number of studies carried out in the 1970s and 1980s (Hunt, 1980; Oakley, 1984; Westwood, 1984). These studies found that women were willing to state these grievances, but usually stopped short of an overall critique of their situation; they rarely dismissed housework as a whole as unrewarding, and were even less likely to challenge the sexual division of labour which made housework their responsibility (Hunt, 1980; Oakley, 1984; Westwood, 1984).[2]

Housework is not merely a set of chores, it is also work which is given meaning through ideas of home and family. Because it is a personal service which involves caring for those a woman cares most about, she is unlikely to see it as just a job and to judge it accordingly. Not only is it difficult to dissociate feelings about the work of caring from feelings about the recipients of that care, but women may also derive considerable satisfaction and a sense of pride from doing this work well, since it is essential to the well-being of all household members. In her classic study of housework,

Ann Oakley (1984) suggested that the contradictions and ambivalences in women's attitudes to housework can be clarified by distinguishing between feelings about housework (as work) and orientation to the 'housewife role'. It is the work itself which is the focus of declared dissatisfactions, whereas 'the housewife role' is more often understood in terms of caring for others and creating a home, and is viewed far more positively. More recent research carried out by Pauline Hunt in the late 1980s suggested that home-building was still central to women's identity (Hunt, 1989, 1995). The continued salience of this activity in many women's lives is indicated by the lasting popularity of those women's magazines which focus on domesticity: the top five women's magazines in Britain in 1994 were all of this type, including *Take a Break* and *Bella*, as well as the long established *Woman* and *Woman's Own*.

It has sometimes been suggested that feminist critiques of housework have only ever held true for white middle-class women. In terms of 'orientation to the housewife role', as opposed to feelings about the work itself, this may have been the case. For example, in her study of women workers in a Leicester factory, Sallie Westwood heard all the usual complaints about housework. Yet the women also saw it as 'their *proper* work' which was invested with meaning and status because it was 'work done for love' and demonstrated their commitment to their families. Hence otherwise boring, routine work was 'transformed into satisfying, caring work' (Westwood, 1984, p. 170).

White feminists' preoccupation with the oppressiveness of domestic labour during the 1970s called forth a spate of criticism from Black feminists who argued that domesticity did not have the same meaning for Black and white women (see, for example, Carby, 1982; hooks, 1982). In a society which is both racist and patriarchal, where Black women are likely to have the least satisfying and worst-paid jobs, family life may be particularly highly valued as a source of more positive identities and relationships (Collins, 1990). Nonetheless, housework itself was still disliked by the Asian women in Sallie Westwood's study. Nicki Thorogood (1987) found a high degree of dissatisfaction with domestic chores among Afro-Caribbean women, and those of them living independently of men felt a major advantage of this arrangement was that it reduced the amount of housework they had to do. More recently, Avtar Brah found that young Pakistani women in Birmingham emphasised the importance of paid work, but some were too overburdened with domestic work to seek employment. This group of women (both single and married) clearly defined housework *as* work and experienced it as onerous: as wives or daughters they were often caring for large households which, because of poverty, lacked the domestic appliances more privileged women take for granted (Brah, 1994). There is little evidence, then, that Black women like housework any more than white women. All the research I have cited indicates that the dislike of housework as work is widespread and is experienced by women irrespective of class, 'race', ethnicity, education or paid occupation, albeit to differing degrees.

A key feature of housework is that it is unpaid; it is not part of the wage economy but takes place within private households. This is related to other specific features of domestic labour. It lacks clear temporal definition because, unlike paid work, it does not involve the sale of labour power for a set number of hours in return for a given wage. The goods and services produced through housework are consumed by a woman's immediate family rather than being destined for the commodity market. The peculiarities of domestic labour arise from these socio-economic relations rather than being intrinsic to the tasks wives (or daughters or sisters) perform. Such tasks can be undertaken as paid jobs and the services wives provide can be purchased on the market. Only when performed within households and without pay does such work become subject to the specific conditions of housework.

It is clear that housework takes place within social relations very different from those of capitalist production, and I would suggest that these relations are patriarchal. The work accomplished within households does, however, connect with the capitalist economy. One aspect of this connection, which has been the subject of much discussion, is the production of labour power. Women do the work which maintains their own and their husband's capacity to work, and they rear the future work force. This was a central focus of the 'domestic labour debate' during the 1970s through which feminists sought to understand the specific location of women in capitalist society (for summaries see Kaluzynska, 1980; Malos, 1980; Walby, 1986; Delphy and Leonard, 1992).

A major limitation of this debate was that it concentrated on the contribution of domestic labour to capitalism and did not consider the extent to which men benefit from it. Some writers did point out that housework took place within relations of production distinct from those of capitalism (Gardiner, Himmelweit and Mackintosh, 1975; P. Smith, 1978), but Marxists and Marxist feminists were unwilling to see these distinctive productive relations as patriarchal. This line of enquiry has subsequently been pursued by Christine Delphy and Sylvia Walby (Delphy, 1984; Delphy and Leonard, 1992; Walby, 1986, 1990). Both these theorists argue that housework takes place within a domestic or patriarchal mode of production in which men exploit women's labour. This has proved very contentious, and Delphy's work in particular was subjected to fierce criticism by Marxist feminists (see Jackson, 1996a).

At the heart of the objection to the concept of the patriarchal mode of production was a refusal to accept that men benefit directly from women's domestic labour (see, for example, Barrett, 1988, pp. 216–17). It is clear from the evidence that I have cited on consumption and leisure that men do gain a great deal from women's household work. Men do not only 'evade' their share of the housework and childcare, as Michèle Barrett put it, but they also have their share done for them. They thus receive services for which they do not pay, beyond contributing to their wives' maintenance. Moreover, a woman is not simply a dependent whom her male partner's wage must support: she contributes to his capacity to earn that wage. She produces his labour power which he exchanges for a wage which he controls (Walby, 1986, 1990). He thus benefits both from the personal services his wife performs for him and the advantages this gives him in freeing his time for both work and leisure. A man may thus be said to appropriate his wife's labour power within a patriarchal mode of production (Delphy and Leonard, 1992; Jackson, 1996a).

The patriarchal mode of production is not a fixed, inflexible structure, and has developed in 'dynamic articulation' with capitalism (Walby, 1986 p. 55). Patriarchal production has also been shaped by the history of colonial exploitation and racism. It does not therefore take the same form in Black and white households. All over the world, Black women and colonised women have often worked within the patriarchal mode of production as other women's servants. This has historically been more common in the USA than in Britain (Nain, 1991). However, with increasing numbers of white middle-class women pursuing careers, domestic service is once again becoming a widespread form of employment for Black and/or working-class women in Britain (Gregson and Lowe, 1994). Nonetheless, it remains the case that across the diverse range of ethnic groups which make up British society, it is commonly accepted that housework is women's work.

There are, however, ethnic variations in the degree to which women live independently of men. There are a higher proportion of female-headed households among Afro-Caribbeans than among those of white European origin, and more among Europeans than among Asians (CSO, 1995). This does suggest that there are differing degrees to which women are subject to patriarchal exploitation within households among different ethnic groups. The history of slavery, institutionalised racism and economic insecurity have ensured that few Afro-Caribbean and Afro-American women have had the chance to be dependent on a male breadwinner (Coonz, 1988; Nain, 1991). Asian women, on the other hand, are often more tightly bound to work within the home. They are, for example, overrepresented in home-working (Phizacklea, 1994), combining underpaid work with their unpaid work, and in work within family businesses. There is a strong tradition of family-based enterprise among Asian communities in Britain. Of those in employment in 1994 over 20 per cent of Pakistani and Bangladeshi people and around 18 per cent of Indian people are self employed (CSO, 1995). A family business provides both an alternative to competing for jobs in a racially segregated labour market and a means of acquiring status within South Asian communities (Westwood and Bhachu, 1988; Afshar, 1989). The existence of such businesses means that, for many South Asian and Chinese women, work within the patriarchal mode of production involves more than just housework. This can intensify the degree of patriarchal exploitation occurring, since kinship obligations can mean women working for little or no remuneration within family enterprises (Baxter and Raw, 1988; Bhachu, 1988; Afshar, 1989; Phizacklea and Ram, 1996).

This is not a situation peculiar to Asian women. The wives of self-employed men, Black or white, from chimney sweeps to lawyers, may provide free labour to their husbands' businesses. There are also grey areas where housework shades into work connected to a husband's business or employment such as, for example, entertaining his colleagues or clients and taking telephone messages. Women can, in many ways, find themselves married to their husband's job (Finch, 1983). All these situations are characteristic of the patriarchal mode of production in which women's unpaid work is expropriated by their husbands (or male kin). Indeed it is a feature of the patriarchal mode of production that the work wives do can be very varied. Because this work is undertaken as a personal service to a woman's husband, the tasks women are called upon to perform depend upon her husband's social position and personal requirements (Delphy and Leonard, 1992). A woman's labour is exploited whether she is the wife of a poor working-class man and her life is one of unremitting toil, or the wife of a prosperous businessman who is freed from physical drudgery in order to concentrate on such wifely duties as planning elaborate dinner parties. Few wives, even among the upper classes, are exempt from providing some form of domestic service (including sexual services) to their husbands. The conditions under which wives labour and their standard of living vary enormously, but they share a similar relation to the means of production within the patriarchal mode of production.

Over the last two decades domestic productive relations have undergone some change:

> Women are no longer necessarily bound to an individual husband who expropriates their labour till death do them part. Instead, increasing numbers of women change husbands, have children without husbands and engage in work for an employer other than their husband. Women spend a smaller proportion of their life-time's labour under patriarchal relations of production. (Walby, 1990, p. 89)

Walby sees these changes as part of a shift from private to public patriarchy, with male control of individual women in families and households giving way to public patriarchal control through the state, the labour market and so on. Walby's analysis suggests that the patriarchal mode of production may be declining in relative importance within the social structure as a whole. If there is a decline, however, it is far from terminal.

Most women still marry or cohabit with men, and most still spend much of their adult lives performing housework for men. Indeed, the fact that most women are now employed could be taken to indicate an intensification of their exploitation. Where wives are earning their own keep they are clearly doing housework for nothing (Delphy and Leonard, 1992).

Why do women enter into a relationship in which they are exploited? Somewhat paradoxically, it is likely to be in their immediate material interests to do so. Because women have been marginalised in the labour market, with adverse effects on their capacity to earn, entering upon the labour contract of marriage may offer them a better chance of economic security than does remaining single. This is particularly the case for working-class women or those with few qualifications, since they often cannot earn enough to support an independent household (Siltanen, 1994). The choice of marrying cannot, however, be explained only in economic terms. Marriage may be a labour relationship, but that is not all it is. Neither women nor men enter into it motivated entirely by economics, and both expect rewards other than material ones from it. It is to these other expectations and desires that I will now turn my attention.

Marriage as a personal relationship

The vast majority of women marry at least once, but since the 1970s there have been distinct changes in patterns of marriage, with a trend towards later marriage and lower overall rates of marriage. The median age of first marriages for British women rose from 21.4 in 1971 to 26 in 1992. In the early 1970s teenage marriage was common and, in the year 1971, 9 per cent of girls aged 16–19 got married, compared with less than 1 per cent who did so in 1992. At the beginning of the 1970s only 4 per cent of women would still be single when they were 50, but by the late 1980s 17 per cent could expect to reach that age without having ever married, and all indications are that this trend is continuing. More women are staying single and more are living with men without formalising their relationship in marriage. Over half of those who marry are already living together (Kiernan and Wicks, 1990; CSO, 1995). Similar trends have been noted throughout Europe, North America and Australasia (United Nations, 1995).[3]

It may be that some women are able to exercise more real choice over whether to marry as a result of greater financial independence. Conversely, it may be that for others high male unemployment has made marriage less economically viable and therefore less attractive. There have also been changes in sexual mores over this period, but studies conducted in the late 1980s indicated that older attitudes to courtship, love and marriage were persisting and co-existed with newer ideas (Mansfield and Collard, 1988; Hutson and Jenkins, 1989). The degree to which things have changed can be overemphasised. Cohabitation may be little different in practice from formal marriage, and most of those who cohabit later marry. The majority of women, in Britain and elsewhere, enter their first marriages by the time they are 30 (CSO, 1995; United Nations, 1995).

Despite increasing numbers opting to delay or eschew marriage, it is still taken for granted by most young women as a normal and inevitable part of their lives (Mansfield and Collard, 1988; Lees, 1993; Sharpe, 1994). This expectation is part of the way in which 'compulsory heterosexuality' (Rich, 1980a) is maintained, making lesbianism appear to be a deviant, unnatural choice. While marriage is generally regarded as desirable there is some ambivalence here, a recognition that 'settling down' might mean losing out on freedom and independence, and young women now hope for greater equality and autonomy in their marriages (Lees, 1993; Sharpe, 1994). 'Settling down' also has its positive aspects, admitting young people to full adult status and the possibility of a home life independent of their parents (Mansfield and Collard, 1988). Although the decision to marry is based upon realistic choices and mundane aspirations, within the Western cultural tradition being 'in love' is seen as an essential basis of marriage.

Marrying other than on the basis of free choice and romantic love, particularly the forms of arranged marriage practised by many Asian people in Britain, are judged very negatively from the standpoint of the dominant white culture. The popular image of arranged marriage is informed by racist stereotypes of Asian women as passive victims forced by unscrupulous parents into marriages of convenience (Parmar, 1988). In fact, Asian parents usually select their daughter's husband with considerable care, and young women have varying degrees of choice in the matter (Westwood, 1984; Afshar, 1989; Sharpe, 1994). The ideal is that love should develop within marriage. While the reality does not always match the ideal, this is equally true of Western style romantic love.

There are no logical or empirical grounds for arguing that choosing a spouse on the basis of romantic love offers any greater guarantee of marital happiness than does having one's marriage arranged. Many a white woman who has married for love can find herself feeling vulnerable, powerless and restricted within marriage. Tales of male violence and exploitation could be told about both love matches and arranged matches. Asian women themselves do not usually attribute unhappy marriages to the fact that they are arranged, but to women's lack of status and power within families (see, for example, Shan, 1985). It is mistaken, and indeed arrogant, to assume that young Asian women necessarily want to emulate their white contemporaries. Haleh Afshar, for example, found that the younger generation of British Pakistani women 'felt strongly that they should be consulted on the choice of future husbands' but still accepted the arranged marriage system and 'were somewhat sceptical about romantic love and Western style marriages' (Afshar, 1989, p. 216). Some do rebel, and can then find themselves isolated from their own families and communities (Afshar, 1994; Sharpe, 1994).

Most research on marital relationships deals with white couples. It is clear from this that marriage on the basis of romantic love does not deliver what it promises. While women do not expect to live out their lives in a state of romantic passion, they do hope for affection and companionship (Mansfield and Collard, 1988). 'Togetherness' is central to the modern Western ideal of marriage, but it is often one-sided. The unity which marriage is supposed to create disguises the two marriages which exist within one union. The distinction which Jessie Bernard (1982) noted between 'his' and 'her' marriages is still with us in the 1990s. The two marriages are not merely different, but fundamentally unequal.

Penny Mansfield and Jean Collard's study of newly-weds, carried out in the 1980s, painted a poignant picture of the disillusionment which is experienced by wives. Although still in the 'honeymoon' period of the first six months of marriage, many felt abandoned by husbands who left them alone too often, and let down by the lack of affection the men demonstrated. Husbands and wives defined the ideal of 'togetherness' differently. The men wanted a home and a wife, a secure physical and emotional base, something and someone to come home to. The women desired 'a close exchange of intimacy which would make them feel valued as a person and not just as a wife'. They 'expected more of their husbands emotionally than these men were prepared, or felt able, to give' (ibid., pp. 179 and 192). In general the men were unaware of this divergence of expectations and far more content with marriage; where they complained about their wives it was often because they saw them as being too emotionally demanding. The only other major source of dissatisfaction was with wives' housekeeping skills. This research suggested that it was the emotional divide which was the most keenly felt source of discontent among women in the early days of marriage. The women seemed, on the whole, willing to accept the inequitable distribution of work and resources in marriage: they asked only to be loved and valued.

These findings are not unique. A number of North American studies of women's experiences of love have found that heterosexual women feel that their emotional needs are not being met by their partners and that men fail to demonstrate affection while relying on women for emotional support (see Cancian, 1990). British studies, too, suggest that women put a great deal of emotional labour, as well as domestic labour, into maintaining marital relationships. Here, as well as in the economic aspects of marriage, they give more than they receive (Duncombe and Marsden 1993, 1995; Langford, 1995). Women are by no means totally powerless within marriage, but structurally and culturally marriage favours men.

One indicator of this, and of women's refusal to accept economic and emotional deprivation within marriage, is divorce. Since divorce was made more widely available in Britain in 1969, and with subsequent further liberalisation of divorce laws, increasing numbers of women have availed themselves of the opportunity to escape from unsatisfactory marriages. Not only have divorce rates risen, but so have the proportion of divorces initiated by women as it has become easier for them to leave and survive outside unsatisfactory marriages. In 1992, more than two and a half times as many divorces were initiated by women as by men (CSO, 1995). This may reflect women's greater need to formalise financial and child custody arrangements once a marriage has broken down (Delphy and Leonard, 1992), as well as their greater marital unhappiness. Overall, divorce is becoming more and more common. In the 1970s divorce rates doubled, but have since increased more slowly, by 11 per cent between 1981 and 1992. By 1992, there was one divorce for every two weddings (CSO, 1995), and on current trends it is likely that up to 2 in 5 marriages will ultimately end in divorce. Divorce, however, only ends a particular marital relationship. It does not necessarily undermine the institution of marriage itself. Most of those who divorce subsequently remarry, or enter into heterosexual cohabitation (many only to separate or divorce again). Women's discontent with marriage does not seem to be experienced as disillusionment with the institution, but rather with a particular relationship.

The legal regulation of marriage and divorce

Marriage in Western society is regarded as the most intimate and private of all relationships, but the fact that it is controlled by the state indicates that it is not just a personal relationship: it is of wider social and political significance. The state does not merely regulate family life; it helps to constitute it by defining what counts as a family (Barrett and McIntosh, 1991). It does so through such provisions as Section 28 of the 1988 Local Government Act and Section 13 of the Human Fertilisation and Embryology Act, 1990, which states that a woman should not have access to certain treatments for infertility 'unless account has been taken of the welfare of the child who may be born as a result of the treatment (including the need of that child for a father)'. Single women and lesbians are thus not regarded as having the same rights to motherhood as women involved in a heterosexual relationship. Marriage, then, is central to this definition of heterosexual family life and establishes patterns of rights and dependencies around which much state policy revolves. Not only are the processes whereby we enter into or terminate a marriage legally prescribed, but the state also defines who may marry whom.

Marriage institutionalises heterosexual monogamy, and privileges only one form of sexuality as a socially and legally valid foundation for family life. A lesbian couple, however long established, can have no recognised relationship to each other. For example, they will not be defined as each other's next of kin as a heterosexual married couple would, and have no automatic rights in relation to each other. A lesbian mother can lose custody of her children and her partner has no legally-sanctioned relationship to a child she has helped to rear unless she has formally been appointed as the child's legal guardian. Lesbian couples are also frequently denied the right to foster or adopt children. Although, from time to time, lesbians win battles in the courts over these issues, the balance of both legislation and legal precedent is against them (*Rights of Women Bulletin*, Spring, 1993). Lesbians may escape the constraints of patriarchal marriage, but they are also denied its privileges.

The reason why marriage is by definition heterosexual lies in its history as a patriarchal institution: a sexual relationship whereby a man established rights in the person and property of his wife (Guillaumin, 1995). Under English common law the rights a man acquired through marriage were extensive. Until the nineteenth century a wife's property became her husband's and she effectively became his property. He had near absolute claims to her labour, her children and her body, and the authority to chastise her if she did not fulfil her obligations. This patriarchal power has only very slowly been eroded (Brophy and Smart, 1981; Smart, 1984).

In 1839 men lost their absolute right to their children, and subsequent legislative change and judicial decisions gradually gave women more chance of keeping their children when a marriage ended. It was not until 1973, however, that both parents became equal in law and, since the late 1980s, changes in legislation and in the pattern of custody decisions threaten once more to empower fathers at the expense of mothers (Smart, 1984, 1989a; Brophy, 1989; Harne, 1993). Married women gained rights to their earnings in 1870 and the right to own property in 1882. Equal divorce rights have existed only since 1923. Family law has moved towards the idea of marriage as a partnership and the establishment of formal equal rights even to the extent that since 1990 the existence of rape in marriage has been recognised in British courts, thus challenging men's ancient rights over their wives' sexuality. Yet while men's power within marriage has been reduced, it has not been totally undermined. The partnership of marriage is, as we have seen, far from being an equal one.

Formal equality before the law has limited effects in a society where women are economically unequal and where other state agencies enforce that inequality. The idea of equality founded on an essentially masculine conception of legal subjects, abstractly equal before the law, conceals material inequalities between men and women (Naffine, 1990; Kingdom, 1991). One example of this is the British 1996 Family Law Act which does away with the idea of 'fault' in divorce and ends quick divorces on grounds such as adultery or unreasonable behaviour. Those seeking divorce must now wait eighteen months, during which mediation is offered, to encourage them to reconsider or at least settle their differences amicably. This move is based on the assumption that marriage is an egalitarian relationship and ignores the real differences of interest and power which divide husbands and wives.

Formal equality can actually erode some rights, such as rights of custody of children, which women have won by virtue of their place within families, specifically as mothers. In practice women's rights within marriage have always been conditional, bound up with the interests of their children and dependent on their being defined as 'good mothers'. Throughout the twentieth century, until the 1980s, custody of children was increasingly awarded to mothers 'in the best interests of the child'. If a mother was deemed 'unfit', however, she might still lose her children. Such women are often those who challenge patriarchal relations: in the 1950s the adulteress, more recently, the lesbian (Smart, 1984, 1989a). Here, there has been a backlash against women in the name of fathers' rights. During the 1980s mothers were still being awarded care and control, but courts were moving towards granting joint custody and greater access to children for fathers. This renders a woman subject to surveillance and possible harassment by her former husband, and can mean that she is effectively rearing the children under his supervision (see Brophy, 1989; Smart, 1989a; Harne, 1993).

The 1989 Children Act effectively enshrined joint custody as the legal norm, giving absent fathers a say in all major decisions concerning the child. It is also assumed that children have the right to maintain 'contact' with the absent parent and, except under exceptional circumstances, parents have a legal obligation to facilitate contact. While couched in terms of the rights of the child, the Act has undermined mothers' rights and causes particular problems for women and children seeking to escape from violent men. In the name of children's 'right' to a relationship with their father, courts have disclosed to violent men the whereabouts of their former partners and children and, in a few cases, have debarred women from taking children to live in refuges (Harne, 1993).

While feminists are rightly concerned about the damaging effects of these developments on women and children, there may be problems in simply asserting that mothers' rights over children should take precedence over those of fathers. Christine Delphy (1992, 1994) has urged caution in pursuing 'maternal demands' on two grounds. In the first place, pleas for mothers' rights rest upon the assumption of women's 'natural difference' from men and therefore undermine women's demands for equality. In her view women's responsibility for childcare is part and parcel of men's individual and collective appropriation of women's labour and hence, in the long term, the recognition of maternal rights might help to perpetuate women's subordination. Second, Delphy argues that mother's rights can easily become rights *over* another category of people: children. She is well aware that in a social situation where men do not do their share of childcare when couples are together, and where assertions of fathers' rights are an extension of male power over women and children, feminist opposition to fathers' rights is just. However, she is worried that feminists are adopting a position which implies that men should never have the right to look after children. This, she suggests, is not about women's liberation, but the corporate rights of mothers, a claim to ownership which maintains the subordinate status of children and ultimately of women too:

> Maybe we will end up with full ownership of children; but I don't think this will help children. It won't be much of an improvement for them, even if the new owner proves better than the old one. Nor do I think it will help to liberate women. It may constitute an increase of power for some women *within the gender system as it exists*; but it will be at the price of renouncing the perspective of one day obliterating this dividing line: of renouncing the objective of having the gender system disappear. (Delphy 1992, p. 19, italics in original)

The state, welfare and the family

The regulation of marriage is one of the ways in which the state perpetuates women's subordination and helps constitute 'the family'.[4] Other aspects of state regulation contribute to this process: welfare provision, through defining women as men's dependants, and immigration policy, through determining which of a person's relatives may be allowed into the country and under what conditions. Other areas of policy (such as housing, health, education and so on) are also informed by assumptions about 'normal' family life.

The state is not a monolithic entity which has consistent effects: it is made up of a number of agencies and apparatuses which do not always work in harmony. There are differences, for example, in the degree to which family law, taxation and the social security system define wives as dependent upon their husbands. Moreover, legislation which affects family relationships is not always formulated purposefully to impose a particular form of family life, although it is underpinned by common-sense ideas about families. During the 1980s and 1990s, however, Britain's Conservative government explicitly identified the family as a target for policy, and sought to promote and defend traditional patriarchal structures (David, 1986; Abbot and Wallace, 1989; Laws, 1994). A change in government is unlikely to alter this situation since, by the mid-1990s, the Labour Party was also adopting a strongly pro-family stance and was endorsing heterosexual marriage and fathers' rights (Harne, 1995).

The welfare state in its modern form dates from the post-war period when all major parties broadly supported it. The growth of welfarism has usually been seen by Marxists as functional for capital, ensuring the efficient reproduction of labour power and a degree of social stability. Support for a particular family form is held to follow this (Barrett, 1988). Such a view ignores the possibility that patriarchal interests are served by the state. As is recognised by many Marxists, the welfare state is in part a response to struggle and represents concessions won by the working class. These struggles were dominated by organised male labour, whose demands for recognition as family breadwinners fitted with a wider patriarchal ideology. Male dominance and female dependency were taken for granted by men of all classes and became enshrined in the welfare state. In its welfare provision, as elsewhere, the state is patriarchal as well as capitalist in that it supports family structures which benefit men (Walby, 1990).

The ways in which welfare policy has defined women as family carers and dependants is well established (see, for example, Ungerson, 1990). Unlike children, who are treated as dependants because they need care, women are regarded as dependants because they provide care. Yet the assumption of dependency applies to women as wives rather than mothers. This underlies the patriarchal interests and assumptions which inform the formulation of state policy. Child benefit is one of the few areas where the British state defines women as mothers rather than wives and pays them, rather than their husbands, a benefit. It is not such a contradiction as it might seem that the 1980s British Conservative administration, ostensibly committed to 'family values', should freeze child benefit for four years. The form of family they have sought to promote is a patriarchal one, hence the recent emphasis on paternal responsibilities. It is quite in keeping with this to refuse to acknowledge the economic inequalities that exist within families and therefore claim that only poor families require benefits for children. This view also happens to coincide with other political aims, notably the reduction of public expenditure and 'welfare dependency'. The patriarchal and capitalist aspects of New Right philosophy do not, however, always fit together so neatly. Aggressive, individualistic economic liberalism sometimes conflicts with pro-family moral authoritarianism, while women's dependence contradicts the principle of individual self-reliance. The resolution usually attempted emphasises an ideal of self-reliant families rather than individuals.

During the last two decades cuts in public expenditure have adversely affected many women. The general trend of recent British welfare legislation has been to increase the dependence of women on men (and also young people on parents). Cuts in non-means-tested benefits paid to women, such as freezing child benefit and the abolition of universal maternity benefit, are examples of measures which particularly affect those who are not employed. While stressing the importance of women staying home to care for young children, the government penalises those who do so. While the Labour Party ostensibly has a more positive approach to welfare provision, both their pro-family stance and the financial constraints faced by any future Labour government make it unlikely that the trends established under the Tories will be reversed.

Gestures towards equality have been made by treating women in employment as individuals rather than as dependants for some purposes (for example, by taxing husbands and wives separately). Other areas of policy, however, assume women's availability for unpaid work in the home. Childcare provision in Britain is appallingly inadequate. A study conducted in the 1980s found that less than half of the parents who would like places for their children were able to find them, most relying on the private sector (Cohen, 1988). Since this study was conducted, public sector provision has declined, although there has been an increase in private provision (CSO, 1995). The emphasis on 'community care' means more women shouldering the burden of care for sick or elderly relatives, with little support. In 1991 one in five women between the ages of 45 and 64 (and 17 per cent of all women) were providing such care (CSO, 1995).

While stressing the importance of family responsibility for care, especially that of mothers of young children, the government has sought to recruit women into the paid labour force. Such conflicts of demand for women's labour both inside and outside the home has sometimes been seen as resulting from contradictions within capitalism, but can also be conceptualised as a tension between patriarchy and capitalism (Walby, 1986, 1990). This tension is at its most acute and obvious in the situation of lone mothers, most of whom live on state benefits. On the one hand there is the aim of reducing what the Conservatives call the 'dependency culture' and the need for the labour of some of these women, while on the other is the patriarchal ideal which holds that mothers should stay home to look after their children. During the 1990s single mothers have been subjected to sustained attacks by government ministers, with their rights to housing and benefits under continual threat (Laws, 1994; Millar, 1994). As Sophie Laws points out, lone mothers are regarded as a social ill in themselves, the message being that no woman has the right to rear children outside the traditional contract within which 'women with children are expected to put up with anything in return for being supported by a man rather than the state' (Laws, 1994, p. 6).

In this context, the solution to the 'problem' of lone mothers has been to plump for the patriarchal option, replacing dependency on the state by dependency on men. The 1992 Child Support Act, which came into effect in 1993, aimed to make fathers maintain their children whether or not they were, or had been, married to the mothers of those children. The Act, along with the Child Support Agency which implements it, has proved unpopular with men, who quickly organised against it, winning concessions which take more account of their current commitments in the setting of maintenance payments. The Act has not proved to be of much help to women, either.

Most of the women affected are no better off, since what they gain in maintenance is deducted pound for pound from their benefits. While some women welcome the prospect of men being made to take some responsibility for their offspring, dependency on a former partner is something many women wish to avoid, particularly where it makes them vulnerable to harassment and violence. Although male violence is the one ground on which women can refuse to disclose the identity of children's fathers, in practice the Agency has demanded more proof than many women are able to provide. Women on benefit are effectively coerced into dependence on individual men since those who do not name the father of their children face having their benefit reduced. Women who have conceived by artificial insemination are in a particularly anomalous situation. Those who avail themselves of an anonymous donor via a private clinic cannot, and are not expected to, reveal the identity of the father; if a woman opts for self-insemination, however, the 'donor' becomes a father and the woman is expected to name him. The Act is also racist in its implications, given that Afro-Caribbean women are more likely to be lone parents than white women, and that Black women already find themselves subject to a greater degree of state surveillance than their white sisters. The assumption under-pinning the Act is that women have no right to rear children independently of men (Laws, 1994; Anderson, 1995). Here, again, we can expect no improvement from a change in government since the Labour Party has endorsed the principles underpinning the Act (Harne, 1995).

The pro-family stance adopted by the British government, and indeed the familial ideology underpinning state policy in general, is not applied universally. The family which successive governments have wished to promote and protect is the white, heterosexual family. This 'family' has long been one of the focal points around which ideas of 'Britishness' have been constructed, so that families of 'others' are seen as suspect and pathological. That the welfare state has been, from its inception, racist as well as patriarchal is exemplified in Lord Beveridge's famous pronounce-ment made in 1942 on the role of British women: 'In the next thirty years housewives as mothers have vital work to do in ensuring the adequate continuance of the British race and of British ideals in the world' (quoted in Deakin and Wicks, 1988, p. 20).

In the post-war era, immigration legislation has consistently threatened the unity of Black families. The Thatcher administration, supposedly committed to the defence of family life, introduced the Nationality Act, the Primary Purposes Rule[5] and tighter visa restrictions for people from specified African and Asian countries. As a result, many families have been split up through deportation. The Primary Purposes Rule, for example, places the onus on a couple to prove their marriage is not a marriage of convenience and results in many being subject to intrusive and humiliating vetting (Jacobs, 1988). These changes in immigration have had particularly negative consequences for young Asian women and their families. Those who had promised their daughters in marriage prior to these new restrictions, in the expectation that their sons-in-law would move to Britain, found themselves in the situation of their daughters having to leave the country (Afshar, 1989).

The racism which results in families being divided cannot be reduced to a side-effect of capitalism. State policy on the family has been shaped by a complex interplay between capitalist, patriarchal and racist interests.

Conclusion

Women are differently located within patriarchal, racist and capitalist society and thus have varying experiences of family life. Some of us are freer to make choices and experience less contradictions than others (Ramazanoglu, 1989). All, however, make choices (albeit within given limits): women are not simply passive victims ensnared into oppressive marriages. It may be that it is becoming easier for some women to live independently of men, and it is certainly the case that marriage no longer ties us to an individual man for life. Given other constraints on women's lives, however, marriage will still seem to many to be an attractive option.

Neither the differences among women in our experience of family life, nor our ambivalent feelings about it, should blind us to the fact that gender divisions remain a ubiquitous and pervasive feature of families, affecting all of us irrespective of class, sexuality, 'race' or ethnicity. Families can be the basis of political solidarity in Black and working-class communities, but they are also central to the reproduction of patriarchal relations and the perpetuation of women's subordination (Nain, 1991).

Notes

1. Here and throughout this chapter, I have given the most recent statistics available for Britain, taken from the Government publications, *Social Trends*. The statistics contained in each annual edition of this publication are the most up-to-date available, but are often for different years depending on their source. For example, the 1995 edition contains data from the 1991 census, but also more recent statistics – for 1992 and 1993 – from surveys which are carried out more frequently than the census. To complicate matters further, the same data is not always available in the same form from year to year. Wherever possible, I have taken my statistics from the 1995 edition of *Social Trends* (CSO, 1995), but have occasionally drawn on older editions.
2. There has been little research on women's feelings about and experiences of housework in recent years, largely because it would be unlikely to reveal anything new. We know that women are still doing most of the domestic chores,

and it is highly improbable that they have suddenly started to find them more rewarding. More recent studies of domestic divisions of labour suggest that women still feel a sense of obligation to ensure that housework gets done and thus take responsibility for making the arrangements necessary to make a dual earner household run smoothly (see, for example, Brannen and Moss, 1991).
3. There are different patterns in other parts of the world. For example, far fewer women remain unmarried in most of North Africa, Asia and the Pacific regions, while far more women remain unmarried in Central and South America and the Caribbean. For further details see the United Nations report, *The World's Women* (United Nations, 1995).
4. The limited ways in which violence within marriage is subject to legal regulation is a further example: here the state has historically condoned male violence and still fails to provide adequate protection for women (see Chapter 8).
5. The Primary Purposes Rule, introduced in 1983, gave immigration officials the power to refuse the foreign spouse of someone living in Britain entry to the country, or to deport them, if it was judged that the 'primary purpose' of the marriage was to secure residence in Britain.

Further reading

Christine Delphy and Diana Leonard, *Familiar Exploitation: A New Analysis of Marriage in Contemporary Western Societies* (Cambridge, Polity, 1992). This book offers a materialist feminist perspective on marriage, arguing that it is a relationship founded on men's exploitation of women's work. It offers a thorough overview of sources of economic inequality within marriage and the family, engages with other theoretical perspectives and backs up the theoretical argument with research findings from Britain and France.

Stevi Jackson and Shaun Moores (eds), *The Politics of Domestic Consumption: Critical Readings* (Hemel Hempstead, Prentice-Hall/Harvester Wheatsheaf, 1995). This reader brings together critical work on the everyday practices of domestic consumption, emphasising the power relations and inequalities governing the distribution of resources in households and families. The readings are arranged into five sections covering economic inequality, food and clothing, leisure and media reception, domestic technologies, and the cultural construction of home.

Diana Gittins, *The Family In Question*, 2nd edn (London, Macmillan, 1993). This is an accessible, introductory overview of debates and research on family life from a feminist perspective. It has a strong historical emphasis and addresses many of the basic questions about women's situation within families.

Jo VanEvery, *Heterosexual Women Changing the Family: Refusing to be a 'Wife'!* (London, Taylor & Francis, 1995). This book is based on a study of heterosexual women who are attempting to develop anti-sexist living arrangements, and also contains some data on lesbians. The findings are set in the context of wider research and theory, and cast interesting light on the constraints women face within heterosexual relationships as well as the ways in which they seek to change them.

Kath Weston, *Families We Choose: Lesbians, Gays, Kinship* (New York, Columbia University Press, 1991). This study, conducted in San Francisco, looks at the ways in which lesbians and gay men negotiate relationships with their families of origin and how they construct new forms of family and kin relations with partners, friends and children. Weston places her research in the context of political debates about lesbian and gay families and assesses the challenges these 'chosen' families pose to conventional heterosexual assumptions.

Most of the reading so far cited deals primarily with white families. There is still a relative paucity of material on Black and ethnic minority families and no single book written from a feminist perspective. Haleh Afshar's three-generation study of Muslim women's family relationships has so far only been published as articles. The most useful are 'Gender roles and the "moral economy of kin" among Pakistani Women in West Yorkshire', *New Community*, 15(2) (1989), pp. 211–25 and 'Muslim women in West Yorkshire: growing up with real and imaginary values amidst conflicting views of self and society', in H. Afshar and M. Maynard (eds) *The Dynamics of Race and Gender: Some Feminist Implications*, (London, Taylor & Francis, 1994. Some other articles in the latter collection also deal with aspects of family life. Some general works on Black women and Black feminism also contain sections on the family, many of which I have cited in this chapter. One of the more thorough ones in this respect is Patricia Collins's *Black Feminist Thought*, London, Routledge, 1990, which deals mainly with women in the USA. Sallie Westwood and Parminder Bhachu's edited collection, *Enterprising Women: Ethnicity, Economy and Gender Relations*, London, Routledge, 1989, covers women working within family enterprises in various ethnic minority communities in Britain. Sallie Westwood's classic study of women workers in a textile factory, though now rather old, raises interesting questions about the similarities and differences in the family lives of white and Asian women: see her *All Day, Every Day: Factory and Family in Women's Lives*, London, Pluto, 1984. An article by Gemma Tang Nain addressing political and theoretical questions about Black and white women's experience of male dominance includes a section on the family. See her 'Black women, sexism and racism: black or anti-racist feminism?' *Feminist Review*, 37 (1991), pp. 1–22. For a discussion of Afro-Caribbean women's experience of housework see Nickie Thorogood, 'Race, class and gender: the politics of housework' in J. Brannen and G. Wilson (eds), *Give and Take in Families: Studies in Resource Distribution*, London, Allen & Unwin, 1987.

16

Women and Reproduction

Jalna Hanmer

Early women's liberation movement theory on reproduction

This chapter is about biological reproduction; how it has and is being theorised and why it is central to some strands of feminist theory and to Women's Studies. The initial questions and issues of concern to women since the 1960s are discussed first. Scientific developments and medical technologies currently restructuring biological reproduction are described next, followed by a description of how this is impacting on rights, choice and self-determination for women. The chapter concludes with crucial issues for an agenda to secure a better future for women in the new millennium.

Feminists in the early 1970s were concerned with basic questions. Why are women oppressed? Who or what is oppressing women? Have women always been oppressed? How can our oppression be overcome? Feminists identified family, marriage, childbearing, children, capitalism and men as basic causes of women's oppression, and biological reproduction was occasionally prioritised (Rose and Hanmer, 1976).

In the early 1970s in Britain, women formed groups around reproductive issues in order to provide advice and practical services in relation to pregnancy testing, contraception, abortion and childbirth. The aim was to gain control over our bodies. But during the 1970s this broad focus on reproduction was overtaken by political actions to retain the provisions of the 1967 Abortion Act. Throughout the 1970s feminist and Left political groups participated actively, as abortion was accepted as a major means of obtaining women's social equality with men, and much of women's political action on reproduction was redirected to retaining our limited right to abortion. From time to time, however, other major single-issue campaigns arose, such as the attempt to retain London's women-only hospital, the Elizabeth Garrett Anderson, and the demonstrations about the management of birthing at the Royal Free Hospital.

The demand to take up broader concerns, including those of Black women, and for a women-only organisation eventually led to a political split within the National Abortion Campaign in 1981. Upon the creation of the Reproductive Rights Campaign with its separate Information Centre, a broader focus on reproduction again became a dominant theme of practical political work: for example, objections to the testing and introduction of Depo-Provera, the long-term contraceptive injectable, was the focus of a sustained campaign. The National Abortion Campaign continued as a single-issue mixed organisation.

Over this period the political emphasis on reproduction shifted from women's liberation to women's rights; but, based on a more critical approach to science and technology, a strand of thought and action rooted in the concepts of oppression and imperialism began to re-emerge in the mid-1980s. The women's liberation movement was initially largely uncritical of science and technology, although the medical establishment received substantial criticism (Ehrenreich and English, 1979). Scientific and medical interventions in conception (for example, the hormonal contraceptive pill) had been welcomed, with few dissenting voices. Women gradually became more critical throughout the 1970s, however, as the immediate and long-term adverse health implications of developments such as the contraceptive pill, and medication prescribed during pregnancy such as DES (diethylstilbestrol), began to surface. Also, it became clearer how science and technology were being used to disempower growing numbers of women by extending interventions initially justified 'in exceptional circumstances only' to routine use. Specific techniques identified from pregnancy and the birthing process include foetal monitoring, hormonal drips, ultrasound, inductions, episiotomies and amniocentesis (Rakusen and Davidson, 1982). Women found they could directly use some very low-tech interventions, such as self-insemination, or pregnancy-testing kits, but as the technology became more developed control passed increasingly into the hands of professionals (as, for example, with IVF, or the genetic testing of embryos).

Although these types of intervention were yet to be successfully used on women, in 1971 Shulamith Firestone in the classic text, *The Dialectic of Sex*, precipitated a debate on artificial reproduction. Her view was that because women bear children it has been possible for men to gain ascendancy over them. The reason she gave for this was that the subjugation of women is rooted in the division of labour which begins with the differing roles males and females have in the reproduction of the species. This division of labour is institutionalised in the family; therefore, to free women, it is necessary to eradicate the family. A transitional stage in the elimination of the family is to develop alternative lifestyles and social institutions. Eventually science will enable the full realisation of this project by reproducing people artificially, thus eliminating the female reproductive function.

Firestone wanted to sketch a future in which women and men could live in harmony with full equality between the sexes. In her theory, science and technology ensure the new utopia by stripping the division of labour at the root of the family (that is, the differential parts played by women and men in human reproduction) of any remaining practical value. The transitional phase includes strategies that are shared by feminist theorists from other perspectives: for example, to open up jobs to satisfy individual social and emotional needs so that the pressure on women to establish family units is not so great, and to encourage alternative lifestyles which imply non-fertility, such as lesbian mothers living on their own or in groups, and gay fathers, as well as collectives. Firestone believed that adopting new forms of living will, over several generations, lead to the obsolescence of the mono-gamous couple and family.

Her clearly-articulated analysis of reproduction both as the cause of and the solution to women's oppression has been criticised for biological reductionism and for her assumption that science, technology and the state are neutral institutions. Historically, her work is important to the feminist process of clarifying what and who is oppressing women, but unfortunately for an understanding of feminist theory, her work continues to be used negatively to caricature all radical feminism as essentialist or biologically determinist (Richardson, 1996; Rowland and Klein, 1996b).

Other theorists were less centrally committed to a single strand of analysis. Juliet Mitchell (1966), who identified herself as a Marxist feminist, sought to specify the separate structures that form the complex total of women's oppression. She identified production, reproduction, sex and socialisation as the four structures, specifying that each of these is to some considerable extent autonomous of the others, and each has its own momentum.

Maria Rosa Dalla Costa (1972) moved the analysis of reproduction in another direction, one that had immense influence in the development of Marxist feminist analyses in Britain. She argued that women are engaged in social production through housework, including childbearing and child-rearing. Dalla Costa expanded the concept of reproduction to include the social reproduction of the paid industrial worker through housework, and of the next generation of workers. She argued that these forms of reproduc-tion are not just private, but create labour power and therefore value, which makes *women* part of the working class.

Although written around the same time, the work of the French radical feminist Christine Delphy (1970) was not translated into English until 1974. She too argued that housework creates value, and that it does not seem to be so because women do not receive a wage for their work as they are trapped in a non-capitalist form of production more closely approximating that of master and slave. Delphy was not concerned with biological reproduction as a form of labour power, while Dalla Costa saw it as intimately linked with domestic work generally, although she made only a brief reference to the need for women to control reproductive science and technology. Dalla Costa's and Delphy's were highly critical works within a Marxist framework, but it was left to Mary O'Brien some years later to develop a materialistic analysis based on biological reproduction (1981, 1989).

Carla Lonzi of the Italian group, Rivolta Feminile (Lanzi, 1972), was another radical feminist profoundly influenced by Marxist analysis, and quite unlike Firestone, who ignored power in analysing the role of science and technology. Like Mitchell, she separated reproduction from sexuality, but unlike Mitchell she did not regard the split between sex and reproduction to be impossible for the dominant social class to accept. Rivolta Feminile argued that a male world is able to turn the separation of reproduction and sexuality to a male and ruling-class advantage. They described men as 'colonizing women through the penis culture', and that while the split between sexuality and reproduction made possible by contraception and abortion tended to aid women, it also increased male power over women. Men obtain sexual satisfaction, and their dominant status is amplified by permissiveness. This issue began to be raised with the development of birth-control and continues to be important for radical feminist writing on sexuality today (Coveney *et al.*, 1984; Jeffreys, 1990; *Feminism and Psychology*, 1992). The conclusion that Rivolta Feminile drew is that women should only consort with men to conceive, while real sexuality and tenderness can be obtained with other women.

While the women's movement all over the world seeks in some general sense to increase women's control over their own bodies as part of the wish to control their own lives, the theoretical analyses of the early 1970s which focused on reproduction were concerned to identify and re-organise the oppressive conditions under which women live in relation to men. These early feminists were writing at a time when fundamentally reshaping women's role in biological reproduction was understood to be utopian, although research and experimentation was rapidly developing and the first IVF conception and birth, in 1978, of Louise Brown was only a few years away. The themes they explored – women's relation to reproductive science and technology and how its use may alter gender relations – retain their relevance for feminist theory. Not only are we living in an era when a technological re-organisation of human reproduction is partially and may become fully possible, but the issues raised by early feminists have not been resolved.

Before going further it is necessary to describe the new reproductive technologies, including recent contraceptive developments.

Scientific developments and medical technologies

To look first at contraception, there are a number of new developments that are based on hormonal interventions as well as inter-uterine devices (IUDs), barrier methods such as the diaphragm, and sterilisation.

- The hormonal contraceptive pill is taken for a number of days each month. It ensures that the embryo does not attach to the lining of the womb and was developed through experimentation on Black women, particularly in Puerto Rico.
- Long-acting hormonal injections that last for three to six months are licensed in Britain and tend to be used on the most vulnerable women: that is, those deemed not sufficiently reliable to use other contraceptives. Working-class and Black women are more likely to be prescribed injections with Depo-Provera, which works by ensuring that the embryo does not attach to the lining of the womb.
- Hormonal implants that last up to five years were tested on women in Latin America and Asia, and although there was opposition, they were accepted for use in the USA and then Britain. The implants are surgically placed, usually in the upper arm, and cannot be removed without surgical intervention. These small hormonal rods slowly release hormones that stop the embryo from implanting in the womb. Now licensed in Britain, implants are more likely to be used on socially-vulnerable women.
- Hormonal abortifacients, such as the 'morning after' pill which is taken after unprotected sexual intercourse (RU486), have been developed. There are also various methods of surgical abortion involving both abdominal and vaginal interventions (Klein, Raymond and Dumble, 1991).
- Vaccination against pregnancy, the so-called immuno-contraceptives, are a new type of contraceptive that induces a reaction against reproductive or pregnancy-related hormones or against egg or sperm cells. This research and the ongoing trials, once again undertaken in Third World countries, are directed at women's bodies, although immuno-contraceptives could be aimed at the bodies of men (Richter, 1996).

As well as for contraception, there is a growing market for hormonal products and services to increase conception. Britain set up the first governmental committee worldwide to consider the new developments in conception and how they might be regulated. The UK Report on Human Fertilisation and Embryology (Warnock Report, 1984) focused on the following techniques and processes.

- Insemination by donor (AID) is a simple procedure in which sperm is introduced into a woman's vagina as close to her cervix as possible. This can easily be performed by a woman herself without a doctor or medical agency/clinic.
- IVF involves a number of procedures. First, hormones are administered to the woman to induce superovulation so that more than one ovum (or

egg) is produced during the monthly cycle. The ova (eggs) are removed surgically by one of several egg-collection procedures. The ova are then fertilised in a laboratory dish and reimplanted in the woman's body. GIFT is a variation of IVF, with the eggs replaced in the Fallopian tube with sperm so that fertilisation takes place there rather than in a laboratory dish.

- Egg or embryo transfer occurs when a woman receiving the ova or the embryo is not the same woman who provided them.
- Egg, sperm and embryo freezing are procedures for saving human genetic material that is surplus to immediate requirements.
- Embryo flushing or lavage is a procedure for washing out a woman's fertilised egg, or embryo, for diagnostic assessment or implantation in another woman, or for experimentation.
- Embryo experimentation involves using 'spare' embryos for research purposes legally, in Britain, for up to 14 days after fertilisation.
- Surrogacy involves a woman entering a contract to produce a child for someone else. She may be subjected to a number of interventions; such as artificial insemination, superovulation and IVF, and may use her own egg(s) or those of another woman.

The only technique discussed above that is unproblematic for women's health is artificial insemination (provided, of course, that the sperm used is not infected with HIV or sexually transmitted diseases). Hormonal stimulation and surgical interventions, including embryo flushing, involve both immediate and long-term health risks to the woman and/or her embryo/child (Holmes, 1989; Rosier, 1989; Rowland, 1992).

- Sex selection involves the identification of the sex of an already existing embryo. There are two basic processes to determine the sex of the embryo; as it develops in a woman's body through amniocentesis, a test of the fluid around the embryo in the sixteenth week, or a less-reliable test earlier on; or by screening an IVF embryo prior to entry into the woman's body. Abortion, or implanting the desired sex only, achieves sex selection. This is happening in Britain and is justified as medically necessary to eliminate certain genetic conditions. In India, amniocentesis followed by selective abortion is widely practised for social reasons in order to achieve the birth of sons, not daughters (Kishwar, 1985).

Other potential interventions that as yet have not received approval in the UK for their use with humans include the following:

- Transgenic species involves mixing the genetic material of different species, including potentially that of human and other animal life.

- Cloning involves splitting the early embryo into separate cells so that genetically identical individuals are produced.

These techniques are currently being used on life forms other than the human. It takes little imagination to understand, for example, the commercial profit to be made by producing via cloning and sex selection, high-milk-producing female calves for dairy and quality-meat producing male calves for beef herds.

Other developments yet to be achieved are outlined below.

- Sex predetermination is an attempt to obtain the desired sex prior to fertilisation of the egg. As the sex of the human species is determined by sperm, various methods of as yet dubious reliability for identifying X- and Y-carrying sperm are being used or are being developed in Britain and elsewhere.
- Ectogenesis will involve conception and pregnancy outside a woman's body in an artificial womb.

To sum up, the techniques and processes of concern to the first governmental committee to consider these issues, the UK Report on Human Fertilisation and Embryology (Warnock Report, 1984), were those that alter human conception through insemination by donor (AID) and IVF and related procedures, or genetic continuity through egg or embryo transfer; embryo, egg and semen freezing and storage; embryo experimentation; embryo flushing; sex selection; so-called surrogacy; and potential practices such as the creation of transgenic species, cloning and sex predetermination.

The Canadian Royal Commission on New Reproductive Technologies expanded the scientific, technical and social areas discussed in the Warnock Report. An extensive public consultation took place. The first of two final volumes reported on social values and attitudes towards technology and the new reproductive technologies, including infertility, prevalence, risks and treatments, while the second included commercial interests in the new reproductive technologies, pre-natal diagnosis and genetic technologies, gene therapy and genetic alteration, the use of foetal tissue and judicial intervention in pregnancy and birth (Royal Commission on New Reproductive Technologies, 1993). These new topics demonstrate rapid growth in reproductive interventions over the decade.

It is essential to look at the developments in genetics to understand fully the future potential of these technologies. Genetic counselling of adults and diagnosis of embryos are practices involving the identification of chromosomes or genes believed to be defective, and assessment, advice or selection based on the eugenic principle of reproducing genetically 'desirable' traits/ individuals. The possibilities for the genetic manipulation of embryos are increasing and the Human Genome Project is of direct relevance in the transformation of human reproduction (Ewing, 1988, 1990a; Kevles and

Hood, 1992). This is a multinational, multibillion dollar, project begun in 1990 to sequence human DNA and to identify all human genes by the year 2005.[1] Genetic counselling is a well established professional activity. The bringing together of reproductive technology and the science of genetics is illustrated by routine interventions in pregnancy, such as screening through amniocentesis and selective abortion of foetuses for particular conditions such as spina bifida. Many women are concerned that these interventions are signs of the growth of a new eugenics (Hanmer and van Wingerden, 1992, 1997). Historically eugenics is a belief in biological superiority and inferiority of peoples of so-called races and of individuals on the basis of physical characteristics related to able-bodiedness. The old eugenics expressed itself through mass murder of Jews and other groups in Germany in the Second World War, and through race hygiene laws in a number of other Western countries (Chorover, 1980; Lifton, 1986). These led to compulsory sterilisations of women, particularly amongst those who were poor or Black or who had learning or physical disabilities. The major argument used by those currently in favour of genetic interventions in reproduction is that the decision to undergo tests and selective abortion is an individual choice, not an action required by the state. Those who define current genetic-based practices and future possibilities as the new eugenics challenge both the social reality of 'free choice' and the role of social forces and institutions, such as science, medicine, law and government, in creating the present situation.

Feminist critiques of the new technologies and genetics

In the West, the birth-control movement was influenced by eugenic ideas and their political expression, as well as being a grass-roots movement to help women space their children in order to protect their health (Gordon, 1977). This double edge of control by women and of women by the state remains an unresolved issue today. Feminist critiques of contraceptive techniques, especially hormonal methods and IUDs, abortifacients, sterilisation, new reproductive technologies and genetic engineering increased during the 1980s.[2] Critical arguments centre on the social experiences of women and the social structures in which gender relations are embedded, contesting the truthfulness of claims of safety for both contraceptives and interventions in conception and, even more basic, of reproductive science as infertility treatment. These arguments offer an alternative analysis that links the technologies of contraception with those of conception on both a practical and a theoretical basis. The same hormonal products in differing combinations are used both to create and to eliminate pregnancy, and the power relations promoting pronatalism mirror those that deliver population control. This developing international analysis challenges the positive claims made by reproductive science and medicine, and the ideological justifications and social forces through which the technologies are directed at women's bodies.

One critique of these technologies challenges the notion of choice for women by arguing that the pressures on women to have children, but only when it is socially acceptable to do so, are so great that it is ridiculous to speak of choice. Women are seen as having no option about whether or not to have babies. They must be prepared to go through any emotional and physical pain, distress and effort to achieve a successful pregnancy. Motherhood is socially compulsory, even in countries with coercive population control policies. This is not the same as arguing that women are passive robots who do not know their own minds; it is because their 'choices' are highly circumscribed.

The new reproductive technologies are used to uphold traditional notions of motherhood and femininity via the selection of those who should or should not be mothers. While contraception and abortion can be seen to play the same social role, until the recent advent of fully medically-controlled contraceptives, many women in the West and North felt they were largely in charge of reproductive decisions. Women in the South and East have been subjected to contraception, including sterilisation, for some years, in conditions that cannot be described as free choice. As in the West, the social factors of class, 'race' and ethnicity, and male domination determine differential treatment of women.

In Britain, we see these social forces at play with the new reproductive technologies; women who are not dependent on men are largely deemed to be unacceptable for motherhood by the medical gatekeepers and the state: that is, lesbians, virgins and women not in stable cohabiting relations with men. Also, the technologies tend to be expensive, with access usually limited to those who can afford to pay or whom doctors deem acceptable for NHS treatment. Restricted access is damaging to women as a group, as it creates divisions between women and reaffirms the patriarchal rule that husbands or male partners and fathers have unrestricted authority over women and children. But in terms of individual experiences, limiting access can be a protection against psychological and physical abuse as the documenting of women's experiences of IVF programmes demonstrate (Crowe, 1985; Williams, 1988, 1990, 1991; Klein, 1989, 1990; Fleischer, 1990; Koch, 1990).

Women's 'choices' to pursue IVF and related technologies are shaped by a variety of factors, including the expectations and demands of others amongst women's families and friends; the presentation of the technologies by medical staff as unproblematic; and, by implication, likely to lead to a child. Clinics, particularly commercial clinics, use a variety of techniques to encourage women to enter programmes (for example, open days) and to continue with programmes, such as newsletters organised by patients in which women tell their stories of repeated attempts and determination to not give up, or support groups with similar aims. Women rarely receive counselling on how they could have a fulfilling life without producing their own biological child.

While hormonal conception contains health risks for women, it is largely reliable. But the new reproductive technologies do not offer as effective a means of having babies as is implied in the media and claimed by medical teams. In the first investigation of success rates, Gena Corea and Susan Ince (1987) found that clinics in the USA (as elsewhere) were including chemical pregnancies (that is, a rise in a woman's blood levels of certain hormones for several days only); pregnancies that spontaneously abort; and still births, as well as living babies. Because the latter is the way in which people in general understand, and therefore interpret, claims of success, the charge is misrepresentation (Klein, 1989).

Registers of children conceived by IVF and associated techniques have been set up in a number of countries, but the National Perinatal Statistics Unit in Australia was the first to report on the worse health outcomes for children born by IVF (Batman, 1988). These include prematurity (26.9 per cent in 1986); delivery by caesarean section (43.9 per cent compared with 15–18 per cent of pregnancies generally); an increase in multiple births and medical problems associated with low birth weight and prematurity; a higher percentage of babies with major abnormalities, primarily neural tube (spina bifida) and cardiac problems (transposition of the great vessels) at 2.2 per cent rather than 1.5 per cent of births generally. The Australian Report concluded that the success rate for an unproblematic live birth was 4.8 per cent: that is, fewer than 5 women from each 100 who undergo IVF would have a completely healthy baby, while another 3 women would have a child with health problems. The remaining 92 per cent would not have a child. Even these success rates are open to challenge, as cases have been reported of women who conceive naturally before their turn for IVF treatment arrives, and even of a child being born who was conceived naturally along with two others inserted through IVF techniques.

The British 'success' rates are very similar. The Voluntary Licensing Authority for Human in Vitro Fertilisation and Embryology (VLA) in 1989 cited the live birth rate per treatment cycle in 1987 as 10.1 per cent; in 1986, 8.6 per cent and 1985, also 8.6 per cent (VLA, 1989, p. 19). Small centres in the UK were identified as achieving 3.1 per cent live births per treatment cycle (VLA, 1989, p. 19), and some clinics had never produced an IVF baby. Their success rate was zero, yet they continue to advertise their services to the public and to intervene in women's bodies as if this were not the case. Described as failed technology, there are demands for its cessation (Klein, 1989), but in Britain the state has responded by setting up a licensing authority for IVF centres and research. The success rates for live births have not increased substantially in the 1990s.

Another line of attack criticises the new reproductive technologies for being about something very different from what is claimed; not about helping women to have children, but rather being an aspect of genetic engineering closely associated with new developments in biotechnology (Bartels, 1988; Shiva, 1988; Hynes, 1989a, 1989b, 1989c; Kollek, 1990). This includes the attempt to map the entire gene pool, beginning with the Human Genome Project, to 'improve' human embryos through genetic testing and ultimately adding and subtracting genetic material (Kaufmann, 1988; Leuzinger and Rambert, 1988). Modifying and eliminating people before birth gives a new twist to eugenics (Bridenthal, Grossman and Kaplan, 1984; Ewing, 1988; Kaupen-Haas, 1988; Degener, 1990; Schleiermacher, 1990; Zimmerman, 1990). It can also be seen to be about men as a class taking control of women's reproductive activities as husbands/male partners/fathers; scientists/medical practitioners; businessmen; and governmental leaders (Hanmer, 1981, 1983, 1985; Hanmer and Allen, 1980). For example, in India there is growing resistance by women to the expanding use of amniocentesis to detect female foetuses, followed by abortion (Patel, 1989; Lingam, 1990; Rothman, 1993).

These critiques also analyse the differential interventions into the bodies of women in the South and East, and the North and West, and find common ground. An analysis of the ways in which governments, aid agencies to the so-called Third World and multinational pharmaceutical companies are intermeshed is slowly gaining momentum, particularly in relation to population-control activities (McDonnell, 1986; Nair, 1989; International Solidarity for Safe Contraception, 1990; Gupta, 1991; UBINIG, 1991b; Akhter 1992; Hartmann, 1994). In Britain, the provision of IVF and other new reproductive technologies is dominated by commercial interests. Bourn Hallam, the largest reproductive technology centre in the world, is owned by the multinational pharmaceutical company, Ares Serono. Ares Serono manufactures, wholesales and, with Bourn Hallam, retails hormonal and other products to women. Bourn Hallam also serves as a research and development centre for Ares Serono, the major world producer of fertility drugs.

A survey of women's perspectives on the ethical, social and legal implications and applications of the human genome analysis was undertaken in the then twelve nations of the EU (Hanmer and van Wingerden, 1992, 1997). Women have both gender-neutral and gender-sensitive views on the Human Genome Project. Gender-sensitive views see women and men as differentially affected by the applications of the project and/or consider women to be more affected than men. The gender-sensitive perspective is visible in six areas of concern: issues for carriers, parenting, reproductive processes, pre-implantation screening, embryo research, reproductive control and autonomy. Gender-neutral approaches are based on a social justice model. This perspective raised a number of issues of concern in the following areas: the organisation and processes of scientific activity; the role of regulation and legislation in the control of science, scientists and scientific products; the lack of information and education for the general public on the human genome analysis; democracy and decision-making. Women were critical and, while there was support for the human genome analysis a cautious approach coupled with limited expectations for effective state control predominated. Women were more likely to fear that genetic development would restrict their personal reproductive control and autonomy rather than increase it.

Conceptualising science, ethics and a woman-centred analysis

Robert Edwards, a key figure in the development of the new reproductive technologies, argued in his popularising work on IVF after the birth of the world's first 'test-tube' baby, Louise Brown, that IVF is medical treatment for infertility (Edwards and Steptoe, 1980). In his later popular work he defended the social desirability of surrogacy and embryo experimentation (Edwards, 1989). These issues may at first sight appear unrelated, but what they have in common is the redefinition of motherhood (Chesler, 1988; Rothman, 1989; Bartels *et al.*, 1990).

Many women are afraid to object to embryo experimentation, whatever their private misgivings, as their greater fear is that to do so will endanger the 'rights' of women to abortion. The reasoning is that if embryos and foetuses up to 20 weeks can be aborted, then there is no logical reason why embryos cannot be experimented upon. From this perspective, to protect embryos from experimentation necessitates protecting embryos and foetuses from abortion. The argument is framed around the concept of 'right to life'.

Edwards too made these connections, but in a different way. He justified embryo experimentation because experimentation on foetal material obtained through abortion is routine, and has been for many years (Edwards, 1989, p. 148). With regulatory guidelines introduced by the state he saw no difficulty in obtaining the full range of foetal material for experimentation, as 'Most studies in vitro can be completed by day 25, and after that the current rules for using tissues from aborted foetuses will suffice. So the time of research in dispute is really very small indeed' (1989, p. 173). The time in dispute is becoming smaller as the new abortive drug, RU486, enables embryonic tissue to become available at 18 to 20 days.

Edwards also dismissed criticisms of embryo experimentation as a new form for the expression of eugenics, or selective breeding. Edwards distinguished between negative and positive eugenics, defining negative eugenics as avoiding the birth of children with defects while positive eugenics is making children superior by changing their characteristics. Eugenics embody value judgements about which types of people and which character-istics are to be preserved and promoted, and which are to be eliminated. In societies dominated by social inequalities, it is inevitable that women, Black people, the disabled, and the poor will be less valued, and that certain physical, mental, personal or social characteristics will be classified as undesirable. Given the implementation of eugenics in Western history it is foolish to imagine that in medicine the line between what is ethical and what is not is clearly demarcated (Chorover, 1980; Lifton, 1986; Hanmer and van Wingerden, 1992, 1997). There are ethically dubious practices taking place in medicine today. For example, the media gave a high profile to a number of issues during the 1990s, such as the debate over post-menopausal mothers conceiving through IVF; the destruction of embryos after the maximum storage date is reached; and the use of embryos for experimental purposes.

IVF is a painful and stressful procedure with low success rates that is applied to fertile as well as infertile women. Male fertility problems are routinely being dealt with by submitting fertile women to these procedures as well as women whose condition remains undiagnosed. Women with children who have undergone sterilisation and later remarry are viewed as appropriate candidates for IVF. There is a tendency within society generally to dismiss the vulnerability of women to men, as biological reproduction becomes progressively under their control, as being negative, or pessimistic, or 'science fiction'. But given these practices we can deduce a social belief that men own women's reproductive function. The social rule is that each woman must produce biological children for a particular man should he so wish it.

Control of women's reproductive processes can be exercised in other ways, however. The most extreme scenario that has been considered is to phase out women altogether or to keep just a few as 'queen bees' for their eggs. Women will become redundant to the process of creating new life once immature eggs (for example, foetal eggs) can be matured, and ectogensis becomes a reality. Less extreme future visions retain women in more-or-less their present numbers to caretake the results of the biological manufacture of human beings to exact specification. Science and technology are systems of social relations resonating with power differentials. We must face the fact that, given the power and interests of men in science and society, those who decide on what is desirable in relation to human reproduction are unlikely to be those most affected (that is, women).

The central contradiction of these developments is that the new repro-ductive technologies are presented as a return to the natural, while replacing a biological activity with technology. Doing this challenges the naturalness of biological processes while claiming to restore to every woman her natural nature. The Warnock Report, for example, did this by justifying the technologies as a response to infertility, even though the report did not consider the causes of infertility, or available and needed infertility services

(Humm, 1988; Pfeffer and Quick, 1988; Solomon, 1988; Rowland, 1992; Raymond, 1993).

Rights, choice and self-determination for women

The struggle of women to claim a personhood that is more than 'nature' or 'natural' pre-dates the French Revolution, with its demands for individual rights. Rights, nature and the natural are shifting terrain in relation to the definition of woman; in particular, in relation to women as wives/heterosexual partners, mothers and sexual beings. More recently these issues have been expressed as a central demand of the post-1968 wave of feminism for control over our bodies through the prescient slogan 'Our Bodies – Ourselves'.

Being a wife, heterosexual and a mother are relational statuses to men. The socially validated uses of the new reproductive technologies illustrate that our relation to men is more fundamental to society than women's relation to the future generation and their specific biological children. The primacy of the relation of these statuses to men surfaces in the re-emergence of demands and legislation around 'fathers' rights' (Stolcke, 1988; Raymond, 1993); in the ways in which women become invisible or are reduced to body parts when the state considers the new reproductive technologies; by the dissociation of embryos and foetuses from women's bodies through so-called 'foetal rights'; in the demands for embryos for experimentation; and in the social opposition to so-called virgin births or lesbian motherhood.

While 'wifehood' as a biological need – that is, to ensure mental and physical healthy functioning – is being denied, and heterosexuality as a natural system is being questioned by feminists, to do so can be seen as leaving women vulnerable (Richardson, 1996e). Andrea Dworkin (1987) argued that Right-wing women understand only too well that to challenge wifehood is to make women vulnerable to servicing not just one man but many, and to economic poverty. Feminists resist these vulnerabilities by demanding a better position for women in the labour market and in society generally, rather than strengthening the idea that being a wife is a natural facet of being female.

With motherhood, however, the issues are not so simple or so well worked out. Not having children was a feminist political issue in the 1970s. Within the women's liberation movement women argued that putting time and energy into other women and feminists were priorities, while others saw this as being anti-mothers. The so-called need to mother can be more complicated for women to confront than any other aspect of life. As with being a wife, it is constructed through heterosexuality as a system of social relations. Within heterosexuality, the issue is seen as contraception, abortion, the sterilisation of women with learning difficulties, eliminating pregnancies by teenagers and unmarried women, or spacing children so that 'every child is a wanted child'; the 'problem' is to control the fertility of women, not men. The hidden agenda is that women remain sexually available to men at all times through the regulation of their fertility and its outcome: pregnancy and birth. Women's fertility is seen as a problem to be addressed through international population control policies – sometimes urging women to have children and sometimes denying women the ability to have children – and not the difficulties women have in controlling the access of men to their bodies. The 'need' to mother and the heterosexuality on which it is based is rarely challenged, but only when, where, how and with whom, as not only are women the biology to be controlled, we are also believed simply to *be* our biology, and therefore we must have children. The media hype is of perfect babies for perfect, and grateful, heterosexual couples.

It is because of the general acceptance of women as their biology, and as the biology to be controlled, that the new reproductive technologies can be presented successfully as a choice for women (Raymond, 1996). The political position that centres on rights is not unlike that of the mainstream because of the strength of the heterosexual belief that women must be available to men, and the pronatalism that permeates all our Western societies, although the arguments take a different form. Surrogacy, for example, can be seen as a way of strengthening women's rights, including the rights of the gestational mother. The view is that surrogacy contracts should be legally enforceable, even if the gestating mother changes her mind, because these contracts recognise legal parenthood as a matter of autonomous decision-making before conception. Money payments should be permitted to gestating mothers because in the resulting transformation of reproductive consciousness male-female biological differences will be transcended and women can reclaim their procreative power (Cohen and Taub, 1989; Shalev, 1989). All the technologies can be seen as unproblematic if the issue of power is not acknowledged; for example, Peter Singer and Deane Wells (1984) argued for new ways of making babies as an unqualified benefit, as choice is being extended. They defined any curtailment of access and future developments (for example, of ectogenesis) as an act of paternalism.

The degree of criticism of science and technology in human reproduction also affects feminist views on the new developments and leads to more positive assessments, albeit with reservations (Stanworth, 1987; Birke, Himmelweit and Vines, 1990; Rose, 1994). If science and technology are seen as neutral, the issue then becomes the social uses to which they are put. To avoid negative outcomes, it is argued that new developments in reproductive technologies require regulation by law, ethical professional practices, and informed consent by the users of the techniques. Meeting these requirements can be thought to provide the necessary safeguards to ensure that technology and science are constructive social forces. The Canadian Royal Commission on New Reproductive Technologies has gone further than any other governmental initiative in exploring these criteria (1993).

Mothers' rights and fathers' rights

The respective 'rights' of women and men in relation to biological reproduction is under constant dispute, and the new reproductive technologies offer opportunities for significant changes. In human reproduction the interests of women and men are not identical, and the physical processes of conception, gestation and birth do not affect women and men in the same way. But how are these differences to be understood? There are two strands to consider. The first is the denaturalising of motherhood through increased medical and scientific intervention in the processes of conception, pregnancy and birth, while utilising an ideology of women's nature as justification for these interventions. Naturalising fatherhood through these same interventions, utilising the ideology of the central importance of the male genetic contribution, is the second.

Mary O'Brien developed a theoretical explanation around these issues by reinterpreting the work of G. W. F. Hegel and Karl Marx on the natural and nature (O'Brien, 1981, 1989). She argued that in childbirth women labour, transforming biological reproduction (the natural) into a human activity. Men do not labour in the same way, as the ejaculation of sperm is the sole contribution to biological reproduction. Mary O'Brien argued that they are alienated at the point of biological reproduction because they do not labour. If we accept this as a premise, it is logical to argue that science and medical technology can become the social process by which men attempt to overcome their alienation. As men labour through science and technology with biological reproduction, of necessity they conflate nature and the natural with women's bodies. The outcome of this fusion is that it is women who are to be transformed as they become the 'natural nature' on which men work. The new reproductive technologies do not alienate men, but overcome their alienation by enabling them to control 'natural nature', while the new reproductive technologies increase women's alienation by intervening with the work process in which women are engaged, as they turn a natural biological process into a social activity, the production of new life. In the shift in alienation from men to women, social power between men and women also shifts. Men gain, women lose.

Mary O'Brien has been criticised by some feminists for producing theory rooted in biology, but the commodifying of things and life processes is structurally related to capitalism and the societies in which it has developed. It is logical in a capitalist economic system that human reproduction and all life processes should be turned into commodities, as ownership is the highest social goal of the individual. However, these same social relations of science and medical technology also were being developed in previous socialist societies in relation to women's bodies and life processes generally. This is because any economic system can restructure its ideology in order to serve its economy and power structures. Gender domination varies its forms as societies alter over time, and it is only now, in the latter part of the twentieth century, becoming possible to intensify control over women through highly-developed technologies based on reproductive biology.

Denaturalising motherhood while naturalising fatherhood begins with the discourse on the new reproductive technologies. This is so powerfully organised that oppositional views are marginalised or totally excluded from public debate. In Britain, it has been particularly difficult to gain popular media attention for viewpoints that challenge the new reproductive technologies as infertility interventions. The media exposure can only be described as free advertising, as smiling IVF doctors and couples with babies, and heart-rending stories of surrogacy, epitomise the coverage. These representations draw primary strength from a particular view of women, whose need to mother is unquestionable.

Reducing women to biology facilitates our social disappearance. These basic assumptions enable government reports, beginning with the Warnock Report in the UK (Warnock Report, 1984), to not mention women, but to write of disembodied parts of women's bodies or of couples. The discourse is of technical processes, in which the differences between the contribution to and impact upon women and men inherent in the new reproductive technologies is absent. When bodies appear it is as couples who make equal contributions to biological reproduction. It is becoming common parlance, for example, to hear of 'pregnant couples'.

Dismembering bodies and reconstituting them in new forms enable embryos to be seen as separate from the women in whose bodies they thrive. Embryo research can then be presented as not affecting women differently from men. The foetus becomes an independent subject whose interests can be defined as in opposition to that of its mother, and further, it may become necessary to protect the foetus from a hostile maternal environment. The arguments can then rage on about when embryos become sufficiently human to be legally granted an independent existence. The embryo as part of the mother, subjectively and objectively, is disengaged, and mothers' rights and fathers' rights cannot be differentiated. (These points also apply to the abortion debate.)

Another form of supposed biological equality between women and men is to equate sperm collection for donor insemination with egg retrieval. The very obvious difference in the methods of obtaining eggs and sperm, however, make it less easy to obscure their different meanings for women and men in terms of health outcomes, bodily interventions, and the commitment of time, energy and psychological resources. Equating selling eggs with selling sperm is less likely to gain social acceptability, as the unsuccessful libel action brought by an IVF doctor in Austria against women who objected to his egg-buying illustrates (Riegler and Weikert, 1988; Riegler, 1989).

A number of important legal actions to regulate the relationships between women, men and their reproductive biologies arising from the new reproductive technologies were brought in 1989. The rights of individual men as well as men as a social group began to be strengthened through legal actions brought by individual men, and through legislation arising out of government reports and European agreements. Individual men began to demand more 'rights' to 'their' children generally (for example, custody and control of children who have been born) and these are receiving legislative support (Hester and Radford, 1996). Legal actions to require women to carry foetuses to full term were first brought in the UK in 1989 (*Observer*, 30 July 1989). Although this legal action was unsuccessful, there are other ways in which men are demanding more control over whether or not 'their' children can be born. For example, again 1989 saw the first custody action in the USA over frozen embryos (the woman wanted to use them but the estranged husband refused on the grounds that his wife wanted to make him a father against his will); this illustrates the extension of legal control in disputes between women and men over children (*Daily Telegraph*, 8 August 1989). The legal arguments are important as they raise fundamental issues about the social construction of the relationship between women, men and their biological reproduction.

The competing claims in the American case tuned on the physical and social impact on women and men of the new technologies. The woman argued that the embryos represented more than eight years of tests and surgery, and a test-tube baby was her only chance of having a child. The man said that it would be 'very unsettling' to bump into his child without knowing it in ten years' time. His lawyer argued that the embryos were joint property to be disposed of like any other assets in a divorce, while hers appealed to tradition based on biology: 'It has never been within the man's power to cancel a pregnancy once an egg has been fertilised' (*Daily Telegraph*, 8 August 1989). Expert witness and law professor comment was that the husband would be the most hurt by losing, and therefore the case should be decided in his favour. The ultimate judgement turned on a principle that disempowers women even though she won the case and was allowed to implant the embryos: that of embryo rights, that is, the right-to-life argument. This disempowers women because embryos are given an existence independent of the maternal environment, even though they cannot at the present time become a child without it.

These individual legal actions are located within the law relating to disputes between women and men over children. For example, when divorce is legally contested, men are likely to extinguish a mother's 'natural' rights, even to very young children. The 'rights' of unmarried men, sperm donors even, began to be established and a woman's 'right' to abortion without the man's permission began to be contested in 1989 (*Observer*, 30 July 1989). These new 'rights' are being gained in a social situation where it is extremely difficult to extinguish a man's rights of access to 'his' children. Men are not expected to take responsibility for the day-to-day care of children. Theirs is a right based on authority, so even a man who kills his wife may be given custody of her children once out of prison. As the exposure of male abuse in families grows, so too does the counter-attack. In Britain, 'Families Need Fathers', and similar organisations of men, vociferously argue that harm is being done to men and to children by the 'unfair' treatment men receive in courts. The attack is on women's 'privileged' position in relation to children.

Law and legislative issues include the development of contract law to severely limit or extinguish women's rights to their biological children, beginning with US surrogacy cases (Raymond, 1988a, 1988b, 1993; Rowland, 1992). In Britain, commercial surrogacy is not legally permitted, but expenses can be paid. Contracts are not legally enforceable, but the Human Fertilisation and Embryology Act 1990 makes it possible to treat a child born as a result of a surrogacy arrangement as the child of the commissioning parents, even though the surrogate mother is the legal mother at birth. In Britain, IVF clinics engage in surrogacy, in secrecy, protected by the courts (*Re* W (Minors) (Surrogacy), 1991).

In the USA the contract takes precedence over a woman's wishes: so if a woman, prior to artificial insemination, has agreed to hand over the child she will gestate, courts will not subsequently allow her to keep the child. With the passage of the 1990 Human Fertilisation and Embryology Act in Britain, this outcome became enforceable in British courts. For example, in 1996 a woman tried through legal action to reverse a surrogacy agreement without success (*The Sunday Times*, 20 June 1996). A single parent with four children who needed the £8000 paid for 'expenses', and with feelings of altruism, allowed herself to be inseminated with the sperm of the man who, with his wife, ultimately legally obtained the child. This case mirrors precisely that of Mary Beth Whitehead, the first US surrogacy case a decade earlier, including the extreme distress experienced by the biological mother. Surrogacy is reconceptualised as a new form of trafficking in women (Raymond, 1993).

The rights of women to their illegitimate children is also changing in Britain. In the past, the threat of non-recognition of the child by the father was an important social and economic control regulating biological reproduction through marriage. As this status becomes less stigmatised, and as the proportion of illegitimate births continues to rise, unmarried men are being given the same rights to children that married men have. This is legally codified within Europe as a result of a Council of Europe agreement, and in Britain via the Children Act 1991.

Spain was the first European country to legislate on the new reproductive technologies, with the Law on Technologies for Assisted Reproduction, 1988 (Varela and Stolcke, 1989). This law substantially implements the recommendations of the UK Warnock Report, although discriminatory treatment of single women was modified so that any woman able to work independently of her marital status and her lifestyle is deemed to be suitable for IVF and other interventions. But, if married, the consent of her husband is required. 'Medical tourism' to obtain access to new reproductive technologies results from differential laws. The introduction of uniform legislation in EU member states is likely (Winkler, 1996).

In Britain legislation arising out of the Warnock Report, the 1990 Human Fertilisation and Embryology Act, means that the consent of husbands and cohabitees is necessary for women to have access to IVF and other treatments, and effectively limits IVF, artificial insemination and other interventions in conception to married or stable cohabiting heterosexual couples. Fathers' rights are clearly specified in the Act.[3] The legislative attempt to criminalise the use of AID for single and lesbian women, however, failed, possibly because of feminist opposition, the difficulty in implementing any such law and the likelihood of its challenge in the European Court of Human Rights.

International feminism: an agenda for the new millennium

We are living in a time of increasing scientific and medical intervention in women's bodies. So-called Third World women are sterilised and given contraceptives dangerous to their health, while 'First World' women are expected to have babies (Parsons, 1990). The Norplant trials in Bangladesh provided one of many examples of coercive population policy activities, in which women were used for experimental purposes without their consent, and 'motivated' to accept the five-year hormonal implants without basic knowledge of the problems that may result and, once these were evident, requests to remove the implants were refused (Akhter, 1988; UBINIG, 1990, 1991b; Reis, 1990).[4] Within 'First World' countries, the same pattern exists between ethnic and racial groups. Thus in Britain, for example, it is easier to get a free NHS abortion if a woman is Black and working class, and much more difficult if white and middle class, although for any individual, sufficient funds to obtain a private-sector abortion will override this problem. 'Race' and ethnicity, sexuality, social class, disability and age converge to weight women's chances of being selected as a 'fit' or 'unfit' reproducer, and a range of techniques are being utilised to ensure the appropriate outcome (Wichterich, 1988).

Surrogacy provides another way in which working-class women serve higher social classes and men (Kane, 1988, 1989; Arditti, 1990; Ewing, 1990b; Rowland, 1990, 1992). The well-reported Mary Beth Whitehead case in the USA, was of a working-class woman who entered a surrogacy contract for altruistic reasons. As her pregnancy advanced and with the birth of her daughter, she resolved to keep the child, but lost her legal case to the middle-class professional man who provided the sperm. Mary Beth Whitehead gave birth to an illegitimate child, but the use of contract law enabled her position as a mother to be largely denied.

Now that it is possible to implant an embryo genetically unrelated to the mother who gives birth, her claims upon the child are likely to be further eroded. In the USA, surrogacy agencies speak of the reproductive use of Black and 'Third World' women as surrogates by economically and socially dominant white people (Raymond, 1989; 1993). The lower fees needed for the reproductive use (abuse) of women from countries of the South and East will spur on this development. In Australia, as well as the USA, surrogacy is being publicly opposed by women, including feminists (Ewing, 1990b; Rowland, 1992; Raymond, 1993).

Women contribute more biologically and socially to the origin and care of children than do men. It is a false equality to attempt to eradicate these physiological and social differences by ideological fiat. Any discussion of ethics which does not recognise these basic factors can only be experienced by women as negative, as denying the basis from which ethical choices are made. But the recognition of difference is not to collapse women into the category of the natural or nature. With respect to the sperm-providing male, a woman's interests may be interlinked with his, but different. Her immediate task is the protection and creation of new life within her body. The male cannot do this and therefore the interests of women and men are different. Mary O'Brien (1981) argued that this is why genetic lineage matters so significantly for the Western male, and was in the past so important in regulating women's sexuality. Ideologically, for a woman-centred perspective to be taken seriously, the masculinist discourse of the various national reports on the new reproductive technologies and embryology must be seen as one-sided, and not representing the interests of women/mothers.

For women to control their reproductive processes, the importance of the power difference between women and men needs to be recognised. For women, choice can only have meaning if women are able to control the access of men to their bodies, and I mean this in a very general sense. This is a general point that arises out of the subordination of women so that, for example, in many countries the law decrees that rape in marriage is not a crime. Ideologically and legally, a woman cannot restrict her husband's access to her body. He can take that which the law defines as rightfully his by force if the woman attempts to deny him. Even in those countries and states where rape in marriage is now recognised as a crime, the prosecution of offenders and the success of these prosecutions is greatly reduced in comparison with stranger rape, because socially it is not fully accepted as crime. Translated into reproductive technology, this difficulty in denying men access to women's bodies is illustrated powerfully through the progressive utilisation of the bodies of fertile women to enable male subfertility to be overcome through IVF.

When a leading North American surrogacy agency was driven out of Germany, women in Europe have shown that it is possible to confront the development of surrogacy and win (Winkler, 1988), but what of embryo research? To resolve how to defend abortion while opposing embryo research is a central issue. Holding both positions at the same time only makes sense when the relationship between the growing cells that will become a child, and the woman who will become a mother, is acknowledged, and neither mother nor embryo is objectified.

While not all feminists object to embryo experimentation and demand that abortion be fully available to all women at any time during pregnancy, the objectification of the embryo/foetus that is implicitly involved in this position is damaging to women's civil status. *Roe* v. *Wade*, the US Supreme Court decision that gave women an unrestricted right to abortion in the first three months, lesser rights in the next three, and no right to abortion in the last three, was hailed a victory by both pro- and anti-abortionists, as it gave women limited rights to abortion as well as establishing the foetus as a person. Legal cases, including that of the frozen embryos described earlier, are now being decided on a principle that disempowers women; that is, that the embryo equals a child. While this can mean that women are allowed to gestate their embryos, the woman becomes an incubator: the subject is the embryo. The principle of foetal personhood is being used to legitimate the artificial split between the woman and her body part, the embryo. The frozen embryo case, for example, could have turned on the principle that the embryo is a part of the mother's body, and therefore hers to gestate or not as the case may be, while a child is a person viable in the environment and separate from the woman's body.

The defence of safe, legal abortion under women's control turns on the same principle. It is not sufficient to reverse the argument defining the embryo as object and woman as subject as this implicitly accepts the split between us. The dynamic relationship between embryo and woman, and her responsibility for the interior growth of the resulting child and, more likely than not, her continued responsibility for its survival and development once born, must be acknowledged. It is these responsibilities that should determine her sole authority to continue or not with the pregnancy. That the state should legally sever women's control over her embryonic material by legally granting the right to others to experiment upon it should be a matter of concern to women. Legislation that protects embryos, degrading women to the status of foetal environment, as in Germany in 1991, is one possible way to further women's social subordination (Roach, 1989; Sadrozinski, 1989; Waldschmidt, 1991).

Women who seek to challenge this dismembering discourse are trying to enter a game with three players; scientists/doctors; theologians; and lawyers.

A feminist, woman-centred perspective is excluded rigorously, as it demands a fundamental re-ordering of knowledge, an epistemology in which woman is subject, her body whole, in one piece with the growing cells that will become a child. Ethical choice can have no meaning for women if our subjectivity is not recognised. The ethical issue for women is how to transform the dominant ethical discourse and practice in order to regain our bodies for ourselves. It can be argued that to control the access of men and their so-called ethics to our bodies is the central problem for women today. The major issue is the dissection of the female body into discrete parts, ideologically and literally, and specifically the severing of the relationship between the embryo and the womb (Mies, 1988; Rowland, 1992). This is central for yet another reason: the social acceptance of the severing of the embryo from the woman is necessary for the next stages of scientific endeavour, genetic manipulation and ectogenesis. Once achieved, new possibilities for reshaping gendered dominance will then be fully realisable and, while the precise form this will take is not predetermined, we currently have no grounds for thinking women will be responding to events other than from a continuing position of social subordination.

Scientists are working on the artificial womb and have made significant progress (*The Sunday Times*, 11 August 1996). The work on human gestation is being carried out by an Anglo-Japanese team in Japan for fear of ethical objections if it were located in Britain. While success in rearing premature foetuses and ultimately embryos to full term outside the mother's body is still thought to be a few years away, animal experimentation led in 1996 to the full-term gestation of an immature goat foetus in a tank of artificial amniotic fluid. The ideological justifications for the artificial womb are being rehearsed in national media; 'gestation tanks would eliminate the emotional trauma of "rent a womb" surrogacy', they would 'save very premature babies that might otherwise die' and 'women [could] have children without the burden of carrying their babies through pregnancy' (*Sunday Times*, 11 August 1996). The potential of ectogenesis in furthering reproductive control of women by men was raised by feminists in the early days of the women's liberation movement (Hanmer and Allen, 1980).

The Feminist International Network of Resistance to Reproductive and Genetic Engineering (FINRRAGE) emerged in 1984, with growing awareness among some feminists that it was time to question the assumption that older and newer forms of contraceptives, the new reproductive technologies and genetic engineering are neutral or even benign (Hanmer and Powell-Jones, 1984; Wichterich, 1988). FINRRAGE links women with common concerns and viewpoints from countries in the North and in the South; from both the so-called First and Third Worlds. Women work within their countries choosing priorities for issues and activities suited to their specific situations, such as critical grass-roots investigation or academic research; providing information to women and the general public; lobbying;

promoting cultural and political forms of opposition; and establishing alternatives for women, for example, counselling or self-help groups.

FINRRAGE seeks to develop a global movement of feminist resistance to population control policies and reproductive and genetic engineering, while confronting the issues that divide women because of differences in their social, economic, political and cultural situations. As with women from the North and West, women from the South and East also have differing politics on population control and the new reproductive technologies. From time to time international meetings, such as the United Nations Conference on Population held in Cairo in 1995, followed by the United Nations Decade for Women Conference held in Beijing in 1995, bring women together from non-governmental organisations to exchange information and to strategise. Women's international meetings are important occasions for both dissent and agreement. Women's experiences of (and attitudes towards) reproductive technologies differ between as well as within countries, and sharing knowledge and participating in confrontations between opposing viewpoints can increase consciousness and move theory and politics forward. These occasions can result in the development of common strategies and analyses with women worldwide (Salomone, 1991; UBINIG, 1991a, 1996).

Crucial issues in the new millennium include women continuing to organise themselves to refuse the new eugenics and the racism, anti-semitism, heterosexism and able-bodiedism on which the new reproductive and genetic technologies are built; to resist the extension of the division of women into body parts, objectified and reduced to the carriers of male genetic material, the beneficiaries of the smiling, whitecoated 'fathers' of hundreds of IVF babies that we see in newspapers and on television; and to build a responsive politics by listening to those whose bodies constitute the prime experimental matter for the control and replication of life processes.

Notes

1. To keep up to date with the latest developments, there are a number of sources for the non-specialist to pursue; for example, the journals *Science* and *Nature*; and in-house publications such as *Human Genome News*, sponsored by the US Department of Energy and the National Institute of Health.
2. Arditti, Klein and Minden (1984); Baruch, D'Adamo and Seager (1988); Conseil du Statut de la Femme (1988); Corea (1985); Corea *et al.* (1985); Hanmer (1981, 1983, 1985); Hanmer and Allen (1980); Hartmann (1987); Homans (1985); Holmes, Hoskins and Gross (1981); Hubbard (1990); *IRAGE* and *RAGE*, all issues; Kirejczyk (1990); McNeil, Varcoe and Yearley (1990); Overall (1987); Spallone (1988); Spallone and Steinberg (1987); Scutt (1988); and Stanworth (1987).

3. The Human Fertilisation and Embryology Act 1990 specifies in Section 1.3.5, 'Conditions of licences for treatment', that 'A woman shall not be provided with treatment services unless account has been taken of the welfare of any child who may be born as a result of the treatment (including the need of that child for a father), and of any other child who may be affected by the birth'; and in Section 1.3.6, women being treated with men may not receive services involving sperm, egg or embryo donation unless the man (but not the woman) has been 'given a suitable opportunity to receive proper counselling about the implications of taking the proposed steps, and [has] been provided with such relevant information as is proper'.
4. The science programme, Horizon, in investigating Norplant found that damage to the eye that could result in blindness was noted in the trials but not listed as a possible side effect when marketed. This programme explored the coercive experiences of women who were used in the test trials.

Further reading

Jocelynne A. Scutt (ed.), *The Baby Machine: Reproductive Technology and the Commercialisation of Motherhood* (London, Greenprint, 1990). A collection of articles on IVF, surrogacy, biotechnology, genetic manipulations, interventions in conception, embryo research, eugenics, infertility, pregnancy, childbirth, motherhood, fathers' rights, women's reproductive choice and rights, law and commerce, and the relation between science, technology and society. This volume offers a view from women, both as objects of these interventions and as critical protagonists. This largely Australian collection exposes the international character of medical, scientific and commercial developments in reproduction.

Robyn Rowland, *Living Laboratories: Women and Reproductive Technologies* (Bloomington, Indiana University Press, 1992). The question of who is in control of motherhood underpins the issues explored in this volume. Reproductive interventions are explained simply using the experiences of women undergoing IVF and other procedures. The commercial involvements are discussed. How the foetus became a person in medicine and law and the implications for women's personhood is another theme. Women explain how they are depersonalised by surrogacy. The values of medical science, the conceptual presentations of the technologies, infertility and desire, set the context for a reconsideration of rights, responsibilities and resistance.

Michelle Stanworth (ed.), *Reproductive Technologies: Gender, Motherhood and Medicine* (Cambridge, Polity, 1987). This largely British collection proceeds from the view that technologies draw their meaning from the cultural and political climate in which they are embedded. The question is, can the cultural and political conditions be created so that reproductive technologies can be employed by women to shape the experience of reproduction according to their own definitions? The authors explore the relation of women to science and medicine; infertility and infertility services in the NHS; the restructuring of motherhood and paternal authority; the social and legal redefinition of the foetus; eugenics; surrogacy; and the various forms taken by technology in human reproduction.

Janice Raymond, *Women as Wombs: Reproductive Technologies and the Battle over Women's Freedom* (San Francisco, Harper, 1993). Are reproductive technologies and genetic interventions issues of reproductive 'choice' or are they a threat to women's basic human rights? This book critiques reproductive liberalism and describes ways reproductive technologies violate the integrity of women's bodies and perpetuate trafficking in women, children and foetuses, and prostitution. Connections are made between (hetero)sexuality and reproduction in order to bring together sexual and reproductive politics. The new reproductive technologies are presented as a form of medical sexualised violence against women, thus extending the ethical and social debate.

17

Motherhood and Women's Lives

Paula Nicolson

Introduction

Motherhood is a central aspect of most women's lives worldwide. For example, in 1994 there were 6.7 million women with children under 16 in the UK: that is, 29 per cent of all women (Church and Sommerfield, 1995). However, the availability of acceptable methods of contraception have made it easier for women to take control of their own fertility. In 1992 for the first time, women in their early thirties were more likely to give birth than women in their early twenties, and the number of women in their forties having babies is also increasing. Although there is an increase in the number of women who do not become mothers, it remains the case that most women *do* have children, although they have fewer than women in previous generations (Church and Sommerfield, 1995).

Patterns of fertility have a complicated connection with women's lives overall. Better educated middle-class women appear to have ensured greater control over when, if and how many children they have than have those women from less privileged backgrounds. Further, control over fertility means more scope for education and employment for women, which in turn provides opportunities for independence and autonomy. Statistics make it clear that more women in the 1990s were divorcing, separating, marrying later and not marrying than was the case in the 1970s and 1980s, and this data is clearly connected to the fact that women's lives are no longer solely prescribed by their role as mother in the traditional family (see Gittins, 1993).

However what women do and social beliefs about what women *should do* are sometimes at odds with each other. Motherhood and womanhood stand in a complex and contradictory relationship with one another, despite the fact that this relationship appears to be changing. While motherhood is still central to women's identity, recent demographic changes appear to suggest that motherhood alone no longer dictates the pattern of women's lives, and may not be such a popular choice for women as it once was (Church and Sommerfield, 1995). Under patriarchy, however, motherhood has a mythological, mysterious and powerful status. Only women are granted this status, and it is one to which all women have been expected to aspire. The reality of mothers' lives, however, often fails to match these aspirations. Motherhood is a challenge; although potentially enjoyable, it is also hard work and routinely stressful (Richardson, 1993). Becoming a mother often means economic dependence on another person or the state, and frequently reduces women's income. It affects relationships with men and other women, and changes occupational, domestic and sexual arrangements. Being a mother influences social and personal identity, and has implications for women's health (Doyal, 1995).

Feminist analyses of the conditions surrounding motherhood have identified its socially prescribed situation as an accompaniment to marriage, heterosexuality, monogamy and economic viability (Gittins, 1993). Further, it has been argued that motherhood is the key means of women's oppression in patriarchal societies (Bleier, 1984). Despite this, many young working-class women still see it as a means of 'liberation' from the prospect of dreary paid employment (Griffin, 1989).

Despite the prominence of motherhood as a social institution, and the almost universal expectation that women will become mothers, the everyday reality of mothering is frequently invisible. For women caught up in the myths that accompany motherhood, failure to achieve that imaginary status is frequently a 'shock' (Parker, 1995). Women who do not have children are also caught in these contradictions and constraints. Women who are not mothers are seen as failed and unfeminine women, and achievements and pleasures gained outside motherhood are condemned within patriarchy as substitutes for 'normal' femininity (Woollett, 1991). In this chapter the consequences of the contradictions surrounding motherhood are explored, with particular emphasis on the ways in which the conditions of motherhood, both social and psychological, have been socially constructed within patriarchy and capitalism.

What is motherhood?

Perceptions of mothers as powerful and influential and the romanticisation and idealisation of the mothering role (Apter, 1993) need to be qualified in the context of women's everyday experiences. Motherhood as an institution includes certain responsibilities and duties, but women's power is limited. Women's power in both the public and private/domestic spheres is subject to the rule of men, both as individuals and as represented by patriarchy. Psychologists have traditionally claimed priority for mothers' power over children, through emphasising the importance of mother-child relationships (Apter, 1993) and through the debate on mothers' responsibilities to their children (Tizard, 1991). However, legal and traditional power over women and children is held by men (Segal, 1990b).

Matriarchy (defined as a society with matriarchal government and descent reckoned through female lineage) is not recognised in most societies and is certainly not an influential means of social organisation. Claims from community and anthropological studies, that matriarchies prevail in certain traditional subcultures – for example, among Black urban American groups (Kitzinger, 1978) or among traditional white working-class communities in British cities (Young and Willmott, 1966) – cannot be upheld in terms of true power in contemporary Western society. Ruth Bleier (1984), reviewing anthropological studies of a large number of cultures, argued that women's roles are always of a lower status compared to those of men, and this continues to be upheld through the enactment of gendered roles (Connell, 1993). In some small, non-industrial societies where men have primary responsibility for aspects of childcare, 'mothering' is taken very seriously and given high status, which is not the case when women do it.

Most mothers in industrial and non-industrial, urban and rural, societies are oppressed. They may have particular responsibilities, but not the accompanying rights to choose how they mother or whether to mother at all. The popular perceptions of maternal influence and power are mythological and the origins of this myth lie within patriarchy. The repercussions of this have had a powerful psychological effect on relationships between mothers and daughters, and affect expectations of mothering from generation to generation.

It is through the everyday experience of the mother-daughter relationship that the contradictions in the myth become clear: 'Belief in the all powerful mother spawns a recurrent tendency to blame the mother on the one hand, and a fantasy of maternal perfectibility on the other' (Chodorow and Contratto, 1982, p. 55). The romanticised and idealised woman, full of love, forgiveness and selflessness, does not and cannot exist, so that all mothers are destined to disappoint their children and themselves.

Mother-blaming occurs on a number of levels, from individual attributions to mothers as the cause of psychological insecurities, to the portrayal of the cold, rejecting, neurotic or inadequate mother in popular culture (Sayers, 1988; Parker, 1995). The patriarchal myth of maternal power renders women culpable, and thus in reality deprives them of effective social influence. Women are consequently perceived as imperfect in their central role, while men as fathers can maintain their own mythological status and claim the admiration of their sons and daughters.

Science and motherhood

How is it, then, that mothers are 'blamed' and seen as both powerful and destructive? These contradictory images of motherhood are constructed and exploited within patriarchy through the medium of 'scientific knowledge', and operate to ensure that many aspects of motherhood are rendered invisible, and that women as mothers are denied the power to change this within existing social structures. The mechanisms through which the status of motherhood are controlled are both social and psychological. Motherhood is often idealised and some argue that men experience 'womb envy': that is, they envy women's ability to become pregnant and give birth. The image of the idealised mother, however, exists in stark contrast to men's apparent unwillingness to become involved in the aspects of infant care that are available to them (Nicolson, 1996) and with the daily lives of the women attempting to mother (Parker, 1995).

The role of 'mother' has not evolved in a 'natural' way, and neither is it outside culture and free from ideology. It has been socially constructed within patriarchy through a complex set of power relations which ensure that women become mothers, and practise motherhood, in narrowly-defined ways. This is achieved in part through the mechanism of 'science', which bolsters existing power relations. Contemporary motherhood is the product of (at least) nineteenth- and twentieth-century medical/biological and psychological/social science, and this can be seen in a number of ways.

Social prescriptions for contemporary motherhood are constantly offered, reinforced and embellished by 'experts' with recourse to 'science', and their versions of what constitutes good mothering practice is the socially received 'wisdom'. Certain kinds of claims to knowledge are given priority over others, and it is those which serve the needs of the socially-powerful (that is, in this case, men: Foucault, 1973a; Philp, 1985) that pass into popular discourse and come to represent our everyday understanding of what we all take for granted as 'truth' or 'facts' (Nicolson, 1995).

In the case of motherhood, while there are potentially myriad dimensions which could be studied to explain and determine mothering practice (that is, the nature of the role itself, what behaviour is appropriate and so on), only a small proportion of what constitutes motherhood has been identified and described. In other words, *normative* behaviour associated with mothering has emerged from the power of the knowledge-claims of scientists which suit the needs of patriarchy (Foucault, 1973a). These knowledge claims have not only informed the ideology of mainstream social and psychological science but, more importantly, the everyday understanding of women themselves. This means that the accompanying stresses of motherhood may be experienced by women as their own 'inadequacies' (Boulton, 1983; Lewis, 1995).

I shall briefly explore some of these knowledge-claims and normative prescriptions, before identifying their manifestations in the social and psychological conditions of contemporary motherhood.

Post-natal depression and the expert view

The concepts surrounding childbirth and motherhood are constructed by medical discourses. Clinicians have defined women's post-natal experience though proposing that well adjusted, normal and thus 'good' mothers are those who are contented; and that mothers who are anxious or depressed are ill (Cox and Holden, 1994). Post-natal depression has been distinguished from other forms of depression by being placed in a causal relation to childbirth. Thereby the concept 'post-natal depression' potentially represents a means of positioning women as potentially vulnerable solely as a consequence of female biology (Nicolson, 1996). But how did this happen? Most women are aware that having a baby is demanding, stressful and potentially depressing at times, so depression should be expected rather than pathologised.

'Post-natal depression' was one of a collection of post-puerperal 'illnesses' identified by the French psychiatrist Marce in the nineteenth century. Although distinctions between the 'blues' (during the first few days after birth), subsequent depression, and psychosis have been made (Cox and Holden, 1994), there is no irrefutable evidence to link any of these conditions *exclusively* to childbirth (Nicolson, 1996). So why is the notion of post-natal depression so commonplace?

The psychiatric profession has engaged in the process of norm-setting in relation to post-natal moods and emotional states, and distinguishes the 'normal' condition (not depressed) from the 'pathological' one (depressed) in a notional ideological manner rather than through statistical analysis, so that the norm-setting bears no relation to recorded frequency of post-natal depression (see below) but rather reflects the knowledge-claims of the medical/clinical discourse (Foucault, 1977). Even so, individuals position themselves according to these knowledge-claims.

Assumptions underlying the construction of the 'post-natal depression' syndrome are encapsulated in the following quotation:

> The majority of women suffering from post natal depression do not even recognise they are ill. They believe they are bogged down by utter exhaustion and irritability. It is all too easy to blame their condition on to the extra work the baby brings to their new life . . . Once the condition has been recognised and treated the husband will be able to declare 'She's once more the woman I married'. (Dalton, 1980, p. 4)

This represents 'post-natal depression' as a 'curable' 'illness' juxtaposed with childbearing and early motherhood as unqualified 'happy' (or at least non-depressing) experiences. This view continues to dominate the scientific and self-help literature, undermining accounts from women who attribute stress and depression to the mothering tasks themselves (Nicolson, 1996).

The persistence of this clinical/medical discourse has been challenged to some extent by a social science discourse which acknowledges the impact of additional life stressors on an individual's psychological well-being and identifies 'post-natal depression' as a realistic response to the tasks surrounding motherhood (Lewis, 1995).

While this social science framework avoids 'illness' as an explanation for depression and gives priority to social support over medication, the focus remains within the discourse that pathologises women's negative responses to mothering. Moreover, there is still an attempt to 'medicalise'. In one recent review of childbirth as a 'life event', the emphasis was upon categorising women into subgroups so that social depression might be distinguished from biological depression, thus reinstating the priority of the medical/clinical framework (Elliot, 1990).

Both kinds of 'expert' accounts, medical and social scientific then, employ the view that 'post-natal depression' can (a) be made available to an 'objective' identification, and (b) is distinct in its quality from other forms of depression that might be experienced by women or men at times other than following childbirth. It is these ideas that have penetrated popular consciousness and predefined women's experiences of the transition to motherhood.

Experts and childrearing: how to become a good mother

The focus of 'experts' on motherhood has been upon the effects of mothering on children and the marital relationship, post-natal adjustment and when reproductive technology to aid fertility is appropriate. This clearly reflects the ideology underlying their claims to scientific knowledge. A number of ways have been suggested by these experts in which maternal behaviour can have potentially dire consequences for children, not only in their infancy and pre-school years, but also through adolescence and into adulthood. John Bowlby's assertions about the mothering role is a good example of this. Mother love in infancy, he claimed, is as important for mental health as vitamins and proteins are for physical health (Bowlby, 1951). Above all else, infants need mothers, and those mothers have to love them. This love, by implication, needs to be ever-available and offered without qualification, regardless of the mother's own needs and circumstances.

The consequent development of the 'maternal deprivation thesis' redefined the responsibilities of women towards their children, although the implications for women's lives were largely ignored. The emphasis in all this work was on the dependency needs of infants, and the psychological implications of separation traumas for the remainder of life. Mothers' needs were invisible.

This thesis not only informed popular ideas about childcare, but also set the parameters for subsequent psychological research on infant/child development, adopting the notion of the 'secure base' as an ideal context for human development. This paradigm emerged as a moral as well as psychological prescription for mental health. The burden for providing the secure base fell upon mothers, regardless of circumstances and abilities (Ainsworth, 1992).

Evidence of the interconnection between science and politics can be seen in Denise Riley's important (1983) study of women's work and day-care in the immediate post-war/post-Bowlby period:

> The reproductive woman at the heart of family policy was surrounded by the language of pronatalism. By pronatalism, I mean that despondency and alarm over the low birth rate, both past and as anticipated by demographers, which took the solution to the problem to be encouraging women to have more children; four per family was a widely agreed target. (Riley, 1983, p. 151)

Riley paints a complex picture, contrasting with some popular contemporary feminist images of women's post-war resistance to leaving the labour market (for example, as in the film *The Life and Times of Rosie the Riveter*). Many women, exhausted by the multiple burdens of childcare, domestic responsibility and work outside the home, appeared to welcome the pronatalist direction of government policy, which included ideas about the dangers for children of anything less than maternal dedication and constant availability. This was accomplished, at least in part, through direct information on film and in childcare manuals, for the specific consumption of women (Richardson, 1993), making it clear that experts know best, but also helping to ensure that women focused their major efforts upon mothering, or the management of mothering.

More recently, attention has been paid to the role of the father. However, the treatment of fatherhood by experts has been explained differently from the motherhood role. In clear contrast to mothers, fathers are represented as adding positive ingredients to the beleaguered and insufficient mother-child relationship. Fathers' involvement has traditionally been seen as improving children's intellectual and social capacities (Parke, 1981; McGuire, 1991). Mothers, it seems, are seen primarily as supplying the basic conditions for survival and maintenance, while experiencing a decline in their own wider capacities. Feminist studies of motherhood clearly show the ways in which the mothering role operates to exclude women's own development; for example, sometimes resulting in a self-defined sense of being unfit for tasks demanding intellectual skills (Kaplan, 1992).

Interest in fathers has led to a further strand of expert concern: the 'family'. Functionalist sociologists have in the past been concerned to divide and stratify family roles/functions in terms of gender and generation, portraying the family as a social microcosm where women were seen as both dependent and nurturant in the home in relation to men and children, and nurturant and dependent in society (Parsons and Bales, 1953). Subsequent sociological studies, as with mainstream psychology, focused upon motherhood as a role or as a variable in predicting marital satisfaction, and it was not until the publication of Hannah Gavron's *The Captive Wife* in 1966 that contemporary sociologists attempted to take seriously women as mothers. Even Elizabeth Bott's (1957) sensitive and influential study, which took class and gender into account, failed to identify and challenge the conditions surrounding women's role in the family and in relation to childcare.

Feminist analysis of the family has redefined the context within which domestic relationships are enacted, dispelling the myth of the traditional nuclear family unit. Single parenthood, domestic violence, divorce and lesbian parenting, all indicate the need to re-evaluate the way 'experts' define and prescribe women's lives (Gittins, 1993).

In contemporary mainstream psychology, expert attention to the family has focused upon the transition to motherhood, and the consequences of becoming a mother for reducing marital intimacy (Kaplan, 1992), for women's impaired physical attractiveness, and for women's rejection of what had been 'normal' pre-pregnancy sexual relations (Reamy and White, 1987; Nicolson, 1991), and for precipitating post-natal or maternal depression which is detrimental to childrearing (Foreman, 1994). These issues have all been taken as indices through which good motherhood/wifehood might be assessed.

Within the social sciences and medicine, mainstream patriarchal values are still given the status of knowledge. Despite feminist critiques, feminist analyses (or woman-focused studies) are less often adopted into the mainstream and so have less impact on popular ideas and beliefs. However, patriarchal frameworks alone do not fully account for women's thinking about their own experience of motherhood. Women draw upon personal experience as well as popular discourses, and this often sets up the contradictions that potentially lead to feminist consciousness.

Becoming a mother

Motherhood is *not* a unitary experience, and neither is it a simple one. To be a mother demands that a woman takes on a complex identity (Richardson, 1993). She is still herself but she is also a mother, with the incumbent roles, responsibilities and relationships which this entails. Becoming a mother has been part of most women's identities since childhood and, although many accept that they did not really know what motherhood was like until they experienced it, the fact of becoming a mother is no surprise in itself.

Why do women become mothers, or at least take the option of becoming a mother so seriously? On an individual level, women recognise their biological capacity to have children and, through socialisation into the female role, come to equate femininity with marriage and motherhood, often seeing women who do not do this as 'inadequate' (Woollett, 1992). Motherhood potentially provides girls/women with entry into womanhood (Woollett, 1987).

> One of the attractions of motherhood is its normative quality. Mother-hood is an expected and normal role for all women. To become a mother is to do what women and those around them expect and want them to do. It is to be the same as other women and not stand out as different. In this ideological context, women's decisions about motherhood are not so much about when to have children, but how many to have and increasingly, in which social context to have them. The mandate for motherhood, as it has been called, means that women opt out of motherhood rather than opting into it. (Woollett, 1987, p. 1)

Many women believe that they can only achieve adult, feminine status through becoming mothers. Ann Phoenix's (1991) research with teenage mothers supports this view, in that their desire for motherhood as entry to womanhood is not so much a biological desire to become pregnant and nurture a child, but an implicit recognition of apparent privilege unavailable to childless women. This system of beliefs is related to the patriarchal idealisation of women as mothers, which is part of women's subordination. The romanticisation of motherhood, and the sets of relationships which accompany it, are dictated by patriarchal power relations. It suits men for women to mother.

The motherhood 'mandate' is 'serviced' by the popular and powerful belief system surrounding the notion of a 'maternal instinct'. This 'instinct' is characterised by two desires: to have children, and to care for them (Figes, 1994). However, it has become increasingly clear that this 'instinct' is a socially constructed myth and that many mothers feel able to express their ambivalence both about their children and the role (Badinter, 1981; Parker, 1995).

The notion of the maternal instinct underpins the contemporary construction of motherhood. It underlies notions of femininity and required maternal behaviour, and its 'absence' is used to explain women's maternal 'failures', such as not protecting children from (or perpetrating) child abuse or neglect. It is also used, in conjunction with theories of attachment, to explain childhood anxieties, subsequent problems in adulthood and in developing childbirth and day-care policies.

The myth of femininity encapsulated by this notion of the 'maternal instinct' is the one through which women's psychology and social role are determined 'scientifically' (Apter, 1993). The myth may be summarised thus.

1. All women have a biological drive towards conceiving and bearing children.
2. This is a precursor to the drive to *nurture* those children.
3. The skills/capacities required to care for infants/children emerge or evolve immediately after the birth without the need for training.

The logical consequence of this 'instinct' would be the knowledge that all women want to (and thus should be enabled to) have children, and are capable of looking after them without training. The 'maternal instinct' cuts across ideas that women are *socialised* into wanting children: it is a biological imperative (Buss, 1994).

Feminist research has challenged such myths by showing contradictions within the idea of a 'maternal instinct': for example, by observing that doctors differentiate between 'possessors' of the maternal instinct (married women) and those without (unmarried women). Married women are encouraged to seek fertility counselling if necessary, and condemned for wanting abortions. Unmarried women (especially lesbians: see Burns, 1992) are challenged for wanting children (Boyle, 1992).

There certainly appears to be little historical or psychological evidence for an innate desire either to bear or nurture children (Parker, 1995). Elisabeth Badinter (1981), for example, distinguished maternal 'instinct' from 'love' in her historically grounded critique of motherhood: 'Maternal love is a human feeling. And like any feelings, it is uncertain, fragile and imperfect. Contrary to many assumptions, it is not a deeply rooted given in women's natures' (Badinter, 1981, p. xxiii). She provided evidence of historical variations in maternal behaviour which sometimes reflect interest in and devotion to the child, and sometimes not (Riley, 1983). Research on women's responses to their newborn infants further challenges the belief about instinctual maternal love (Crouch and Manderson, 1995), but does identify the influence of the scientific experts' advice, through the fact that women expect to feel this and experience guilt and distress when they do not (Nicolson, 1996).

What is apparent is that when women have children (whether or not the children are planned) they usually try their best to care for them and often grow to love them. Many evaluate their personal worth through this relationship and discharge their responsibilities as well as they are able.

The motherhood role, contrary to the ideology of the maternal instinct, appears to be one for which most women are ill-prepared. However, it is an experience which seems to be reproduced from generation to generation of women, and women continue to mother. Why should this be the case? Nancy Chodorow (1978) suggested in a key text, that this 'reproduction' of mothering within the context of patriarchy, although not a biological imperative, is in one sense both 'natural' and 'inevitable' for women given the dominant social structures. Women's mothering is not only a product of biology, but also causally related to historical conditions and the way that childcare and the division of labour have evolved. She argued that girls/ women and boys/men develop in a context which encourages the psychological capacities and commitments to participate in the existing social relations and structures. The dominant structures, whereby women mother and men work outside the home, are accompanied by appropriate psychological capacities which underlie these tasks, and these are reproduced at both conscious and unconscious levels:

> Women as mothers, produce daughters with mothering capacities and the desire to mother. These capacities and needs are built into and grow out of the mother-daughter relationship itself. By contrast, women as mothers (and men as not-mothers) produce sons whose nurturant capacities and needs have been systematically curtailed and suppressed. (Chodorow, 1978, p. 7)

Many radical feminists have challenged this view, proposing that men avoid sharing childcare because they do not want to, not because they are incapable of it. Further, by focusing upon the personality dimension, Nancy Chodorow failed to explore social, economic and other psychological aspects of parenting which might be changed to make shared parenting more of a reality (Richardson, 1993). Chodorow's analysis implies a determinism, with an emphasis on childhood socialisation, which potentially enables men themselves to employ the 'excuse' that they have not been brought up to be good at childcare! Childcare is not mysterious or part of early developmental psychology; it is learnt in adulthood, often following childbirth.

Earlier, Sue Sharpe (1976) had proposed a very different view of how girls choose and learn to mother, and adopt the accompanying behaviour and beliefs associated with being a woman. Her study, which focused on white, Afro-Caribbean and Asian girls living in London, identified ways in which cultural stereotyping was used to represent the typical or ideal characteristics of women and men so that, despite class differences and changes over time, certain fundamental qualities and beliefs are pervasive and represented as feminine or masculine 'natures'.

School, family and the media all act to reinforce these images of the norm which, on the whole, still designate men to have the more socially desirable traits. Sharpe (1994) found nearly 20 years later that traditional female images of wife, mother and homemaker are now mixed with more overt sexuality. Cute pretty media image of women have been replaced by more assertive, sexual ones. This co-exists with the expansion of masculinity to include a nurturant side (see also Segal, 1990b). Seventy-five per cent of the girls in Sue Sharpe's original study had said they would have chosen to have been girls, and part of their choice was 'the anticipated joys and satisfactions of becoming wives and mothers and caring for homes and children' (Sharpe, 1976, p. 206). She suggested that all the girls had been presented with an idealised image of motherhood, and many appeared unaware of the oppressive conditions so that 'motherhood remains one of the most positive aspects of the feminine role for many girls'. Any conflicts between their futures as housewives and mothers and the low social status of this role did not seem to arise. Some clue to this might be their perceived potential of life as a worker outside the home. The limited possibilities in employment, particularly for working-class girls and, because of racism, Black girls, contrasted with the possible fulfilment, satisfaction and apparent relative freedom and adult status which comes with the housewife/mother role. So, despite the struggles the girls in this study witnessed in their own mothers' lives, the perceived satisfaction from mothering potentially outweighed the lack of satisfaction they saw in paid employment or unemployment.

Twenty years later girls and boys were experiencing severely reduced prospects of employment. However, girls now appear to have a greater set of possibilities beyond the role of wife and mother. Working-class girls frequently move into white-collar clerical and secretarial occupations more easily than previously, and better educated girls could opt for professional life more acceptably than in the 1970s. This is reinforced by the higher achievements that many girls experience in school compared with their male contemporaries (see Chapter 14).

This then may result in delaying parenthood, but girls still want to include motherhood in their lives. Hazel Beckett (1986) and Chris Griffin (1989, 1993) both observed the impact of gender socialisation on young women and men. Hazel Beckett suggests that marriage and motherhood were part of almost all her respondents' eventual aims. However, 'The question of motherhood versus career seems, for the majority, to have been stably resolved in the direction of combining them. They seem to have made a unanimous and unconflicted choice to experience occupational involvement, marriage and motherhood' (Beckett, 1986, p. 47). From this, she argued that female gender identity contains a flexibility that traditional theorists have ignored.

Chris Griffin's (1986) study of young women from a variety of backgrounds leaving school indicates similarly that 'Marriage and motherhood were seen as distant events which might occur some ten years in the future, but they were also seen as inevitable for most young women. Few financially feasible or socially acceptable alternatives were available, particularly for young working class women' (1986, p. 181).

This remains the case as Terri Apter (1993) and Sue Sharpe (1994) observe. Women mother, on the whole, because the motherhood 'parcel' is the one most open to them; other ways of life for women are not as well rewarded. Women are often (unless, for example, they are lesbian or single women) made to feel that there must be something wrong with them if they do not choose to be a mother. Men, on the other hand, although encouraged into a particularly well-defined masculine role which precludes 'mothering', remain more able to choose whether, or how far, to involve themselves in childrearing (Apter, 1993).

The experience of motherhood

Early sociological studies in the 1960s and 1970s indicated that the mother/housewife role (more common then) was not the ideal that women had been led to believe awaited them (Friedan, 1963). Gavron's (1966) study suggested that this cuts across social class groups. She found that expectations of marriage and motherhood contradicted the actual experience, which led to confusion surrounding women's roles. This affected her respondents' attitudes to marriage: 'For some wives of both classes marriage was seen as a kind of freedom; yet when it was combined with motherhood it became a kind of prison and they felt their freedom had been restricted before they had really been free at all' (Gavron, 1966, p. 136).

Ann Oakley (1976) found a similar pattern of disillusion and suggested that while marriage and motherhood are seen as potentially providing the greatest life satisfaction for women, in reality they provide disappointment: 'Before they become mothers, women have a highly romanticised picture of what motherhood is . . . before motherhood is experienced they want more children than they do later' (Oakley, 1976, p. 189).

Motherhood still appears to be perceived by young women as 'more pliable, more mutable than it turns out to be' (Apter, 1993, p. 55). Despite some high profile changes in the fatherhood role, in two-parent, hetero-sexual families, motherhood is tied to the role of the housewife/homemaker (Apter, 1993). This is the case whether or not the woman works, and it cuts across social class groupings (Lewis, 1995).

What makes images of marriage and motherhood so appealing while remaining problematic in reality? Each step in women's 'normal' lives – finding a male partner, marriage and having children – increases the disappointment. The more women fulfil their destiny the more pernicious, it seems, is the trap. Why do women appear not to learn the lessons of their foremothers?

It is difficult for us to believe that our biological 'destiny' and 'instinctual drives' lead us to such a confusing end! It is often not until we come face to face with motherhood itself that we realise, through experience, that this idealised image is a patriarchal myth. What is it that causes this confusion? If motherhood is so bad, why do women not just opt out?

To understand this it is necessary to look in more detail at what mothering entails. Some studies have focused upon changes in role and social status following childbirth which demonstrate the re-orientation of women's domestic and working lives once they have had a baby (Oakley, 1989); others focus on more psychological dimensions, examining it as a life transition which requires psychological adjustment in identity (Nicolson, 1996). Although arguably a woman's identity as a mother starts in childhood, the process of actually giving birth to and caring for a baby changes most women's sense of themselves and also their values and beliefs. Many women report that it is not until they do become mothers that this change becomes a reality (Nicolson, 1988). The initial transition to motherhood is a shock in a number of ways, both physically and emotionally (Oakley, 1980), and this does not appear to diminish with second or subsequent births. Each time the pressures, hard work and need to relearn childcare skills confronts each woman anew. With each child, women are expected, and expect themselves, to take primary childcare responsibility regardless of their other responsibilities or their specific abilities (Apter, 1993).

The practice of mothering (that is, the day-to-day experience of childcare and associated tasks) can be difficult and may lead to depression and unhappiness (Parker, 1995). However, motherhood is not always a negative, stressful, tiring, depressing experience brought about through an oppressive set of social structures; it can also be an exciting, rewarding and emotionally stimulating one. It is inherent paradoxes such as these that produce what Adrienne Rich has described as 'the suffering of ambivalence: the murderous alternation between bitter resentment and raw-edged nerves and blissful gratification and tenderness. Sometimes I seem to myself, in my feelings towards these tiny guiltless beings, a monster of selfishness and intolerance' (Rich, 1984, p. 21).

Rozsika Parker (1995) more recently reiterates this: 'Much of the guilt with which mothers are familiar stems from difficulties in weathering the complicated and contradictory feelings provoked by maternal ambivalence' (Parker, 1995, p. 1). It is the children themselves who produce rewards, and the motherhood role includes the power, responsibility, satisfaction and independence that childrearing brings, as well as the boredom, hard work and pain. Motherhood can introduce meaning and purpose into life as well as bringing new opportunities for exploring a woman's own capacities and forming relationships: 'Having children can bring greater vitality, fun and humour into our lives, as well as providing us with a different insight into the world' (Richardson, 1993, p. 1). Supporting this view, Sian Lewis (1995) found that several mothers reported their children to be rewarding companions which, provided they were financially secure and emotionally supported by a partner or friends, helped them overcome much of the negative experiences of routine childcare.

Motherhood certainly does qualitatively change women's lives, for better and worse. Even so, motherhood remains a low-status role in patriarchal society. Further, the image of the 'mother', things that mothers do, qualities they are perceived to have, and their additional strengths and achievements are often treated with a degree of disdain, although this co-exists with the idealised view that motherhood is the most important job in the world (Figes, 1994).

While there is no evidence that women are innately endowed with special maternal qualities, the experience of mothering does enable women (and men) to develop skills and capacities which can be generalised to other activities. Also, being a mother may stimulate particular ways of perceiving and explaining the world. This is what Sarah Ruddick has called 'maternal thinking' which, she claims, evolves through the very experience of being a mother who of necessity engages in the universal and culturally prescribed practices needed to maintain a child's life and nurture it. Socially and psychologically, mothers develop a distinctive way of seeing and being in the world in order to accomplish this, and mothers frequently adopt a style of 'humility' and 'cheerfulness' to cope with their priority activities. However, 'Because in the dominant society "humility" and "cheerfulness" name virtues of subordinates, and because these virtues have in fact developed in conditions of subordination, it is difficult to credit them, and easy to confuse them with self-effacement and cheery denial that are degenerative forms' (Ruddick, 1982, p. 81).

In fact, Ruddick argues, far from motherhood being a humble activity, 'maternal thinking' demonstrates resilience and strength. Mothers need to be strong to cope with mothering and with the social conditions surrounding that role: childrearing; running the home; managing complementary childcare arrangements; and maintaining relationships with their partners, family, friends and others. They have to be strong in order to maintain a sense of their own identity and fulfil some of their own needs and negotiate their way through the associated social subordination. A feminist consciousness and feminist analysis of motherhood helps to enable this to happen, and makes women's strengths explicit (Apter, 1993).

The social conditions of contemporary motherhood

Contemporary motherhood, as argued above, traditionally exists within the clearly prescribed social context of heterosexuality and marriage, the Western patriarchal parcel of rules for appropriate sexual relations and

behaviour between men and women. However, long/medium-term heterosexual monogamy now appears to be substituted in many cases for marriage
(Gittins, 1993), with 12 per cent of women between the ages of 25 and 34
living with a partner but not married (Church and Sommerfield, 1995).
However, over two-thirds of women in all age groups believed that people
who wanted children should be married first. Between 1993 and 1994, 56 per
cent of women in all age groups were married and 5 per cent cohabiting;
women between the ages of 35 and 44 were most likely to live in two-adult-
plus-children households (Church and Sommerfield, 1995).

Each one of those conditions – heterosexuality, 'marriage' or motherhood
– entails a form of oppression. Social class, 'race', ethnicity, sexuality and
economic status further impinge upon the social conditions of mothering for
individual women and differentially influence their experiences. For example, the experience of some Asian women in Britain includes arranged
marriages and different expectations and experiences in relation to their
husbands, children and extended families, than that of many white middle-
class women (Dosanj-Matwala and Woollett, 1990). Among ethnic minority
groups of women, those belonging to the Pakistani/Bangladeshi groups in
the UK were more likely to be married or cohabiting than any other ethnic
group (Church and Sommerfield, 1995). This suggests that this group is less
willing or able to end unhappy and/or violent marriages.

Women who are married are expected to have children (Gittins, 1993) and
most fulfil, or want to fulfil, this expectation in that by 1994 around
6 733 000 women in Britain were mothers (Church and Sommerfield,
1995). Women who do not have children may be seen as odd or abnormal,
whether they fail to conceive by choice or through infertility (Woollett,
1992), as are married women seeking abortion (Boyle, 1992). Although it
has been argued that voluntary childlessness among married women has
begun to carry less stigma than before, motherhood is still the most popular
option (Woollett, 1992).

Lesbians do not manage to escape male power over their fertility and,
along with other unmarried women seeking fertility counselling, are often
assessed as 'sick' or abnormal. Such women who succeed in becoming
pregnant are treated with official caution (Burns, 1992), and attempts at
targeting policy towards preventing pregnancy among this group are
applied enthusiastically. For example, the case of the so-called 'virgin births'
(reported widely in Britain during March 1991) illustrated the vehemence of
professional and popular opinion towards those who choose to seek
maternity without having sex with a man and without the intention of
marriage (Nicolson, 1991).

There is no evidence, however, that women who *do* fulfil the obligations in
this 'patriarchal parcel' necessarily live 'happily ever after'. Indeed, although
the 'dream' has been accomplished, the experience frequently fails in its
promise. Betty Friedan (1963), in the early 1960s describing the experience

of primarily white, married, middle-class, non-working mothers, expressed this as the 'problem with no name':

> It was a strange stirring, a sense of dissatisfaction, a yearning that women suffered in the middle of the twentieth century in the United States. Each suburban wife struggled with it alone. As she made the beds, shopped for groceries, matched slip cover material, ate peanut butter sandwiches with her children, chauffeured Cub Scouts and Brownies, lay beside her husband at night, she was afraid to ask, even of herself, the silent question: 'is this all?' (Friedan, 1963, p. 13)

It was this feeling that began to awaken a feminist consciousness among some American women. How far, though, were such feelings representative of all mothers? What of other social groups: single parents, Black mothers, working mothers, lesbians, the poor and the working class? In what ways do they experience motherhood now? The model of the married heterosexual two-parent, 2.4 children household may no longer be the norm, although it is still the most powerful image of the family (Apter, 1993).

In the USA since the 1970s, the number of lone-parent families has increased (Millar, 1994). Similarly, in England and Wales there has been a sharp increase in the number of one-parent families, from 8 per cent in 1971 to 14 per cent in 1983 (OPCS, 1988). In 1988, 16 per cent of families in England and Wales were headed by lone mothers, of which the majority were single or divorced rather than widowed, which would have been more likely to have been the case during the 1970s. By 1994, one in five (20 per cent), mothers in the UK were lone parents (Church and Sommerfield, 1995). These lone mothers are more likely to have no academic or professional qualifications (48 per cent had none at all) and fewer qualifications than women who were married or cohabiting. Lone mothers are also more likely to have dependent children under school age and younger than those in the care of a lone father. All lone parents are more likely to live in rented rather than owner-occupied accommodation (Church and Sommerfield, 1995). This suggests that lone mothers are likely to be suffering economic hardship, poor housing and are unlikely to be able to exercise much choice over employment, both because they are poorly qualified and because they are more likely to have young children dependent on them. As Brown and Harris's (1978) classic large-scale study of depression in London clearly demonstrated, such conditions are all factors associated with long-term depression.

The divorce rates in the UK, Europe and the USA have also been steadily increasing over the past two decades. During the 1970s, the rate of divorce doubled in the UK, from 6 per 1000 to 12 per 1000 of the population. During the 1980s about 150 000 couples a year divorced compared with 51 000 in the 1960s. In 1992, 173 000 marriages were ended by divorce, and by 1994 about 14 per cent of women in the 35 to 44 age group were divorced or separated, although the rate is directly influenced by social and religious factors (religious beliefs have an impact on the marriage, divorce and cohabitation figures in Northern Ireland where fewer women cohabit or divorce: see Church and Sommerfield, 1995). Black women are more likely to be single overall than white women, and Asian women are more likely to be married (Church and Sommerfield, 1995). So for an increasing number of mothers and their children, the married, heterosexual parenthood dream is a myth!

Further, for an increasing larger group of women, parenthood does not necessarily mean marriage. During the 1980s in the UK there was a marked rise in children born outside marriage from 77 000 in 1980 to 177 000 in 1988. (Most were born to women under 25.) In fact, 28.9 per cent of births in England and Wales in 1989 were outside marriage (Birth Statistics, 1989). In 1992–3 this figure rose by 0.6 per cent compared with a fall of 3.7 per cent for births inside marriage. Thus, in 1993 extra-marital births counted for 32.2 per cent of all live births (compared with 31.2 per cent in 1992 and 15.8 per cent in 1983: OPCS, 1995). This varies across countries. In Sweden 50 per cent of births are outside marriage, while in Italy it is only 10 per cent. England and Wales are most similar to the USA (32 per cent) in this respect, and these figures clearly reflect religious and cultural similaries and differences (OPCS, 1995).

For married women, the mean age for having children increased to 28.4 years during 1989, slipping slightly to 28.1 in 1994 (OPCS, 1995), which was the highest mean age since 1952 (calculated for all births not just first children). In fact in 1992, for the first time, it was more likely that women in their early thirties than in their early twenties would have a first baby, although women aged 25–29 are still the most likely age group to give birth (Church and Sommerfield, 1995).

Another dramatic change has been an increase in childlessness. For women born in 1946, 11 per cent were childless in 1989; and for those born in 1951, 18 per cent were childless in 1989. For women born in 1948, 13 per cent were still childless by the age of 35, while for women born in 1958, 26 per cent were still childless by the age of 35 (OPCS, 1995). It is expected that over a fifth of women born in England and Wales in 1967 will still be childless when they reach 40. Also, the proportion of women aged 16 to 49 who said that they expected to remain childless doubled between 1986 and 1991 from 5 per cent to 10 per cent (Church and Sommerfield, 1995). This may be because of later marriage and a high level of marital breakdown as well as reasons of infertility and decisions not to have children.

However, the fertility rates of women in their early forties (40 to 44 years of age) has increased in the decade up to 1994 (Church and Sommerfield, 1995). This may account to some degree for the apparent decrease in fertility. While two-thirds of births to older women in the UK were to women between 40 and 44, and only 5 per cent of the births to women over 40, it must be noted that there have been isolated cases of post-menopausal women receiving medical treatment resulting in successful conception (see Chapter 16). Also the number of children born to each woman in England and Wales has decreased from 2.4 in the 1960s to 1.88 in 1993 and a slightly greater interval between births has been noted (OPCS, 1995). Fertility rates also vary between countries. Currently, it is 2 in Sweden, 2.002 in Eire, 1.25 in Italy and 1.39 in West Germany (OPCS, 1995).

Finally, the model nuclear family with the husband as breadwinner is challenged by the large number of women with dependent children who are also working outside the home in the UK, a trend mirrored in the USA (Apter, 1993). Between 1973 and 1988 in England and Wales there was an increase of 47–56 per cent, which was characterised by an increase in part-time working. In 1994, 12 million women were economically active in the UK (Church and Sommerfield, 1995). Before 1986, lone mothers had been less likely to be working outside the home, but since that time they too have been more frequently involved in part-time employment (OPCS, 1988). The reasons women gave for wanting to remain at work were: liking their jobs; enjoying getting out of the house; and avoiding the boredom and frustration of the daily housework-childcare routine. Such reasons emerge time and again in other studies, although of course the type of employment and occupational/social class are important factors influencing reasons for working and how that relates to the day-to-day experience of being a mother (Glover and Arber, 1995).

However, working mothers do not experience comparable conditions to those experienced by working men. They are not nurtured or 'serviced' in the way the 'traditional' breadwinner expects to be. To be a working mother produces a range of additional stresses and problems for women. For instance, it continues to be primarily women who shop, cook, clean and manage the house, as well as make childcare arrangements (Lewis, 1986; Nicolson, 1996). Delivering and collecting children from childminders and nurseries still falls mainly to women, often because they work fewer hours outside the home, or do shift work to fit in with childcare arrangements. They manage to combine their roles as mothers, housewives and workers, but often at a cost to their health and the quality of their own lives.

Working mothers need good and adequate day-care provision for their children. This means that not only should the quality of the provision in relation to the children's care be stimulating and appropriate, but it should be available when needed and physically accessible. Many women need to leave their children with a substitute carer early in the morning, or until late at night, because they have shift work, or cleaning or factory jobs. Council and private day-care facilities are not normally flexible in this way. Even if they were to be, their availability is severely limited by the number of places, another limiting factor is the cost. State-run nurseries in Britain have strict criteria for allocating places, normally related to the interests of the child, so that mothers who do not have acute social or psychological problems will not qualify. In 1988, day-nursery places were available for only 2 per cent of children under five in England and Wales (Equal Opportunities Commission, 1990). Between the mid-1970s and mid-1980s, there was an increase in births[1] and the number of women with dependent children who were working. Alongside this there have been the continued cuts in public spending, suggesting that pressure on day-care places is still acute.

Informal reliance on the extended family and friends, or upon child-minders (approved or unapproved), is common, and although studies have shown that most mothers would prefer good-quality nursery provision (Tizard, 1991), childminders and informal arrangements are often more flexible. Women wanting to work 'unconventional' hours, who cannot afford day-nursery fees, are thus more likely to use childminders. Child-minders themselves are usually mothers of pre-school children who thus work long, extended hours, often for low pay. It is a complex and vicious cycle. Nannies, au-pairs and nanny-shares are normally confined to more affluent mothers, as they not only require a salary or 'pocket money' but often accommodation and food. However, such childcare arrangements may carry their own problems: ill-trained, homesick teenage 'nannies' often need mothering themselves.

Even if the provision for childcare were adequate, it would not be the end of the organisational problem for mothers. Working mothers consistently experience pressure from almost every sphere of their lives. First, there is the difficulty of dealing with their own emotional reactions to working. Despite the financial/emotional/psychological need to work, and the satisfaction that working might bring, many mothers who do paid work suffer from guilt prompted by the continued claims that maternal deprivation arises when mothers go to work (Tizard, 1991; Richardson, 1993).

Another pressure is that the worlds of work and home are often in conflict. Where do priorities lie? Can mothers afford to spend extra hours doing overtime, attending union meetings or other extra work-related activities? There is often pressure from employers on women to convince them that their loyalties lie at work and not at home (Figes, 1994).

Mothers' relationships with partners (or attempts to find a new partner) are also likely to suffer because of the overall increase in workload, and the inherent conflicts often do not leave much energy for social or emotional life (Cooper and Lewis, 1993). There is also the question of division of labour in the home, particularly in relation to women living with male partners. The 'new man' has been demonstrated to be a myth and though there is some evidence of an increase in fathers' interest and involvement in parenting, it seems this does not stretch to the daily childcare routine, or equal participation in activities such as nappy changing or taking time off work when a child is ill (Segal, 1990b).

Men are selective about what they will do and it is often middle-class men, who demonstrated the greatest 'promise' prior to becoming fathers, who are most likely to let their partners down, with their reluctant or non-existent participation in domestic and childcare activities (Nicolson, 1990). In single-parent male households, most of the men appear to seek female support in order to limit their domestic roles. This varies from female friends and relatives to housekeepers, depending upon financial resources (Segal, 1990b). While women are more likely to have to cope alone, there is some evidence that lone mothers may be less stressed than unhappily-married ones, and that they experience greater autonomy and satisfaction from coping alone (Brown *et al.*, 1986), although this may depend on their economic situation.

Feminism and motherhood: towards the future

[T]he aim of feminism is not to free women from motherhood but from the conditions in which they find motherhood oppressive. (Richardson, 1993, p. 124)

Despite the research by sociologists, psychologists and other 'experts', it has been primarily through the effects of feminist writers that the reality of mothers' lives, and the impact of the idealisation of motherhood and the family upon girls'/women's experience, that the conditions of motherhood were made explicit.

Feminist writers have paid sustained attention to the experience of being a woman and the ways in which motherhood impinges upon women's lives. Accounts of childbirth prior to the work of Ann Oakley tended to be either 'medical' or to extol the joys and fulfilment of childbirth for the truly 'feminine' woman. Feminist writers, while not denying the pleasures of children and the various experiences of childbirth, explored the medicalisation of birth and the ways in which women's control (both as professionals and mothers) had been eroded (Oakley, 1980; Nicolson, 1988). Recognition of patriarchal control of women's bodies inspired women's action in a number of ways over childbirth (for instance, the 'right' to homebirths and the challenge to routine induced deliveries which were fashionable in the mid-1970s).

Understanding the daily lives of mothers with young children was first made explicit by Hannah Gavron (1966), and was followed by other writers who have made further contributions towards explaining the conditions of motherhood (Boulton, 1983; Sharpe, 1994). Gavron specifically explored issues of class and motherhood, and noted the way that for both working- and middle-class women, becoming a mother changed their lives as they lost their independence. However, her work also clarified the ways in which social class differences are exacerbated with the transition to motherhood, as social class is, in part, determined through men's levels of income and, as mothers, married and cohabiting women are more likely to be dependent on men.

Almost 20 years later, Mary Boulton's (1983) study supported the view that experiences of motherhood are to some extent class-related. Although all the mothers in her study reported positive and negative aspects of mothering: 'A large house and domestic conveniences . . . can lighten the burden of childcare and give a woman the time and space for her interests apart from the children; a car and telephone can also help her maintain these interests as well as reduce her sense of isolation at home' (Boulton, 1983, p. 205). For the vast majority of women, these may only be obtained with the help of a partner and even then are clearly subject to social and economic status. Lone mothers, as argued above, are still more likely to be poor, in bad housing and less well educated, so for them the oppressive conditions of motherhood remain unalleviated.

The married woman, however, despite the possibility of greater affluence, does not avoid oppression. As Friedan found (1963), there are still issues about the lack of satisfaction in her relationship with her partner and the sense of pointlessness in her life when she realises she has been pursuing a myth. This myth of marriage and motherhood has been sustained despite some changes in domestic roles. Since the 1970s much attention has been paid to men's fathering. The representations by experts of the benefits to men and their children of being an active father were discussed earlier, along with the evidence that men's fathering is usually on their own terms. Popular ideas about the fatherhood role have changed so that men are expected to, and expect themselves to, enjoy children. The idea that (particularly middle-class) men would take an equal part in domestic activities after becoming parents has, however, been challenged by a number of studies (see, for example, Lewis, 1986). As Lynne Segal (1990b) argues, men will be persuaded to be more involved in fathering when conditions of parenting become more flexible, ensuring maximum choice in terms of childcare, and domestic and employment arrangements.

Despite the centrality of motherhood in women's lives, and the contributions of feminist writers to challenging the invisibility of women's own experience as mothers, feminist analysis has had an ambivalent relationship with motherhood. This may be due in part to the overemphasis upon middle-class white heterosexual women which emerged from early work such as Friedan's, and perhaps a failure to understand the covert pressures towards maternity. Perhaps many feminist writers lost patience with the problems faced by 'comfortable' mothers when there were potentially more pressing political issues.

Women do still opt for motherhood, however, and feminism has made the experience of lone mothers, lesbians, Black and working-class mothers more visible (Griffin, 1989). It is the influence of these groups that has clarified the conditions under which motherhood exists and also the ways in which, paradoxically, motherhood may still be the best option for many. However, more recently attention has been drawn to the benefits as well as the pressures of motherhood in lesbian relationships, and the role of the family in relation to childcare in Black families (Richardson, 1993). Consciousness of feminism may not necessarily change potential choices, but it can make women from all groups aware of discrimination at work, and the lack of domestic equality in the home, as well as the added discrimination experienced by Black women and lesbians.

Conclusion

The influence of feminism has meant that women no longer have to see motherhood, heterosexuality and marriage as the only possible lifestyle, and myths portraying women's happiness as being confined within these parameters have now been exploded. This is not to say that issues of inequality have been removed from women's lives but, through analysis of the motherhood role and its consequences, women and men have access to feminist ideas as dynamic forces of social criticism and change.

Investigations by feminists of mothering in the 1960s identified the hard work and isolated conditions characteristic of most women's lives, in contrast to traditional studies which ignored women in favour of the 'family' and child development. The impact of scientific ideas about childcare and the 'maternal deprivation thesis' had meant that women not only struggled in their tasks individually, but also felt guilty for wanting anything for themselves beyond the home, and inevitably 'failed' as mothers. However, gradually these negative individualistic images of motherhood, which presented a sense of hopelessness, were replaced through a focus upon the social and economic conditions of mothering. This served to unite women in an awareness that the 'failure' was not personal but was a consequence of capitalism and gender inequalities. Also, women began to identify the special and important qualities associated with the motherhood role, which strengthened their ability to cope in a number of spheres.

Such confidence has led to feminist campaigns for change, including ones for better and more flexible day-care, maternity benefits, equal opportunities and improved employment conditions for women generally. Women are increasingly working for wages outside the home, re-entering the education system and gaining qualifications. They are also having fewer children and putting off the age at which they first become mothers. This is a consequence of women feeling they have greater choice as to whether or not to have children, or marry, or to opt out of heterosexual relationships altogether. Motherhood and womanhood, although still linked, no longer prescribe women's lives as they did in the 1950s, although the ideological and material conditions of motherhood are still concerns for feminist theory and practice.

Note

1.   More recently, though, the birth-rate in England and Wales has fallen by 6 000 between 1988 and 1989, to 6 877 000 and to 673 000 000 in 1993. This is a 2 per cent decrease from the previous year and represents the third successive fall (OPCS, 1995).

Further reading

Paula Nicolson and Jane Ussher, *The Psychology of Women's Health and Health Care* (London, Macmillan, 1992). This volume, with essays by feminist psychologists, focuses specifically upon the ways in which mainstream psychology seeks to pathologise women's health and health care, particularly in relation to sexuality and reproduction. It includes chapters on infertility, pregnancy, abortion and health-care provision in relation to childbirth and early motherhood. It also explores the ways in which traditional psychological images of femininity equate with expectations of women's mothering.

Diane Richardson, *Women, Motherhood and Childrearing* (London, Macmillan, 1993). This provides a lucid account of all aspects of mothering from a feminist perspective, drawing upon sociological, historical and psychological ideas. It identifies the complex and often contradictory emotions surrounding the experience of mothering. It is also useful in clarifying the different ways in which feminists have conceptualised motherhood and the changes that the women's movement has brought about in women's lives.

Elizabeth Bortolaia Silva (ed.) *Good Enough Mothering? Feminist Perspectives on Lone Motherhood* (London, Routledge, 1996). This edited collection provides accounts of historical patterns of mothering and ideologies of the family, cross-national comparisons of policies and experiences of lone mothers in developed and developing countries. It analyses recent social policies and legislative changes in family law, the Child Support Act and discourses about the creation of an underclass in Britain and the United States.

Ann Phoenix, Anne Woollett and Eva Lloyd (eds), *Motherhood: Meanings, Practices and Ideologies* (London, Sage, 1991).This collection of essays focuses on particular aspects of mothering practice, concentrating upon the ways in which motherhood is socially constructed and how that construction affects the ways in which women become mothers. Chapter topics include an analysis of childcare manuals, and the messages that those convey, as well as exploring infertility, the experience of teenage motherhood and becoming a mother later in life. The influence of developmental psychology on the expectations about motherhood practice is also discussed.

Rozsika Parker's *Torn in Two: The Experience of Maternal Ambivalence* (London, Virago, 1995) takes a feminist psychoanalytic view of maternal ambivalence. She uses interviews from her clinical work with mothers to look at the joy, pain and guilt associated with mothering. She challenges the traditional psychoanalytic view that mothers are to 'blame' for all a child and adults' ills, and shows how society springs an emotional trap through juxtaposing ideas about femininity, women's roles and childcare.

Bibliography

Aaron, Jane and Sylvia Walby (eds) (1991) *Out of the Margins: Women's Studies in the Nineties* (London, Falmer Press).

Abbott, Pamela (1991) 'Feminist perspectives in sociology: the challenge to "mainstream" orthodoxy', in Jane Aaron and Sylvia Walby (eds), *Out of the Margins: Women's Studies in the Nineties* (London, Falmer Press).

—— and Claire Wallace (1989) 'The family', in P. Brown and R. Sparks (eds), *After Thatcher: Social Policy, Politics and Society* (Buckingham, Open University Press).

—— and Claire Wallace (1990), *An Introduction to Sociology: Feminist Perspectives*, 2nd edn 1996 (London, Routledge).

Abelove, Henry, Michèle Aina Barale and David M. Halperin (eds) (1993) *The Lesbian and Gay Studies Reader* (London, Routledge).

Abraham, John (1995) *Divide and School: Gender and Class Dynamics in Comprehensive Education* (London, Falmer Press).

ABSWAP (Association of Black Social Workers & Allied Professionals) (1983) *Black Children in Care*, Evidence to House of Commons Social Services Committee (London, ABSWAP).

Abu-Lugod, Leila (1990) 'Can there be a feminist ethnography?', *Women and Performance*, 5, 7–27.

Acker, Joan (1990) 'Hierarchies, jobs and bodies: a theory of gendered organizations', *Gender and Society*, 4(2) 139–58.

—— (1992) 'Gendering organisational theory', in A. J. Mills and P. Tancred (eds), *Gendering Organizational Analysis* (London, Sage).

Acker, Sandra (1994) *Gendered Education* (Buckingham, Open University Press).

Adams, Carol (1994) *Neither Man nor Beast: Feminism and the Defence of Animals* (New York, Continuum).

Adams, Maurianne (1977) 'Jane Eyre: Woman's Estate', in Arlyn Diamond and Lee R. Edwards (eds), *The Authority of Experience: Essays in Feminist Criticism* (Amherst, Mass., University of Massachusetts Press).

Adams, Stephanie (1996) 'Women returners and fractured identities', in Nickie Charles and Felicia Hughes-Freeland (eds), *Practising Feminism: Identity Difference Power* (London, Routledge).

Adas, Michael (1989) *Machines as the Measure of Men: Science, Technology and Ideologies of Western Dominance* (London, Cornell University Press).

Adkins, Lisa (1995) *Gendered Work: Sexuality, Family and the Labour Market* (Milton Keynes, Open University Press).

—— (1997) 'Feminist Theory and Economic Change', in Stevi Jackson and Jackie Jones (eds), *Contemporary Feminist Theory* (Edinburgh, Edinburgh University Press).

—— and Celia Lury (1996) 'The cultural, the sexual and the gendering of the labour market', in L. Adkins and V. Merchant (eds), *Sexualizing the Social: Power and the Organization of Sexuality* (London, Macmillan).

Afshar, Haleh (1989) 'Gender roles and the "moral economy of kin" among Pakistani Women in West Yorkshire', *New Community*, 15(2) 211–25.

—— (1994) 'Muslim women in West Yorkshire: growing up with real and imaginary values amidst conflicting views of self and society', in H. Afshar and M. Maynard (eds), *The Dynamics of Race and Gender: Some Feminist Implications* (London, Taylor & Francis).

—— (ed.) (1996) *Women and Politics in the Third World* (London, Routledge).

Agarwal, Bina (1992) 'Cold hearths and barren slopes: the woodfuel crisis in the Third World', in G. Kirkup and L. S. Keller (eds), *Inventing Women* (London, Polity/Open University Press).

Ainsworth, M. D. (1992) 'Attachments and other affectional bonds across the life cycle', in J. Stevenson-Hinde and T. Marris (eds), *Attachment Across the Life Cycle* (New York, Routledge).

Akhter, Farida (1988) 'The state of contraceptive technology in Bangladesh', *Reproductive and Genetic Engineering: Journal of International Feminist Analysis*, 1(2) 153–8.

—— (1992) *Depopulating Bangladesh: Essays on the Politics of Fertility* (Dhaka, Bangladesh, Narigrantha Prabartana [Feminist Bookstore]).

Al-Khalifa, Elisabeth (1988) 'Pin money professionals? Women in teaching', in A. Coyle and J. Skinner (eds), *Women in Work; Positive Action for Change* (London, Macmillan).

Alexander, Jacqui (1991) 'The post-colonial state: the Sexual Offences Bill of Trinidad and Tobago', in C. Mohanty, A. Russo, and L. Torres (eds), *Third World Women and the Politics of Feminism* (Bloomington, Indiana University Press).

Alexander, Sally (1977) 'Women's work in nineteenth-century London: a study of the years 1820–1850', in Juliet Mitchell and Ann Oakley (eds), *The Rights and Wrongs of Women* (Harmondsworth, Penguin).

—— (1980) 'Review Essay', *Capital and Class*, 11, Summer, 138–43.

—— (1984) 'Women, class and sexual differences in the 1830s and 1840s: some reflections on the writing of a feminist history', *History Workshop Journal*, 17, Spring, 125–49.

—— and Barbara Taylor (1981) 'In defence of patriarchy', in Raphael Samuel (ed.), *People's History and Socialist Theory* (London, Routledge & Kegan Paul).

Alexander, Ziggi (1990) 'Let it lie upon the table: the status of Black women's biography in the U.K.', *Gender and History*, 2(1), Spring, 22–33.

Alic, Margaret (1986) *Hypatia's Heritage: A History of Women in Science from Antiquity to the Late Nineteenth Century* (London, The Women's Press).

Allen, Isobel (1988) *Any Room at the Top* (London, Policy Studies Institute).

Allen, Katherine and Kristine Baber (1992) 'Ethical and epistemological tensions in applying a postmodern perspective to feminist research', *Psychology of Women Quarterly*, 16(1), 1–15.

Allen, Sheila and Carol Wolkowitz (1987) *Homemaking: Myths and Realities* (London: Macmillan).

Alonso, Ana Maria (1988) 'The effects of truth: re-presentations of the past and the imagining of community', in *Journal of Historical Sociology*, 1(1) 33–57.

Alvares, Claude (1991) *Decolonizing History: Technology and Culture in India, China and the West 1492 to the Present Day* (New York: Apex Press).

Amir, Menachem (1971) *Patterns in Forcible Rape* (Chicago University Press).

Anderson, Lucy (1995) 'Child support changes – an absent fathers' charter', *Rights of Women Bulletin*, Summer, 6–9.

Ang, Ien (1985) *Watching Dallas* (London, Methuen).

—— (1995) 'I'm a feminist but . . . "other" women and postnational feminism', in Barbara Caine and Rosemary Pringle (eds), *Transitions: New Australian Feminisms* (New York, St Martin's Press).

Ang-Lygate, Magdalene (1996) 'Women who move: experiences of diaspora', in Mary Maynard and June Purvis (eds), *New Frontiers in Women's Studies: Knowledge, Identity and Nationalism* (London, Taylor & Francis).
—— Chris Corrin and Millsom Henry (eds) (1996) *Desperately Seeking Sisterhood: Still Challenging and Building* (London, Taylor & Francis).
Anthias, Floya and Nira Yuval-Davis (1992) *Racialized Boundaries: Race, Nation, Gender, Colour and Class and the Anti-Racist Struggle* (London, Routledge).
Anwell, Maggie (1988) 'Lolita meets the werewolf: *The Company of Wolves*', in Lorraine Gamman and Margaret Marshment (eds), *The Female Gaze* (London, The Women's Press).
Appleton, Helen, M. E. Fernandez, C. L. M. Hill and C. Quiraz (1995) 'Claiming and using indigenous knowledge', in Gender Working Group, United Nations Commission on Science and Technology for Development, *Missing Links: Gender Equity in Science and Technology for Development* (London, Intermediate Technology Publications).
Apter, T. (1993) *Professional Progress: Why Women Still Don't Have Wives* (London, Macmillan).
Arber, Sara and Jay Ginn (1991) *Gender and Later Life: A Sociological Analysis of Resources and Constraints* (London, Sage).
—— and Jay Ginn (eds) (1995) *Connecting Gender and Ageing: A Sociological Approach* (Buckingham, Open University Press).
Arditti, Rita (1990) 'Surrogacy in Argentina', *Issues in Reproductive and Genetic Engineering: Journal of International Feminist Analysis*, 3(1) 35–43.
——, Renate Duelli Klein and Shelley Minden (eds) (1984) *Test Tube Women: What Future For Motherhood?* (London, Pandora).
Armitt, Lucie (ed.) (1991) *Where No Man Has Gone Before: Women and Science Fiction* (London and New York, Routledge).
Armstrong, Nancy (1987) *Desire and Domestic Fiction: A Political History of the Novel* (New York and Oxford, Oxford University Press).
Arnot, Madeleine (1985) *Race and Gender* (Oxford, Pergamon).
—— (1987) 'Political lip-service or radical reform? Central government responses to sex equality as a policy issue', in Madeleine Arnot and Gaby Weiner (eds), *Gender and the Politics of Schooling* (London, Hutchinson).
—— (1992) 'Feminism, education and the New Right', in Madeleine Arnot and Len Barton (eds), *Voicing Concerns* (Wallingford, Triangle).
—— and Len Barton (eds) (1992) *Voicing Concerns* (Wallingford, Triangle).
—— and Gaby Weiner (eds) (1987) *Gender and the Politics of Schooling* (London, Hutchinson).
Arpad, Susan (1993) 'The personal cost of the feminist knowledge explosion', in Cheris Kramarae and Dale Spender (eds), *The Knowledge Explosion: Generations of Feminist Scholarship* (London, Harvester Wheatsheaf).
Askew, Sue and Carol Ross (1988) *Boys Don't Cry* (Milton Keynes, Open University Press).
Atkinson, Kate (1996) *Behind the Scenes at the Museum* (London, Black Swan).
Attar, Dena (1995) 'Boys: from sea-cooks to catering managers', in Janet Holland and Maud Blair with Sue Sheldon (eds), *Debates and Issues in Feminist Research and Pedagogy* (Clevedon, Multilingual Matters).
Atwood, Margaret (1985) *The Handmaid's Tale* (London, Virago).
—— (1989) *Cat's Eye* (London, Bloomsbury).
—— (1993) *The Robber Bride* (London, Virago).
Azim, Firdous (1993) *The Colonial Rise of the Novel* (London, Routledge).
Baca-Zinn, Maxine and Bonnie Thornton-Dill (eds) (1994) *Women of Color in U.S. Society* (Philadelphia, Temple University Press).

Badinter, E. (1981) *The Myth of Motherhood* (London, Souvenir Press).

Baeher, Helen and Ann Gray (eds) (1996) *Turning It On: A Reader in Women and Media* (London, Arnold).

Bailey, Angela (1988) 'Sex-stereotyping in primary school mathematics schemes', *Research in Education*, 39, 39–46.

Ball, Stephen (1994) *Education Reform* (Buckingham, Open University Press).

Balsamo, Anne (1996) *Technologies of the Gendered Body* (Durham, N. Carolina, and London, Duke University Press).

Banks, Olive (1981) *Faces of Feminism* (Oxford, Martin Robertson).

Barad, Karen (1995) 'A feminist approach to teaching quantum physics', in Rosser (ed.), *Teaching the Majority* (New York, Teachers' College Press).

Barker, Pat (1991) *Regeneration* (Harmondsworth, Penguin).

—— (1993) *The Eye in the Door* (Harmondsworth, Penguin).

—— (1995) *The Ghost Road* (London, Viking).

Barrett, Michèle (1980) *Women's Oppression Today: Problems in Marxist – Feminist Analysis* (London, Verso).

—— (1982) 'Feminism and the Definition of Cultural Politics', in R. Brunt and C. Rowan (eds), *Feminism, Culture and Politics* (London, Lawrence & Wishart).

—— (1986) 'The soapbox', *Network* (British Sociological Association newsletter) 35, 20.

—— (1987) 'The concept of "difference"', *Feminist Review*, 26, 29–41.

—— (1988), *Women's Oppression Today*, 2nd edn (London, Verso).

—— (1992) 'Words and Things: Materialism and Method in Contemporary Feminist Analysis', in Michèle Barrett and Ann Phillips (eds), *Destabilising Theory: Contemporary Feminist Debates* (Cambridge, Polity).

—— and Mary McIntosh (1980) 'The "family wage": some problems for socialists and feminists', *Capital and Class*, 2.

—— and Mary McIntosh (1991) *The Anti-Social Family*, 2nd edn (London, Verso).

Barry, Kathleen (1995) *The Prostitution of Sexuality: The Global Exploitation of Women* (London, New York University Press).

—— (1996) 'Deconstructing deconstructionism (or, whatever happened to feminist studies?)', in Diane Bell and Renate Klein (eds), *Radically Speaking: Feminism Reclaimed* (Melbourne, Spinifex Press).

Bartels, Ditta (1988) 'Built-in obsolescence: women, embryo production and genetic engineering', *Reproductive and Genetic Engineering: Journal of International Feminist Analysis*, 1(2) 141–52.

Bartels, M. Dianne, Reinhard Priester, Dorothy E. Vawter and Arthur L. Caplan (eds) (1990) *Beyond Baby M: Ethical Issues in New Reproductive Techniques* (New Jersey, Humana Press).

Barthes, Roland (1975) The Pleasure of the Text (New York, Hill & Wang).

—— (1977) 'The death of the author', first published 1968 in Roland Barthes, *Image-Music-Text*, trans. and ed. Stephen Heath (London, Fontana).

Bartky, Sandra (1977) 'Toward a phenomenology of feminist consciousness', in Mary Vetterling-Braggin, Frederick Elliston and Jane English (eds), *Feminism and Philosophy* (New Jersey, Littlefield Adams).

Baruch, Elaine Hoffman, Armadeo F. D'Adamo and Joni Seager (eds) (1988) *Embryos, Ethics and Women's Rights: Exploring the New Reproductive Technologies* (New York, The Haworth Press).

Basen, Gwynne, Margaret Eichler and Abby Lippman (eds) (1993) *Misconceptions: The Social Construction of Choice and New Reproductive and Genetic Technologies* (Quebec, Voyageur Publishing).

Batman, Gail (1988) *Commonwealth Perspective in IVF Funding* (Canberra Commonwealth Department of Community Services and Health, Australia).

Baum Duberman, Martin, Martha Vicinus and George Chauncey (1991) *Hidden from History: Reclaiming the Gay and Lesbian Past* (Harmondsworth, Penguin).

Baxter, Sue and Geoff Raw (1988) 'Fast food, fettered work: Chinese women in the ethnic catering industry', in S. Westwood and P. Bhachu (eds), *Enterprising Women: Ethnicity, Economy and Gender Relations* (London, Routledge).

Beck, Ulrich (1992) *Risk Society: Towards a New Modernity* (London, Sage).

—— and Elizabeth Beck-Gersheim (1995) *The Normal Chaos of Love* (Cambridge, Polity).

Beckett, H. (1986) 'Cognitive developmental theory in the study of adolescent development', in S. Wilkinson (ed.), *Feminist Social Psychology: Developing Theory and Practice* (Milton Keynes, Open University Press).

Beckett, K. (1996) 'Culture and Politics of Signification: The Case of Child Sexual Abuse', *Social Problems*, 443(1) 57–75.

Beddoe, Deirdre (1983) *Discovering Women's History: A Practical Manual* (London, Pandora).

Beechey, Veronica (1977) 'Some notes on female wage labour in capitalist production', *Capital and Class*, 3, 45–66.

—— (1986) 'Introduction', in Veronica Beechey and Elizabeth Whitelegg (eds), Women in Britain Today (Milton Keynes, Open University Press).

—— (1987) *Unequal Work* (London, Verso).

Begum, Nasa (1992a) 'Disabled women and the feminist agenda', in Hilary Hinds, Ann Phoenix and Jackie Stacey (eds), *Working Out: New Directions For Women's Studies* (London, The Falmer Press).

Begum, Nasa (1992b) 'Disabled women and the feminist agenda', *Feminist Review*, 40, 70–84.

Behar, Ruth (1993) *Translated Woman Crossing the Border with Esperanza's Story* (Boston, Mass., Beacon Press).

Bell, David and Gill Valentine (eds) (1995) *Mapping Desire. Geographies of Sexualities* (London, Routledge).

Bell, Diane and Renate Klein (eds) (1996) *Radically Speaking: Feminism Reclaimed* (Melbourne, Spinifex Press, London, Zed).

Bell, Vicki (1993) *Interrogating Incest, Feminism, Foucault and the Law* (London, Routledge).

Belotti, Elena Gianni (1975) *Little Girls* (London, Writers and Readers Publishing Cooperative).

Belsey, Catherine (1994) *Desire: Love Stories in Western Culture* (Oxford, Basil Blackwell).

—— and Jane Moore (eds) (1989) *The Feminist Reader: Essays in Gender and the Politics of Literary Criticism* (London, Macmillan).

Bem, Sandra Lipsitz (1993) *The Lenses of Gender: Transforming the Debate on Sexual Inequality* (New Haven and London, Yale University Press).

Benjamin, Jessica (1990) *The Bonds of Love* (London, Virago).

Bennett, Judith (1993) 'Women's history: a study in continuity and change', *Women's History Review*, 2(2) 173–84.

Bennett, Paula (1990) 'The pea that duty locks: lesbian and feminist-heterosexual readings of Emily Dickinson's poetry', in Karla Jay and Joanne Glasgow (eds), *Lesbian Texts and Contexts: Radical Revisions* (New York, New York University Press).

Benston, Margaret Lowe (1992) 'Women's voices/men's voices: technology as language', in G. Kirkup and L. S. Keller (eds), *Inventing Women* (London, Polity/Open University Press).

Berg, Maxine (1993) 'What difference did women's work make to the Industrial Revolution?,' *History Workshop Journal*, 35, 22–44.

—— and Pat Hudson (1992) 'Rehabilitating the Industrial Revolution', *Economic History Review*, 45, 24–50.

Berger, Bridget and Peter Berger (1983) *The War Over the Family: Capturing the Middle Ground* (London, Hutchinson).

Berger, John (1972) *Ways of Seeing* (Harmondsworth, Penguin).

Bernard, Jessie (1982) *The Future of Marriage*, 2nd edn (Newhaven, Conn., Yale University Press).

Bernard, Miriam, Catherine Itzin, Chris Phillipson and Julie Skucha (1995) 'Gendered work, gendered retirement', in Sara Arber and Jay Ginn (eds), *Connecting Gender and Ageing* (Buckingham, Open University Press).

Beveridge, William (1942) *Social Insurance and Allied Services* (The Beveridge Report) (London, HMSO).

Bezucha, Rober J. (1985) 'Feminist pedagogy as a subversive activity', in Margo Culley and Catherine Portuges (eds), *Gendered Subjects: The Dynamics of Feminist Teaching* (London, Routledge & Kegan Paul).

Bhachu, Parminder (1988) 'Apni, marzi, kardhi. Home and work: Sikh women in Britain', in S. Westwood and P. Bhachu (eds), *Enterprising Women: Ethnicity, Economy and Gender Relations* (London, Routledge).

Bhatt, Chetan (1995) 'New Foundations: Contingency, Interdeterminary and Black Translocality', in Jeffrey Weeks (ed.) *The Lesser Evil and the Greater Good. The Theory and Politics of Social Diversity* (London, Rivers Oram Press).

Bhavnani, K.-K. (1990) 'What's power got to do with it? Empowerment and social research', in I. Parker and J. Shotter (eds), *Deconstructing Social Psychology* (London, Routledge).

—— (1993a) 'Talking racism and the editing of Women's Studies', in Diane Richardson and Victoria Robinson, *Introducing Women's Studies: Feminist Theory and Practice*, 1st edn (London, Macmillan).

—— (1993b) 'Tracing the Contours: Feminist Research and Feminist Objectivity', *Women's Studies International Forum*, 16(2).

—— (1996) 'If the Glove Fits . . . O. J. Simpson and the US Imaginary'. Opening keynote address for The Body Politic Conference, Johannesburg, South Africa, September.

—— and Reena Bhavnani (1985) 'Racism and resistance in Britain', in David Coates, Graham Johnstone and Ray Bush (eds), *A Socialist Anatomy of Britain* (Cambridge, Polity).

—— and Margaret Coulson (1986) 'Transforming socialist feminism: the challenge of racism', *Feminist Review*, 23, 81–92.

—— and Ann Phoenix (eds) (1994) *Shifting Identities, Shifting Racisms – A Feminism and Psychology Reader* (London, Sage).

Bhopal, Kalwant (1995) 'Women and feminism as subjects of Black study: the difficulties and dilemmas of carrying out re-search', *Journal of Gender Studies*, 4(2), 153–68.

Biology and Gender Group (1989) 'The importance of feminist critique for Contemporary Cell Biology', in N. Tuana (ed.), *Feminism and Science* (Bloomington, Indiana University Press).

Birke, Lynda (1986) *Women, Feminism and Biology* (Brighton, Wheatsheaf).

—— (1991) ' "Life" as we have known it: feminism and the biology of gender', in M. Benjamin (ed.), *Science and Sensibility* (Oxford, Basil Blackwell).

—— (1994a) *Feminism, Animals and Science: The Naming of the Shrew* (Buckingham, Open University Press).

—— (1994b) 'Interventions in hostile territory', in Gabriele Griffin, Marianne Hester, Shirin Rai and Sasha Roseneil (eds), *Stirring It: Challenges for Feminism* (London, Taylor & Francis).

—— (1997) 'Our bodies, ourselves? Feminism and biology', in A. Jaggar and I. Young (eds), *Companion to Feminist Philosophy* (Oxford, Basil Blackwell).

——, Susan Himmelweit and Gail Vines (1990) *Tomorrow's Child, Reproductive Technologies in the 90s* (London, Virago).

Birkett, Dea and Julie Wheelwright (1990) ' "How could she?" Unpalatable facts and feminist heroines', *Gender and History*, 2(1) 49–57.

Birth Statistics (1989) Series FMI, No. 16 (London, HMSO).

Bjørhoude, Gerd (1993) 'Women's Studies in Norway', *Journal of Gender Studies*, 2 (1) 159–65.

Blackwell, Antoinette Brown (1875) extract in Alice Rossi (1974), *The Feminist Papers* (New York, Bantam).

Blair, Maud (1995) ' "Race", class and gender in school research', in Janet Holland and Maud Blair with Sue Sheldon (eds), *Debates and Issues in Feminist Research and Pedagogy* (Clevedon, Multilingual Matters).

Blakemore, Ken and Anthea Symonds (1993) 'Health policy in Britain', in Steve Taylor and David Field (eds), *Sociology of Health and Health Care* (Oxford, Basil Blackwell Scientific Publications).

Bland, Lucy (1986) 'Marriage laid bare: middle-class women and marital sex c.1880–1914', in Jane Lewis (ed.), *Labour and Love: Women's Experience of Home and Family* (Brighton, Wheatsheaf).

—— (1995) *Banishing the Beast: English Feminism and Sexual Morality, 1885–1914* (Harmondsworth, Penguin).

Blaxter, Mildred (1990) *Health and Lifestyles* (London, Routledge).

—— and Elizabeth Paterson (1982) *Mothers and Daughters: Women's Experiences of Home and Family* (Brighton, Wheatsheaf).

Bleier, Ruth (1984) *Science and Gender: A Critique of Biology and Its Theories on Women* (Oxford, Pergamon).

Bleys, Rudi C. (1996) *The Geography of Perversion: Male-to-Male Sexual Behaviour outside the West and the Ethnographic Imagination 1750–1918* (London, Cassell).

Bly, Robert (1990) *Iron John* (Reading, Mass., Addison-Wesley).

—— (1991) *Iron John: A Book about Men* (Shaftesbury, Element Books).

Bobo, Jacqueline (1988) 'The Color Purple: Black Women as Cultural Readers', in E. D. Pribram (ed.) *Female Spectators: Looking at Film and Television* (London, Verso).

Bock, Giselda (1989) 'Women's history and gender history: aspects of an international debate', *Gender and History*, 1(1) 7–30.

—— and Pat Thane (eds) (1991) *Maternity and Gender Policies: Women and the Rise of European Welfare States, 1880–1950* (London, Routledge).

Bogus, S. Diane A. (1990) 'The "Queen B" figure in Black literature', in Karla Jay and Joanne Glasgow (eds), *Lesbian Texts and Contexts: Radical Revisions* (New York University Press).

Bolderston, Helen (1994) 'What they don't teach you on clinical psychology training courses', *Feminism and Psychology*, 4(2), 293–7.

Booth, Charles (1902–3) *Life and Labour of the People in London*, 3rd edn (London, Macmillan).

Bornat, Joanna, Charmaine Pereira, David Pilgrim and Fiona Williams (1990) *Community Care: A Reader* (London, Macmillan).

Bortolaia Silva, Elizabeth (ed.) (1996) *Good Enough Mothering? Feminist Perspectives on Lone Motherhood* (London, Routledge).

Boston Women's Health Collective (1973) *Our Bodies, Ourselves* (New York, Simon & Schuster).

Bott, E. (1957) *Family and Social Network* (London, Tavistock).

Boulton, M. G. (1983) *On Being a Mother* (London, Tavistock).

Boumelha, Penny (1990) *Charlotte Brontë* (Hemel Hempstead, Harvester Wheatsheaf).

Boutilier, Mary and Lucinda San Giovanni (1985) 'Women and sports: reflections on health and policy', in E. Lewin and V. Olesen (eds), *Women, Health and Healing* (London, Tavistock).

Bouvard, Marguerite Guzman (1996) *Women Reshaping Human Rights: How Extraordinary Activists are Changing the World* (Wilmington, Delaware, Scholarly Resources Inc).

Bowlby, J. (1951) *Maternal Care and Mental Health* (Geneva, World Health Organisation monograph).

Bowles, Gloria (1983) 'Is Women's Studies an academic discipline?', in Gloria Bowles and Renate Duelli Klein (eds), *Theories of Women's Studies* (London, Routledge & Kegan Paul).

—— and Renate Duelli Klein (eds) (1983) *Theories of Women's Studies* (London, Routledge & Kegan Paul).

Boyd, Julia A. (1990) 'Ethnic and cultural diversity in feminist therapy: the key to power', in E. White (ed.), *The Black Women's Health Book. Speaking for Ourselves* (Seattle, Seal Press).

Boyle, M. (1992) 'The abortion debate', in P. Nicolson and J. M. Ussher (eds), *The Psychology of Women's Health and Health Care* (London, Macmillan).

Bradley, Harriet (1989) *Men's Work, Women's Work* (Cambridge, Polity Press).

—— (1996) *Fractured Identities: Changing Patterns of Inequality* (Cambridge, Polity Press).

Brah, Avtar (1991) 'Questions of difference and international feminism', in Jane Aaron and Sylvia Walby (eds), *Out of the Margins: Women's Studies in the Nineties* (London, Falmer Press).

—— (1992) 'Difference, diversity and differentiation', in James Donald and Ali Rattansi (eds), *'Race', Culture and Difference* (London, Sage).

—— (1994) ' "Race" and "culture", in the gendering of labour markets: South Asian young women and the labour market', in H. Afshar and M. Maynard (eds), *The Dynamics of Race and Gender: Some Feminist Implications* (London, Taylor & Francis).

—— and Rosemary Deem (1986) 'Towards anti-sexist and anti-racist schooling', *Critical Social Policy*, 16, 66–79.

Braidotti, Rosi (1991) 'Plenary Address', Women's Studies Network Annual Conference, London.

—— (1992) 'Origin and development of gender studies in Western Europe', paper given at the European Network for Women's Studies 'Establishing Gender Studies in Central and Eastern European Countries' Workshop, Wassenaar, The Netherlands, 5–8 November.

—— (1994) *Nomadic Subjects: Embodiment and Sexual Difference in Contemporary Feminist Theory* (New York, Columbia University Press).

—— with Judith Butler (1994) 'Feminism by any other name', *differences: A Journal of Feminist Cultural Studies* 6, Summer–Fall, 27–61.

Brannen, Julia and Peter Moss (1987) 'Dual earner households: women's financial contribution after the birth of the first child', in J. Brannen and G. Wilson (eds), *Give and Take in Families: Studies in Resource Distribution* (London, Allen & Unwin).

—— and Peter Moss (1991) *Managing Mothers* (London, Unwin Hyman).

—— and G. Wilson (eds) (1987) *Give and Take in Families: Studies in Resource Distribution* (London, Allen & Unwin).

Braverman, H. (1974) *Labour and Monopoly Capitalism* (New York and London, Monthly Review Press).

Bray, R. (1991) 'Taking Sides Against Ourselves', *New York Times*, 17 November.

Braybon, Gail and Penny Summerfield (1987) *Out of the Cage: Women's Experiences in Two World Wars* (London, Pandora).

Brehony, Kevin (1984) 'Co-education: perspectives and debates in the early twentieth century', in Rosemary Deem (ed.), *Co-education Reconsidered* (Milton Keynes, Open University Press).

Brewer, Rose (1993) 'Black studies transformed: a consideration of gender, feminism, and Black women's studies', in Cheris Kramarae and Dale Spender (eds), *The Knowledge Explosion: Generations of Feminist Scholarship* (London, Harvester Wheatsheaf).

Bridenthal, Renate, Atina Grossman and Marion Kaplan (eds) (1984) *When Biology Became Destiny: Women in Weimar and Nazi Germany* (New York, Monthly Review Press).

Bright, Suzie and Jill Posener (eds) (1996) *Nothing But the Girl. The Blatant Lesbian Image. A Portfolio and Exploration of Lesbian Erotic Photography* (London, Cassell).

Brighton Women and Science Group (1980) *Alice Through the Microscope: The Power of Science over Women's Lives* (London, Virago).

Brimstone. Lyndie (1991) 'Out of the margins and into the soup: some thoughts on incorporation', in Jane Aaron and Sylvia Walby (eds), *Out of the Margins: Women's Studies in the 1990s* (London, Falmer Press).

Brittan, Arthur (1989) *Masculinity and Power* (Oxford, Basil Blackwell).

Brod, Harry (ed.) (1987) *The Making of Masculinities* (Boston, Mass., Allen & Unwin).

Bronfen, Elisabeth (1992) *Over Her Dead Body: Death, Femininity and the Aesthetic* (Manchester University Press).

Brontë, Charlotte (1847) *Jane Eyre* (reprinted 1966), Q. D. Leavis (ed.) (Harmondsworth, Penguin).

Brophy, Julia (1989) 'Custody law, child care and inequality in Britain', in C. Smart and S. Sevenhuijsen (eds), *Child Custody and the Politics of Gender* (London, Routledge).

—— and Carol Smart (1981) 'From disregard to disrepute: the position of women in family law', *Feminist Review*, 9.

—— and Carol Smart (eds) (1985) *Women in Law* (London, Routledge & Kegan Paul).

Brown, Barbara Packer (1995) 'Irrigating the sacred grove: stages of gender equity development', in Louise Morley and Val Walsh (eds), *Feminist Academics: Creative Agents For Change* (London, Taylor & Francis).

Brown, G. and T. Harris (1978) *The Social Origins of Depression* (London, Tavistock).

Brown, G. W., B. Andrews, T. O. Harris, Z. Adler and L. Bridge (1986) 'Social Support, Self-Esteem and Depression', *Psychological Medicine*, 16, 813–31.

Browne, Naima (ed.) (1991) *Science and Technology in the Early Years* (Buckingham, Open University Press).

Brownmiller, Susan (1976) *Against Our Will* (Harmondsworth, Penguin).

Bruegel, Irene (1979) 'Women as a reserve army of labour: a note on recent British experience', *Feminist Review*, 3, 12–23.

—— (1989) 'Sex and race in the labour market', *Feminist Review*, 32, 49–68.

Brunet, Ariane and Louise Turcotte (1988) 'Separatism and radicalism', in Sarah Lucia Hoagland and Julia Penelope (eds), *For Lesbians Only: A Separatist Anthology* (London, Onlywomen Press).

Brunsden, Charlotte (1986) *Films for Women* (London, BFI).

Brunt, Rosalind and Caroline Rowan (eds) (1982) *Feminism, Culture and Politics* (London, Lawrence and Wishart).

Bryan, Beverley, Stella Dadzie and Suzanne Scafe (1985) *The Heart of the Race: Black Women's Writing in Britain* (London, Virago).

Bryson, Lois, Michael Bittman and Sue Donath (1994) 'Men's welfare state, women's welfare state: tendencies to convergence in practice and theory?', in Diane Sainsbury (ed.), *Gendering Welfare States* (London, Sage).

Bullard, D. and S. Knight (1981) *Sexuality and Physical Disability: Personal Perspectives* (St Louis, Mosby).

Burman, Erica (ed.) (1990) *Feminists and Psychological Practice* (London, Sage).

Burman, Sandra (ed.)(1979) *Fit Work for Women* (London, Croom Helm).

Burns, J. (1992) 'The psychology of lesbian health care', in P. Nicolson and J. M. Ussher (eds), *The Psychology of Women's Health and Health Care* (London, Macmillan).

Burton, Antoinette (1994) 'Rules of thumb: British history and "imperial culture" in nineteenth and twentieth-century Britain', *Women's History Review*, 3(4) 483–500.

—— (1995) *Burdens of History: British Feminism, Indian Women and Imperial Culture 1865–1915* (Bloomington, Indiana University Press).

Busfield, Joan (1989) 'Sexism and psychiatry', *Sociology*, 23(3) 343–64.

Buss, D. M. (1994) 'The strategies of human mating', *American Scientists*, 82, 238–49.

Butler, Judith (1990) *Gender Trouble: Feminism and the Subversion of Identity* (New York and London, Routledge).

—— (1993) *Bodies that Matter: On the Discursive Limits of 'Sex'* (New York and London, Routledge).

—— and Joan Scott (eds) (1992) *Feminists Theorize. The Political* (London, Routledge).

Butterworth, Diane (1993) 'Wanking in Cyberspace: the development of computer porn', *Trouble and Strife*, 27, 33–7.

Buzawa, E. and C. Buzawa (1990) *Domestic Violence: The Criminal Justice Response* (Newbury Park, CA, Sage).

Byrne, Eileen (1978) *Women and Education* (London, Tavistock).

Cahn, Dudley D. and Sally A. Lloyd (1996) *Family Violence from a Communications Perspective* (London, Sage).

Cain, Maureen (1990) 'Realist philosophies and standpoint epistemologies or feminist criminology as a successor science', in Loraine Gelsthorpe and Allison Morris (eds), *Feminist Perspectives in Criminology* (Buckingham, Open University Press).

Caine, Barbara (1992) *Victorian Feminists* (Oxford University Press).

Cairns, Joyce and Bill Inglis (1989) 'A content analysis of ten popular history textbooks for primary schools with particular emphasis on the role of women', *Educational Review*, 41(3) 221–6.

Callaway, Helen (1993) ' "The most essentially female function of all": giving birth', in S. Ardener (ed.), *Defining Females* (London, Croom Helm).

Came, B. and B. Bergman (1990) 'Victims in the home: domestic violence in Quebec', *Canada*, 22 October, 18.

Cameron, Deborah (1989) ' "Released into language": the study of language outside and inside academic institutions', in Ann Thompson and Helen Wilcox (eds), *Teaching Women: Feminism and English Studies* (Manchester University Press).

—— (1992) *Feminism and Linguistic Theory*, 2nd edn; 1st edn 1985 (London, Macmillan).

—— and Elizabeth Frazer (1992) 'On the question of pornography and sexual violence: moving beyond cause and effect', in Catherine Itzin (ed.), *Pornography: Women, Violence and Civil Liberties* (Oxford University Press).

Campbell, Anne (1993) *Out of Control: Men, Women and Aggression* (London, Pandora).

Campbell, Beatrix (1980) 'A feminist sexual politics: now you see it, now you don't', *Feminist Review*, 5, 1–18.

—— (1988) *Unofficial Secrets* (London, Virago).

—— (1993) *Goliath: Britain's Dangerous Places* (London, Methuen).

Campbell, Carole A. (1990) 'Women and AIDS', *Social Science and Medicine*, 30(4) 407–515.

Campbell, Kate (ed.) (1992) *Critical Feminism: Argument in the Disciplines* (Buckingham, Open University Press).

Campbell, M. A. and R. K. Campbell-Wright (1995) 'Toward a feminist algebra', in S. Rosser (ed.), *Teaching the Majority* (New York, Teachers College Press).

Canaan, Joyce E. and and Christine Griffin (1990) 'The new men's studies: part of the problem or part of the solution?', in Jeff Hearn and David Morgan, *Men, Masculinities and Social Theory* (London, Unwin Hyman).

Cancian, Francesca (1990) *Love in America* (Cambridge, Cambridge University Press).

Caplan, Pat (ed.) (1987) *The Cultural Construction of Sexuality* (London, Routledge).

Carabine, Jean (1992) 'Constructing women: women's sexuality and social policy', *Critical Social Policy*, 34, 23–37.

—— (1995) 'Invisible sexualities: sexuality, politics and influencing policy-making', in Angelia R. Wilson (ed.), *A Simple Matter of Justice* (London, Cassell).

—— (1996a) 'A straight playing field or queering the pitch: centring sexuality in social policy', *Feminist Review*, 54, 31–64.

—— (1996b) 'Heterosexuality and social policy', in Diane Richardson (ed.), *Theorising Heterosexuality: Telling it Straight* (Buckingham, Open University Press).

Carby, Hazel V. (1982) 'White woman listen! Black feminism and the boundaries of sisterhood', in Centre for Contemporary Cultural Studies (eds), *The Empire Strikes Back: Race and Racism in 70s Britain* (London, Hutchinson).

—— (1987) *Reconstructing Womanhood: The Emergence of the Afro-American Woman Novelist* (New York and Oxford, Oxford University Press).

Carlen, Pat, Denis Gleeson and Julia Wardhaugh (1992) *Truancy: The Politics of Compulsory Schooling* (Buckingham, Open University Press).

Carmen, Gail, Shaila and Pratibha (1984) 'Becoming visible: Black lesbian discussions', *Feminist Review*, 17, Autumn, 53–74.

Carpenter, Mary Wilson (1996) 'Female grotesques in academia: ageism, antifeminism, and feminists on the faculty', in VèVè Clark, Shirley Nelson Garner, Margaret Higonnet and Ketu H. Katrak (eds), *Antifeminism in the Academy* (New York and London, Routledge).

Carr, Helen (ed.) (1989) *From My Guy to Sci-Fi: Genre and Women's Writing in the Post-modern World* (London, Pandora).

Carter, Angela (1979) *The Bloody Chamber and Other Stories*, reprinted 1981 (Harmondsworth, Penguin).

—— (1992) *Wise Children*, reprinted 1992 (London, Vintage).

Cartwright, Ann and Robert Anderson (1981) *General Practice Revisited* (London, Tavistock).

Cartwright, Lisa (1995) *Screening the Body: Tracing Medicine's Visual Culture* (Minneapolis and London, University of Minnesota Press).

Castle, Terry (1993) *The Apparitional Lesbian: Female Homosexuality and Modern Culture* (New York, Columbia University Press).

Cavendish, Ruth (1982) *Women on the Line* (London, Routledge & Kegan Paul).

Cavin, Susan (1985) *Lesbian Origins* (San Francisco, ism Press).

Central Statistical Office (CSO) (1993) *Social Trends*, 23 (London, HMSO).

—— (1994) *Social Trends*, 24 (London, HMSO).

—— (1995) *Social Trends*, 25 (London, HMSO).

—— (1996) *Social Trends*, 26 (London, HMSO).

Chakravarthy, Radha (1992) 'Science, technology and development: the impact on the status of women', in G. Kirkup and L. S. Keller (eds), *Inventing Women* (London, Polity/Open University Press).

Chambers, Deborah (1986) 'The constraints of work and domestic schedules on women's leisure', *Leisure Studies*, 5, 309–25.

(charles), Helen (1992) 'Whiteness – The relevance of politically colouring the "non"', in Hilary Hinds, Ann Phoenix and Jackie Stacey (eds), *Working Out: New Directions For Women's Studies* (London, Falmer Press).

Charles, Nickie (1993) *Gender Divisions and Social Change* (Hemel Hempstead, Harvester Wheatsheaf).

—— (1996) 'Feminist practices: identity, difference, power', in Nickie Charles and Felicia Hughes-Freeland (eds), *Practising Feminism: Identity Difference Power* (London, Routledge).

—— and Felicia Hughes-Freeland (eds) (1996) *Practising Feminism: Identity Difference Power* (London, Routledge).

Chaudhuri, Nupur and Margaret Strobel (eds) (1992) *Western Women and Imperialism: Complicity and Resistance* (Bloomington Indiana, Indiana University Press).

Chesler, Phyllis (1972) *Women and Madness* (London, Allen Lane).

—— (1988) *Scared Bond: Motherhood Under Siege* (New York, Times Books; and London, Virago, 1990).

Chester, Gail and Julienne Dickey (eds) (1988) *Feminism and Censorship* (London, Prism Press).

Chisholm, Diane (1992) 'The uncanny', in Elizabeth Wright (ed.), *Feminism and Psychoanalysis: A Critical Dictionary* (Oxford, Basil Blackwell).

Chodorow, N. (1978) *The Reproduction of Mothering* (Berkeley, University of California Press).

—— (1992) *Feminism and Psychoanalytic Theory* (London, Yale University Press).

—— and S. Contratto (1982) 'The fantasy of the perfect mother', in B. Thorne and M. Yalom (eds), *Rethinking the Family: Some Feminist Questions* (New York, Longman).

Chorover, Stephen (1980) *From Genesis to Genocide: The Meaning of Human Nature and the Power of Behaviour Control* (Cambridge, Mass., MIT).

Christian, Barbara (1987) 'The race for theory' *Cultural Critique*, Spring, 51–63.

—— (1990) 'The race for theory', in Karen V. Hansen and Ilene J. Philipson (eds), *Women, Class and Feminist Imagination: A Socialist-Feminist Reader* (Philadelphia, Temple University Press).

Christian Smith, Linda (ed.) (1993) *Texts of Desire: Essays on Fiction, Femininity and Schooling* (London, Falmer Press).

Church, J. and C. Sommerfield (1995) *Social Focus on Women*, Central Statistical Office (London, HMSO).

Cixous, Hélène (1981) 'The laugh of the Medusa', in Elaine Marks and Isobel de Courtivron (eds), *New French Feminisms* (Brighton, Harvester).

—— (1989) 'Sorties: out and out: attacks/ways out/forays', in Catherine Belsey and Jane Moore (eds), *The Feminist Reader: Essays in Gender and the Politics of Literary Criticism* (London, Macmillan).

Clark, Alice (1968) *Working Life of Women in the Seventeenth Century*, 1st edn 1919 (London, Frank Cass).

Clark, Anna (1988) *Women's Silence, Men's Violence, Sexual Assault in England, 1770–1845* (London, Pandora).

—— (1995) *The Struggle for the Breeches. Gender and the Making of the British Working Class* (London, Rivers Oram).

Clarke, Adele (1994) 'Subtle forms of sterilisation abuse: a reproductive rights analysis', in A. Jaggar (ed.), *Living with Contradictions: Controversies in Feminist Social Ethics* (Oxford, Westview Press).

Clarke, June, Mandy Merck and Diana Simmonds (1982) 'Doris Day case study: stars and exhibition', *Star Signs: Papers from a Weekend Workshop* (London, BFI).

Clarke, VèVè, Shirley Nelson Garner, Margaret Higonnet and Ketu H. Katrak (eds) (1996) *Antifeminism in the Academy* (New York and London, Routledge).

Clarricoates, Katherine (1978) 'Dinosaurs in the classroom – a re-examination of some of the aspects of the "hidden curriculum", in primary schools', *Women's Studies International Quarterly*, 1, 353–64.

—— (1980) 'The importance of being Ernest . . . Emma . . . Tom . . . Jane. The perception and categorisation of gender conformity and gender deviation in primary schools', in Rosemary Deem (ed.), *Schooling for Women's Work* (London, Routledge & Kegan Paul).

—— (1987) 'Child culture at school: a clash between gendered worlds?', in A. Pollard (ed.), *Children and their Primary School* (Lewes, Falmer).

Clegg, Sue (1985) 'Feminist methodology – fact or fiction?', *Quality and Quantity*, 19, 83–97.

Cobbe, Francis Power (1987) 'Wife torture in England' (first published in 1878), in Sheila Jeffreys (ed.), *The Sexuality Debates* (New York, Routledge & Kegan Paul).

Cockburn, Cynthia (1981) 'The material of male power', *Feminist Review*, 9, 41–8.

—— (1983) *Brothers: Male Dominance and Technological Change* (London, Pluto).

—— (1991) *In The Way of Women: Men's Resistance to Sex Equality in Organisations* (Basingstoke, Macmillan).

—— and Susan Ormrod (1993) *Gender and Technology in the Making* (London, Sage).

Code, Lorraine (1991) *What Can She Know?* (Ithaca, NY, Cornell University Press).

Coffey, Amanda and Sandra Acker (1991) ' "Girlies on the warpath": addressing gender in initial teacher education', *Gender and Education*, 3(3) 249–61.

Cohen, Bronwen (1988) *Caring for Children: Services and Policies for Childcare and Equal Opportunities in the UK*. Report for the European Commission's Childcare Network (London, Family Policy Studies Centre).

Cohen, Sherrill and Nadine Taub (eds) (1989) *Reproductive laws for the 1990s* (New Jersey, Humana Press).

Colley, Ann, Chris Comber and David J. Hargreaves (1994) 'School subject preferences of pupils in single sex and co-educational secondary schools', *Educational Studies*, 20(3) 379–85.

Collins, Patricia Hill (1990) *Black Feminist Thought: Knowledge, Consciousness and the Politics of Empowerment* (London, HarperCollins).

—— (1996) 'Black women and the sex/gender hierarchy', in Stevi Jackson and Sue Scott (eds), *Feminism and Sexuality: A Reader* (Edinburgh University Press). Reprinted from Patricia Hill Collins (1990), *Black Feminist Thought: Knowledge, Consciousness and the Politics of Empowerment* (London, HarperCollins).

Collinson, David and Margaret Collinson (1989) 'Sexuality in the workplace: the domination of men's sexuality', in J. Hearn *et al.* (eds), *The Sexuality of Organisation* (London, Sage).

Colmina, Beatriz (ed.) (1992) *Sexuality and Space* (New York, Princeton Architectural Press).

Combahee River Collective (1981) 'A Black feminist statement', in Cherrie Moraga and Gloria Anzaldua (eds), *This Bridge Called my Back* (Watertown, Mass., Persephone Press).

Commeyras, Michelle and Donna E. Alvermann (1996) 'Reading about women in world history textbooks from one feminist perspective', *Gender and Education*, 8(1) 31–48.

Communicable Disease Report (1993) 3(4) *AIDS and HIV in the United Kingdom: Monthly Report*, 17–20.

Connell, R. W. (1993) *Gender and Power* (Cambridge, Polity).

Conseil Du Statut De La Femme (1988) *Sortir la Maternité du Laboratoire* (Quebec, Gouvernement du Quebec).

Cook, Judith (1983) 'An interdisciplinary look at feminist methodology', *Humboldt Journal of Social Relations*, 10, 127–52.

—— and Mary Fonow (1986) 'Knowledge and women's interests: issues of epistemology and methodology in feminist sociological research', *Sociological Inquiry*, 56, 2–29.

Cook, Pam and Philip Dodd (eds) (1994) *Women and Film: A Sight and Sound Reader* (London, BFI/Scarlett Press).

Coons, Phillip, E. S. Bowman, T. A. Pellow and P. Schneider (1989) 'Post traumatic aspects of the treatment of victims of sexual abuse and incest', *Psychiatric Clinics of North America*, 12(2) 325–35.

Coonz, Stephanie (1988) *The Social Origins of Family Life: A History of American Families 1600–1900* (London, Verso).

Cooper, C. and S. Lewis (1993) *The Workplace Revolution: Managing Today's Dual Career Families* (London, Kogan Page).

Cooper, Davina (1994) *Sexing the City* (London, Rivers Oram).

Cooper, Fiona (1988) *Rotary Spokes* (London, Brilliance Books).

Coote, Anna and Beatrix Campbell (1982) *Sweet Freedom* (London, Pan), 2nd edn (Oxford, Basil Blackwell, 1987).

Corea, Gena (1985) *The Mother Machine: Reproductive Technologies from Artificial Insemination to Artificial Wombs* (New York, Harper & Row; and London, The Women's Press, 1988).

—— and Susan Ince (1987) 'Report of a survey of IVF clinics in the US', in Pat Spallone and Deborah Lynn Steinberg (eds), *Made to Order* (Oxford, Pergamon).

—— *et al.* (1985) *Man-Made Woman: How New Reproductive Technologies Affect Women* (London, Hutchinson; and Indiana University Press, 1987).

Cornillon, Susan Koppelman (ed.) (1972) *Images of Women in Fiction: Feminist Perspectives* (Bowling Green, Ohio, Bowling Green University Popular Press).

Cornwall, Andrea and Nancy Lindisfarne (eds) (1994) *Dislocating Masculinity: Comparative Ethnographics* (London, Routledge).

Cornwell, Jocelyn (1984) *Hard Earned Lives: Accounts of Health and Illness from East London* (London, Tavistock).

Corrin, Chris (1992) 'Women's Studies in Central and Eastern Europe', in Hilary Hinds, Ann Phoenix and Jackie Stacey (eds), *Working Out: New Directions For Women's Studies* (London, The Falmer Press).

Cosslett, Tess, Alison Easton and Penny Summerfield (eds) (1996) *Women, Power and Resistance: An Introduction to Women's Studies* (Buckingham, Open University Press).

Coulson, Margaret and Kum-Kum Bhavnani (1990) 'Making a difference – questioning women's studies', in Erica Burman (ed.), *Feminists and Psychological Practice* (London, Sage).

Coveney, Lal, Margaret Jackson, Sheila Jeffreys, Leslie Kaye and Pat Mahony (1984) *The Sexuality Papers: Male Sexuality and the Social Control of Women* (London, Hutchinson).

Coward, Rosalind (1980) 'Are women's novels feminist novels?', *Feminist Review*, 5.

—— (1983) *Patriarchal Precedents: Sexuality and Social Relations* (London, Routledge & Kegan Paul).

—— (1989) 'The true story of how I became my own person' (first published 1984) in Catherine Belsey and Jane Moore (eds), *The Feminist Reader: Essays in Gender and the Politics of Literary Criticism* (London, Macmillan).

—— and John Ellis (1977) *Language and Materialism: Developments in Semiology and the Theory of the Subject* (London, Routledge & Kegan Paul).

—— and Linda Semple (1989) 'Tracking down the past: women and detective fiction', in Helen Carr (ed.), *From My Guy to Sci-Fi* (London, Pandora).

Cox, J. and J. Holden (eds) (1994), *Perinatal Psychiatry: Use and Misuse of the Edinburgh Postnatal Depression Scale* (London, Gaskell/Royal College of Psychiatrists).

Cramer, Patricia and Ann Russo (1993) 'Toward a multicentered Women's Studies in the 1990s', in Cheris Kramarae and Dale Spender (eds), *The Knowledge Explosion: Generations of Feminist Scholarship* (London, Harvester Wheatsheaf).

Cranny-Francis, Anne (1990) *Feminist Fiction: Feminist Uses of Generic Fiction* (Cambridge, Polity).

Creed, Barbara (1993) *The Monstrous – Feminine: Film, Feminism and Psychoanalysis* (London, Routledge).

Crompton, Rosemary and Kay Sanderson (1989) *Gendered Jobs and Social Change* (London, Allen & Unwin).

Crouch, M. and L. Manderson (1995) 'The social life of bonding theory', *Social Science and Medicine*, 41(6) 837–44.

Crowe, Christine (1985) 'Women want it: in vitro fertilization and women's motivations for participation', *Women's Studies International Forum*, 8(6).

Crowley, Helen and Susan Himmelweit (1992) *Knowing Women, Feminism and Knowledge* (Cambridge, Oxford and Buckingham, Polity, Basil Blackwell and Open University Press).

Crowther Report (1959) *15 to 18, A Report of the Central Advisory Council for Education* (London, HMSO).

Crumpacker, Laurie and Eleanor Vander Haegen (1987) 'Pedagogy and prejudice: strategies for confronting homophobia in the classroom' *Women's Studies Quarterly*, XV(3 and 4), Fall/Winter, 65–73.

CSO: *see under* Central Statistical Office.

Cullingford, Cedric (1993) 'Children's views on gender issues in school', *British Educational Research Journal*, 19(5) 555–63.

Currie, Dawn (1988) 'Re-thinking what we do and how we do it', *Canadian Review of Sociology and Anthropology*, 25, 231–53.

—— and Hamida Kazi (1987) 'Academic feminism and the process of de-radicalisation', *Feminist Review*, 25, 77–98.

Dalla Costa, Maria Rosa (1972) 'Women and the subversion of the community', in Maria Della Costa and Selma James, *The Power of Women and the Subversion of the Community* (Bristol, Falling Wall Press).

Dalley, Gillian (1988) *Ideologies of Caring: Rethinking Community and Collectivism* (London, Macmillan).

Dalton, K. (1980) *Depression After Childbirth: how to recognize and treat postnatal illness* (Oxford University Press).

Daly, Mary (1978) *Gyn/Ecology: The Metaethics of Radical Feminism* (Boston, Mass., Beacon Press; and London, The Women's Press, 1979).

Daniels, Arlene Kaplan (1975) 'Feminist perspectives in sociological research', in Marcia Millman and Rosabeth Kanter (eds), *Another Voice* (New York, Anchor Books).

David, Miriam (1986) 'The moral and the maternal: the family and the new right', in R. Levitas (ed.), *The Ideology of the New Right* (Cambridge, Polity).

—— (1992) 'Parents and the state: how has social research informed educational reforms', in Madeleine Arnot and Len Barton (eds), *Voicing Concerns* (Wallingford, Triangle).

Davidoff, Leonore (1973) *The Best Circles: Society, Etiquette and the Season* (London, Croom Helm).

—— and Catherine Hall (1987) *Family Fortunes: Men and Women of the English Middle Class 1780–1850* (London, Hutchinson).

Davies, Bronwyn (1989) *Frogs and Snails and Feminist Tales* (London, Allen & Unwin).

—— and Chas Banks (1995) 'The gender trap: a feminist poststructuralist analysis of primary school children's talk about gender', in Janet Holland and Maud Blair with Sue Sheldon (eds), *Debates and Issues in Feminist Research and Pedagogy* (Clevedon, Multilingual Matters).

Davies, Carole Boyce (1994) *Black Women, Writing and Identity: Migrations of the Subject* (London, Routledge).

Davies, Celia and Penny Holloway (1995) 'Troubling transformations: gender regimes and organizational culture in the academy', in Louise Morley and Val Walsh (eds), *Feminist Academics: Creative Agents for Change* (London, Taylor & Francis).

Davies, Emily (1868) 'Special Systems of Education for Women', in Dale Spender (ed.) (1987), *The Education Papers: Women's Quest for Equality in Britain 1850–1912* (London, Routledge & Kegan Paul).

Davies, Lynn (1984) *Pupil Power: Deviance and Gender at School* (Lewes, Falmer Press).

Davin, Anna (1972) 'Women and history', in Micheline Wandor (comp.), *The Body Politic. Women's Liberation in Britain 1969–1972* (London, Stage 1).

—— (1978) 'Imperialism and motherhood', *History Workshop Journal*, 5, 9–65.

—— (1981) 'Feminism and labour history', in Raphael Samuel (ed.), *People's History and Socialist Theory* (London, Routledge & Kegan Paul).

Davis, Angela (1971) 'Reflections on the role of the black woman in the community of slaves', *Black Scholar*, December 3–15.

—— (1982) *Women, Race and Class* (London, The Women's Press).

—— (1990) 'Sick and tired of being sick and tired: the politics of Black women's health', in Evelyn White (ed.) *The Black Women's Health Book. Speaking for Ourselves* (Seattle, Seal Press).

Dawtrey, Liz, Janet Holland and Merril Hammer with Sue Sheldon (eds) (1995) *Equality and Inequality in Education Policy* (Clevedon, Multilingual Matters/Open University Press).

Daykin, Norma and Jennie Naidoo (1995) 'Feminist critiques of health promotion', in Robin Bunton, Sara Nettleton and Roger Burrows (eds), *The Sociology of Health Promotion* (London, Routledge).

de Beauvoir, Simone (1949) *The Second Sex* (reprinted 1972) ((Harmondsworth, Penguin).

de Francis, Vincent (1969) *Protecting the Child Victims of Sex Crimes Committed by Adults* (Denver, Colorado, African Humane Society).

de Groot, Joanna (1994) 'Roses and thorns: modest thoughts on prickly issues', in Gabriele Griffin (ed.), *Changing Our Lives: Doing Women's Studies* (London, Pluto).

—— and Mary Maynard (1993) 'Doing things differently? A context for women's studies in the next decade', in Joanna de Groot and Mary Maynard (eds), *Women's Studies in the 1990s. Doing Things Differently?* (London, Macmillan).

de Lauretis, Teresa (1991) 'Queer Theory: lesbian and gay sexualities: an introduction', *differences: A Journal of Feminist Cultural Studies*, 3(2) iii–xviii.

—— (1994) *The Practice of Love: Lesbian Sexuality and Perverse Desire* (Bloomington, Indiana University Press).

de Lyon, Hilary and Frances Migniuolo (eds) (1989) *Women Teachers* (Milton Keynes, Open University Press).

Deakin, Nicholas and Malcom Wicks (1988) *Families and the State* (London, Family Policy Studies Centre).

Deem, Rosemary (ed.) (1980) *Schooling for Women's Work* (London, Routledge & Kegan Paul).

—— (1981) 'State policy and ideology in the education of women 1914–1980', *British Journal of Sociology of Education*, 2(2) 131–43.

—— (1995) 'Do methodology and epistemology still matter to feminist educational researchers?,' paper presented to European Conference of Educational Researchers, University of Bath, Sept. 1995.

Degener, Theresia (1990) 'Female self-determination between feminist claims and "voluntary" eugenics, between "rights" and ethics', *Issues in Reproductive and Genetic Engineering: Journal of International Feminist Analysis*, 3(2) 87–99.

Delamont, Sara (1990) *Sex Roles and the School*, 2nd edn (London, Routledge and Methuen).

Delphy, Christine (1970) 'Liberation des femmes année zero', Partisans, 50/51, Maspero. Translated in mimeo form, Edinburgh Women's Liberation Conference 1974.

—— (1984) *Close to Home: A Materialist Analysis of Women's Oppression* (London, Hutchinson).

—— (1992) 'Mother's union?', *Trouble and Strife*, 24, 12–19.

—— (1994) 'Changing women in a changing Europe: is "difference" the future for feminism?', *Women's Studies International Forum*, 17 (2/3) 187–201.

—— and Diana Leonard (1992) *Familiar Exploitation: A New Analysis of Marriage in Contemporary Western Societies* (Cambridge, Polity).

DeLynn, Jane (1990) *Don Juan in the Village* (London, Serpent's Tail).

Denfield, R. (1995) *The New Victorians: A Young Woman's Challenge to the Old Feminist Order* (New York, Simon & Schuster).

Department for Education, *Statistics of Education; Teachers in Service*, England and Wales 1992 (London, HMSO).

—— *Statistical Bulletin 24/93: Public Examinations GCSE and GCE 1993* (London, HMSO).

Department for Education and Employment, *Statistical Bulletin 6/95: GCSE and GCE A/AS Examination Results 1993/94* (London, HMSO).

Department of Health (1994) *Health and Personal Social Services Statistics for England* (London, HMSO).

Dhavernas, Marie-Jo (1996) 'Hating masculinity not men', in Stevi Jackson and Sue Scott (eds), *Feminism and Sexuality. A Reader* (Edinburgh University Press). Reprinted from Claire Duchen (ed.), *French Connections* (London, Unwin Hyman, 1987).

DHSS (1983) *NHS Management Inquiry* (Griffiths Report) (London, HMSO).

Diamond, Irene (1994) *Fertile Ground: Women, Earth and the Limits of Control* (Boston, Mass., Beacon Press).

Dick, Leslie (1987) *Without Falling* (London, Serpent's Tail).

—— (1989) 'Feminism, writing, postmodernism', in Helen Carr (ed.), *From My Guy to Sci-Fi: Genre and Women's Writing in the Post-modern World* (London, Pandora).

Dickens, Linda (1995) 'Legal update: UK part-time employees and the law – recent and potential developments', *Gender, Work and Organisation*, 2(4) 207–15.

Doan, Laura (ed.) (1994) *The Lesbian Postmodern* (New York, Columbia University Press).

Dobash, Rebecca and Russell Dobash (1987) 'The response of the British and American women's movement to violence against women', in Jalna Hanmer and Mary Maynard (eds), *Women, Violence and Social Control* (London, Macmillan).

—— and Russell Dobash (1992) *Women, Violence and Social Control* (London, Routledge).

Dollimore, Jonathan (1991) *Sexual Dissidence: Augustine to Wilde, Freud to Foucault* (Oxford, Clarendon Press).

Donovan, Josephine (1991) 'Animal rights and feminist theory', *Signs*, 15, 350–75.

Dosanj-Matwala, N. and A. Woollett (1990) 'Asian women's ideas about contraception, family size and composition', *Journal of Reproductive and Infant Psychology*, 8, 231–2.

Douglas, Carol Anne (1990) *Love and Politics: Radical Feminist and Lesbian Theories* (San Francisco, ism Press).

Douglas, Jenny (1992) 'Black women's health matters: putting black women on the research agenda', in Helen Roberts (ed.), *Women's Health Matters* (London, Routledge).

Downing, Hazel (1983) 'On being automated', *Aslib Proceedings*, 35(1) 38–51.

Doyal, Lesley (1985) 'Women and the National Health Service: the carers and the careless', in E. Lewin and V. Olesen (eds), *Women, Health and Healing* (London, Tavistock).

—— (1995) *What Makes Women Sick? Gender and the Political Economy of Health* (London, Macmillan).

—— and Mary Ann Elston (1986) 'Women, health and medicine', in V. Beechey and E. Whitelegg (eds), *Women in Britain Today* (Buckingham, Open University Press).

—— Jennie Naidoo and Tamsin Wilton (1994) *AIDS: Setting a Feminist Agenda* (London, Taylor & Francis).

Drake, Barbara (1920) *Women and Trade Unions* (London, Labour Research Department).

Dreifus, Claudia (ed.) (1977) *Seizing Our Bodies: The Politics of Women's Health* (New York, Vintage Books).

Driver, Emily (1989) 'Introduction', in Emily Driver and Audrey Droisen (eds), *Child Sexual Abuse* (London, Macmillan).

Droisen, Audrey (1989) 'Racism and anti-semitism', in Emily Driver and Audrey Droisen (eds), *Child Sexual Abuse* (London, Macmillan).

du Cille, Ann (1994) 'The occult of true Black womanhood: critical demeanor and Black feminist studies', *Signs*, 19(3) 591–629.

Duchen, Claire (1986) *Feminism in France* (London, Routledge).

Duncombe, Jean and Dennis Marsden (1993) 'Love and intimacy: the gender division of emotion and "emotion work"', *Sociology*, 27 (2) 221–41.

—— and Dennis Marsden (1995) '"Can men love?" "Reading", "staging" and "resisting" the romance', in Lynne Pearce and Jackie Stacey (eds), *Romance Revisited* (London, Lawrence & Wishart).

Dunn, Sara (1990) 'Voyages of the Valkyries: recent lesbian pornographic writing', *Feminist Review*, 34, 161–70.

Dunne, Gillian (1996) *Lesbian Lifestyles: Women's Work and the Politics of Sexuality* (London, Macmillan).

Dworkin, Andrea (1981) *Pornography: Men Possessing Women* (London, The Women's Press).

—— (1987) *Right-wing Women: The Politics of Domesticated Females*, first published New York, Perigree Books (London, The Women's Press).

—— (1991) Interview, *The Guardian*, 5 December, 21.

—— (1996) 'Dworkin on Dworkin', in Diane Bell and Renate Klein (eds), *Radically Speaking: Feminism Reclaimed* (Melbourne, Spinifex).

Dyer, Richard *et al.* (1981) *Coronation Street* (London, BFI monograph).

Dyhouse, Carol (1981) *Girls Growing Up in Late Victorian and Edwardian England* (London, Routledge & Kegan Paul).

Echols, Alice (1989) *Daring to Be Bad: Radical Feminism in America 1967–75* (University of Minnesota Press).

Edholm, Felicity (1982) 'The unnatural family', in E. Whitelegg, M. Arnot, E. Bartels, V. Beechey and L. Birke (eds), *The Changing Experience of Women* (Oxford, Martin Robertson).

Edwards, Robert (1989) *Life Before Birth: Reflections on the Embryo Debate* (London, Hutchinson).

—— and Patrick Steptoe (1980) *A Matter of Life: The Story of a Medical Breakthrough* (London, Hutchinson).

Edwards, Rosalind (1993) *Mature Women Students* (London, Taylor & Francis).

Edwards, Susan (1981) *Female Sexuality and the Law* (Oxford, Martin Robertson).

—— (1993) 'Battered woman syndrome', in *Justice for Women Information Pack* (London, The London Justice for Women Collective).

Ehrenreich, Barbara and Deirdre English (1979) *For Her Own Good: 150 Years of the Experts' Advice to Women* (London, Pluto).

—— Elizabeth Hess and Gloria Jacobs (1987) *Re-making Love: The Feminization of Sex* (London, Fontana).

Eichler, Margrit (1980) *The Double Standard* (London, Croom Helm).

—— (1985) 'And the work never ends: feminist contributions', *Canadian Review of Sociology and Anthropology*, 22, 619–44.

Eisenstein, Hester (1984) *Contemporary Feminist Thought* (London, Unwin).

Eisenstein, Zillah (1994) *The Color of Gender: Reimaging Democracy* (Berkeley, University of California Press).

Elliot, S. A. (1990), 'Commentary on "Childbirth as a Life Event",' *Journal of Reproductive and Infant Psychology*, 8, 147–59.

Elliott, Michele (1993) 'Introduction', in Michele Elliott (ed.), *Female Sexual Abuse of Children: The Ultimate Taboo* (Harlow, Longman).

Ellman, Mary (1968) *Thinking about Women* (New York, Harcourt Brace Jovanovich).

Elston, Mary Ann (1987) 'Women and anti-vivisection in Victorian England', in N. Rupke (ed.), *Vivisection in Historical Perspective* (London, Routledge).

Enloe, Cynthia (1990) *Bananas, Beaches And Bases: Making Feminist Sense Of International Politics* (Berkeley, University of California Press).

Epstein, Debbie (ed.) (1994) *Challenging Lesbian and Gay Inequalities in Education* (Buckingham, Open University Press).

—— (1995) 'In our (new) right minds: the hidden curriculum and the academy', in Louise Morley and Val Walsh (eds), *Feminist Academics: Creative Agents For Change* (London, Taylor & Francis).

Epstein, Julia (1995) *Altered Conditions: Disease, Medicine, Storytelling* (London, Routledge).

—— and Kristina Straub (eds) (1991) *Body Guards: the Cultural Politics of Gender Ambiguity* (London, Routledge).

Equal Opportunities Commission (1990) *Women and Men in Great Britain 1990* (HMSO, London).

—— (1991) *Women and Men in Britain* (London, HMSO).

—— (1994) *Black Women in the Labour Market: A Research Review by Reena Bhavnani* (Manchester, EOC).

—— (1996) *Facts About Women 1996* (Manchester, EOC).

Escoffier, Jeffrey (1990) 'Inside the ivory closet: the challenges facing lesbian and gay studies', *Out/Look*, Fall, 40–8.

Esping-Andersen, G. (1990) *The Three Worlds of Welfare Capitalism (Cambridge, Polity)*.

—— (1993) *Changing Classes* (London, Sage).

European Women's Lobby (1993) *Confronting the Fortress: Black and Migrant Women in the European Community*. Report written by Emma Franks of the European Forum of Left Feminists (Brussels, European Women's Lobby).

Evans, David (1993) *Sexual Citizenship: The Material Construction of Sexualities* (London, Routledge).

Evans, Mary (1991) 'The problem of gender for women's studies', in Jane Aaron and Sylvia Walby (eds), *Out of the Margins: Women's Studies in the Nineties* (London, Falmer Press).

—— (ed.) (1994) *The Woman Question*, 2nd edn (London, Sage).

—— (1995) 'Culture and class', in Maud Blair and Janet Holland with Sue Sheldon (eds), *Identity and Diversity* (Clevedon, Multilingual Matters).

—— (1996) *Introducing Contemporary Feminist Thought* (Cambridge, Polity Press).

Evanson, E. (1980) *Just Me and the Kids: A Study of Single-Parent Families in Northern Ireland* (Belfast, Equal Opportunities Commission of Northern Ireland).

Everywoman (1988) *Pornography and Sexual Violence: Evidence of Links* (London, Everywoman).

Ewing, Christine M. (1988) 'Tailored genes: IVF, genetic engineering and eugenics', *Reproductive and Genetic Engineering: Journal of International Feminist Analysis*, 1(1) 31–40.

—— (1990a) 'Australian perspectives on embryo experimentation: an update', *Issues in Reproductive and Genetic Engineering: Journal of International Feminist Analysis*, 3(2) 119–23.

—— (1990b) 'Draft report on surrogacy issued by the Australian National Bioethics Consultative Committee', *Issues in Reproductive and Genetic Engineering: Journal of International Feminist Analysis*, 3(2) 143–6.

Faderman, Lillian (1981) *Surpassing the Love of Men: Romantic Friendship and Love Between Women from the Renaissance to the Present* (London, Junction Books).

Faludi, Susan (1991) *Backlash, The Undeclared War Against Women* (London, Chatto & Windus).

Family Policy Studies Centre (1990) *Family Policy Bulletin*, No.8.

Farrell, Wayne (1994) *The Myth of Male Power* (London, Fourth Estate).

Farwell, Marilyn R. (1990) 'Heterosexual plots and lesbian subtexts: toward a theory of lesbian narrative space', in Karla Jay and Joanne Glasgow (eds), *Lesbian Texts and Contexts: Radical Revisions* (New York University Press).

Faulkner, Wendy and E. Arnold (1985) *Smothered by Invention* (London, Pluto).

Fausto-Sterling, Anne (1985) *Myths of Gender* (reprinted 1992) (New York, Basic Books).

Feldberg, Roslyn and Evelyn Nakano Glen (1979) 'Male and female: job versus gender models in the sociology of work', *Social Problems*, 26(5) 524–38.

Felski, Rita (1989) *Beyond Feminist Aesthetics: Feminist Literature and Social Change* (London, Hutchinson Radius).
Feminism and Psychology, Special Issue on Heterosexuality, 2(3), October 1992.
Ferguson, Marjorie (1983) *Forever Feminine: Women's Magazines and the Cult of Femininity* (London, Heinemann).
Figes, K. (1994) *The Myth of Equality for Women in Britain* (London, Macmillan).
Finch, Janet (1983) *Married to the Job: Wives' Incorporation into Men's Work* (London, George Allen & Unwin).
—— (1984) 'Community care: developing non-sexist alternatives', *Critical Social Policy*, 9.
—— and Dulcie Groves (1980) 'Community Care and the Family: A Case for Equal Opportunities', *Journal of Social Policy*, 9(4) 487–511.
—— and Dulcie Groves (1983) *A Labour of Love: Women, Work and Caring* (London, Routledge & Kegan Paul).
Findlen, B. (ed.) (1995) *Listen Up: Voices from the Next Feminist Generation* (Seattle, Seal Press).
Finkelhor, David, G. Hotaling, I. A. Lewis and C. Smith (1990) 'Sexual abuse in a national survey of adult men and women: prevalence, characteristics and risk factors', *Child Abuse and Neglect*, 14, 19–28.
Firestone, Shulamith (1971) *The Dialectic of Sex: The Case for Feminist Revolution* (London, Jonathan Cape).
Fisher, June (1994) 'The case for girls-only schools', *Education Review*, 8(2) 49–50.
Fiske, John (1996) *Media Matters: Race and Gender in U.S. Politics* (Minneapolis, University of Minnesota Press).
Fleischer, Eva (1990) 'Ready for any sacrifice? Women in IVF programmes', *Issues in Reproductive and Genetic Engineering: Journal of International Feminist Analysis*, 3(1) 1–11.
Flint, Kate (1993) *The Woman Reader: 1837–1914* (Oxford, Clarendon Press).
Flying Boot (1994) (London, Nelson).
Folbre, Nancy (1994) *Who Pays for the Kids? Gender and the Structures of Consent* (London, Routledge).
Foley, Roz (1993) 'Zero tolerance', *Trouble and Strife*, 27, 16–20.
Fonow, Mary and Judith Cook (eds) (1991) *Beyond Methodology* (Buckingham, Open University Press).
Foran, John, Linda Klouzal, and J.-P. Rivera (1996) 'Race, class and gender in the Mexican, Cuban and Nicaraguan Revolutions', *Research in Social Movements, Conflict and Change*.
Foreman, D. (1994) 'Beyond the Edinburgh Postnatal Depression Scale: other rating scales and standardised interviews of use in assessing disturbed parents and their children', in J. Cox and J. Holden (eds), *Perinatal Psychiatry: Use and Misuse of the Edinburgh Postnatal Depression Scale* (London, Gaskell/Royal College of Psychiatrists).
Forna, Aminatta (1992) 'Pornography and Racism: Sexualizing Oppression and Inciting Hatred', in Catherine Itzin (ed.), *Pornography: Women, Violence and Civil Liberties* (Oxford University Press).
Foster, Peggy (1995) *Women and the Health Care Industry: An Unhealthy Relationship?* (Buckingham, Open University Press).
Foucault, Michel (1973a) *The Archaeology of Knowledge* (London, Tavistock).
—— (1973b) *The Birth of the Clinic: An Archaeology of Medical Knowledge* (trans. Alan Sheridan) (London, Tavistock).
—— (1977) *Discipline and Punish: The Birth of The Prison* (Harmondswoth, Penguin).
—— (1979) *The History of Sexuality*, Vol. 1 (London, Allen Lane).

Frankenberg, Ruth (1993) *White Women: Race Matters* (London, Routledge).

Franklin, Sarah, Celia Lury and Jackie Stacey (1997, forthcoming) *Second Nature: Body Techniques in Global Culture*.

—— and Maureen McNeil (1991) 'Science and technology: questions for cultural studies and feminism', in Sarah Franklin, Celia Lury and Jackie Stacey (eds), *Off-Centre: Feminism and Cultural Studies* (London, HarperCollins/Routledge).

—— and Maureen McNeil (1993) 'Procreation stories', *Science as Culture*, 3(4) 477–83.

Fraser, Nancy (1989) *Unruly Practices – Power, Discourse and Gender In Contemporary Social Theory* (Minneapolis, University of Minnesota Press).

Freire, Paulo (1970) *Pedagogy of the Oppressed* (New York, Seabury Press).

French, Jane and Peter French (1984) 'Gender imbalances in the primary classroom', *Educational Research*, 26(2) 127–36.

—— and Peter French (1986) *Gender Imbalances in Infant School Classroom Interaction* (Manchester, EOC).

French, Marilyn (1977) *The Women's Room* (reprinted 1978) (London, Sphere).

Friedan, B. (1963) *The Feminine Mystique* (London, Gollancz; Harmondsworth, Penguin, 1965).

Frith, Gill (1993) 'Women, writing and language: making the silences speak', in Diane Richardson and Victoria Robinson (eds), *Introducing Women's Studies: Feminist Theory and Practice*, 1st edn (London, Macmillan).

Frith, Ruth and Pat Mahony (eds) (1994) *Promoting Quality and Equality in Schools* (London, David Fulton).

Fuller, Mary (1980) 'Black girls in a London comprehensive school', in Rosemary Deem (ed.), *Schooling for Women's Work* (London, Routledge & Kegan Paul).

Fuss, Diana (1990) *Essentially Speaking: Feminism, Nature and Difference* (New York and London, Routledge).

—— (ed.) (1991) *Inside Out: Lesbian Theories, Gay Theories* (London, Routledge).

Gaard, Greta (1993) *Ecofeminism: Women, Animals, Nature* (Philadelphia, Temple University Press).

Gabaccia, Donna (1994) *From the Other Side: Women, Gender and Immigrant Life in the U.S. 1820–1990* (Bloomington, Indiana University Press).

Gagné, Patricia (1996) 'Identity, strategy, and feminist politics: clemency for battered women who kill', *Social Problems*, 43(1) 77–93.

Gagnon, John H. and William Simon (1973) *Sexual Conduct* (London, Hutchinson).

Gallup, Jane (1982) *Feminism and Psychoanalysis: The Daughter's Seduction* (London, Macmillan).

Game, Ann (1991) *Undoing the Social* (Buckingham, Open University Press).

Gamman, Lorraine and Margaret Marshmment (eds) (1988) *The Female Gaze* (London, The Women's Press).

Garber, Marjorie (1993) *Vested Interests: Crossdressing and Cultural Anxiety* (Harmondsworth, Penguin).

Gardiner, Jean, Susan Himmelweit and Maureen Mackintosh (1975) 'Women's domestic labour', *Bulletin of the Conference of Socialist Economists*, 4, 1–11.

Garfinkel, Harold (1967) *Studies in Ethnomethodology* (Englewood Cliffs, NJ, Prentice-Hall).

Garner, Lesley (1984) *Stepping Stones to Women's Liberty: Feminist Ideas in the Women's Suffrage Movement, 1900–1918* (London, Heinemann).

Gavron, H. (1966) *The Captive Wife* (Harmondsworth, Penguin).

Gawanas, Bience (1993) 'Violence against women in Tanzania', *Review of African Political Economy*, 56, March.

Gelles, Richard J. (1983) 'An exchange/social control theory of family', in David Finklehor *et al.* (eds), *The Dark Side of Families* (California, Sage).

—— and Clark Cornell (1985) *Intimate Violence in Families* (California, Sage).

Gelsthorpe, Loraine (1990) 'Feminist methodology in criminology: a new approach or old wine in new bottles?', in Loraine Gelsthorpe and Allison Morris (eds), *Feminist Perspectives in Criminology* (Buckingham, Open University Press).

—— (1992) 'Response to Martyn Hammersley's paper "On feminist methodology"', *Sociology*, 26, 213–18.

Gender and History (1990) Special Issue on Autobiography and Biography, 2(1), Spring.

Gender Working Group (1995) *Missing Links: Gender Equity in Science and Technology for Development* (London, Intermediate Technology Publications).

Gerhardi, Sylvia (1995) *Gender and Organisational Symbolism* (London, Sage).

Gerrard, Nicci (1989) *Into the Mainstream: How Feminism Has Changed Women's Writing* (London, Pandora).

Gever, Martha, Pratibha Parmar and John Greyson (eds) (1994) *Queer Looks: Perspectives on Lesbian and Gay Film and Video* (London, Routledge).

Ghandi, Nandita and Nandita Shah (1992) *The Issues at Stake: Theory and Practice in the Contemporary Women's Movement in India* (New Delhi, Kali For Women)

Giddens, A. (1992) *The Transformation of Intimacy: Sexuality, Love and Eroticism in Modern Societies* (Cambridge, Polity).

Giddings, Paula (1984) *When and Where I Enter: the Impact of Black Women on Race and Sex in America* (New York, Bantam Books).

Gilbert, Sandra M. and Susan Gubar (1979) *The Madwoman in the Attic: The Woman Writer and the Nineteenth-Century Literary Imagination* (New Haven and London, Yale University Press).

—— and Susan Gubar, *No Man's Land: The Place of the Woman Writer in the Twentieth Century*: Vol. 1, *The War of the Words* (1988) (New Haven, Conn. and London, Yale University Press); Vol. 2, *Sexchanges* (1989) (New Haven, Conn., and London, Yale University Press); Vol. 3, *Letters from the Front* (1994) (New Haven, Conn., and London, Yale University Press).

—— and Pam Taylor (1991) *Fashioning the Feminine: Girls, Popular Culture and Schooling* (London, Allen and Unwin).

Gill, Isobel (1989) 'Trying not just to survive: a lesbian teacher in a boys' school', in Lesley Holly (ed.), *Girls and Sexuality* (Milton Keynes, Open University Press).

Gilligan, Carol (1982) *In a Different Voice. Psychological Theory and Women's Development* (Cambridge, Massachusetts, Harvard University Press).

Gipps, Caroline and Patricia Murphy (1994) *A Fair Test?: Assessment, Achievement and Equity* (Buckingham, Open University Press).

Gittins, Diana (1979) 'Oral history, reliability and recollection' unpublished paper given to Annual British Sociological Association Conference.

—— (1993) *The Family In Question*, 2nd edn (London, Macmillan).

Glaser, D. and S. Frosh (1993) *Child Sexual Abuse* (London, Macmillan).

Glendinning, Caroline (1992) '"Community care": the financial consequences for women', in Caroline Glendinning and Jane Millar (eds), *Women and Poverty in Britain: The Nineties* (Hemel Hempstead, Harvester Wheatsheaf).

—— and Jane Millar (eds) (1987) *Women and Poverty in Britain* (Brighton: Wheatsheaf).

—— and Jane Millar (1992a) '"It all really starts in the family": gender divisions and poverty', in Caroline Glendinning and Jane Millar (eds), *Women and Poverty in Britain: The Nineties* (Hemel Hempstead, Harvester Wheatsheaf).

—— and Jane Millar (eds) (1992b) *Women and Poverty in Britain: The Nineties* (Hemel Hempstead: Harvester Wheatsheaf).

Glover, J. and Arber, S. (1995) 'Polarisation in mothers' employment', *Gender, Work and Organisation*, 2, 4, 165–79.

Gluck, Sherna B. and Daphne Patai (1991) *Women's Words: The Feminist Practice of Oral History* (London, Routledge).

Glucksmann, Miriam (1990) *Women Assemble: Women Workers and the New Industries in Inter-War Britain* (London, Routledge).

Goddard-Spear, Margaret (1989) 'Differences between the written work of boys and girls', *British Educational Research Journal*, 15(3) 271–7.

Goffman, Erving (1976) *Gender Advertisements* (London, Macmillan).

Goldsack, Laura (1994) 'The insecure home', paper presented at 'Ideal Homes? Towards a Sociology of Domestic Architecture and Interior Design Conference', School of Human Studies, University of Teesside (mimeo).

Gordon, Linda (1977) *Birth Control in America: Woman's Body, Woman's Right* (Harmondsworth, Penguin).

—— (1990) *Women, the State and Welfare* (Wisconsin, University of Wisconsin Press).

—— and Ellen DuBois (1992) 'Seeking ecstasy on the battlefield: danger and pleasure in the nineteenth-century feminist sexual thought', in Carole S. Vance (ed.), *Pleasure and Danger: Exploring Female Sexuality* (London, Pandora).

Gove, Walter and Jeannette Tudor (1973) 'Adult sex roles and mental illness', *American Journal of Sociology*, 78, 812.

Grace, Sharon (1995) *Policing Domestic Violence in the 1990s* (London, HMSO).

Graham, Hilary (1983) 'Caring: a labour of love', in Janet Finch and Dulcie Groves (eds), *A Labour of Love: Women, Work and Caring* (London, Routledge & Kegan Paul).

—— (1985) *Women, Health and Healing* (Brighton, Wheatsheaf).

—— (1987a) 'Being poor: perceptions and coping strategies of lone mothers', in J. Brannen and G. Wilson (eds), *Give and Take in Families: Studies in Resource Distribution* (London, Allen & Unwin).

—— (1987b) 'Women, health and illness', *Social Studies Review*, 3(1) 15–20.

—— (1987c) 'Women's poverty and caring', in C. Glendinning and J. Millar (eds), *Women and Poverty in Britain* (Brighton, Wheatsheaf).

—— (1990) 'Feminist perspectives of care', in Joanna Bornat, Charmaine Pereira, David Pilgrim and Fiona Williams (eds), *Community Care: A Reader* (London, Macmillan).

Gray, Ann (1987) 'Behind closed doors': video recorders in the home', in H. Baehr and Gillian Dyer (eds), *Boxed In* (London, Pandora).

Green, Eileen, Sandra Hebron and Diana Woodward (1990) *Women's Leisure, What Leisure?* (London, Macmillan).

Greer, Germaine (1971) *The Female Eunuch*, first published 1970 (London, Paladin).

—— (1984) *Sex and Destiny* (Harmondsworth, Penguin).

—— (1988) 'The proper study of womankind', *The Times Literary Supplement*, 3–9 June, 616 and 629.

Gregson, Nicky and Michelle Lowe (1994) 'Waged domestic labour and the renegotiation of the domestic division of labour within dual career households', *Sociology*, 28(1) 55–78.

Grewal, Shabnum, Jackie Kay, Liliane Landor, Gail Lewis, and Pratibha Parmar (1988) (eds), *Charting the Journey: Writings by Black and Third World Women* (London, Sheba Feminist Publishers).

Griffin, C. (1986) 'Qualitative methods and female experience: young women from school to the job market', in S. Wilkinson (ed.), *Feminist Social Psychology: Developing Theory and Practice* (Milton Keynes, Open University Press).

—— (1989) 'I'm not a women's libber but . . . feminism, consciousness and identity', in S. Skevington and D. Baker (eds), *The Social Identity of Women* (London, Sage).

—— (1993) *Representations of Youth: The Study of Youth and Adolescence in Britain and America* (Cambridge, Polity).

Griffin, Gabriele (1994a) 'The desire for change and the experience of Women's Studies', in Gabriele Griffin (ed.), *Changing Our Lives: Doing Women's Studies* (London, Pluto).

—— (ed.) (1994b) *Changing Our Lives: Doing Women's Studies* (London, Pluto).

—— (ed.) (1995) *Feminist Activism in the 1990s* (London, Taylor & Francis).

—— Marianne Hester, Shirin Rai and Sasha Roseneil (eds) (1994) *Stirring It: Challenges For Feminism* (London, Taylor & Francis).

Grimstad, K. and S. Rennie (1973) *The New Woman's Survival Catalog* (New York, Coward McCann & Geoghegan).

Grosz, Elizabeth (1990) *Jacques Lacan: A Feminist Introduction* (London, Routledge).

—— (1991) 'Lesbian fetishism', *Differences*, 3(2) 39–54.

—— (1992) 'Julia Kristeva', in Elizabeth Wright (ed.), *Feminism and Psychoanalysis: A Critical Dictionary* (Oxford, Basil Blackwell).

—— (1994) *Volatile Bodies: Towards a Corporeal Feminism* (Bloomington, Indiana University Press).

—— and Elspeth Probyn (eds) (1995) *Sexy Bodies: The Strange Carnalities of Feminism* (London, Routledge).

Groth, N. (1979) *Men Who Rape* (New York, Plenum).

Guillaumin, Colette (1995) *Racism, Sexism, Power and Ideology* (London, Routledge).

Gunaratnam, Yasmin (1990) 'Breaking the silence: Asian carers in Britain', in Joanna Bornat Charmaine Pereira, David Pilgrim and Fiona Williams (eds), *Community Care: A Reader* (London, Macmillan).

Gupta, Jyotsna Agnihotri (1991) 'Women's bodies: the site for the ongoing conquest by reproductive technologies', *Issues in Reproductive and Genetic Engineering: Journal of International Feminist Analysis*, 4(2) 93–107.

Guy, Camille (1996) 'Feminism and sexual abuse', *Feminist Review*, 52, Spring, 154–68.

Hageman-White, Carol (1987) 'Gendered modes of behaviour – a sociological strategy for empirical research', Paper presented at the Third International Interdisciplinary Congress on Women, July, Dublin, Ireland.

Hague, Gill and Ellen Malos (1993) *Domestic Violence: Action for Change* (Cheltenham, New Clarion Press).

Hakim, Catherine (1979) *Occupational Segregation: A Comparative Study of the Degree and Patterns of the Differentiation between Men's and Women's Work in Britain, the United States and other countries*, Department of Employment Research Paper (London, HMSO).

—— (1992) 'Explaining trends in occupational segregation: the measurement, causes, and consequences of the sexual division of labour', *European Sociological Review*, 8(2) 127–52.

—— (1993) 'Segregated and integrated occupations: a new approach to analysing social change', *European Sociological Review*, 9(3) 289–314.

Halford, Susan, Mike Savage and Anne Witz (1997) *Gender, Careers and Organisations* (London, Macmillan).

Hall Carpenter Archives/Lesbian Oral History Group (eds) (1989) *Inventing Ourselves: Lesbian Life Stories* (London, Routledge).

Hall, Catherine (1991) 'Politics, post-structuralism and feminist history', *Gender and History*, 3(2) 204–10.

—— (1992) *White, Male and Middle Class: Explorations in Feminism and History* (Cambridge, Polity).

Hall, E. J. (1993) 'Waitering/Waitressing: engendering the work of table servers', *Gender and Society*, 7(3) 329–46.

Hall, Marny (1989) 'Private experience in the public domain', in J. Hearn *et al.* (eds), *The Sexuality of Organisation* (London, Sage).

Hall, Radclyffe (1928) *The Well of Loneliness* (reprinted 1982) (London, Virago).

Hall, Ruth (1985) *Ask Any Woman* (Bristol, Falling Wall Press).

Hallet, Christine (1996) *Women and Social Policy: An Introduction* (London, Prentice-Hall and Harvester Wheatsheaf).

Hamer, Diane (1990) 'Significant others: lesbians and psychoanalytic theory', *Feminist Review*, 34, 134–51.

—— and Belinda Budge (eds) (1994) *The Good, the Bad and the Gorgeous: Popular Culture's Romance with Lesbianism* (London, Pandora).

Hammersley, Martyn (1992) 'On feminist methodology', *Sociology*, 26, 187–206.

Hanmer, Jalna (1978) 'Violence and the social contral of women', in Gary Littlejohn *et al.* (eds), *Power and the State* (London, Croom Helm).

—— (1981) 'Sex predetermination, artificial insemination and the maintenance of male dominated culture', in Helen Roberts (ed.), *Women, Health and Reproduction* (London, Routledge & Kegan Paul).

—— (1983) 'Reproductive technology: the future for women', in Joan Rothchild (ed.) *Machina Ex Dea: Feminist Perspectives on Technology* (New York, Pergamon).

—— (1985) 'Transforming consciousness: women and the new reproductive technologies', in Gena Corea *et al.*, *Man-Made Women: How the New Reproductive Technologies Affect Women* (London, Hutchinson).

—— (1990) 'Men, power and the exploitation of women', in Jeff Hearn and David Morgan (eds), *Men, Masculinities and Social Theory* (London, Unwin Hyman).

—— (1991) 'Women's Studies – A transitional programme', in Jane Aaron and Sylvia Walby (eds), *Out of the Margin: Women's Studies in the Nineties* (London, Falmer).

—— and Pat Allen (1980) 'Reproductive engineering: the final solution?', in Sandra Best and Linda Birke (eds), *Alice Through the Microscope: The Power of Science over Women's Lives* (London, Virago).

—— and Mary Maynard (eds) (1987) *Women, Violence and Social Control* (London, Macmillan).

—— and Elizabeth Powell-Jones (1984) 'Who's holding the test-tube?' *Trouble and Strife*, 3, Summer, 44–9.

—— Jill Radford and Elizabeth Stanko (eds) (1989) *Women, Policing and Male Violence* (London, Routledge).

—— and Sheila Saunders (1984) *Well-Founded Fear* (London, Hutchinson).

—— and Ineke van Wingerden (1992) 'Women's perspectives on the ethical, social and legal', European Union DGXII, Nr. GENO-0036–GB (EASE).

—— and Ineke van Wingerden (1997) 'Power, policy and health: European women's perspectives on human genome analysis', in Susan Baker and Anneka van Doorne-Huiskes (eds), *Women and Public Policy: The Shifting Boundaries between the Public and Private* (Buckingham, Open University Press).

Hannam, June (1989) *Isabella Ford, 1855–1924* (Oxford, Basil Blackwell).

—— (1992) 'Women and the ILP, c. 1890–1914', in David James, Tony Jowitt and Keith Laybourn (eds), *The Centennial History of the Independent Labour Party* (Halifax, Ryburn).

Hantrais, L. (1995) *Social Policy in the European Union* (London, Macmillan).

Hapke, Laura (1995) 'A wealth of possibilities: workers, texts, and reforming the English Department', *Women's Studies Quarterly*, XX111(1)&(2) 142–54.

Haraway, Donna (1988) 'Situated knowledges: the science question in feminism and the privilege of partial perspective', *Feminist Studies* 14, 575–99.

—— (1989) *Primate Visions: Gender, Race and Nature in the World of Modern Science* (London, Routledge).

—— (1990) 'Reading Buchi Emecheta: contests for women's experience in women's studies', in Mary Evans (ed.), *The Woman Question*, 2nd edn, 1994 (London, Sage).

—— (1991) *Simians, Cyborgs and Women: The Reinvention of Nature* (New York, Routledge).

Harding, Sandra (1986) *The Science Question in Feminism* (Milton Keynes, Open University Press).

—— (ed.) (1987) *Feminism and Methodology* (Buckingham, Open University Press).

—— (1990) 'Feminism and theories of scientific knowledge', in Mary Evans (ed.), *The Woman Question*, 2nd edn, 1994 (London, Sage).

—— (1991) *Whose Science? Whose Knowledge?* (Ithaca, Cornell University Press).

—— (1992a) 'The instability of the analytical categories of feminist theory', in Helen Crowley and Susan Himmelweit (eds), *Knowing Women, Feminism and Knowledge* (Cambridge, Oxford and Buckingham, Polity, Basil Blackwell and Open University Press).

—— (1992b) *Whose Science? Whose Knowledge?*, (Buckingham, Open University Press).

Hareven, Tamara (1982) *Family Time and Industrial Time: The Relationship between Family and Work in a New England Industrial Community* (Cambridge University Press).

Hargreaves, Jennifer (1985) 'Where's the virtue? Where's the grace' A discussion of the social production of gender relations in and through sport', *Thesis Eleven*, 12, 109–21.

Harne, Lynne (1993) 'Families and fathers: the effects of the Children Act 1989', *Rights of Women Bulletin*, 5–6.

—— (1995) 'Labour's proposals for women', *Rights of Women Bulletin*, 19.

Harris, Chris (1990) *Kinship* (London, Routledge).

Harris, Simon (1990) *Lesbian and Gay Issues in the English Classroom* (Milton Keynes, Open University Press).

Hart, Barbara (1986) 'Lesbian battering: an examination', in Kerry Lobel (ed.), *Naming the Violence: Speaking Out about Lesbian Battering* (Washington, Seal Press).

Hartman, Mary and Lois Banner (eds) (1974) *Clio's Consciousness Raised* (London, Harper).

Hartmann, Betsy (1987, 1994) *Reproductive Rights and Wrongs: The Global Politics of Population Control and Contraceptive Choice* (Boston, Mass., South End Press).

Hartmann, Heidi (1979) 'Capitalism, patriarchy and job segregation by sex', in Z. Eisenstein (ed.), *Capitalist Patriarchy and the Case for Socialist Feminism* (New York, Monthly Review Press).

—— (1981) 'The unhappy marriage of Marxism and feminism: towards a more progressive union', in Lydia Sargent (ed.), *Women and Revolution* (London, Pluto).

Haskell, Molly (1973) *From Reverence to Rape: The Treatment of Women in the Movies* (Harmondsworth, Penguin).

Hatty, Suzanne (1989) 'Policing and male violence in Australia', in J. Hanmer *et al.* (eds), *Women, Policing and Male Violence* (London, Routledge).

Haug, Frigga (ed.) (1987) *Female Sexualisation* (London, Verso).

Hawkes, Gail (1996) *A Sociology of Sex and Sexuality* (Buckingham, Open University Press).

Hearn, Jeff and David Morgan (eds) (1990) *Men, Masculinities and Social Theories* (London, Unwin Hyman).

—— and Wendy Parkin (1986) 'Sex' at 'Work': The Power and Paradox of Organizational Sexuality (London, Sage).

—— Deborah Sheppard, Peta Tancred-Sheriff, and Gibson Burrell (eds) (1989) *The Sexuality of Organisation* (London, Sage).

Heelas, Paul, Scott Lash, and Peter Morris (eds) (1996) *Detraditionalization: Critical Reflections on Authority and Identity* (Oxford, Basil Blackwell).

Henderson, Mae Gwendolyn (1990) 'Speaking in tongues: dialogics dialectics, and the Black woman writer's literary tradition', in Cheryl A. Wall (ed.), *Changing Our Own Words* (London, Routledge).

Hennegan, Alison (1988) 'On becoming a lesbian reader', in S. Radstone (ed.), *Sweet Dreams: Sexuality, Gender and Popular Fiction* (London, Lawrence & Wishart).

Henriques, Julian, Wendy Hollway, Cathy Urwin, Couze Venn and Valerie Walkerdine (eds) (1984) *Changing the Subject* (London, Methuen).

Hepburn, Cuca with Bonnie Gutierrez (1988) *Alive and Well. A Lesbian Health Guide* (New York, The Crossing Press).

Herbert, Carrie (1989) *Talking of Silence: The Sexual Harassment of Girls* (Lewes, Falmer Press).

Hester, Marianne, Liz Kelly and Jill Radford (eds) (1995) *Women, Violence and Male Power; Feminist Research Activism and Practice* (Buckingham, Open University Press).

—— and Lorraine Radford (1996) *Domestic Violence and Child Contact in England and Denmark* (Joseph Rowntree Foundation and The Policy Press, Bristol).

Higginbotham, Elizabeth and Sarah Watts (1988) 'The new scholarship on Afro-American women', *Women's Studies Quarterly*, XV1(1 & 2) Spring/Summer, 12–21.

Higginbotham, Evelyn (1990) 'Beyond the sound of silence: Afro-American women's history', *Gender and History*, 1(1) 50–67.

Hill, Bridget (1993) 'Women's history: a study in change, continuity or standing still?', *Women's History Review*, 2(2) 173–84.

Hills, Leslie (1995) ' "The Senga Syndrome": Reflections on twenty-one years in Scottish education', in Maud Blair and Janet Holland with Sue Sheldon (eds), *Identity and Diversity* (Clevedon, Multilingual Matters).

Hillyer, Barbara (1993) *Feminism and Disability* (Norman, University of Oklahoma Press).

Hinds, Hilary, Ann Phoenix and Jackie Stacey (eds) (1992) *Working Out: New Directions For Women's Studies* (London, Falmer Press).

—— Ann Phoenix and Jackie Stacey (1992) 'Introduction: working out: new directions for Women's Studies', in Hilary Hinds, Ann Phoenix and Jackie Stacey (eds), *Working Out: New Directions for Women's Studies* (London, Falmer Press).

Hirshfield, Clare (1990), 'A fractured faith: Liberal Party women and the suffrage issue in Britain, 1892–1914', *Gender and History*, 2(2) 173–97.

HMSO (1985) *General Household Survey* (London, HMSO).

HMSO (1994) *Criminal Statistics for England and Wales* (London, HMSO).

HMSO (1996) *Social Trends 1996* (London, Central Statistical Office).

Ho, Mae Wan (1988) 'On not holding nature still: evolution by process, not by consequence', in M.W. Ho and S.W. Fox (eds), *Evolutionary Processes and Metaphors*, (Chichester, Wiley).

Hobby, Elaine (1989) 'Women returning to study', in Ann Thompson and Helen Wilcox (eds), *Teaching Women: Feminism and English Studies* (Manchester University Press).

Hobson, Barbara (1994) 'Solo mothers, solo policy regimes and the logics of gender', in Diane Sainsbury, *Gendering Welfare States* (London, Sage).

Hochschild, Arlie (1983) *The Managed Heart* (Berkeley, California University Press).

Hockey, Jenny (1993) 'Women and health', in Diane Richardson and Victoria Robinson (eds), *Introducing Women's Studies: Feminist Theory and Practice*, 1st edn (London, Macmillan).

Hodgeon, Julia (1988) 'A woman's world? A report on a project in Cleveland nurseries on sex differentiation in the early years', unpublished report sponsored jointly by Cleveland Education Committee and the EOC.

Hoff, Joan (1994) 'Gender as a post modern category of paralysis', *Women's History Review*, 3(2) 149–68.

Holland, Janet, Caroline Ramazanoglu, Sue Scott, Sue Sharpe and Rachel Thomson (1992) 'Pressure, resistance, empowerment: young women and the negotiation of safer sex', in Peter Aggleton, Peter Davies and Graham Hart (eds), *AIDS: Rights, Risk and Reason* (London, Falmer Press).

—— Caroline Ramazanoglu, Sue Scott and Rachel Thomson (1994) 'Desire, risk and control: the body as a site of contestation', in Lesley Doyal, Jennie Naidoo and Tamsin Wilton (eds), *AIDS: Setting a Feminist Agenda* (London, Taylor & Francis).

—— Caroline Ramazanoglu and Rachel Thomson (1996) 'In the same boat? The gendered (in)experience of first heterosex', in Diane Richardson (ed.), *Theorising Heterosexuality: Telling it Straight* (Buckingham, Open University Press).

—— and Maud Blair with Sue Sheldon (eds) (1995) *Debates and Issues in Feminist Research and Pedagogy* (Clevedon, Multilingual Matters/Open University Press).

Hollibaugh, Amber (1996) 'Desire for the future: radical hope in passion and pleasure', in Stevi Jackson and Sue Scott (eds), *Feminism and Sexuality. A Reader* (Edinburgh University Press).

Hollis, Karyn L. (1995) 'Autobiography and reconstructing subjectivity at the Bryn Mawr Summer School for women workers, 1921–1938', *Women's Studies Quarterly*, XX111(1)&(2) 71–100.

Hollis, Patricia (1979) *Women in Public: The Women's Movement 1850–1900* (London, Allen & Unwin).

—— (1987) 'Women in council: separate spheres, public space', in Jane Rendall (ed.), *Equal or Different? Women's Politics, 1800–1914* (Oxford, Basil Blackwell).

Hollway, Wendy (1984) 'Gender difference and the production of subjectivity', in Julian Henriques, Wendy Hollway, Cathy Urwin, Couze Venn and Valerie Walkerdine (eds), *Changing the Subject* (London, Methuen).

—— (1989) *Subjectivity and Method in Psychology* (London, Sage).

—— (1993) 'Theorizing heterosexuality; a response', *Feminism and Psychology*, 3(3) 412–17.

—— (1996) 'Recognition and heterosexual desire', in Diane Richardson (ed.), *Theorising Heterosexuality: Telling it Straight* (Buckingham, Open University Press).

Holly, Lesley (1985) 'Mary, Jane and Virginia Woolf: ten year old girls talking', in Gaby Weiner (ed.), *Just a Bunch of Girls* (Milton Keynes, Open University Press).

—— (1989) *Girls and Sexuality* (Milton Keynes, Open University Press).

Holmes, Helen Bequaert (1989) 'Hepatitis – yet another risk of in vitro fertilization?', *Reproductive and Genetic Engineering: Journal of International Feminist Analysis*, 2(1) 29–37.

—— Betty Hoskins and Michael Gross (eds) (1981) *The Custom-Made Child? Women-Centred Perspectives* (New Jersey, Humana Press).

Holmes, Ronald M. and Stephen T. Holmes (1994) *Murder in America* (Thousand Oaks, CA and London, Sage).

Holton, Sandra (1986) *Feminism and Democracy* (Cambridge, Cambridge University Press).

—— (1996) *Suffrage Days: Stories from the Women's Suffrage Movement* (London, Routledge).

Homans, Hilary (ed.) (1985) *The Sexual Politics of Reproduction* (Aldershot, Gower).

Homans, Margaret (1986) *Bearing the Word: Language and Female Experience in Nineteenth-Century Women's Writing* (Chicago and London, University of Chicago Press).

hooks, bell (1982) *Ain't I a Woman? Black Women and Feminism* (London, Pluto).

—— (1989) *Talking Back: Thinking Feminist – Thinking Black* (London, Sheba).

—— (1992) *Black Looks: Race and Representation* (Boston, Mass., South End Press).

—— (1996) 'Continued devaluation of Black womanhood', in Stevi Jackson and Sue Scott (eds), *Feminism and Sexuality. A Reader* (Edinburgh University Press).

—— (Gloria Watkins) (1991) 'Sisterhood: political solidarity between women', in Sneja Gunew (ed.), *A Reader in Feminist Knowledge* (London, Routledge).

Hooper, Carol-Ann (1987) 'Getting him off the Hook – the Theory and Practice of Mother-Blaming in Child Sexual Abuse', *Trouble and Strife*, 12.

—— (1992) *Mothers Surviving Child Sexual Abuse* (London, Routledge).

Hubbard, Ruth (1990) *The Politics of Women's Biology* (New Brunswick, NJ, Rutgers University Press).

—— M. S. Henifin and B. Fried (1979) *Women Look at Biology Looking at Women* (Cambridge, Mass., Schenkman).

—— and E. Wald. (1993) *Exploding the Gene Myth: How Genetic Information is Produced and Manipulated by Scientists, Physicians, Employers, Insurance Companies, Educators and Law Enforcers* (Boston, Mass., Beacon Press).

Hudson, Pat (1995) 'Women and industrialization', in June Purvis (ed.) *Women's History: Britain, 1850–1945* (London, UCL).

—— and Robert Lee (eds) (1990) *Women's Work and the Family Economy in Historical Perspective* (Manchester University Press).

Hull, Gloria T., Patricia Bell Scott and Barbara Smith (eds) (1982) *All the Women are White, All the Blacks are Men, But Some of Us Are Brave: Black Women's Studies* (New York, The Feminist Press).

Humm, Maggie (1986) *Feminist Criticism: Women as Contemporary Critics* (Brighton, Harvester).

—— (1988) 'Amenorrhea and autobiography', *Reproductive and Genetic Engineering: Journal of International Feminist Analysis*, 1(2) 159–65.

—— (1989) 'Subjects in English: autobiography, women and education', in Ann Thompson and Helen Wilcox (eds), *Teaching Women: Feminism and English Studies* (Manchester University Press).

—— (1991) '"Thinking of things in themselves": theory, experience, Women's Studies', in Jane Aaron and Sylvia Walby (eds), *Out of the Margins: Women's Studies in the Nineties* (London, Falmer).

—— (1994a) *A Reader's Guide to Contemporary Feminist Literary Criticism* (Hemel Hempstead, Harvester Wheatsheaf).

—— (1994b) 'Tropisms, tape-slide and theory', in Gabriele Griffin (ed.), *Changing Our Lives: Doing Women's Studies* (London, Pluto).

—— (1995a) *Practising Feminist Criticism: An Introduction* (Hemel Hempstead, Prentice-Hall/Harvester Wheatsheaf).

—— (1995b) *The Dictionary of Feminist Theory*, 2nd edn (Columbus, Ohio State University Press).

Humphries, Jane (1983) 'The emancipation of women in the 1970s and the 1980s: from the latent to the floating', *Capital and Class*, 20, 6–28.

—— (1995) 'Women and Paid Work', in June Purvis (ed.), *Women's History: Britain, 1850–1945* (London, UCL).

—— and Jill Rubery (1988) 'Recession and exploitation: British women in a changing workforce, 1979–1985', in J. Jenson, E. Hagen and C. Reddy (eds), *Feminization of the Labour Force: Paradoxes and Promises* (Cambridge, Polity).

Hunt, Karen (1996) *Equivocal Feminists. The Social Democratic Federation and the Woman Question, 1884–1911* (Cambridge, Cambridge University Press).

Hunt, Pauline (1980) *Gender and Class Consciousness* (London, Macmillan).

—— (1989) 'Gender and the Construction of Home Life', in Graham Allen and Graham Crow (eds), *Home and Family: Creating the Domestic Sphere* (London, Macmillan).

—— (1995) 'Gender and the construction of home life', in S. Jackson and S. Moores (eds), *The Politics of Domestic Consumption: Critical Readings* (Hemel Hempstead, Prentice-Hall/Harvester Wheatsheaf).

Hutcheon, Linda (1989) *The Politics of Postmodernism* (London, Routledge).

Hutchins, Barbara (1915) *Women in Modern Industry* (London, G. Bell).

Hutson, Susan and Richard Jenkins (1989) *Taking the Strain: Families, Unemployment and the Transition to Adulthood* (Buckingham, Open University Press).

Hynes, H. Patricia (1989a) 'Biotechnology in agriculture: an analysis of selected technologies and policy in the United States', *Reproductive and Genetic Engineering: Journal of International Feminist Analysis*, 2(1) 39–49.

—— (ed.) (1989b) *Reconstructing Babylon: Essays on Women and Technology* (London, Earthscan).

—— (1989c) *The Recurring Silent Spring* (New York, Pergamon Press).

Illich, Ivan (1975) *Medical Nemesis: The Expropriation of Health* (London, Caldar & Boyars).

Ingrisch, Doris (1995) 'Conformity and resistance as women age', in Sara Arber and Jay Ginn (eds), *Connecting Gender and Aging: A Sociological Approach* (Buckingham, Open University Press).

International Solidarity for Safe Contraception, Amsterdam and X-Y Movement, Amsterdam (1990) *Report of a Working Day on Changing Trends in Population Control, Impact on Third World Women and the Role of the World Health Organisation* (Amsterdam, International Solidarity for Safe Contraception and X-Y Movement).

Irigary, Luce (1985a) *Speculum of the Other Woman* (Ithaca, NY, Cornell University Press).

—— (198b) *This Sex Which Is Not One*, trans. Catherine Porter with Carolyn Burke, first published 1977 (Ithaca, NY, Cornell University Press).

Islam, Sharmeen (1993) 'Towards a Global Network of Asian Lesbians', in Rakesh Ratti (ed.), *A Lotus of Another Color* (Boston, Mass., Alyson).

Israel, Kali (1990) 'Writing inside the kaleidoscope: re-representing Victorian women public figures', *Gender and History*, 2 (1) 40–8.

Itzin, Catherine (ed.) (1993) *Pornography: Women, Violence and Civil Liberties* (Oxford University Press).

Jackson, David (1995) *Destroying the Baby in Themselves: Why did the Two Boys Kill James Bulger?* (Nottingham, Mushroom).

Jackson, Margaret (1994) *The Real Facts of Life: Feminism and the Politics of Sexuality, c.1850–1940* (London, Taylor & Francis).

Jackson, Stevi (1982) *Childhood and Sexuality* (Oxford, Basil Blackwell).

—— (1992a) 'The amazing deconstructing woman', *Trouble and Strife*, 25, 25–31.

—— (1992b) 'Towards a historical sociology of housework: a materialist feminist analysis', *Women's Studies International Forum*, 15(2) 153–72.

—— (1996a) *Christine Delphy* (London, Sage).

—— (1996b) 'Heterosexuality and feminist theory', in D. Richardson (ed.), *Theorising Heterosexuality: Telling it Straight* (Buckingham, Open University Press).

—— (1996c) 'Heterosexuality as a problem for feminist theory, in Lisa Adkins and Vicki Merchant (eds), *Sexualising the Social: Power and the Organisation of Sexuality* (London, Macmillan).

—— and Shaun Moores (eds) (1995) *The Politics of Domestic Consumption: Critical Readings* (Hemel Hempstead, Prentice-Hall/Harvester Wheatsheaf).

—— and Sue Scott (1996a) *Feminism and Sexuality. A Reader* (Edinburgh University Press).

—— and Sue Scott (eds) (1996b) 'Sexual skirmishes and feminist factions. Twenty five years of debate on women and sexuality', in Stevi Jackson and Sue Scott (eds.), *Feminism and Sexuality. A Reader* (Edinburgh University Press).

—— and Momin Rahman (1997) 'Up against nature: sociological thoughts on sexuality', in John Gubbay, Chris Middleton and Chet Ballard (eds), *Student Companion to Sociology* (London, Blackwell).

Jacobs, Brian (1988) *Racism in Britain* (London, Croom Helm).

Jacobs, Harriet (1861) *Incidents in the Life of a Slave Girl*, reprinted 1988 (New York and Oxford, Oxford University Press).

Jacobus, Mary (1981) 'Review of The Madwoman in the Attic', *Signs*, 6 (3) 517–23.

Jaggar, Alison and Paula Rothenberg (1993) *Feminist Frameworks*, 3rd edn (New York, McGraw Hill).

James, Stanlie and Abena Busia (eds) (1993) *Theorizing Black Feminisms: The Visionary Pragmatism of Black Women* (New York, Routledge).

Janet and John (1949) (Welwyn, Nisbet).

Jarrett, Juliette (1996) 'Black women in British art schools', in Delia Jarrett-Macauley (ed.), *Reconstructing Womanhood, Reconstructing Feminism: Writings on Black Women* (London, Routledge).

Jarrett-Macauley, Delia (ed.) (1996) *Reconstructing Womanhood, Reconstructing Feminism: Writings On Black Women* (London, Routledge).

Jay, Karla and Joanne Glasgow (eds) (1990) *Lesbian Texts and Contexts: Radical Revisions* (New York and London, New York University Press).

Jeffreys, Sheila (1985) *The Spinster and Her Enemies: Feminism and Sexuality, 1880–1930* (London, Pandora).

—— (1990) *Anti Climax: A Feminist Perspective on the Sexual Revolution* (London, The Women's Press).

—— (1994) *The Lesbian Heresy: A Feminist Perspective on the Lesbian Sexual Revolution* (London, The Women's Press).

—— (1995) 'Women and sexuality', in June Purvis (ed.), *Women's History: Britain, 1850–1945* (London, UCL).

—— (1996) 'Heterosexuality and the desire for gender', in Diane Richardson (ed.), *Theorising Heterosexuality: Telling it Straight* (Buckingham, Open University Press).

Jewish Women in London Group (1989) *Gerations of Memories: Voices of Jewish Women* (London, The Women's Press).

Joekes, Susan, P. (1987) *Women in the World Economy*, United Nations International Research and Training Institute for the Advancement of Women (Oxford University Press).

Joffe, L. and D. Foxman (1984) 'Assessing Mathematics: 5. Attitudes and sex differences', *Mathematics in School*, 13(4) 95–107.

John, Angela (ed.) (1986) *Unequal Opportunities: Women's Employment in England 1800–1918* (Oxford, Blackwell).

—— (1995) Elizabeth Robbins: Staging A Life, 1862–1952 (London, Routledge).

Jones, Alison (1993) 'Becoming a "girl": Post-structuralist suggestions for educational research', *Gender and Education*, 5(2) 157–66.

Jones, Ann Rosalind (1986) 'Writing the body: toward an understanding of *l'Ecriture féminine*', in Elaine Showalter (ed.), *The New Feminist Criticism: Essays on Women, Literature and Theory* (London, Virago).

Jones, Carol (1985) 'Sexual tyranny in mixed-sex schools: an in-depth study of male violence', in Gaby Weiner (ed.), *Just a Bunch of Girls* (Milton Keynes, Open University Press).

—— and Pat Mahony (eds) (1989) *Learning our Lines: Sexuality and Social Control in Education* (London, The Women's Press).

Jones, L. G. and L. P. Jones (1989) 'Context, confidence and the able girl', *Educational Research*, 31(3) 189–94.

Joshi, Heather (1992) 'The cost of caring', in C. Glendinning and J. Millar (eds), *Women and Poverty in Britain: The Nineties* (Hemel Hempstead, Harvester Wheatsheaf).

Judt, Tony (1979) 'A crown in regal purple: social history and the historians', *History Workshop Journal*, 7, Spring, 66–94.

Jung, Nora (1994) 'Eastern European women with Western eyes', in Gabriele Griffin, Marianne Hester, Shirin Rai and Sasha Roseneil (eds), *Stirring It: Challenges For Feminism* (London, Taylor & Francis).

Kaahumanu, L. and L. Hutchins (eds) (1991) *Bi In Any Other Name: Bisexual People Speak Out* (Boston, Mass., Alyson).

Kabeer, Naila (1992) 'Feminist perspectives in development: a critical review', in Hilary Hinds, Ann Phoenix and Jackie Stacey (eds), *Working Out: New Directions For Women's Studies* (London, Falmer Press).

—— (1995) '*Reversed Realities: Gender Hierarchies in Development Thought* (London, Verso).

Kaluzynska, Eva (1980) 'Wiping the floor with theory: a survey of writings on housework', *Feminist Review*, 6, 27–54.

Kane, Elizabeth (1988) *Birth Mother: The Story of America's First Legal Surrogate Mother* (San Diego, Calif., Harcourt Brace Jovanovich).

—— (1989) 'Surrogate parenting: a division of families, not a creation', *Reproductive and Genetic Engineering: Journal of International Feminist Analysis*, 2(2) 105–9.

Kaplan, Cora (1986a) 'Language and gender' (first published 1976) in Cora Kaplan, *Sea Changes: Essays on Culture and Feminism* (London, Verso).

—— (1986b) 'Pandora's Box: subjectivity, class and sexuality in socialist feminist criticism', in Cora Kaplan, *Sea Changes: Essays on Culture and Feminism*, first published 1985 (London, Verso).

—— (1986c) *Sea Changes: Essays on Culture and Feminism* (London, Verso).

Kaplan, E. A. (ed.) (1978) *Women in Film Noir* (London, BFI).

Kaplan, M. M. (1992) *Mothers' Images of Motherhood* (London, Routledge).

Kauffman, Linda (1993) *American Feminist Thought at Century's End: A Reader* (Cambridge, Mass., Blackwell).

Kaufman, Caroline L. (1988) 'Perfect mothers, perfect babies: an examination of the ethics of fetal treatment', *Reproductive and Genetic Engineering: Journal of International Feminist Analysis*, 1(2) 133–9.

Kaupen-Haas, Heidrun (1988) 'Experimental obstetrics and national socialism: the conceptual basis of reproductive technology today', *Reproductive and Genetic Engineering: Journal of International Feminist Analysis* 1(2) 127–32.

Kay, Jackie (1993) *Other Lovers* (Newcastle upon Tyne, Bloodaxe Books).

Keith, Lois (1990) 'Caring Partnership', *Community Care*, 22 February, v–vi.

Keller, Evelyn Fox (1985) *Perspectives on Gender and Science* (New Haven, Conn., Yale University Press).

—— (1992) *Secrets of Life, Secrets of Death: Essays on Language, Gender and Science* (London, Routledge).

—— (1995) *Refiguring Life: Metaphors of Twentieth-century Biology* (New York, Columbia University Press).

Kelly, Alison (1996) 'Comparing like with like', *Education*, 187/1, 14–15.

—— Barbara Smails and Judith Whyte (1984) *Girls into Science and Technology: Final Report* (Manchester, Equal Opportunities Commission).

Kelly, Joan (1983) 'The doubled vision of feminist theory', in Judith Newton *et al.* (eds), *Sex and Class in Women's History* (London, Routledge & Kegan Paul).

Kelly, Liz (1985) 'Feminists v feminists – legislating against porn in the USA', *Trouble and Strife*, 7, 4–10.

—— (1988a) *Surviving Sexual Violence* (Cambridge, Polity Press).

—— (1988b) 'What's in a name?: defining child sexual abuse', *Feminist Review*, 28, Spring.

—— (1992a) 'Not in front of the children: responding to right wing agendas on sexuality and education', in Madeleine Arnot and Len Barton (eds), *Voicing Concerns: Sociological Perspectives on Contemporary Education Reforms* (Wallingford, Triangle Books).

—— (1992b) 'Sex exposed. Sexuality and the pornography debate', *Spare Rib*, 237, August/September, 19–20.

—— and Sara Scott (1989) 'With our own hands 2', *Trouble and Strife*, 16, 28–9.

—— *et al.* (1991) *An Exploratory Study of the Prevalence of Sexual Abuse in a Sample of 16–21 year olds* (London, Polytechnic of North London).

Kennedy, Mary, Cathy Lubelska and Val Walsh (eds) (1993) *Making Connections: Women's Studies, Women's Movements, Women's Lives* (London, Taylor & Francis).

—— and Brec'hed Piette (1991) 'Issues around Women's Studies on adult education and access courses', in Jane Aaron and Sylvia Walby (eds), *Out of the Margins: Women's Studies in the Nineties* (London, Falmer Press).

Kenney, Janet W. and Donna T. Tash (1993) 'Lesbian childbearing couples, dilemmas and decisions', in Phyllis Noerager Stern (ed.), *Lesbian Health. What are the Issues?* (Washington, DC, Taylor & Francis).

Kenrick, Penelope (1994) 'Video practice within the academy', in Gabriele Griffin (ed.), *Changing Our Lives: Doing Women's Studies* (London, Pluto).

Kent, Susan Kingsley (1996), 'Mistrals and diatribulation: a reply to Joan Hoff', *Women's History Review*, 5 (1) 9–18.

Kessler, Sandra, Dean Ashenden, Bob Connell and Gary Donsett (1987) 'Gender relations in secondary schooling', in Madeleine Arnot and Gaby Weiner (eds), *Gender and the Politics of Schooling* (London, Unwin Hyman).

Kevles, D. and L. Hood (eds) (1992) *The Code of Codes: Scientific and Social Issues in the Human Genome Project* (Cambridge, Mass., Harvard).

Keyssar, Helene (1984) *Feminist Theatre: An Introduction to Plays of Contemporary British and American Women* (London, Macmillan).

Khanum, Saeeda (1995) 'Education and the Muslim Girl', in Maud Blair and Janet Holland with Sue Sheldon (eds), *Identity and Diversity* (Clevedon, Multilingual Matters).

Kiernan, Kathleen and Malcom Wicks (1990) *Family Change and Future Policy* (London, Family Policy Studies Centre).

Kimmel, Michael (1988) 'The gender blender', *The Guardian*, 29 September, 20.

King, Alison (1992) 'Mystery and imagination: the case of pornography effects studies', in Alison Assiter and Carol Avedon (eds), *Bad Girls and Dirty Pictures* (London, Pluto).

Kingdom, Elizabeth (1991) *What's Wrong with Rights? Problems for a Feminist Politics of Law* (Edinburgh University Press).

Kingston, Maxine Hong (1977) *The Woman Warrior: Memoirs of a Girlhood among Ghosts*, first published 1976 (Harmondsworth, Penguin).

Kingston, Paul and Bridget Penhale (ed.) (1995) *Family Violence and the Caring Professions* (London, Macmillan).

Kirejczyk, Marta (1990) 'A question of meaning? Controversies about the new reproductive technologies in the Netherlands', *Issues in Reproductive and Genetic Engineering: Journal of International Feminist Analysis*, 3(1) 23–33.

Kirkup, Gill (1992) 'The social construction of computers: hammers or harpsichords?', in G. Kirkup and L. S. Keller (eds), *Inventing Women* (Cambridge Polity/ Open University Press).

—— and L. S. Keller (eds) (1992) *Inventing Women: Science, Technology and Gender* (Cambridge, Polity).

Kirkwood, Katherine (1993) *Leaving Abusive Partners, From the Scars of Survival to the Wisdom for Change* (London, Sage).

Kishwar, Madhu (1985) 'The continuing deficit of women in India and the impact of amniocentesis', in Gena Corea *et al.*, *Man-Made Women: How the New Reproductive Technologies Affect Women* (London, Hutchinson, 1985; Bloomington, Indiana University Press, 1987).

—— and Ruth Vanita (1984) *In Search of Answers* (London, Zed).

Kitzinger, Celia (1990) 'Resisting the discipline', in Erica Burman (ed.), *Feminists and Psychological Practice* (London, Sage).

—— (1994) 'Experiential authority and heterosexuality', in Gabriele Griffin (ed.), *Changing Our Lives: Doing Women's Studies* (London, Pluto).

—— and Sue Wilkinson (1993),'Theorizing heterosexuality', in Sue Wilkinson and Celia Kitzinger (eds), *Heterosexuality: A Feminism and Psychology Reader* (London, Sage).

Kitzinger, Jenny and Kate Hunt (1994) *Zero Tolerance of Male Violence: A Report on Attempts to Change the Social Context of Sexual Violence through a Public Awareness Campaign* (Edinburgh District Council).

Kitzinger, S. (1978) *Women as Mothers* (Glasgow, William Collins).

Klein, Renate Duelli (ed.) (1989) *Infertility: Women Speak out about their Experiences of Reproductive Medicine* (London, Pandora).

—— (1990) 'IVF research: a question of feminist ethics', *Issues in Reproductive and Genetic Engineering: Journal of International Feminist Analysis*, 3(3) 234–51.

—— (1991) 'Passion and politics in Women's Studies in the 1990s', in Jane Aaron and Sylvia Walby (eds), *Out of the Margins: Women's Studies in the Nineties* (London, Falmer Press).

——, Janice G. Raymond and Lynetter J. Dumble (1991) *RU 486: Misconceptions, Myths and Morals*, first published by Spinifex Press, Melbourne (Dhaka, Bangladesh, Narigrantha Prabartana [The Feminist Bookstore]).

—— and Robyn Rowland (1988) 'Women as test-sites for fertility drugs: clomiphene citrate and hormonal cocktails', *Reproductive and Genetic Engineering: Journal of International Feminist Analysis*, 3 (3) 235–42.

Koch, Lene (1990) 'IVF: an irrational choice?' *Issues in Reproductive and Genetic Engineering: Journal of International Feminist Analysis*, 3(3) 235–42.

Koedt, Anne (1974) 'The myth of the vaginal orgasm', in The Radical Therapist Collective (eds), *The Radical Therapist* (Harmondsworth, Penguin).

—— (1996) 'The myth of the vaginal orgasm', in Stevi Jackson and Sue Scott (eds), *Feminism and Sexuality. A Reader* (Edinburgh University Press). Reprinted from Anne Koedt, *Radical Feminism* (Quadrangle, 1972).

Kollek, Regine (1990) 'The limits of experimental knowledge: a feminist perspective on the ecological risks of genetic engineering', *Issues in Reproductive and Genetic Engineering: Journal of International Feminist Analysis*, 3(2) 125–35.

Kondo, Dorinne (1991) *Crafting Selves Power, Gender and Discourses of Identity in a Japanese Workplace* (Chicago, The University of Chicago).

Koso-Thomas, Olayinka (1987) *The Circumcision of Women, A Strategy for Eradication* (London, Zed).

Kramarae, Cheris (1988) *Technology and Women's Voices: Keeping in Touch* (London, Routledge).

—— and Dale Spender (eds) (1993) *The Knowledge Explosion: Generations of Feminist Scholarship* (London, Harvester Wheatsheaf).

—— and Dale Spender (eds) (1997) *The Feminist Encyclopedia* (4 vols) (London, Prentice-Hall).

Krauss, Rosalind (1993) 'Film stills', in Rosalind Krauss (ed.), *Cindy Sherman, 1975–1993* (New York, Rizzoli).

Kristeva, Julia (1982) *Powers of Horror: An Essay on Abjection*, trans. Leon Raudiez (New York, Columbia University Press).

Kristeva, Julia (1986) *The Kristeva Reader*, ed. Toril Moi (Oxford, Basil Blackwell).

Kuhn, Annette (1995) *Family Secrets: Acts of Memory and Imagination* (London, Verso).

Kupryashkina, Svetlana (1996) 'Possibilities for Women's Studies in post-communist countries: where are we going?', in Mary Maynard and June Purvis (eds), *New Frontiers in Women's Studies: Knowledge, Identity and Nationalism* (London, Taylor & Francis).

Ladas, Alice Kahn, Beverley Whipple and John D. Perry (1982) *The G-Spot* (New York, Holt, Rinehart & Winston).

Lamos, Colleen (1994) 'The postmodern lesbian position: on our backs', in Laura Doan (ed.), *The Lesbian Postmodern* (New York, Columbia University Press).

Land, Hilary (1983) 'Who still cares for the family? Recent developments in income maintenance, taxation and family law' in Jane Lewis (ed.), *Women's Welfare, Women's Rights* (London, Croom Helm).

Landry, Donna and Gerald MacLean (1993) *Materialist Feminisms* (Cambridge, Mass., Blackwell).

Langan, M. and I. Ostner (1991) 'Gender and Welfare: Towards a Comparative Framework', in G. Room (ed.), *Towards a European Welfare State?* (Bristol, SAUS Publications).

—— and Lesley Day (1992) *Women, Oppression and Social Work* (London, Routledge).

Langford, Wendy (1995) 'The subject of love', PhD thesis, Lancaster University.

Larkin, June (1994) 'Walking through walls: the sexual harassment of high school girls', *Gender and Education*, 6(3) 263–80.

Lash, Scott and John Urry (1994) *Economies of Signs and Space* (London, Sage).

Lather, Patti (1991) *Getting Smart: Feminist Research and Pedagogy With/In The Postmodern* (New York, Routledge).

Laws, Sophie (1994) 'Undervalued families: standing up for single mothers', *Trouble and Strife*, 28, 5–11.

Lee, Dorothy (1990) 'Chatterboxes', *Child Education*, 67(7) 26–7.

Lee, So-Hee (1995) 'The prospects and problems of Korean Women's Studies: women's studies and women's movement' and 'Women's Studies in an international context: debates and controversies', *Journal of Gender Studies*, 4 (1) 73–6.

Lees, Sue (1986) *Losing Out: Sexuality and Adolescent Girls* (London, Hutchinson).

—— (1991) 'Feminist politics and Women's Studies: struggle, not incorporation', in Jane Aaron and Sylvia Walby (eds), *Out of the Margins: Women's Studies in the Nineties* (London, Falmer Press).

—— (1993) *Sugar and Spice: Sexuality and Adolescent Girls* (Harmondsworth, Penguin).

Lefanu, Sarah (1988) *In the Chinks of the World Machine: Feminism and Science Fiction* (London, The Women's Press).

Leidner, Robin (1991) 'Serving hamburgers and selling insurance: gender work and identity in interactive service jobs', *Gender and Society*, 5, 154–77.

Lennon, Kathleen (1995) 'Gender and Knowledge', *Journal of Gender Studies*, 4 (2) 133–43.

Lerner, Gerda (1981) *The Majority Finds its Past* (Oxford University Press).

—— (1986) *The Creation of Patriarchy* (Oxford University Press).

Leuzinger, Monika and Bigna Rambert (1988) '"I can feel it – my baby is healthy": women's experiences with prenatal diagnosis in Switzerland', *Reproductive and Genetic Engineering: Journal of International Feminist Analysis*, 1(3) 239–49.

Levine, Phillippa (1987) *Victorian Feminism, 1850–1900* (London, Hutchinson).

—— (1990) Feminist Lives in Victorian England (Oxford, Basil Blackwell).

Levitin, T. E. and J. D. Chananie (1972) 'Responses of female primary school teachers to sex-typed behaviours in male and female children', *Child Development*, 43, 1309–16.

Lewallen, Avis (1988) '"Lace": pornography for women?', in Lorraine Gamman and Margaret Marshment (eds), *The Female Gaze* (London, The Women's Press).

Lewenhak, Sheila (1977) *Women and Trade Unions* (London, Benn).

Lewin, Ellen and Virginia Olesen (1985) 'Occupational health and women: the case of clerical work', in E. Lewin and V. Olesen (eds), *Women, Health and Healing* (London, Tavistock).

Lewis, Gail (1990) 'Audre Lorde: vignettes and mental conversations', *Feminist Review*, 34, Spring, 100–14.

—— (1993) 'Black women's employment and the British economy', in Winston James and Clive Harris (eds), *Inside Babylon: The Caribbean Diaspora in Britain* (London: Verso).

Lewis, Jane (1981) 'Women lost and found: the impact of feminism on history', in Dale Spender (ed.), *Men's Studies Modified: The Impact of Feminism on the Academic Disciplines* (Oxford, Pergamon).

—— (ed.) (1986) *Labour and Love: Women's Experience of Home and Family* (Oxford, Blackwell).

—— (1991) *Women and Social Action in Victorian and Edwardian England* (Aldershot, Edward Elgar).

—— (1992) 'Gender and the development of welfare regimes', *Journal of European Social Policy*, 2(3) 159–73.

Lewis, Reina (1996) Gendering *Orientalism: Race, Femininity and Representation* (London, Routledge).

Lewis, S. E. (1995) 'The social construction of depression: experience, discourse and subjectivity', Unpublished PhD thesis, University of Sheffield.

Liddington, Jill and Jill Norris (1978) *One Hand Tied Behind Us: The Rise of the Women's Suffrage Movement* (London, Virago).

Lifton, Robert Jay (1986) *The Nazi Doctors: Medical Killing and the Psychology of Genocide* (New York, Basic Books).

Light, Alison (1984) ' "Returning to Manderley" – Romance fiction, female sexuality and class' Feminist Review, 16, Summer, 7–25.

Lilly, Mark (ed.) (1990) *Lesbian and Gay Writing* (London, Macmillan).

Lingam, Lakshmi (1990) 'New reproductive technologies in India: a print media analysis', *Issues in Reproductive and Genetic Engineering: Journal of International Feminist Analysis*, 3(1) 13–21.

Lister, Ruth (1993) 'Tracing the contours of women's citizenship', *Policy and Politics* 21(1) 3–16.

—— (1994) 'Citizenship and difference', paper presented at 4th ESRC Gender and Welfare Seminar, Bath, December.

—— (1997) Citizenship: Feminist Perspectives (London, Macmillan).

Littlewood, Roland and Maurice Lipsedge (1988) 'Psychiatric illness among British Afro-Caribbeans', *British Medical Journal*, 296, 950–1.

Lobban, Glenys (1975) 'Sex roles in reading schemes', *Educational Review*, 27(3) 202–10.

Lobel, Kerry (ed.) (1986) *Naming the Violence: Speaking Out about Lesbian Battering* (Seattle, The Seal Press).

London Feminist History Group (1986) *The Sexual Dynamics of History: Men's Power, Women's Resistance*, 2nd edn (London, Pluto).

Longino, Helen (1990) *Science as Social Knowledge: Values and Objectivity in Scientific Inquiry* (Princeton University Press).

—— (1993) 'Feminist standpoint theory and the problems of knowledge, *Signs* 19(1) 201–12

—— and E. Hammonds (1990) 'Conflicts and tensions in the study of gender and science', in M. Hirsch and E. F. Keller (eds), *Conflicts in Feminism* (London, Routledge).

Lonsdale, Susan (1990) *Women and Disability: The Experience of Physical Disability Among Women* (London, Macmillan).

Lonzi, Carla (1972) *Sputiamo su Hegel* (Milan, Scritti di Rivolta Feminile). Available in English (mimeo) London; reprinted as 'Let's spit on Hegel', in Paola Bono and Sandra Kemp (eds) (1991), *Italian Feminist Thought: A Reader* (Oxford, Basil Blackwell).

Lorde, Audre (1982) *Zami: A New Spelling of My Name* (New York, The Crossing Press).

—— (1984a) *Sister Outsider: Essays and Speeches* (New York, The Crossing Press).

—— (1984b) 'The master's tools will never dismantle the master's house', in Audre Lorde, *Sister Outsider: Essays and Speeches* (New York, The Crossing Press).

—— (1992) 'Age, race, class and sex: women redefining difference', in Helen Crowley and Susan Himmelweit (eds), *Knowing Women: Feminism and Knowledge* (Cambridge, Oxford and Buckingham, Polity, Blackwell and Open University Press).

Lovell, Terry (1987) *Consuming Fiction* (London, Verso).

Lowe, Marian and Margaret Lowe Benston (1991) 'The uneasy alliance of feminism and academia', in Sneja Gunew (ed.), *A Reader in Feminist Knowledge* (London, Routledge).

Lubelska, Cathy (1991) 'Teaching methods in Women's Studies: challenging the mainstream', in Jane Aaron and Sylvia Walby (eds), *Out of the Margins: Women's Studies in the Nineties* (London, Falmer Press).

Luddy, Maria (1992) 'An agenda for women's history in Ireland, 1500–1900. Part 2 1800–1900', *Irish Historical Studies*, XXVIII, 109, May, 19–37.

—— (1995) *Women and Philanthropy in Nineteenth-Century Ireland* (Cambridge University Press).

Lugones, Maria C. (in collaboration with Pat Alake Rosezelle) (1993) 'Sisterhood and friendship as feminist models', in Cheris Kramarae and Dale Spender (eds), *The Knowledge Explosion: Generations of Feminist Scholarship* (Hemel Hempstead, Harvester Wheatsheaf).

Lyndon, Neil (1992) *No More Sex War: The Failures of Feminism* (London, Sinclair-Stevenson).

Lyotard, Jean François (1984) *The Postmodern Condition: A Report on Knowledge* (trans. Geoff Bennington and Brian Massumi) (Manchester University Press).

Mac an Ghaill, Mairtin (1988) *Young, Gifted and Black: Student Teacher Relations in the Schooling of Black Youth* (Milton Keynes, Open University Press).
—— (1994) *The Making of Men; Masculinities, Sexualities and Schooling* (Buckingham, Open University Press).
—— (1995) '(In)visibility: "Race", Sexuality and Masculinity in the School Context', in Maud Blair and Janet Holland with Sue Sheldon (eds), *Identity and Diversity* (Clevedon, Multilingual Matters).
—— (ed.) (1996) *Understanding Masculinities* (Buckingham, Open University Press).
MacCabe, Colin (1976) 'Realism and cinema: notes on some Brechtion theses', *Screen*, 17, Autumn (3).
MacCormack, Carol P. (1989) 'Technology and women's health in developing countries', *International Journal of Health Services*, 19(4) 681–92.
MacCurtain, Margaret and Mary O'Dowd (1992) 'An agenda for women's history in Ireland, 1500–1900. Part 1 1500–1800', *Irish Historical Studies*, XXVIII, 109, May, 1–19.
MacDonald, Barbara with C. Rich (1984) *Look Me in the Eye: Old Women, Ageing and Ageism* (London, The Women's Press).
Macguire, Sara (1993) 'The law in relation to women killing violent men', in *Justice for Women Information Pack* (London, The London Justice for Women Collective).
MacKeith, Nancy (1978) *The New Women's Health Handbook* (London, Virago).
MacKinnon, Catharine A. (1982) 'Feminism, Marxism, method and the state: an agenda for theory', *Signs*, 7(3) 515–44.
—— (1989) *Towards a Feminist Theory of the State* (Cambridge, Mass., Harvard University Press).
—— (1996) 'Feminism, Marxism, method and the state: an agenda for theory', in Stevi Jackson and Sue Scott (eds), *Feminism and Sexuality. A Reader* (Edinburgh University Press).
—— and Andrea Dworkin (1996) 'Statement on Canadian customs and legal approaches to pornography', in Diane Bell and Renate Klein (eds), *Radically Speaking: Feminism Reclaimed* (Melbourne, Spinifex).
MacKinnon, Catherine (1978) *Sexual Harassment of Working Women: A Case of Sex Discrimination* (New Haven, Conn., Yale University Press).
Maclean, Mavis and Dulcie Groves (1991) *Women's Issues in Social Policy* (London, Routledge).
Macleod, Mary and Esther Saraga (1988) 'Challenging the orthodoxy: towards a feminist theory and practice', *Feminist Review*, 28, Spring.
Madoc-Jones, Beryl and Jennifer Coates (eds) (1996) *An Introduction To Women's Studies* (Oxford, Basil Blackwell).
Maher, Frances A. and Mary Kay Thompson Tetreault (1994) *The Feminist Classroom* (New York, Basic Books).
Mahony, Pat (1983) 'Boys will be boys: teaching Women's Studies in mixed sex groups', *Women's Studies International Forum*, 6(3) 331–4.
—— (1985) *Schools for the Boys? Co-education Reassessed* (London, Hutchinson).
Mair, Lucy (1972) *Marriage* (New York, Pica Press).
Malečková, Jitka (1996) 'Gender, nation and scholarship: reflections on gender: Women's Studies in the Czech Republic', in Mary Maynard and June Purvis (eds), *New Frontiers in Women's Studies: Knowledge, Identity and Nationalism* (London, Taylor & Francis).
Malos, Ellen (ed.) (1980) *The Politics of Housework* (London, Allison & Busby).
Mama, Amina (1989) *The Hidden Struggle: Statutory and Voluntary Sector Responses to Violence against Black Women in the Home* 2nd edn 1993 (London, London Race and Housing Research Unit).
—— (1995) *Beyond the Masks: Race, Gender and Subjectivity* (London, Routledge).

Mani, Lata (1990) 'Multiple mediations: feminist scholarship in the age of multi-national reception', in *Feminist Review*, 35, Summer, 24–41.

Mansfield, Penny and Jean Collard (1988) *The Beginning of the Rest of Your Life: A Portrait of Newly-Wed Marriage* (London, Macmillan).

Margolies, David (1982) 'Mills and Boon – guilt without sex', *Red Letters*, 14.

Mark-Lawson, Jane and Anne Witz (1986) 'From "family labour" to "family wage"? The case of women's labour in 19th-century coal mining', *Social History*, 13(2) 151–74.

—— and Anne Witz (1990) 'Familial control or patriarchal domination? The case of the family system of labour in 19th century coal mining', in Helen Corr and Lynn Jamieson (eds), *Politics of Everyday Life: Continuity and Change in Work and the Family* (London, Macmillan).

Marks, Elaine and Isabelle de Courtivron (eds) (1981) *New French Feminisms: An Anthology* (Brighton, Harvester).

Marks, Lara V. (1991), 'Carers and servers of the Jewish community: the margin-alised heritage of Jewish women in Britain', *Immigrants and Minorities*, 10 (1,2), 106–27.

—— (1994) *Model Mothers: Jewish Mothers and Maternity Provision in East London, 1870–1939* (Oxford, Clarendon).

Marland, Michael (ed.) (1983) *Sex Differentiation and Schooling* (London, Heine-mann).

Marshall, T. H. (1950) *Citizenship and Social Class and Other Essays* (Cambridge, Cambridge University Press).

Martin, Emily (1987) *The Woman in the Body: A Cultural Analysis of Reproduction* (Boston, Mass., Beacon Press).

—— (1994) *Flexible Bodies: The Role of Immunity in American Culture – from the Days of Polio to the Age of AIDS* (Boston, Mass., Beacon Press).

Marx, Karl and Frederick Engels (1970) *The German Ideology* (London, Lawrence & Wishart).

Marxist Feminist Literature Collective (1978) 'Women's writing: Jane Eyre, Shirley, Villette, Aurora Leigh', in Francis Barker *et al.* (eds), *1848: The Sociology of Literature* (University of Essex).

Mason, Carol (1995) 'Terminating bodies: toward a cyborg history of abortion', in J. Halberstam and I. Livingston (eds), *Posthuman Bodies* (Bloomington, Indiana University Press).

Mason-John, Valerie (ed.) (1995) *Talking Black: Lesbians of African and Asian Descent Speak Out* (London, Cassell).

—— and Ann Khambatta (1993) *Making Black Waves* (London, Scarlet Press).

Masters, Judith C. (1995) 'Revolutionary theory: reinventing our origin myths', in L. Birke and R. Hubbard (eds), *Reinventing Biology* (Bloomington, Indiana University Press).

Mavolwane, Sibusiso and Jill Radford (1993) 'We'll be freeing all the women', in *Justice for Women Information Pack* (London, The London Justice for Women Collective).

May, Margaret and Edward Brunsden (1996) 'Women and private welfare', in Christine Hallett (ed.) *Women and Social Policy: An Introduction* (London, Prentice-Hall and Harvester Wheatsheaf in association with the Social Policy Association Women and Social Policy Group).

Mayhew, Pat, Natalie Aye Maung and Catriona Mirrlees-Black (1993) *The 1992 British Crime Survey* (London, HMSO).

Maynard, Mary (1989) 'Privilege and patriarchy: feminist thought in the nineteeth century', in Susan Mendus and Jane Rendall (eds), *Sexuality and Subordination* (London, Routledge & Kegan Paul).

—— (1994) 'Race, gender and the concept of difference in feminist thought', in Haleh Afshar and Mary Maynard (eds), *The Dynamics of 'Race' and Gender: Some Feminist Interventions* (London, Taylor & Francis).

—— (1995) 'Beyond the 'Big Three': the development of feminist theory into the 1990s', *Women's History Review*, 4(3) 259–81.

—— (1996) 'Challenging the boundaries: towards an anti-racist Women's Studies', in Mary Maynard and June Purvis (eds), *New Frontiers in Women's Studies: Knowledge, Identity and Nationalism* (London, Taylor & Francis).

—— and June Purvis (eds) (1994) *Researching Women's Lives from a Feminist Perspective* (London, Taylor & Francis).

—— and June Purvis (eds) (1996) *New Frontiers in Women's Studies: Knowledge, Identity and Nationalism* (London, Taylor & Francis).

Mayo, Marjorie and Angela Weir (1993) 'The future for feminist social policy', in Robert Page and John Baldock (eds), *Social Policy Review 5* (Canterbury: Social Policy Association).

McCann, Kathy (1985) 'Battered women and the law', in Julia Brophy and Carol Smart (eds), *Women-in-Law* (London, Routledge & Kegan Paul).

McClintock, Anne (1995) *Imperial Leather: Race, Gender and Sexuality in the Colonial Contest* (London, Routledge).

—— (1996) 'Ethnicity, "race" and empire', in June Purvis (ed.), *Women's History: Britain, 1850–1945* (London, UCL).

McDonnell, Kathleen (1986) *Adverse Effects: Women and the Pharmaceutical Industry* (Penang, Malaysia, International Organization of Consumers Unions Regional for Asia and the Pacific).

McGuire, J. (1991) 'Sons and daughters', in A. Phoenix, A. Woollett and E. Lloyd (eds), *Motherhood: Meanings, Practices and Ideologies* (London, Sage).

McIntosh, Mary (1968) 'The homosexual role', *Social Problems*, 16(2) 182–92.

—— (1978) 'The state and the oppression of women', in Annette Kuhn and Anne Marie Wolpe (eds), *Feminism and Materialism* (London, Routledge & Kegan Paul).

—— (1993a) 'Queer Theory and the war of the sexes', in Joseph Bristow and Angelia R. Wilson (eds), *Activating Theory: Lesbian, Gay and Bisexual Politics* (London, Lawrence & Wishart).

—— (1993b) 'The homosexual role', in Edward Stein (ed.) *Forms of Desire: Sexual Orientation and the Social Constructionist Controversy* (London and New York, Routledge).

—— (1996) 'Liberalism and the contradictions of oppression', in Stevi Jackson and Sue Scott (eds), *Feminism and Sexuality. A Reader* (Edinburgh University Press). Reprinted from Lynne Segal and Mary McIntosh (eds) (1992) *Sex Exposed: Sexuality and the Pornography Debate* (London, Virago).

McMullin, Julie (1995) 'Theorising age and gender relations', in Sara Arber and Jay Ginn (eds), *Connecting Gender and Aging: A Sociological Approach* (Buckingham, Open University Press).

McNay, Lois (1992) *Foucault and Feminism* (Cambridge, Polity).

McNeil, Maureen (ed.) (1987) *Gender and Expertise* (London, Free Association Books).

—— (1992) 'Pedagogical praxis and problems: reflections on teaching about gender relations', in Hilary Hinds, Ann Phoenix and Jackie Stacey (eds), *Working Out: New Directions For Women's Studies* (London, Falmer Press).

—— (1997 forthcoming) *Science and Popular Culture*.

—— Ian Varcoe and Steven Yearly (eds) (1990) *The New Reproductive Technologies* (New York, St Martin's Press).

McRobbie, A. (1989) 'Second-hand dresses and the role of the ragmarket', in McRobbie, A. (ed.), *Zoots Suits and Second-Hand Dresses: An Anthology of Fashion and Music* (London: Unwin Hyman).

Measor, Lynda and Patricia Sikes (1992) *Gender and Schools* (London, Cassell).

Merchant, Carolyn (1982) *The Death of Nature* (London, Wildwood).

Messing, Karen and D. Mergler (1995) '"The rat couldn't speak, but we can": inhumanity in occupational health research', in L. Birke and R. Hubbard (eds), *Reinventing Biology* (Bloomington, Indiana University Press).

Michie, Elsie B. (1993) *Outside the Pale: Cultural Exclusion, Gender Difference and the Victorian Woman Writer* (Ithaca and London, Cornell University Press).

Middleton, Chris (1983) 'Patriarchal domination and the rise of English Capitalism', in E. Gamarnikow, D. Morgan, J. Purvis and D. Taylorson (eds), *Gender, Class and Work* (London, Hutchinson).

Middleton, Chris (1988) 'The familiar fate of the famulae: gender division in the history of wage labour', in R. Pahl (ed.) *On Work: Historical, Comparative and Theoretical Approaches*, (Oxford, Blackwell).

Midgley, Clare (1992) *Women Against Slavery: The British Campaigns, 1780–1870* (London, Routledge).

—— (1995) 'Ethnicity, "race" and empire', in June Purvis (ed.), *Women's History: Britain, 1850–1945* (London, UCL).

Miedzian, Myriam (1992) *Boys will be Boys: Breaking the Link between Masculinity and Violence* (London, Virago).

Mies, Maria (1986) *Patriarchy and Accumulation on a World Scale: Women in the International Division of Labour* (London, Zed Books).

—— (1988) 'From the individual to the dividual: in the supermarket of 'Reproductive Alternative'', *Reproductive and Genetic Engineering: Journal of International Feminist Analysis*, 1(3) 225–37.

Miles, Sheila and Chris Middleton (1995) 'Girls' education in the balance: the ERA and inequality', in Liz Dawtrey, Janet Holland and Merril Hammer with Sue Sheldon (eds), *Equality and Inequality in Education Policy* (Clevedon, Multilingual Matters).

Millar, Jane (1992) 'Lone parents and poverty', in Caroline Glendinning and Jane Millar (eds), *Women and Poverty in Britain: The Nineties* (Hemel Hempstead: Harvester Wheatsheaf).

Miller, Nancy (1991) *Getting Personal: Feminist Occasions and Other Autobiographical Acts* (London, Routledge).

Millett, Kate (1970) *Sexual Politics*, reprinted 1977 (London, Virago).

—— (1992) 'Beyond politics? Children and sexuality', in Carol Vance (ed.), *Pleasure and Danger: Exploring Female Sexuality*, first published in 1984 (London, Pandora).

Mills, Arthur and Peta Tancred (eds) (1992) *Gendering Organizational Analysis* (London, Sage).

Mills, Sara and Lynne Pearce (1996) *Feminist Readings/Feminists Reading*, 2nd edn; 1st edn 1989 (Hemel Hempstead, Harvester Wheatsheaf).

Mirza, Heidi (1995) 'Life in the classroom', in Janet Holland and Maud Blair with Sue Sheldon (eds), *Debates and Issues in Feminist Research and Pedagogy* (Clevedon, Multilingual Matters).

—— (1995a) 'Black women in higher education: defining a space/finding a place', in Louise Morley and Val Walsh (eds), *Feminist Academics: Creative Agents For Change* (London, Taylor & Francis).

Mitchell, Juliet (1966) 'Women: the longest revolution', *New Left Review*, 40, 11–37.

—— (1971) *Woman's Estate* (Harmondsworth, Penguin).

—— (1974) *Psychoanalysis and Feminism* (Harmondsworth, Penguin).

—— and Jacqueline Rose (1982) *Feminine Sexuality: Jacques Lacan and the Ecole Freudienne* (London, Macmillan).

Mitter, Swasti (1995) 'Who benefits?', in Gender Working Group, United Nations Commission on Science and Technology for Development, *Missing Links: Gender Equity in Science and Technology for Development* (London, Intermediate Technology Publications).

Modleski, Tania (1982) *Loving with a Vengeance: Mass-produced Fantasies for Women*, reprinted 1988 (London, Routledge).

Moers, Ellen (1978) *Literary Women*, first published 1976 (London, The Women's Press).

Mohanty, Chandra Talpade (1988) 'Under Western eyes: feminist scholarship and colonial discourses', *Feminist Review*, 30, Autumn, 61–89.

Moi, Toril (1985) *Sexual/Textual Politics: Feminist Literary Theory* (London and New York, Methuen).

—— (ed.) (1986) *The Kristeva Reader* (Oxford, Basil Blackwell).

—— (ed.) (1987) *French Feminist Thought: A Reader* (Oxford, Basil Blackwell).

Montefiore, Han (1987) *Feminism and Poetry: Language, Experience, Identity in Women's Writing* (London and New York, Pandora).

Moore, Henrietta (1988) *Feminism and Anthropology* (Cambridge, Polity).

—— (1994) *A Passion for Difference: Essays in Anthropology and Gender* (Bloomington, Indiana University Press and Cambridge, Polity Press).

Moraga Cherrie and Gloria Anzaldua (eds) (1981) *This Bridge Called my Back: Writings By Radical Women of Colour* (Watertown, Mass., The Persephone Press).

Morgan, David (1992) *Discovering Men* (London, Routledge).

Morgan, Debi (1995) 'Invisible women: young women and feminism', in Gabriele Griffinn (ed.), *Feminist Activism in the 1990s* (London, Taylor & Francis).

Morgan, Valerie and Seamus Dunn (1990) 'Management strategies and gender differences in nursery and infant classrooms', *Research in Education*, 44, 81–91.

Morley, Louise (1995a) 'Measuring the muse: feminism, creativity and career development in higher education', in Louise Morley and Val Walsh (eds), *Feminist Academics: Creative Agents for Change* (London, Taylor & Francis).

—— (1995b) 'The micropolitics of Women's Studies: feminism and organizational change in the academy', in Mary Maynard and June Purvis (eds), *(Hetero)sexual Politics* (London, Taylor & Francis).

—— and Val Walsh (eds) (1995) *Feminist Academics: Creative Agents for Change* (London, Taylor & Francis).

Morley, Rebecca and Audrey Mullender (1994) *Preventing Domestic Violence to Women*, Crime Prevention Unit Series: Paper No. 48 (London, Home Office Police Department).

Morris, Jenny (1991) *Pride Against Prejudice: Transforming Attitudes to Disability* (London, The Women's Press).

—— (1993) *Independent Lives? Community Care and Disabled People* (London, Macmillan).

Morris, Lydia (1990) *The Workings of the Household* (Cambridge, Polity).

Morrison, Toni (1973) *Sula*, reprinted 1982 (London, Triad Granada).

—— (1987) *Beloved*, reprinted 1988 (London, Picador).

—— (1993a) *Playing in the Dark: Whiteness and the Literary Imagination*, first published 1992 (London, Picador).

—— (ed.) (1993b) *Race-ing Justice, En-Gendering Power: Essays on Anita Hill, Clarence Thomas and the Construction of Social Reality* (London, Chatto & Windus).

Mrazek, Patricia Beezley, Margaret Lynch and Arnon Bentovim (1981) 'Recognition of child sexual abuse in the United Kingdom', in Patricia Beezley Mrazek and Henry C. Kempe (eds), *Sexually Abused Children and Their Families* (Oxford, Pergamon Press).

Mulvey, Laura (1975) 'Visual pleasure and narrative cinema', *Screen*, 16(3), reprinted in Laura Mulvey (1989), *Visual and Other Pleasures* (London, Macmillan).

—— (1991) 'A phantasmagoria of the female body: the work of Cindy Sherman', *New Left Review*, 188, July–August, 136–51.

Muntemba, Shimwaayi and R. Chimedza (1995) 'Women spearhead food security', in Gender Working Group, United Nations Commission on Science and Technology for Development *Missing Links: Gender Equity in Science and Technology for Development* (London, Intermediate Technology Publications).

Murray Charles (1990) *The Emerging British Underclass* (London, IEA Health and Welfare Unit).

Myers, Kathy (1989) 'Towards a feminists erotica', *Camerawork*, 24, 14–16 and 19.

Nadel, Jennifer (1993) *Sara Thornton: The Story of a Woman who Killed* (London, Victor Gollancz).

Naffine, N. (1990) *Law and the Sexes: Explorations in Feminist Jursiprudence* (Sydney, Allen & Unwin).

Nain, Gemma Tang (1991) 'Black women, sexism and racism: black or anti-racist feminism?', *Feminist Review*, 37, 1–22.

Nair, Sumati (1989) *Imperialism and the Control of Women's Fertility: New Hormonal Contraceptives Population Control and the WHO* (Amsterdam, Campaign Against Long Acting Hormonal Contraceptives).

Namjoshi, Suniti (1985) *The Conversations of Cow* (London, The Women's Press).

Nandy, Ashis (1988) 'Science as a reason of state', in A. Nandy (ed.) *Science, Hegemony and Violence* (Oxford University Press).

Nash, K. (1994) 'State, family and personal responsiblity; the changing balance for lone mothers in the United Kingdom', *Feminist Review*, 47.

Nathanson, Constance A. (1975) 'Illness and the feminine role: a theoretical review', *Social Science and Medicine*, 9, 57–62.

Naylor, Bronwyn (1995) 'Women's crime and media coverage: making explanations', in R. Emerson Dobash, Russell P. Dobash and Lesley Noaks (eds), *Gender and Crime* (Cardiff, University of Wales Press).

Naylor, K. (1994) 'Part-time working in Great Britain – an historical analysis', *Employment Gazette*, December, 473–84.

Nelson, Sarah (1987) *Incest: Fact and Myth* (Edinburgh, Stramullion).

Nestle, Joan (1996) *A Restricted Country* (London, Pandora Press).

Nettleton, Sarah (1995) *The Sociology of Health and Illness* (Cambridge, Polity).

New, Caroline and Miriam David (1985) *For the Children's Sake: Making Childcare more than Women's Business* (Harmondsworth, Penguin).

Newsom Report (1963) *Half Our Future: A Report of the Central Advisory Council for Education* (London, HMSO).

Newton, Judith, Mary Ryan and Judith Walkowitz (eds) (1983) *Sex and Class in Women's History* (London, Routledge & Kegan Paul).

Nichols, Grace (1984) *The Fat Black Woman's Poems* (London, Virago).

Nicholson, Linda J. (ed.) (1990) *Feminism/Postmodernism* (London, Routledge).

Nicolson, Paula (1988) 'The Social Psychology of Postnatal Depression', unpublished PhD Thesis, University of London.

—— (1990) 'Brief report of women's expectations of men's behaviour in the transition to motherhood', *Counselling Psychology Quarterly*, 3(4) 353–61.

—— (1991) 'Virgins and wise women', *Psychology of Women Section of the British Psychological Society Newsletter*, 7, 5–8.

—— (1992) 'Feminism and academic psychology: towards a psychology of women?', in Kate Campbell (ed.), *Critical Feminism: Argument in the Disciplines* (Buckingham, Open University Press).

—— and Jane Ussher (1992) *The Psychology of Women's Health and Health Care* (London, Macmillan).

—— (1994) 'Interpreting gender', *Signs*, 20(1) 79–105.

—— (1995) 'Public values and private beliefs: why do women refer themselves for sex therapy?', in J. M. Ussher and C. D. Baker (eds), *Psychological Perspectives on Sexual Problems* (London, Routledge).

—— (1996) *Post Natal Depression: Psychology, Science and the Transition to Motherhood* (Hemel Hempstead, Harvester).

Northam, Jean (1982) 'Girls and boys in primary maths books', *Education*, 3–13, 10(1) 11–14.

Oakley, Ann (1974) *The Sociology of Housework* (Oxford, Martin Robertson).

—— (1976) *Housewife* (Harmondsworth, Penguin).

—— (1980) *Women Confined: Towards a Sociology of Childbirth* (Oxford, Martin Robertson).

—— (1984) *The Sociology of Housework*, 2nd edn (Oxford, Basil Blackwell).

—— (1989) 'Smoking in pregnancy: smokescreen or risk factor? Towards a materialist analysis', *Sociology of Health and Illness*, 11 (4).

—— (1995) *Public Visions, Private Matters* (London, Institute of Education, University of London).

O'Brien, Mary (1981) *The Politics of Reproduction* (London, Routledge & Kegan Paul).

—— (1989) *Reproducing the World: Essays in Feminist Theory* (Boulder, Col., Westview Press).

O'Connor, Margaret Ann (1987) 'Health/illness in healing/caring – a feminist perspective', in J. Orr (ed.), *Women's Health in the Community* (Chichester, John Wiley).

Offen, Karen, Ruth Roach Pierson and Jane Rendall (eds) (1991) *Writing Women's History: International Perspectives* (London, Macmillan).

Onlywomen Press (eds) (1981) *Love Your Enemy? The Debate between Heterosexual Feminism and Political Lesbianism* (London, Onlywomen Press).

OPCS (Office of Population Censuses and Surveys) (1988) *General Household Survey*, No. 19 (London, HMSO).

OPCS (1995) *1993 Birth Statistics England and Wales* (HMSO, London).

Orloff, Ann (1993) 'Gender and the social rights of citizenship: the comparative analysis of gender relations and welfare states', *American Sociological Review*, 58(3) 303–28.

O'Rourke, Rebecca (1979) 'Summer reading', *Feminist Review*, 2.

—— (1989) *Reflecting on* The Well of Loneliness (London and New York, Routledge).

Osler, Audrey (1994) 'Still hidden from history? The representation of women in recently published history textbooks', *Oxford Review of Education*, 20(2) 219–35.

Ostrowski (1996) letter to *US National Women's Studies Association Newsletter*, Spring.

Oudshoorn, Nelly (1994) *Beyond the Natural Body: An Archeology of Sex Hormones* (London, Routledge).

Overall, Christine (1987) *Ethics and Human Reproduction: A Feminist Analysis* (London, Allen & Unwin).

Ozga, Jenny (ed.) (1993) *Women in Educational Management* (Buckingham, Open University Press).

Pahl, Jan (1985) *Private Violence and Public Policy* (London, Routledge & Kegan Paul).

—— (1989) *Money and Marriage* (London, Macmillan).

—— (1990) 'Household spending, personal spending and the control of money in marriage', *Sociology* 24(1) 119–38.

Palmer, Paulina (1989) *Contemporary Women's Fiction: Narrative Practice and Feminist Theory* (Hemel Hempstead, Harvester Wheatsheaf).

—— (1990) 'Contemporary lesbian feminist fiction: texts for everywoman', in L. Anderson (ed.), *Plotting Change: Contemporary Women's Fiction* (London/Melbourne/Auckland, Edward Arnold).

—— (1993) *Contemporary Lesbian Writing: Dreams, Desire, Difference* (Buckingham and Philadelphia, Open University Press).

Parke, R. D. (1981) *Fathering* (Glasgow, Fontana).

Parker, Julia (1988) *Women and Welfare: Ten Women in Public Social Service* (London, Macmillan).

Parker, R. (1995) *Torn in Two: The Experience of Maternal Ambivalence* (London, Virago).

Parker, R. and Griselda Pollock (1981) *Old Mistresses: Women, Art and Ideology* (London, Pandora).

Parmar, Pratibha (1988) 'Gender, race and power: the challenge to youth work practice', in P. Cohen and H. S. Bains (eds), *Multi-Racist Britain* (London, Macmillan).

Parsons, Claire D. F. (1990) 'Drugs, science and ethics: lessons from the Depo-Provera story', *Issues in Reproductive and Genetic Engineering: Journal of International Feminist Analysis*, 3(2) 101–10.

Parsons, T. and R. F. Bales (1953) *Family Socialisation and Interaction Process* (New York, Free Press).

Pascall, Gillian (1986) *Social Policy: A Feminist Analysis* (London, Tavistock).

—— and Roger Cox (1993) *Women Returning to Higher Education* (Buckingham, SRHE and Open University Press).

Patel, Vibhuti (1989) 'Sex-determination and sex pre-selection tests in India: recent techniques in femicide', *Reproductive and Genetic Engineering: Journal of International Feminist Analysis*, 2(2) 111–19.

Pearce, Lynne (1994a) 'Reading as autobiography', in Gabriele Griffin (ed.), *Changing Our Lives: Doing Women's Studies* (London, Pluto).

—— (1994b) '"Written on tablets of stone": Roland Barthes, Jeanette Winterson and the discourse of romantic love', in Suzanne Raitt (ed.), *Volcanoes and Pearl Divers: Essays in Lesbian Feminist Studies* (London, Onlywomen Press).

—— (1997 forthcoming) *Feminism and the Emotional Politics of Reading* (London, Edward Arnold).

Penna, Sue and Martin O'Brien (1996) 'Postmodernism and social policy: a small step forwards?', *Journal of Social Policy*, 25(1) 39–61.

Perkin, Harold (1976) 'Social history in Britain', *Journal of Social History*, 10(2), Winter, 129–43.

Pfeffer, Naomi and Allison Quick (1988) *Infertility Services: A Desperate Case* (London, Greater London Association of Community Health Councils).

Philips, Deborah and Ella Westland (1992) 'Men in Women's Studies classrooms', in Hilary Hinds, Ann Phoenix and Jackie Stacey (eds), *Working Out: New Directions For Women's Studies* (London, Falmer Press).

—— and Jill Rakusen (eds) (1978) *Our Bodies, Ourselves*, 2nd edn 1989 (Harmondsworth, Penguin).

—— and Barbara Taylor (1980) 'Sex and skill: notes towards a feminist economics', *Feminist Review*, 6, 79–88.

Phillips, Angela (1993) *The Trouble with Boys* (London, Pandora).

Phillips, Ann (1993) *Democracy and Difference* (Cambridge, Polity Press).

Philp, M. (1985) 'Madness, truth and critique: Foucault and anti-psychiatry', *PsychCritique*, 1, 155–70.

Phizacklea, Annie (1994) 'A single or segregated labour market? Gendered and racialized divisions', in H. Afshar and M. Maynard (eds), *The Dynamics of 'Race' and Gender* (London, Taylor & Francis).

—— and M. Ram (1996) 'Being your own boss: ethnic minority entrepreneurs in comparative perspective', *Work, Employment and Society*, 10(2), 319–39.

—— and Wolkowitz, Carol (1995) *Homeworking Women. Gender, Racism and Class at Work* (London, Sage).

Phoenix, A. (1991) 'Mothers under twenty: the outsider and insider views', in A. Phoenix, A. Woollett and E. Lloyd (eds), Motherhood: Meanings, Practices and Ideologies (London, Sage).

—— (1994) 'Practising feminist research: the intersection of gender and "race" in the research process', in Mary Maynard and June Purvis (eds), *Researching Women's Lives from a Feminist Perspective* (London, Taylor & Francis).

——, A. Woollett and E. Lloyd (1991) *Motherhood: Meanings, Practices and Ideologies* (London, Sage).

Pierce-Baker, Charlotte (1990) 'A quilting of voices: diversifying the curriculum/canon in the traditional humanities', *College Literature*, 17(2)-(3) 152–61.

Pill, Roisin and Nigel C.H. Stott (1982) 'Concepts of illness causation and responsibility: some preliminary data from a sample of working class mothers', *Social Science and Medicine*, 60, 43–52.

Place, Janey (1980) 'Women in film noir', in E. Ann Kaplan (ed.), *Women in Film Noir*, first published 1978 (London: BFI).

Plant, Sadie (1996) *Greek Girls* (Internet).

Pleck, Elizabeth (1987) *Domestic Tryanny* (Oxford University Press).

Plummer, Kenneth (ed.) (1992) *Modern Homosexualities: Fragments of Lesbian and Gay Experience* (London, Routledge).

—— (1995) *Telling Sexual Stories. Power, Change and Social Worlds* (London, Routledge).

Plumwood, Val (1993) *Feminism and the Mastery of Nature* (London, Routledge).

Poland, Fiona (1990) 'Breaking the rules: assessing the assessment of a girls work project', in Liz Stanley (ed.), *Feminist Praxis: Research, Theory and Epistemology in Feminist Sociology* (Routledge, London).

Politi, Jina (1982) 'Jane Eyre classified', *Literature and History*, 8(1), Spring, 56–66.

Polity Reader in Gender Studies (1994) (Cambridge, Polity).

Pollert, Anna (1981) *Girls, Wives, Factory Lives* (London, Macmillan).

Pollock, Griselda (1977) 'What's wrong with images of women?', *Screen Education*, 24, Autumn, reprinted in Rosemary Betterton (ed.) 198, *Looking On: Images of Feminity in the Visual Arts and Media* (London, Pandora).

Poovey, Mary (1988) *Uneven Developments: The Ideological Work of Gender in Mid-Victorian Britain* (Chicago University of Chicago Press).

Porter, Eugene (1986) *Treating the Young Male Victim of Sexual Assault* (Safer Society Press).

Potts, Maggie and Rebecca Fido (1990) *A Fit Person to be Removed* (Plymouth, Northcote Press).

Potts, Tracey and Janet Price (1995) ' "Out of the Blood and Spirit of Our Lives": the place of the body in academic feminism', in Louise Morley and Val Walsh (eds), *Feminist Academics: Creative Agents for Change* (London, Taylor & Francis).

Pringle, Keith (1990) *Managing to Survive* (London, Barnardos).

—— (1992) 'Child sexual abuse perpetrated by welfare personel and the problem of men', *Critical Social Policy*, 36, 4–19.

—— (1995) *Men, Masculinities and Social Welfare* (London, UCL).

Pringle, Rosemary (1989) *Secretaries' Talk: Sexuality, Power and Work* (London: Verso).

Probyn, Elspeth (1993) *Sexing the Self: Gendered Positions in Cultural Studies* (London, Routledge).

Prochaska, Frank (1980) *Women and Philanthropy in Nineteenth-Century England* (Oxford, Clarendon Press).

Purvis, June (1991) *A History of Women's Education in England* (Buckingham Open University Press).

—— (1995a) 'From "women worthies" to poststructuralism? Debate and controversy in women's history in Britain', in June Purvis (ed.), *Women's History: Britain, 1850–1945* (London, UCL).

—— (1995b) 'Women and education: a historical account, 1800–1914', in Liz Dawtrey, Janet Holland and Merril Hammer with Sue Sheldon (eds), *Equality and Inequality in Education Policy* (Clevedon, Multilingual Matters).

Rack, Philip (1982) *Race, Culture and Mental Disorder* (London, Tavistock).

Radcliffe, Richards, Janet (1982) The Sceptical Feminist (Harmondsworth, Penguin).

Radford, Jill (1993) 'Self preservation', in *Justice for Women Information Pack* (London, The London Justice for Women Collective).

—— and Rita Rupal (1993), 'Child Support Act 1991: What's it about and why does it matter?', *Rights of Women Bulletin*, Spring, 2–4.

—— (1994) 'History of women's liberation movements in Britain: a reflective personal history', in Gabriele Griffin, Marianne Hester, Shirin Rai and Sasha Roseneil (eds), *Stirring It: Challenges for Feminism* (London, Taylor & Francis).

—— and Diana E. H. Russell (eds) (1992) *Femicide: The Politics of Women Killing* (Buckingham, Open University Press).

Radicalesbians (1973) 'The woman-identified woman', in Anne Koedt, Ellen Levine and Anita Rapone (eds), *Radical Feminism* (New York, Quadrangle Books).

Radstone, Susannah (ed.) (1988) Sweet Dreams: Sexuality Gender and Popular Fiction (London, Lawrence & Wishart).

Radway, Janice (1987) *Reading the Romance: Women, Patriarchy, and Popular Literature*, first published 1984 (London, Verso).

Rakusen, Jill and Nick Davidson (1982) *Out of Our Hands: What Technology Does to Pregnancy* (London, Pan).

Ramazanoglu, Caroline (1987) 'Sex and violence in academic life or you can keep a good woman down', in Jalna Hanmer and Mary Maynard (eds), *Women, Violence and Social Control* (London, Macmillan).

—— (1989) *Feminism and the Contradictions of Oppression* (London, Routledge).

—— (1992) 'On feminist methodology: male reason versus female empowerment' *Sociology*, 26, 207–12

—— (1993a) 'Theorizing heterosexuality: a response to Wendy Hollway', in Sue Wilkinson and Celia Kitzinger (eds), *Heterosexuality: A Feminism and Psychology Reader* (London, Sage).

—— (ed.) (1993b) *Up Against Foucault: Explorations of Some Tensions between Foucault and Feminism* (London, Routledge).

—— (1995) 'Back to basics: heterosexuality, biology and why men stay on top', in Mary Maynard and June Purvis (eds), *(Hetero)sexual Politics* (London, Taylor & Francis).

Rassool, Naz (1995) 'Black women as the "Other" in the academy', in Louise Morley and Val Walsh (eds), *Feminist Academics: Creative Agents For Change* (London, Taylor & Francis).

Ratti, Rakesh (ed.) (1993) *A Lotus of Another Color* (Boston, Alyson).

Raymond, Janice (1988a) 'At issue: in the matter of baby M; rejudged', *Reproductive and Genetic Engineering: Journal of International Feminist Analysis*, 1(2) 175–81.
—— (1988b) 'The spermic market: surrogate stock and liquid assets', *Reproductive and Genetic Engineering: Journal of International Feminist Analysis*, 1(1) 65–75.
—— (1989) 'The international traffic in women: women used in systems of surrogacy and reproduction', *Reproductive and Genetic Engineering: Journal of International Feminist Analysis*, 2(1) 51–7.
—— (1993) *Women as Wombs: Reproductive Technologies and the Battle over Women's Freedom* (San Francisco, Harper).
—— (1996) 'Connecting reproductive and sexual liberalism', in Diane Bell and Renate Klein, *Radically Speaking: Feminism Reclaimed* (Melbourne, Spinifex; London, Zed).
Re W (1991) (Minors) (Surrogacy) Family Division, Family Law, 180, 1FLR, 385.
Reading 360 (1994) (Aylesbury, Ginn).
Reamy, K. J. and S. E. White (1987) 'Sexuality in the puerperium: a review', *Archives of Sexual Behaviour*, 16(2) 165–87.
Reay, Diane (1991) 'Intersections of gender, race and class in the primary school', *British Journal of Sociology of Education*, 12(2) 163–82.
Reich, Michael, David M. Gordon and Richard C. Edwards (1980) 'A theory of labour market segmentation', in Alice Amsden (ed.), *The Economics of Women and Work* (Harmondsworth, Penguin).
Reinharz, Shulamit (1979) *On Becoming a Social Scientist* (San Francisco, Jossey-Bass).
—— (1992) *Feminist Methods in Social Research* (Oxford University Press).
Reis, Regina Gomes dos (1990) 'Norplant in Brazil: implantation strategy in guise of "scientific research"', *Issues in Reproductive and Genetic Engineering: Journal of International Feminist Analysis*, 3(2) 111–18.
Rendal, Margherita (1985) 'The winning of the Sex Discrimination Act', in Madeleine Arnot (ed.), *Race and Gender*, (Oxford, Pergamon).
Rendall, Jane (1985) *The Origins of Modern Feminism* (London, Macmillan).
—— (1990) 'Review article: women's history: beyond the cage?', *History*, 75, February, 63–72.
—— (ed.) (1987) *Equal or Different? Women's Politics, 1800–1914* (Oxford, Basil Blackwell).
—— (1994) 'Citizenship, culture and civilisation: the languages of British suffragists, 1866–1874', in Caroline Daley and Melanie Nolan (eds), *Suffrage and Beyond: International Feminist Perspectives* (Auckland, New Zealand, Auckland University Press).
Renzetti, Clare M. (1992) *Violent Betrayal: Partner Abuse in Lesbian Relationships* (Newbury Park, Sage).
Reskin, Barbara and Irene Padavic (1994) *Women and Men at Work* (London, Pine Forge Press).
—— and Barbara Roos (1990) *Job Queues, Gender Queues: Explaining Women's Inroads Into Male Occupations* (Philadelphia, Temple University Press).
Reynolds, Margaret (ed.) (1991) *Erotica: An Anthology of Women's Writing* (London, Pandora).
Rhys, Jean (1968) *Wide Sargasso Sea*, first published 1966 (Harmondsworth, Penguin).
Rich, Adrienne (1977) *Of Woman Born: Motherhood as Experience and Institution*, first published 1976 (London, Virago).
—— (1980a) 'Compulsory heterosexuality and lesbian existence', *Signs*, 5(4) 631–60. Also published 1981, London, Onlywomen Press.

—— (1980b) 'Jane Eyre: the temptations of a motherless woman', in Adrienne Rich, *On Lies, Secrets, and Silence: Selected Prose 1966–1978*, (London, Virago).

—— (1980c) *On Lies, Secrets and Silence: Selected Prose 1966–1978* (London, Virago).

—— (1980d) 'When we dead awaken: writing as re-vision' (1971), in Adrienne Rich, *On Lies, Secrets and Silence: Selected Prose 1966–1978* (London, Virago).

—— (1981) 'Disobedience is what NWSA is potentially about', *Women's Studies Quarterly*, 9(3) Fall, 4–5.

—— (1984) 'Compulsory heterosexuality and lesbian existence', in Ann Snitow, Christine Stansell and Sharon Thompson (eds), *Desire: The Politics of Sexuality* (London, Virago).

—— (1986) *Blood, Bread and Poetry* (New York, W.W. Norton).

Rich, Ruby B. (1994) 'Reflections on a queer screen', *GLQ: A Journal of Lesbian and Gay Studies*, 1(1) 83–92.

Richardson, Diane (1989) *Women and the AIDS Crisis*, 2nd edn (London, Pandora).

—— (1992) 'Constructing lesbian sexualities', in Kenneth Plummer (ed.), *Modern Homosexualities* (London, Routledge).

—— (1993) *Women, Motherhood and Childrearing* (London, Macmillan).

—— (1996a) 'Contradictions in discourse: gender, sexuality and HIV/AIDS', in Janet Holland and Lisa Adkins (eds), *Sex, Sensibility and the Gendered Body* (London, Macmillan).

—— (1996b) 'Deconstructing feminist critiques of radical feminism', in Magdalene Ang-Lygate, Chris Corrin and Millsom Henry (eds), *Desperately Seeking Sisterhood: Still Challenging and Building* (London, Taylor & Francis).

—— (1996c) 'Heterosexuality and social theory', in Diane Richardson (ed.), *Theorising Heterosexuality: Telling it Straight* (Buckingham, Open University Press).

—— (1996d) 'Misguided, dangerous and wrong: on the maligning of radical feminism', in Diane Bell and Renate Klein (eds), *Radically Speaking: Feminism Reclaimed* (Melbourne, Spinifex Press, London, Zed).

—— (ed.) (1996e) *Theorising Heterosexuality: Telling it Straight* (Buckingham, Open University Press).

—— and Victoria Robinson (eds) (1993) *Introducing Women's Studies: Feminist Theory and Practice* (London, Macmillan).

—— and Victoria Robinson (1994) 'Theorising Women's Studies, gender studies and masculinity: the politics of naming', *European Journal of Women's Studies*, 1(1) 11–27.

Richie, Beth E. (1996) *Compelled to Crime: The Gender Entrapment of Battered Black Women* (New York, Routledge).

Richter, Judith (1996) *Vaccination Against Pregnancy: Miracle or Menace?* (Melbourne, Spinifex; London, Zed).

Riegler, Johanna (1989) 'IVF doctor sues: updates from Austria', *Reproductive and Genetic Engineering: Journal of International Feminist Analysis*, 2(3) 251.

—— and Aurelia Weikert (1988) 'Product egg: egg selling in an Austrian IVF clinic', *Reproductive and Genetic Engineering: Journal of International Feminist Analysis*, 1(3) 221–3.

Rights of Women Bulletin (1994) 'Zero tolerance', *Rights of Women Bulletin*, Spring, 23–4.

Riley, D. (1983) *The War in the Nursery: Theories of the Child and Mother* (London, Virago).

Riley, Denise (1988) *Am I That Name? Feminism and the category of 'Women' in History* (London, Macmillan).

Riska, Elianne and Katarina Wegar (1993) *Gender, Work and Medicine: Women and the Medical Division of Labour* (London, Sage).

Ritvo, Harriet (1987) *The Animal Estate: the English and Other Creatures in the Victorian Age* (Harmondsworth, Penguin).

Roach, Sharyn L. (1989) 'New reproductive technologies and legal reform', *Reproductive and Genetic Engineering: Journal of International Feminist Analysis*, 2(1) 11–27.

Roberts, Elizabeth (1984) *A Woman's Place: An Oral History of Working-Class Women* (Oxford, Basil Blackwell).

Roberts, Michèle (1978) *A Piece of the Night* (London, The Women's Press).

—— (1994) *Flesh and Blood* (London, Virago).

Roberts, Mike (1994) 'Sauce for goose, sauce for the gender', *The Times Higher Education Supplement*, 4 February.

Robinson, Kathryn (1996) 'Mail-order brides and "Boys' Own" tales: representations of Asian-Australian marriages', *Feminist Review*, 52, Spring, 53–68.

Robinson, Lillian S. (1993) 'A good man is hard to find: reflections on men's studies', in Cheris Kramarae and Dale Spender (eds), *The Knowledge Explosion: Generations of Feminist Scholarship* (Hemel Hempstead, Harvester Wheatsheaf).

Robinson, Victoria (1993) 'Heterosexuality: beginnings and connections', in Sue Wilkinson and Celia Kitzinger (eds), *Heterosexuality: A Feminism and Psychology Reader* (London, Sage).

—— (1996) 'Heterosexuality and masculinity: theorising male power or the male wounded psyche?', in Diane Richardson (ed.), *Theorising Heterosexuality: Telling it Straight* (Buckingham, Open University Press).

—— and Diane Richardson (1994) 'Publishing feminism: re-defining the women's studies discourse', *Journal of Gender Studies*, 3(1) 87–94.

—— and Diane Richardson (1996) 'Repackaging women and feminism: taking the heat off patriarchy', in Diane Bell and Renate Klein (eds), *Radically Speaking: Feminism Reclaimed* (Melbourne, Spinifex Press, London, Zed).

Rodgerson, Gillian and Elizabeth Wilson (eds) (1991) *Pornography and Feminism by Feminists against Censorship* (London, Lawrence & Wishart).

Rogers, Marigold (1994) 'Growing up lesbian: the role of the school', in Debbie Epstein (ed.), *Challenging Lesbian and Gay Inequalities in Education* (Buckingham, Open University Press).

Roper, Michael (1992) *Masculinity and the British Organisational Man since 1945* (Oxford University Press).

Rose, Hilary (1981) 'Re-reading Titmuss: the sexual division of welfare', *Journal of Social Policy*, 10(4).

—— (1994) *Love Power and Knowledge: Towards a Feminist Transformation of the Sciences* (Cambridge, Polity Press).

—— and Jalna Hanmer (1976) 'Women's liberation, reproduction and the technological fix', in Diana Leonard Barker and Sheila Allen (eds), *Sexual Divisions and Society: Process and Change* (London, Tavistock).

Rose, Jacqueline (1986) *Sexuality in the Field of Vision* (London, Verso).

Rose, Sonya (1988) 'Gender antagonism and class conflict: exclusionary strategies of male trade unionists in nineteenth-century Britain', *Social History*, 13, May, 191–208.

—— (1992) *Limited Livelihoods: Gender and Class in Nineteenth-Century England* (Berkeley, California, California University Press).

—— (1993) 'Gender and labour history: the nineteenth-century legacy', *International Review of Social History*, 38, 145–62.

Roseneil, Sasha (1996) 'Transgressions and transformations: experience, consciousness and identity at Greenham', in Nickie Charles and Felicia Hughes-Freeland (eds), *Practising Feminism – Identity Difference Power* (London, Routledge).

Rosenfelt, D. (1984) 'What women's studies programs do that mainstreaming can't', *Women's Studies International Forum*, 7(3) 167–76.

Rosier, Pat (1989) 'The speculum bites back: feminists spark an inquiry into the treatment of carcinoma in situ at Auckland's National Women's Hospital', *Reproductive and Genetic Engineering: Journal of International Feminist Analysis*, 2 (2) 121–32.

Ross Muir, Anne (1988) 'The status of women working in film and television', in Lorraine Gammon and Margaret Marshment (eds), *The Female Gaze* (London, The Women's Press).

Rosser, Sue. and B. Kelly (1994) *Educating Women for Success in Science and Mathematics* (Columbia, University of South Carolina).

Rossiter, Margaret (1982) *Women Scientists in America* (Baltimore, Md, Johns Hopkins University Press).

Rothman, Barbara Katz (1989) *Recreating Motherhood: Ideology and Technology in a Patriarchal Society* (New York, W.W. Norton).

Rowbotham, Sheila (1973) *Women's Consciousness, Man's World* (Harmondsworth, Penguin).

—— (1982) 'The trouble with patriarchy', in Mary Evans (ed.), *The Women Question* (London, Fontana).

—— (1990a) *Hidden from History*, 1st edn 1973 (London, Pluto).

—— (1990b) *The Past is before Us: Feminism in Action since the 1960s* (Harmondsworth, Penguin).

Rowland, Robyn (1990) 'Response to draft report of the National Bioethics Consultative Committee, Surrogacy', *Issues in Reproductive and Genetic Engineering: Journal of International Feminist Analysis*, 3(2) 147–57.

—— (1992) *Living Laboratories: Women and Reproductive Technologies* (Bloomington, Indiana University Press).

—— and Renate Klein (1996) 'Radical feminism: history, politics, action', in Diane Bell and Renate Klein (eds), *Radically Speaking: Feminism Reclaimed* (Melbourne, Spinifex Press, London, Zed).

Royal Commission on New Reproductive Technologies (1993) *Proceed with Care: Final report of the Royal Commission on New Reproductive Technologies*, Volumes 1 and 2 (Ottawa, Canada Communications Group).

Rubery, Jill and Colette Fagan (1995) 'Gender segregation in societal context', *Work, Employment and Society*, 9(2) 213–40.

Rubin, Gayle (1984) 'Thinking sex; notes for a radical theory of the politics of sexuality', in Carole S. Vance (ed.), *Pleasure and Danger: Exploring Female Sexuality* (London, Routledge & Kegan Paul).

Ruddick, S. (1982) 'Maternal thinking', in B. Thorne and M. Yalom (eds), *Rethinking the Family: Some Feminist Questions* (London, Longman).

Rule, Jane (1975) *Lesbian Images*, also published 1982 (Trumansburg, New York, The Crossing Press).

Rumbold, Judy (1991) 'My vile bodies', *The Guardian*, 10 January.

Russ, Joanna (1975) *The Female Man* (reprinted 1985) (London, The Women's Press).

Russell, Denise (1995) *Women, Madness and Medicine* (Cambridge, Polity).

Russell, Diana (ed.) (1993) *Making Violence Sexy: Feminist Views on Pornography* (Buckingham, Open University Press).

Saadawi, Nawal el (1980) *The Hidden Face of Eve* (London, Zed).

Sack, F. (1992) *Romance to Die For* (Deerfield Beach, FL, Health Communications Inc.).

Sacks, Harvey (1963) 'Sociological description', *Berkeley Journal of Sociology*, 8, 1–16

Sadrozinski, Renate (1989) '"Kinder oder keine-entscheiden wir alleine": on the abolition of the law against abortion and the patriarchal needs to protect embryos', *Reproductive and Genetic Engineering: Journal of International Feminist Analysis*, 2(1) 1–9.

Said, Edward (1978) *Orientalism* (London, Routledge & Kegan Paul).

Sainsbury, Diane (1994) *Gendering Welfare States* (London, Sage).

Salisbury, Jonathan and David Jackson (1996) *Challenging Macho Values* (London, Falmer Press).

Salomone, Jo (1991) 'Report on the 6th International Women and Health Meeting, November 3–9 1990, Manila, Philippines', *Issues in Reproductive and Genetic Engineering: Journal of International Feminist Analysis*, 4(1) 77–85.

Samuel, Raphael (ed.) (1981) *People's History and Socialist Theory* (London, Routledge & Kegan Paul).

Sanders, Sue and Gill Spraggs (1989) 'Section 28 and Education', in Carol Jones and Pat Mahony (eds), *Learning our Lines: Sexuality and Social Control* (London, The Women's Press).

Sandoval, C. (1991) 'U.S. Third World feminism: the theory and method of oppositional consciousness in the postmodern world', *Genders*, 10, Spring, 1–23.

Sangari, K. K. and S. Vaid (1989) *Recasting Women: Essays on Colonial History* (New Delhi, Kali).

Sargent, Lydia (ed.) (1981) *The Unhappy Marriage of Marxism and Feminism: A Debate on Class and Patriarchy* (London, Pluto).

Sashidharan, Sashi P. and Errol Francis (1993) 'Epidemiology, ethnicity and schizophrenia', in Waqar Ahmad (ed.), *'Race' and Health in Contemporary Britain* (Buckingham, Open University Press).

Savage, Mike and Anne Witz, (eds) (1992) *Gender and Bureaucracy* (Oxford, Basil Blackwell).

Sayers, J. (1988) 'Feminist therapy: forgetting the father?', *Psychology of Women Section of the British Psychological Society Newsletter*, 2, 18–22.

Schiebinger, Londa (1989) *The Mind has No Sex? Women in the Origins of Modern Science* (Cambridge, Mass., Harvard University Press).

Schiebinger, Londa (1994) *Nature's Body, Sexual Politics and the Making of Modern Science* (London, Pandora).

Schilb, John (1985) 'Pedagogy of the oppressors?', in Margo Culley and Catherine Portuges (eds), *Gendered Subjects: The Dynamics of Feminist Teaching* (London, Routledge Kegan Paul).

Schleiermacher, Sabine (1990) 'Racial hygiene and "deliberate parenthood": two sides of demographer Hans Harmsen's population policy', *Issues in Reproductive and Genetic Engineering: Journal of International Feminist Analysis*, 3(3) 201–10.

School Curriculum and Assessment Authority (SCAA) (1996) *Inform*, February.

Schor, Naomi and Elizabeth Weed (eds) (1974) *The Essential Difference* (Bloomington, Indiana University Press).

Schulman, Sarah (1990) *After Delores*, first published 1988 (London, Sheba).

Scott, Joan (1988) *Gender and the Politics of History* (New York, Columbia University Press).

Scott, Marion (1980) 'Teach her a lesson: sexist curriculum in patriarchal education', in Dale Spender and Elizabeth Sarah (eds), *Learning to Lose* (London, The Women's Press).

Scott, Sara (1987) 'Sex and Danger: Feminism and AIDS', *Trouble and Strife*, 11.

Scutt, Jocelynne A. (1988) (ed.) *The Baby Machine: Commercialisation of Mother-hood* (Carlton, Australia, McCulloch; London, Greenprint, 1990).

Seccombe, Wally (1986) 'Patriarchy stabilized: the construction of the male bread-winner wage norm in nineteenth-century Britain', *Social History*, 11 (1) 53–76.

Seccombe, Wally (1992) *A Millennium of Family Change* (London, Verso).

Sedgwick, Eve Kosofsky (1985) *Between Men: English Literature and Male Homo-social Desire* (New York, Columbia University Press).

—— (1990) *Epistemology of the Closet* (Berkeley, University of California Press).

—— (1994) *Tendencies* (Durham, Duke University Press).

Segal, Lynne (1987) *Is the Future Female? Troubled Thoughts on Contemporary Feminism* (London, Virago).

—— (1989) 'Slow change or no change?: Feminism, socialism and the problem of men', *Feminist Review*, 31, Spring, 5–21.

—— (1990a) 'Pornography and violence: what the "experts" really say', *Feminist Review*, 36

—— (1990b) *Slow Motion: Changing Masculinities, Changing Men* (London, Vir-ago).

—— (1994) *Straight Sex: Rethinking the Politics of Pleasure* (London, Virago).

—— and Mary McIntosh (eds) (1992) *Sex Exposed: Sexuality and the Pornography Debate* (London, Virago).

Serbin, Lisa (1983) 'The hidden curriculum: academic consequences of teacher expectations', in Michael Marland (ed.), *Sex Differentiation and Schooling* (Lon-don, Heinemann).

Sex Education Forum (1992) *A Framework for School Sex Education* (London, National Children's Bureau).

Seymour, Julie (1992) 'Women's time as a household resource', *Women's Studies International Forum*, 15(2).

Shalev, Carmel (1989) *Birth Power: The Case for Surrogacy* (New Haven, Conn., and London, Yale University Press).

Shan, Sharan-Jeet (1985) *In My Own Name: An Autobiography* (London, The Women's Press).

Shape, Jenny (1993) *Allegories of Empire: The Figure of Woman in the Colonial Text* (Minneapolis, University of Minnesota Press).

Sharpe, Sue (1976) *Just Like a Girl* (Harmondsworth, Penguin).

—— (1994) *'Just Like a Girl'. How Girls Learn to be Women: From the Seventies to the Nineties* (Harmondsworth, Penguin).

Sheridan, Susan (1990) 'Feminist knowledge, women's liberation and Women's Studies', in Sneja Gunew (ed.), *Feminist Knowledge: Critique and Construct* (London, Routledge).

—— (1991) 'From margin to mainstream, situating Women's Studies', in Sneja Gunew (ed.), *A Reader in Feminist Knowledge* (London, Routledge).

—— (1996) 'Cancer and women: some feminist ethics concerns', in Carolyn Sargent and Caroline Brettell (eds), *Gender and Health. An International Perspective* (Englewood Cliffs, NJ, Prentice-Hall).

Sherwin, Susan (1996) 'Cancer and women: some feminist ethics concerns', in Carolyn Sargent and Caroline Brettell (eds) *Gender and Health: An International Perspective* (Englewood Cliffs, NJ, Prentice-Hall).

Shiva, Vandana (1988) *Staying Alive: Women, Ecology and Development* (London, Zed).

—— (1993) *Monocultures of the Mind* (Penang, Third World Network).

—— (1995) 'Democratizing biology: reinventing biology from a feminist, ecological and third world perspective', in L. Birke and R. Hubbard (eds), *Reinventing Biology* (Bloomington, Indiana University Press).

Showalter, Elaine (1978) *A Literature of Their Own: British Women Novelists from Brontë to Lessing*, first published 1977 (London, Virago).

—— (ed.) (1979) 'Towards a feminist poetics', in Mary Jacobus (ed.), *Women Writing and Writing about Women* (London, Croom Helm).

—— (1986) *The New Feminist Criticism: Essays on Women, Literature and Theory* (London, Virago).

—— (1987) 'Critical cross-dressing: male feminists and the Woman of the Year', in Alice Jardine and Paul Smith (eds), *Men in Feminism* (London, Methuen).

Siltanen, Janet (1994) *Locating Gender: Occupational Segregation, Wages and Domestic Responsibilities* (London, UCL Press).

Simmonds, Felly Nkweto (1992) 'Difference, power and knowledge: black women in academia', in Hilary Hinds, Ann Phoenix and Jackie Stacey (eds), *Working Out: New Directions For Women's Studies* (London, Falmer Press).

Simon, William (1996) *Postmodern Sexualities* (London, Routledge).

Simson, Rennie (1984) 'The Afro-American female: the historical context of the construction of sexual identity', in Ann Snitow, Christine Stansell and Sharon Thompson (eds), *Desire: The Politics of Sexuality* (London, Virago).

Singer, Peter and Deane Wells (1984) *The Reproduction Revolution: New Ways of Making Babies* (Oxford University Press).

Siraj-Blatchford, Iram (ed.) (1993) '*Race*', *Gender and the Education of Teachers* (Buckingham, Open University Press).

—— (1995) 'Racialized and gendered discourses in teacher education', in Liz Dawtrey, Janet Holland and Merril Hammer with Sue Sheldon (eds), *Equality and Inequality in Education Policy* (Clevedon, Multilingual Matters).

Skeggs, Beverley (1995) 'Introduction', in *Feminist Cultural Theory: Process and Production* (Manchester University Press).

Skelton, Christine (1987) 'A study of gender discrimination in a primary programme of teacher training', *Journal of Education for Teaching*, 13(2) 163–75.

—— (ed.) (1989) *Whatever Happens to Little Women?: Gender and Primary Schooling* (Milton Keynes, Open University Press).

—— (1988) 'Demolishing "The House That Jack Built": anti-sexist initiatives in the primary school', in Bruce Carrington and Barry Troyna (eds), *Children and Controversial Issues* (Lewes, Falmer).

—— (1995) 'New names, new faces – same old stereotypes?', *Language and Learning*, Sept./Oct., 2–4.

—— (1997) 'Revisiting gender issues in reading schemes, *Education*, 3–13

Skocpol, Theda (1979) *States and Social Revolution* (Cambridge, Mass., Harvard University Press).

Smart, Carol (1984) *The Ties That Bind: Law, Marriage and the Reproduction of Patriarchal Relations* (London, Routledge & Kegan Paul).

—— (1989a) *Feminism and the Power of the Law* (London, Routledge).

—— (1989b) 'Power and the politics of child custody', in C. Smart and S. Sevenhuijsen, *Child Custody and the Politics of Gender* (London, Routledge).

—— (1992) 'Disruptive bodies and unruly sex: the regulation of reproduction and sexuality in the nineteenth century', in Carol Smart (ed.), *Regulating Womanhood: Historical Essays on Marriage, Motherhood and Sexuality* (London, Routledge).

—— (1995) *Law, Crime and Sexuality: Essays in Feminism* (London, Sage).

—— (1996a) 'Collusion, collaboration and confession: on moving beyond the heterosexuality debate', in Diane Richardson (ed.), *Theorising Heterosexuality: Telling it Straight* (Buckingham, Open University Press).

—— (1996b) 'Desperately seeking post-heterosexual woman', in Janet Holland and Lisa Adkins (eds), *Sex, Sensibility and the Gendered Body* (London, Macmillan).

Smith, Barbara (1982) 'Racism and Women's Studies', in G. Hull *et al.* (eds), *But Some of Us Are Brave* (Old Westbury, New York, The Feminist Press).

—— (1986) 'Toward a Black feminist criticism' (first published 1977) in Elaine Showalter (ed.), *The New Feminist Criticism: Essays on Women, Literature and Theory* (London, Virago).

Smith, Dorothy (1974a) 'Theorising as ideology', in Roy Turner (ed.), *Ethnomethodology* (Penguin, Harmondsworth).

—— (1974b) 'Women's perspective as a radical critique of sociology' *Sociological Quarterly*, 44, 7–13.

—— (1978) 'A peculiar eclipsing: women's exclusion from men's culture', *Women's Studies International Quarterly*, 1, 281–96

—— (1987) *The Everyday World as Problematic* (Milton Keynes, Open University Press).

—— (1993) *Texts, Facts, and Femininity: Exploring the Relations of Ruling*, first published 1990 (London and New York, Routledge).

Smith, Lorna (1989) *Domestic Violence: An Overview of the Literature* (London, HMSO).

Smith, Paul (1978) 'Domestic labour and Marx's theory of value', in A. Kuhn and A. M. Wolpe (eds), *Feminism and Materialism: Women and Modes of Production* (London, Routledge & Kegan Paul).

Smith, Valerie (1990) 'Black feminist theory and the representation of the "other" ', in Cheryl A. Wall (ed.), *Changing Our Own Words* (London, Routledge).

Smithers, Alan and Pamela Robinson (1995) *Co-educational and Single Sex Schooling* (Manchester University Press).

Smyth, Ailbhe (1995) 'Haystacks in my mind or how to stay SAFE (Sane, Angry and Feminist) in the 1990s', in Gabriele Griffin (ed.), *Feminist Activism in the 1990s* (London, Taylor & Francis).

Smyth, Cherry (1990) 'The pleasure threshold: looking at lesbian pornography on film', *Feminist Review*, 34, 152–9.

Snitow, Anne (1983) 'Mass Market Romance: Pornography for Women is Different', in A. Snitow, C. Stansell and S. Thompson (eds), *Powers of Desire: The Politics of Sexuality* (New York, Monthly Review Press).

——, Christine Stansell and Sharon Thompson (eds) (1984) *Desire: The Politics of Sexuality* (London, Virago).

Snock, Diedrick (1985) 'A male feminist in a women's college classroom', in Margo Culley and Catherine Portuges (eds), *Gendered Subjects: The Dynamics of Feminist Teaching* (London, Routledge & Kegan Paul).

Solomon, Alison (1988) 'Integrating infertility crisis counselling into feminist practice', *Reproductive and Genetic Engineering: Journal of International Feminist Analysis*, 1(1) 41–9.

Sontag, Susan (1983) *Illness as Metaphor* (Harmondsworth, Penguin).

Southall Black Sisters (1993) 'Domestic violence and immigration law: an urgent need for reform', in *Justice for Women Information Pack* (London, The London Justice for Women Collective).

Spallone, Patricia (1988) *Beyond Conception: The New Politics of Reproduction* (London, Macmillan).

—— and Deborah Lynne Steinberg (eds) (1987) *Made to Order: The Myth of Reproductive and Genetic Progress* (Oxford, Pergamon).

Spanier, Bonnie. (1995) *Im/partial Science: Gender Ideology in Molecular Biology* (Bloomington, Indiana University Press).

Spelman, Elizabeth (1988) *Inessential Woman. Problems of Exclusion in Feminist Thought* (Boston, Mass., Beacon Press).

Spencer, Jane (1986) *The Rise of the Woman Novelist: From Aphra Behn to Jane Austen* (Oxford and New York, Basil Blackwell).

Spender, Dale (1978) 'Educational research and the feminist perspective', unpublished paper presented at the British Educational Research Association Conference on 'Women, Education and Research', University of Leicester.

—— (1980) *Man Made Language* (London, Routledge & Kegan Paul).

—— (ed.) (1981) *Men's Studies Modified: The Impact of Feminism on the Academic Disciplines* (Oxford, Pergamon).

—— (1982) *Invisible Women: The Schooling Scandal* (London, Writers and Readers Publishing Co-operative).

—— (ed.) (1983a) *Feminist Theorists: Three Centuries of Women's Intellectual Traditions* (London, The Women's Press).

—— (1983b) *Women of Ideas (and What Men have Done to Them)* (London, Ark).

—— (1986) *Mothers of the Novel: 100 Good Women Novelists Before Jane Austen* (London, Pandora).

—— (ed.) (1987) *The Education Papers: Women's Quest for Equality in Britain 1850–1912* (London, Routledge & Kegan Paul).

—— (1993) 'The entry of women to the education of men', in Cheris Kramarae and Dale Spender (eds), *The Knowledge Explosion: Generations of Feminist Scholarship* (Hemel Hempstead, Harvester Wheatsheaf).

—— (1994) 'Women and madness: a justifiable response', *Feminism and Psychology*, 4(2) 280–3.

Spivak, G. C. (1987) *In Other Worlds: Essays in Cultural Politics* (London, Methuen).

—— (1988) 'Can the Subaltern Speak', in K. Grossberf and C. Nelson (eds), *Marxism and the Interpretation of Culture* (Chicago: University of Illinois Press).

—— (1989) 'Three women's texts and a critique of imperialism', in Catherine Belsey and Jane Moore, *The Feminist Reader: Essays in Gender and the Politics of Literary Criticism* (London, Macmillan).

—— (1994) 'In a word. Interview', in Naomi Shor and Elizabeth Weed (eds), *The Essential Difference* (Bloomington, Indiana University Press).

Squire, Corinne (1990) 'Feminism as antipsychology: learning and teaching in feminist psychology', in Erica Burman (ed.), *Feminists and Psychological Practice* (London, Sage).

Squirrell, Gillian (1989) 'Teachers and issues of sexual orientation', *Gender and Education*, 1(1) 17–34.

Stables, Andrew and Sian Stables (1995) 'Gender differences in students' approaches to A-level subject choices and perceptions of A-level subjects', *Educational Research*, 37(1) 39–51.

Stacey, Jackie (1991) 'Promoting normality: Section 28 and the regulation of sexuality', in Sarah Franklin, Celia Lury and Jackie Stacey (eds), *Off Centre: Feminism and Cultural Studies* (London, Unwin Hyman).

—— (1993) 'Untangling feminist theory', in Diane Richardson and Victoria Robinson (eds), *Introducing Women's Studies: Feminist Theory and Practice*, 1st edn (London, Macmillan).

—— (1994) *Stargazing: Hollywood Cinema and Female Spectatorship* (London, Routledge).

—— (1997 forthcoming) *Teratologies: A Cultural Study of Cancer* (London, Routledge).

Stacey, Margaret (1988) *The Sociology of Health and Healing* (London, Routledge).

Staddon, Patsy (1995) 'Lesbian studies: an opportunity not to be missed', in Mary Maynard and June Purvis (eds), *(Hetero)sexual Politics* (London, Taylor & Francis).

Stafford, Barbara Maria (1993) *Body Criticism: Imaging the Unseen in Enlightenment Art and Science* (Boston, Mass., Zone Books, MIT Press).

Stanko, Betsy (1988) 'Keeping women in and out of line: sexual harassment and occupational segregation', in S. Walby (ed.), *Gender Segregation at Work* (Milton Keynes, Open University Press).

—— (1991) 'Angst and academia' *Trouble and Strife*, 22, 19–21.

Stanko, Elizabeth A. (1985) *Intimate Intrusions* (London, Routledge & Kegan Paul).

Stanley, Autumn (1982) 'Women hold up two thirds of the sky: notes for a revised history of technology', in J. Rothschild (ed.), *Machina Ex Dea* (New York, Pergamon Press).

Stanley, Jo (1995) 'Pain(t) for healing: the academic conference and the classed/embodied self', in Louise Morley and Val Walsh (eds), *Feminist Academics: Creative Agents For Change* (London, Taylor & Francis).

Stanley, Liz (1985) 'Feminism and friendship: two essays on Olive Schreiner', *Studies in Sexual Politics*, 8 (Manchester University).

—— (1987) 'Biography as microscope or kaleidoscope? The case of "Power", in Hannah Cullwick's relationship with Arthur Munby', *Women's Studies International Forum*, 10 (1) 19–31.

—— (1990a) 'Feminist praxis and the academic mode of production', in Liz Stanley (ed.), *Feminist Praxis* (London, Routledge).

—— (ed.) (1990b) *Feminist Praxis: Research Theory and Epistemology in Feminist Sociology* (London, Routledge).

—— (1990c) 'Recovering women in history from feminist deconstructionism', *Women's Studies International Forum*, 13(1/2) 151–8.

—— (1992a) 'Romantic friendship: some issues in researching lesbian history and biography', *Women's History Review*, 1(2) 193–216.

—— (1992b) *The Auto/Biographical I. The Theory and Practice of Feminist Auto/Biography* (Manchester University Press).

—— (1993) 'The impact of feminism on sociology in the last 20 years', in Cheris Kramarae and Dale Spender (eds), *The Knowledge Explosion: Generations of Feminist Scholarship* (Hemel Hempstead, Harvester Wheatsheaf).

—— (1995a) 'My mother's voice? On being "a native in academia"', in Louise Morley and Val Walsh (eds), *Feminist Academics: Creative Agents For Change* (London, Taylor & Francis).

—— (1995b) 'Women have servants and men never eat: issues in reading "gender", in Mass-Observation's 1937 day-diaries', *Women's History Review*, 3, 85–101.

—— (ed.) (1996) *Knowing Feminisms* (London, Sage).

Stanley, Liz and Wise, Sue (1979) 'Feminist research, feminist consciousness and experiences of sexism', *Women's Studies International Quarterly*, 2, 259–74.

—— and Sue Wise (1983) *Breaking Out: Feminist Consciousness and Feminist Research* (London, Routledge).

—— and Sue Wise (1990) 'Method, methodology and epistemology in feminist research processes', in Liz Stanley (ed.), *Feminist Praxis: Research, Theory and Epistemology in Feminist Sociology* (London, Routledge).

—— and Sue Wise (1993) *Breaking Out Again: Feminist Ontology and Epistemology* (London, Routledge).

Stanworth, Michelle (1981) *Gender and Schooling* (London, Hutchinson).

—— (ed.) (1987) *Reproductive Technologies: Gender, Motherhood and Medicine* (Cambridge, Polity Press).

Stears, D. and S. Clift (1990) *A Study of AIDS Education in Secondary Schools* (Horsham, Avert).

Steedman, Carolyn (1986) *Landscape for a Good Woman: The Story of Two Lives* (London, Virago).

—— (1990) *Childhood, Culture and Class in Britain: Margaret McMillan, 1860–1939* (London, Virago).

—— (1992) *Past Tenses: Essays on Writing Autobiography and History* (London, Rivers Oram).

Stein, Edward (1992) *Forms of Desire: Sexual Orientation and the Social Constructionist Controversy* (London and New York, Routledge).

Stern, Phyllis Noerager (1993) *Lesbian Health. What are the Issues?* (Washington and London, Taylor & Francis).

Stimpson, C. (1988) *Where the Meanings Are: Feminism and Cultural Spaces* (New York, Routledge).

Stolcke, Verena (1988) 'New reproductive technologies: the old quest for fatherhood', *Reproductive and Genetic Engineering: Journal of International Feminist Analysis*, 1(1) 5–19.

Stone, Maureen (1985) *The Education of the Black Child: The Myth of Multicultural Education* (London, Fontana).

Strathern, Marilyn (1992) *After Nature: English Kinship in the Late Twentieth Century* (Cambridge University Press).

Straus, Murray (1980) 'A sociological perspective on the causes of family violence', in Michael Green (ed.), *Violence in the Family* (Boulder, Colorado, Westview Press).

Strom, Linda (1995) 'Reclaiming our working-class identities: teaching working-class studies in a blue-collar community, course syllabi: working-class women writers, working-class experiences in American fiction', *Women's Studies Quarterly*, XX111 (1)&(2) 131–41.

Stuart, Andrea (1988) 'The Color Purple: In Defence of Happy Endings', in L. Gamman and M. Marshment (eds), *The Female Gaze* (London, The Women's Press).

Summerfield, Penny (1995) 'Women and war in the twentieth century', in June Purvis (ed.), *Women's History: Britain, 1850–1945* (London, UCL).

Sydie, Rosalind A. (1987) *Natural Women Cultured Men: A Feminist Perspective on Sociological Theory* (Milton Keynes, Open University Press).

Taking Liberties Collective (1989) *Learning The Hard Way: Women's Oppression in Men's Education* (London, Macmillan).

Tan, Amy (1989) *The Joy Luck Club* (reprinted 1990) (London, Minerva).

Tandon, K. (1987) 'Lumps and bumps in racism and sexism', in S. O'Sullivan (ed.), *Women's Health: A Spare Rib Reader* (London, Pandora).

Tasker, Yvonne (1993) *Spectacular Bodies: Gender, Genre and the Action Cinema* (London, Routledge).

Taylor, Helen (1989) *Scarlett's Women: Gone with the Wind and its Female Fans* (London, Virago).

Taylor, Jill McLean, Carol Gilligan and Amy Sullivan (1995) *Between Voice and Silence: Women and Girls, Race and Relationship* (Cambridge, Mass., Harvard University Press).

Taylor, Joelle and Tracey Chandler (1995) *Lesbians Talk: Violent Relationships* (London, Scarlet Press).

Terry, Jennifer and Jacqueline Urla (eds) (1995) *Deviant Bodies* (Bloomington, Indiana University Press).

Third World Network (1995) *The Need for Greater Regulation and control of Genetic Engineering* (Penang, Third World Network).

Thom, Deborah (1992), 'A lop-sided view: feminist history or the history of women', in Kate Campbell (ed.), *Critical Feminism: Argument in the Disciplines* (Milton Keynes, Open University Press).

Thomas, David (1993) *Not Guilty: In Defence of the Modern Man* (London, Weidenfeld & Nicolson).

Thompkins, Jane (1989) 'Me and my shadow', in Linda Kauffman (ed.), *Gender and Theory: Dialogues on Feminist Criticism* (New York, Basil Blackwell).

Thompson, Becky (1994) *A Hunger So Wide and So Deep* (Minneapolis, University of Minnesota Press).

—— and Sangeeta Tyagi (eds) (1996) *Names We Call Home: Autobiography on Racial Identity* (New York, Routledge).

Thompson, Denise (1991) *Reading between the Lines: A Lesbian Feminist Critique of Feminist Accounts of Sexuality* (Sydney, Lesbian Studies and Research Group, The Gorgon's Head Press).

—— (1996) 'The self-contradiction of "post-modernist" feminism', in Diane Bell and Renate Klein (eds), *Radically Speaking: Feminism Reclaimed* (Melbourne, Spinifex Press; London, Zed).

Thompson, Edward (1968) *The Making of the English Working Class* (Harmondsworth, Penguin).

Thomson, Rachel (1995) 'Unholy alliances: the recent politics of sex education', in Liz Dawtrey, Janet Holland and Merril Hammer with Sue Sheldon (eds), *Equality and Inequality in Education Policy* (Clevedon, Multilingual Matters).

Thorne, Barrie (1993) *Gender Play: Girls and Boys in School* (Buckingham, Open University Press).

Thorogood, Nicki (1987) 'Race, class and gender: the politics of housework', in J. Brannen and G. Wilson (eds), *Give and Take in Families: Studies in Resource Distribution* (London, Allen & Unwin).

Tizard, B. (1991) 'Employed mothers and the care of young children', in A. Phoenix, A. Woollett and E. Lloyd (eds), *Motherhood: Meanings, Practices and Ideologies* (London, Sage).

Tremain, Rose (1990) *Restoration*, first published 1989 (London, Sceptre).

Trenchard, Lorraine and Hugh Warren (1984) *Something to Tell You* (London, London Gay Teenage Group).

Trivedy, Parita (1984) 'To deny our fullness: Asian women in the making of history', in *Feminist Review*, 17, 37–52.

Troyna, Barry (ed.) (1987) *Racial Inequality in Education* (London, Tavistock).

—— (1993) *Racism and Education* (Buckingham, Open University Press).

Trujillo, Carla (1991) *Chicana Lesbians: The Girls Our Mothers Warned Us About* (Berkeley Third World Womens Press).

Turkle, Sherry (1995) *Life on the Screen: Identity in the Age of the Internet* (New York, Simon & Schuster).

Turnbull, Annmarie, Jan Pollock and Sue Bruley (1983) 'History', in Janie Whyld (ed.), *Sexism in the Secondary Curriculum* (London, Harper & Row).

Twigg, Julia and Karl Atkin (1994) *Carers Perceived: Policy and Practice in Informal Care* (Buckingham, Open University Press).

UBINIG (1990) 'Research report: Norplant: the five year needle: an investigation of the Norplant trial in Bangladesh from the user's perspective', *Issues in Reproductive and Genetic Engineering: Journal of International Feminist Analysis*, 3(3) 211–28.

—— (1991a) *Declaration of Comilla: Proceeding of FINRRAGE-UBINIG International Conference, 1989* (Bangladesh, UBINIG).

—— (1991b) '"The Price of Norplant is TK.2000! You cannot remove it." Clients are refused removal of Norplant trial in Bangladesh', *Issues in Reproductive and Genetic Engineering: Journal of International Feminist Analysis*, 4(1) 45–6.

—— (1996) 'Declaration of people's perspectives on "population" symposium', in Diane Bell and Renate Klein (1996) *Radically Speaking: Feminism Reclaimed* (Melbourne, Spinifex; London, Zed).

Ungerson, Claire (1987) *Policy is Personal: Sex, Gender and Informal* Care (London, Tavistock).

—— (1988) *The Times Higher Education Supplement*, 3 June, 22 and 24.

—— (1990) *Gender and Caring* (Hemel Hempstead, Harvester Wheatsheaf).

United Nations (1995) *The World's Women 1995: Trends and Statistics* (New York, United Nations).

Ussher, Jane (1991) *Women's Madness. Misogyny or Mental Illness?* (Amherst, Mass., University of Massachusetts Press).

—— (1994) 'Women and madness: a voice in the dark of women's despair', *Feminism and Psychology*, 4(2) 288–92.

van den Wijngaard, Marianne (1991) 'Reinventing the sexes', doctoral thesis, University of Amsterdam.

Vance, Carole S. (ed.) (1984) *Pleasure and Danger: Exploring Female Sexuality* (London, Routledge & Kegan Paul).

—— (1989) 'Social construction theory: problems in the history of sexuality', in Dennis Altman *et al.*, *Which Homosexuality?* (London, Gay Men's Press).

—— (ed.) (1992) *Pleasure and Danger: Exploring Female Sexuality* (London, Pandora).

VanEvery, Jo (1995) *Heterosexual Women Changing the Family: Refusing to be a 'Wife'!* (London, Taylor & Francis).

—— (1996) 'Heterosexuality and domestic life', in Diane Richardson (ed.), *Theorising Heterosexuality: Telling it Straight* (Buckingham, Open University Press).

Varela, Maria Jose and Verena Stolcke (1989) 'The new Spanish law: a model for Europe?', *Reproductive and Genetic Engineering: Journal of International Feminist Analysis*, 2(3) 231–5.

Vellacott, Jo (1993) *From Liberal to Labour with Women's Suffrage. The Story of Catherine Marshall* (Montreal, McGill-Queen's University Press).

Versluysen, Margaret Connor (1981) 'Midwives, medical men and poor women labouring of child: lying-in hospitals in eighteenth century London', in Helen Roberts (ed.), *Women, Health and Reproduction* (London, Routledge & Kegan Paul).

Vicinus, Martha (ed.) (1981) *Suffer and Be Still: Women in the Victorian Age* (London, Methuen).

—— (1985) *Independent Women: Work and Community for Single Women, 1850–1920* (London, Virago).

Viinikka, Simmy (1989) 'Child sexual abuse and the law', in Emily Driver and Audrey Droisen (eds), *Child Sexual* Abuse (London, Macmillan).

Vincent, John (1995) *Inequality and Old Age* (London, UCL).

Violence Against Children Study Group (1990) *Taking Child Abuse Seriously* (London, Unwin Allen).

Visram, Rosina (1986) *Ayahs, Lascars and Princes* (London, Pluto Press).

Voluntary Licensing Authority (VLA) (1989) *IVF Research in the UK: A Report on Research Licensed by the Interim Licensing Authority (ILA) for Human In Vitro Fertilisation and Embryology 1985–1989* (London, ILA). See Annual Reports from 1986.

Wajcman, Judy (1991) *Feminism Confronts Technology* (Cambridge, Polity).

Walby, Sylvia (1986) *Patriarchy at Work* (Cambridge, Polity).

—— (1990) *Theorising Patriarchy* (Oxford, Basil Blackwell).

—— (1992) 'Post-post-modernism? Theorizing social complexity', in M. Barrett and

A. Phillips (eds), *Destabilizing Theory: Contemporary Feminist Debates* (Cambridge, Polity).
—— (1994) 'Is citizenship gendered?', *Sociology*, (2) 379–95.
—— (1997) *Gender Transformations* (London, Routledge).
Waldby, Cathy, Clancy Atosha, Jan Emetchi, Caroline Summerfield for Dympna House (1989) 'Theoretical perspectives on father–daughter incest', in Emily Driver and Audrey Droisen (eds), *Child Sexual Abuse* (London, Macmillan).
Waldschmidt, Anne (1991) 'The embryo as a legal entity – woman as a fetal environment. The new German laws on reproductive engineering and embryo research', *Issues in Reproductive and Genetic Engineering: Journal of International Feminist Analysis*, 4(3) 209–22.
Walford, Geoffrey (1980) 'Sex bias in physics textbooks', *School Science Review*, 1(62) 224–5.
Walker, Alice (1982) *The Color Purple*, reprinted 1983 (London, The Women's Press).
—— (1984) 'In search of our mothers' gardens', in Alice Walker, *In Search of Our Mothers' Gardens: Womanist Prose* (London, The Women's Press).
Walker, Linda (1987) 'Party political women: a comparative study of Liberal women and the Primrose League, 1890–1914', in Jane Rendall (ed.), *Equal or Different? Women's Politics, 1800–1914* (Oxford, Blackwell).
Walkerdine, Valerie (1986) 'Video replay: families, films and fantasy', in Victor Burgin, James Donald and Cora Kaplan (eds), *Formations of Fantasy* (London, Methuen).
—— (1989) *Schoolgirl Fictions* (London, Verso).
Walklate, Sandra (1995) *Gender and Crime* (Hemel Hempstead, Prentice-Hall/Harvester Wheatsheaf).
Walkling, Philip and Chris Brannigan (1986) 'Anti-sexist/anti-racist education: a possible dilemma', *Journal of Moral Education*, 15(1) 16–25.
Walkowitz, Judith (1980) *Prostitution and Victorian Society: Women, Class and the State* (Cambridge University Press).
—— (1992) *City of Dreadful Delight: Narratives of Sexual Danger in Late-Victorian London* (London, Virago).
Wall, Cheryl A. (ed.) (1990) *Changing Our Own Words: Essays on Criticism, Theory and Writing by Black Women* (London, Routledge).
Walsh, Val (1995) 'Transgression and the academy: feminists and institutionalization', in Louise Morley and Val Walsh (eds), *Feminist Academics: Creative Agents For Change* (London, Taylor & Francis).
Walter, Natasha (1994) 'An agenda of gender', *The Guardian*, 23 October.
Ward, Elizabeth (1984) *Father–Daughter Rape* (London, The Women's Press).
Ware, Vron (1992) *Beyond the Pale: White Women, Racism and History* (London, Verso).
Warner, M. (ed.) (1993) *Fear of a Queer Planet: Queer Politics and Social Theory* (Minneapolis, University of Minnesota Press).
—— (1994) *Managing Monsters: Six Myths of Our Time* (London, Vintage).
—— (1995) *From the Beast to the Blonde: On Fairy Tales and Their Tellers* (first published 1994) (London, Vintage).
(Warnock Report) Department of Health and Social Security (1984) *Report of the Committee of Inquiry into Human Fertilisation and Embryology*, Cmnd 9314 (London, HMSO).
Warwick, Alex and Rosemary Auchmuty (1995) 'Women's Studies as feminist activism', in Gabriele Griffin (ed.), *Feminist Activism in the 1990s* (London, Taylor & Francis).

Waterhouse, L., J. Carnie, and R. Dobash (1993) 'The abuser under the microscope', *Community Care*, 24 June, 24.

Watney, Simon (1987) *Policing Desire: Pornography, AIDS and the Media* (Minneapolis, University of Minnesota Press).

Watt, Shantu and Juliet Cook (1991) 'Racism: whose liberation? Implications for Women's Studies', in Jane Aaron and Sylvia Walby (eds), *Out of the Margins: Women's Studies in the Nineties* (London, Falmer Press).

Weed, Elizabeth (ed.) (1989) *Coming to Terms: Feminism, Theory, Politics* (London, Routledge).

Weedon, Chris (1987) *Feminist Practice and Post-structuralist Theory* (Oxford, Basil Blackwell).

Weeks, Jeffrey (1990) *Sex, Politics and Society*, 2nd edn (London, Longman).

Weightman, Jane (1989) 'Women in management', *Educational Management and Administration*, 17(3) 119–22.

Weiler, Kathleen and Candace Mitchell (eds) (1992) *What Schools Can Do: Critical Pedagogy and Practice* (Albany, State University of New York Press).

Weiner, Gaby (ed.) (1985) *Just a Bunch of Girls* (Milton Keynes, Open University Press).

—— (1986) 'Feminist education and equal opportunities: unity or discord?', *British Journal of Sociology of Education*, 7(3) 265–74.

—— (1994) *Feminisms in Education* (Buckingham, Open University Press).

—— and Madeleine Arnot (eds) (1987) *Gender Under Scrutiny* (London, Hutchinson).

Weldon, Fay (1977) *Female Friends*, first published 1975 (London, Picador).

West, Candice and Don Zimmerman (1987) 'Doing Gender', *Gender and Society*, 1, 125–51.

West, Jackie (1978) 'Women, sex and class', in A. Kuhn and A. M. Wolpe (eds), *Feminism and Materialism* (London, Routledge & Kegan Paul).

Weston, Kath (1991) *Families We Choose: Lesbians, Gays, Kinship* (New York, Columbia University Press).

Westwood, Sallie (1984) *All Day, Every Day: Factory and Family in the Making of Women's Lives* (London, Pluto Press).

—— and Parminder Bhachu (eds) (1988) *Enterprising Women: Ethnicity, Economy and Gender Relations* (London, Routledge).

White, Evelyn (1990) *The Black Women's Health Book. Speaking for Ourselves* (Seattle, The Seal Press).

Whitty, Geoff (1991) 'Making sense of urban education after Thatcher', seminar paper, University of Liverpool, Department of Education, 1 May.

Whyld, Janie (ed.) (1983) *Sexism in the Secondary Curriculum* (London, Harper & Row).

Whyte, Judith (1986a) *Beyond the Wendy House: Sex Role Stereotyping in Primary Schools* (York, Longman for Schools Council).

—— (1986b) *Girls into Science and Technology* (London, Routledge).

Wichterich, Christa (1988) 'From the struggle against "overpopulation" to the industrialization of human production', *Reproductive and Genetic Engineering: Journal of International Feminist Analysis*, 1(1) 21–30.

Wieringa, Saskia (1995) *Subversive Women: Women's Movements in Africa, Asia, Latin America and the Caribbean* (London, Zed Press).

Wilkinson, Sue (ed.) 1986 *Feminist Social Psychology: Developing Theory and Practice* (Milton Keynes, Open University Press).

—— (1991) 'Why psychology (badly) needs feminism', in Jane Aaron and Sylvia Walby (eds), *Out of the Margins: Women's Studies in the Nineties* (London, Falmer).

—— and Celia Kitzinger (1993) *Heterosexuality: A Feminism and Psychology Reader* (London, Sage).

—— and Celia Kitzinger, (1994) *Women and Health: Feminist Perspectives* (London, Taylor & Francis).

Williams, Anne (1987) 'Making sense of feminist contributions to women's health', in J. Orr (ed.), *Women's Health in the Community* (Chichester, John Wiley).

—— (1993) 'Diversity and agreement in feminist ethnography', *Sociology*, 27, 575–89.

Williams, Fiona (1989) *Social Policy: A Critical Introduction. Issues of Race, Gender and Class* (Cambridge, Polity).

—— (1992a) 'Women with learning difficulties are women, too', in Mary Langan and Lesley Day (eds), *Women, Oppression and Social Work* (London, Routledge).

—— (1992b) 'Somewhere over the rainbow: universality and diversity in social policy', in N. Manning and R. Page (eds), *Social Policy Review 4* (Canterbury, Social Policy Association).

—— (1995) 'Race/ethnicity, gender and class in welfare states: a framework for comparative analysis', *Social Politics: International Studies in Gender, State and Society*, (2) 127–59.

—— (1996) 'Postmodernism, feminism and the question of difference', in Nigel Parton (ed.), *Social Work, Social Theory and Social Change* (London, Routledge).

Williams, Jenny (1987) 'The construction of women and black students as educational problems: re-evaluating policy on gender and "race"', in Madeleine Arnot and Gaby Weiner (eds), *Gender and the Politics of Schooling* (London, Hutchinson).

Williams, Linda (1988) 'It's gonna work for me', *Birth*, 15 March, 153–6.

—— (1990) 'Wanting children badly: A study of Canadian women seeking in vitro fertilization and their husbands', *Issues in Reproductive and Genetic Engineering: Journal of International Feminist Analysis*, 3(3) 229–34.

—— (1991) 'Motherhood, ideology, and the power of technology: in vitro fertilization use by adoptive mothers', *Women's Studies International Forum*, 13(6) 543–52.

Williamson, Judith (1986) *Consuming Passings: The Dynamics of Popular Culture* (London, Marion Boyars).

Willis, Susan (1990) *Specifying: Black Women Writing the American Experience*, first published 1987 (London, Routledge).

Wilson, Amrit (1978) *Finding A Voice: Asian Women in Britain* (London, Virago).

Wilson, Barbara (1986) Sisters of the Road (London, The Women's Press).

Wilson, Elizabeth (1977) *Women and the Welfare State* (London, Tavistock).

—— (1982) *Mirror Writing* (London, Virago).

—— (1983) *What is to be Done about Violence Against Women?* (Harmondsworth, Penguin).

—— (1985) *Adorned in Dreams: Fashion and Modernity* (London, Virago).

—— (1988) 'Tell it like it is: women and confessional writing', in S. Radstone (ed.) *Sweet Dreams: Sexuality, Gender and Popular Fiction* (London, Lawrence & Wishart).

—— (1993a) 'Is Transgression Transgressive?', in Joseph Bristow and Angelia R. Wilson (eds), *Activating Theory: Lesbian, Gay, Bisexual Politics* (London, Lawrence & Wishart).

—— (1993b) *The Lost Time Café* (London, Virago).

—— (1995) *Poisoned Hearts* (London, Virago).

Wilson, G. (1987) 'Patterns of responsibility and irresponsibility in marriage', in J. Brannen and G. Wilson (eds), *Give and Take in Families: Studies in Resource Distribution* (London, Allen & Unwin).

Wilton, Tamsin (1994) 'Silences, absences and fragmentation', in Lesley Doyal, Jennie Naidoo and Tamsin Wilton (eds), *AIDS: Setting a Feminist Agenda* (London, Taylor & Francis).

―― (1995a) *Lesbian Studies: Setting An Agenda* (London, Routledge).

―― (1995b) 'On invisibility and mortality', in Tamsin Wilton (ed.), *Immortal, Invisible: Lesbians and the Moving Image* (London, Routledge).

―― (1996) 'Which one's the man? The heterosexualisation of lesbian sex', in Diane Richardson (ed.), *Theorising Heterosexuality: Telling it Straight* (Buckingham, Open University Press).

Windass, Andrew (1989) 'Classroom practices and organization', in Christine Skelton (ed.), *Whatever Happens to Little Women?: Gender and Primary Schooling* (Milton Keynes, Open University Press).

Wings, Mary (1986) *She Came Too Late* (London, The Women's Press, 1986).

Winkler, Ute (1988) 'New U.S. know-how in Frankfurt – a "surrogate mother" agency', *Reproductive and Genetic Engineering: Journal of Intrernational Feminist Analysis*, 1(12) 205–7.

―― (1996) 'Reproductive technologies in Germany: an issue for the European Union', in R. Amy Elman, (ed.) *Sexual Politics and the European Union: The New Feminist Challenge* (Providence RI, Berghahn). Also published in *Reproductive and Genetic Engineering: Journal of International Feminist Analysis*, 1(2) 205–7.

Winship, Janice (1987) *Inside Women's Magazines* (London, Pandora).

Winterson, Jeanette (1985) *Oranges Are Not the Only Fruit* (London, Pandora).

―― (1987) *The Passion* (Harmondsworth, Penguin).

―― (1993) *Written on the Body*, first published 1992 (London, Vintage).

Wittig, Monique (1992) *The Straight Mind and Other Essays* (Hemel Hempstead, Harvester Wheatsheaf).

―― (1996) 'The straight mind', in Stevi Jackson and Sue Scott (eds), *Feminism and Sexuality. A Reader* (Edinburgh University Press).

Witz, Anne (1992) *Professions and Patriarchy* (London, Routledge).

―― (1994) 'The challenge of nursing', in J. Gabe *et al.* (eds), *Challenging Medicine* (London, Routledge).

Wolfers, Olive (1992) 'Same abuse, different parent', *Social Work Today*, 23, 26.

―― (1993) 'The paradox of women who sexually abuse children', in Michele Elliott (ed.), *Female Sexual Abuse of Children: The Ultimate Taboo* (Harlow, Longman).

Wolpe, Ann-Marie (1988) *Within School Walls* (London, Routledge & Kegan Paul).

Women and AIDS Project (1991) (New York, New York State Division for Women).

Women of the South Asian Diaspora (eds) (1993) *Our Feet Walk the Sky* (San Francisco, Aunt Lute Books).

Woods, Peter (1990) *The Happiest Days? How Pupils Cope with School* (Basingstoke, Falmer Press).

Woodward, Kathleen (1994) 'From virtual cyborgs to biological time-bombs: technocriticism and the material body', in *Culture on the Brink: Ideologies of Technology* (Seattle, Bay Press).

Woolf, Virginia (1929) *A Room of One's Own*, reprinted 1977 (London, Grafton).

―― (1938) *Three Guineas*, reprinted 1986 (London, Hogarth Press).

Woollacott, Angela (1994) *On Her Their Lives Depend: Munitions Workers in The Great War* (Berkeley, California, University of California Press).

Woollett, A. (1987) 'Why motherhood is popular: an analysis of accounts of mothers and childless women', paper presented at the second Women and Psychology Conference, Brunel University Uxbridge.

—— (1991) 'Having children: accounts of childless women and women with reproductive problems', in A. Phoenix, A. Woollett, and E. Lloyd, (eds), *Motherhood: Meanings, Practices and Ideologies* (London, Sage).

—— (1992) 'Psychological aspects of infertility and infertility investigation', in P. Nicolson and J. M. Ussher (eds), *The Psychology of Women's Health and Health Care* (London, Macmillan).

Wright, Cecile (1987) 'The relations between teachers and Afro-Caribbean pupils: observing multi-racial classrooms', in Gaby Weiner and Madeleine Arnot (eds), *Gender under Scrutiny* (London, Hutchinson).

Wynn, Barbara (1983) 'Home economics', in Janie Whyld (ed.), *Sexism in the Secondary Curriculum* (London, Harper & Row).

Yanagisako, Sylvia and Carol Delaney (eds) (1995) *Naturalising Power: Essays in Feminist Cultural Criticism* (London, Routledge).

Yeandle, Susan (1984) *Women's Working Lives: Patterns and Strategies* (London, Tavistock).

Yllo, Kersti and Michele Bograd (eds) (1988) *Feminist Perspectives on Wife Abuse* (California, Sage).

Young, D. (1994) 'Single sex schools and physics achievement: are girls really advantaged?', *International Journal of Science Education*, 16(3) 315–25.

Young, Iris Marion (1988) 'Abjection and oppression: unconscious dynamics of racism, sexism and homophobia' paper presented at the Society of Phenomenology and Existential Philosophy Meetings, Northwestern University.

—— (1990) *Justice and the Politics of Difference* (Princeton, NJ, Princeton University Press).

Young, Lola (1990) 'A nasty piece of work: a psychoanalytic study of sexual and racial difference in "Mona Lisa"', in J Rutherford, (ed.) *Identity, Community, Culture, Difference* (London, Lawrence & Wishart).

—— (1996) *Fear of the Dark: 'Race', Gender and Sexuality in the Cinema* (London and New York, Routledge).

Young, M. and P. Willmott (1966) *Family and Kinship in East London* (Harmondsworth, Penguin).

Young, Shelagh (1988) 'Femininism and the Politics of Power: Whose Gaze is it Anyway?', in L. Gamman and M. Marshment (eds), *The Female Gaze* (London, The Women's Press).

Young, Val (1993) 'Women abusers: a feminist view', in Michele Elliott (ed.), *Female Sexual Abuse of Children: The Ultimate Taboo* (Harlow, Longman).

Yuval-Davis, Nira (1996) 'Women, citizenship and difference', Paper presented at Conference on Women and Citizenship, University of Greenwich, London, 16–19 July.

Zimmerman, Susan (1990) 'Industrial capitalism's "hostility to childbirth", "responsible childbearing" and eugenic reproductive politics in the first third of the 20th century', *Issues in Reproductive and Genetic Engineering: Journal of International Feminist Analysis*, 3(3) 191–200.

Zimmermann, Bonnie (1986) 'What has never been: an overview of lesbian feminist literary criticism', first published 1981 in Elaine Showalter, *The New Feminist Criticism: Essays on Women, Literature and Theory* (London, Virago).

—— (1992) *The Safe Sea of Women: Lesbian Fiction 1969–1989* (London, Onlywomen Press).

Zmroczek, Christine and Claire Duchen (1991) 'What are those women up to? Women's Studies and feminist research in the European Community', in Jane Aaron and Sylvia Walby (eds), *Out of the Margins: Women's Studies in the Nineties* (London, Falmer Press).

Zoonen, Liesbet Van (1994) *Feminist Media Studies* (London: Sage).

Author Index

Subject Index